THE ONE SHOW

THE ONE SHOW

THE
55TH ANNUAL
OF ADVERTISING,
EDITORIAL,
AND
TELEVISION
ART AND DESIGN
WITH THE
16TH ANNUAL
COPY
AWARDS

Art Director/Designer	**Martin Solomon**
Art Editor	**Ted Bernstein**
Editors	**Jennifer Place**
	Glenda Spencer
Writer, Hall of Fame	**Jo Yanow**
Graphic Production	**Frank DeLuca**
Editorial Assistants	**Connie Buckley**
	Jackie Weir
	Caroline Von Huguley
Art Assistant	**Steve Feldman**
Design & Mechanicals	**Ralph Smith**
	Carol Moore
	James Craig
	Bob Niland
Typographers	**Gerard Associates**
	Royal Composing Room, Inc.
Printing and Binding	**Interstate Book Manufacturing**
4/Color Seps.	**Lehigh Press**
Camera Work	**Pre Press Company**
Paper	**70 pound Patina**
Cover Material	**Joanna Buckram**
Endpapers	**New England Book Components**

The 55th Annual of Advertising, Editorial,
and Television Art and Design with the 16th Annual Copy Awards
Copyright 1976 by the Art Director's Club Inc.
Published by Watson-Guptill Publications
a Division of Billboard Publications Inc.
1515 Broadway, New York, N.Y. 10036
Library of Congress Catalog Number 22 5058
ISBN 0-8230-1908-X

THE ONE SHOW

CONTENTS

THE GOLD AWARDS

10

ART DIRECTOR Carl Stewart
WRITER Joan McArthur
DESIGNER Carl Stewart
ARTIST Charles Slackman
PHOTOGRAPHER Klaus Lucka
AGENCY Scali, McCabe, Sloves
CLIENT Barney's

57

ART DIRECTOR Allan Beaver
WRITER Larry Plapler
PHOTOGRAPHERS Cailor/Resnick
AGENCY Levine, Huntley, Schmidt,
Plapler, and Beaver
CLIENT Lesney Products

When it comes to buying an engagement ring, don't let love get in the way.

There you are, crazy in love, and you want to buy the moon for your love. Unfortunately, that's not the most discerning mood to be in when you're about to spend hundreds or thousands of dollars.

So, how do you buy the best diamond for the best possible price? How do you make sure you won't be taken advantage of?

Diamonds should be mysterious, buying them shouldn't be.

At Fortunoff we tell you everything about a diamond before you buy it. In detail.

We give you all the time you need, and all the facts. We want you to walk away with a diamond you love. And loving it isn't enough. It has to be a spectacular value as well.

Four simple rules.

A diamond's worth is determined by four simple things

which jewelers call the "4 c's": color, clarity, cut and carat weight.

At Fortunoff we carefully analyze each of these for you. So you'll know exactly what goes into the price of every diamond you're considering.

Color.

The closer a diamond comes to colorless, the more valuable it is. And the very few diamonds

which are perfectly colorless are usually found in museums, not on fingers.

Clarity.

A diamond's clarity tells how free from flaws it is. Most diamonds have slight marks called 'inclusions,' but they're normal and most can't be seen by the human eye.

That's why we let you use our Gemolite to study your diamond. This instrument magnifies a diamond up to 40 times under intense light, and lets you see the diamond exactly as we see it. Exactly as a gemologist would study it.

Cut.

A diamond's brilliance is determined by its cut. When perfectly proportioned, its facets maximize the light and reflect it up through the top of the diamond making it

bright, fiery and brilliant. In an improperly cut diamond the light is 'leaked,' and the stone has little sparkle, no life and lesser value.

The shape however is up to you. All shapes are valuable when properly cut. So choose the one that looks the most beautiful to you.

Carat weight.

This measures a diamond's size by weight. Each carat is equal to 1/5 of a gram and divided into 100 points.

A fingerprint of your diamond.

Because we want you to know exactly what you're buying, we give you a specific gemological breakdown of every diamond you're considering. A document on which the diamond is scientifically rated. The cut and carat weight are described exactly, and the clarity and color are graded on precise scales.

This system was initiated by the Gemological Institute, and it's like a

fingerprint of your diamond. As a matter of fact, it's Fortunoff's absolute warranty on your stone.

We take care of you and your diamond.

So now that you know what to ask about, go ahead. Grill us. Talk to any of our over 25 diamond experts. Staff members who studied at the Gemological Institute of America. Ask them to evaluate every stone you're considering. And ask us about our complete refund policy. And our modern service center.

Come see us. We're proud of our diamonds. Our selection. And our prices. We believe the more you know the better. Because the more you know, the more you'll be able to appreciate us.

Fortunoff, the source.

WESTBURY, L.I. 1300 Old Country Road at the Raceway. (516) 334-9000. Open daily 10 AM to 10 PM.
NEW YORK. 124 East 57th Street between Park and Lex. (212) 758-6660. Open daily 10 AM to 6:30 PM, Thursday to 8:30 PM, Saturday to 6 PM.
PARAMUS, N.J. Paramus Park Mall between Route #17 and Garden State Parkway. (201) 261-8900. Open daily 10 AM to 9:30 PM.

One day Henry G. Reed and Charles E. Barton went quietly and magnificently berserk.

Ever since 1828 Henry Reed and Charles Barton have been known for their refined taste, dedication to perfection, and excellent craftsmanship. But in 1900, when Reed and Barton designed Labors of Cupid, they entered the realms of insanity. Inspired, magnificent, spectacular insanity.

The silver that's art.

Labors of Cupid is a sterling silver pattern that goes beyond being forks, knives and spoons. It goes beyond being beautiful. It goes beyond being exquisite. It goes all the way to art, pure art.

The sixteen Labors of Cupid.

Etched, carved and embossed into the

handles of Labors of Cupid are cupids. Cupids doing things. Not one, two or three things. But sixteen completely

different things! Each handle is an entire little world, and in that world is a story told in silver.

On the tablespoon two cupids are seated at a table, on the oyster fork they're dredging oysters, on the butter spreader they're churning butter, on the salad fork they're eating salad, on the berry spoon they're gathering berries and on the fish fork they're fishing.

All of this amidst swirls of flowers, leaves, fruit, vegetables, arabesques and curls of silver.

The better, the slower.

When you have a design as magnificent as Labors of Cupid, you don't stamp it out by machine, or mass produce it. Not if you're Reed and Barton.

Each piece is completely hand cut. One intricate detail at a time. One cupid at

a time. One flower at a time. One leaf at a time.

Of course it takes a long time, but who's being practical? This is art!

That's just the beginning.

After you've looked at Labors of Cupid, look up and look around you.

We have more silver, stainless and pewter flatware than you've probably ever seen in one place. We have all the great American silversmiths. Gorham, Towle, International and more. And our own special silver which we import ourselves from all over the world. And all at the best prices you can find anywhere. We guarantee it.

Then, there are our gifts. Aisles and aisles of them. Silver rattles, gold hoop earrings, sterling candelabra, onyx cuff links,

digital watches, magnificent sparkling

diamonds.

Not to mention the silver ice buckets, golden bowls, Victorian jewelry, pearls from Hong Kong and chains from Italy.

And we'll even gift wrap them for free. Beautifully and luxuriously.

And if it sounds like a lot, it is. It has to be. After all, we are the source.

Fortunoff, the source.

WESTBURY, L.I. 1300 Old Country Road at the Raceway. (516) 334-9000. Open daily 10 AM to 10 PM. NEW YORK. 124 East 57th Street between Park and Lex. (212) 758-6660.
Special holiday hours: Mon., and Thurs., 10 AM to 8:30 PM. Tues., Wed., Fri., 10 AM to 6:30 PM. Sat. 10 AM to 6 PM. PARAMUS, N.J. Paramus Park Shopping Center between
Route #17 and Garden State Parkway. (201) 261-8900. **Special holiday hours:** Open daily Dec. 18th 9:30 AM to 10:30 PM;
Mail and phone Orders: Call (212) 695-0413, Ext. 454 or 455, or (516) 334-9000, Ext. 454 or 455. Write P.O. Box 132, Westbury, N.Y. 11590.

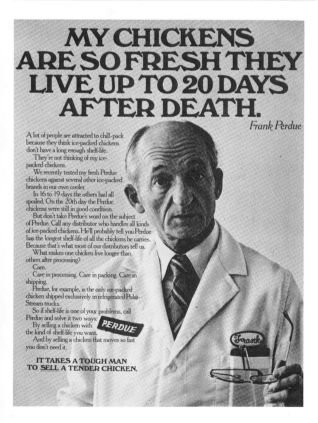

MY CHICKENS ARE SO FRESH THEY LIVE UP TO 20 DAYS AFTER DEATH.

Frank Perdue

A lot of people are attracted to chill-pack because they think ice-packed chickens don't have a long enough shelf-life.

They're not thinking of *my* ice-packed chickens.

We recently tested my fresh Perdue chickens against several other ice-packed brands in our own cooler.

In 16 to 19 days the others had all spoiled. On the 20th day the Perdue chickens were still in good condition.

But don't take Perdue's word on the subject of Perdue. Call any distributor who handles all kinds of ice-packed chickens. He'll probably tell you Perdue has the longest shelf-life of all the chickens he carries. Because that's what most of our distributors tell us.

What makes one chicken live longer than others after processing?

Care.

Care in processing. Care in packing. Care in shipping.

Perdue, for example, is the only ice-packed chicken shipped exclusively in refrigerated Polar-Stream trucks.

So if shelf-life is one of your problems, call Perdue and solve it two ways:

By selling a chicken with the kind of shelf-life you want.

And by selling a chicken that moves so fast you don't need it.

IT TAKES A TOUGH MAN TO SELL A TENDER CHICKEN.

21
ART DIRECTOR Arnold Arlow
WRITER Jennifer Berne
DESIGNER Jim Clarke
PHOTOGRAPHER Michael Harris
AGENCY Martin Landey, Arlow
CLIENT Fortunoff

93
ART DIRECTOR Sam Scali
WRITER Ed McCabe
DESIGNER Sam Scali
PHOTOGRAPHER Alan Dolgins
AGENCY Scali, McCabe, Sloves
CLIENT Perdue Farms

VOLVO 242
$5,925

AUDI 100LS
$6,002

BMW 2002
$5,940

FIAT 131
$3,958

It not only goes faster than the others. It gets there $2,000 cheaper.

When we had an independent testing company test the new Fiat 131 against the Audi, the Volvo, and the BMW, we hoped the Fiat would manage to keep up.

After all, for a $4,000 car to just keep up with $6,000 cars would be quite a feat.

As it turned out, the three $6,000 cars didn't quite manage to keep up with us.

In four separate acceleration tests, the Fiat ran away from all of them. In fact, from 40-70 mph the Fiat beat the Volvo by the incredible margin of 157 feet.

The results of these acceleration tests were no fluke. In separate tests of cornering, steering, road-holding ability, and overall responsiveness, the Fiat proved itself to be every bit the equal of the Audi, the Volvo, and the BMW.

Does all this surprise you? It should. It surprised us.

FIAT

A lot of car. Not a lot of money.

All prices 1975 East Coast POE. Inland transportation, dealer preparation and local taxes additional.
Fiat overseas delivery and leasing arranged through your dealer.

46
ART DIRECTOR   Amil Gargano
WRITER   David Altschiller
PHOTOGRAPHER   Peter Papadopolous
AGENCY   Carl Ally
CLIENT   Fiat Distributors

It takes nerve to compare a $4,000 car with $6,000 cars.
It also takes some $4,000 car.

Audi 100LS $6,002.

Volvo 242 $5,925.

BMW 2002 $5,940.

Fiat 131 $3,958.

We knew we had an exceptional car in the new Fiat 131. So when it came time to test it, we didn't put it up against other $4,000 cars.

Instead, we asked an independent testing company to pit our car against three $6,000 cars that had big reputations for performance: the BMW 2002, the Audi 100 LS, and the Volvo 242.

They ran 3 different kinds of handling tests, and 4 different acceleration tests.

The results surprised even us. In separate tests of cornering, steering, road-holding ability and overall responsiveness, the Fiat was the equal of the BMW, the Audi, and the Volvo.

And in 4 separate acceleration tests, the Fiat ran away from all the others. In fact, from 40-70 mph it beat the Volvo by an astonishing 157 feet.

But there's one test the scientists didn't do. They didn't put their hands in their pockets and come out with a $2,000 saving on the Fiat.

We're saving that test for you.

All prices 1975 East Coast POE. Inland transportation, dealer preparation, and local taxes additional. Fiat overseas delivery and leasing arranged through your dealer.

FIAT
A lot of car. Not a lot of money.

The new Fiat 131.
It's not a dream car. It's a reality car.

Part of the American dream has always been the American dream car. Bigger than it had to be, more powerful than it had to be, more expensive than it had to be. More a symbol of having arrived than a practical means of getting somewhere.

The way things are today, you'd assume that the dream car would have seen its end. But somehow it persists. Despite all the whoopla you've been hearing, in 1975 the average American car will weigh 4,000 pounds and get 13 miles a gallon.

At Fiat, we never shared the idea of the American dream car. Being Italian, we didn't have to.

Instead, we've built our cars to deal with the world as it really is.

The new Fiat 131 is our latest and most advanced extension of this idea.

The 131 squarely faces the problem of survival. If you've gotten used to trading in your car every 2 or 3 years, the 131 should come as a pleasant surprise.

The engine was tested for over a million miles. The valves last twice as long as ordinary valves. The rings are plated with chromium. They last far longer than ordinary rings.

The Fiat 131 faces the problem of rust. Its entire underbody is sealed against the elements. The exhaust system is made of a special steel, impervious to corrosion. The wheels offer the most advanced

protection against rust in the world today.

The 131 faces up to the inevitability of accidents. The passenger compartment has been designed with particular attention to passenger safety. It is protected by steel rings at the floor, waist and roof. The gas tank is tucked away behind the back seat, protected by the wheels and trunk. In a head-on collision, the steering wheel collapses.

The 131 gives passengers in the front seat more legroom than the $9,000 Chrysler Imperial. Yet it's shorter than a Vega. It deals very nicely with parking and traffic.

Last, the 131 faces the spiraling costs of owning a car. It's designed to be economical not just on gas, but on day-to-day maintenance and repair.

In times like these, isn't the reality car starting to sound more and more like a dream?

Based on U.S. Environmental Protection Agency fuel economy test results. Overseas delivery and leasing arranged through your dealer.

FIAT

73
ART DIRECTOR Amil Gargano
WRITER David Altschiller
PHOTOGRAPHERS Tony Petrucelli
Peter Papadopolous
AGENCY Carl Ally
CLIENT Fiat Distributors

141

ART DIRECTOR	Amil Gargano
WRITER	David Altschiller
PHOTOGRAPHER	Tony Petrucelli
AGENCY	Carl Ally
CLIENT	Fiat Distributors

366

ART DIRECTOR	Steve Heller
DESIGNER	Steve Heller
ARTIST	Brad Holland
EDITOR	Charlotte Curtis
PUBLISHER	The New York Times
AGENCY	The New York Times

Which car is bigger?

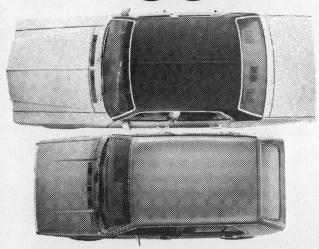

That mid-sized car in the picture above looks a lot bigger than the Rabbit, right?

Well, the Volkswagen Rabbit actually has as much headroom and legroom as that bigger car. And as far as luggage space goes, with the rear seat folded down it holds as much as a Cadillac Fleetwood.

It's merely our front and rear that are smaller.

Our front is smaller because we put the engine in sideways. And our rear is smaller because of our ingeniously designed hatchback and rear seat that adjusts to three different luggage positions.

Incredible? Sure. But then, just about everything about this car is incredible.

For example, the standard transmission Rabbit got an EPA-estimated 39 miles per gallon on the highway (and 25 in the city), yet it goes from 0 to 50 in 8.2 seconds. (Actual mileage may vary depending on type of driving, driving habits, car's condition and optional equipment.)

Stop in for a test drive and you'll see what we mean.

Better yet, bring the wife and kids. And try the whole car on for size.

The Amazing Rabbit 🅥

---

7 out of 10 Rabbit Tests are positive.

Our research shows that 70% of all the people who buy the Rabbit say that it was the test drive that made up their minds for them.

It's no wonder. The Rabbit drives like no other car you've ever driven before.

You see, in designing the Rabbit, we didn't just stop at things like front-wheel drive and rack-and-pinion steering. We created a totally unique "independent stabilizer rear axle" that greatly increases the stability of the car on rough roads. And therefore the safety.

And speaking of safety, we gave the Rabbit features that you'll find on few other cars in the world. Like "negative steering roll radius," for example, which helps bring the car to a straight stop in the event of a front-wheel blowout.

But the two big things that everyone who drives the Rabbit really marvels at are: one, the amount of head and leg room (as much as some mid-sized cars); and two, its incredible pickup (0 to 50 in 8.2 seconds). Which is pretty amazing for a car that rates an EPA-estimated 39 mpg on the highway—and 25 in the city, with standard transmission. (Actual mileage may vary depending on type of driving, driving habits, car's condition and optional equipment.)

But don't just take our word for it. Stop in and take a Rabbit Test today.

The Amazing Rabbit 🅥

Seat belts that put themselves on.

It's like magic. You just get in the Rabbit and close the door, and voilà! Your seat belt's on.

This remarkable feature, found on the deluxe model of the Rabbit, is just one of many many safety precautions that we've built into this amazing car.

We also have something called an "independent stabilizer rear axle," which increases the stability of the car on rough roads.

"Negative steering roll radius," which helps bring the car to a straight stop in the event of a front-wheel blowout.

"Dual diagonal brakes," which means that if either brake circuit fails, directional stability is maintained.

But perhaps one of the most significant safety features of all is the Rabbit's extraordinary peppiness (0 to 50 in 8.2 seconds) which can help you avoid trouble.

We could go on and on about all the other safety devices we've built into this revolutionary automobile, but we'll mention just one more. Because it kind of symbolizes the attention we paid to safety in designing the Rabbit.

Would you believe a padded ignition key?

The Amazing Rabbit 🅥

152
ART DIRECTOR John Caggiano
WRITER Mike Mangano
DESIGNER John Caggiano
PHOTOGRAPHER Nick Samardge
AGENCY Doyle Dane Bernbach
CLIENT Volkswagen

"Pioneer, innovator, visionary . . . all describe Paul Rand, but none measures the
             true meaning of his many contributions to the contemporary scene.
He was a graphic designer before the concept 'graphic design' existed.
He is an artist who has brought high standards of art to the world of business, and proved their value.
And he is a presence whose achievements prod all of us in the visual arts to do better.
There could be no more fitting subject for a graphic arts publication such
             as The Printing Salesman's Herald than Paul Rand and his exciting work."

Edward Russell Jr., Vice President, Marketing Services, Champion Papers

Champion Papers
The Printing Salesman's Herald
Book 35

Special Issue on Paul Rand

396
DESIGNER Paul Rand
PHOTOGRAPHER Paul Rand
WRITER Paul Rand
PUBLISHER Champion Papers
AGENCY Champion Papers

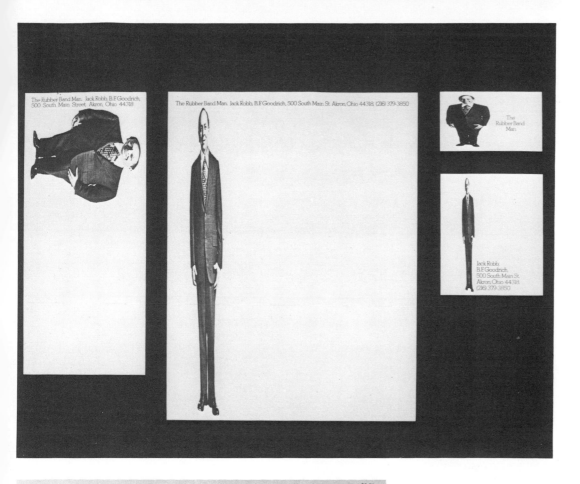

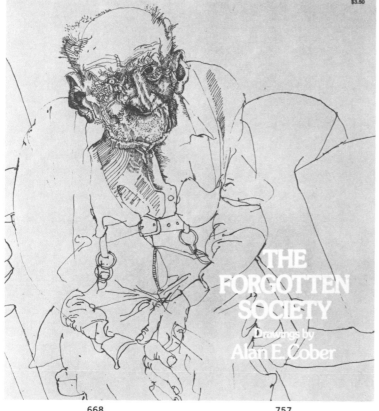

	668		757
ART DIRECTOR	Bob Kwait	**ART DIRECTOR**	Paul Kennedy
DESIGNER	Bob Kwait	**DESIGNERS**	Sam Antupit
PHOTOGRAPHERS	Bob Bender		Alan E. Cober
	Geoff Whittaker	**ARTIST**	Alan E. Cober
AGENCY	Griswold-Eshleman	**PUBLISHER**	Dover Publishing
CLIENT	B. F. Goodrich	**AGENCY**	Alan E. Cober

At around 90°F, workers evaporate.

65°F. He's okay.

72°F. He's feeling warm.

78°F. He's hot and bothered.

80°F. He can't concentrate.

85°F. He's fading fast.

90°F. He's disappeared.

It's a sad fact of life that the 'Disappearing Workers' actually exist in large numbers throughout Britain.

And if you're in any doubt about it, try spending an hour or two on the factory floor one sunny afternoon.

The chances are, you'll find that a number of employees aren't to be seen. And of those who are, many will be present in body but not in spirit.

The reason will hit you full blast the moment you step in the door. It is, quite simply, the hot, sweltering atmosphere caused by bad ventilation.

It's unpleasant to walk around in, it's damned near impossible to work in. And if you subject a man to these conditions, his will to work dies.

His productivity drops like a stone, his attitude to management takes a very fast turn for the worse. In his eyes, you actually become the cause of his misery – for it's an industrial fact he can only work at his best in a temperature of 60°F to 72°F.

So what's to be done about it? The answer that over 60,000 British companies have found is to call us at Colt.

We carry out a detailed survey at your factory, then report in full and without charge, showing how the right use of ventilation can create healthier, safer, altogether better working conditions (and, incidentally, help to keep you within the Act).

It can only do good for your company's profits – and even the tax-man shoulders a fair share of the capital outlay.

Write or phone. It's the one sure way you have of making a very real problem disappear.

Colt International Limited (Heating, Ventilation and Industrial Access). Havant, Hants. Havant 6411. Telex 86219.

People work better in Colt conditions.

805
ART DIRECTOR John Wood
WRITER Geoff Horne
DESIGNER John Wood
PHOTOGRAPHER John Thornton
AGENCY Davidson, Pearce, Berry & Spottiswoode England
CLIENT Colt International

Yesterday at Belmont Lucky Lady won, Do-It-Again placed, and Anita Baron showed.

Taking a chance on a horse is one thing.

But taking a chance on the wrong zipper is really gambling.

Anita found that out yesterday in the sixth race.

Lucky Lady was coming up fast. The crowd was going wild. And in the stretch, Anita's zipper opened up. Right in front of thousands of people.

That's when she realized how important it is to have a dependable zipper at all times.

Like the Talon Zephyr® zipper. Its quality has been proven in millions and millions of garments. That's why women look for the Talon name when they buy.

From now on, Anita will put her money on dresses with Talon® zippers.

She knows the odds are the rest of the dress will be well made, too.

Talon
THE WORLD'S QUALITY ZIPPER

The Talon Zephyr zipper says a lot about what it's in.

TALON A Textron COMPANY ©1975

The New York Times Magazine/June 29, 1975   7

164
ART DIRECTOR Al Weintraub
WRITER Richard Schiera
DESIGNER Al Weintraub
PHOTOGRAPHER Bob Salomon
AGENCY The Bloom Agency
CLIENT Jax Brewing Co.

When you're 2½ years old, everything in a bottle, box or can is fair game.

And it explains why a half million kids were poisoned last year by common products you'll find in every home.

Yet we parents go about setting deadly little traps. Unwittingly but effectively. Leaving soaps, paints, powders, gasoline, medicines in reach of unsuspecting, curious kids.

If you think a child has swallowed something possibly poisonous, dishwasher detergent for example, you might save a life or a throat or a stomach if you'll remember what you're reading.

First thing to remember—do nothing to treat the child yourself, without medical advice. Induced vomiting or giving milk or water may be right. Or dead wrong.

Immediately, get whatever is still in the child's mouth out. Get the container the child got into, to identify toxicity. Call a poison control center or doctor.

It's a good idea to keep Syrup of Ipecac around in case induced vomiting is recommended. It'll save critical time.

Finally, keep the parent quiet. If you lose your head, you could lose a kid.

When you're 2½, you can't spell poison. When you're 20 or 30, you should know better.

LIBERTY NATIONAL
LIFE INSURANCE COMPANY
HOME OFFICE: BIRMINGHAM, ALABAMA

Cleaning fluid looks just like ginger ale when you're 2½.

170
ART DIRECTOR   Rock Obenchain
WRITER   Bob Richardson
PHOTOGRAPHER   Jerome Drown
AGENCY   Luckie & Forney
CLIENT   Liberty National Life
Insurance

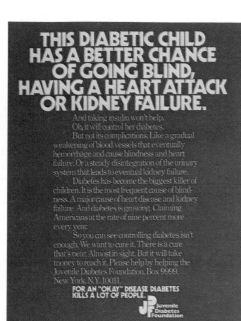

THIS DIABETIC CHILD HAS A BETTER CHANCE OF GOING BLIND, HAVING A HEART ATTACK OR KIDNEY FAILURE.

And taking insulin won't help.

Oh, it will control her diabetes.

But not its complications. Like a gradual weakening of blood vessels that eventually hemorrhage and cause blindness and heart failure. Or a steady disintegration of the urinary system that leads to eventual kidney failure.

Diabetes has become the biggest killer of children. It is the most frequent cause of blindness. A major cause of heart disease and kidney failure. And diabetes is growing. Claiming Americans at the rate of nine percent more every year.

So you can see controlling diabetes isn't enough. We want to cure it. There is a cure that's near. Almost in sight. But it will take money to reach it. Please help by helping the Juvenile Diabetes Foundation, Box 9999, New York, N.Y. 10011.

FOR AN "OKAY" DISEASE DIABETES KILLS A LOT OF PEOPLE.

JDF Juvenile Diabetes Foundation

Redbook's Quick and Easy Wise Woman's Diet

This is a hearty Seasoup. For more—including delicious dieting desserts— turn the page.

178
ART DIRECTOR Richard Brown
WRITER Steve August
PHOTOGRAPHERS Robert Monroe
Steve Steigman
Joe Morello
DESIGNER Richard Brown
AGENCY McCann-Erickson
CLIENT Juvenile Diabetes Foundation

375
ART DIRECTOR Bill Cadge
DESIGNER Ed Sobel
PHOTOGRAPHER Jerry Sarapochiello
PUBLISHER Redbook Publishing Co.
AGENCY Redbook Publishing Co.

The Icons of California:
The season's new body-defining black swimsuits
take shape against
the state's spectacular natural contours.

Photographs by Silano

The High Sierras

Yosemite National Park

387
ART DIRECTOR Ed Hamway
DESIGNER Ed Hamway
PHOTOGRAPHER Silano
EDITOR Mary Louise Ransdell
PUBLISHER Town & Country
AGENCY Town & Country

THE INTERNATIONAL MAGAZINE FOR WOMEN   APRIL 75 $1.25

VIVA

CONFESSIONS
OF THE NEWEST
SEX QUEEN,
VALERIE PERRINE

IUD VS. THE PILL:
WHICH ONE
IS SAFER??

THE SEXIEST
FANTASIES:
HIS AND HERS

COMPATABILITY QUIZ:
IS HE RIGHT FOR YOU?

PLUS: ROMANTIC
FICTION, BITCHY GOSSIP,
FABULOUS FASHIONS,
BEAUTIFUL BODIES,
AND MUCH,
MUCH MORE

Australia $1.35/Belgie 75 frs./Danmark 12 Kr. inkl. moms/France 8 NF/Israeli 7.00 Israeli Pounds/Italy 1250 Lire/Japan 6.50 Yen/Nederland 6 Fl./
New Zealand $1.25/Norge 11 N kr./Oesterreich 40 Sch/Philippines 12 Pesos/Schweiz 6.60 frs./Sverige 8.50 kr. inkl. moms/United Kingdom 50 p

390
ART DIRECTOR Rowan Johnson
DESIGNERS   Claire Victor
              George Moy
PHOTOGRAPHER Richard L. Shaefer
PUBLISHER   Viva International
AGENCY   Viva International

REHABILITATION

Two Perspectives

She looks like any other pretty sixteen year old girl — faded jeans, pink knit top, a red bandana covering her hair. Then she starts talking . . .

She was twelve when she started taking pills — uppers, downers, anything the schoolyard pusher had to offer. Last year she became addicted to heroin, ran away from home and turned to prostitution to support her habit. She was arrested and put into a cell with three other women prisoners. Before bail could be posted all the horror stories she had heard about being in jail came true.

But, terrible as they were, those few hours in jail did one thing that the desperation of a $150 a day habit and nine months on the street hadn't — she decided to get help.

As far removed from the lives of most people as this young woman's story may seem, she is not a unique case. Young alcoholics and drug abusers roam most city streets. Many say they do not want or need help. But a number of them do wake up and realize that they must straighten out their lives and that they can't do it alone. Once that decision is made, help has to be available — and fast — before the overwhelming desire for a drink or a fix erases the thought of getting help . . . maybe forever.

394
ART DIRECTOR Al Gluth
DESIGNER Al Gluth
PHOTOGRAPHER Joe Baraban
WRITER Charlie McBroom
PUBLISHER Exxon Chemicals Magazine
AGENCY Baxter & Korge

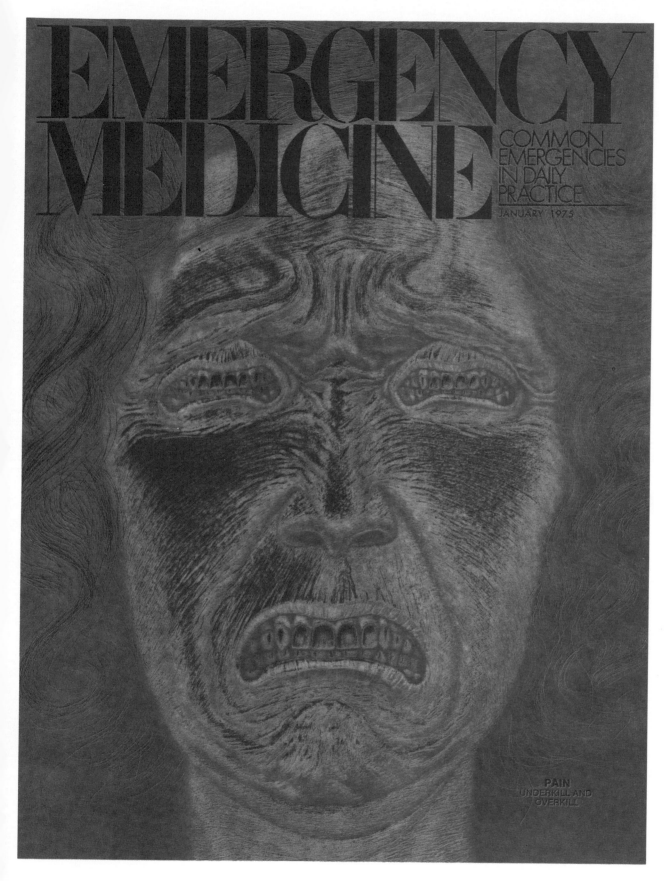

EMERGENCY MEDICINE

COMMON
EMERGENCIES
IN DAILY
PRACTICE

JANUARY 1975

PAIN
UNDERKILL AND
OVERKILL

400
ART DIRECTORS   Ira Silberlicht
                Tom Lennon
DESIGNER   Tom Lennon
ARTIST   Ed Soyka
EDITOR   Irving J. Cohen
PUBLISHER   Emergency Medicine
AGENCY   Fischer Medical
                Publications

409
ART DIRECTOR McRay Magleby
PUBLISHER Brigham Young
University Library
WRITERS Louise Hansen
Philip J. Spartano
Chad J. Flake
AGENCY Graphic Communications
Dept.

BEARDS

Reginald Reynolds

The fascinating history of beards through the ages.
"First-rate entertainment." — San Francisco Chronicle

432

ART DIRECTOR Harris Lewine
DESIGNER Alan Peckolick
ARTIST Alan Peckolick
PUBLISHER Harcourt Brace
Jovanovich
AGENCY Lubalin, Smith, Carnese &
Peckolick

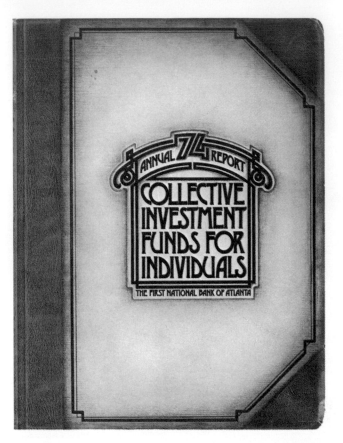

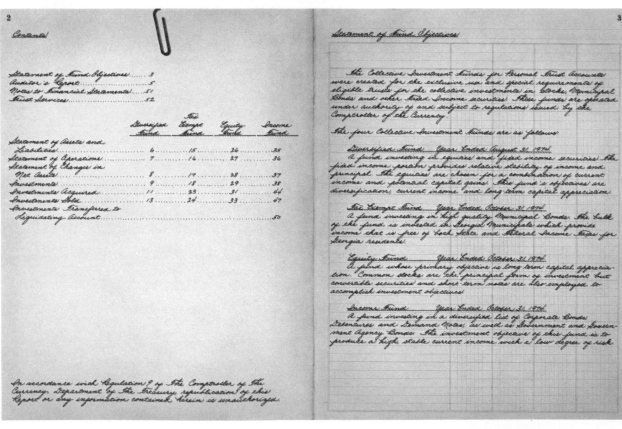

520
ART DIRECTOR Bob Wages
DESIGNER The Workshop, Inc.
ARTIST The Workshop, Inc.
AGENCY McDonald & Little
CLIENT The First National Bank of Atlanta

**CAMPBELL TAGGART, INC.
1974 ANNUAL REPORT**

523
ART DIRECTOR   Ad Directors
DESIGNERS   Don Crum
               Tom Melnichek
               Jack Reed
ARTIST   Don Crum
PHOTOGRAPHER   Gary Blockley
WRITER   Mike Moon
AGENCY   Ad Directors
CLIENT   Campbell Taggart

Our Problem

To create
a bottle for
Cutty Sark's
12 year old
Scotch
that dramatizes
its lightness,
distinguishes
it from
regular
Cutty Sark,
yet maintains
the traditional
Cutty Sark
'feel.'

Our Solution

First the name:
Cutty 12.
A swift
separation from
Cutty Sark.
Next:
Maintaining
the traditional
'feel' of
Cutty Sark.
We delved
into
nautical lore
and adapted
the most
exciting use
of glass
that involves
ships:
the brilliant
prisms that
send light
flashing from
lighthouses.

And here's
what our
prismatic bottle
accomplishes.

1. It looks
unlike
Chivas Regal,
Johnnie
Walker Black,
or any other
Scotch bottle.

2. The prisms
actually gather
in light,
then reflect
it out,
in a
sparkling,
multifaceted
demonstration
of
Cutty 12's
lightness.

3. The
jewel-like
look supports
the necessarily
higher price
of a
12 year old
Scotch.

Finally,
we enriched
the familiar
Cutty Sark
yellow label
with an
elegant
embossed print
on a luxurious
gold foil.

Note

The ecstasy
(and the agony)
of designing
glass bottles
is in finding
fresh,
original
expressions
that make
economic
sense,
can stand
the rigors
of automated
conveyors,
and be
labelled with
existing
machinery.
We passed
every
aesthetic,
practical and
monetary test.

532

ART DIRECTOR Kurt Weihs
DESIGNER Kurt Weihs
PHOTOGRAPHER Tom Weihs
WRITER Ron Holland
AGENCY Lois Holland Callaway
CLIENT Buckingham Corp.

537

ART DIRECTORS Primo Angeli,
Roger Shelly
DESIGNER Primo Angeli
ARTISTS Primo Angeli,
Tandy Belew
AGENCY Steedman, Cooper &
Busse
CLIENT Boudin Bakeries

565
ART DIRECTOR John Berg
DESIGNER John Berg
PHOTOGRAPHER Joel Baldwin
AGENCY CBS Records
CLIENT CBS Records

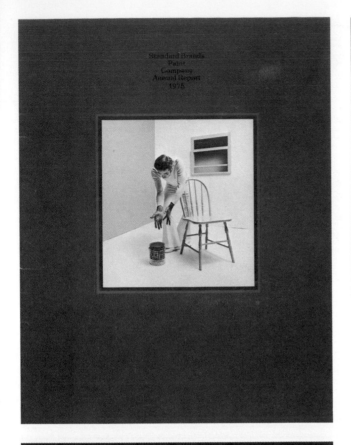

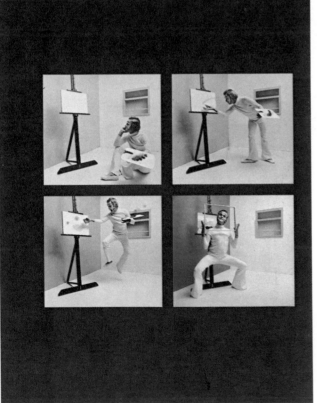

AIRPLANE
60-second

STEW: Magazine, sir?

BERT: Ah, yes. *Time* Magazine, please, stewardess.

STEW: Oh, golly, that man across the aisle just took the last copy of *Time* we have.

BERT: Oh . . .

STEW: Sorry! Magazines?

BERT: Uh, pardon me?

DICK: Yes?

BERT: I notice you haven't started reading your *Time* yet . . . could I . . .

DICK: No, you couldn't.

BERT: But, you haven't . . .

DICK: I'm writing a letter to my mother and when I'm finished, I'm going to enjoy *Time* . . . Don't try to peek inside of it, sir!

BERT: Stewardess!

STEW: Yes, sir?

BERT: This man isn't reading the *Time* Magazine you gave him.

DICK: I'm writing a letter first . . .

BERT: To his *Mommy*

DICK: Don't be nasty.

BERT: All I want . . .

STEW: Sir, couldn't this gentleman here . . .

BERT: Just lemme glance at the theatre section?

DICK: No

BERT: Modern Living?

DICK: No.

BERT: One little book review?

DICK: Look, I know how enjoyable *Time* Magazine is to read. He'll start reading one article, then another, and by the time he's finished, we'll be in Budapest.

BERT: I have a speed reading diploma, sir!

CAPTAIN: Problem here, stewardess?

STEW: Not really, Captain . . . this man here has the last copy of *Time* Magazine, but he's writing a letter to his mommy!

CAPTAIN: Sir, you'll have to give up one or the other.

BERT: Yes.

DICK: All right . . . here!

CAPTAIN: Dear mommy . . . I'm up in a big airplane . . .

ANNCR: *Time* makes everything more interesting, including you.

759
ART DIRECTOR Don Weller
DESIGNER Don Weller
ARTISTS Don Weller,
Alan Williams
PHOTOGRAPHER Roger Marshutz
WRITER Sheldon Weinstein
PUBLISHER Standard Brands
Paint Co.
AGENCY The Weller Institute for
the Cure of Design

217
WRITERS Dick Orkin
Bert Berdis
Woody Woodruff
DIRECTORS Dick Orkin
Bert Berdis
PRODUCER Jim Coyne
PRODUCTION CO. Dick & Bert
AGENCY Young & Rubicam
CLIENT Time

LEAPING
60-second

BERT: You grabbed *Time* magazine right out of my hand.

DICK: I know that, sir. I had to.

BERT: Why?

DICK: Because you're reading it wrong—all out of order.

BERT: What?

DICK: You should read it in order.

BERT: Read . . . .

DICK: See, you opened it to the book section in the back, then leapt forward to the people section, and *then* doubled back to science.

BERT: Well, that's how I read *Time*—by leaping here and there, see.

DICK: Acrobats flip, sir.

BERT: Each week, T-*Time* is . . . is filled with great stories of people, places and events, so I . . . .

DICK: In order! In order and by page number!

BERT: All right, but some stories *interest* me more than others, so I naturally dip into those stories, first, and then I—

DICK: Crackers dip, sir.

BERT: What?

DICK: Forget that one. My point is this. If you want to read Helter Skelter, Higgeldy-Piggedly, read the Willy-Nilly weekly. Not *Time*, the weekly news magazine.

BERT: Look, I'll read—j-just don't grab my *Time* again!!

DICK: Then, stop page-jumping!

BERT: I'll jump if I want to!

DICK: Checkers jump!

BERT: I'm gonna jump you, right here on the bus.

DICK: This looks like my stop, here. Yes, this is my stop, definitely.

BERT: C'mon, put 'em up . . . c'mon, c'mon . . .

ANNCR: *Time* makes everything more interesting, including you.

FU-CHI MANOLI
60-second

AIRPLANE
60-second

SISTINE CHAPEL
60-second

MICHAELANGELO: Is this the Sistine Chapel?

HIS GRACE: Yes.

MICHAELANGELO: Hi, my name is Michaelangelo and you wanted me to stop by and give you an estimate on fixing the place up a little.

HIS GRACE: Yes, I wanted you to look at the main chapel. Right this way.

MICHAELANGELO: Nice place you got here.

HIS GRACE: We like it. Ah, here we are.

MICHAELANGELO: Wow—that's some floor!

HIS GRACE: I beg your pardon.

MICHAELANGELO: That's a great floor.

HIS GRACE: Oh.

MICHAELANGELO: But, you're right. You do need a new floor covering. I'd recommend GAFSTAR Sheet Vinyl Flooring. It comes in hundreds of patterns and colours and never needs scrubbing or waxing. It's made by GAF.

HIS GRACE: That's G-A-F.

MICHAELANGELO: No, it's GAF, G-A-F spells GAF.

HIS GRACE: Are you arguing with us?

MICHAELANGELO: No, no, no, of course not, your Grace. Uh?

HIS GRACE: Good, then it's settled. It's G-A-F. Now, what do you think about the ceiling?

MICHAELANGELO: Well, the ceiling. See, I don't do ceilings, I do floors. No ceilings, no windows, and half a day on Saturday.

HIS GRACE: Are you arguing with us again?

MICHAELANGELO: No, no, I—I'll start in the morning, your Grace.

(MUSIC: Capture your great moments—great moments with G-A-F)

257
WRITERS Dick Orkin
Bert Berdis
Woody Woodruff
DIRECTORS Dick Orkin
Bert Berdis
PRODUCER Jim Coyne
PRODUCTION CO. Dick & Bert
AGENCY Young & Rubicam
CLIENT Time

827
WRITERS Miles Ramsay.
Doug Linton
PRODUCERS Miles Ramsay.
Evelyn Arthur
PRODUCTION CO. Griffiths. Gibson
AGENCY Goodis. Goldberg. Soren
Canada
CLIENT GAF Canada

PERFORMING
30-second

MUSIC UNDER

ANNCR: The Volvo 242.

The BMW 2002.

The Audi 100LS.

The new Fiat 131.

In handling, the Fiat is the equal of all of them.

In acceleration . . . the Fiat is faster than all of them.

But what's incredible,

. . is that Fiat does all this about $2000 cheaper than all of them.

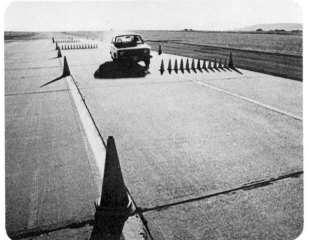

306

ART DIRECTOR	Amil Gargano
WRITER	David Altschiller
DIRECTOR	Neil Tardio
PRODUCER	Maureen Kearns
PRODUCTION CO.	Lovinger, Tardio, Melsky
AGENCY	Carl Ally
CLIENT	Fiat Distributors

SHOWROOM
30-second

ANNCR: Last year was a rotten year for cars. Volkswagen sales were down.

Vega down.

Pinto down.

Toyota down.

Gremlin down.

Datsun down.

Capri, Opel, Mazda . . . down.

Of these leading small cars, last year . . . only one was up. Fiat. It was our best year ever.

LIVE WITH IT
30-second

337
ART DIRECTOR Amil Gargano
WRITER David Altschiller
DIRECTORS Steve Horn
  Michael Cuesta
  Neil Tardio
PRODUCERS Janine Marjollet
  Vera Samama
  Maureen Kearns
PRODUCTION COS. Steve Horn
  Griner Cuesta
  Lovinger, Tardio, Melsky
AGENCY Carl Ally
CLIENT Fiat Distributors

CAR REPAIRS
10-second
_____

MAN: Do you have any books on car repairs?
CLERK: Sorry, have you tried Barnes & Noble?
MAN: Barnes & Noble. Of course, of course!
SUPER: *Barnes & Noble*
Of course
Of course

DOG TRAINING
10-second
EARLY READERS
10-second
ELECTRICAL WIRING
10-second

346
ART DIRECTOR Jim Adair
WRITER Steve Olderman
DIRECTOR Mike Elliot
PRODUCER Doria Steedman
PRODUCTION CO. EUE Screen Gems
AGENCY Geer, DuBois
CLIENT Barnes & Noble
Bookstores

MONKS
90-second

MUSIC UNDER: (Baroque)

ANNCR: Ever since people started recording information, there's been a need to duplicate it.

FATHER: Very nice work, Brother Dominick.

BROTHER: Thank you.

FATHER: Now, I'd like 500 more sets!

BROTHER: (muttering painfully) 500 more sets?

STEPHENS: Brother Dominick, what can I do for you?

MONK: Could you do a big job for me?

ANNCR: Xerox has developed an amazing machine that's unlike anything we've ever made.

The Xerox 9200 Duplicating System. It automatically feeds and cycles originals . . .

Has a computerized programmer that coordinates the entire system.

Can duplicate, reduce, and assemble a virtually limitless number of complete sets . . .

And does it all at the incredible rate of 2 pages per second.

BROTHER: Here are your sets, Father.

FATHER: What?

BROTHER: The 500 sets you asked for.

FATHER: It's a miracle!

SUPER: Xerox

347
ART DIRECTOR Allen Kay
WRITER Steve Penchina
DIRECTOR Neil Tardio
PRODUCER Syd Rangell
PRODUCTION CO. Lovinger, Tardio, Melsky
AGENCY Needham, Harper & Steers
CLIENT Xerox

ANNE SULLIVAN
60-second

Anne Sullivan was a child without promises, orphaned and almost sightless. But she spent her adult life bringing understanding and illumination to those trapped in darkness and silence. She taught the deaf and the blind.

And her greatest achievement of all was that she enabled those minds cut off from sight and sound to find expression.

Her pioneering teaching methods brought the music of understanding to the ears of the deaf and the eyes of the blind.

Hers was a life of compassion, tenderness, patience and love;

And her most illustrious pupil, Helen Keller, went on to become one of the great women of our time. We salute Anne Sullivan for her great achievement in teaching and helping the handicapped.

The Spirit of Achievement is the Spirit of America.

This message was brought to you by Exxon in commemoration of the American Bicentennial.

SUPER: *The spirit of achievement is the spirit of America.*

SUPER: *Exxon*

MARK TWAIN
60-second

358
ART DIRECTOR Ken Demme
Don Tortoriello
John Jenkins
Gavino Sanna
WRITER Nick Pisacane
DIRECTORS Norm Griner
Steve Horn
PRODUCER John Jenkins
PRODUCTION COS. Griner Cuesta
Steve Horn
AGENCY McCann-Erickson
CLIENT Exxon

TEDDY
60-second

MAN: I might be saving my buddy's life.

He was all ready to drive home when I said, "Teddy, I think you had too much to drink."

He says, "Come on, a couple of beers."

I said, "Teddy, nine beers. That could be like nine mixed drinks. I'll drive ya. Better yet park yourself on the couch."

He says, "Come on, give me a cup of coffee and I'll get out of here."

I said, "Teddy, your kidding yourself. Coffee's not gonna sober you up, no way."

So we talked it over some more. Finally I convinced him. Simple. I hid his car keys. Hey, I never did anything like this before.

Ya know, I figured he was gonna give me an argument. But then I thought, how many best friends does a guy have?

Sleeping beauty over there, he's gonna have some head in the morning. But me, I'm gonna feel terrific.

There are no more excuses.

Friends don't let friends drive drunk.

Find out how else you can help. Please write.

361
ART DIRECTOR Anthony Angotti
WRITER Harold Karp
DIRECTOR Judd Maze
PRODUCER Maura Dausey
PRODUCTION CO. Flickers
AGENCY Grey Advertising
CLIENT National Highway Traffic Safety Admin.

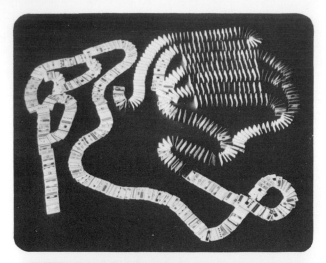

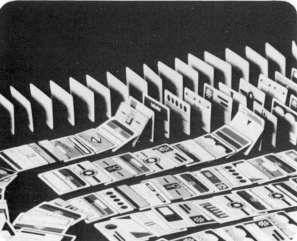

DOMINOES
30-second

ANNCR: There are a lot of credit cards in the line-up these days.

Cards that will get you clothes, but not gas. . . cards that will get you gas, but not meals. . . cards that will get you meals, but not furniture. . . cards that will get you furniture, but not clothes. And then, there's a card that will get you just about anything.

Master Charge. It's number one. . .because it's used by more people, for more things, than any other card in the world.

SUPER: *No. 1 in the world.*

842

ART DIRECTORS	Barry Stringer	**PRODUCERS**	Barry Smith
	Barry Olson		Barry Olson
WRITERS	Kearney Freeman	**PRODUCTION CO.**	Falby-Blum
	Mary-Lynn Durrant	**AGENCY**	Vickers & Benson
	Barry Olson		Canada
DESIGNER	Barry Smith	**CLIENT**	Bank of Montreal
DIRECTOR	Rick Okada		

STRANGE LEGEND
60-second

SUPER: *The legend of chipmonks*

ANNCR: Long before they even had black-and-white TV, all the monks in the monasteries made something. . .like jam, or bread, or bagels, or wine. It seems they all had some kind of schtick . . .except one. All they had was potatoes. . . which ain't exactly earth shattering.

Now one day, one of the bright young monks was fooling around with some potatoes when he suddenly discovered something terrific to eat. So he named them "chips" after his dog. He tried them on a few of his pals; they were a big hit. . .

And in no time they were cranking them out.

Pretty soon, the place was in the chips.

Now naturally, it's a very old secret recipe only recently made available to the general public. . . that's you.

You get two whole stacks in every package and somehow or other every potato chip is perfectly formed. . .which is weird.

Today you can ask for them just the way they did centuries ago. . .

ABBOT: "Gimme a chip, monk."

ANNCR: Ye olde Chipmonks, from Christie's.

858
ART DIRECTORS Brian Harrod
Mel McKelvie
WRITER Alan Marr
DIRECTOR Paul Herriott
PRODUCER Karen Hayes
PRODUCTION CO. Paul Herriott Productions
AGENCY McCann-Erickson
Canada
CLIENT Christie, Brown

PRINT ADVERTISING

VOLVO 242
$5,925

AUDI 100LS
$6,002

BMW 2002
$5,940

FIAT 131
$3,958

It not only goes faster than the others. It gets there $2,000 cheaper.

When we had an independent testing company test the new Fiat 131 against the Audi, the Volvo, and the BMW, we hoped the Fiat would manage to keep up.

After all, for a $4,000 car to just keep up with $6,000 cars would be quite a feat.

As it turned out, the three $6,000 cars didn't quite manage to keep up with us.

In four separate acceleration tests, the Fiat ran away from all of them. In fact, from 40-70 mph the Fiat beat the Volvo

by the incredible margin of 157 feet.

The results of these acceleration tests were no fluke. In separate tests of cornering, steering, road-holding ability, and overall responsiveness, the Fiat proved itself to be every bit the equal of the Audi, the Volvo, and the BMW.

Does all this surprise you? It should. It surprised us.

FIAT
A lot of car. Not a lot of money.

All prices 1975 East Coast POE. Inland transportation, dealer preparation and local taxes additional.
Fiat overseas delivery and leasing arranged through your dealer.

1
ART DIRECTOR Amil Gargano
WRITER David Altschiller
PHOTOGRAPHER Peter Papadopolous
AGENCY Carl Ally
CLIENT Fiat Distributors

When it comes to buying an engagement ring, don't let love get in the way.

There you are, crazy in love, and you want to buy the moon for your love. Unfortunately, that's not the most discerning mood to be in when you're about to spend hundreds or thousands of dollars.

So, how do you buy the best diamond for the best possible price? How do you make sure you won't be taken advantage of?

Diamonds should be mysterious, buying them shouldn't be.

At Fortunoff we tell you everything about a diamond before you buy it. In detail.

We give you all the time you need, and all the facts. We want you to walk away with a diamond you love. And loving it isn't enough. It has to be a spectacular value as well.

Four simple rules.

A diamond's worth is determined by four simple things

which jewelers call the "4c's": color, clarity, cut and carat weight.

At Fortunoff we carefully analyze each of these for you. So you'll know exactly what goes into the price of every diamond you're considering.

Color.

The closer a diamond comes to colorless, the more valuable it is. And the very few diamonds which are perfectly colorless are usually found in museums, not on fingers.

Clarity.

A diamond's clarity tells how free from flaws it is. Most diamonds have slight marks called 'inclusions,' but they're normal and most can't be seen by the human eye.

That's why we let you use our Gemolite to study your diamond. This instrument magnifies a diamond up to 40 times under intense light, and lets you see the diamond exactly as we see it. Exactly as a gemologist would study it.

Cut.

A diamond's brilliance is determined by its cut. When perfectly proportioned, its facets maximize the light and reflect it up through the top of the diamond making it

bright, fiery and brilliant. In an improperly cut diamond the light is 'leaked,' and the stone has little sparkle, no life and lesser value.

The shape however is up to you. All shapes are valuable when properly cut. So choose the one that looks the most beautiful to you.

Carat weight.

This measures a diamond's size by weight. Each carat is equal to 1/5 of a gram and divided into 100 points.

A fingerprint of your diamond.

Because we want you to know exactly what you're buying, we give you a specific gemological breakdown of every diamond you're considering. A document on which the diamond is scientifically rated. The cut and carat weight are described exactly, and the clarity and color are graded on precise scales.

This system was initiated by the Gemological Institute, and it's like a

fingerprint of your diamond. As a matter of fact, it's Fortunoff's absolute warranty on your stone.

We take care of you and your diamond.

So now that you know what to ask about, go ahead. Grill us. Talk to any of our over 25 diamond experts. Staff members who studied at the Gemological Institute of America. Ask them to evaluate every stone you're considering. And ask us about our complete refund policy. And our modern service center.

Come see us. We're proud of our diamonds. Our selection. And our prices.

We believe the more you know the better. Because the more you know, the more you'll be able to appreciate us.

Fortunoff, the source.

WESTBURY, L.I. 1300 Old Country Road at the Raceway. (516) 334-9000. Open daily 10 AM to 10 PM.
NEW YORK. 124 East 57th Street between Park and Lex. (212) 758-6660. Open daily 10 AM to 6:30 PM, Thursday to 8:30 PM, Saturday to 6 PM.
PARAMUS, N.J. Paramus Park Mall between Route #17 and Garden State Parkway. (201) 261-8900. Open daily 10 AM to 9:30 PM.

2

2
ART DIRECTOR   Arnold Arlow
WRITER   Jennifer Berne
DESIGNER   Jim Clarke
PHOTOGRAPHER   Michael Harris
AGENCY   Martin Landey, Arlow
CLIENT   Fortunoff

Everyone has his own interpretation of Spring.

No matter what feelings Spring awakens in you, one thing is for certain.

If you choose to express what you feel inside, outside, there is only one place to go. Barney's.

Would you enjoy spending a lazy Spring afternoon in an outdoor café sipping an apéritif? Then you'd probably enjoy it in a linen-blended suit by Cardin. Or a vested gabardine by Yves Saint Laurent.

Are you ready to experiment with color? Then you're ready for Piattelli's unique floral ties. Or Cacharel's color-oriented sportswear.

Are you ready for more? Then you'll want to stroll through all five floors of our International House and see how all the world's great designers have interpreted Spring.

Of course, you may be more traditional-minded than this. And still wish to express your personal feelings about Spring. In which case you'll feel at home on the second floor of our America House. The Madison Room.

Here you'll be able to choose from every important expression of traditional, natural shouldered clothing.

By such respected names as Linett, Stanley Blacker and H. Freeman.

Demitasse? Barney's Designer Den.

Dining out elegantly? Barney's International House.

Any one of their new textured weaves in soft shades of blue, beige or light gray will brighten up even the dullest of business meetings.

If you see Spring as an excuse to don the elegance of imported silk, go no further than our Imperial Room. An entire floor devoted to the most elegant, hand-tailored fashions in America.

Here you'll find such necessary extravagances as a silk sport coat by Baker or the new peaked-lapel suits by GGG. Even a masterfully hand-stitched leisure suit by Louis Roth. In a silky gabardine.

And you shouldn't leave Barney's without learning how to translate Spring into English.

Our English Room is the one place on this continent where you can see the complete collections of the best of the Empire's clothiers: Burberrys, Daks, Rodex, Aquascutum and Kilgour, French & Stanbury.

So come to Barney's and wander through the most comprehensive collection of Spring fashions in the world.

We think you'll find that no matter how you feel about Spring, we feel exactly the same way.

April showers? Barney's Rainmaker Room.

Sightseeing or daydreaming? Barney's Leather and Suede Shop.

June wedding? Barney's RSVP Room.

Tennis anyone? Barney's Sportswear Den.

Barney's

7th Avenue & 17th Street. Open 9AM to 9:30 PM.
Free Parking. Free alterations. We honor the American Express Card, Master Charge and BankAmericard.

3

ART DIRECTOR Lou Colletti
WRITER Mike Lichtman
DESIGNER Lou Colletti
ARTIST R&V Studio
PHOTOGRAPHER Hal Davis
AGENCY Scali, McCabe, Sloves
CLIENT Barney's

HOW TO WRITE AN AD FOR THE YELLOW PAGES.

HEADLINE
This is the most-read part of any ad. Make a promise you can keep. And make it an important benefit for the consumer.

BODY COPY
Yes, people do read body copy. This is where you must convince the reader. If you have research facts supporting a claim, include them.

NAME-LOGO-ADDRESS
Tell shoppers who you are and where you are. If a diagram, picture or landmark helps locate you, use it.

HOURS OF BUSINESS
Shoppers are looking for this information. It may mean the difference between a sale or a customer who goes elsewhere.

CREDIT CARDS ACCEPTED
Cash is a disappearing commodity. Make sure people know which credit cards you accept. A picture is the quickest way.

BAKERY GOODS SO FRESH THEY'LL BRING YOU BACK TO MOTHER'S.

No matter what time of day you buy bakery goods from us, they're always fresh from Your Mother's Oven.

We get up at four in the morning like other bakers. But instead of baking all our goods at once, we bake a few at a time. All day long.

It's this attitude toward freshness that's helped us earn our four-star rating from the American Institute of Bakers.* The same attitude that keeps bringing you back to Your Mother's Oven.

*A.I.B. rates member bakers each year. Four stars is the highest rating given.

YOUR MOTHER'S OVEN
CUSTOM CAKES DELIVERED THROUGHOUT THE CITY.

59 West St. 914-4952
Open 8am-6pm Except Sunday

BAKED FRESH ALL DAY LONG.

ILLUSTRATION
Make sure your picture carries out or reinforces your promise. It's worth 1000 words. Note how things like the rolling pin give that "just-baked" feeling.

SUPPORT STATEMENT
Authenticity is assured when you state the research source for your claims.

PHONE NUMBER
Make it stand out. That's the main reason you're here.

SPECIAL SERVICES, BRANDS AVAILABLE
If you do something other people in your line of business don't do, be sure to say it. If the brand names or lines you carry are important to the consumer, mention them.

SLOGAN
This doesn't always have to be a clever line. Better to have a message you want people to remember and to associate with your business.

The Yellow Pages is more than just a book of phone numbers.

It's an opportunity to present your strongest message at the time consumers are ready to make a purchase.

Never underestimate the pulling power of your Yellow Pages ad.

It's the most readily available and reliable source of information for newcomers moving into your town.

Overall, the Yellow Pages reaches more people than any daily paper, radio show or television program.

Three out of four people turn to the Yellow Pages for shopping information. They use it an average of 40 times per year—nearly once a week.

Eighty-nine percent of these references are followed by action. Either a visit, phone call or letter.

Most importantly, your ad runs every day of the year. That way you are certain to reach people when they are interested in and ready to purchase the type of product or service you offer.

Just try to think of another advertising medium that can work this hard for you. Even

The Advertising Medium Where You Can Afford To Stand Out Every Day.

if you're already using another medium, think how valuable a good Yellow Pages ad can be in tying your other advertising together at that crucial step just before the consumer makes a purchase decision.

That's why it's so important for you to have a strong, effective ad.

Make your Yellow Pages ad big. Make it bold. Make it stand out. And consider running it under more than one business or product classification if you have more than one important product or service to sell. Or if more than one category applies to your type of business.

Do all this and you won't have to worry about going down in people's minds as just a number.

⌂ Southwestern Bell

4

ART DIRECTORS Richard Brown / Sue Weaver
WRITER Donn Carstens
DESIGNERS Richard Brown / Sue Weaver
ARTIST Bill Vann
AGENCY Gardner Advertising
CLIENT Southwestern Bell Telephone

OUR SPORTS CAR CAME IN FIRST JUST STANDING STILL.

The Fiat X 1/9. Winner of Motor Trend's 1975 Award for Styling.

Of the 120 cars Motor Trend judged, this one was judged the best for style. But to buy it for its looks alone would be to sell it short.

The Fiat X1/9 is a high-performance sports car in every sense of the word. It has a fully-synchromeshed, 4-speed gear box, 4-wheel disc brakes, and all-

independent suspension.

Like all Fiats, our mid-engine X1/9 handles exceptionally well.

And because it's the creation of Nuccio Bertone, designer of Lamborghinis and Maseratis, its body is an uncanny blend of form and function.

It has integral roll bars, a front

spoiler, removable roof, luggage compartments in front and rear, and all the instrumentation you'd expect. At a price you wouldn't expect. Under $5,000.

F I A T

5

5
ART DIRECTOR Joe Cappadona
WRITER Carla Carlotti
PHOTOGRAPHER Peter Papadopolous
AGENCY Carl Ally
CLIENT Fiat Distributors

You'll pray for rain.

If you'd like to shine on even the gloomiest of days, we suggest you visit Barney's Rainmaker Room.

You won't just find a sprinkling of raincoats here, but the largest selection of rainwear, anywhere.

By such distinguished names as Piattelli (above), Givenchy, Yves Saint Laurent, Pierre Cardin, Nino Cerruti, Burberrys, Aquascutum, Cortefiel, Gleneagles, London Fog and Harbormaster.

These coats are so distinctive, you may even want to save them for a sunny day.

Barney's Rainmaker Room

6

ART DIRECTOR	Lou Colletti
WRITER	Mike Drazen
DESIGNER	Lou Colletti
AGENCY	Scali, McCabe, Sloves
CLIENT	Barney's

6

A FEW WORDS FOR THE PEOPLE WHO KEEP REFERRING TO US AS "THAT LITTLE OUTFIT OUT OF MEMPHIS."

It was 3 years ago that Federal Express went into business.

We didn't exactly get off to a flying start.

People thought we were crazy to buy an entire airline just to carry packages around. "What's wrong with the freight forwarders?" they asked.

But we didn't let that get us down.

And we went from 6 packages on opening night, April 17, 1973, to over 15,000 a night today.

From handling less shipments than anybody to handling more shipments than Emery Air Freight.

And from around $80 in sales the first night to over $80,000,000 for this year.

So who's crazy.

"...ONE OF THE BIGGEST AND BEST IDEAS TO COME ALONG IN YEARS."

– Forbes Magazine.

Like all great ideas, this one's simple.

Instead of shipping packages on airlines designed primarily for people, we designed a system especially for packages.

With a route structure designed not to take people somewhere, but rather to get packages delivered from one city to another overnight.

To and from big cities like New York and Los Angeles.

And smaller cities, like Macon and Albuquerque, Peoria and Rochester, and 5,000 other combinations, many of which are virtually impossible to connect with overnight on the passenger airlines.

A ROUTE SYSTEM FOR PACKAGES, NOT PEOPLE.

Here's how it works: Each night our planes take off from all over the country and head for Memphis, making scheduled stops along the way to pick up packages.

In Memphis, the packages are unloaded, sorted, and put back on the appropriate plane. Then around 3:00 a.m., they take off and fly back where they came from, dropping off packages along the way.

Our trucks meet our planes as they land and deliver the packages by noon.

It all happens overnight, while 75% of the passenger planes are "asleep" on the ground.

It's a totally enclosed system. The package is picked up, flown, and delivered all by the same company.

Unlike the freight forwarder/passenger airline system, *the package never leaves our hands.* The idea is as simple as that, and from what we hear, it's got more than a few freight forwarders shaking in their trucks.

FASTER AND CHEAPER THAN EMERY.

To see how this idea works in reality, we hired an independent research organization* to test us against Emery, the granddaddy of the air freight forwarders.

Identical packages were sent between 47 cities at Emery's regular rates and ours.

Emery, for years regarded as the best in the business, delivered an average of 42% of their packages the next day.

Our average: 93%.

And we were *cheaper.*

Not only that, according to mandatory reports submitted to the CAB for the last quarter and Federal Express' records, our claim rate for stolen, lost, and damaged packages was 5 times better than Emery's.

Let's see: faster, cheaper, and more reliable than Emery.

Not bad for a newcomer to the business.

DISTRIBUTION, RE-THOUGHT.

The Federal Express idea has many other applications. One we've already put into effect is the Federal Express Courier Pak.

It's a waterproof, tearproof envelope, and anything you put in it, documents, contracts, tapes, etc., up to 2 lbs., will go from your desk today to practically any desk in the country tomorrow. For only $10.

A more revolutionary application is what we call the Federal Express PartsBank.

It does away with the need for a lot of regional warehouses and the expensive inventory that's had to go into them.

Located in Memphis, the "air center" of the country, it's a warehouse and an airline combined.

And once you put your parts there, there's no faster, more efficient way for machines scattered all over the country to get the parts they need.

OUT OF THE RED AND INTO THE BLACK.

Today, Federal Express is the fastest growing major air freight company in the country.

In terms of domestic, unduplicated route miles, Federal Express is over twice the size of United Airlines, the world's largest air carrier.

We operate airport terminals in 72 major U.S. cities, serving 125 major markets and 10,000 satellite communities, which account for more than 95% of all air freight activity.

We have over 20,000 regular customers, including most of the Fortune 500.

And we're one of the few airlines today making a profit.

So our idea wasn't such a bad one after all.

Maybe the people who still refer to us as "that little outfit out of Memphis" wish they'd thought of it first.

FEDERAL EXPRESS

7

7
ART DIRECTOR Michael Tesch
WRITER Patrick Kelly
PHOTOGRAPHER John Danza
AGENCY Carl Ally
CLIENT Federal Express Corp.

He'll walk by 1, talk by 2, and die by 38.

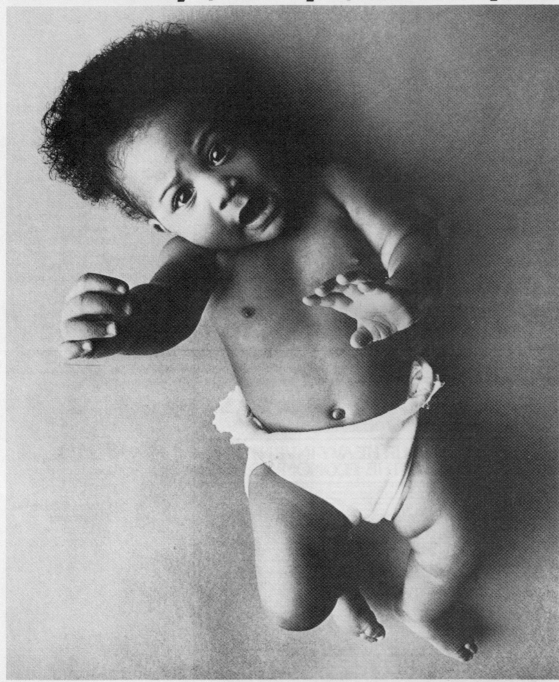

Each day the residents of our black community face a terrible killer. Each other.

Of all the people murdered in the metroplex last year, more than 60% were black. That's more than twice the number of whites that were killed. And more than triple the number of Chicanos.

What's more, statistics show that in 72% of all cases of rape, robbery and assault committed by blacks last year, a black was the victim as well. And the number of victims is rising every day.

What can you do about it?
Well to begin with, you can watch News-eight's five part series on "Why Blacks Die Young." A special in-depth investigation, beginning on Channel 8 at 5 p.m. tonight.

In the series, Byron Harris talks to blacks about the problem. To sociologists about the solution. And to police about what all of us can do to help:

"Why Blacks Die Young," on News 8 tonight. Because, we better find a way to eliminate the problem. Before we eliminate each other.

"Why Blacks Die Young." A special in-depth report on News⑧, beginning at 5 p.m. tonight.

8

8
ART DIRECTOR   Pete Coutroulis
WRITER   Jim Weller
DESIGNER   Pete Coutroulis
PHOTOGRAPHER   Moses Almos
AGENCY   Clinton E. Frank
CLIENT   WFAA-TV

 SILVER

EUROPE FOR $6.50

A trip to Europe used to be only for the very rich and the very well-traveled.

That's changed.

Now you can see England, France, and Germany just minutes from Williamsburg, Virginia. At Busch Gardens—The Old Country. And you can visit any Saturday or Sunday for no more than $6.50.

Meet a bobbie at Busch Gardens.

Enter Elizabethan England. It's a world of cobbled streets, wandering troubadours, bobbies and beefeaters.

In the Shakespearean Globe Theatre, you can see an exciting 30-minute magical show. And on the breathtaking skyride, you can get a bird's-eye view of the grounds.

Then cross the brooding moors into Scotland. Here, you can meet the mighty Clydesdales and take a ride on a real live-steam train.

For fast-paced adventure, visit nearby Hastings. There's an arcade of antique games. A fun palace. An old-fashioned shooting gallery. A puppet theatre, where world-famous Sid and Marty Krofft pull strings daily. And a body-scrambling dark ride which catapults you through medieval history.

Become an American in Paris.

Browse through an open-air marketplace where vendors sell their wares, sidewalk artists paint your portrait, and chefs concoct French delicacies.

For entertainment, see trained animal acts at the Three Musketeers Theatre. And enjoy the Anheuser-Busch® Bird Circus at La Jolie Plume outdoor arena.

At Le Mans, you can take the wheel of a vintage motorcar and race a compatriot down the stretch.

And just beyond the trees, discover New France. You'll find live music,

bygone crafts, and the scariest log flume ever built. It plunges into a whirring sawmill for an unforgettable, hair-raising finale.

Join the excitement of Old Germany.

Roving oompah bands keep you company as you explore the shops, restaurants, and old-world attractions.

Enjoy famous Anheuser-Busch hospitality in the 19th century-style Willkommenhaus.

Kids can pet and feed baby animals, and ride the galloping horses of a brightly colored antique carousel.

There's a 20-minute boat cruise down the legendary Rhine River. And for the brave, a German steel roller coaster with slopes as sharp as an Alpine toboggan run.

One low price covers it all.

Take a whirlwind tour of Europe right here in America. At Busch Gardens—The Old Country. You can enjoy all the rides, shows, music and adventures for one low daily admission price. Just $6.50 for adults. $5.50 for children ages 4-11. Children under four are admitted free.

Visit this weekend. It may be more exciting than Europe itself.

And it's certainly a lot more affordable.

PRICES:
Adults, $6.50. Children 4-11, $5.50. Children under 4 are admitted free.

HOURS:
Open weekends of May 10 and May 17, 10:00 a.m. to 6:00 p.m.
Open daily May 24 through June 13, 10:00 a.m. to 6:00 p.m.
June 14 through Labor Day, 10:00 a.m. to 10:00 p.m.

DIRECTIONS:
Take Highway 60, five miles east of Williamsburg, Virginia.

GROUP RATES AVAILABLE:
Just write: Sales Manager, The Old Country, Busch Gardens, P.O. Drawer FC, Williamsburg, Virginia 23185. Phone: (804) 220-1510.

For a free, full-color travel book on The Old Country, write Busch Gardens—Williamsburg, P.O. Box 77, Williamsburg, Virginia 23185.

Name
Address
City
State
Zip

The Old Country
Busch Gardens, Williamsburg, Va.

9

9
ART DIRECTOR James F. McComb
WRITER John Nieman
DESIGNER James F. McComb
PHOTOGRAPHER Claude Chassagne
AGENCY Gardner Advertising
CLIENT Busch Gardens

10

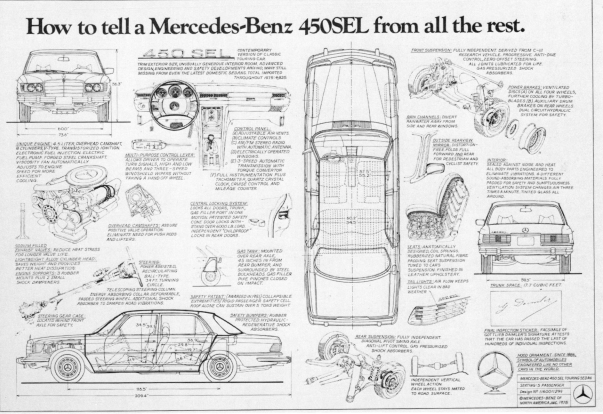

11

	10		**11**
ART DIRECTOR	Carl Stewart	**ART DIRECTOR**	Jim Corrieri
WRITER	Joan McArthur	**WRITER**	J. Roy McKechnie
DESIGNER	Carl Stewart	**ARTIST**	Ken Dallison
ARTIST	Charles Slackman	**AGENCY**	Ogilvy & Mather
PHOTOGRAPHER	Klaus Lucka	**CLIENT**	Mercedes-Benz
AGENCY	Scali, McCabe, Sloves		
CLIENT	Barney's		

GOLD

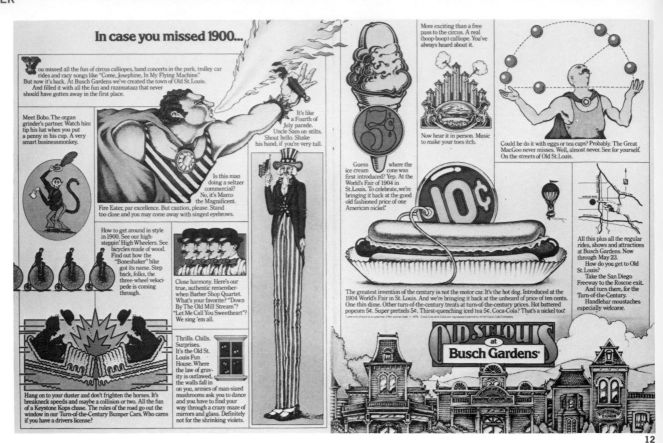

In case you missed 1900...

You missed all the fun of circus calliopes, band concerts in the park, trolley car rides and racy songs like "Come, Josephine, In My Flying Machine." But now it's back. At Busch Gardens we've created the town of Old St. Louis. And filled it with all the fun and razzmatazz that never should have gotten away in the first place.

Meet Bobo. The organ grinder's partner. Watch him tip his hat when you put a penny in his cup. A very smart businessmonkey.

Is this man doing a seltzer commercial? No, it's Marco the Magnificent. Fire Eater, par excellence. But caution, please. Stand too close and you may come away with singed eyebrows.

It's like a Fourth of July parade. Uncle Sam on stilts. Shout hello. Shake his hand, if you're very tall.

How to get around in style in 1900. See our high-steppin' High Wheelers. See bicycles made of wood. Find out how the "Boneshaker" bike got its name. Step back, folks, the three-wheel veloci-pede is coming through.

Close harmony. Here's our true, authentic remember-when Barber Shop Quartet. What's your favorite? "Down By The Old Mill Stream"? "Let Me Call You Sweetheart"? We sing 'em all.

Thrills. Chills. Surprises. It's the Old St. Louis Fun House. Where the law of grav-ity is outlawed, the walls fall in on you, armies of man-sized mushrooms ask you to dance and you have to find your way through a crazy maze of mirrors and glass. Definitely not for the shrinking violets.

Hang on to your duster and don't frighten the horses. It's breakneck speeds and maybe a collision or two. All the fun of a Keystone Kops chase. The rules of the road go out the window in our Turn-of-the-Century Bumper Cars. Who cares if you have a drivers license?

More exciting than a free pass to the circus. A real (boop-boop) calliope. You've always heard about it.

Now hear it in person. Music to make your toes itch.

Guess where the ice cream cone was first introduced? Yep. At the World's Fair of 1904 in St. Louis. To celebrate, we're bringing it back at the good old fashioned price of one American nickel.*

Could he do it with eggs or tea cups? Probably. The Great MacGoo never misses. Well, almost never. See for yourself. On the streets of Old St. Louis.

The greatest invention of the century is not the motor car. It's the hot dog. Introduced at the 1904 World's Fair in St. Louis. And we're bringing it back at the unheard of price of ten cents. One thin dime. Other turn-of-the-century treats at turn-of-the-century prices. Hot buttered popcorn 5¢. Super pretzels 5¢. Thirst-quenching iced tea 5¢. Coca-Cola? That's a nickel too.*

*Limit one of each to a customer. Offer expires Sept. 1, 1976. Coca-Cola and Coke are registered trademarks of the Coca-Cola Company.

All this plus all the regular rides, shows and attractions at Busch Gardens. Now through May 23. How do you get to Old St. Louis? Take the San Diego Freeway to the Roscoe exit. And turn there, for the Turn-of-the-Century. Handlebar moustaches especially welcome.

OLD ST. LOUIS at Busch Gardens

12

12
ART DIRECTOR Lee Clow
WRITER Blake Hunter
ARTIST Dick Drayton
AGENCY Chiat/Day
CLIENT Busch Gardens

Take away our clothes and what have you got?

Lots of free parking.

When you come to Barney's, you can take your car along for the ride, without having to worry about parking. Just leave it in either one of our two convenient parking lots. Free.

A helping hand and a smiling face.

At our entrance, and on all five floors, there are hostesses waiting to greet you with real smiles.

They're there to help you. If you have a general idea of what you're looking for, they'll point you in the right direction. If you seem lost, they'll tell you in no time where in Barney's you'll find yourself.

The freedom to browse in peace.

If you just want to look, the hostess at the door will provide you with one of our "Just Looking" buttons. This lets you roam through all 23 of our shops and dens without being interrupted by a salesman. Without even having to say you're just looking.

Just looking. Barney's

A great lunch.

If you're trying to sandwich some shopping in on your lunch hour, Barney's will see to it that you're well-fed, too. Drop in any day between 11:45 and 2 PM and we'll serve you a generous portion of thick English-cut roast beef carved by our chef, salad, a wedge of apple cake and a cup of coffee. All for just $2.50 including tip. At that price it's a lot more profitable for you than it is for us.

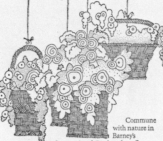

The Hanging Gardens of Barney's.

Commune with nature in Barney's International Garden, three floors above 17th Street. Or plant yourself on a comfortable sofa facing the garden and just plain relax.

Salesmen who know what they're talking about.

Barney's salesmen don't say too much (when you have the world's most complete selection of men's fashions at your disposal, you don't have to talk anybody into anything). But when you want their advice, you'll discover that Barney's salesmen don't just sell fashion, they understand it.

The Espresso Bar.

How about a mid-shopping lift while you talk things over with your wife or salesman? Barney's Espresso Bar donates your fifty cents to The Fresh Air Fund which helps send thousands of underprivileged kids to the country each summer.

One lump? Or two?

Tailors who know what they're doing.

Across the street from Barney's we have a building that houses 232 of the finest tailors a lot of money can buy. Here, these old world craftsmen give what you select all the care and attention it deserves. Free of charge. We believe one of the best ways to make sure you'll come back to Barney's is to make sure what you bought doesn't have to.

Barney's
7th Avenue & 17th Street

Open 9 AM to 9:30 PM. Free parking. Free alterations. We honor the American Express Card, Master Charge and BankAmericard.

13

13
ART DIRECTOR Sam Scali
WRITER Mike Drazen
DESIGNER Sam Scali
ARTIST Push Pin Studios
AGENCY Scali, McCabe, Sloves
CLIENT Barney's

THE EUROPEAN WEEKEND.

Beginning May 10, you can see England, France and Germany any weekend just minutes from Williamsburg, Virginia. At Busch Gardens, The Old Country. This new 300-acre family entertainment center features all the spirit, romance and excitement of America's mother countries.

There'll be old-world shops. Shows. Live music. Good food. And spectacular European-style rides. All for one low price.

See the Best of Britain at Busch Gardens.

You enter through the heather-strewn countryside into a world of cobbled streets, chimney-topped shops, and Elizabethan merriment.

Visit the Shakespearean Globe Theatre, where you can see a 30-minute magical drama. Then soar 90 feet above the ground on the high-flying skyride.

In nearby Scotland, you can meet the mighty Clydesdales, and chug through the forest on a real live-steam train.

If you long for adventure, explore Hastings. There's a body-scrambling Catapult Ride. An old-fashioned shooting gallery. An arcade of antique games. A puppet theatre. And a fun house that'll please even the most errant knave.

Be an American in Paris. Right Here in America.

Old France is a land of gaiety and romance. At Le Petit Monmartre, you'll find souvenirs, fresh flowers, and equally fresh artists (watch out —they pinch).

Escape into town, where you can lunch in a sidewalk café. And enjoy trained animal acts at your choice of two theatres.

Then tour the French countryside in a vintage Le Mans-replica race car.

Just beyond the trees lies New France—complete with log cabins, live music, and bygone crafts. Plus the most terrifying

flume ride you'll ever ride. It zooms into a lumber-mill, towards a 7-foot buzz saw for a truly hair-raising finale.

Join a German Oktoberfest in May.

The hub of Old Germany is the 19th century-style Willkommenhaus. Here you can relax, while you enjoy food, drink, oompah music, and polka dancing. Kids can pet and feed baby animals. And ride the galloping stallions of an antique carousel.

There's a Rhine River Cruise which plies a 60-acre waterway. And a thrilling steel roller coaster ride with slopes as sharp as an Alpine toboggan run.

Bring the Whole Family to The Old Country.

There's plenty to do and see for kids of all ages. And one low admission covers it all. Plan a visit this weekend. Bring the whole family to The Old Country, just five minutes from Williamsburg. It may be more exciting than Europe itself.

PRICES:
Adults, $6.50. Children 4-11, $5.50. Children under four, free.
HOURS:
Open weekends of May 10 and May 17, 10:00 a.m. to 6:00 p.m.
Open daily May 24 through June 13, 10:00 a.m. to 6:00 p.m.
June 14 through Labor Day, 10:00 a.m. to 10:00 p.m.
DIRECTIONS:
Take Highway 60, five miles east of Williamsburg, Va.
GROUP RATES AVAILABLE:
Just write: Sales Manager, The Old Country, Busch Gardens, P.O. Drawer FC, Williamsburg, Virginia 23185. Phone (804) 220-1510.

Please send me a free, full-color travel book on The Old Country. Write: Busch Gardens—Williamsburg, P.O. Box 77. Williamsburg, Virginia 23185.

Name _____
Address _____
City _____
State, Zip _____

The Old Country
Busch Gardens,
Williamsburg, Va.

14

14
ART DIRECTOR James F. McComb
DESIGNER James F. McComb
WRITER John Nieman
PHOTOGRAPHER Claude Chassagne
AGENCY Gardner Advertising
CLIENT Busch Gardens

OW TO S UP FOR A NEW AIR FREIGHT COMPANY WHEN YOU WERE PERFECTLY HAPPY WITH YOUR OLD ONE.

If you were an REA customer, chances are you were a very satisfied customer.

REA was that kind of company.

The same guys would pick your packages up. At just about the same time every day. You could almost set your clock by them. Seldom were they late. And you never had to call them.

Not only were they easy to take, they'd take your package practically anywhere. For a price that wasn't hard to handle.

In fact, with all the service they gave you the last thing you'd ever want to do is change the way you did business with your air freight company.

Which is why you should consider doing business with Emery Air Freight.

We're that kind of company, too.

YOUR NEW AIR FREIGHT COMPANY SHOULD GO TO AS MANY PLACES AS YOUR OLD ONE. OR MORE.

Emery has 83 offices in the United States.

And over 100 all over the world.

What's more, Emery services U.S. towns and cities with over 1000 planes a day going to 191 airports.

That's more places than any air freight company goes to. Even more than REA.

All of which is worth considering.

After all, when you have an emergency package to ship you don't want to have to look all over the place to find an air freight company that goes all over the place.

IT SHOULD GET YOUR PACKAGE ON THE BEST FLIGHT, NOT THE ONLY ONE.

With some air freight shippers, your package has to hang around the airport, waiting for the one plane a day that's going its way.

It wasn't like that with REA.

It's not like that with Emery, either.

As regular passengers on practically every airplane that carries freight, we can almost always get your package to where it's going the quickest, most economical way.

Which may be one reason why Emery carries more freight than the next five air freight shippers combined.

AND IT SHOULDN'T TAKE YOU FOR A RIDE, EITHER.

If you have a package of one pound or less that has to be somewhere tomorrow, you pay only $7.07 with Emery. Plus pick up and delivery. And that's the only plus.

For packages of five pounds or less, you pay only $7.47. Plus pick up and delivery.

And you don't have to watch your size or weight with Emery because we'll pick up a package no matter how heavy it is.

At Emery, we think price is something worth weighing when you're weighing an air freight company.

NO MATTER WHERE ON EARTH YOUR PACKAGE GOES YOUR AIR FREIGHT COMPANY SHOULD KNOW WHERE IT IS.

Emery has a computerized tracking system.

And we have more people working on it than most air freight companies have on their payroll.

What it means is that we can tell you just exactly where your package is, when it was picked up, what flight it made, when it'll be delivered. And we can do all that in less than ten seconds, from the time you ask. No matter how many times you ask. No matter what time of the day or night you ask.

And because of this machine, our customer service people can act far more human to our customers.

Nobody in the air freight business has any control remotely resembling this. Not even REA.

BECAUSE YOUR PACKAGE HAS TO LAND, YOUR AIR FREIGHT COMPANY SHOULD HAVE BOTH ITS FEET ON THE GROUND.

Emery has more people than any other air freight company.

What's more, we have more trucks. We even have bikes.

If you have a package that's going overseas, we can help keep you from getting grounded in customs. Or by paperwork.

A lot of air freight companies treat surface transportation pretty superficially.

REA wasn't like that.

Neither is Emery.

YOUR AIR FREIGHT COMPANY SHOULD ACT LIKE A TRAVEL AGENT FOR YOUR PACKAGE.

Emery gives a package a choice of ways to fly.

For example, in addition to our regular service there are a variety of priority services. Including one where we even ride shotgun for your package.

What's more, if you're the consignee and you request Emery's Air Procurement Service, we can keep you and anybody else involved up to date on what's up with your package.

And not only do we take a package that takes up a foot, now that we have an air charter service we'll also take a package that takes up a plane.

YOUR AIR FREIGHT COMPANY SHOULD DELIVER ITSELF QUICKLY.

In less than 90 minutes from the time you call us, we'll be at your front door. Or you can bring your package to our front door. For Emery has drop centers conveniently located in some major cities.

All of which means that you don't have to spend your valuable time or money carrying your valuable packages out to the airport.

In fact, if you like, we'll even have the same guys stop by your office for your packages at the same time every day.

Just like REA did.

EMERY AIR FREIGHT
The shortest distance between two points.

15

15
ART DIRECTOR Jim Perretti
WRITER Neil Drossman
DESIGNER Jim Perretti
AGENCY Della Femina, Travisano & Partners
CLIENT Emery Air Freight

What's the world come to when a backseat is considered optional equipment?

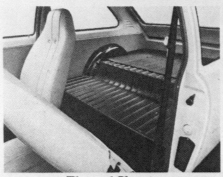

**The 1976 Chevette.
The new idea from Detroit.**

As incredible as it may seem, on the 1976 Chevette Scooter, for your $2,899,* you don't get a backseat. You get a space where a backseat could go. If you want a backseat, it costs you an extra $199.

It's part of a trend in the auto industry. Things that people once considered important to the design and safety of a car are now considered luxuries.

On many cars, radial-ply tires are now optional. Padded steering wheels are optional. Power-assisted brakes are optional. Even day/night rearview mirrors are optional.

And many of the things that make a car look better are anything but standard.

For example, on the standard VW Rabbit, armrests, vinyl interior trim and vinyl seats, and bright metal exterior trim, and carpeting are yours. But only at extra cost. They've even left off the rubber pads on the brake and gas pedals. Those are optional, too.

On the standard Chevette Scooter, the door panels are embossed cardboard and the bumpers and hubcaps aren't aluminum or chrome. They're metal painted gray.

Why are we telling you this?

Because even today a few cars still give you a great deal of standard equipment for your money. And we're happy to say one of them is Fiat.

On the standard Fiat 128, our least expensive model, the door panels are vinyl not cardboard. The seats are vinyl instead of cloth. The bumpers are aluminum and rubber instead of painted metal. There are front door armrests. Passenger-assist handles. An electric windshield washer. A day/night rearview mirror. All standard.

Radial-ply tires, which cost $100 to $200 extra on many cars, are standard on the Fiat. Power-assisted front disc brakes are standard. Rack-and-pinion steering is standard.

And then you get things standard on the Fiat you couldn't get on most cars even as options: front-wheel drive, 4-wheel independent suspension, a transverse-mounted overhead cam engine.

Instead of a long list of options we give you a long list of standards.

Now that you know all this, we hope that when you go out to buy a car you'll take the time to figure out the real price of the car, the price that includes everything you want on it. And that you won't fall for the stripped-down price on the sticker. It will save you a fortune. And it's been known to make us a few customers.

A lot of car. Not a lot of money.

*1976 Manufacturer's suggested retail price POE. Inland transportation, dealer preparation and local taxes additional. Fiat car rental, leasing, and overseas delivery arranged through your participating dealer.

16

16
ART DIRECTORS Amil Gargano
    Paul Wollman
WRITER David Altschiller
PHOTOGRAPHER Boulevard Photographic
AGENCY Carl Ally
CLIENT Fiat Distributors

Barney's Imperial Room. For the demanding ones.

Stepping into the Imperial Room is almost like stepping back into time. For the dedication to excellence and elegance that exists here is that of a bygone era.

Take, for example, the suit shown by Baker. Its fabric, simply, is the richest there is. Silk. Its tailoring, impeccable.

What makes the Imperial Room the Imperial Room , though, is that as exceptional as this suit is, it's not an exception.

Here you'll be able to select from the finest fashions in America—Hickey Freeman, GGG, Delton, Lebow, Louis Roth. .

And when you're ready to be fitted, one of our Imperial Room fitters will also be ready. Each is a custom tailor in his own right. And perfectly attuned to the subtleties these fashions require .

So when you come to the Imperial Room, we not only expect you to be demanding. We demand it.

Barney's, 7th Avenue and 17th Street. Open 9 AM to 9:30 PM. Free parking. We honor the American Express Card, Master Charge and BankAmericard.

Character of El Exigente® is a registered trademark of S.A. Schonbrunn & Co., Inc.

17

17
ART DIRECTOR Sam Scali
WRITER Mike Drazen
DESIGNER Sam Scali
AGENCY Scali, McCabe, Sloves
CLIENT Barney's

18
ART DIRECTOR Bob Czernysz
WRITER Richard Olmsted
DESIGNER Bob Czernysz
PHOTOGRAPHER Editorial Photographs
AGENCY Young and Rubicam
CLIENT Time Inc.

SILVER

In 1966 he made half as much and it was twice as easy to save.

It's ironic. In the past ten years salaries have increased dramatically, while for many people saving has become harder and harder.

Part of the problem is inflation. The money you made ten or fifteen years ago was simply worth more then. But part of the problem is also rising expectations: you want and expect more today than you did then.

Whatever the reasons, however, the bottom line is that saving money may seem more impossible now than ever.

We realize the problems of saving. That's why we're prepared not only to offer a variety of savings plans, but also a variety of saving tips to help you save.

Tips like saving your next raise. After your next raise, simply put the additional money you make into savings each month. Since you haven't grown used to it, you won't miss it. And over the years it will grow.

We have other tips, too. Tips that may not make saving easy, but will make it possible. Tips you may not have thought about, but we make it our business to think about.

Because one thing is for certain: even though saving may be tough, it's just as important now as it ever was.

The Merchants National Bank and Trust Co.
505 Second Avenue N., Fargo   Phone 293-0511, Member F.D.I.C.

It's hard to think about saving for tomorrow when you can't make ends meet today.

The Merchants National Bank and Trust Co.

When a man spends a lifetime working the land, he shouldn't have to retire dirt poor.

The Merchants National Bank and Trust Co.

20

20
ART DIRECTOR   Ron Anderson
WRITER   Tom McElligott
DESIGNER   Ron Anderson
PHOTOGRAPHERS   Tom Berthiaume
St. Paul Historical Society
AGENCY   Bozell & Jacobs
CLIENT   First Bank System

The source is proud to present the life's work of *Mr. Henry G. Reed* and *Mr. Charles E. Barton.*

In 1824 Reed and Barton began. A few craftsmen in a little silver shop in Massachusetts.

Millions of knives, forks, spoons and pitchers later, Reed & Barton is still here.

And, after 150 years of exquisite craftsmanship, you can see the results of it all at the source. At Fortunoff.

Reed & Barton & Reed & Barton & Reed & Barton.

We have Reed & Barton silver from lemon forks to gravy boats. From butter knives to candle snuffers. From cake breakers to olive dishes.

One beautiful piece of Reed & Barton after another. Like a museum of fine silver. Only you can touch it, hold it, and best of all, you can take it home with you if you want. Which you probably will. It's pretty irresistible.

150 years of craftsmanship.

To give you an example of the kind of craftsmanship and love that goes into each piece of Reed & Barton, we'll tell you about Francis First. A sterling silver pattern based on 16th century Renaissance design. Classic, elegant and ornate.

The spoons alone take over 40 separate steps to make. And a piece like a creamer passes from hand to hand until over 180 steps are completed.

And the intricate Renaissance fruit designs on the handles come in 15 different variations. It's like 15 patterns in one.

So the handle of the fish knife has an apple, peach and orange on it, while the handle of the sugar tongs has a pineapple, orange, tangerine and grapes on it.

And Francis First comes with 68 different serving pieces. Everything from cream forks to baby spoons.

Kettles and candelabra.

Of course Reed & Barton makes beautiful holloware. Holloware to match Francis First. And holloware to go with their other patterns. Sterling and silverplate.

Kettles. Sugar bowls.

Almond dishes. Pitchers. And more and more.

Just come look at it. It's so gorgeous, a description wouldn't do it justice.

Modern to antique.

Then there are all the Reed & Barton patterns you can choose from.

Silver flatware patterns that range from modern to the most intricate, lacy, swirly antique designs. Baroque patterns, 18th century patterns. Spanish. English. Everything.

Patterns that are right at home with caviar. Patterns that can even make macaroni seem elegant.

And that's just the beginning.

Reed & Barton is just one beautiful example of what you can see at the source.

We have a 72 foot wall just covered with flatware. Over 1000 patterns for you to choose from.

Including many of our own silver patterns. Silver made exclusively by us at our 300 factories all over the world.

So come to the source.

You won't find a better selection or better prices anywhere.

And that goes for more than our silver. It goes for our gifts and jewelry and watches too. And our pewter, ivory, jade, diamonds, rubies, lapis lazuli, gold, onyx, crystal, sapphires, and moonstones.

We could go on and on. Because so does the source.

But to really appreciate it all, you have to see it.

If it sounds good here, believe us, it's even better in real life.

Fortunoff, the source.

When it comes to buying an engagement ring, don't let love get in the way.

There you are, crazy in love, and you want to buy the moon for your love. Unfortunately, that's not the most discerning mood to be in when you're about to spend hundreds or thousands of dollars.

So, how do you buy the best diamond for the best possible price? How do you make sure you won't be taken advantage of?

Diamonds should be mysterious, buying them shouldn't be.

At Fortunoff we tell you everything about a diamond before you buy it. In detail.

We give you all the time you need, and all the facts. We want you to walk away with a diamond you love. And loving it isn't enough. It has to be a spectacular value as well.

Four simple rules.

A diamond's worth is determined by four simple things which jewelers call the "4c's": color, clarity, cut and carat weight.

At Fortunoff we carefully analyze each of these for you. So you'll know exactly what goes into the price of every diamond you're considering.

Color.

The closer a diamond comes to colorless, the more valuable it is. And the very few diamonds which are perfectly colorless are usually found in museums, not on fingers.

Clarity.

A diamond's clarity tells how free from flaws it is. Most diamonds have slight marks called 'inclusions,' but they're normal and most can't be seen by the human eye.

That's why we let you use our Gemolite to study your diamond. This instrument magnifies a diamond up to 40 times under intense light, and lets you see the diamond exactly as we see it. Exactly as a gemologist would study it.

Cut.

A diamond's brilliance is determined by its cut. When perfectly proportioned, its facets maximize the light and reflect it up through the top of the diamond making it bright, fiery and brilliant. In an improperly cut diamond the light is 'leaked,' and the stone has little sparkle, no life and lesser value.

The shape however is up to you. All shapes are valuable when properly cut. So choose the one that looks the most beautiful to you.

Carat weight.

This measures a diamond's size by weight. Each carat is equal to 1/5 of a gram and divided into 100 points.

A fingerprint of your diamond.

Because we want you to know exactly what you're buying, we give you a specific gemological breakdown of every diamond you're considering. A document on which the diamond is scientifically rated. The cut and carat weight are described exactly, and the clarity and color are graded on precise scales.

This system was initiated by the Gemological Institute, and it's like a fingerprint of your diamond. As a matter of fact, it's Fortunoff's absolute warranty on your stone.

We take care of you and your diamond.

So now that you know what to ask about, go ahead. Grill us. Talk to any of our over 25 diamond experts. Staff members who studied at the Gemological Institute of America. Ask them to evaluate every stone you're considering. And ask us about our complete refund policy. And our modern service center.

Come see us. We're proud of our diamonds. Our selection. And our prices.

We believe the more you know the better. Because the more you know, the more you'll be able to appreciate us.

Fortunoff, the source.

One day Henry G. Reed and Charles E. Barton went quietly and magnificently berserk.

Ever since 1828 Henry Reed and Charles Barton have been known for their refined taste, dedication to perfection, and excellent craftsmanship. But in 1900, when Reed and Barton designed Labors of Cupid, they entered the realms of insanity. Inspired, magnificent, spectacular insanity.

The silver that's art.

Labors of Cupid is a sterling silver pattern that goes beyond being forks, knives and spoons. It goes beyond being beautiful. It goes beyond being exquisite. It goes all the way to art, pure art.

The sixteen Labors of Cupid.

Etched, carved and embossed into the handles of Labors of Cupid are cupids. Cupids doing things. Not one, two or three things. But sixteen completely different things!

Each handle is an entire little world, and in that world is a story told in silver.

On the tablespoon two cupids are seated at a table, on the oyster fork they're dredging oysters, on the butter spreader they're churning butter, on the salad fork they're eating salad, on the berry spoon they're gathering berries and on the fish fork they're fishing.

All of this amidst swirls of flowers, leaves, fruit, vegetables, arabesques and curls of silver.

The better, the slower.

When you have a design as magnificent as Labors of Cupid, you don't stamp it out by machine, or mass produce it. Not if you're Reed and Barton.

Each piece is completely hand cut. One intricate detail at a time. One cupid at a time. One flower at a time. One leaf at a time.

Of course it takes a long time, but who's being practical? This is art!

That's just the beginning.

After you've looked at Labors of Cupid, look up and look around you.

We have more silver, stainless and pewter flatware than you've probably ever seen in one place. We have all the great American silversmiths. Gorham, Towle, International and more. And our own special silver which we import ourselves from all over the world. And all at the best prices you can find anywhere. We guarantee it.

Then, there are our gifts. Aisles and aisles of them. Silver rattles, gold hoop earrings, sterling candelabra, onyx cuff links, digital watches, magnificent sparkling diamonds.

Not to mention the silver ice buckets, golden bowls, Victorian jewelry, pearls from Hong Kong and chains from Italy.

And we'll even gift wrap them for free. Beautifully and luxuriously.

And if it sounds like a lot, it is. It has to be. After all, we are the source.

Fortunoff, the source.

21

Atlanta's Geography Was All I Needed to Convince Me That This Was Home.

GEOFFREY H. BOURNE
Director, YERKES REGIONAL PRIMATE RESEARCH CENTER

Years ago, when I was teaching at the University of London, the people at Emory University offered me a post as head of their anatomy department. I had no real intention of leaving England, so they suggested I simply treat the trip as a vacation.

I flew out on a typically damp, cold November day. When I arrived in Atlanta, the sun was shining, the trees were green, the temperature was in the seventies, and Emory had itself a new department head.

Since then, my work in primate research has taken me around the world several times, but I wouldn't move to any other city whatever sum of money was offered. I have all the educational and scientific advantages of London along with Atlanta's superb environment.

There is so much open country here, and what with the nearby lakes and mountains and our appealing physical climate, I'm able to enjoy the outdoors throughout the year.

In watching the great apes at Yerkes Primate Center thrive to the point that we now have the largest collection in the world, it's evident to me that Atlanta has been good for all of us.

ATLANTANS
People Shaping a City.

For more about Atlanta, contact: Atlanta Chamber of Commerce, 1333 Commerce Bldg., Atlanta, Georgia 30303/404 521 0845.

Atlanta Helped Make Us A Winner from the Day We Moved Here.

BERNIE GEOFFRION
Coach, THE ATLANTA FLAMES

When the Atlanta hockey franchise was first awarded three years ago, the word was that the people down South wouldn't go near ice unless you put it in a mint julep.

But Atlanta showed them. They packed the house, and we made the playoffs in our second year. No NHL expansion team ever had that kind of success before.

And if you think the Atlanta fans are crazy about their Flames, you ought to hear how the players feel about this city. Of the nineteen guys on the club, nine live here throughout the year. That's a far cry from the other teams where the players pack up and go home to Canada after the season.

As far as I'm concerned, hockey or no hockey, I'm going to make Atlanta my home. The lifestyle is great. You can't beat the climate. And the people are so friendly and enthusiastic, especially the children. We had two hundred kids in our hockey school last year, and with more room, we could have had six hundred.

Now there's a new pee wee hockey team up North calling themselves the Toronto Flames. So I guess you could say we've really arrived.

ATLANTANS
People Shaping a City.

For more about Atlanta, contact: Atlanta Chamber of Commerce, 1363 Commerce Bldg., Atlanta, Georgia 30303/404 521 0845.

When Atlanta Kept Its Cool in the Hot Sixties, I Knew No Problem Was Too Big for This City to Solve.

ANDREW YOUNG
U.S. Congressman, 5TH DISTRICT GEORGIA

There are two things about Atlanta that stand out above all the rest for me. In the first place, Atlanta doesn't live by its fears and anxieties. It lives by its hopes and aspirations. And it doesn't matter what color the leadership is. The important thing is that we have people who are willing to work together. And that we have people with decent ideas who can rally support for those ideas.

In the second place, there is no better organized city anywhere. And basically this means that the bankers sit down with the poor folks. The businesses, the civic groups, the black community and the middle class neighborhoods openly communicate with each other in Atlanta.

That's the only way to anticipate a city's problems and get them solved. And in Atlanta, it's been a tradition for at least twenty years.

ATLANTANS
People Shaping a City.

For more about Atlanta, contact: Atlanta Chamber of Commerce, 1373 Commerce Bldg., Atlanta, Georgia 30303/404 521 0845.

Atlanta's Spirit of Cooperation Between Business and Government is Higher Than Any I've Ever Seen.

JULE SUGARMAN
Chief Administrative Officer, CITY OF ATLANTA

There is no psychology of failure here. Atlanta is very fortunate in that we're not overburdened with high unemployment, unmanageable density or an outdated physical plant.

Instead you find an indefatigable optimism that only pride in the business community and dynamic political leadership can generate.

The people in this city who are in a position to make a city work are not only aware of their problems and willing to come to grips with them, they're convinced they'll succeed.

And I've been around enough to know that if it's going to happen anywhere, it will happen here.

ATLANTANS
People Shaping a City.

For more about Atlanta, contact: Atlanta Chamber of Commerce, 1313 Commerce Bldg., Atlanta, Georgia 30303/404 521 0845.

22

ART DIRECTOR Tony Anthony
WRITER Mack Kirkpatrick
DESIGNER Tony Anthony
PHOTOGRAPHERS Al Clayton
Randy Miller
Allen Matthews
AGENCY Tucker Wayne
CLIENT Atlanta Chamber of
Commerce

Either this car is a miracle or this ad is a lie.

From the time we're very small, we're all taught to believe that when you pay more for something, you can expect to get more.

Which is why what you are about to read will be very hard to accept.

The car you see above is the new Fiat 131. It costs $4,092.*

When we asked an independent testing company to test it, however, we said, "Don't compare it to other $4,000 cars. Instead, put it up against $6,000 cars. And let's see what happens."

So they tested the Fiat against three $6,000 cars that have big reputations for performance: the BMW 2002, the Audi 100LS, and the Volvo 242. They ran three different handling tests and four different acceleration tests.

In separate tests of cornering, steering, road-holding ability, and overall responsiveness, the Fiat was every bit the equal of the BMW, the Audi, and the Volvo.

And in four separate acceleration tests, the Fiat ran away from all of them. In fact, from 40-70 mph it beat the Volvo by the astounding margin of 157 feet.

But the new 131 wasn't just made to drive well. It was made to keep driving well. The engine was tested for over a million miles. The valves last twice as long as ordinary valves. The rings last far longer than ordinary rings. The exhaust system is impervious to corrosion. The wheels offer the most advanced protection against rust in the world today.

Now you might ask, "How can a car that has so much going for it cost so little?" To which we might ask, "How can all those other cars cost so much?"

FIAT
A lot of car. Not a lot of money.

*1975 Manufacturer's suggested retail price POE. Inland transportation, dealer preparation and local taxes additional. Overseas delivery and leasing arranged through your dealer.

What's the world come to when a backseat is considered optional equipment?

**The 1976 Chevette.
The new idea from Detroit.**

As incredible as it may seem, on the 1976 Chevette Scooter, for your $2,899,* you don't get a backseat. You get a space where a backseat could go. If you want a backseat, it costs you an extra $199.

It's part of a trend in the auto industry. Things that people once considered important to the design and safety of a car are now considered luxuries.

On many cars, radial-ply tires are now optional. Padded steering wheels are optional. Power-assisted brakes are optional. Even day/night rearview mirrors are optional.

And many of the things that make a car look better are anything but standard.

For example, on the standard VW Rabbit, armrests, vinyl interior trim and vinyl seats, and bright metal exterior trim, and carpeting are yours. But only at extra cost. They've even left off the rubber pads on the brake and gas pedals. Those are optional, too.

On the standard Chevette Scooter, the door panels are embossed cardboard and the bumpers and hubcaps aren't aluminum or chrome. They're metal painted gray.

Why are we telling you this?

Because even today a few cars still give you a great deal of standard equipment for your money. And we're happy to say one of them is Fiat.

On the standard Fiat 128, our least expensive model, the door panels are vinyl not cardboard. The seats are vinyl instead of cloth. The bumpers are aluminum and rubber instead of painted metal. There are front door armrests. Passenger-assist handles. An electric windshield washer. A day/night rearview mirror. All standard.

Radial-ply tires, which cost $100 to $200 extra on many cars, are standard on the Fiat. Power-assisted front disc brakes are standard. Rack-and-pinion steering is standard.

And then you get things standard on the Fiat you couldn't get on most cars even as options: front-wheel drive, 4-wheel independent suspension, a transverse-mounted overhead cam engine.

Instead of a long list of options we give you a long list of standards.

Now that you know all this, we hope that when you go out to buy a car you'll take the time to figure out the real price of the car, the price that includes everything you want on it. And that you won't fall for the stripped-down price on the sticker. It will save you a fortune. And it's been known to make us a few customers.

FIAT
A lot of car. Not a lot of money.

*1976 Manufacturer's suggested retail price POE. Inland transportation, dealer preparation and local taxes additional. Overseas delivery and leasing arranged through your dealer.

It not only goes faster than the others. It gets there $2,000 cheaper.

When we had an independent testing company test the new Fiat 131 against the Audi, the Volvo, and the BMW, we hoped the Fiat would manage to keep up.

After all, for a $4,000 car to just keep up with $6,000 cars would be quite a feat.

As it turned out, the three $6,000 cars didn't quite manage to keep up with us.

In four separate acceleration tests, the Fiat ran away from all of them. In fact, from 40-70 mph the Fiat beat the Volvo by the incredible margin of 157 feet.

The results of these acceleration tests were no fluke. In separate tests of cornering, steering, road-holding ability, and overall responsiveness, the Fiat proved itself to be every bit the equal of the Audi, the Volvo, and the BMW.

Does all this surprise you? It should. It surprised us.

FIAT
A lot of car. Not a lot of money.

All prices 1975 East Coast POE. Inland transportation, dealer preparation and local taxes additional. Fiat overseas delivery and leasing arranged through your dealer.

23

ART DIRECTOR Amil Gargano
WRITER David Altschiller
PHOTOGRAPHERS Tony Petrucelli
Peter Papadopolous
Boulevard Photographic
AGENCY Carl Ally
CLIENT Fiat Distributors

7 out of 10 Rabbit Tests are positive.

Our research shows that 70% of all the people who buy the Rabbit say that it was the test drive that made up their minds for them.

And it's no wonder. The Volkswagen Rabbit drives like no other car you've ever driven before.

You see, in designing the Rabbit, we didn't just stop at things like front-wheel drive (for better tracking) and sports car rack-and-pinion steering—though they make the car handle so well, we probably could have.

We created, for example, a totally unique "independent stabilizer rear axle." This axle greatly increases the stability of the car on rough roads. And therefore the safety.

And speaking of safety, we gave the Rabbit features that you'll find on few other cars in the world. Like "negative steering roll radius," for ex-

ample, which helps bring the car to a straight stop in the event of a front-wheel blowout.

But it seems the two big things that everyone who drives the Rabbit really marvels at are: one, the amount of headroom and legroom (as much as some mid-sized cars); and two, its incredible pickup. 0 to 50 in 8.2 seconds. Which is pretty extraordinary for a car that rates an EPA-estimated 39 miles per gallon on the highway—and 25 in the city, with standard transmission. (Actual mileage may vary depending on type of driving, driving habits, car's condition and optional equipment.)

But don't just take our word for it. Stop in and take a Rabbit Test today.

The Amazing Rabbit 🆅

Seat belts that put themselves on.

It's like magic. You just get in the Rabbit and close the door, and voilà! Your seat belt's on.

This remarkable feature, found on the deluxe model of the Rabbit, is just one of many many safety precautions that we've built into this amazing car.

We also have something called an "independent stabilizer rear axle," which increases the stability of the car on rough roads.

"Negative steering roll radius," which helps bring the car to a straight stop in the event of a front-wheel blowout. "Dual diagonal brakes," which means that if either

brake circuit fails, directional stability is maintained.

But perhaps one of the most significant safety features of all is the Rabbit's extraordinary peppiness (0 to 50 in 8.2 seconds) which can help you avoid trouble.

Regretfully, we don't have the space right now to go into all the other safety devices that we've built into this revolutionary automobile. However, there's one more feature that we think you should know about—because it kind of symbolizes the attention we paid to safety in designing the Rabbit.

Would you believe a padded ignition key?

The Amazing Rabbit 🆅

Which car is bigger?

The outside of an automobile can be somewhat deceiving.

Take the mid-sized car in the picture above. Looks like it's a lot bigger than the Rabbit, right?

Well, the Volkswagen Rabbit actually has as much headroom and legroom as that bigger car. And as far as luggage space goes, with the rear seat folded down it holds as much as a Cadillac Fleetwood.

It's merely our front and rear that are smaller (which, by the way, makes handling and parking a pleasure).

Our front is smaller because we put the engine in sideways. And our rear is smaller because of our ingeniously designed hatchback and rear seat that adjusts to three differ-

ent luggage positions. (If you have nobody sitting in back, you can actually turn the Rabbit into a station wagon.)

Incredible? Sure. But then, just about everything about this car is incredible.

For example, the standard transmission Rabbit got an EPA-estimated 39 miles per gallon on the highway (and 25 in the city), yet it goes from 0 to 50 in 8.2 seconds. No other car gives you this kind of power with so much economy. (Actual mileage may vary depending on type of driving, driving habits, car's condition and optional equipment.)

Stop in for a test drive and you'll see what we mean.

Better yet, bring the wife and kids. And try the whole car on for size.

The Amazing Rabbit 🆅

24

ART DIRECTOR John Caggiano
WRITER Mike Mangano
DESIGNER John Caggiano
PHOTOGRAPHER Nick Samardge
AGENCY Doyle Dane Bernbach
CLIENT Volkswagen

When it comes to fashion, a few men set the standard for the world.

In the last few years, some of the top designers of women's fashion have challenged the established order of men's fashion.

And in doing so, allowed men to dress with an individuality and elegance once reserved for women.

To find the designers whose individual statements express you best, you can go to their own shops scattered throughout Europe. You can even find an occasional designer or two in stores scattered throughout New York.

Or you can come to Barney's International House. Where you'll find, arranged throughout five floors, the collections of all the most important designers in the world.

Only at Barney's can you compare the classic tailoring of Dimitri's camel hair blazer with the more relaxed fit of Bill Blass' version. Or the closely shaped styling of the one designed by Pierre Cardin.

Here you can try on Rafael's multi-zippered jumpsuit, and in the next instant, a velvet suit by Yves Saint Laurent. Or Meledandri's luxurious cashmere wrap coat. And then see the newest interpretations by such masters as Givenchy, Gilbert Feruch, Cacharel, Nino Cerruti, Emilio Pucci, Phillipe Venet, Renoma and Carlo Palazzi.

There is only one place in the world where you'll find them all under one roof.

Barney's International House. Also setting a standard for the world.

Barney's International House

We're big enough to treat you as an individual.

7th Avenue and 17th Street. Open 9AM to 9:30PM. Free parking. We honor the American Express Card, Master Charge and BankAmericard. And, of course, your Barney's Card.

Until he was five years old, the father of our country dressed like his mother.

Barney's invites you to the Brooklyn Museum's review of men's and boys' fashions, 1750 to 1975, "Of Men Only." Opening Sept. 18th.

After you see the classics of yesterday, see the classics of today. At Barney's.

Barney's

Once a year, Barney's becomes the world's largest women's store.

25

ART DIRECTOR	Carl Stewart
WRITERS	Mike Drazen
	Joan McArthur
	Mike Lichtman
DESIGNER	Carl Stewart
ARTIST	Charles Slackman
PHOTOGRAPHERS	Klaus Lucka
	Hal Davis
AGENCY	Scali, McCabe, Sloves
CLIENT	Barney's

Put it where you want to be kissed.

Distributed by Rorer International Cosmetics, Ltd. 730 Fifth Avenue, New York City, N.Y. 10019

26

26
ART DIRECTOR Phil Mazzurco
WRITER Dan Bingham
PHOTOGRAPHER Phil Mazzurco
AGENCY Dan Bingham
CLIENT Rorer International
Cosmetics

IRONICALLY, THE MOST IMPORTANT INVESTOR ON WALL STREET HAS ALWAYS HAD THE LEAST AMOUNT OF HELP.

The individual investor has always been the most important person on Wall Street. It's a widely held view that when his capital is invested in securities, the market

flourishes. When it's not, the market suffers.

Yet, while institutional and big investors have always had the advantage of a money manager, the smaller investor has usually had to manage on his own.

At Sanford C. Bernstein & Co., Inc., we've built our business on making professional money management available to individual investors.

Our philosophy is simple. When we make investment decisions, they're based on more than just the likelihood of a stock going up. They're based on how well specific stocks can meet the individual's specific financial goals. Sometimes that means being in more than just stocks. It may mean using bonds, options or other investment alternatives, including short selling, depending upon your financial objectives.

And of course, all our clients get this same personalized attention. No matter what the size of their account.

If you'd like more information as to how this traditionally institutional way of investing can better help you meet your financial goals, please send the coupon to: Sanford C. Bernstein & Co., Inc., 717 Fifth Avenue, New York, New York, or call (212) 486-6723. After all, the most important person on Wall Street should get the most amount of help.

Sanford C. Bernstein & Co., Inc.

Investment Research and Management

Member, New York Stock Exchange, Inc.

717 Fifth Avenue, New York, New York 10022

Dear Sirs:

☐ Please send me more information about your firm.

☐ I would like you to review my financial situation and my investment portfolio.

☐ Please have a member of your firm contact me.

Name _____ Tel _____

Address _____

City _____ State _____ Zip _____

SANFORD C. BERNSTEIN & CO., INC. MONEY MANAGEMENT FOR THE INDIVIDUAL.

27

27
ART DIRECTOR Paul Jervis
WRITER Jay Taub
ARTIST Joan Berg Victor
AGENCY Cox & Co.
CLIENT Sanford C. Bernstein & Co.

Now you can copy in small, medium and large.

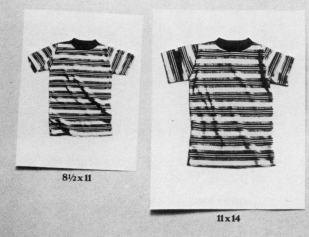

8½ x 11

11 x 14

14 x 18

The best thing about the Xerox 3100 LDC isn't that it makes incredibly clear, sharp copies. Or that it's portable. Or that it can copy light originals, bulky bound volumes, or even photographs.

It's not even that it has easy-to-load paper cassettes and a document feeder.

It's the fact that it can make size-for-size copies from documents as small as 8½ x 11 to as large as 14 x 18. And any size in between.

So now you can copy letters, ledger sheets, even oversize computer printout, all with one machine.

The Xerox 3100 Large Document Copier. Because one size doesn't fit all.

XEROX

XEROX® and 3100 are trademarks of XEROX CORPORATION

Reproductions of actual Xerox 3100 LDC copies.

28

Either this car is a miracle or this ad is a lie.

From the time we're very small, we're all taught to believe that when you pay more for something, you can expect to get more.

Which is why what you are about to read will be very hard to accept.

The car you see above is the new Fiat 131. It costs $4,092.*

When we asked an independent testing company to test it, however, we said, "Don't compare it to other $4,000 cars. Instead, put it up against $6,000 cars. And let's see what happens."

So they tested the Fiat against three $6,000 cars that have big reputations for performance: the BMW 2002, the Audi 100LS, and the Volvo 242. They ran three different handling tests and four different acceleration tests.

In separate tests of cornering, steering, road-holding ability, and overall responsiveness, the Fiat was every bit the equal of the BMW, the Audi, and the Volvo.

And in four separate acceleration tests, the Fiat ran away from all of them. In fact, from 40-70 mph it beat the Volvo by the astounding margin of 157 feet.

But the new 131 wasn't just made to drive well. It was made to keep driving well. The engine was tested for over a million miles. The valves last twice as long as ordinary valves. The rings last far longer than ordinary rings. The exhaust system is impervious to corrosion. The wheels offer the most advanced protection against rust in the world today.

Now you might ask, "How can a car that has so much going for it cost so little?" To which we might ask, "How can all those other cars cost so much?"

FIAT
A lot of car. Not a lot of money.

*1975 Manufacturer's suggested retail price POE. Inland transportation, dealer preparation and local taxes additional. Overseas delivery and leasing arranged through your dealer.

29

	28		**29**	
ART DIRECTOR	Jeff Cohen		ART DIRECTOR	Amil Gargano
WRITER	Steve Penchina		WRITER	David Altschiller
PHOTOGRAPHER	Steve Steigman		PHOTOGRAPHER	Tony Petrucelli
AGENCY	Needham, Harper & Steers		AGENCY	Carl Ally
CLIENT	Xerox		CLIENT	Fiat Distributors

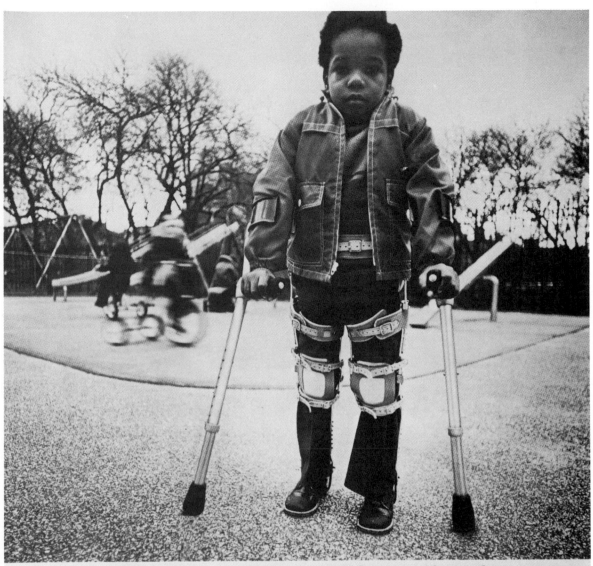

If you forget to have your children vaccinated, you could be reminded of it the rest of your life.

There's no gentle way of putting it.

Parents who don't have their children immunized against polio are risking a senseless tragedy. We only raise the point here because that's exactly what many parents seem to be doing.

In 1963, for example, 84% of all preschoolers had three or more doses of polio vaccine. Ten years later the number had plummeted to 60%—which is simply another way of saying that 2 out of every 5 children have not been immunized against polio.

And polio isn't the only childhood disease people seem to be ignoring.

Immunization against diphtheria has been so neglected that not long ago there was an epidemic of it in Texas.

In 1974, reports show there were 57,407 cases of mumps, 22,085 of measles, 94 of tetanus, and 1,758 of whooping cough—all preventable.

What about your children? Are they protected against these diseases?

The best way to make sure is to see your family doctor. He can help you check on which immunizations your children may have missed, and then see that your children get them.

Of course, one of the best weapons

in preventing any disease is knowledge. So to help you learn about immunization in greater detail, we've prepared a booklet. You can get it by writing: "Immunization," Metropolitan Life, One Madison Avenue, New York, N.Y. 10010.

Our interest in this is simple. At Metropolitan Life, literally everything we do is concerned with people's futures. And we'd like to make sure those futures are not only secure, but healthy and long.

❄ Metropolitan Life
Where the future is now

30

30
ART DIRECTOR Robert Engel
WRITER Tom Thomas
PHOTOGRAPHER Carl Fischer
AGENCY Young and Rubicam
CLIENT Metropolitan Life
Insurance Co.

XEROX® and TELECOPIER® are trademarks of XEROX CORPORATION.

"Did anyone see the 2 rabbits that were due in Des Moines, Tuesday?"

All too often freight in the terminal gets mishandled or misplaced.

Usually it's due to faulty communications.

Which is why at Xerox we have Transportation Specialists who can show you better ways to help control the movement on your docks, and keep track of your shipments.

How to use our duplicators to color-code dock paper flow so you avoid mix-ups.

How to reduce and reproduce exact copies of bills of lading onto pre-printed freight bill forms. (Since there's no retyping there's less chance of error.)

Or how by using a Xerox Telecopier transceiver and your own telephone you can send copies of any document to any terminal, instantly.

Xerox Transportation Specialists.

They'll help you keep track of what's coming in, going out, and going on.

XEROX

31

31
ART DIRECTOR Jeff Cohen
WRITERS Lester Colodny
Allen Kay
PHOTOGRAPHER Menken/Seltzer
AGENCY Needham, Harper &
Steers
CLIENT Xerox

Most people who make small cars really want to sell you something else.

Have you noticed how many small cars are coming out today that bear no resemblance to anything small?

There's a good reason for this. Big cars make big profits. And simple, practical, unencumbered small cars make small profits.

At Fiat, we learned how to make a living out of small cars a long time ago. And we've spent the last 40 years making sense out of them.

The Fiat 128 below is about 4 feet shorter than the Skylark, the Fury, or the Monarch. But it has more legroom than any of them. In fact, it has more legroom than the Big Three's "big" cars: the Imperial, the Continental, and the Eldorado.*

Instead of making the 128 low and sleek like the others, we've given it more headroom than a Rolls-Royce.**

Instead of loading it down with all sorts of gadgetry, we've given it things that actually make it perform better.

Rack-and-pinion steering, front-wheel drive, and an all-independent suspension are standard equipment.

None of which are even available on the Skylark, Fury, or Monarch.

Last, the Fiat 128 costs between $400 and $700 less than they do.

You see, when the Big Three said these were small cars, they never said they had small prices.

That's where the automobile is going.

*Automotive News, November 4, 1974. **Automotive News Almanac 1974.

211.1"
The small Plymouth Fury: Is this Chrysler's idea of a small car?

200.3"
The small Buick Skylark: Can this be GM's idea of a small car?

199.9"
The Mercury Monarch: Is this Ford's idea of the precision size for today?

157.2"
The Fiat 128: Instead of naming it small, we made it small.

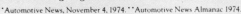

Overseas delivery arranged through your dealer.

32

32
ART DIRECTOR Amil Gargano
WRITER David Altschiller
PHOTOGRAPHER Tony Petrucelli
AGENCY Carl Ally
CLIENT Fiat Distributors

Avis is a registered trademark of Avis Rent A Car System, Inc. ©

"Don't look now, but we're about to get another complaint about the air conditioner in LB-5468."

You can end up in a dirty car. You can end up in a faulty car. You can end up in an old car.

Avis doesn't want you to end up this way.

That's why Avis rents newer automobiles, on the average, than even our biggest competitor. And Avis sets the highest of standards for maintenance and cleanliness.

(Remember, we're the ones who started it all with a clean ashtray.)

We're the Avis System, renting all make automobiles, featuring those engineered by Chrysler.

More importantly, we're the people of Avis, trying harder and caring more.

And part of trying harder and caring more, is getting you a car you'd be proud to own yourself.

I want my Avis.

33

33
ART DIRECTOR Roy Grace
WRITER John Noble
DESIGNER Roy Grace
ARTIST George Price
AGENCY Doyle Dane Bernbach
CLIENT Avis Rent-A-Car

It's easier to remember where we don't go.

Our apologies to the Antarctica Tourist Board.

For despite the fact we have the world's largest fleet of 747s.

And despite the fact we have 28,000 people who've made a profession out of taking Americans to foreign lands.

And despite the fact we have a route structure that takes in 96 cities in 65 countries.

There's still one continent we don't fly to.

Of course, tastes may change radically.

In which case, we'll open Antarctica to air travel.

Even as we opened every other continent.

And take the apology back and start taking tourists.

⊕ PAN AM

America's airline to the world.

34

34
ART DIRECTOR Michael Tesch
WRITERS Tom Messner
Jim Durfee
PHOTOGRAPHER Time/Life Photos
AGENCY Carl Ally
CLIENT Pan American World
Airways

CONSUMER MAGAZINE

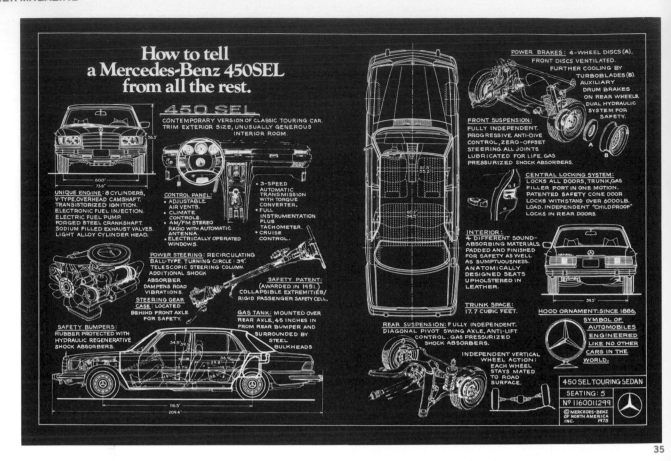

35

Which house is covered by your present homeowners policy? The one you bought or the one you own?

Chances are, it's somewhere in between.

Because over the years, it was easy to overlook the one thing that affects the value of a home more than all the money you put into it. Inflation.

Today, your house, like so many houses, is probably worth more than the insurance that covers it.

But if you're insured by The Travelers, we can help you offset the effects of an unpredictable economy.

Every year, we'll check your coverage against replacement costs in your area. If the price of raw materials and the cost of labor are higher than they were last year, we'll adjust your policy to reflect those changes.

This service is only one part of what may be the most comprehensive homeowners protection you can buy.

If you'd like to know more about it, see your own Travelers agent or check the Yellow Pages for one near you.

That way, if something happens to your house, you might have to rebuild or replace it at today's prices, but you won't have to do it with yesterday's coverage.

THE TRAVELERS
Maybe we can help.

36

35
ART DIRECTOR Jim Corrieri
WRITER J. Roy McKechnie
ARTIST Ken Dallison
AGENCY Ogilvy & Mather
CLIENT Mercedes-Benz

36
ART DIRECTOR Howard Benson
WRITERS Ron Berger / Ed Butler
PHOTOGRAPHER Peter Papadopolous
AGENCY Carl Ally
CLIENT The Travelers Insurance Co's.

Avis is a registered trademark of Avis Rent A Car System, Inc. ©

"I'd like to make an obscene phone call to Bonzo-Rent-A-Car in Pepper Pike, Ohio."

Terrific. You're now 5 minutes late for a meeting and 5 miles from nowhere in a broken-down rent a car.

Avis does not want you to go through this.

That's why Avis rents newer automobiles, on the average, than even our biggest competitor.

It only seems logical. The newer the car you drive, the fewer the problems you're likely to have.

We're the Avis System, renting all make automobiles, featuring those engineered by Chrysler.

More importantly, we're the people of Avis, trying harder and caring more.

And part of trying harder and caring more, is renting newer.

I want my Avis.

37

37
ART DIRECTOR Roy Grace
WRITER John Noble
DESIGNER Roy Grace
ARTIST Lee Lorenz
AGENCY Doyle Dane Bernbach
CLIENT Avis Rent-A-Car

It takes nerve to compare a $4,000 car with $6,000 cars. It also takes some $4,000 car.

Audi 100LS $6,002.

Volvo 242 $5,925.

BMW 2002 $5,940.

Fiat 131 $3,958.

We knew we had an exceptional car in the new Fiat 131. So when it came time to test it, we didn't put it up against other $4,000 cars.

Instead, we asked an independent testing company to pit our car against three $6,000 cars that had big reputations for performance: the BMW 2002, the Audi 100 LS, and the Volvo 242.

They ran 3 different kinds of handling tests, and 4 different acceleration tests.

The results surprised even us. In separate tests of cornering, steering, road-holding ability and overall responsiveness, the Fiat was the equal of the BMW, the Audi, and the Volvo.

And in 4 separate acceleration

tests, the Fiat ran away from all the others. In fact, from 40-70 mph it beat the Volvo by an astonishing 157 feet.

But there's one test the scientists didn't do. They didn't put their hands in their pockets and come out with a $2,000 saving on the Fiat.

We're saving that test for you.

All prices 1975 East Coast POE. Inland transportation, dealer preparation, and local taxes additional. Fiat overseas delivery and leasing arranged through your dealer.

FIAT

A lot of car. Not a lot of money.

We Hope You've Enjoyed Our Services This Sunday.

As any of our customers know, when you bank at Fulton National, you get an added blessing. The Fultime Banker. A machine that provides you with 11 different banking services at the push of a button. 24 hours a day. 7 days a week. Including Sunday. Miraculous? Our customers think so.

FULTON NATIONAL BANK
Atlanta, Georgia

	38		39
ART DIRECTOR	Amil Gargano	ART DIRECTOR	Lee Stewart
WRITER	David Altschiller	WRITER	Jim Walsh
PHOTOGRAPHER	Tony Petrucelli	DESIGNER	Lee Stewart
AGENCY	Carl Ally	PHOTOGRAPHER	Phillip Vullo
CLIENT	Fiat Distributors	AGENCY	Lawler Ballard Little
		CLIENT	Fulton National Bank

Instead of giving up on buying a new car, maybe you should give up on the kind of car you've been buying.

A lot of people have finally become fed up with cars. They've given up on big cars. Because today big cars just don't make any sense.

And they've given up on small cars. Because they aren't willing to give up everything they like about big cars just to make sense.

What people seem to be looking for is a different kind of car. A car that offers them the advantages of big cars without many of the disadvantages of small ones.

And that's just the kind of car we make.

The Fiat 128. A small car that's designed differently than most cars you've ever driven.

Eighty percent of the 128 is for passengers and luggage. Only twenty percent is for the engine. As a result, the 128 has more legroom for passengers in the front seat than even Detroit's "Big Three": the Imperial, the Continental and the Eldorado.

Instead of making the 128 sleek and sexy outside, we made it high and roomy inside. You don't get that claustrophobic feeling so common to small cars.

Instead of loading down the car with expensive gadgets and gizmos, we've loaded it down with things that actually make the car perform better.

Rack-and-pinion steering, front-wheel drive, an all-independent suspension, and front-disc brakes aren't options. They're standard equipment.

The 128 isn't at all sluggish. It'll go faster than you'll ever care to go. And the way it handles is nothing short of extraordinary.

It's the kind of car that may start you liking cars all over again.

Overseas delivery and leasing arranged through your dealer.

41

Send yourself cross country in four minutes or less.

With a Xerox Telecopier transceiver and an ordinary telephone, you can send copies of letters, memos, orders, even pictures anywhere in the country in less time than it takes you to finish your morning coffee.

Just put the document into the Telecopier unit, call the place you want it to go, and minutes later an exact copy is there.

Xerox offers you three models to choose from:

The portable Telecopier 400.

The Telecopier 410, which can automatically send and receive as many as 75 documents even when no one's there.

And for people who have to send a lot of information, there's the new Telecopier 200, which can automatically send documents in just two minutes or less.

For more information, contact your local Xerox Telecopier sales representative.

Imagine. With a Xerox Telecopier transceiver you can arrive with important information at an out-of-town office without ever leaving yours.

XEROX

40

	40		41
ART DIRECTOR	Allen Kay	**ART DIRECTOR**	Amil Gargano
WRITER	Steve Penchina	**WRITER**	David Altschiller
PHOTOGRAPHER	Steve Steigman	**PHOTOGRAPHER**	Steve Horn
AGENCY	Needham, Harper & Steers	**AGENCY**	Carl Ally
CLIENT	Xerox	**CLIENT**	Fiat Distributors

One thing about the U.S. Open never changes.

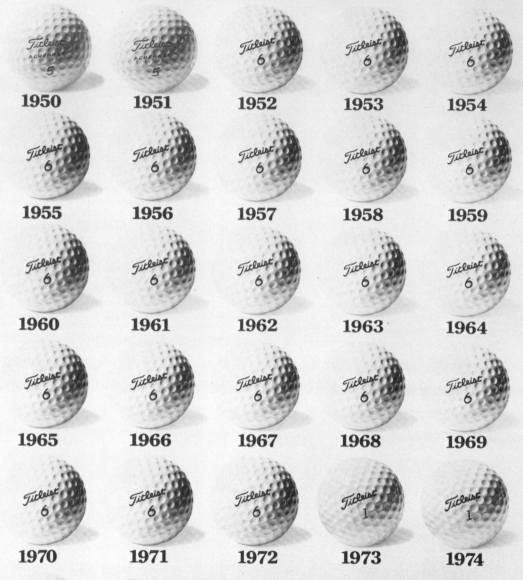

1950 1951 1952 1953 1954

1955 1956 1957 1958 1959

1960 1961 1962 1963 1964

1965 1966 1967 1968 1969

1970 1971 1972 1973 1974

1975

Titleist has been the most played ball at every U.S. Open since 1950. And of the 150 golfers competing this year at Medinah, 86 were playing a Titleist. That's more than all the other balls combined.

After 26 straight years, you'd think winning might lose some of its excitement. It hasn't. Because if the U.S. Open is still the toughest test of a golfer, it's still the toughest test of a ball.

ACUSHNET GOLF EQUIPMENT
Sold thru golf course pro shops only

This advertisement appeared in Golf World, June 27, 1975.

42

ART DIRECTOR Dick Gage
WRITER Jack Wallwork
DESIGNER Dick Gage
PHOTOGRAPHER Bill Bruin
AGENCY Humphrey Browning MacDougall
CLIENT Acushnet Golf Equipment

Donald Brooks
designs a classic collection
for Maidenform.

It's a shame you have to
cover it up.

Padded down underdressings for every body. Stretchiest lace.
Softest crepe. Light and gentle Lycra® spandex. Smooth, luxurious Antron nylon.
In whites, pales, and flowers. Bras from $6. Bikinis from $4.
Donald Brooks for Maidenform®.

Available at Garfinckel's, Goldwaters, Lord & Taylor, I. Magnin and other fine stores in the U.S. & Canada.

44

Introducing the
who-said-what-when Sony.

Sony's new Confer-Corder™ is the first 4-track simultaneous recording/transcribing system to work on a standard cassette. Whew!

Actually, this simply means people can now do what comes naturally in a meeting. Talk all at once. Afterwards, the Confer-Corder tells them—and the transcribing secretary—what they said. Amazing someone didn't think of this before.

The Confer-Corder has four undirectional microphones, each recording onto its own track. For playback or transcribing, the machine neatly separates the voices into their own individual channels.

The Sony Automatic Gain Control equalizes voice sounds, so he who shouts loudest doesn't drown out those who don't shout at all.

So much for who said what. To know when they said it, just touch the index button to mark the indexing strip.

If the meeting's a marathon, Confer-Corder signals you when it's time to change cassettes. Or you can buy the complete Confer-Corder package and record continuously on and on and on. But that's another story, and we'll go on and on and on about it if you'll just send us the coupon below.

Sony Information Center—Business Products Div.
P.O. Box 1624, Trenton, N.J. 08607

NAME _____
PLEASE PRINT
COMPANY _____ TITLE _____
ADDRESS _____ PHONE _____
CITY _____ STATE _____ ZIP ____
© 1975 Sony Corp. of America
SONY is a trademark of Sony Corp.

"IT'S A SONY."

43

	43		44
ART DIRECTOR	Tony Romeo	**ART DIRECTOR**	Brett Shevack
WRITER	Diane Till	**WRITER**	Len Leokum
DESIGNER	Tony Romeo	**DESIGNER**	Brett Shevack
PHOTOGRAPHER	Cailor/Resnick	**PHOTOGRAPHER**	Richard Avedon
AGENCY	Doyle Dane Bernbach	**AGENCY**	Daniel & Charles Associates
CLIENT	Sony	**CLIENT**	Maidenform

YOU MAY BE GIVING THE GOVERNMENT MONEY THE GOVERNMENT WANTS YOU TO KEEP.

If you are, you're not alone.

Every year, literally millions of men and women fail to take advantage of a legitimate tax break. They're people in business for themselves. Doctors, lawyers, shopkeepers, people who put in twelve to fourteen hours a day to make a success of something.

If you run your own business, The Travelers can help you save some money. Money you might otherwise pay out in Federal income taxes.

Under a plan enacted by Congress called HR-10, pre-tax income can be set aside each year for your retirement. If you have a few people working for you,

the plan benefits them as well.

If you'd like to know more about this easy way to prepare for tomorrow, just check the Yellow Pages for your local Travelers Agent.

Because if you run your own business, the day will come when you might like to slow down or step aside. And when that time comes, it's not much consolation to find out that you've succeeded at business but failed at retirement.

THE TRAVELERS
Maybe we can help.

45

45
ART DIRECTOR Michael Tesch
WRITER Ed Butler
AGENCY Carl Ally
CLIENT The Travelers Insurance Co's

It not only goes faster than the others. It gets there $2,000 cheaper.

When we had an independent testing company test the new Fiat 131 against the Audi, the Volvo, and the BMW, we hoped the Fiat would manage to keep up.

After all, for a $4,000 car to just keep up with $6,000 cars would be quite a feat.

As it turned out, the three $6,000 cars didn't quite manage to keep up with us.

In four separate acceleration tests, the Fiat ran away from all of them. In fact, from 40-70 mph the Fiat beat the Volvo

by the incredible margin of 157 feet.

The results of these acceleration tests were no fluke. In separate tests of cornering, steering, road-holding ability, and overall responsiveness, the Fiat proved itself to be every bit the equal of the Audi, the Volvo, and the BMW.

Does all this surprise you? It should. It surprised us.

F I A T

A lot of car. Not a lot of money.

All prices 1975 East Coast POE. Inland transportation, dealer preparation and local taxes additional.
Fiat overseas delivery and leasing arranged through your dealer.

46

46
ART DIRECTOR Amil Gargano
WRITER David Altschiller
PHOTOGRAPHER Peter Papadopolous
AGENCY Carl Ally
CLIENT Fiat Distributors

GOLD

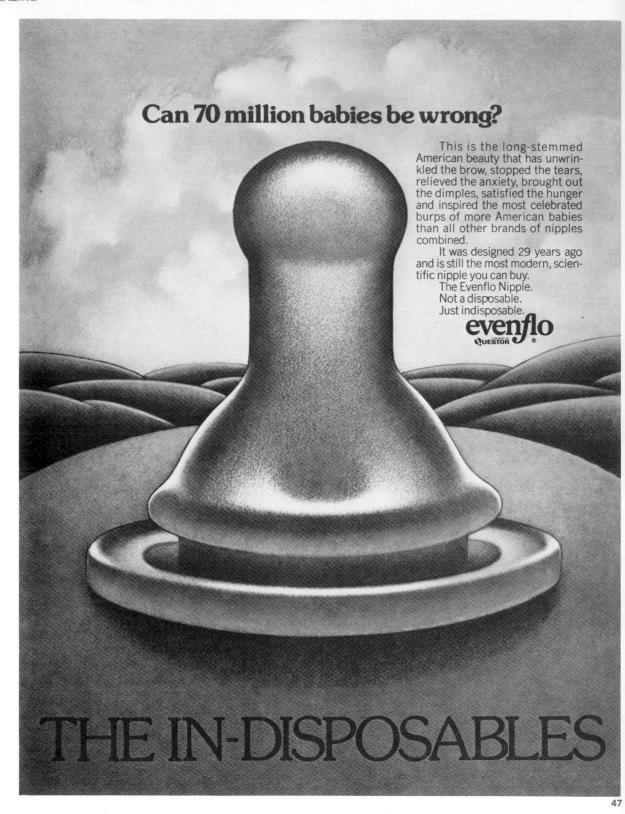

Can 70 million babies be wrong?

This is the long-stemmed American beauty that has unwrinkled the brow, stopped the tears, relieved the anxiety, brought out the dimples, satisfied the hunger and inspired the most celebrated burps of more American babies than all other brands of nipples combined.

It was designed 29 years ago and is still the most modern, scientific nipple you can buy.
The Evenflo Nipple.
Not a disposable.
Just indisposable.

evenflo
QUESTOR ®

THE IN-DISPOSABLES

47
ART DIRECTOR Tony Apilado
WRITER John Paul Itta
DESIGNER Tony Apilado
ARTIST Peter Shaumann
AGENCY John Paul Itta
CLIENT Questor Juvenile
Products

3. Cruel bumps

2. Twisting stairs

4. Wicked curves

Every Peugeot goes through hell to get to America.

When a Peugeot 504 comes off the assembly line, we don't just drive it off to the nearest parking lot.

We take it for a little ride on a devilishly-designed test track outside our factory.

Not just a few Peugeots picked at random, *but every single one of them.* What exactly do we test? Practically everything.

We test the entire electrical system, from the headlights to the taillights and everything in between.

We check all the gauges on the dash and test the speedometer for accuracy.

5. Nasty cobblestones We listen for wind noise around the windows and doors. And we listen for any strange sounds rising out of the transmission.

We test the turn signals to make sure they turn off after completing a turn.

We test the engine for acceleration. And the brakes for deceleration —at a speed of 50 miles an hour, with no hands on the steering wheel. (If the car doesn't stop

6. Fiendish ribs

straight, we check it out and test it again.)

We test the steering system around a few wicked curves. And the suspension system over more than a few bumps and ribs and cobblestones.

And the whole time we're testing to make sure everything works, we're listening to make sure nothing rattles.

In all, a Peugeot has to pass a full hour of tests and inspections before we'll put it on the boat for America.

Why do we go to such extremes to test our cars?

Because since 1889, the year we built the first Peugeot, we've believed in building cars that can take a lot of punishment.

That's why Peugeot won the world's first re- corded auto race in 1894.

And why Peugeot won the 3,075-mile East Afri- can Safari—the world's most brutal test of an auto- mobile—in 1975.

1. Mean moguls

As a result, we're so sure any Peugeot—sedan or wagon, gas or diesel—can pass any test you put it to, we'll let you take one for a 24-hour Trial through any participating Peugeot dealer.

The Peugeot 504. We put it through hell on our test track so it doesn't put you through hell on the road.

PEUGEOT
A different kind of luxury car.

© 1975 Peugeot Inc.

If you really want to save gas, buy a car that doesn't burn any.

PEUGEOT

48
ART DIRECTOR Joe Shansky
WRITERS Don Dickison
Douglas Houston
DESIGNER Joe Shansky
PHOTOGRAPHER Frank Moscati
AGENCY Van Leeuwen
CLIENT Peugeot

Presenting the Royal Camouflage suit in green.

Looks good, doesn't it.
With that handy drawstring hood, elastic parka cuffs and matching pants with take-in leg snaps, it's hard to find a better hunting outfit.
Notice the functional batwing shoulder—that stretches when you stretch. And the waterproof FLEXNET material—that bends when you bend.

Note that big roomy pocket.
Those tough double zippers.
And that convenient jacket length.
Now, add to this those natural splotches of green, and you've got just what you've been looking for.
And now that you've seen it in green, look on the next page—to see it in brown.

And here it is in brown.

It certainly looks the same.
With that handy drawstring hood, elastic parka cuffs and matching pants with take-in leg snaps, you'd think Royal's brown one was just like the green one.
Notice the familiar batwing shoulder—that stretches when you stretch. And that comfortable FLEXNET material—that bends when you bend.
Now, check out the parka.

Note that it's long like a coat instead of short like a jacket. But no matter. Because when you add to it those natural shades of brown, it oddly resembles what you've been looking for in green.
"OK, OK. But where can I find them?"
In the photographs, about dead center.
But for a closer look, try a sporting goods store.
Or turn to page 00.

49

This is a 4.39 carat oval solitaire.
(Enlarged for detail.)

How do you put a price on a miracle?

Born from the earth through volcanic eruptions, all diamonds seem to be a fluke of nature, but here's why a diamond like this is a miracle. And why it is so valuable.

First seen. This diamond might never have seen the light of day if it weren't for man's perseverance. It was trapped in the hardest of rock ore at a De Beers mine near Kimberly. When dug up, special equipment was used to free this stone. Nature just did not want to let it go.

A rare find. When the hard rock was finally split apart, it revealed this rough 8.2 carat diamond. An important discovery, because large diamonds are becoming scarcer every day.

Cut by a master. Some cutters study a miracle like this for a month, others give it a year. They explore all possibilities. Wrestling with weighty decisions. Should this rough diamond be cut in two. Two small round cuts. Or one large oval. This time, the cutter lost almost half the weight of that original rough diamond, and he created one large magnificent oval, worth about $80,000.*

A masterpiece. Reflecting and refracting light in its own inimitable way, there is no other diamond like this in the entire universe. It is one-of-a-kind. As all diamonds are. Each one has a history, a personality and a value all its own. And anyone who is fortunate enough to call a diamond like this his very own, is someone who possesses something nobody else can ever own.

A diamond is forever.
*This price refers to this specific stone. Other stones of the same size can vary in price, according to the individual characteristics of each stone. De Beers Consolidated Mines, Ltd.

50

	49		50
ART DIRECTOR	William J. Urban	ART DIRECTORS	Richard Brown
WRITER	Robert Saxon		Agi Clark
DESIGNER	William J. Urban	WRITER	Libby Daniel
PHOTOGRAPHER	Mathias Oppersdorff	PHOTOGRAPHER	Henry Sandbank
AGENCY	McCann-Erickson	AGENCY	N. W. Ayer
CLIENT	Uniroyal	CLIENT	Du Beers Diamonds

Money can't buy this kind of advertising:

Esquire
THE MAGAZINE FOR MEN AUGUST 1975

VW's new Rabbit is significant because it is a complete departure for Volkswagen, and also because it is the specific type of car that Detroit will be building in the 1980's.

The statistics speak for themselves: accommodation for four, a seventy-horsepower engine, fuel consumption of thirty-eight mpg and a weight of under two thousand pounds.

What they came up with was "a car that doesn't have an ounce of fat, one which provides excellent operating economy, as well as performance and value."

VW's note: The 1976 EPA estimates for the standard shift model are 39 mpg on the highway, 25 mpg in the city. Your actual mileage may vary, depending on the type of driving you do, your driving habits, your car's condition and optional equipment.

Volkswagen is evidently confident in its new model, because it is covered by the VW Owner's Security Blanket, which is as good as you can get.

Personally, I think that VW's Rabbit is one very good idea ahead of its time.

ROAD & TRACK
MAY 1975

The winner, and not by a hare (sorry, couldn't resist). This car does it all: it's small, light, roomy and fast, with nimble and responsive steering, ride and handling. A modern and sophisticated car with a handsome Guigiaro-designed hatchback body, the Rabbit offers one of the most space-saving mechanical layouts we've seen yet: front-wheel drive, transverse engine and a unique, independent rear suspension featuring an integral anti-roll bar and using so little space it's remarkable.

Seats are firm in the German manner and you sit high, viewing the world through an expansive greenhouse.

The Rabbit has a solid feel and an ultramodern look to it. Best of all it is almost sinfully enjoyable to drive.

Popular Mechanics
APRIL 1975

The most important new import for 1975 is the VW Rabbit.

The 1800-pound Rabbit is a mechanical masterpiece. It gets up to 60 mph in about 12 seconds—giving it the edge on some V8 subcompacts. Its hatchback design provides 24.7 cubic feet of luggage capacity with the rear seat folded.

VW got the greatest possible amount of usable interior space into the smallest possible outer shell—and an exterior with some style.

Popular Science
JUNE 1975

A totally new kind of small car. Volkswagen's Rabbit, may make things difficult for U.S. small-car makers in the coming months.

Its speed through the maneuvering courses matched or exceeded the best times of the other test cars, and the feeling of control is ever present, even at high speed and in extreme turning tests.

Economy means light weight, small engines. VW has it now. The others have a way to go.

ROAD TEST
JULY 1975

The Volkswagen Rabbit should be recognized as a true worldcar; it would be as at home commuting in Los Angeles, on a ski trip in the Alps, or chasing kangaroos across Australia. It is the finest example to date of a totally integrated passenger car, useful anywhere in the world and is qualified as no other imported car of 1975 for the Road Test Engineering Award.

CAR and DRIVER
APRIL 1975

Whole populations of drivers will live for years with this car, strongly impressed by its generally nimble disposition and its sensitive feel of the road through the steering wheel and brake pedal. It slips through city traffic like a bicycle and thrives on the parking-space remnants most cars pass by. You can stuff enough groceries for a football team through the rear hatch while the back seat folds and pivots forward out of the way. The only thing you'll need a trailer for is objects too heavy to boost across the high lift-over.

VW-RABBIT

51

The Breaks of the Game.

You couldn't resist that adorable little tennis dress. But how were you to know that when you attacked at the net, your zipper would be the one to surrender?

You should have made sure the dress had a zipper you could rely on. Like the Talon Zephyr® Nylon zipper. Its performance has been proven for years on tennis courts all over the world.

That's why Talon is known as a quality zipper. And why it's your clue that the rest of the dress is well-made, too. The next time you buy a tennis dress (or any active sportswear), look for the Talon name.

Even if you have an undependable volley, at least you'll have a dependable zipper.

Talon THE WORLD'S QUALITY ZIPPER

The Talon Zephyr Nylon Zipper says a lot about what it's in.

52

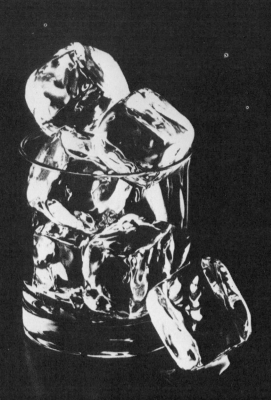

The road to success is paved with rocks.
Let us smooth them for you.

JOHNNIE WALKER® BLACK LABEL 12 YEAR OLD BLENDED SCOTCH WHISKY, 86.8 PROOF. BOTTLED IN SCOTLAND. IMPORTED BY SOMERSET IMPORTERS, LTD., N.Y.

53

ART DIRECTOR	Ivan Sherman
WRITER	Murray Klein
PHOTOGRAPHER	Henry Sandbank
AGENCY	Smith/Greenland
CLIENT	Somerset Importers

Before I discovered McCormick/Schilling the only one who ate well was Ralph.

Each night when our family sat down to dinner, there was a lot of begging at the table. But it never made much difference. My family wouldn't touch my food with a ten-foot fork. No matter how much I begged.

Not that they complained, mind you. When it came to the subject of the dinners I made, my family generally kept their mouth shut. Especially between soup and dessert. But, whenever I told them to come and get it, the only one who did was Ralph. And Ralph never had any taste.

Of course, taste can be a relative thing. In fact, one of my relatives used to say that when it comes to judging taste, leave it to the tongue. Because the tongue always knows. Of course, the nose knows. But nothing knows as much as the tongue. And believe me, if my family's tongues could talk, they could tell you a lot about my cooking. Which was sometimes pretty hard for me to swallow.

Until I discovered McCormick/Schilling. You know, McCormick/Schilling are the spice and flavor people. So when it comes to great spices, seasonings, extracts, and flavors, they come from McCormick/Schilling.

Take their Season-All, for example. Season-All does a lot more than regular seasoning salts. Because it's a lot more than just seasoned salt. It's like a whole spice rack in a single bottle. With a delicate mixture of more than 11 different spices, herbs and special flavorings, that can add a special flavor to almost anything you make.

Raw or cooked vegetables. Salads. Soups and stews. Cheese or egg dishes. Sauces and gravies. Not to mention some of the important basics like seafood, poultry and meats. Just sprinkle a little Season-All, and you've got it made.

Which made a big difference in the meals I made. And the way my family ate. Except for Ralph, of course. He's still eating the way he always did. Sitting under the table.

McCormick/Schilling flavor makes all the difference in the world.

McCormick/Schilling

54

YOU'VE WORN YOUR LAST PRUNE.

For the first time in your life, you can actually own 100% cotton denim jeans and jackets that don't come out of the dryer looking like a prune.

Sedgefield calls them "Do-Nothing" jeans and jackets because you do nothing and they don't wrinkle.

You do nothing and they don't pucker.

Sedgefield jeans and jackets are made of the first 100% cotton denim that shrinks less than 1%. Which means they stay the size you bought.

What's more, they fade beautifully and get softer faster than any jeans and jackets you or anybody else have ever owned.

And they'll last longer.

All because we took 100% cotton denim and added Sanfor-Set. Only Sedgefield has it!

So get your smooth, young body out of the prune you're wearing. (After all, if nature had intended pants to look like prunes, she would have made them with pits.)

What do you have to do to have perfect jeans and jackets from now on? Nothing.

Sedgefield Sportswear Company, 350 Fifth Avenue, N.Y. 10001.

SEDGEFIELD
DO-NOTHING JEANS AND JACKETS WITH SANFOR-SET.

55

	54		55
ART DIRECTOR	Peter Coutroulis	ART DIRECTOR	Merv Shipenberg
WRITER	Jim Weller	WRITER	Martin Shaw
DESIGNER	Peter Coutroulis	DESIGNER	Merv Shipenberg
PHOTOGRAPHERS	Menken/Seltzer	ARTIST	Ray Domingo
AGENCY	Clinton E. Frank	AGENCY	Altman, Stoller, Weiss
CLIENT	McCormick/Schilling	CLIENT	Sedgefield Sportswear

To the host it's half empty. To the guest it's half full.

56
ART DIRECTOR Charles Gennarelli
WRITER Larry Levenson
PHOTOGRAPHER Edward Berger
AGENCY Doyle Dane Bernbach
CLIENT General Wine & Spirit

EVERYTHING IN THE WORLD SHOULD BE MADE THIS GOOD. ONLY BIGGER.

MATCHBOX.

57

Yesterday at Belmont Lucky Lady won, Do-It-Again placed, and Anita Baron showed.

Taking a chance on a horse is one thing.

But taking a chance on the wrong zipper is really gambling.

Anita found that out yesterday in the sixth race.

Lucky Lady was coming up fast. The crowd was going wild.

And in the stretch, Anita's zipper opened up. Right in front of thousands of people.

That's when she realized how important it is to have a dependable zipper at all times.

Like the Talon Zephyr® zipper.

Its quality has been proven in millions and millions of garments. That's why women look for the Talon name when they buy.

From now on, Anita will put her money on dresses with Talon® zippers.

She knows the odds are the rest of the dress will be well made, too.

Talon®
THE WORLD'S QUALITY ZIPPER

The Talon Zephyr zipper says a lot about what it's in.

The New York Times Magazine/June 29, 1975   7

58

	57		58
ART DIRECTOR	Allan Beaver	**ART DIRECTOR**	Ron Becker
WRITER	Larry Plapler	**WRITER**	Anita Baron
PHOTOGRAPHER	Cailor/Resnick	**DESIGNER**	Ron Becker
AGENCY	Levine, Huntley, Schmidt, Plapler and Beaver	**PHOTOGRAPHERS**	Cailor/Resnick
CLIENT	Lesney Products	**AGENCY**	DKG
		CLIENT	Talon

GOLD

SEE THE LANDSCAPE THAT INSPIRED THE LANDSCAPE.

France. Known throughout the world for great artists and great art. And known by great artists for its breathtaking light and magnificent countryside.

For as much as you will appreciate French museums, châteaux, and cathedrals, you'll discover one of the greatest masterpieces in France is the country itself.

On a "Fly-Drive" tour, you can fly to Paris the French way on Air France, and see the treasured works of the masters. Then drive to the country and see the works of nature that inspired them.

Or you can tour the country in the comfort of the French Railroads, without cramping your legs or your wallet.

And you'll see why the world's greatest artists, poets and dreamers made France their home. Or wished that they could.

The French Government Tourist Office, Box 477,
New York, N.Y. 10011
Please send me the information about your "Fly-Drive" tours Quickly.

Name
Street
City
State   Zip

France

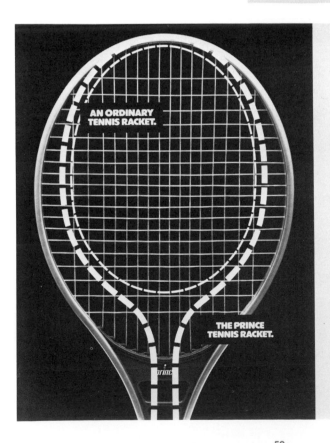

AN ORDINARY TENNIS RACKET.

THE PRINCE TENNIS RACKET.

WITHOUT BREAKING ANY RULES, WE BROKE ALL THE RULES.

With the help of Howard Head, we've created a tennis racket with a 50% larger hitting area. This new racket weighs no more and offers no more wind resistance than an ordinary racket. What's more it is entirely acceptable to both the USPTA and USTA.

This ingenious new racket is called the Prince. Here are just a few of its advantages:

A LARGER SWEET SPOT.
A sweet spot, as if you didn't know, is the high response zone of the strings. A sweet spot 3½ times as large as that of an ordinary racket has an obvious and enormous benefit for any player—from a rank beginner to a Wimbledon champion.

MORE ACCURACY. LESS EFFORT.
The shape of the Prince racket places more of the head's mass further from the center of the racket. This makes the racket less vulnerable to twisting in a player's hand. Which in turn leads to truer, more controlled shots with less effort.

MORE UNIFORM BALL RESPONSE.
The cross strings and the main strings of the Prince have much less proportionate variation than a conventional racket. This consistency of length, offers a more consistent ball response off the strings.

IT'S EASIER TO HIT THE BALL HARDER.
Because there's a much larger high velocity zone on the strings you naturally hit more high velocity shots. In short, you'll find you get more pace on the ball, more often.

GUT-LIKE RESPONSE WITH NYLON.
Conventionally, nylon strings are less responsive than gut. But by stringing nylon over greater lengths at slightly higher tensions, it becomes a different animal. The increased stretch allows the strings to bend back like a drum head and offers better contact with the ball—which means better control.

THE IDEAL RACKET HAS AN IDEAL PRICE.
Not only will the Prince give you a competitive advantage, it's also competitively priced. It sells for $65; a price no higher than that of some ordinary rackets. And now that we've told you a little about the Prince you probably want to see our amazing new tennis racket for yourself.

Toll free, call (800) 257-9480 or, in New Jersey, (800) 792-8697, for the pro shop or tennis shop nearest you.

Discover the many advantages of the Prince racket—before your opponent does.

prince
TENNIS RACKET

	59		**60**
ART DIRECTOR	Allen Kay	**ART DIRECTOR**	Allan Beaver
WRITER	Jan Chinard	**WRITER**	Larry Plapler
ARTIST	Vincent Van Gogh	**ARTIST**	Gabor Kiss
AGENCY	Needham, Harper & Steers	**PHOTOGRAPHERS**	Cailor/Resnick
CLIENT	French Government Tourist Office	**AGENCY**	Levine, Huntley, Schmid, Plapler and Beaver
		CLIENT	Prince

BEFORE YOU TAKE YOUR VOWS, LET US MAKE YOU A FEW PROMISES.

Our promises have a lot to do with those vows.

Because marriage vows are symbolized by the rings you wear. Your engagement ring. And your wedding band.

If they're made of platinum, we can make you quite a few promises. You see, platinum is the most precious metal you can own. The purest. And the toughest.

Because it's precious you'll want the most important stone you'll ever own set in it.

Because it's pure, it can perfectly reflect the beauty and flawlessness of your diamond.

And because it's tough, it will not only hold your stone firmly, but will also resist nicks, scratches and tarnishing.

Naturally, the only thing that can complement the beauty of your platinum engagement ring is a platinum wedding band.

And naturally, the best person to help you select your platinum rings is your jeweler.

Platinum. For rings that are as strong, beautiful and long-lasting as your vows themselves.

Platinum
625 Madison Ave., New York, N.Y. 10022

61

WHY A LOT OF PEOPLE THINK WHEAT GERM TASTES LIKE MEATLOAF

It's unfortunate, but true.

Some people's total wheat germ experience can be summed up in one word.

Meatloaf.

Now, granted, the idea of using Kretschmer Wheat Germ instead of bread crumbs is a good one. It makes a very nutritious meatloaf. It even makes a better tasting one.

But lest you forget, we'd like to say a few words about Kretschmer as a cereal. The world's most nutritious natural cereal.

Natural cereals.

Generally, there are two kinds of cereals. Fortified. And natural. Fortified means vitamins and minerals have been added. And natural cereals contain only natural ingredients.

However, just because a cereal says it's natural, doesn't make it particularly nutritious. (Read a few labels and you'll see what we mean.)

Ounce for ounce, you get a lot more from Kretschmer.

Just an ounce (roughly a quarter of a cup) of Regular Kretschmer Wheat Germ provides 15% of your Recommended Daily Allowance of protein. (More than any of the new "natural" cereals.) And more B Vitamins, iron and Vitamin E than the "naturals" provide.

A matter of taste.

Naturally if your only wheat germ experience is "wheat germ in something else," you have no idea how good it tastes.

Regular Kretschmer has a slightly nutty taste. Something like a cross between bran and toasted walnuts.

Kretschmer Cinnamon Raisin is our idea of what to have for breakfast instead of Danish pastry.

Kretschmer Caramel Apple is so delicious a lot of people eat it by the handful. Right out of the jar.

And Kretschmer Sugar & Honey is so sweet to begin with that all you add is milk.

It doesn't come in a box. So already you know it's different.

Kretschmer Wheat Germ comes in a jar, not a box. This is to keep it fresh, and preserve its nutrients. (The same reason vitamins come in a jar.)

However, you'll still find it in the cereal section of your store. Right next to the cereal boxes.

Because it is a cereal.

A delicious cereal.

Not some secret ingredient.

Ⓜ INTERNATIONAL MULTIFOODS

KRETSCHMER WHEAT GERM. THE WORLD'S MOST NUTRITIOUS NATURAL CEREAL.

62

"I CAN'T BELIEVE THAT'S FUZZY STANDISH"

Somehow, suddenly, he's not a cute boy anymore. He's a very attractive man. Is it the prom? Is it the tux? Is it the end of one kind of life and the beginning of a new time for both of you? It's all of those things. Memories and expectations. All intertwined in one indelible moment. And at times like these all through life, After Six always seems to be there.

Visit the After Six Formal Wear Rental Specialist near you. After Six Formals, 1290 Avenue of the Americas, New York; 22nd and Market Streets, Philadelphia. A prom's not a prom unless it's formal.

after Six FORMALS

CALL (800) 523-4554 TOLL FREE FOR FULL INFORMATION ON FORMAL WEAR FOR PROMS.

65

THE PIONEERS' UNDERWEAR WAS MADE BY THE PIONEERS OF UNDERWEAR.

One hundred years ago rugged men were pushing west. Dynamic men were industrializing the east. And behind the scenes, we too were creating an American institution.

JOCKEY

Jockey International, Inc., Kenosha, Wisconsin, 53140, U.S.A.   Century of Quality/1876-1976

66

	65		66
ART DIRECTOR	Joseph Nissen	ART DIRECTOR	Allan Beaver
WRITER	Edwin Hanft	WRITER	Larry Plapler
DESIGNER	Joseph Nissen	ARTIST	Bettmann Archives
PHOTOGRAPHER	Carl Fischer	AGENCY	Levine, Huntley, Schmidt,
AGENCY	Chalk, Nissen, Hanft		Plapler and Beaver
CLIENT	After Six	CLIENT	Jockey

How to grow a cat.

If you've already got a little kitten, you're lucky.

Now what you need is a little patience. They don't grow-up as fast as you may think they do.

A kitten is a kitten for his whole first year. Because it takes 12 full months of growing before a kitten is a cat.

Even when they look grown-up on the outside (at say six months or so) they've still got to finish growing-up on the inside. Filling out their bodies.

Growing-up isn't easy.

They need all the help they can get. From lots of extra nutrition.

So Purina® Kitten Chow® kitten food (that's the special food for your kitten's whole first year), has the complete and balanced diet they need. With extra vitamins. For keen, bright eyes. Extra calcium. For strong teeth and bones. And plenty of protein. For building healthy muscles.

Kitten Chow tastes so delicious, that if your kitten can't stop eating it after his first year is up, it's okay.

Let him eat. It's good for him.

So even if you've never grown a cat before, now you're an expert. You know how to turn a little kitten into a beautiful grown-up cat.

Kitten Chow. The special food for your kitten's whole first year.

For your pet's health, see your veterinarian regularly

6

Play the ball the pros ignore.

Why should you play our golf ball when most touring pros play another? Because what they play is professional golf. And what *you* play is golf.

Introducing the perfect golf ball for the imperfect golfer.

A pro can make *any* ball play well. He can make it fade or hook at will. He can make it fly high and back up on the green. He hits it consistently farther and consistently better than the average golfer. To anyone who's watched a great pro in action, it looks like a different game.

That's why the average golfer needs Royal® Plus 6 LT. Our tests proved it carries farther than any other golf ball. So you don't have to try to kill the ball to get long yardage. And that means you take better shots.

Pros spend years practicing to get the right trajectory on a golf shot and to make it hold when they hit the green. The Royal Plus 6 LT's unique design and trajectory make it easier for every kind of golfer to do the same.

Consistency and durability.

Pros care a lot about consistency in a golf ball. That's why they handpick their balls and occasionally test them for compression. On the other hand, they *don't* care about durability. They rarely miss-hit a ball so badly that it cuts, and get all their golf balls free anyway.

But most golfers can't afford to play a ball that cuts too easily. That's why we make the Royal Plus 6 with a Surlyn® cover. And when the average golfer does put a perfect swing together, he wants the ball to perform the way he expects it to, without having to test every golf ball he buys. The Royal Plus 6 is a consistent ball and a durable ball—a ball made for the game *you* play.

If we can improve your "inner" game, we can improve your game.

In golf, the most important part of your body is your mind. When you have the right equipment *for you*, the extra confidence that comes with it can make a big difference in your game. When you're playing the Royal Plus 6 LT, you know you're playing the golf ball that carries farther than any other. A durable golf ball. A golf ball that will help keep you out of trouble. So you can relax a little and concentrate on the finer points.

Everyone would like to play flawless golf, but until you do, play the golf ball the pros ignore—Royal Plus 6 LT. The extraordinary golf ball for the ordinary golfer.

Royal UNIROYAL
The perfect golf ball for the imperfect golfer.

(Sold through golf professional shops. Available in 90 and 100 compressions.)

6

	67		68
ART DIRECTOR	Phil Parker	**ART DIRECTOR**	Al Scully
WRITER	Ginni Stern	**WRITER**	Jeff Mullen
PHOTOGRAPHER	Don Mack	**DESIGNER**	Al Scully
AGENCY	Avrett, Free & Fischer	**PHOTOGRAPHER**	Burt Glinn
CLIENT	Ralston Purina	**AGENCY**	McCann-Erickson
		CLIENT	Uniroyal

THERE'S A BIG DIFFERENCE BETWEEN THESE TWO RINGS.

IN TEN YEARS YOU'LL BE ABLE TO SEE IT.

The ring on the left has a band and setting of white gold.

The one on the right has a band and setting of platinum.

Right now, probably only a jeweler could tell the difference.

But in ten years, just about anybody will be able to tell.

Because in ten years both rings are going to go through a lot of wear and tear. And one of them is going to show it.

The white gold one.

You see, as good as white gold is, it doesn't have the properties of platinum.

Platinum is the most precious metal you can own. And the toughest. So it resists things that plague other types of metals. Things like nicks, scratches and tarnishing. Which means you're spared years of cleaning and polishing.

In fact, platinum is so strong, you don't have to worry about your stone coming loose in its setting. Platinum will keep it there. For keeps.

Last but not least, only platinum, because of its purity, can perfectly

reflect the beauty and flawlessness of your diamond.

Platinum. For a ring that will be as bright and beautiful ten years from now as it is today.

Platinum

625 Madison Ave., New York, N.Y. 10022

69

ART DIRECTOR Ed Rotundi
WRITER Kay Kavanagh
DESIGNER Ed Rotundi
PHOTOGRAPHER Phil Marco
AGENCY Della Femina Travisano & Partners
CLIENT Matthey Bishop

© VOLKSWAGEN OF AMERICA, INC.

The Rabbits of Lahaska, Pennsylvania.

It's true.

Meet Peter Rabbit.

His wife, Bunny Rabbit.

Their son, Jay Rabbit.

And their brand-new Volkswagen Rabbit.

Now when we read about them in the newspaper, we couldn't wait to ask the big question:

"What was it that got you to add another Rabbit to the family? The 38 miles to the gallon?*

The incredible acceleration?

The handling ease?

The head and leg room inside of some mid-size cars?

The Hatchback, at no extra charge? VW engineering? The low price?"

"It was all those things," answered Peter Rabbit.

"Plus something I've been fond of for 14 years," added Bunny.

"What's that?" we asked.

"My last name," she smiled.

rabbit

VW

*38 mpg Highway—24 mpg City. Based on the 1975 Model Federal E.P.A. report.

70

ART DIRECTOR John Caggiano
WRITER John Noble
DESIGNER John Caggiano
PHOTOGRAPHER George Hausman
AGENCY Doyle Dane Bernbac
CLIENT Volkswagen

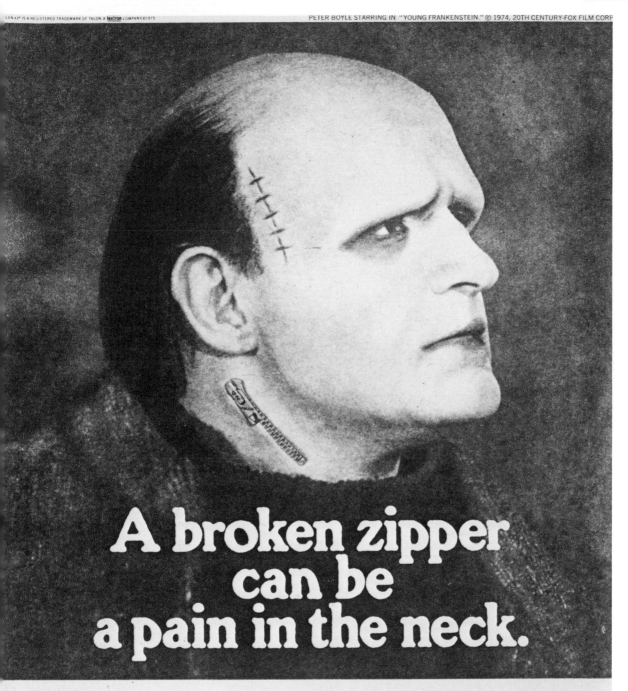

A broken zipper can be a pain in the neck.

When you're making something very strong, you have to hold it together with a zipper that's even stronger.

Like the Talon 42* metal zipper which was designed for strength.

We made it specifically for jeans and work pants, which means it's a zipper that can take the roughest wear and endless washings.

The proof of its toughness is the way the Talon 42 has performed in millions and millions of jeans and work pants. (It also happens to be an excellent zipper for monsters.)

The next time you buy jeans, look for the Talon 42 zipper. It will tell you the manufacturer put as much care into his creation as Young Frankenstein put into his.

Talon
THE WORLD'S QUALITY ZIPPER

The Talon 42 zipper says a lot about the jeans it's in.

The New York Times Magazine/May 18, 1975   21

71

71

ART DIRECTOR	Ron Becker
WRITER	Anita Baron
DESIGNER	Ron Becker
ARTIST	Arton Associates
PHOTOGRAPHER	20th Century Fox
AGENCY	DKG
CLIENT	Talon

PAY MORE, GET MORE.
Plus other compelling arguments for buying a Steinway vertical.

A Steinway vertical piano costs more than other verticals. A little more than some. A lot more than others.

Yet the demand for a fine smaller piano is great enough that half the Steinways® built this year will be vertical models.

Here are some of the compelling arguments that stand behind their popularity.

The 'nuts and bolts' argument.
A Steinway vertical is essentially a Steinway with strings that run up and down instead of back and forth.

It is built with the same care and attention lavished on every Steinway grand.

It is fitted with hammers identical in quality to those in a Steinway grand—made in the same factory with specially prepared felt.

It has Steinway's uniquely responsive Accelerated Action.®

It has Steinway's exclusive Diaphragmatic® Soundboard, 3 millimeters thinner at the edges

This topographical map of a Steinway grand soundboard shows how all Steinway soundboards—grand and vertical alike—are tapered from center to edge. It's one of the reasons only a Steinway sounds like a Steinway.

than in the center, that helps produce a strong, clean, characteristically Steinway sound.

Its tuning pins are set in the patented Steinway Hexagrip Wrestplank...a 6 layer rock maple block that holds the instrument in tune longer.

It is built in the same place, by the same people, of the same materials, to the same standards, as every other Steinway.

It is a smaller Steinway, and emphatically not a compromise.

The 'it's a great investment' argument.
Some pianos are like automobiles.

The moment you get them out of the showroom they begin depreciating like mad. But a Steinway piano holds its value because of its qualities as an instrument and because of its sheer physical endurance.

Look at the back of a Steinway vertical.

Check the dimensions of the back posts.

Note that they are joined invisibly and without resort to metal connectors. The posts are actually mortised into the foot piece, inserted and wedged at the top.

This neat fortress of select maple, birch and spruce is more than capable of bearing the 35,000 odd pounds of pull generated by more than 220 strings under tension.

It is typical of construction found throughout every Steinway, and one of your assurances that, given proper care, your Steinway will last for as long as you care to own it.

The pin-block of every Steinway piano is built of six maple layers, set at 45° to one another, to grip the tuning pins throughout their circumference.

When you compare vertical pianos, look for the hidden features, like back construction. The things you seldom see make a tremendous difference.

Steinway hammers are drilled and 'compression wired' in the Steinway factory. Nobody else makes hammers this way. They'd make any piano sound better.

It is also one of the reasons that if you should want to trade up to a larger piano in the future or simply sell the one you've bought, a Steinway will be worth a greater percentage of what you paid initially, than instruments of lesser quality.

The 'money isn't everything' argument.
This is a musical instrument and as a musical instrument the Steinway vertical has no equal for its size and price.

Its touch and sensitivity and sound are beyond what other verticals are capable of.

It can, in fact, be favorably compared with some small grand pianos which are not Steinways.

Is price really what you're looking for in this kind of purchase?

The 'beautiful furniture' argument.
The style and proportions of a Steinway are authentic, and classically correct.

As a result, the one you buy today will not become 'dated' as you own it. You've probably seen for yourself 100-year-old Steinways that are quite at home in contemporary surroundings.

And as for the tiny details that make the difference between mere cabinetwork and artistry, we simply suggest that you look at a Steinway and compare it with anything else.

A keen eye will tell you more than we can here.

The 'don't short-change the kids' argument.
A vertical is sometimes a first piano for the children.

A poor one is merely a machine for reproducing sound. A fine one can be an inspiration.

And, on a purely technical level, a Steinway opens students' eyes to nuances of touch and tone as no other vertical piano can.

If you're buying the kids a piano just for fooling around, you can get by with less than a Steinway.

But there's always the chance that with the Steinway, they may end up doing a lot more than just fooling around.

For more information write to John H. Steinway, 109 West 57th Street, New York 10019.

STEINWAY & SONS

YOUR LAST PIANO.
Some pianos cost more than others.

But, frankly, none of them is cheap.

So, a careful analysis of what you're getting for your money is not a bad idea.

In a Steinway piano you are getting an instrument which is unquestionably the world standard of how a piano should sound and perform.

You are getting an instrument which is built so carefully and solidly that with reasonable care you can expect to pass it on to your children, even your grandchildren.

And, you are buying a musical objet d'art ...a solid, sculptural piece of cabinetwork that has been designed and built to transcend the whims of decorating style.

No other piano has the qualities you will find in a Steinway piano-a subtle suggestion that you may enjoy more years of good music and make a better investment too, by making your last piano your first piano.

For more about Steinway pianos please write to John H. Steinway, 109 West 57th Street, New York, New York 10019.

STEINWAY & SONS

BUILDING THEM ISN'T EASY EITHER.
It takes 12 months to build a Steinway grand.

There is no way that year can be fully described or recreated on a single magazine page.

It involves feats of craft and patience that boggle the mind.

Imagine.

A soundboard precisely tapered so that it is 8 millimeters thick at its center and 5 millimeters thick at the edges.

An action composed of thousands of tiny reciprocating parts which must operate in utter silence so that all you hear is music. Yet it must be able to hurl 88 hammers at more than 220 strings and return them to rest in fractions of a second.

A wrestplank which must be built to anchor all those strings under 35,000 lbs. tension.

Incredibly, the craft has changed little since Henry E. Steinway first set up shop in 1853.

It is still a job for individuals.

It is still a job of creating instruments one by one.

Admittedly, some delivery techniques have changed. But there is still only one way to build a Steinway.®

For information write to John H. Steinway, 109 West 57th Street, New York, New York 10019.

STEINWAY & SONS

ART DIRECTOR Cathie Campbell
WRITERS Arthur Einstein
Richard Goodman
DESIGNER Cathie Campbell
PHOTOGRAPHERS Sam Varnedoe
David Langley
AGENCY Lord, Geller, Federico
CLIENT Steinway & Sons

SILVER

It takes nerve to compare a $4,000 car with $6,000 cars.
It also takes some $4,000 car.

Audi 100LS $6,002.

Volvo 242 $5,925.

BMW 2002 $5,940.

Fiat 131 $3,958.

We knew we had an exceptional car in the new Fiat 131. So when it came time to test it, we didn't put it up against other $4,000 cars.

Instead, we asked an independent testing company to pit our car against three $6,000 cars that had big reputations for performance: the BMW 2002, the Audi 100 LS, and the Volvo 242.

They ran 3 different kinds of handling tests, and 4 different acceleration tests.

The results surprised even us. In separate tests of cornering, steering, road-holding ability and overall responsiveness, the Fiat was the equal of the BMW, the Audi, and the Volvo.

And in 4 separate acceleration tests, the Fiat ran away from all the others. In fact, from 40-70 mph it beat the Volvo by an astonishing 157 feet.

But there's one test the scientists didn't do. They didn't put their hands in their pockets and come out with a $2,000 saving on the Fiat.

We're saving that test for you.

All prices 1975 East Coast POE. Inland transportation, dealer preparation, and local taxes additional. Fiat overseas delivery and leasing arranged through your dealer.

FIAT
A lot of car. Not a lot of money.

The new Fiat 131.
It's not a dream car. It's a reality car.

Part of the American dream has always been the American dream car. Bigger than it had to be, more powerful than it had to be, more expensive than it had to be. More a symbol of having arrived than a practical means of getting somewhere.

The way things are today, you'd assume that the dream car would have seen its end. But somehow it persists. Despite all the whoopla you've been hearing, in 1975 the average American car will weigh 4,000 pounds and get 13 miles a gallon.

At Fiat, we never shared the idea of the American dream car. Being Italian, we didn't have to.

Instead, we've built our cars to deal with the world as it really is.

The new Fiat 131 is our latest and most advanced extension of this idea.

The 131 squarely faces the problem of survival. If you've gotten used to trading in your car every 2 or 3 years, the 131 should come as a pleasant surprise.

The engine was tested for over a million miles. The valves last twice as long as ordinary valves. The rings are plated with chromium. They last far longer than ordinary rings.

The Fiat 131 faces the problem of rust. Its entire underbody is sealed against the elements. The exhaust system is made of a special steel, impervious to corrosion. The wheels offer the most advanced protection against rust in the world today.

The 131 faces up to the inevitability of accidents. The passenger compartment has been designed with particular attention to passenger safety. It is protected by steel rings at the floor, waist and roof. The gas tank is tucked away behind the back seat, protected by the wheels and trunk. In a head-on collision, the steering wheel collapses.

The 131 gives passengers in the front seat more legroom than the $9,000 Chrysler Imperial. Yet it's shorter than a Vega. It deals very nicely with parking and traffic.

Last, the 131 faces the spiraling costs of owning a car. It's designed to be economical not just on gas, but on day-to-day maintenance and repair.

In times like these, isn't the reality car starting to sound more and more like a dream?

Based on U.S. Environmental Protection Agency fuel economy test results. Overseas delivery and leasing arranged through your dealer.

FIAT

73

ART DIRECTOR Amil Gargano
WRITER David Altschiller
PHOTOGRAPHERS Tony Petrucelli
Peter Papadopolous
AGENCY Carl Ally
CLIENT Fiat Distributors

GOLD

CONSUMER MAGAZINE

The Saab Philosophy, No. 2 in a Series:

"WE BELIEVE HOW FAST A CAR GOES SLOW IS AS IMPORTANT AS HOW FAST A CAR GOES FAST."

When you're heading down the highway at 55 mph, you probably don't think about how fast you can stop. Until somebody stops in front of you.

We thought about it, however, when we first designed the Saab. And that's why we equipped it with big, power-assisted disc brakes on all four wheels (not just two like a lot of cars.) They can take a Saab from 60 mph to 0 mph in only 175 feet.

Of course, braking is only important if you're going, so we gave the Saab a strong, two-liter, fuel-injected, over head cam engine to get it going—from 0 mph to 60 mph in 9.5 seconds.

And with manual transmission, it gets an estimated 30 mpg on the highway and 21 mpg in the city based on EPA tests. The actual mileage you get will vary depending on the type of driving you do, your driving habits, your car's condition and optional equipment.

And to make the driver and passengers feel even more secure, the Saab has front wheel drive, rack-and-pinion steering and roll-cage construction, six solid steel posts, door impact panels, and a body designed to absorb impact in case you can't avoid an accident.

To really appreciate the Saab Philosophy, however, you must drive the result, the new Saab 99 GL. It will make you a believer... fast.

SAAB
IT'S WHAT A CAR SHOULD BE.

The Saab Philosophy, No. 1 in a Series:

"WE BELIEVE A CAR SHOULD HELP CORRECT THE DRIVER'S MISTAKES. NOT VICE VERSA."

When you're heading straight down an open road, we think that's where you should go. No constant correcting. No weaving in the wind. That's why we build every Saab with front-wheel drive.

Front-wheel drive improves directional stability under almost any condition, because the wheels that drive the car are the wheels that steer the car. And the weight of the engine is over those wheels to improve traction.

Front-wheel drive also helps you out in the corners. Even when you enter a fast turn, there is less of a tendency to skid than in rear wheel drive cars, because the front wheels pull you through the turn and the rear wheels tend to follow.

Of course, Saab has many other features that can help a driver: rack-and-pinion steering for precise control, power-assisted disc brakes on four wheels, not just two, and a 2-liter, fuel-injected engine, which with manual transmission, gets an estimated 32 mpg on the highway and 22 mpg in the city based on EPA tests. (The actual mileage you get will vary depending on the type of driving you do, your driving habits, your car's condition and optional equipment.)

In case you can't avoid an accident, Saab also has roll-cage construction, and a body designed to absorb impact to protect the driver and passengers.

To really appreciate a Saab, however, you should drive one. Once you've done that, you'll see that a little philosophy can help you go a long way.

SAAB
IT'S WHAT A CAR SHOULD BE.

The Saab Philosophy, No. 3 in a Series:

"WE BELIEVE THAT SAFETY MEANS AVOIDING ACCIDENTS. NOT JUST SURVIVING THEM."

You never know what's around the next corner until you get there. That's why we designed the Saab to give you every chance to avoid whatever surprise you might find.

We do it with what we call *"active safety devices"*: front-wheel drive for stability, rack-and-pinion steering for precise control, four-wheel power-assisted disc brakes for quick, fade-free stops, and a powerful, fuel-injected 2-liter engine for fast acceleration. Together, they give every Saab exceptional performance.

Of course, if you can't avoid an accident, we've also built every Saab with the *"passive safety devices"* that have made Saab a leader in automotive safety for years. There's roll-cage construction, six solid steel posts to support the roof, door impact panels, and a body designed to absorb impact to protect the driver and passengers.

Every part of the interior of a Saab has also been designed with the safety of the driver and passengers in mind. For example, Saab was first with seats with integral, see-through head restraints. First with a heated driver seat. And first with the ignition key protectively hidden between the front seats.

But you can't really appreciate the confidence and security you get in a Saab, until you drive one.

So take a test drive. It's one thing you'll be glad you didn't miss.

SAAB
IT'S WHAT A CAR SHOULD BE.

74

74
ART DIRECTORS Paul Jervis
Alan Zwiebel
WRITERS Michael Cox
Alan Zwiebel
PHOTOGRAPHER Carl Furuta
AGENCY Cox & Co.
CLIENT Saab-Scania

76

ART DIRECTOR Jim Perretti
WRITERS Neil Drossman
Frank Anton
DESIGNER Jim Perretti
ARTIST Whistlin' Dixie
AGENCY Della Femina, Travisano
& Partners
CLIENT Emery Air Freight

CONSUMER MAGAZINE

With the Martex Master Plan, you don't get · our kind of room. You get your kind of room.

The most important part of your room isn't the furniture. Or the colors on the wall. Or the carpet on the floor.

It's you.

That's why the sheets, towels, blankets and comforters in the Martex Master Plan come in a range of designs wide enough to reflect any personality. Even one that changes with the season.

Take, for example, our Bakuba Collection from the Design Works of Bedford Stuyvesant. It includes enough colors, patterns, and—most important—combinations of colors and patterns, to carry off any look.

Whether it's a country bedroom like the one on the upper left. An urbane music room. Or a bath as individual as the one shown here.

In fact, that's the very essence of our Master Plan: to give you everything it takes to make your room look like your room.

Martex.
We change more than just your bed.

The Martex Master Plan. Now you can · be daring without taking the slightest risk.

Mixing patterns is risky business at best. Done well, the results can be magnificent. But, anything done less than well may not look very attractive.

The Martex Master Plan helps eliminate this risk.

The Master Plan lets you mix patterns daringly, yet with assurance that the results will be enchanting.

How do we achieve this seeming paradox? By designing patterns and colors within each collection to work beautifully with the other patterns and colors in that collection.

Our new China Seas Collection, inspired by the Orient, is a worthy example.

Every sheet, pillowcase, towel, comforter and bedspread works beautifully by itself. Mix them and they become infinitely more dramatic.

Another nice thing about the Martex Master Plan is that you can use our sheets for decorating

throughout the house. Here we've chosen to highlight an otherwise serene gazebo and a jungle like bathroom.

The Master Plan can even add drama to an already dramatic bedroom.

Perhaps the nicest thing of all is how you can make the Plan work for you.

Use it lavishly and it can make any setting tastefully daring. Use it sparingly and it can make any setting simply terrific.

Martex.
We change more than just your bed.

77

ART DIRECTOR Martin Lipsitt
WRITERS Barry Greenspon
Neil Calet
DESIGNER Martin Lipsitt
PHOTOGRAPHER Jerry Abromowitz
AGENCY DKG
CLIENT West Point Pepperell

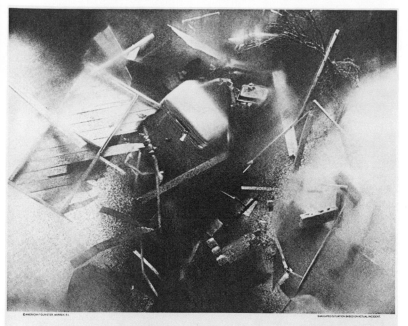

"Dear American Tourister: You got hit by a tornado."

On April 3, 1974, the following happened.

A tornado slammed into an Alabama trailer court, demolishing Wilfred Gileau's house trailer and everything in it.

On April 4, 1974, the following happened.

Under piles of wreck and rubble, Wilfred Gileau found the one thing the tornado hadn't destroyed. His American Tourister. It was a little scuffed, a little scraped, but in good working order.

Mr. Gileau was amazed. And frankly, so are we. Because we don't build American Touristers to do things like ride out tornados.

When we take the toughest materials we can find to mold our cases, and wrap each case with a strong stainless steel frame, and put in nonspring locks designed not to spring open on impact, we do it for just one reason.

So that year after year and mile after mile, your American Tourister will go through all the everyday perils of everyday traveling.

We don't intend American Touristers to survive tornados.

We do intend them to survive your next trip to Wichita.

American Tourister

78

"Dear American Tourister: They should build cars like you build suitcases."

When Mr. and Mrs. Neil Arveschoug stopped their car behind a truck, the car that was following them kept on going.

Right into the Arveschougs' car.

Which, in Mrs. Arveschoug's words, "folded up like an accordion". It had to be sold for junk.

But the Arveschougs' American Tourister held up a little better. Even though it was caught in the crunch, it didn't pop open or fall apart. It just bent a little.

Now, this is very nice to hear. But honesty compels us to tell you that we don't build American Touristers to survive extraordinary things like automobile crashes.

We mold our cases of 16 different strong materials, and give them tough stainless steel frames.

We reinforce them with fiberglass, not just here and there, but through and through.

We put in nonspring locks designed not to spring open on impact. And we do all this for just one reason.

So your American Tourister will survive the ordinary perils of ordinary travel, year after year, and mile after mile.

Detroit, is that such a bad idea?

American Tourister

"Dear American Tourister: Thanks to you I sleep better."

Hey.

Some of you out there aren't using your American Touristers quite the way we meant them to be used.

Like Mrs. Diane Helmick. For three years, ever since the leg broke on her big double bed, she used her American Tourister to hold the whole thing up. After all, she wrote us, "it was the only thing sturdy enough around the house."

Thank you, Mrs. Helmick. But we want all of you out there to know that we don't build American Touristers to hold up beds. We just build them to hold up.

We use the strongest materials available to mold each case.

We wrap each case with a tough stainless steel frame. (Not just to protect the outside, but to protect what's inside.)

We even put in nonspring locks designed not to spring open on impact.

We do everything we can to give you a suitcase that can survive the ordinary hazards of ordinary travel. Year after year. Mile after mile.

American Tourister wants you to know you can rest easy, in more ways than one.

American Tourister

78

ART DIRECTOR Jack Mariucci
WRITER Marica Bell Grace
PHOTOGRAPHERS Henry Sandbank
Cosimo
Dick Stone
AGENCY Doyle Dane Bernbach
CLIENT American Tourister

Careful investigation proves Top Choice chopped burger looks amazingly like hamburger.

It's elementary! Gaines® Top Choice® Chopped Burger For Dogs looks almost identical to hamburger.

And there's no mystery why. Top Choice is made with beef by-products and real beef, so it's moist and meaty. It even holds together just like hamburger.

But it's better for your dog than hamburger, because it also contains vegetables, vitamins and minerals for a fully balanced diet.

Which brings us to Country Style Top Choice. The only chopped burger for dogs with real cheese flavor and protein-rich egg, the equivalent of a quarter of an egg in every serving.

Original Top Choice and Country Style Top Choice. You don't need an investigation to prove they're both great for your dog.

Original Top Choice® and Country Style® Top Choice.® For dogs who love hamburger, they're better for them.

Gaines

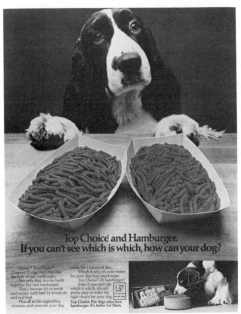

Top Choice and Hamburger. If you can't see which is which, how can your dog?

Gaines® Top Choice® Chopped Burger For Dogs has the look of real hamburger.

Not only that, it even holds together like real hamburger.

That's because it's so moist and meaty, with beef by-products and real beef.

Plus all of the vegetables, vitamins and minerals your dog needs for a balanced diet.

Which is why it's even better for your dog than hamburger.

Top Choice? Or hamburger? Even if you can't see which is which, it's still pretty easy to make the right choice for your dog.

Top Choice. For dogs who love hamburger. It's better for them.

If your dog could read labels, we think he'd buy our chopped burger.

If your dog could read the ingredients label on a package of Gaines® Top Choice® he'd really learn something.

Real Beef.

He'd learn, for instance, that Top Choice has real beef in it, not just beef by-products. *(Does the chopped burger you feed your dog have any beef?)*

A Balanced Diet.

He'd also learn that along with beef by-products and real beef, Top Choice also contains vegetables, vitamins and minerals.

All the things he needs for a completely balanced diet. And that's not all.

Moist and Meaty.

If your dog continued reading the rest of our package he'd find out that Top Choice is also moist and meaty. So moist and meaty it even holds together like real hamburger.

Yes, if your dog could read our package, he'd find some things that aren't on the packages of other chopped burgers for dogs.

Ah, but everyone knows dogs can't read. But at least their owners can.

No wonder it's called Top Choice.®

GF GENERAL FOODS

79

79
ART DIRECTOR Howard Brody
WRITER Neal Dearling
DESIGNER Howard Brody
PHOTOGRAPHER Nick Samardge
AGENCY Young & Rubicam
CLIENT General Foods

A Peugeot isn't a Peugeot until it's passed some 46,000 inspections.

These are some of the people who do the inspecting. There are thousands more.

Because one out of every 10 people who work in the Peugeot factory works in quality control.

It's a very big job.

Practically every single part of every single Peugeot is inspected at least once after it's made. Then it's stamped or signed by the inspector who inspected it.

Every part that affects passenger safety is inspected at least three times—visually, under ultraviolet light, and electronically to expose any otherwise invisible flaws.

Every engine is bench-tested for 12 minutes. Every transmission is sound-tested in a special booth by an inspector whose hearing is tested *everyday*.

In fact, we're so fussy about the quality of our car, the last 75 feet of every assembly line is devoted entirely to inspection.

And still we're not satisfied.

So we take every single Peugeot for a ride on a test track to make sure everything that's supposed to work works the way it's supposed to. We even take it through a rain tunnel to make sure it doesn't leak.

Of course, tests and inspections are only part of a well-built car. That's why we're equally tough about the parts that go into a Peugeot.

Take the shock absorbers. They're designed to be good for at least 60,000 miles of normal driving. The body is welded in 7,000 places, so there's virtually no place for rattles. Critical working parts are made of costly forged or cast steel instead of stamped steel.

Reports Road Test magazine: "Nowhere in the bone, sinew and muscle of the Peugeot can be found the slightest bit of corner-cutting to enable it to sell for thousands less than the above named cars [BMW, Mercedes-Benz and the Porsche 911]. Yet somehow it does."

If you'd like to inspect a Peugeot—gas or diesel, 4-door sedan or 5-door wagon—stop by your local Peugeot dealer. Chances are, he'll also let you take one for a 24-hour Trial.

If you'd like more information, write Peugeot, Inc., Dept. A, 300 Kuller Road, Clifton, N.J. 07015.

PEUGEOT
A different kind of luxury car.

© 1975 Peugeot Inc.

80

ART DIRECTORS Roger Mosconi / Joe Shansky
WRITERS Don Dickison / Douglas Houston
DESIGNERS Roger Mosconi / Joe Shansky
ARTIST Whistl'n Dixie
PHOTOGRAPHERS Dick Miller / David Langley / Frank Moscati
AGENCY Van Leeuwen
CLIENT Peugeot

80

CONSUMER MAGAZINE

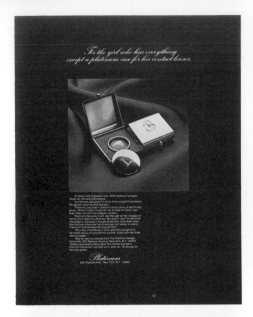

81

ART DIRECTOR Mark Yustein
WRITER Helen Nolan
DESIGNER Mark Yustein
PHOTOGRAPHER Phil Marco
AGENCY Della Femina, Travisano
& Partners
CLIENT Matthey Bishop

The Fisher-Price Dolls welcome Joey, the new boy on the block.

Joey has freckles, rowdy hair and rugged blue jeans. But someone still has to tie his sneakers for him. And help him on and off with his football jacket. Maybe your own child will show him how.

Like our other little lapsitters, Jenny, Mary, Elizabeth, Natalie, Audrey and Baby Ann, our Joey has a huggable body, hands and face that can be washed and hair that doesn't mind a combing.

And because he's a Fisher-Price Doll, he can take all the cuddling and spanking and rough-house that a well-loved doll is given. Because when dolls turn into best friends, you want them to be with you a long, long time.

Look for Fisher-Price Dolls in your favorite Fisher-Price toy center.

82

Fisher-Price knows that a good truck should go through rain, snow, sand and mud puddles, and still look new.

So we built these great galumphing construction trucks. With big grab handles and cranks and scoops. To dig and lift and dump lots of good earth. And each one can come clean with a garden hose. So it can stay overnight in the yard, and still have the run of the house.

There's a Dump Truck, a Scoop Loader and a Shovel Digger. Each with its own one- or two-member crew.

Each with a job of its own. All they need are a few children to get them working together.

And because we think like parents, every Fisher-Price truck is smooth, tough, rust-proof and practically indestructible. With what they're going to go through they have to be.

Look for new Fisher-Price Trucks in your favorite Fisher-Price toy center.

Fisher-Price knows it takes more than a bottle, a bath, and some cuddling to keep a baby happy.

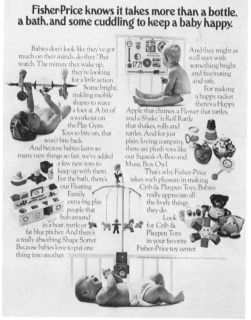

Babies don't look like they've got much on their minds, do they? But watch. The minute they wake up, they're looking for a little action. Some bright, tinkling mobile shapes to wave a foot at. A bit of a workout on the Play Gym. Toys to bite on, that won't bite back.

And because babies learn so many new things so fast, we've added a few new toys to keep up with them. For the bath, there's our Floating Family, extra-big play people that bob around in a boat, turtle or fat blue pitcher. And there's a really absorbing Shape Sorter. Because babies love to put one thing into another.

And they might as well start with something bright and fascinating and safe.

For making a happy racket there's a Happy Apple that chimes, a Flower that rattles, and a Shake 'n Roll Rattle that shakes, rolls and rattles. And for just plain loving company, there are plush toys like our Squeak-A-Boo and Music Box Owl.

That's why Fisher-Price takes such pleasure in making Crib & Playpen Toys. Babies really appreciate all the lively things they do.

Look for Crib & Playpen Toys in your favorite Fisher-Price toy center.

82

ART DIRECTOR	Rafael Morales
WRITER	Francesca Blumenthal
DESIGNER	Rafael Morales
PHOTOGRAPHERS	David Langley
	Arnold Beckerman
AGENCY	Waring & LaRosa
CLIENT	Fisher-Price Toys

The next time you have guests for dinner, entertain the idea of Salton Hotray.

Nothing throws women into panic quite like entertaining guests for dinner.

Does the scented soap in the powder room clash with the air freshener? Was it a mistake to invite both the vegetarian and the butcher? Are the professionally lettered placecards a touch too overboard?

Certainly not the least of the traumas of putting a formal or informal dinner party together is the dinner itself.

Will the hot buffet turn into a lukewarm buffet if one before-dinner cocktail stretches to three? Will your 20 lb. turkey slowly shrink itself to a miniscule morsel in the oven while everyone is lingering over the hors d'oeuvres? Should latecomers be thrown out rather than be subjected to food that has dried out?

Cold salads are one way around the problem. But Salton has a better idea for you to entertain: Hotray.

It keeps your food as hot and fresh as if it just came out of the oven. Even if it just came out of the oven hours before.

The temperature of its shatter-resistant glass surface is thermostatically controlled to keep food just under the cooking point. On Hotray, your food neither continues to cook, nor stands around growing cold. It just sits there, waiting patiently for whenever you and your guests are ready to eat. Without losing a shred of flavor, a degree of temperature.

This way, you can prepare your food, place it on Hotray and join the party. Maintaining some semblance of cool, secure in the knowledge that your food is remaining hot and tasty.

Even if you're anti-social, you should be pro-Hotray.

Of course, you don't have to invite a group of people over to reap the benefits of Hotray. It's just as functional for everyday use.

Preparing breakfast frees you of the dilemma of which gets done first: the pancakes or the sausage? You can make both independently and place each on Hotray as it's done. And they'll taste like they were done at precisely the same second.

For lunch, dedicated mothers can prepare lunch early and sit down with their kids and enjoy a hot lunch. Lazy mothers can leave Hotray plugged in all morning and serve hot leftover pancakes and sausage.

And if the telephone invariably rings just as you're taking the dinner roast out of the oven and you don't even have to answer it to know it's your husband saying he'll be late for dinner, no problem. On Hotray, it'll keep perfectly.

With Hotray, you also need not trot back and forth from kitchen to dining room serving your family dinner. It (and you) can sit nicely by the dining room table throughout the entire meal.

Hotray is available in varying degrees.

Although every Hotray performs the same function, there are a number of them to choose from. Shown here is Hotray model H930, $34.95.

There's also the utterly simple model at $10.95. All the way up to the elaborate Hotable at $300 that's as much an elegant serving cart as it is a place to keep food hot.

Some come with a feature called Sun-spot that keeps beverages piping hot, and some have adjustable thermostatically-controlled temperature settings.

You can get one with a drawer for hot buns. And Hotray under a covered dome for outdoor dining.

For a complete Salton Catalog and our "After-You-Cook Book" write to Salton, Inc., 1265 Zerega Avenue, Bronx, New York 10462.

Salton

Four gifts from Salton that make peanut butter, yogurt, ice cream and sense.

Salton Peanut Butter Machine. Using no oil, salt, or emulsifiers, this ingenious new contraption turns peanuts into freshly-ground peanut butter that's actually warm. And it's the one gift that you can be sure that no one already has. $29.95.

Salton Yogurt Maker. It makes yogurt as light or creamy as you like. In whatever fresh flavor you choose to add to it. For about 70% less than what it would cost you for store-bought yogurt that doesn't taste nearly as good. $11.95.

Salton Ice Cream Machine. Put an end to the pounds of crushed ice and salt that other ice cream makers ask you to use. With Salton, you prepare your favorite ice cream recipe (from the recipe booklet included), pour it into the machine, place it in the freezer and in one hour, you have a quart of fresh, naturally rich ice cream. $24.95.

Salton Hotray.® This doesn't make anything but a great deal of sense. Because it keeps breakfast, lunch and dinner hot and flavorful, without drying out or turning cold long after it comes off the stove or out of the oven. In a wide variety of sizes and models from $10.95.

For a complete catalog of products write Salton, Inc., 1268 Zerega Ave., Bronx, N.Y. 10462.

Salton

The New York Times Magazine/December 7, 1975   91

Now you can make the stuff that sticks to the roof of your mouth under your own roof.

If you're a proponent of the theory that if you want something done right, you have to do it yourself, take heed.

Salton, the company that makes do-it-yourself yogurt and do-it-yourself ice cream possible, has done it again.

The ingenious little contraption pictured is the Salton Peanut Butter Machine. For just $29.95, you can own the only machine of its kind that allows you to make peanut butter at home. And the process is so simple, that even a seven-year-old can (and undoubtedly will) operate it.

All you add are peanuts. Flick a switch, adjust the dial to chunky or smooth, and through a miracle of advanced scientific technology, out comes the goo. Freshly-ground peanut butter, that's actually warm. (And as any purist will tell you, any peanut butter worth its salt contains no added oils or emulsifiers. Or no added salt.) So it tastes far better than any peanut butter that comes in a jar.

For a complete catalog of products write Salton, Inc., 1268 Zerega Ave., Bronx, N.Y. 10462.

The Salton Peanut Butter Machine

83

ART DIRECTOR	Ron Brello
WRITER	Hy Abady
DESIGNER	Ron Brello
PHOTOGRAPHER	Michael O'Neill
AGENCY	Sacks and Rose
CLIENT	Salton

84

ART DIRECTOR Helmut Krone
WRITERS Michael Mangano
Robert Levenson
DESIGNER Helmut Krone
ARTIST Roger Metcalf
PHOTOGRAPHER Guy Morrison
AGENCY Doyle Dane Bernbach
CLIENT Volkswagen

GOLD

We expect that fertilizer is fertilizer to most people. They put some down in the Spring, still have those little bare spots all Summer, and figure that's life.

Here on our grass research farm in Marysville, Ohio, we actually make bare spots come and go by how we use fertilizer.

Take two of the chief reasons for bare spots. The first is that one feeding in the Spring won't give your lawn enough food for the Summer. Thick green grass takes more nitrogen, phosphorus and potash than soil has in it.

The second is that the average fertilizer doesn't give your lawn enough food, either. You get a quick flash of green and think you've got something, and then three weeks later all the activity simply quits. That was all the food your fertilizer had.

When it comes to lawn food, and especially the way it feeds your grass, the best fertilizer we've made in 100 years is *New Super Turf Builder*.

Grass like this takes more food than most soil has.

If you aren't just plain glad you used this new fertilizer, we don't want to keep your money.

We make this with fast and slow release nitrogen. You'll see your lawn green up the very first week. By the third week, when ordinary fertilizers usually run out of gas, your lawn will be a deeper, more intense green than you ever thought you'd get. And by now, our slow-release nitrogen takes over, feeding your lawn for up to five weeks after that.

Now, this one feeding will start thousands of new grass plants in your lawn in a few weeks. But if you'll spend 30 minutes with your spreader every couple of months, you won't be able to see the ground through the grass you'll have.

Your Scotts retailer can tell you all about New Super Turf Builder. (It's the one that comes in a box.) Or you can call us toll-free: (800) 543-1415. From Ohio (800) 762-4010, from the Dakotas and Nebraska West: (800) 543-0091.

You might also like to get our quarterly, Lawn Care. It's free and it's filled with ideas. Just write us here in Marysville, Ohio. We've been in this business 100 years. We'll get you a lawn.

The dandelion is one of nature's prettiest villains. It's not only good to eat, there was a time when people took it as medicine.

But here in Marysville, Ohio, where we have our main grass research farms, it's just another weed.

In fact, it's a bully. It pushes the good grass out of the way and takes the food in the soil for itself. This is one weed that doesn't die every year. It's a tough perennial with roots that go down as far as 2 feet.

And that pretty yellow blossom turns into a white puffball full of seeds that the wind carries all over your lawn.

You can't stop dandelions from coming in, the way you can with crabgrass.

You have to get this pest to get rid of it. But it's easy to lick.

Leave one bit of its root and the dandelion will be back.

We'll get these dandelions out of your lawn and that's a promise.

And don't make it hard on yourself by trying to dig it out. Leave one bit of that root and back she'll come.

But just spend 30 minutes with your spreader and our *Turf Builder Plus-2*. Your dandelion population (and a lot of other weeds) will be on the way out in a matter of days. That's our promise.

And the *Turf Builder* in this is our own slow-release fertilizer. It will also feed your lawn for up to 2 months.

In fact, if you also spend 30 minutes with our straight Turf Builder—say once in July and once again in September—your grass will be so thick there won't even be room for weeds to come in. Good thick turf helps crowd weeds out.

Your Scotts retailer can tell you all about weeds. (We've probably even had him out here to see how we do it.) But you can call us toll-free if you like: (800) 543-1415. From Ohio: (800) 762-4010, from the Dakotas and Nebraska West call: (800) 543-0091.

You might also like to get our quarterly, Lawn Care. It's free and it's filled with good things to know about grass.

Just write us here in Marysville, Ohio. You don't need a street address. We've been here since just after the Civil War.

Get rid of the seeds now and you won't get the crabgrass in August.

Here in the good earth of Marysville, Ohio, where we have our main grass research farms, we also grow just about every weed you will ever see.

And the first thing you might like to know is that you don't have any crabgrass right now. What you have are seeds. We're going to get rid of the crabgrass you would have had by August.

This weed is also called finger grass because its joints grow roots, so it spreads like fingers growing other fingers. It dies with the first frost and that's when it spreads its seeds.

Over 1,000,000 from just one plant.

By late May, up they come, all ready to choke out your good grass. So right now is the time to stop them, and it won't take you more than 30 minutes with a spreader and some of our *Halts Plus*.

We spent 10 years just developing and using Halts Plus here in Marysville. This stuff not only stops crabgrass seeds, it also won't hurt your good grass or your hedge.

And yet the best thing about it isn't just the Halts, it's the Plus. A big dose of our Turf Builder.

A thick healthy turf will help crowd crabgrass out. We do something special with our fertilizer for this. It has slow-release nitrogen that will go on feeding your lawn for up to 2 months.

In fact, if you spend just 30 minutes every couple of months with our straight *Turf Builder* you'll have thicker grass than you ever dreamed of. And it isn't all that much work.

But right now, put down Halts Plus. It's easy work, not like mowing. Just a walk around with a spreader does it.

We'll keep crabgrass from growing in your lawn and we put that in writing.

If you have any questions about weeds or whatnot, call us toll-free: (800) 543-1415. From Ohio: (800) 762-4010, from the Dakotas and Nebraska West call: (800) 543-0091. Or ask your Scotts retailer. Chances are he's spent a little time with us here in the country.

You might also like to get our quarterly, Lawn Care. It's free and it's filled with good things to know about grass.

Just write us here in Marysville, Ohio. You don't need a street address. We've been here since just after the Civil War.

In just two weeks, bugs so small you can't even see them can finish off a whole lawn. So call this a kind of short lesson in bugs.

While our main grass research farms are here in Marysville, Ohio, we got to know the different bugs in the country by going where they are.

Mole crickets in Florida. Chinchbugs in Connecticut. There are Texas bugs, California bugs, special bugs everywhere.

The closest thing there is to a national bug is the chinchbug. This is a vampire. It slips its beak into the grass plant, lets loose with a toxin, and drains off the plant's juices. The toxin does it. That grass is dead.

Let's start with the good news. The same treatment that takes care of one bug—sod webworms, say—also takes care of other bugs. Grubs, armyworms, most any bugs you have.

You'd better get him before he gets your lawn.

That tiny moving object eating your lawn is a goner, or we pay for this bag.

There are two main kinds of bugs to worry about. The surface kind lives down in the thatch and either chews or sucks fluid out of your grass. Most of these generally grow up to be moths.

The other kind lives underground, eats your grass roots and usually becomes a beetle.

In fact, dead grass is the first clue you've got bugs. You're a lot better off doing something before they start.

Our *Lawn Insect Control* will handle just about any bug you can get, and one treatment lasts about 8 weeks. We also have *New Kwit* for towns where chinchbugs are an out-and-out epidemic.

And a feeding of Scotts' fertilizer will help your lawn come back after an attack. All our fertilizers are summer-safe and give your damaged lawn the slow-release feeding it needs.

Your Scotts retailer can tell you all you want to know. (Use lots of water when you're treating chinchbugs, for instance.)

But if you want to call us toll-free with any questions, dial: (800) 543-1415. From Ohio: (800) 762-4010, from the Dakotas and Nebraska West: (800) 543-0091.

You might also like to get our quarterly, Lawn Care. It's free and it's filled with good things to know. Just write: Scotts, Marysville, Ohio. We want to see that lawn grow as much as you do.

85

ART DIRECTOR Helmut Krone
WRITER Jack Dillon
DESIGNER Helmut Krone
ARTIST Jerry Cosgrove
AGENCY Doyle Dane Bernbac
CLIENT O. M. Scott & Sons

The Breaks of the Game.

You couldn't resist that adorable little tennis dress. But how were you to know that when you attacked at the net, your zipper would be the one to surrender?

You should have made sure the dress had a zipper you could rely on. Like the Talon Zephyr® Nylon zipper.

Its performance has been proven for years on tennis courts all over the world.

That's why Talon is known as a quality zipper. And why it's your clue that the rest of the dress is well-made, too. The next time you buy a tennis dress (or any active sportswear), look for the Talon name.

Even if you have an undependable volley, at least you'll have a dependable zipper.

Talon®

The Talon Zephyr Nylon Zipper says a lot about what it's in.

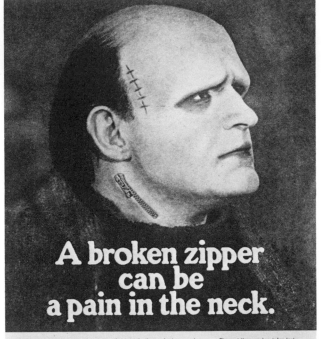

A broken zipper can be a pain in the neck.

When you're making something very strong, you have to hold it together with a zipper that's even stronger.

Like the Talon 42™ metal zipper which was designed for strength.

We made it specifically for jeans and work pants, which means it's a zipper that can take the roughest wear and endless washings.

The proof of its toughness is the way the Talon 42 has performed in millions and millions of jeans and work pants. (It also happens to be an excellent zipper for monsters.)

The next time you buy jeans, look for the Talon 42 zipper. It will tell you the manufacturer put as much care into his creation as Young Frankenstein put into his.

Talon®

The Talon 42 zipper says a lot about the jeans it's in.

The New York Times Magazine/May 18, 1975   21

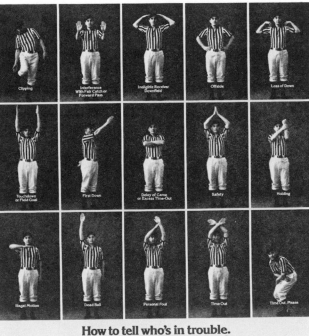

How to tell who's in trouble. Your team, their team, or the referee.

With Talon, you won't be penalized for a broken zipper.

A Talon® zipper says a lot about what it's in.

Talon®

Yesterday at Belmont Lucky Lady won, Do-It-Again placed, and Anita Baron showed.

Taking a chance on a horse is one thing.

But taking a chance on the wrong zipper is really gambling.

Anita found that out yesterday in the sixth race.

Lucky Lady was coming up fast. The crowd was going wild.

And in the stretch, Anita's zipper opened up. Right in front of thousands of people.

That's when she realized how important it is to have a dependable zipper at all times.

Like the Talon Zephyr® zipper. Its quality has been proven in millions and millions of garments. That's why women look for the Talon name when they buy.

From now on, Anita will put her money on dresses with Talon® zippers.

She knows the odds are the rest of the dress will be well made, too.

Talon®

The Talon Zephyr zipper says a lot about what it's in.

86

86
ART DIRECTOR Ron Becker
WRITER Anita Baron
DESIGNER Ron Becker
PHOTOGRAPHERS Cailor/Resnick
20th Century Fox
Denny Tillman
Jerry Abromowitz
AGENCY DKG
CLIENT Talon

SILVER

The key to Sony's success is taking a big idea and making it smaller.

The Sony story started in 1946 when two men named Akio Morita and Masaru Ibuka opened a company called Tokyo Telecommunications Electronics Corporation.

Their first venture was the tape recorder. Which resulted in a modest but encouraging 10,000 sales.

Buoyed by this success, Morita and Ibuka took their first small step.

By changing a big name, Tokyo Telecommunications Electronics Corporation, to a small one. Sony.

A word derived from the Latin "sonus" meaning sound.

In 1954, Sony took its second small step.

It was when we got the right to make the first transistors in Japan from Western Electric. And combined it with some Far Eastern know-how.

As a result of this combination, the listening habits of millions of people were changed forever.

Because in 1955, Sony came out with the first all-transistor radio in Japan.

And quickly followed it with the world's first pocket-size all-transistor radio.

As you might expect, by this time everyone knew Sony was a company to be reckoned with.

What they didn't know was how much more reckoning there would be.

Because in 1961, Sony introduced the world's first transistorized video tape recorder. And a few years later, the first all-transistor VTR for the home.

And there was still more to come.

For example, take a look at our televisions. You'll see the results of over 15 years of solid-state TV experience that started when Sony introduced all-transistor television with an 8" set.

And, as Sony televisions got smaller, Sony got bigger.

In 1962, we introduced a highly successful 5" TV. And in 1964, a 4" one.

Then in 1969, Sony passed its toughest test with flying colors. It was when we introduced our revolutionary 12" Trinitron TV. Which, even though it was almost half the size of other color TV's, was quickly accepted as the standard by which all were judged.

And, finally, this year, Sony took its first small step in the hi-fi business. By introducing our vertical field-effect transistors that have literally set the audio world on its ear.

So in looking back over the last 25 years, you can see how taking big ideas and making them smaller has truly been the key to our success.

But there's really much more to Sony than just that.

Because while the day might come when we can't make things smaller than anybody else, the day will never come when we won't make them better.

SONY

© 1975 Sony Corp. of America. Sony, 9 W. 57 St., N.Y., N.Y. 10019.
SONY and TRINITRON are trade marks of Sony Corporation.

The only thing it won't do is take the final.

Bored of education?

Well, with a Sony TC-67 cassette recorder, you can go right to the head of your class without even being there.

It has a highly sensitive, built-in electret condenser microphone that we were the first to make.

It has our unique Sonymatic recording system that adjusts to different voice levels.

It has an automatic shut-off switch that eliminates worrying about when the tape runs out.

And it's priced so reasonably you won't have to get a part-time job to pay for it.

But the best thing of all is that the TC-67 cassette recorder comes with something nobody else can offer you: the Sony name.

So you can be sure it won't fail even if you do.

SONY

When Western Electric told us the first transistors could only work in hearing aids we didn't hear them.

So, we packed the transistors up and took them back to Japan with us.

The rest is history.

Because one year later, in 1955, Sony came out with the first all-transistor radio.

In 1959, Sony introduced the world to all-transistor television.

And in 1961, we came out with the world's first transistorized stereo tape recorder.

Then 6 years later, we put everything we had learned into our first transistorized receiver.

A receiver made not only with our own transistors but our own filters and circuitry, as well.

Of course, through the years Sony receivers have changed, but the way we make them hasn't.

We still use our own field-effect transistors, our own solid-state filters and our own integrated circuitry.

All designed or made by our own engineers.

And if you take the time to listen to our receivers, you'll hear the difference that experience makes.

For example, in our STR-7065A, you'll hear a receiver that delivers 65 watts minimum RMS continuous power per channel at 8 ohms, 20-20,000Hz with no more than 2% total harmonic distortion.

It has exceptionally high selectivity so it easily picks up weak stations even when they're on the dial next to strong ones.

It has phase locked loop for low distortion and high stereo separation.

It's made with solid-state ceramic i.f. filters, called "forever filters," because that's about how long they last.

And it's made with true complementary push-pull circuitry and direct speaker coupling to ensure a purer quality of sound.

So if you're thinking about buying a receiver, stop into a Sony dealer. That's right, Sony.

Because by our not listening to what Western Electric said 21 years ago, millions of people are listening to us today.

SONY

© 1975 Sony Corp. of America. Sony, 9 W. 57 St., N.Y., N.Y. 10019 SONY is a trademark of Sony Corp.

87
ART DIRECTOR Don Slater
WRITER Ron Berger
DESIGNER Don Slater
PHOTOGRAPHERS Mr. Yasunami
Michael O'Neill
Joe Toto
AGENCY Rosenfeld, Sirowitz & Lawson
CLIENT Sony

This year, logic will drive many thinking people to Volvo showrooms. Because Volvo has a reputation for being one of the world's most intelligently thought out cars. But not all these people will drive out with the same Volvo.

For 1976, we have six different Volvos to choose from. If you're interested in spending less money, you can choose one of our basic Volvo 240s.

Either our 2-or 4-door sedan. Or our roomy 5-door wagon. While you may be getting the lower end of our line, you won't be getting the short end as far as a car is concerned.

Every Volvo 240 comes loaded with standards that are well above the standard. You get a quiet, responsive overhead cam fuel-injected engine. 4-speed manual transmission. 4-wheel power disc brakes and rack and pinion steering.

NOT ALL PEOPLE WHO THINK, THINK ALIKE.

Also on the Volvo 240s, you get steel-belted radials. And orthopedically designed front bucket seats with adjustable lumbar supports.

If you want to exceed these standards, you can order options like air conditioning, power steering with automatic transmission, overdrive and a sunroof.

Of course, for some people even these options won't be enough.

So for them, there's another option.

For thoughtful car buyers to whom money is not as big an object, we have the three objects on your immediate right.

The luxurious new Volvo 260s.

You can choose either the 2- or 4-door sedan. Or, if you carry many of your worldly possessions around with you, a 5-door luxury wagon. The Volvo 260s come with everything the Volvo 240s do and more.

You get a bigger engine: an overhead cam fuel-injected V-6. You also get power steering and your choice of automatic transmission or 4-speed manual with overdrive, all at no extra cost.

In the 260 GL sedans, you'll find many other luxuries that people of means consider necessities. Things like air conditioning. Real leather to sit on. Power front windows. A sunroof. A heated driver's seat. And metallic paint. All standard.

We realize that by giving you six Volvos to choose from, we haven't made things easy for you.

But look at it this way: when you're intelligent enough to make the basic decision to buy a Volvo, you're intelligent enough to decide just how basic that Volvo should be.

88

VOLVO CREATES A WORKING CAR FOR THE LEISURE CLASS.

Even those who can afford life's luxuries must occasionally carry them home. A fact apparently of minor concern to practically every prestige car maker in the world. They've shown a dramatic lack of interest in station wagons.

The Volvo 265 overcomes this oversight. It can be likened to a limousine with the world's largest trunk. But unlike most limousine drivers, the Volvo chauffeur gets more consideration than his cargo.

The front seat cushions raise, lower and tilt. The seat backs recline. The area at the small of your back adjusts from "soft" to "firm."

Air conditioning and automatic transmission are standard equipment, of course.

Driving is silent, smooth and effortless. Steering and braking are power-assisted. And a fuel-injected, light alloy, overhead cam V-6 provides ample performance for the most sporting driver.

Quite naturally, a car this generously endowed does not come cheap. But when you think about it, Volvo does offer extra incentives for paying the price.

All the things we've put into the Volvo 265. And all the things you'll be able to.

VOLVO 265

WHEN YOU SPEND $10,000 FOR A CAR, YOU SHOULDN'T BE AFRAID TO DRIVE IT.

Any man who has traveled the highway to success shouldn't feel he has to detour around potholes.

Yet it seems many big, expensive cars today are better prepared for country club driveways than city streets and back roads.

The elegant new Volvo 264 is not your commonplace rich man's car. It offers more than luxury. It's engineered to afford you the privilege of abusing it.

A new front suspension combining springs *and* struts absorbs jolts and increases stability by reducing roll. Thousands upon thousands of spot-welds (each one strong enough to support the entire weight of the car) fuse body and frame into one solid, silent unit.

The Volvo 264 is extremely agile. A new light alloy, fuel-injected overhead cam V-6 cuts weight. (The 264 is 1,100 pounds lighter and almost a foot shorter than the new "small" Cadillac Seville. Not to mention almost $4,000 smaller in price.)

The 264 GL is also the most lavishly equipped Volvo we make. Leather everywhere you sit. A heated driver's seat. Power front windows. Sunroof. And air conditioning.

So if you're thinking about buying a luxury car, give some thought to the Volvo 264.

You've worked hard to afford the best. You deserve a car that can take the worst.

VOLVO 264

88
ART DIRECTOR   John Danza
WRITER   Tom Nathan
DESIGNER   John Danza
PHOTOGRAPHER   Phil Mazzurco
AGENCY   Scali, McCabe, Sloves
CLIENT   Volvo

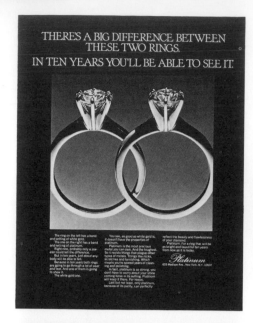

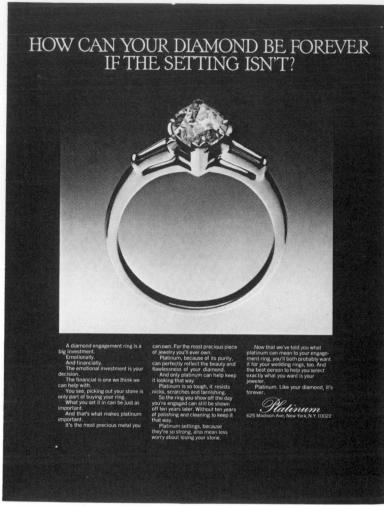

89

ART DIRECTORS	**89**
	Ed Rotundi
	Ken Lombardo
WRITER	Kay Kavanagh
DESIGNERS	Ed Rotundi
	Ken Lombardo
PHOTOGRAPHER	Phil Marco
AGENCY	Della Femina, Travisano & Partners
CLIENT	Matthey Bishop

Ellen Cioni paints roses for us. And abstracts for herself.

"The part I like best is what happens to the dull paints after they're fired."

Artists like Ellen decorate every piece of our Earthenware by hand. We think that's one reason why Franciscan is a part of so many American homes. And why more people have enjoyed more meals from Desert Rose than from any other pattern.

Ellen and 20 other women and men have a direct hand in making each Desert Rose plate. They mix the clay and minerals to our special recipe, shape it, and hand-paint the roses and leaves. They glaze it and fire it. And its brilliant colors will never fade or craze.

Along the way, 5 inspectors make sure it's good enough to be Franciscan.

Maybe machines could do some of these things. But not like Ellen.

The California Craftsmen since 1875.

FRANCISCAN

90

Art Thomas puts the handles on our cups and pitchers with a sculptor's hands.

It almost looks simple. He picks up a handle in one hand, dips a finger into the bowl of slip (liquid clay), and puts some on both ends. Then he picks up an unfired pitcher. He eyeballs where the handle should go, then presses it into place.

Finally, he takes a sponge, wipes away any excess slip, and sends the pitcher on to the decorators.

Simple? Not as simple as Art makes it look. He's been doing it for 27 years. So he knows just how high the handle goes. Just how to line it up with the spout. Just how much pressure to use.

In his spare time, Art's a sculptor. Which helps.

Art Thomas and 22 other men and women make the Sundance coffee pot here. They mix the clay and minerals to our special Earthenware recipe and mold the pot. They glaze it, decorate it, and fire it. And its brilliant colors will never fade, never craze.

Machines can't do all this. Only people like Art Thomas can.

The California Craftsmen since 1875.

FRANCISCAN

Ory Garlow's hands make our china plates.

As the wheel turns, his hands read the clay. They know almost by instinct whether it's shaping right.

If Ory uses too much pressure, he'll stress the clay and the plate will crack in the kiln. Too little, the plate will be defective and will have to be discarded.

During the shaping, Ory keeps the clay damp and malleable. If his sponge is too dry, the clay starts to roll and lump. Too wet, it won't shape into the thin, strong, translucent beauty of our Masterpiece China. But Ory does all this by instinct, the way fine potters have for centuries.

From Ory, the raw plate goes on to finishers, kiln masters, glazers, decorators. It will be fired as many as 5 times, at heats as high as 2,500° F., for as long as 18 hours.

Seven inspectors must agree it's perfect. In all, 37 people work on the Shalimar plate here.

In 1961, Mrs. Kennedy chose our china for Air Force One. And Mrs. Nixon selected it for the Presidential yacht. That made us all feel very proud.

The California Craftsmen since 1875.

FRANCISCAN

90
ART DIRECTORS   Michael Kiernan
                John Feeley
WRITER   Terry McFadden
DESIGNER   Michael Kiernan
PHOTOGRAPHER   Reid Miles
AGENCY   Dailey & Associates
CLIENT   Franciscan
                Dinnerware/Interpace

Your friends say they'll keep in touch. But you know they won't.
Your teachers say come back and see them. And you know you won't.
Maybe someday it won't matter. But, right now, it hurts a little.

Kodak film. For the times of your life.

91

When you learn that
plants have to eat
stuff they find in
the dirt, you're awfully
glad you weren't
born a carrot.

Kodak film.
For the times of
your life.

I had a great game, Mom. I went 3 for 4, threw out a runner
at home plate and I think the shortstop likes me.

Kodak film. For the times of your life.

91
ART DIRECTOR Fred Kittel
WRITER Bill Lane
DESIGNER Fred Kittel
PHOTOGRAPHER Tom McCarthy
AGENCY J. Walter Thompson
CLIENT Eastman Kodak

THE FACT THAT SOME PEOPLE ADD OUR CEREAL TO THEIR CEREAL DOESN'T SAY MUCH FOR THEIR CEREAL.

Over the years, the American woman has done a lot of things with our cereal.

The most popular use she puts it to, is to put it into other people's cereals.

And while we won't go out of our way to stop this (after all, a sale is a sale), the whole idea leaves a lot to be desired.

So we'd like to take this opportunity to remind some people that Kretschmer Wheat Germ is the world's most nutritious natural cereal. All by itself.

Other people's cereals vs. ours.

Generally, there are two kinds of cereals. Fortified. And natural. Fortified means vitamins and minerals have been added. And natural cereals contain only natural ingredients.

Those are, however, just labels. (And speaking of labels, we encourage you to read theirs and ours.)

Because Kretschmer isn't just a natural cereal. It's a nutritious cereal.

An ounce (roughly a quarter of a cup) of Regular Kretschmer Wheat Germ provides 15% of your Recommended Daily Allowance of protein. (More than any of the new "natural" cereals.) And more B Vitamins, iron and Vitamin E than any of the "naturals" provide.

Ounce for ounce, you get a lot more from Kretschmer.

Good things come in original packages.

One big advantage to looking for Kretschmer in a store is that you don't have to look very hard. We're the only cereal that

doesn't come in a box. Kretschmer comes in a jar. To keep it fresh, and preserve its nutrients.

Good breakfast tastes.

Of course, if you're one of those people who've only tasted Kretschmer Wheat Germ in someone else's cereal, you've never really tasted Kretschmer.

Regular Kretschmer has a slightly nutty taste. Something like a cross between bran and toasted walnuts.

And if you want to start your day on a slightly sweeter note, try Kretschmer Sugar & Honey. We've made it so good to begin with, all you add is milk.

When you try Kretschmer Wheat Germ on its own, you'll realize that for years we haven't just been making other cereals more nutritious.

We've been making some of them taste a lot better than they really are.

KRETSCHMER WHEAT GERM. THE WORLD'S MOST NUTRITIOUS NATURAL CEREAL.

CONSIDERING THE SNEAKY THINGS YOUR MOTHER DID WITH WHEAT GERM NO WONDER YOU'RE SUSPICIOUS OF ITS TASTE.

Remember the lengths your mother went to in order to hide the Kretschmer Wheat Germ?

There it would be. Somewhere between the pudding and the whipped cream. Or floating around in among your corn flakes. Even mixed up in the ice cream sundaes she made.

That's simply because in your mother's day, they truly believed that if something was good for you, you probably wouldn't like it.

So they hid it. And never bothered to taste it. Which bothers us a lot. Because Kretschmer is not only the world's most nutritious natural cereal, it's one of the world's most delicious natural cereals.

What's in it for you?

The reason your mother wanted to get some Kretschmer in you is because Kretschmer Wheat Germ is naturally loaded with vitamins and minerals.

Just an ounce (roughly a quarter of a cup) of Regular Kretschmer Wheat Germ provides

15% of your Recommended Daily Allowance of protein. (More than any of the new "natural" cereals.) And more B Vitamins, iron and Vitamin E than any of the "naturals" provide.

Ounce for ounce, you get a lot more from Kretschmer.

Cinnamon, Raisins, Apples, Honey & Wheat Germ.

Naturally, if the joys of eating Kretschmer have been hidden from you all your life, you have no idea how good it tastes.

Regular Kretschmer has a slightly nutty taste. Something

like a cross between bran and toasted walnuts.

Kretschmer Cinnamon Raisin is our idea of what to have for breakfast instead of Danish pastry.

Kretschmer Caramel Apple is so delicious a lot of people eat it by the handful. Right out of the jar.

And Kretschmer Sugar & Honey is so sweet to begin with that all you add is milk.

Our unique one-of-a-kind container.

Unlike ordinary, average cereals, Kretschmer Wheat Germ comes in a jar, not a box. That's because it isn't an ordinary, average cereal. That's also to keep it fresh, and preserve Kretschmer's nutrients.

If you want to find it, however, all you have to do is look in the cereal section of your store.

And we assume you will want to find it.

After having a good thing like Kretschmer hidden from you all these years.

KRETSCHMER WHEAT GERM. THE WORLD'S MOST NUTRITIOUS NATURAL CEREAL.

92

ART DIRECTOR Jim Perretti
WRITER Helen Nolan
DESIGNER Jim Perretti
PHOTOGRAPHERS Cailor/Resnick
AGENCY Della Femina, Travisano & Partners
CLIENT International Multifoods
92

MY CHICKENS ARE SO FRESH THEY LIVE UP TO 20 DAYS AFTER DEATH.

Frank Perdue

A lot of people are attracted to chill-pack because they think ice-packed chickens don't have a long enough shelf-life.

They're not thinking of *my* ice-packed chickens.

We recently tested my fresh Perdue chickens against several other ice-packed brands in our own cooler.

In 16 to 19 days the others had all spoiled. On the 20th day the Perdue chickens were still in good condition.

But don't take Perdue's word on the subject of Perdue. Call any distributor who handles all kinds of ice-packed chickens. He'll probably tell you Perdue has the longest shelf-life of all the chickens he carries. Because that's what most of our distributors tell us.

What makes one chicken live longer than others after processing?

Care.

Care in processing. Care in packing. Care in shipping.

Perdue, for example, is the only ice-packed chicken shipped exclusively in refrigerated Polar-Stream trucks.

So if shelf-life is one of your problems, call Perdue and solve it two ways:

By selling a chicken with the kind of shelf-life you want.

And by selling a chicken that moves so fast you don't need it.

IT TAKES A TOUGH MAN TO SELL A TENDER CHICKEN.

PERDUE

93

Are you ready for Nixon's drummer?

Charlotte Rampling's role in the S-M shocker, *The Night Porter*, didn't hurt her a bit. Suddenly she's Europe's hottest star...and filming *Jackpot* with Richard Burton.

Ron Ziegler, at this point in time, is about to hit the college lecture circuit to talk on The Presidency—and defend his old boss. Tough job, but the $2,500 *per* helps. Meanwhile, back in lonely San Clemente, he tools around on a Honda, practices his new drums, works with Love and Hate boxes on his desk. An exclusive People story.

Honest George Kaufman, all Lincolned-up for a costume party. People dips into a loving new book on the playwright—with many a sample of his beautifully knit wit.

Billie Jean King can still electrify a crowd. But with a take of $800,000 a year, she's turning her smashing energy elsewhere. "I don't want to be just a tennis player. That's not where I'm at anymore." So all hail Queen Chrissie.

Albert Capraro has designs on Betty Ford—like the soft chiffon number the model's wearing. The First Lady picked the unknown American designer after spotting his dresses in a newspaper. Hers will be mostly off-the-rack and retail priced. Whip Inflation Now!

Norton Simon says this 10th-century bronze of Siva is his. After all, he paid a million for it. No, says India, it was smuggled out. So far, two ambassadors and Scotland Yard have entered the tug-of-war.

Helen Reddy may be the voice of Women's Lib, but there's a man behind hits like "I Am Woman." Ms. No. 1 says she owes it all to husband-manager Jeffrey Wald. "It's *our* career." Last year, such togetherness brought in over $2 million.

Philip Agee really bugs the CIA. An agent turned socialist, he's blown covers all over Latin America with his *CIA Diary*...calls the Agency "political police...an instrument of repression."

Photographs by: Harry Benson, Alain Dejean/Sygma, Alfred Eisenstaedt, Terence Spencer, The New York Times, Stanley Tretick and Wide World.

People your life again. The human magazine is here, brimming with people-to-know.

Singer Barry Manilow, for instance, riding high on the year's first biggie, "Mandy." Secretary General Kurt Waldheim, riding herd on a Mid-East peace. Ex-con Daniel Peterson, orating his way toward a national title. A Who's Who of dance turns out for angel Lucia Chase. Marvelous Marvin meets the meanest sheriff in Texas.

"Professor" Red Smith. Sharpshooter Catherine Deneuve. Groom-to-be Johnny Bench. Genius Susan Reynolds. Bridget, Bernie and Baby. They're all in the cast of the brightest, sassiest magazine in town. No wonder People is so much fun to read. It's 100% living, breathing humanity.

Just about every kind of advertising *feels right* in this fresh, warm environment. Young, affluent, educated men and women dig People's world. When they're into it, they're wide open to new ideas about living better. So if you have some suggestions, here's the ideal place to make them. At incredibly low CPMs.

Time Inc.'s newest magazine has zoomed to 1,250,000 in a mere ten months. It's hot—because it's so warm. So why not do some raking off with People?

Join the fun. Start Peopling your ads. In the magazine where fun and efficiency come together.

People weekly

People weekly

Fun **and** efficiency.

94

	93		94
ART DIRECTOR	Sam Scali	**ART DIRECTOR**	Bob Czernysz
WRITER	Ed McCabe	**WRITER**	Richard Olmsted
DESIGNER	Sam Scali	**DESIGNER**	Steve Ong
PHOTOGRAPHER	Alan Dolgins	**PHOTOGRAPHER**	Editorial
AGENCY	Scali, McCabe, Sloves	**AGENCY**	Young and Rubicam
CLIENT	Perdue Farms	**CLIENT**	Time

GOLD

To sell a car in New York, you need the right vehicle.

What you need, especially these days, is a vehicle that can give you the most mileage for your money.

Like the Daily News.

With nearly twice the circulation of any major daily in the nation and over 5,000,000 readers, the Daily News is the big wheel among newspapers in the nation's number one market.

And it doesn't take a back seat to TV, either. In fact, nothing on the tube can give you more penetration. Not All in the Family, Sanford and Son, or Rhoda.

And don't think News readers just ride the IRT. In New York and the suburbs, 38% of the adults in families owning cars are News readers. That's twice as many as The Times. Of the adults in 2-or-more-car families, 33% are News readers. Compared to only 20% for The Times.

What's more, the Daily News is the driving force no matter what kind of car you're pushing. (Imported, domestic, luxury, economy, new, used, compact or station wagon.)

If you'd like to get specific, call your nearest Daily News representative. Or call Mark Meyers in Detroit at (313) 356-3487. Our on-line computerized service (IMD) can help you keep tabs on your traffic and your competitor's traffic. And you can cross-tab, too. For almost all automotive products and services.

But call soon. Before you take yourself for a ride.

DAILY ⊕ NEWS
NEW YORK'S PICTURE NEWSPAPER

Today...you *really* need it!

Source: 1974 Markets in Focus

95

The minute Ron Becker stepped off the train, his zipper went off the track.

96

"Never in the history of mankind has so little done so much for so many"
—Cole of California

97
ART DIRECTOR Israel Liebowitz
WRITER Janet Carlson
DESIGNER Israel Liebowitz
PHOTOGRAPHER Irving Penn
AGENCY Carlson/Liebow
CLIENT Cole of Californi

Introducing 27 small bites of the Big Apple.

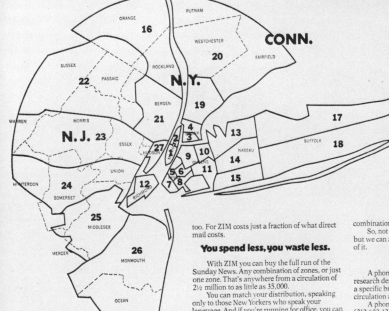

For a small businessman, New York can be a big place. Even for a businessman who's not so small.

So, the New York News, New York's largest newspaper, has taken it upon itself to cut the New York market down to size.

More accurately, we've cut it down to sizes. 27 of them. Now an advertiser can have a preprint inserted in the Sunday News and have that preprint delivered only to the market or markets vital to him.

We call this new marketing concept ZIM.

Who's ZIM?

ZIM stands for Zoned Insert Marketing.

It marries the ever increasing power and popularity of inserts with the precision and flexibility of direct mail.

So, while we may call it ZIM, we think you'll call it terrific.

ZIM vs. the P.O.

When you insert a message in an envelope and send it through the mail, you can hardly count on its reaching all your customers at virtually the same time.

You can count on that with ZIM, however. And you can count on spending less money

too. For ZIM costs just a fraction of what direct mail costs.

You spend less, you waste less.

With ZIM you can buy the full run of the Sunday News. Any combination of zones, or just one zone. That's anywhere from a circulation of 2½ million to as little as 35,000.

You can match your distribution, speaking only to those New Yorkers who speak your language. And if you're running for office, you can speak to your constituents without having to speak to anyone else's.

So you're not biting off more of the Big Apple than you can chew.

ZIM lets you test. Anything.

You can test copy with ZIM by running different strategies in similar zones.

You can test zones with ZIM. By running the same copy strategies in different zones.

You can also change according to local conditions and regulations.

Add all that to the couponing capabilities inherent in inserts and you have a testing device that truly makes the grade.

Us and ZIM.

It's appropriate that the newspaper that can give you more New Yorkers than anyone else can also give you as few as you want.

But that's not the whole News story.

We can give you the highest level of penetration in the city, the highest level of penetration in the suburbs. Or both.

And with our Instant Market Data service, our on-line computer facility, we can tell you an awful lot about our readers by income, occupation and product use.

What's more, we can particularize census data by zip code information for any zone or

combination of zones.

So, not only do we offer you the use of ZIM, but we can also help you make even better use of it.

You and ZIM.

A phone call to your News sales rep or our research department (212-682-1234) can get you a specific breakdown for each zone by population, circulation and percent of household coverage.

A phone call to Jim (ZIM) Ruddy (212-682-1234) can get you information on the maximums, the minimums, the costs and the variety of insert sizes, from catalogs on down. Also, the uses, applications and combinations available with ZIM.

Maybe ZIM is just the thing to help keep you from getting chewed up in the Big Apple.

SUNDAY NEWS
NEW YORK'S PICTURE NEWSPAPER

Today... you **really** need it!

99

99
ART DIRECTOR Mark Yustein
WRITER Neil Drossman
DESIGNER Mark Yustein
PHOTOGRAPHER Jerry Friedman
AGENCY Della Femina, Travisano & Partners
CLIENT Daily News

PETER BOYLE STARRING IN "YOUNG FRANKENSTEIN." © 1974, 20TH CENTURY-FOX FILM COR

A broken zipper can be a pain in the neck.

When you're making something very strong, you have to hold it together with a zipper that's even stronger.

Like the Talon 42® metal zipper which was designed for strength.

We made it specifically for jeans and work pants, which means it's a zipper that can take the roughest wear and endless washings.

The proof of its toughness is the way the Talon 42 has performed in millions and millions of jeans and work pants. (It also happens to be an excellent zipper for monsters.)

When your customers buy jeans, they'll be looking for the Talon 42 zipper. It will tell them you put as much care into your creation as Young Frankenstein put into his.

Talon
THE WORLD'S QUALITY ZIPPER

The Talon 42 zipper says a lot about the jeans it's in.

100

XEROX® and TELECOPIER® are trademarks of XEROX CORPORATION.

"Thank you so much for the insurance money on my stolen Ferrari. But what's a Ferrari?"

With all the paperwork an insurance company has to handle, it's no wonder mix-ups like this happen.

At Xerox, we have people who can show you how to prevent these mix-ups, and help your communications run more efficiently. The Xerox Insurance Specialists.

They can show you how to use a Xerox duplicator and overlays, to copy all the documents of a claim report onto one sheet of paper, so there's no chance of transcription errors.

How to use our reduction duplicator to reduce oversize forms to uniform 8½ x 11 pages.

Or how to use a Xerox Telecopier transceiver, to send documents from field locations to headquarters in just minutes.

No matter what kind of insurance business you're in, a Xerox Insurance Specialist can show you ways to make your paperwork more manageable, and mistakes less likely.

So that the next time you send out a draft for a claim settlement you won't have to ask for it back.

XEROX

101

"I read Playboy and found God."

When The Order Of The Most Holy Trinity needed new recruits, they called on PLAYBOY to do God's work.

It all started when the good Fathers decided to run an ad in PLAYBOY.

Up until that time a total of five new students a year was considered average and ten was exceptional. And ads in church publications, news magazines and newspapers couldn't seem to change that.

In fact, $10,000 worth of advertising in a major magazine didn't get a single inquiry.

So the Fathers had little more than their faith to sustain them when the PLAYBOY ad appeared. But just a few weeks later, the Trinitarians had 600 new applicants.

What other magazine could get so many new recruits for an old religious order?

Only PLAYBOY.

What other magazine gets to 76% of all the college men in America, plus some of the biggest spenders in or out of school?

Only PLAYBOY.

So if you're serious about reaching young men, our story has a fairly obvious moral.

If one ad can make the good Fathers believe, it can do the same for you.

ONLY PLAYBOY

102
ART DIRECTOR   Paul A. Basile
WRITERS   Robert Elgort
          Tony Isidore
DESIGNER   Paul A. Basile
PHOTOGRAPHERS   Cailor/Resnick
AGENCY   Isidore Lefkowitz Elgort
CLIENT   Playboy Enterprises

Has America had it?

As America's 200th birthday approaches, some people are saying she's old and tired.

The system, they're saying, doesn't work anymore.

True? False? Or in between? Next April, the editors of Fortune are going to look for the answers. In a remarkable single-subject issue devoted to "The American System."

Why now? Because now, more than at any time in several decades, the nation is groping for new goals and missions. Fundamental questions are being asked about the way America works. Currents of change are sweeping America and the world forward into uncharted territory, and it's fair to ask—can our system keep up?

"The American System" is Fortune's contribution to the country's bicentennial. It will be one of the most important issues we've ever published.

The April Fortune will come at "The American System" from all directions...economic, political, and social. What are its strengths and its weaknesses? Where is it working and where does it need fixing? What's the future of...the free market, our political institutions, our common goals and aspirations, our role as a world leader?

Certainly it's a vast subject to tackle. A country-sized subject. But Fortune, alone among magazines, has the resources to take it on and make sense of it. And the commitment to advocate what needs to be changed—and what needs to be left alone.

We're telling you about "The American System" this far ahead so you'll have time to be part of it. The bicentennial Fortune is going to be the most talked-about issue of any magazine in 1975...and maybe the most important for years to come. If you have something important to say to America, this is the place to say it.

Closing dates for advertising in "The American System" are: four-color, February 21; black and white and two-color, February 26.

Join us for this major publishing event.

"The American System"
Fortune's bicentennial issue. April, 1975

103

103
ART DIRECTOR Bob Czernysz
WRITER Richard Olmsted
DESIGNER Bob Czernysz
ARTIST Gary Overacre
AGENCY Young and Rubicam
CLIENT Time

The Vocal Cord.

The Technicolor® Superloop system gives silent films a voice by linking an audio cassette with a silent loop projector. So now, a three-minute loop can be extended to a thirty-minute lesson using exciting new sound-assisted programs.

The best part is, Superloop doesn't obsolete your present materials. Show your current silent loops with the Superloop projector. Or play your current tapes with the Superloop cassette player. Or use the projector and cassette player with Superloop materials being produced by Doubleday, BFA and others; many with bilingual capability.

Call your Technicolor dealer for a no-obligation demonstration.

Technicolor makes film work harder.

Technicolor® Audio Visual Systems, 299 Kalmus Drive, Costa Mesa. CA 92626.

104

104
ART DIRECTOR Tom Cordner
WRITER Carolyn Johnson
DESIGNER Tom Cordner
PHOTOGRAPHER Mark Feldman
AGENCY Cochrane Chase and Co.
CLIENT Technicolor Audio-Visual Systems

We're going to never been flyed fly you like you've before.

Since most men need two different kinds of pants (casual and dress pants are one, jeans and work pants the other), Talon makes two different kinds of pants zippers.

And each is by far the largest-selling in its field.

Our Channel Zip nylon zipper was designed especially for casual and dress pants. Not only did we make it exceptionally strong, we made it beautifully slim and flexible. No other zipper combines so much strength with so much style and comfort.

The Talon 42 metal zipper was designed specifically for jeans and work pants. It's a strong, rugged zipper made to take the worst kind of punishment. And looks it. Which is exactly what your customers want in their jeans. (We know, because in a recent consumer study, they told us.)

So much for our superior zippers. Now for our superior service.

The largest sales force.

Talon has more salesmen to serve you than any other zipper company in the United States.

Their knowledge and experience can help determine the best zippers for your pants, as well as the best application equipment for your production methods.

Talon salesmen don't only sell zippers.

They *know* zippers.

Every Talon salesman can fly.

Every Talon salesman attends Fly School.

Before he can call on you, he must go through an intensive training course, in which he learns of the latest developments in Talon zippers and application equipment.

And since Fly School is an ongoing program, each

Channel Zip

Talon 42

salesman is constantly kept up to date.

That's why you can depend on him to come up with the right solutions to your zipper problems.

The fastest zipper in America.

Since you need faster service than ever, Talon will give you better delivery than ever.

That's because we have more warehouses throughout the United States than any other zipper company.

Wherever your factory is, there's an inventory of Talon zippers nearby.

Computerized inventory.

We have one of the most advanced computer systems

available.

It keeps tabs on every zipper in our inventory, as well as in production.

At any given moment — right now, if you like — the computer knows exactly how many of what style in what sizes and colors are where.

A quick phone call and your zippers are on their way.

We make our own equipment.

To make sure our zippers are properly applied, we make our own application equipment.

From a simple bottom-stop unit to the most sophisticated fully-automatic in-line machines.

What's more, we

The Talon Flyers.

have a staff of sales service technicians to advise you which machines are best for your particular production methods.

They'll install and service the equipment for you, and, through regularly scheduled calls, they'll make sure it's running at peak efficiency.

It all comes down to this.

In addition to providing you with the best and most dependable pants zippers, we have a nation-wide system that gives you the most dependable service.

So, to get your pants orders out faster and more efficiently, it makes more sense than ever for you to fly with Talon.

Talon
THE WORLD'S QUALITY ZIPPER

Talon zippers say a lot about the pants they're in.

Channel Zip for casual and dress pants.

Talon 42 for jeans and work pants.

105

Even if you never own one, a Nikon will touch your life.

Today, the photographer at work with his Nikon has become part of the everyday scene. Even the seasoned professional, however, would be surprised to discover that the Nikon equipment he knows and uses so well is only part of the Nikon story. Few of us, in fact, ever become aware of even a few of the roles that Nikon plays in our lives.
The Fashion Photographer
Click-whirr. Click-whirr. The fashion photographer moves about the model, firing off frame after frame with his motor-driven Nikon. One of the shots will appear in an advertisement, in dozens of national magazines, where it will be seen by millions of people. The camera is a Nikon, of course. But, that is the Nikon everyone knows.
The Astronaut
Floating, weightless in space, the astronaut photographs the earth's ozone layer. He is using a special ultra-violet lens, researching ozone's vital ability to absorb radiation. This is only one of many scientific experiments conducted by Apollo men in which a camera has played a vital role. Later, one will record the historic moment when a Soyuz Cosmonaut shakes hands with an Apollo Astronaut. The name on the astronaut's camera is the same as on the fashion photographer's Nikon. It is little changed from off-the-shelf models, and was the only 35mm slr camera in the space program. In fact, the only microscope on Skylab was a Nikon Model H.
The Plastic Surgeon
For perhaps the tenth time in as many months, the plastic surgeon photographs the pretty young girl's face. It had been disfigured in an accident, now it is perfect once again. The progress has been recorded with scientific accuracy, even including essential data right on the film. For, the surgeon's Nikon has the unique Medical Nikkor lens.
Thousands of amateurs who are serious about photography as a means of expression, as an art form, also demand Nikon. For the same reasons: incomparable quality, both optical and mechanical, proven reliability, constant innovation without obsolescence. But, each profession — and each amateur's specialty — places its own very special demands on the camera. And the Nikon System, virtually alone in photography, is equal to the challenge.
Your own unique photographic requirements are also within the scope of Nikon. Your dealer would be glad to discuss them with you.

Nikon Inc., Garden City, N.Y. 11530.
Subsidiary of Ehrenreich Photo-Optical Industries, Inc.
(In Canada: Anglophoto Ltd., PQ.)

Nickel and dime your way to success.

Fill your vending machines with Clark, Zagnut and Clarconut bars. Then watch them empty.
Nickel and dime, nickel and dime. Over and over again. We've seen it happen. For years now, Clark and Zagnut bars have been two of the really fast movers and strong profit-makers in the 15¢ field.
And our newer Clarconut bars promise to be right on the money, too. They're boxed by the gross and seem to sell by the jillion.
We have bigger bars, too. Priced at 20¢ and two bits. 120 to the case. So stock your vending machines with Clark, Zagnut and Clarconut bars.
You'll really notice the change they make.
The D. L. Clark Company
Pittsburgh, Pa. and Evanston, Ill.

	106		**107**
ART DIRECTOR	Roy Tuck	**ART DIRECTOR**	William Werme
WRITER	Bill Irvine	**WRITER**	James Murphy
DESIGNER	Roy Tuck	**ARTIST**	Elwyn Mehlman
PHOTOGRAPHER	Richard Noble	**AGENCY**	Ketchum, MacLeod & Grove
AGENCY	Gilbert, Felix & Sharf		
CLIENT	Nikon	**CLIENT**	D. L. Clark Company

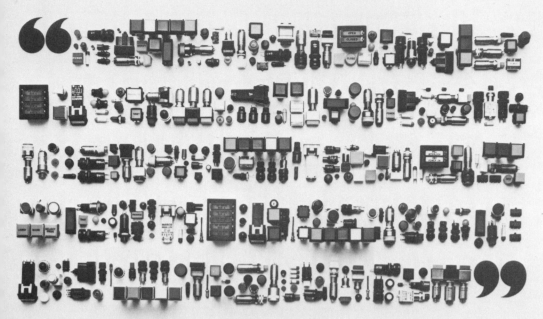

No one else can make this statement.
The Products of Marco-Oak

108

IS THE WORLD NOW READY FOR THE CABBAGE CIGARETTE?

For years now, researchers from all over the world have been seeking substitutes for tobacco.

The materials that they've tried read like a grocery shopping list:

Cabbage, tomato leaves, lettuce, spinach, wild hydrangea.

Recently, cocoa beans and wood cellulose have joined the list.

The success or failure of these efforts depends on several factors:

Can tastes acceptable to today's smokers be developed?

Will the future smoker demand such new approaches as these?

What new technology will have to be developed, if some revolutionary breakthrough does occur?

Just how these questions will be answered, no one knows for sure.

But, at Monk, there's one thing we do know. Whatever happens, we're confident of the long-range viability of the world tobacco industry.

And we believe that leaf tobacco will always continue to be the essential ingredient of blends that the smokers of the world prefer.

Because of that belief, we have committed substantial funds to new plants and equipment.

Industry experts described the results as "the world's most advanced tobacco processing facility."

We have developed technology to maintain the highest possible level of quality and efficiency.

Because we think that's the only level you should be asked to accept.

For a long time now, we've been encouraging pre-placement of orders.

To make sure you'll be able to get tobacco to your exact specifications, at a reasonable cost.

Altogether, approaches like these have resulted in business relationships with over 70% of the manufacturers of cigarettes in the world today.

And also in a confidence that, no matter what the world's future smokers may be ready for, Monk will be ready for it, too. **MONK**

A.C. Monk & Company, Leaf Tobacco Suppliers, Farmville, North Carolina, U.S.A.

109

	108		109
ART DIRECTOR	Douglas Hoppe Stone	ART DIRECTOR	Charles McKinney
WRITER	Tom Bardeen	WRITER	Charlie Ashby
DESIGNER	Douglas Hoppe Stone	PHOTOGRAPHER	Carl Fischer
ARTIST	Douglas Hoppe Stone	AGENCY	McKinney Silver & Rockett
PHOTOGRAPHER	Harry Chamberlain	CLIENT	A. C. Monk & Co.
AGENCY	Rose & Stone		
CLIENT	Marco-Oak		

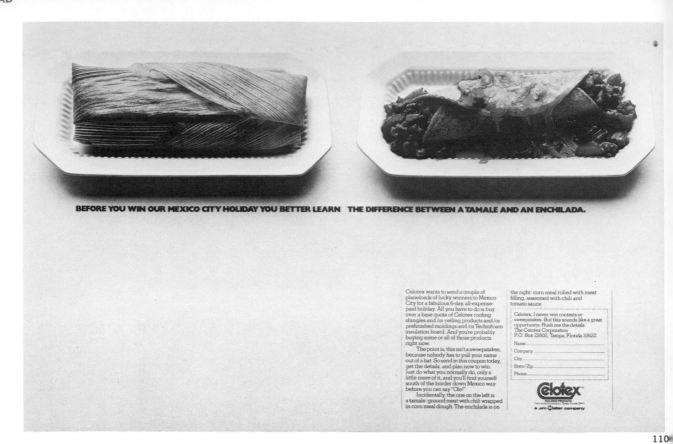

BEFORE YOU WIN OUR MEXICO CITY HOLIDAY YOU BETTER LEARN THE DIFFERENCE BETWEEN A TAMALE AND AN ENCHILADA.

Celotex wants to send a couple of planeloads of lucky winners to Mexico City for a fabulous 6-day, all-expense-paid holiday. All you have to do is buy over a base quota of Celotex roofing shingles and/or ceiling products and/or prefinished moldings and/or Technofoam insulation board. And you're probably buying some or all of those products right now.

The point is, this isn't a sweepstakes, because nobody has to pull your name out of a hat. So send in this coupon today, get the details, and plan now to win. Just do what you normally do, only a little more of it, and you'll find yourself south of the border down Mexico way before you can say "Ole!"

Incidentally, the one on the left is a tamale: ground meat with chili wrapped in corn meal dough. The enchilada is on the right: corn meal rolled with meat filling, seasoned with chili and tomato sauce.

Celotex, I never win contests or sweepstakes. But this sounds like a great opportunity. Rush me the details.
The Celotex Corporation
P.O. Box 22602, Tampa, Florida 33622

Name
Company
City
State/Zip
Phone

Celotex
BUILDING PRODUCTS
The Celotex Corporation, Tampa, Florida 33622
a *Jim Walter* company

110

Who do the police call for protection?

Now more than ever, police need help.

Crime has become big business. The only thing that's rising faster than the crime rate is the demand for people to help lower it.

Law enforcement agencies are asking for more and better equipment and technology to help them protect people. And even to help protect themselves.

They expect the design engineer to come up with the answers. Computers to assist Columbo. Machines that can sniff out narcotics faster than a bloodhound.

More sophisticated crime prevention and criminal detection equipment.

And crime is only one problem keeping the design engineer busy.

Even in this economy, the design engineer is working overtime to solve the technological problems of energy, food shortages, medicine, conservation, and even inflation.

But it's going to mean changes. Right now, 720,000 design engineers are developing new products. Redesigning old ones. Looking for new equipment. Throwing away much of the old.

If you advertise to the OEM, make sure your product is part of the design engineer's plans for the future.

Advertise now, in the only magazine you need to reach the OEM—Machine Design. It's read and respected by more design engineers than any other magazine.

And since it helps design engineers solve problems, it helps advertisers feel safe at night.

Machine Design, a Penton Publication, Penton Plaza, Cleveland, Ohio 44114.

MACHINE DESIGN
For The Problem Solvers

111

	110		111
ART DIRECTOR	Larry Leblang	**ART DIRECTOR**	Tom Gilday
WRITER	Mel Richman	**WRITER**	Mike Faems
PHOTOGRAPHER	Charlie Gold	**DESIGNER**	Tom Gilday
AGENCY	Mike Sloan	**PHOTOGRAPHER**	Jan Czyrba
CLIENT	Celotex	**AGENCY**	Griswold-Eshleman
		CLIENT	Machine Design

The Arabs have the oil.
America has the corn.

Just about everyone knows that the Arabs produce the largest share of the world's oil, close to 40 percent.

But few people realize that, in a sense, American farmers are the "Arabs of corn."

Close to 50 percent of the world's corn is grown in America. It's our single most important agricultural commodity, not to mention one of American industry's major natural resources.

Close to six billion bushels of corn are expected in 1975. Yet only 5 to 6 percent of this harvest will be used by the corn-refining industry in the wet-milling process to produce food and non-food ingredients. So availability of this home-grown raw material is virtually never a problem (as it may be with raw food materials whose supply lines start halfway around the world).

All of this should make sweet news for the processor looking for an economical sweetener with a secure source of supply.

There's practically no application where a corn sweetener cannot replace sugar to reduce your product's cost without sacrificing quality.

To help you make up your own mind about corn, we've prepared a special booklet. There are sections on corn starch as well as all the corn-derived sweeteners, plus other useful information.

For your free copy, write: Corn Products, International Plaza, Englewood Cliffs, N.J. 07632.

Corn Products
a Unit of CPC International Inc.

112

THE PIONEERS' UNDERWEAR
WAS MADE BY THE PIONEERS
OF UNDERWEAR.

JOCKEY

113

	112		113
ART DIRECTOR	Milt Marcus	**ART DIRECTOR**	Allan Beaver
WRITERS	Jack Trout	**WRITER**	Larry Plapler
	Al Ries	**ARTIST**	Bettmann Archives
PHOTOGRAPHER	Dave Edmunds	**AGENCY**	Levine, Huntley, Schmidt,
AGENCY	Ries Cappiello Colwell		Plapler and Beaver
CLIENT	Corn Products	**CLIENT**	Jockey

Our readers don't come to us for economic forecasts, pretty women, current events, "how-to" articles, sports prognostication, political analysis, diet plans, recipes, management tips, or interviews with celebrities.

They come to us to buy.

New Equipment Digest
Where Industry comes to shop.

A Penton Publication. Penton Plaza. Cleveland, Ohio 44114

114

Is plastic all it's cracked up to be?

Plastic or zinc? Design engineers have long been trying to answer that question.

But now, there's a third side to the coin: a new high-strength-to-weight-ratio material called thin-wall zinc.

Snap. Crackle. Pop.

Consumers are demanding gas economy these days. But they're also demanding durability and good looks.

That means you need parts that last, and sacrificing zinc's strength and appearance in critical "high visibility" areas could be a real mistake.

Especially when you consider that new technology has made zinc cheaper than ever before.

Parts may be easy to replace. Satisfied customers aren't.

Thin-wall zinc advantages.
Due to thin-wall technology, zinc is competitive with any material. Competitive in weight. As well as cost.

It's stronger than molded plastics. It has four times the tensile strength. It has higher impact strength and greater dimensional stability.

It also costs less to plate zinc than it does to plate plastics. And chrome-plated thin-wall displays a bright, beautifully crisp appearance. It looks good, feels good, and when exposed to the elements, thin-wall zinc lasts a lot longer than plated plastics.

New technology for a traditional metal. New thin-wall technology makes it possible to produce zinc die-castings as thin as 0.030 of an inch. Instead of using a uniform, standard thickness, wall stock is carefully calculated according to product function.

This means design engineers can now achieve substantial weight and cost savings, without compromising the quality of a component.

Thin-wall die casting capabilities are rapidly increasing among U.S. die casters, too. More than 50 of the largest die casters have already tooled up. And as a result, they've lowered material costs to their customers while improving productivity.

Think thin. Think zinc.
For more information concerning thin-wall zinc, or for a list of U.S. die casters with thin-wall technology, contact Texasgulf.

If what you've specified isn't what it's cracked up to be, maybe thin-wall zinc can help you pick up the pieces.

Zinc.
It costs less than you think.

Texasgulf

115

	114		115
ART DIRECTOR	Bob Kwait	ART DIRECTOR	Milt Marcus
WRITER	Walt Woodward	WRITER	Tom McGuire
DESIGNER	Bob Kwait	PHOTOGRAPHER	Andrew Unangst
PHOTOGRAPHER	Charles Coppins	AGENCY	Ries Cappiello Colwell
AGENCY	Griswold-Eshleman	CLIENT	Texasgulf
CLIENT	New Equipment Digest		

If the design engineer can't figure out how to feed 10 billion people, he'll have to figure out how to bury them.

The problems of too many people and too little food have a lot of people in the world worried sick. (And the rest? They're already too sick to even think about it.)

Even more frightening than hunger is the fact that no one has the technology to solve the problem. For example, one cold night can waste an entire season's crop.

Yet that doesn't mean it's a problem that can't be solved.

The technology to start a green revolution that will feed the world's

hungry *is* being developed. Now. As are new tools to fight crime, protect our environment, and conserve our energy resources.

These tools are being created by the man who's involved in every crisis. The design engineer.

But it's going to mean changes. At this very moment, 720,000 design engineers are developing new products. Redesigning old ones. Looking for new equipment. Throwing away much of the old.

That's why you can't let the de-

sign engineer design your product out of the picture.

If you advertise to the OEM, advertise now; in the only magazine you need to reach the OEM—Machine Design. It's read and respected by more design engineers than any other magazine.

Not only does it help design engineers solve problems, it helps advertisers solve problems, too.

A Penton Publication, Penton Plaza, Cleveland, Ohio 44114.

MACHINE DESIGN
FOR THE PROBLEM SOLVERS

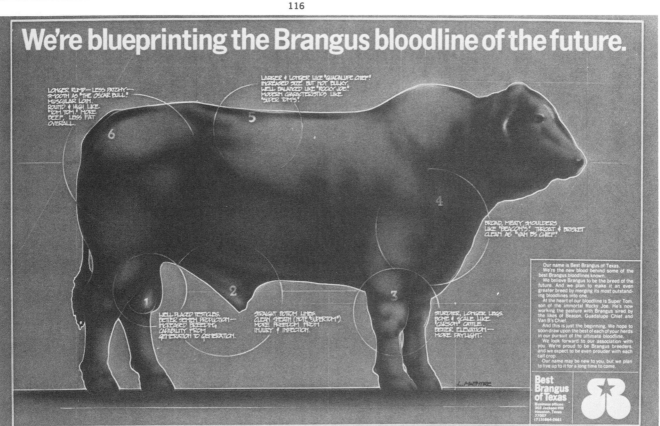

We're blueprinting the Brangus bloodline of the future.

	116		**117**
ART DIRECTOR	Tom Gilday	ART DIRECTOR	Jay Loucks
WRITER	Mike Faems	WRITER	Bruce Davis
DESIGNER	Tom Gilday	DESIGNER	Jay Loucks
PHOTOGRAPHER	Jan Czyrba	ARTIST	Larry McEntire
AGENCY	Griswold-Eshleman	AGENCY	Bruce Henry & Davis
CLIENT	Machine Design	CLIENT	Best Brangus of Texas

TRADE AD

There will always be a place in the American home for bad products.

When consumers get their hands on a bad product these days, watch out.

That's when they start writing unhappy letters, forming groups, passing laws.

And the way we see it, that isn't good for business. It's *great* for business.

Great because, like any reputable manufac-turer, we think quality occupies the most impor-tant place in the consumer's mind. And home.

Which is one of the reasons we've just come out with the following defect-free guarantee: On any approved manufacturer's defect on first-quality goods, we'll reimburse the authorized dealer (when such defects are submitted in ac-cordance with prescribed claim procedures) 50¢ per square yard for the labor to remove the car-pet, and $1.00 per square yard to reinstall new carpet. And, of course, we'll replace the defective product absolutely free of charge, freight included.

We're convinced that this is the sort of pro-gram that will pay off for our dealers. Because satisfied customers will return with repeat orders instead of repeated complaints.

True, a shoddy product can occasionally enjoy short term success in any business. But there's more to it than that.

So we're doing everything possible to live faithfully with an attitude we set out with four years ago: Before you decide to make it big, de-cide to make it good.

Otherwise, people are likely to put you in your place.

Horizon Carpets

P.O. Box 1709, Dalton, Ga. (404) 277-2222. Outside of Ga., call toll free (800) 241-4085

118

EVERYTHING IN THE WORLD SHOULD BE MADE THIS GOOD. ONLY BIGGER.

MATCHBOX.

119

118		**119**	
ART DIRECTOR	William L. Sweney	ART DIRECTOR	Allan Beaver
WRITER	Russ Dymond	WRITER	Larry Plapler
DESIGNER	William L. Sweney	PHOTOGRAPHERS	Cailor/Resnick
PHOTOGRAPHER	Richard Hoflich	AGENCY	Levine, Huntley, Schmidt, Plapler, and Beaver
AGENCY	Cole Henderson Drake	CLIENT	Lesney Products
CLIENT	Horizon Industries		

GOLD

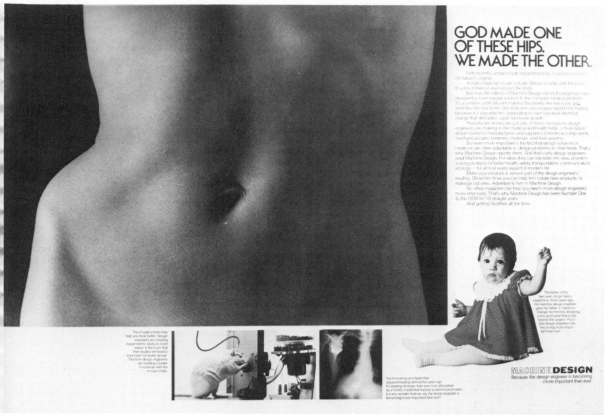

120

120
ART DIRECTOR Tom Gilday
WRITER Mike Marino
DESIGNER Tom Gilday
PHOTOGRAPHER Jan Czyrba
AGENCY Griswold-Eshleman
CLIENT Machine Design

 SILVER

There once was a U.S. President who loved the life he was leading—and led it exceedingly well.

"To any man, but especially to a journalist, it is exciting to consider the prospect that a friend and neighbor might, just possibly, become President of the United States. It is also vaguely rattling."
"Conversations with Kennedy," a memoir by Benjamin C. Bradlee

"Valerie, who never took an acting lesson, finds it hard to believe her rapid ascent. 'Look at me,' she says in disbelief, 'do I look like a sex symbol?'"
Oscar-nominee Valerie answers her own question photographically in "Perrine as in Queen"

"Lenny was a tester, a heavyweight tester. I've never done anything as extreme as he did, but I'm something of a tester, too."
Dustin Hoffman recalls Lenny Bruce in the "Playboy Interview"

That kind of heavy reader involvement creates the perfect selling environment. So much so that, as the recent Media Insight study proved, people pay more attention to the advertising in PLAYBOY than in any other major medium, print or broadcast.

But then, that's what you'd expect from the most powerful male marketing force in the world.

PLAYBOY
In A Class By Itself.

80 million hours in the ring.

"No physical activity is so vain as boxing. A man gets into the ring to attract admiration. In no other sport, therefore, can you be more humiliated. Ali would use every effort to make Foreman look clumsy."
From "The Fight" by Norman Mailer.

"T-shirts are good just to hang out in or out of, depending on who you are or where you are. This girl, for example, thinks she is an automobile." From "'T' Formations" pictorial proof that the proletarian skivvy has come a long way, baby.

What Ali makes, Simon takes: The man who keeps America's bundle tries to pin down the problem of money. Treasury Secretary William Simon is the subject of this month's candid "Playboy Interview."

PLAYBOY
In A Class By Itself.

"I don't like to win against men. It doesn't make me feel good at all."

"I don't like to win against men. It doesn't make me feel good at all. I know it's probably because of my conditioning." —BILLIE JEAN KING

"Who's afraid of hard times? Anybody with good sense. So until the government shows some, make sure you look out for number one."
—WILLIAM E. SIMON

"I spent most of my adolescence trying to change myself to look like Miss January. When I grew up I stopped all that. And now what happens, along comes PLAYBOY wanting to photograph me. OK, I said, I'll show 'em what a real woman looks like." —MARGOT KIDDER

PLAYBOY
In A Class By Itself.

"It was like I had to make God laugh."

"I would be damned if anybody would write anything funnier than I would. I had to get to the ultimate punch line, the cosmic joke that all the other jokes came out of. It was like I was screaming at the universe to pay attention. Like I had to make God laugh."

"Uncle Joe was a philosopher, very deep, very serious. He'd come up and zap you on the arm while you were playing stickball. 'Marry a fat gohl,' he'd whisper. 'They strong. Woik f'ya. Don't marry a face. Put ya under.'"

"I might as well be honest. I'm crowding six, one. Got a mass of blond hair, sensational eyes, bluer than Newman's. Muscular but whippy, like Redford. Only trouble is I have no.... It fell off."

Playboy Interviews are always probing, candid and topical. This month's is insane.

It's with Mel Brooks, a practicing maniac and possibly the greatest comic genius of our time.

PLAYBOY
In A Class By Itself.

121

ART DIRECTOR Richard Manzo
WRITERS Robert Carr
Irwin Kornblau
Emery Smyth
DESIGNER Richard Manzo
ARTISTS Dave Gaadt
Don Ivan Punchatz
PHOTOGRAPHERS Phillip Dixon
Carl Iri
Douglas Kirkland
Terry O'Neill
J. Barry O'Rourke
Ed Streeky
AGENCY Playboy Enterprises
CLIENT Playboy Magazine

We're going to never been flyed fly you like you've before.

Since most men need two different kinds of pants (casual and dress pants are one, jeans and work pants the other), Talon makes two different kinds of pants zippers.

And each is by far the largest-selling in its field.

Our Channel Zip nylon zipper was designed especially for casual and dress pants. Not only did we make it exceptionally strong, we made it beautifully slim and flexible. No other zipper combines so much strength with so much style and comfort.

Channel Zip   *Talon 42*

The Talon 42 metal zipper was designed specifically for jeans and work pants. It's a strong, rugged zipper made to take the worst kind of punishment. And looks it. Which is exactly what your customers want in their jeans. (We know, because in a recent consumer study, they told us.)

So much for our superior zippers. Now for our superior service.

The largest sales force.
Talon has more salesmen to serve you than any other zipper company in the United States.

Their knowledge and experience can help determine the best zippers for your pants, as well as the best application equipment for your production methods.

Talon salesmen don't only sell zippers. They *know* zippers.

Every Talon salesman can fly.
Every Talon salesman attends Fly School.

Before he can call on you, he must go through an intensive training course, in which he learns of the latest developments in Talon zippers and application equipment.

And since Fly School is an ongoing program, each

The Talon Flyers.

Channel Zip for casual and dress pants.   *Talon 42 for jeans and work pants.*

salesman is constantly kept up to date.

That's why you can depend on him to come up with the right solutions to your zipper problems.

The fastest zipper in America.
Since you need faster service than ever, Talon will give you better delivery than ever.

That's because we have more warehouses throughout the United States than any other zipper company.

Wherever your factory is, there's an inventory of Talon zippers nearby.

Computerized inventory.
We have one of the most advanced computer systems

available.

It keeps tabs on every zipper in our inventory, as well as in production.

At any given moment — right now, if you like — the computer knows exactly how many of what style in what sizes and colors are where.

A quick phone call and your zippers are on their way.

We make our own equipment.
To make sure our zippers are properly applied, we make our own application equipment.

From a simple bottom-stop unit to the most sophisticated fully-automatic in-line machines.

What's more, we

have a staff of sales service technicians to advise you which machines are best for your particular production methods.

They'll install and service the equipment for you, and, through regularly scheduled calls, they'll make sure it's running at peak efficiency.

It all comes down to this.
In addition to providing you with the best and most dependable pants zippers, we have a nation-wide system that gives you the most dependable service.

So, to get your pants orders out faster and more efficiently, it makes more sense than ever for you to fly with Talon.

Talon
THE WORLD'S QUALITY ZIPPER

Talon zippers say a lot about the pants they're in.

122

Yesterday at Aqueduct Lucky Lady won, Do-It-Again placed and Anita Baron showed.

Taking a chance on a horse is one thing.

But taking a chance on the wrong zipper is really gambling.

Anita found that out yesterday in the sixth race.

Lucky Lady was coming up fast. The crowd was going wild. And in the stretch, Anita's zipper opened up. Right in front of thousands of people.

That's when she realized how important it is to have a dependable zipper at all times.

Like the Talon Zephyr zipper. Its quality has been proven in millions and millions of garments. That's why your customers look for the Talon name when they buy.

From now on, Anita will put her money on dresses with Talon zippers.

She knows the odds are the rest of the dress will be well made, too.

Talon
THE WORLD'S QUALITY ZIPPER

The Talon Zephyr zipper says a lot about what it's in.

Just as Ron's train reached the station, his zipper started another trip.

It rode down to the end of the line, creating a wide gap. (If you think the train was steaming, you should have seen Ron.)

But it was a good lesson. Now he knows how important it is to have a dependable zipper at all times.

Like Talon's Channel Zip nylon zipper.

It was designed specifically for the active life-style of so many men. That's why it was made strong yet stylish.

The next time Ron goes looking for well-made slacks or dress pants he'll look for the Talon name on the zipper.

It will be a sign that he's on the right track.

Talon
THE WORLD'S QUALITY ZIPPER

The Talon Channel Zip zipper says a lot about the pants it's in.

The minute Ron Becker stepped off the train, his zipper went off the track.

122

ART DIRECTOR	Ron Becker
WRITER	Anita Baron
DESIGNER	Ron Becker
ARTIST	Arton Associates
PHOTOGRAPHERS	Cailor/Resnick
	Bob Gelberg
	20th Century Fox
AGENCY	DKG
CLIENT	Talon

GOLD

Converse introduces training shoes for the body.

To an athlete, comfortable feet are a necessity. The slightest restrictions can cause circulation problems, which can cause tired feet, which can cause a tired body. "My feet are killing me" isn't an idle expression. Put simply, if feet aren't comfortable, the body won't last.

What makes a training shoe comfortable?

Flex: If a training shoe feels supple when you flex your foot, it's not good enough. You shouldn't be able to feel anything. Wearing Converse All Star® training

shoes is like wearing a pair of socks. That is, they fit next to your skin, but you don't feel a thing. The uppers are made with a nylon that is as light as air, soft suede and supple, glove-like leather. The shoe clings to your foot, supporting it without smothering it.

Shock absorption: A sprinting athlete comes down on his heel, then springs off the ball of his foot. Research has shown that pressures of over 5,000

pounds are exerted on the foot during typical jogging exercises. All Star® training shoes have a protective wedge-lifted heel and midsole; a layer of foam rubber tapering from the back of the shoe to the middle. This elevated heel reduces extension of the Achilles tendon, cushioning the jolt and absorbing it. The flared heel-wrap stabilizes the foot during the heel strike and helps reduce roll injuries.

Stress absorption: There are certain points where a shoe rubs particularly hard against a running foot. The All Star eases the stress at these points with a full-length, extra thick sponge insole, a padded nylon tongue, a foam-padded collar, and a padded arch support.

The Converse All Star Training Shoe, built to help the body do better. Available in both men's and women's sizes.

Selected for use by the U.S. Team for the 1976 Olympic Games in Montreal.

How Converse built the quick tennis shoe.

We asked a group of professional tennis players* what would give a tennis shoe an edge in quickness. Some of their answers were enlightening. Here are those answers, built into a wonderfully quick new All Star® Tennis Shoe.

Bounce: Good players bounce continuously. If they don't bounce, they don't move quickly. The Converse All Star design includes a cushion crepe wedge heel. Among other things, this inclines the center of gravity toward the ball of the foot, where the bounce is. The shoe is wide at the toe so the foot can spread, and grab . . . and bounce. It's made with materials that are light and very springy.

Lightness: Obviously, the less feet have to carry, the quicker they can move. There are a variety of outsoles for this new shoe, but they are all made with incredibly light compound materials. The uppers come in light deertone leather, suede, and cool cotton fabrics.

Traction: Tennis players move forward, backward, sideways and even straight up. And they do it suddenly. Above all, a tennis shoe must give excellent traction. Converse designers have spent years perfecting outsoles for different court surfaces. No matter what surface you're playing on, there is a Converse All Star with the right traction for that surface.

A side aspect of traction is the wearing effect on the shoe caused by friction. Converse has compensated for this with extra

reinforcement in all the high-abrasion areas. Reinforced toe bumpers and specially compounded toe plates are examples.

Comfort: It's one thing to be quick at the start of a match. It's quite another to still be quick in the third set. The new All Star gives the kind of comfort that helps prevent fatigue. The cushion crepe wedge heel, the one we mentioned before, absorbs shock from the heel through the arch. It also lends extra support to the arch and midsole area. The uppers are designed not just to fit but to lend support under stress. The ankle collar and tongue are thickly padded with sponge rubber. The insoles have excellent

perspiration absorption qualities, and they are made with non-slip materials that help prevent chafing and blisters.

Converse All Star Tennis Shoes are available in men's and women's styles and colors to match your tennis outfit.

As you can see, the quick tennis shoe gives you a lot more besides.

*Tom Gorman, Roscoe Tanner, Bob Lutz, Charlie Pasarell, Harold Solomon, Ismael El Shafei, Brian Gottfried, Jim McManus, Paul Gerken, Eric Van Dillen.

The Quick American Tennis Shoe

123

ART DIRECTOR Ralph Moxcey
WRITER Derald Breneman
DESIGNER Ralph Moxcey
PHOTOGRAPHER Bill Bruin
AGENCY Humphrey Browning MacDougall
CLIENT Converse Rubber Co.

To sell a car in New York, you need the right vehicle.

What you need, especially these days, is a vehicle that can give you the most mileage for your money.

Like the Daily News.

With nearly twice the circulation of any major daily in the nation and over 5,000,000 readers, the Daily News is the big wheel among newspapers in the nation's number one market.

And it doesn't take a back seat to TV, either. In fact, nothing on the tube can give you more penetration. Not All in the Family, Sanford and Son, or Rhoda.

And don't think News readers just ride the IRT. In New York and the suburbs, 38% of the adults in families owning cars are News readers. That's twice as many as The Times. Of the adults in 2-or-more-car families, 33% are News readers. Compared to only 20% for The Times.

What's more, the Daily News is the driving force no matter what kind of car you're pushing. (Imported, domestic, luxury, economy, new, used, compact or station wagon.)

If you'd like to get specific, call your nearest Daily News representative. Or call Mark Meyers in Detroit at (313) 356-3487. Our on-line computerized service (IMD) can help you keep tabs on your traffic and your competitor's traffic. And you can cross-tab, too. For almost all automotive products and services.

But call soon. Before you take yourself for a ride.

DAILY ⊕ NEWS
NEW YORK'S PICTURE NEWSPAPER

Today... you really need it!

Source: 1974 Markets in Focus

This ring could change your emotions about the Daily News.

Last month in our Sunday News, Alexander's Department Stores ran an ad for their new Mood Ring. They ran it only in The News. By Monday afternoon they ran out of rings. Which put them in a very good mood. And by Monday night, after restocking, they had sold 8,000 rings.

It was the best day Alexander's costume jewelry department ever had.

And although it came as a big surprise to them, it was no surprise to us. Because when it comes to putting your finger on the ring market (or any market), we know we ran rings around all our competitors. Including The Times.

First of all, the New York Daily News is read by more than 5 million people (the Sunday News is read by 6 million). That's more than twice the coverage of The New York Times. So when you place an ad in The News, you'll be selling where most readers are shopping.

And speaking of shopping, our readers have more money to shop with. We give you 55% more adults in families earning between $15,000 and $25,000 than The Times.

What all this is trying to tell you is what Alexander's already knows. If you want your product to be noticed, you have to put it in the right setting.

DAILY ⊕ NEWS
Today...you really need it!

Millions of New Yorkers have left town because of us.

We hope it's nothing we said. But the fact is that after reading the travel ads in our newspaper the immediate reaction of many New Yorkers is to get out of town. Any way they can.

In fact, last year 953,000 Sunday News readers took U.S. vacations by air compared to only 896,000 Sunday Times readers.

And in the last five years, 728,000 Sunday News readers took a combination air-sea cruise compared to only 542,000 Sunday Times readers.

Obviously, regardless of what newspaper moves the travel trade, when it comes to moving the travel market The News leaves The Times behind.

Which isn't surprising. After all, the New York News has more than twice as many readers as the New York Times. And 55% more readers in families earning between $15,000 and $25,000.

See for yourself if we can't give you more customers at a lower cost. Run an ad in The News, daily or Sunday, and key the coupons. Do the same for your other papers.

A good time to do it might be the July 13th midsummer vacation issue which closes July 8th, the August 10th Fall vacations issue which closes August 5th or the September 21st Fall and Winter cruises issue which closes September 16th.

For reservations call Robert Staats, News Travel and Resort Manager, at (212) 682-1234 or your local News representative.

When you see the results, we think you'll agree that the New York News is just the ticket.

DAILY ⊕ NEWS
Today...you really need it!

Source: 1974 Markets in Focus

Circle 1 on Reply Card, page 33.

124

124

ART DIRECTOR Dick Capell
WRITERS Neil Drossman
Jay Taub
DESIGNER Dick Capell
ARTIST Tom Stoerrle
AGENCY Della Femina, Travisano & Partners
CLIENT Daily News

"When I first asked the Board of Education for a Xerox duplicator, the response was overwhelming."

Actually I could tell that they were just suppressing their enthusiasm.

Of course they knew how valuable it would be as an instructional device, allowing teachers to easily create and reproduce their own lesson materials on a regular basis.

"Perhaps," they retorted.

How we could use it to reduce oversize papers like maps and charts onto regular-size paper. And save paper and money by copying on both sides of the same sheet.

"Possibly," they replied.

And how with the special educational pricing plan we'd even get a half-cent rate for the fifth copy on, made from one original.

"Hmmm," they answered.

And that's why we've had a Xerox duplicator in our school for the last two years.

And the Board of Education is delighted they came up with the idea.

XEROX

Circuits aren't the only things that get overloaded.

People do. And at Xerox, we have people who are specially trained to help you handle your communications more efficiently.

We can show you how to use a Xerox duplicator to reduce the load of your next rate case filing.

How to color-code entries by the day, so that the service orders you get on Monday will be processed before the ones you get on Tuesday.

How to reduce engineering drawings so they'll be easier to handle.

Or how to use a Xerox Telecopier transceiver to instantly send service requests from a remote service area to your main office.

Now our Xerox Utilities Specialist can't tell you how much power to sell, or what switches to throw, but he can help keep your communications systems running smoothly.

And your people from blowing their fuses.

XEROX

"Did anyone see the 2 rabbits that were due in Des Moines, Tuesday?"

Occasionally, freight in a terminal can get mishandled or misplaced.

Usually it's due to faulty communications.

Which is why many trucking companies are using Xerox duplicators.

By simply color-coding dock paper flow, for example, they can avoid mix-ups and help control the movement on their loading docks.

And by reducing and reproducing exact copies of bills of lading onto pre-printed freight bill forms, they can avoid transcription errors.

Just as Xerox duplicators are helping people in the transportation industry, they're helping businessmen in all industries.

For more information, call Xerox. We'll help you keep things moving.

XEROX

125

ROLLING STONE

What is Rolling Stone doing on swank East 56th street?

Adding a whole new floor.
From now on, it's Upstairs. Downstairs at Rolling Stone East, a few doors off snotty Park Avenue. We've doubled our space. We need more room. For Polaroid. For Toyota. For Roots and Clark. For Johnson & Johnson and Colgate-Palmolive and Wells Fargo Bank. For Seagram's Gin and Schaefer Beer and Tequila Sauza and Chartreuse. For Sony and Panasonic and Memorex and Samsui —

And we need new spaces for all our new faces. For our new Advertising Director, Don Welsh (ex-Fortune). For Jeff Martini (from Pioneer Electronics) and Flip Powers (from Broadcasting) who have joined Rolling Stone Sales. For a flock of new editorial people — Marianne Partridge (from Rolling Stone West) and Dave Marsh (from Newsday), and people in research (hello, Jeanne Theis) and marketing.

Today, two floors, tomorrow the whole damn building.

ROLLING STONE, 78 EAST 56TH STREET NEW YORK 10022. (212) 486-9560/ WASHINGTON/CHICAGO/SAN FRANCISCO/LOS ANGELES/LONDON

ROLLING STONE

Toyota: Welcome to Rolling Stone
Polaroid: Welcome to Rolling St
Sony: Welcome to Rolling Stone
Colgate-Palmolive: Welcome to
Seagram's Gin: Welcome to Rolli
Johnson & Johnson: Welcome to
Panasonic: Welcome to Rolling S
Wells Fargo Bank: Welcome to R
Clark Shoes: Welcome to Rolling
Tequila Sauza: Welcome to Rolli
Roots: Welcome to Rolling Ston
Southern Comfort: Welcome to
Old Gold: Welcome to Rolling S
Chartreuse: Welcome to Rolling
BOAC: Welcome to Rolling Ston
Memorex: Welcome to Rolling S
More Cigarettes: Welcome to Ro
Nectarose: Welcome to Rolling
Playboy: Welcome to Rolling St

ROLLING STONE

We're way up in Billings.

In '74, we had a whopping 50% gain in advertising revenues. First quarter of '75: up again. 53% ahead in billings. Why? Because more and more major advertisers are finding out that they can't reach our more than 2 million bright, young readers as efficiently, as effectively any other way.

To talk powerfully, personally, to this intensely loyal 18-25 year old crowd, Rolling Stone is where you have to be.

Call Joe Armstrong. (212) 486-9560 78 East 56th St. New York, N.Y. 10022.

ROLLING STONE/NEW YORK, CHICAGO, SAN FRANCISCO, LOS ANGELES, LONDON.

ROLLING STONE

The Rolling Stone sales team is a great bunch of bright, happy, enthusiastic, savvy, energetic peddlers. They have a terrific product to sell, they deeply believe in it, and they're selling it for all it's worth. With spectacular results. More and more big advertisers keep signing on.

We're really rolling. Get aboard.

Up, up, up, Rolling Stone ended up 1974 a whopping *50% ahead* in ad billings (to $3.5 million). And for the first quarter of '75, we're up again. 53% up. Up in pages. Up in dollars. Way ahead in color.

Recession? We sure as hell aren't having one around here. What has Rolling Stone got that you need? More than two million active young readers who can't be reached as efficiently, as effectively, as personally and powerfully *any other way.* We have some remarkable advertising success stories we'd like to share with you. Let us know when, and we'll pedal right over.

Hey, Joe, get on your bicycle and come see me. Could be that Colgate-Palmolive, Heublein, Seagram's, Time-Life, R.J.Reynolds and *all* the major home entertainment manufacturers have learned something about *selective selling* that I should know.

Joe Armstrong
Rolling Stone   NAME
78 East 56th St.   TITLE
New York, N.Y.
10022   COMPANY
   TELEPHONE

126

ART DIRECTOR Dick Thomas
WRITER Whit Hobbs
ARTIST Bob Deschamps
AGENCY Blue Green
CLIENT Rolling Stone

126

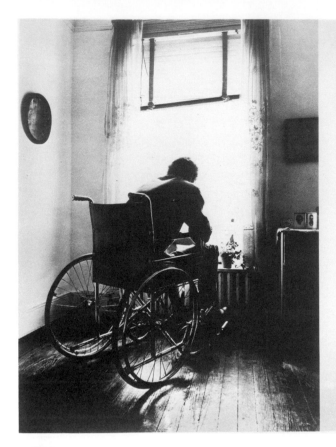

DISCRIMINATION IS HIS BIGGEST HANDICAP.

Storer stations are concerned and are doing something about it.

Over 11,000,000 Americans ages 16 to 64 are physically or mentally handicapped. Some are paralyzed. Some physically deformed, retarded, deaf or blind.

320,000 are disabled veterans of the Vietnam War.

Employer trepidation, plus ignorance of their capabilities, frequently keep these handicapped people from being hired for jobs. So some 21% live below the poverty level compared with 14% for the U.S. population as a whole.

Yet experience shows the handicapped make top-notch workers in many fields. For example, the U.S. Postal Service employs deaf workers as distribution clerks where the noise level is high. And in a large chemical concern, a study of 1400 handicapped employees revealed that 91% rated average-or-better in job perfor-

mance compared with other employees.

Storer feels that these people, too, deserve full, productive lives. That's why in programming and editorials, Storer stations regularly devote air time to their problems.

KGBS-Radio, Los Angeles, for instance brought together the chairman of Volunteers with the Committee for the Employment of the Handicapped, a state senator, an employment counselor with Goodwill Industries and a special assistant to a U.S. Senator. Focus of the show: the dual issues of training and employment of the handicapped.

Another KGBS program gathered a pediatrician, the mother of a handicapped child and the heads of two institutions. This special dealt with the problems of handicapped children and the importance of early diagnosis and training so the child can better cope with his problems.

In Atlanta, the General Man-

ager of WAGA-TV recently spent a day in a wheelchair so he could bring to Atlanta viewers an understanding of what it means to be handicapped. To quote from his editorial, "A curb becomes a mountain, a flight of stairs approximates outer space, a narrow door becomes a forbidding wall."

In a recent 4-month period, WGBS-Radio, Miami aired 143 announcements on the handicapped and their employment. And this is typical of Storer stations across the nation.

The way we see it, the more effective we are in our communities, the more effective we are for our advertisers, and the more effective we are for ourselves.

Broadcasting that serves.
THE
STORER STATIONS
STORER BROADCASTING COMPANY

WAGA-TV Atlanta/WSBK-TV Boston/WJW-TV Cleveland/WJBK-TV Detroit/WITI-TV Milwaukee/KCST-TV San Diego/WSPD-TV Toledo
WJW Cleveland/KGBS Los Angeles/WGBS Miami/WHN New York/WSPD Toledo

WHERE THOUSANDS OF BREADWINNERS BECOME LOSERS EACH YEAR.

Storer stations are concerned and are doing something about it.

America's highways are like bloody battlefields. In 1973 alone, they were the scene of over 20,000,000 accidents and 55,600 fatalities.

And, while safety experts are cheered by the improvement the 55-mph speed limit has made, the carnage in 1974 still totaled an estimated 44,500 dead.

By far most of the fatalities are men—many at an age when young families are vitally dependent on their support. This makes the toll on American life go well beyond anything the grisly statistics reveal.

For this reason, Storer stations feel they must relentlessly press the attack against this deadly killer. So you'll find Storer stations across the country regularly devoting important air time to programs and editorials that stress highway safety.

KCST-TV in San Diego, for example, recently tackled a fre-

quent cause of accidents—the drunken driver. In a 30-minute special, KCST-TV brought together for discussion the municipal judge who originated San Diego's Rehabilitation Program for Alcoholics; the area commander of the California Highway Patrol; the executive director of the San Diego Traffic Safety Council; and a practicing attorney.

On the day following this program, KCST-TV's Eyewitness News took viewers for a ride in a Highway Patrol car and gave a filmed account of what happens on an actual drunken driver arrest.

Scores of people are killed at railroad crossings. Yet Georgia law doesn't require drivers to stop at crossings unless there's a stop sign. Many crossings have no signs. And of those that do, many have no bells and lights. So in a hard-hitting series of editorials, WAGA-TV in Atlanta pushed to make stops at all crossings a law, and to get signals at important crossings.

In Toledo, a fatal trailer-

truck accident occurred at an intersection just off a busy interstate highway exit. WSPD-TV, aware that it was the scene of several other bad accidents, interviewed witnesses who live nearby. They learned that trucks regularly ran the light. Truck drivers checked said that the light was so short, they couldn't stop. WSPD-TV informed the city traffic department and the light was re-timed.

Involvement like this in the affairs of their communities is typical of all Storer stations.

We feel the more effective we are in our communities, the more effective we are for our advertisers, and the more effective we are for ourselves.

Broadcasting that serves.
THE
STORER STATIONS
STORER BROADCASTING COMPANY

WAGA-TV Atlanta/WSBK-TV Boston/WJW-TV Cleveland/WJBK-TV Detroit/WITI-TV Milwaukee/KCST-TV San Diego/WSPD-TV Toledo
WJW Cleveland/KGBS Los Angeles/WGBS Miami/WHN New York/WSPD Toledo

127

127
ART DIRECTOR John Cenatiempo
WRITER Andrew Isaacson
PHOTOGRAPHER Cailor/Resnick
AGENCY Gaynor & Ducas
CLIENT Storer Broadcasting Co.

What good is a guarantee on the muffler when your tailpipe goes?

There's more to an exhaust system than a muffler. There's a tailpipe, exhaust pipe, clamps and hangers. And statistics tell us that the tailpipe often goes before the muffler.

Yet most of the people who repair exhaust systems only give a lifetime guarantee on their mufflers. If you have to buy a tailpipe and it goes, guess who pays? And you could pay as much as $35.

That's not the case at your Scotti Muffler Center. At Scotti, we guarantee any and every part of the exhaust system we install. Pipes, muffler, you name it. And any of the 650 Scotti dealers coast to coast, will replace any Scotti part free of charge for as long as you own your car. And we'll do it while you wait.

Yet with all this we charge about the same as places with less of a guarantee. So at Scotti you get off a lot cheaper in the long run.

SCOTTI MUFFLER CENTER
COAST TO COAST

We give you a 100% guarantee on 100% of our work.

Address, Telephone

If you ever have to collect on a muffler guarantee, this is what could be collected from you.

$50. crossover pipe
$1. clamp
$1. hanger
$26. exhaust pipe
$1. hanger
$0. muffler
$1. clamp
$22. tailpipe

Lots of places are willing to repair your exhaust system. But not too many are willing to guarantee any more than the muffler. Which means if you have to replace any other part of the exhaust system they installed (like the tailpipe, exhaust pipe, clamps, hangers, etc.) you'll have to pay the piper. What you pay depends on what kind of car you drive. The approximate prices in the example above are just for a 1970 Chevy Impala V-8.

Now at Scotti, we're willing to guarantee each and every part of the exhaust system we install. Which means if you should ever have to replace part of a Scotti exhaust system, you'll never have to pay for any parts, or labor, for as long as you own the car. And any of the 650 Scotti dealers coast to coast will honor that guarantee.

And with a guarantee like that you can be certain we're going to give you the best muffler and pipes money can buy. If we didn't, we could end up spending all our time replacing them and working for nothing.

Yet you don't pay any more at Scotti than you would at one of those other places. After all, what's the good of giving you all this, if we couldn't get you into a Scotti Muffler Center in the first place?

SCOTTI MUFFLER CENTER
COAST TO COAST

We give you a 100% guarantee on 100% of our work.

Address, Telephone

How a free muffler at Midas can cost you up to $102.

If a Midas muffler wears out, they'll replace it free for the life of your car.

THE MIDAS TOUCH.

But come back to collect that free muffler and you'll find that the muffler is just one part of your exhaust system. There are also clamps, hangers, a tailpipe, exhaust pipe, etc.

These, unfortunately, are not guaranteed for the life of your car at Midas. So if they go, Midas could touch you for $22 for a tailpipe, $26 for an exhaust pipe, $50 for a crossover pipe or $4 for clamps and hangers.

And that's just for a 1970 Chevy Impala V-8. If you have a fancier car, you could have a fancier bill.

THE SCOTTI GUARANTEE.

Now there is a way to avoid all this. Come to a Scotti Muffler Center. When one of our 650 dealers repairs your exhaust system he guarantees every part he installs, not just the muffler.

Should you ever have to return for a replacement, there's no charge for parts, or labor. Which means you get off Scot-free.

And amazingly enough, the prices for exhaust repairs at Scotti compare favorably to the Midas prices. Of course, that's on your first visit. After that, there's no comparison.

SCOTTI MUFFLER CENTER
COAST TO COAST

We give you a 100% guarantee on 100% of our work.

Address, Telephone

128
ART DIRECTOR Ray Alban
WRITER Steve Smith
DESIGNER Ray Alban
ARTIST Charles White III
AGENCY Scali, McCabe, Sloves
CLIENT Scotti Muffler Centers

SILVER

129

ART DIRECTORS	Allan Beaver
	Bill Kamp
	Ken Sausville
WRITERS	Larry Plapler
	John Russo
	Frank Anton
PHOTOGRAPHERS	Peter Papadopolous
	Cailor/Resnick
	Menken Seltzer
AGENCY	Levine, Huntley, Schmidt, Plapler and Beaver

It's the car that should go quickly, not the gas.

A bewildered Rabbit customer was recently overheard asking himself the following question: "Everything's right with this car. What's wrong?"

Quite honestly, nothing.

The standard shift Rabbit got incredible EPA estimates of 39 miles per gallon on the highway and 25 in the city. (Actual mileage may vary, depending on your type of driving, your car's condition and optional equipment.)

But what's truly remarkable is that the Rabbit delivers this economy without sacrificing performance. It hops from 0 to 50 in just 8.2 seconds. No other car in the world gives you that kind of power with that kind of gas economy.

So if you're tired of burning up money and falling behind, trade your car for a Rabbit. It's a sure way to come out ahead.

The Amazing Rabbit ⓋⓌ

©VOLKSWAGEN OF AMERICA, INC.

130

The good news is that Blacks aren't being lynched in Mississippi any more.

The bad news is that they still have to live in Mississippi.

Eleven years ago Philadelphia, Mississippi, a town named after the city of brotherly love, became famous when three civil rights workers were murdered nearby.

What's the deep South like today? We wanted to find out. So we sent Al Austin and photographer Les Solin down to Mississippi. What they saw wasn't necessarily heartening.

Mississippi is officially fully integrated today. Which means if you're a Black person, you have just as much right to live in a shack with fifteen other people as a white person does.

And Blacks don't do dull, unskilled work on plantations and live in substandard housing any more. Because today, all cotton picking is mechanized. So the Blacks have gone away to other towns, where they do dull, unskilled work in factories and live in substandard housing.

There has been progress. There are now Black mayors and Black police in towns around Mississippi. But poverty and illiteracy are still rampant.

Beginning October 6th, we're going to begin broadcasting this special four-part report on "The Scene Tonight."

Watch "Mississippi: Pride and Prejudice." It may make you glad you aren't a Black man in Mississippi. Or a white man, for that matter.

Mississippi: Pride and Prejudice. 4 WCCO TV
The Scene Tonight at 10

NOTHING WILL SELL YOU A NEW VOLVO LIKE A TEST DRIVE IN A USED ONE.

During a ten minute test drive, any new car will shine.

But how do you know a few thousand hard miles won't turn `000014` that shiny new VS. car into a rattling old heap? `030149`

Volvo builds cars to stay tight and quiet. And to prove it, we'll have you test drive two.

A used Volvo with at least 30,000 miles on it. And a new Volvo equipped the way you want.

In uncertain times like these, one thing is certain. Before you spend a lot of money on a new car, you should know how good it can be when it's old.

See us today...for "The Test Drive for People Who Think." **VOLVO**
© 1975 VOLVO OF AMERICA CORPORATION. LEASING AVAILABLE.

DEALER NAME

131   132

Go where this newspaper won't follow.

Tahiti

Moorea

No billboards. No crowds. No freeways. No smog.

And for $698 we can take you on Pan Am's Tahitian Long Weekend. The price includes round trip flight based on individual economy tour basing fare. Hotel accommodations (double occupancy) for 3 nights on Tahiti and 4 nights on Moorea. Transportation between airport and hotel. Motor launch to Moorea (and back). And sightseeing on both islands.

One more thing. Because you'll be on Pan Am's Flight #815 (the only through-plane service to Tahiti) leaving on Friday or Saturday at 10:50 a.m., you'll have a nice lunch and get there in plenty of time for dinner that evening in Papeete.

If this sounds like a good way to escape, send in this coupon or call your travel agent and ask about Pan Am's Tahitian Bali Hai vacation.

Pan Am Tour Brochure Department
1 California Street
San Francisco, California 94111
Name_____
Address_____
City_____State_____Zip_____
My travel agent is_____

PAN AM.
The Spirit of '75

See your travel agent.

133

If you ever have to collect on a muffler guarantee, this is what could be collected from you.

$50. crossover pipe

$26. exhaust pipe

$1. clamp

$1. hanger

$1. hanger

$0. muffler

$1. clamp

$22. tailpipe

Lots of places are willing to repair your exhaust system. But not too many are willing to guarantee any more than the muffler. Which means if you have to replace any other part of the exhaust system they installed (like the tailpipe, exhaust pipe, clamps, hangers, etc.) you'll have to pay the piper. What you pay depends on what kind of car you drive. The approximate prices in the example above are just for a 1970 Chevy Impala V-8.

Now at Scotti, we're willing to guarantee each and every part of the exhaust system we install. Which means if you should ever have to replace part of a Scotti exhaust system, you'll never have to pay for any parts, or labor, for as long as you own the car. And any of the 650 Scotti dealers coast to coast will honor that guarantee.

And with a guarantee like that you can be certain we're going to give you the best muffler and pipes money can buy. If we didn't, we could end up spending all our time replacing them and working for nothing.

Yet you don't pay any more at Scotti than you would at one of those other places. After all, what's the good of giving you all this, if we couldn't get you into a Scotti Muffler Center in the first place?

SCOTTI MUFFLER CENTER
COAST TO COAST

We give you a 100% guarantee on 100% of our work.

Address, Telephone

134

TONIGHT'S SHOW IS GARBAGE.

6-8 PACKS 48–7 OZ BOTTLES

And with New Yorkers producing 28,000 tons of garbage every day, this town is full of it. Tonight, you'll follow its journey from the cans to the trucks, to the barges and then on to its final burial ground—the landfills. Like Fresh Kills in Staten Island, where 5 miles of mountainous garbage make it the world's biggest dump.

But we're running out of places to dump it. New, imaginative solutions are needed. Fast. Because one thing is clear. Left unsolved, New York's garbage problem could bury us all.

"YOU CAN SMELL FOREVER." NARRATED BY ROGER GRIMSBY. A CHANNEL 7 SPECIAL REPORT TONIGHT AT 6:30.

136

When I was sentenced to 197 years in prison, even my father felt that if a jury found me guilty, then I must be guilty.

So I understand when perfect strangers automatically assume that I was the killer of 3 people in a New Jersey tavern. Luckily, my father lived long enough to see the principal 'eyewitnesses' against me admit they lied. Now I'm seeking a re-trial so I can convince everyone of my innocence.

RUBIN "HURRICANE" CARTER, NO. 45475 TRENTON STATE PRISON

135

ART DIRECTOR	Nathan Fiarman	**ART DIRECTOR**	Ray Alban	
WRITER	Carla Carlotti	**WRITER**	Steve Smith	
AGENCY	Carl Ally	**DESIGNER**	Ray Alban	
CLIENT	Pan American World Airways	**ARTIST**	Charles White III	
		AGENCY	Scali, McCabe, Sloves	
		CLIENT	Scotti Muffler Centers	

133
ART DIRECTOR Nathan Fiarman
WRITER Carla Carlotti
AGENCY Carl Ally
CLIENT Pan American World Airways

134
ART DIRECTOR Ray Alban
WRITER Steve Smith
DESIGNER Ray Alban
ARTIST Charles White III
AGENCY Scali, McCabe, Sloves
CLIENT Scotti Muffler Centers

135
ART DIRECTOR George Lois
WRITER Ron Holland
DESIGNER Dennis Mazzella
AGENCY Lois Holland Callaway
CLIENT The Hurricane Fund

136
ART DIRECTOR Eugene Calogero
WRITER Mike Glass
PHOTOGRAPHER George Ehrlich
AGENCY Rosenfeld, Sirowitz & Lawson
CLIENT American Broadcasting Co's.

7 out of 10 Rabbit Tests are positive.

Our research shows that 70% of all the people who buy the Rabbit say that it was the test drive that made up their minds for them.

It's no wonder. The Rabbit drives like no other car you've ever driven before.

You see, in designing the Rabbit, we didn't just stop at things like front-wheel drive and rack-and-pinion steering. We created a totally unique "independent stabilizer rear axle" that greatly increases the stability of the car on rough roads. And therefore the safety.

And speaking of safety, we gave the Rabbit features that you'll find on few other cars in the world. Like "negative steering roll radius," for example, which helps bring the car to a straight stop in the event of a front-wheel blowout.

But the two big things that everyone who drives the Rabbit really marvels at are: one, the amount of head and leg room (as much as some mid-sized cars); and two, its incredible pickup (0 to 50 in 8.2 seconds). Which is pretty amazing for a car that rates an EPA-estimated 39 mpg on the highway—and 25 in the city, with standard transmission. (Actual mileage may vary depending on type of driving, driving habits, car's condition and optional equipment.)

But don't just take our word for it. Stop in and take a Rabbit Test today.

The Amazing Rabbit ⓥ

137

ART DIRECTOR John Caggiano
WRITER Mike Mangano
DESIGNER John Caggiano
PHOTOGRAPHER Nick Samardge
AGENCY Doyle Dane Bernbach
CLIENT Volkswagen

THE ECONOMY HAS MADE THE STANDARD TEST DRIVE OBSOLETE.

If you plan to live with your next car for the next few years, you should know what you're getting into.

Americans are considered to be intelligent, well-informed people. Yet the most common large investment made in this country is nothing more than a hunch bet.

Often, a person buying a new car will gamble thousands of dollars based on a five minute once-over.

In these shaky times, Volvo considers this not only risky, but foolish.

Today, any purchase as important as a new car calls for a second look, and more.

That's what Volvo gives you.

Naturally, we'll have you test drive one of our brand new Volvos. But before you spend your hard-earned money, we'll

give you a good hard look at a used Volvo. One with at least 30,000 miles on it.

Slam the doors. See how tight the body still is. Sit in the seats. They still support your back, instead of sagging under your weight. Kick the tires: the hubcaps stay on.

Then, take the keys and give it a workout. You'll find that what makes a Volvo stand out is how well it stands up.

Volvo knows that these days, any car you buy will have to be a used car a lot longer than it's a new one.

So we build accordingly.

See for yourself at the Volvo dealer who invites you to take "The Test Drive for People Who Think."

VOLVO
The car for people who think.

139

They're standing in their new driveway.

These people had a choice: get a new driveway or get away for a week in the sun. They decided to park themselves on the beach. They're Psychology Today readers.

In fact, Simmons shows that more PT women travel to Europe, Bermuda or the Caribbean than the male readers of Time, Newsweek and Playboy! And PT men travel even more than PT women.

Our readers are secure about the future. But today is where they live.

PT's 4½ million readers.
They live their dreams today, not tomorrow.

Psychology Today
A Ziff-Davis Publication

Source: Simmons 1974/75

138

TO KEEP A COMPANY TRIM, TRY A LOW FATHEAD DIET.

When business goes bad, companies trim the fat.

We say, "Trim the fathead, instead".

Sloppy thinking can kill a company just as dead as sloppy spending.

Industry Week helps its readers stay on a low fathead diet. It prods them. Stimulates them. Provides efficient, workable answers to difficult and nasty problems.

Industry Week does the same for its advertisers. It's the most efficient answer to the problem of selling ideas, products and services to industry managers. It talks to 1.3 million managers each week and tells them about your company and its products. For less than two cents per reader, according to TGI.

Managers like IW's low fathead diet. So do advertisers.

INDUSTRY WEEK
The magazine managers read.

140

	138		**139**		**140**
ART DIRECTOR	Lew-Dave-Marv	**ART DIRECTOR**	Bob Reitzfeld	**ART DIRECTOR**	Bob Kwait
WRITER	Lew-Dave-Marv	**WRITERS**	Ed McCabe	**WRITER**	Mike Marino
PHOTOGRAPHER	Michael Dakota		Tom Nathan	**DESIGNER**	Bob Kwait
AGENCY	KSW&G	**DESIGNER**	Bob Reitzfeld	**AGENCY**	Griswold-Eshleman
CLIENT	Psychology Today	**PHOTOGRAPHER**	Henry Sandbank	**CLIENT**	Industry Week
		AGENCY	Scali, McCabe, Sloves		
		CLIENT	Volvo		

"I WAS TEN WHEN MY FATHER STARTED SAVING FOR MY COLLEGE EDUCATION.
I WAS ELEVEN WHEN HE DIED."

Sometimes the saddest thing about a man's death is to watch his dreams die with him. His dreams for his family. His hopes for making their lives a little easier, a little more satisfying than his own.

If you have dreams for your family, don't let anything happen to them if something happens to you. Talk to us, MONY, Mutual Of New York. We can sit down with you now and work out a life insurance plan that can protect your family's future.

It will be a sound, sensible plan because we'll work hard to make it that way. But most important, it will keep your dreams for your family alive no matter what might happen to you.

MONY
FOR THE FUTURE.
The Mutual Life Insurance Company Of New York

AGENCY NAME • ADDRESS • PHONE NUMBER

(F.U.'s Name) (F.U.'s Name) (F.U.'s Name) (F.U.'s Name) (F.U.'s Name)

143

Either this car is a miracle or this ad is a lie.

FIAT A lot of car. Not a lot of money.

141

Counting today, I have sat in prison 3,135 days for a crime I did not commit.

If I don't get a retrial, I have 189 years to go. 6 months ago the "eye-witnesses," who testified they saw me leaving a bar in which 3 people had been killed, admitted they gave false testimony. Despite this, the judge who sentenced me won't give me a retrial. Why?

RUBIN "HURRICANE" CARTER, NO. 45475 TRENTON STATE PRISON

142

	141		142		143
ART DIRECTOR	Amil Gargano	ART DIRECTOR	George Lois	ART DIRECTOR	Ed McCabe
WRITER	David Altschiller	WRITER	Ron Holland	WRITER	Charles Glass
PHOTOGRAPHER	Tony Petrucelli	DESIGNER	Dennis Mazzella	PHOTOGRAPHER	Cailor/Resnick
AGENCY	Carl Ally	AGENCY	Lois Holland Callaway	AGENCY	The Marschalk Co.
CLIENT	Fiat Distributors	CLIENT	The Hurricane Fund	CLIENT	Mutual Of New York

GOLD

I was asleep for 29 years.

I woke up one day, and realized that nothing happens in your life unless you make it happen. Whether it's shopping for a new color TV, or making vacation reservations.

Now I go after what I want, because you have to live your life today, even though you're always planning for tomorrow.

In fact, I feel secure about the future. But today is where I live.

PT readers live their dreams today, not tomorrow.

Psychology Today
A Ziff-Davis Publication

146

Which car is bigger?

That mid-sized car in the picture above looks a lot bigger than the Rabbit, right?

Well, the Volkswagen Rabbit actually has as much headroom and legroom as that bigger car. And as far as luggage space goes, with the rear seat folded down it holds as much as a Cadillac Fleetwood.

It's merely our front and rear that are smaller.

Our front is smaller because we put the engine in sideways. And our rear is smaller because of our ingeniously designed hatchback and rear seat that adjusts to three different luggage positions.

Incredible? Sure. But then, just about everything about this car is incredible.

For example, the standard transmission Rabbit got an EPA-estimated 39 miles per gallon on the highway (and 25 in the city), yet it goes from 0 to 50 in 8.2 seconds. (Actual mileage may vary depending on type of driving, driving habits, car's condition and optional equipment.)

Stop in for a test drive and you'll see what we mean.

Better yet, bring the wife and kids. And try the whole car on for size.

The Amazing Rabbit ⓋⓌ

144

"We guarantee to double your money in less than nine years.* How many companies on this page can make that statement?"

*It's actually 8 years 10 months.

The Provident
Institution for Savings

145

	144		145		146
ART DIRECTOR	John Caggiano	**ART DIRECTOR**	Janice Hawkins	**ART DIRECTOR**	Lew-Dave-Marv
WRITER	Mike Mangano	**WRITER**	Peter Caroline	**WRITER**	Lew-Dave-Marv
DESIGNER	John Caggiano	**AGENCY**	Humphrey Browning MacDougall	**PHOTOGRAPHER**	Michael Dakota
PHOTOGRAPHER	Nick Samardge	**CLIENT**	Provident Institution For Savings	**AGENCY**	KSW&G
AGENCY	Doyle Dane Bernbach			**CLIENT**	Psychology Today
CLIENT	Volkswagen				

At this price, no wonder it goes so fast.

The 1976 Fiat 124 Spider. $5,759.

F I A T
A lot of car. Not a lot of money.

1976 Manufacturer's suggested retail price East Coast POE. Inland transportation, dealer preparation and local taxes additional. Car rental, leasing, and overseas delivery arranged through your participating dealer.

147

Not all the pyramids are along the Nile.

Our apologies to the Pharaohs of Egypt. But the ancient Mayan civilization, built literally hundreds of pyramids 2000 years ago in northern Guatemala.

Now we don't expect this to deter you from visiting the "real" pyramids.

But if Guatemala's spring climate doesn't send you, or you don't find her Indian markets, like Chichicastenango, intriguing, or if you can call your life complete without seeing volcano-ringed Lake Atitlan, maybe Guatemala's pyramids alone are enough to attract you.

And if the Mayan pyramids, or the modern hotels, or the thousands of quiet lakes aren't

enough, we've got one last good reason for you to visit Guatemala.

Pan Am has 3 flights a week to Guatemala.
Flight #541 leaves every Monday, Wednesday, and Friday at 1:05 in the afternoon. It's the only non-stop service from Washington to Guatemala.

Make sure to ask your travel agent for Pan Am's Flight #541.

Because if you just ask for the pyramids, he might send you to the wrong ones.

PAN AM
The Spirit of '75.

See your travel agent.

149

There's a good reason why we have you speaking Spanish sooner.
We don't let you speak English.

Whether you're learning Spanish or any other language at Berlitz, you'll speak only that language, right from the start of your very first lesson.

You'll learn without tedious grammar drills and, in almost every case, with the help of a native instructor.

The atmosphere is warm and friendly, and with the Berlitz Method, you'll learn to think in the language, as well as to speak it.

We know because we've helped 21 million students to master a second language at Berlitz.

All because we refused to communicate in their first one.

1414 North Central Avenue **252-6566** **BERLITZ**®

148

Seat belts that put <u>themselves</u> on.

It's like magic. You just get in the Rabbit and close the door, and voilà! Your seat belt's on.

This remarkable feature, found on the deluxe model of the Rabbit, is just one of many many safety precautions that we've built into this amazing car.

We also have something called an "independent stabilizer rear axle," which increases the stability of the car on rough roads.

"Negative steering roll radius," which helps bring the car to a straight stop in the event of a front-wheel blowout.

"Dual diagonal brakes," which means that if either brake circuit fails, directional stability is maintained.

But perhaps one of the most significant safety features of all is the Rabbit's extraordinary peppiness (0 to 50 in 8.2 seconds) which can help you *avoid* trouble.

We could go on and on about all the other safety devices we've built into this revolutionary automobile, but we'll mention just one more. Because it kind of symbolizes the attention we paid to safety in designing the Rabbit.

Would you believe a padded ignition key?

The Amazing Rabbit ⊗

150

Pasta time 12:30 Posta time 1:30

Monday is Italian Day at Suffolk Downs and that means lots of Italian food, pre-race entertainment by East Boston's own Paul Penta Trio, and the Italian Jockey Invitational Handicap. Get here early!

ITALIAN DAY AT Suffolk Downs

10 races — 1 daily double — 4 perfectas — first race 1:30

15

	150		151
ART DIRECTOR	John Caggiano	ART DIRECTOR	Bill Murphy
WRITER	Mike Mangano	WRITER	Betsy Clark
DESIGNER	John Caggiano	AGENCY	Ingalls Associate
PHOTOGRAPHER	Nick Samardge	CLIENT	Suffolk Downs
AGENCY	Doyle Dane Bernbach		
CLIENT	Volkswagen		

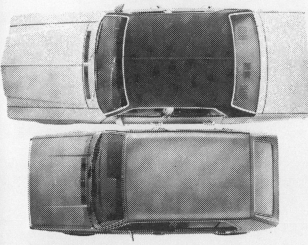

152
ART DIRECTOR John Caggiano
WRITER Mike Mangano
DESIGNER John Caggiano
PHOTOGRAPHER Nick Samardge
AGENCY Doyle Dane Bernbach
CLIENT Volkswagen

GOLD

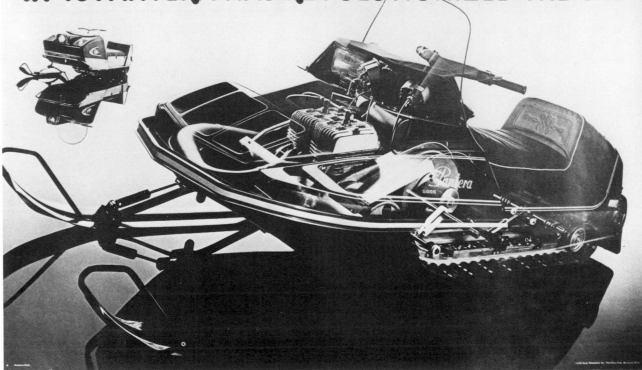

153
ART DIRECTOR James Lotter
WRITER Duane Johnson
PHOTOGRAPHER Vern Hammarlun
AGENCY Carmichael/Lync
CLIENT Arctic Enterprise

154

154
ART DIRECTOR Larry Sheridan
WRITER Jan Busselle
DESIGNER Larry Sheridan
ARTIST Arnold Varga
AGENCY Campbell-Ewald
CLIENT General Motors

155

ART DIRECTOR Vincent R. Longo
PHOTOGRAPHER Paul Frankian
AGENCY Doremus & Company
CLIENT East River Savings Bank

"Some of my favorite performers are horses!"

156

THE PIONEERS' UNDERWEAR WAS MADE BY THE PIONEERS OF UNDERWEAR.

157

	156		157
ART DIRECTOR	Kurt Weihs	ART DIRECTOR	Allan Beaver
WRITER	Wally Weis	WRITER	Larry Plapler
DESIGNER	Kurt Weihs	ARTIST	Bettmann Archives
AGENCY	Lois Holland Callaway	AGENCY	Levine, Huntley, Schmidt, Plapler, and Beaver
CLIENT	Off Track Betting Corp.	CLIENT	Jockey

See Ford's Van Go!

FORD

15

How to tell who's in trouble.
Your team, their team, or the referee.

Offside

Holding

Time Out

Time Out, Please

With Talon, you won't be penalized for a broken zipper.

Talon
THE WORLD'S QUALITY ZIPPER

TALON, A textron COMPANY,©1975

1

158
ART DIRECTOR George Schoenberger
WRITER Fred Bishop
ARTIST Skidmore Sahratian
AGENCY J. Walter Thompson
CLIENT Ford Motor Company

159
ART DIRECTOR Ron Becker
WRITER Anita Baron
DESIGNER Ron Becker
PHOTOGRAPHER Jerry Abromow
AGENCY DKG
CLIENT Talon

161

161
ART DIRECTOR Ozzie Hawkins, Jr.
WRITER Robert Taylor
DESIGNER Ozzie Hawkins, Jr.
ARTISTS Dan Burback
Art Graphics Associates
AGENCY J. Walter Thompson
CLIENT Seven Up

A BURRITO BUILT FOR TWO.

NACHOS ARE A GIRL'S BEST FRIEND.

REMEMBER THE CHILI RELLENO.

162
ART DIRECTOR Marty Neumeier
WRITER Garth De Cew
DESIGNER Marty Neumeier
AGENCY Garth De Cew Group
CLIENT Dos Pesos Restaurants

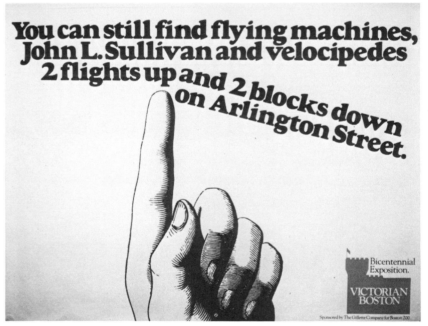

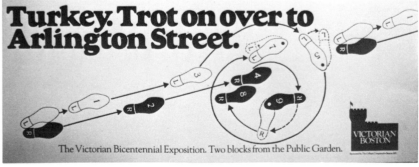

163

163
ART DIRECTOR Tony Viola
WRITERS Jim Pappademas
Jay Hill
DESIGNER Tony Viola
AGENCY Hill, Holliday,
Connors, Cosmopule
CLIENT Boston 200

JAX & JILL.

JAX FROST.

JAX IN A BOX.

164

	164
ART DIRECTOR	Al Weintraub
WRITER	Richard Schiera
DESIGNER	Al Weintraub
PHOTOGRAPHER	Bob Salomon
AGENCY	The Bloom Agency
CLIENT	Jax Brewing Co.

 GOLD

GOVERNMENT CENTER

STBOUND KENMORE PARK

Two of our critics have died of boredom so you could avoid dull movies.

Don't let their sacrifice be in vain.

The Real Paper

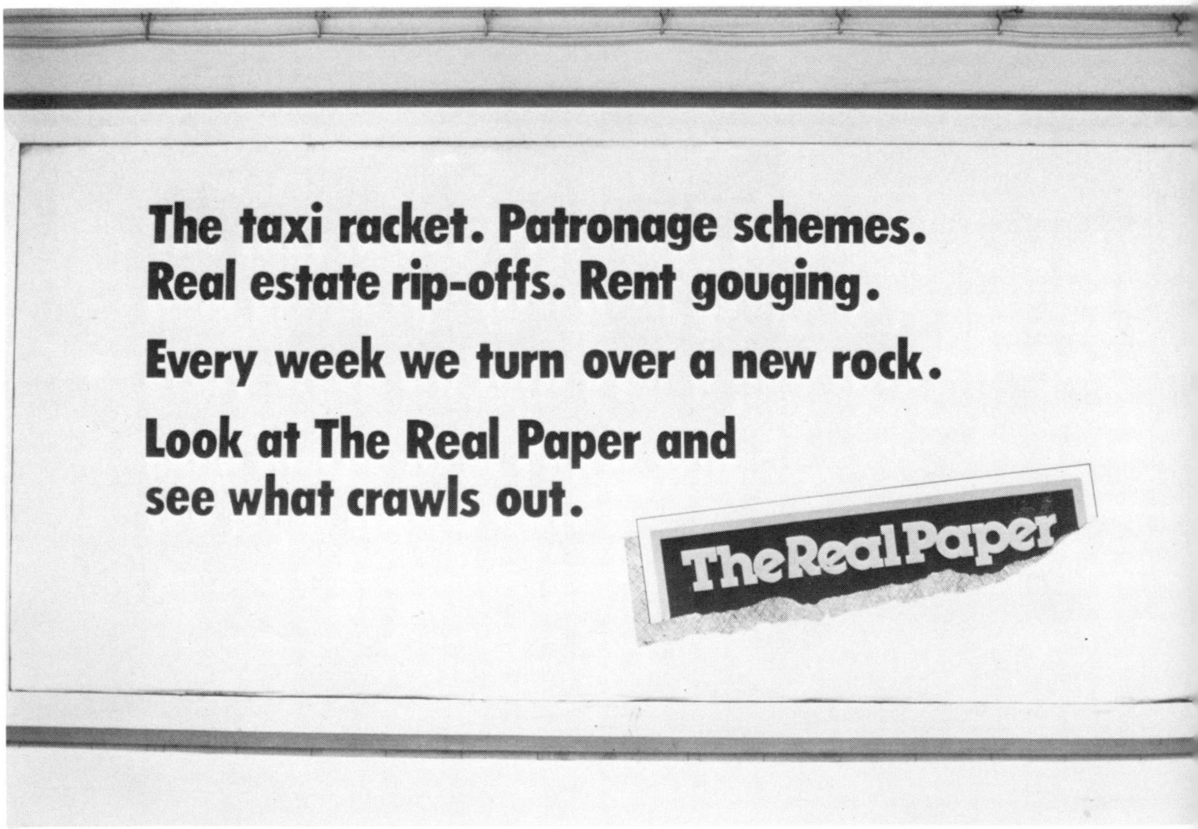

The taxi racket. Patronage schemes. Real estate rip-offs. Rent gouging.

Every week we turn over a new rock.

Look at The Real Paper and see what crawls out.

The Real Paper

165
ART DIRECTOR Ralph Moxcey
WRITER Reilly Fletcher
DESIGNER Ralph Moxcey
AGENCY Humphrey Browning
MacDougall
CLIENT The Real Paper

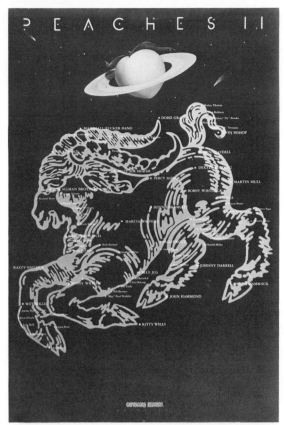

ART DIRECTOR	Diana Kaylan
DESIGNER	Dave Bhang
ARTIST	Bill Imhoff
PHOTOGRAPHER	David Alexander
AGENCY	Capricorn Records
CLIENT	Capricorn Records

166

167
ART DIRECTOR Marty Neumeier
WRITER Garth De Cew
DESIGNER Marty Neumeier
AGENCY Garth De Cew Grou
CLIENT Santa Barbara
Metropolitan
Transit District

Last year, more money was donated to the Society for the Prevention of Cruelty to Animals than to the Society for the Prevention of Cruelty to Children.

Today we at the Queensboro Society for the Prevention of Cruelty to Children are still years behind the Society for the Prevention of Cruelty to Animals.

We need money.

We need money to continue helping abused children. By giving them food, clothing, and shelter. And to help heal the wounds on the inside, psychological help.

We need money to take them out of a home, if it can't be saved, and find them a new one.

To provide legal assistance for children who can't defend themselves.

And we don't stop there. We want to prevent child abuse. So, we help parents, too. By helping them understand child abuse and how to stop it before it begins.

We're working hard so that someday you can give all your money to the Society for the Prevention of Cruelty to Animals. Because, hopefully, there'll be no need for a Society for the Prevention of Cruelty to Children.

An abused child's worst scars are on the inside.

The Queensboro Society for the Prevention of Cruelty to Children. 105-16 Union Hall Street, Jamaica, N.Y. 11433

168

168
ART DIRECTOR Nick Gisonde
WRITER John Russo
DESIGNER Nick Gisonde
PHOTOGRAPHER Stan Smilow
AGENCY Della Femina, Travisano & Partners
CLIENT Queensboro Society for the Prevention of Cruelty to Children

 SILVER

How to tell a heart attack from a toothache.

A severe toothache, or a sore jaw, can be an early warning sign of heart attack. So can a shooting pain in one or both arms, a bellyache that feels like acute indigestion, and a pain in the center of the chest.

If you experience any of these accompanied by sweating, shortness of breath or nausea, it's a strong sign you are having a heart attack.

Don't tell yourself it'll go away. Call your Emergency Number for help. In Anson County it's 694-2167.

Call immediately. Minutes count.

NORTH CAROLINA HEART ASSOCIATION, INC.

16

169
ART DIRECTOR Robert Boggs
WRITER George Dusenbury
DESIGNER Robert Boggs
AGENCY Carmichael & Company
CLIENT North Carolina Heart Association

When you're 2½ years old, everything in a bottle, box or can is fair game.

And it explains why a half million kids were poisoned last year by common products you'll find in every home.

Yet we parents go about setting deadly little traps. Unwittingly but effectively. Leaving soaps, paints, powders, gasoline, medicines in reach of unsuspecting, curious kids.

If you think a child has swallowed something possibly poisonous, dishwasher detergent for example, you might save a life or a throat or a stomach if you'll remember what you're reading.

First thing to remember— do nothing to treat the child yourself, without medical advice. Induced vomiting or giving milk or water may be right. Or dead wrong.

Immediately, get whatever is still in the child's mouth out. Get the container the child got into, to identify toxicity. Call a poison control center or doctor.

It's a good idea to keep Syrup of Ipecac around in case induced vomiting is recommended. It'll save critical time.

Finally, keep the parent quiet. If you lose your head, you could lose a kid.

When you're 2½, you can't spell poison. When you're 20 or 30, you should know better.

LIBERTY NATIONAL
LIFE INSURANCE COMPANY
HOME OFFICE: BIRMINGHAM, ALABAMA

Cleaning fluid looks just like ginger ale when you're 2½.

170
ART DIRECTOR Rock Obenchain
WRITER Bob Richardson
PHOTOGRAPHER Jerome Drown
AGENCY Luckie & Forney
CLIENT Liberty National Life Insurance

GOLD

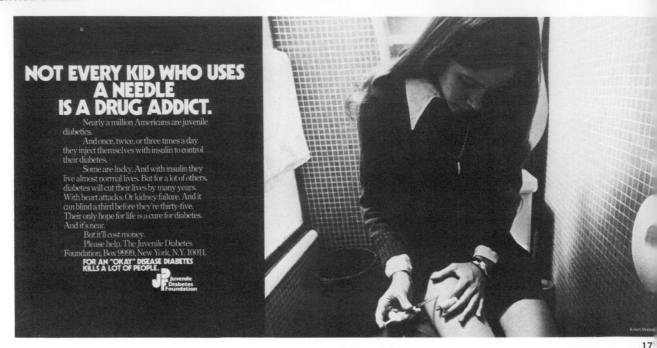

NOT EVERY KID WHO USES A NEEDLE IS A DRUG ADDICT.

Nearly a million Americans are juvenile diabetics.

And once, twice, or three times a day they inject themselves with insulin to control their diabetes.

Some are lucky. And with insulin they live almost normal lives. But for a lot of others, diabetes will cut their lives by many years. With heart attacks. Or kidney failure. And it can blind a third before they're thirty-five. Their only hope for life is a cure for diabetes. And it's near.

But it'll cost money.

Please help. The Juvenile Diabetes Foundation, Box 9999, New York, N.Y. 10011.

FOR AN "OKAY" DISEASE DIABETES KILLS A LOT OF PEOPLE.

Juvenile Diabetes Foundation

17

DUE TO A LACK OF FUNDS, THERE WILL BE A SHORTAGE OF JUSTICE THIS YEAR.

The Legal Aid Society is kind of a law firm for the poor.

We defend them in cases of consumer fraud or discrimination. We help those who have problems with immigration, social security or welfare.

We defend them against landlords who try to evict so they can double the rent with new tenants. And against landlords who don't go through this formality, and simply gouge the tenants they already have.

We defend them against landlords who provide little or no heat or hot water, subjecting tenants to conditions that are not only unliveable but illegal.

We do everything other law firms do, except charge money. Our services are free. And since they are, we're the only lawyers the poor can afford.

But after 100 years of helping poor people, suddenly *we're* poor.

And if we don't get help soon, thousands of poor people might have no one to turn to, to see that their rights aren't denied.

Please help us. Send what you can. (Donations are tax deductible.)

We're not asking you to help rid the world of poverty. We're asking you to help give poor people the chance to fight within the system for their rights.

All they ask is a fair fight.

And if we can't guarantee them that much, then there *is* no justice.

Give to the Legal Aid Society. The disease we're trying to cure is injustice.

17

171
ART DIRECTOR Richard Brown
WRITER Steve August
DESIGNER Richard Brown
PHOTOGRAPHER Robert Monroe
AGENCY McCann-Erickson
CLIENT Juvenile Diabetes Foundation

172
ART DIRECTOR Robert Engel
WRITER Tom Thomas
PHOTOGRAPHER Jeff Lovinger
AGENCY Young and Rubicam
CLIENT Legal Aid Society

As you light the Chanukah candles, remember.

Remember the first Chanukah. Against overwhelming odds, the Maccabees defeated their enemies and rededicated the Temple of Jerusalem. And for eight days the light miraculously burned.

Remember those Jews throughout history who have been persecuted for no other reason than that they were Jews.

Remember the UN resolution of November 10th, thirty-seven years to the day after Nazis attacked Jewish homes, shops and synagogues.

Remember in these difficult days how many Jews are in desperate need of help both here in New York and in countries throughout the world.

Remember that today thousands of immigrants in Israel need food, clothing, housing, shelter and jobs.

Remember that today thousands of Jews in New York are troubled, sick, frightened, poor, old and alone in this time of crisis in our city.

Remember that today thousands of Jews in foreign lands have even less hope now to live in freedom and dignity.

Remember, above all, what we have learned again and again: whatever happens to one Jew anywhere affects all Jews everywhere. Those who can must help those who cannot help themselves. It is our tradition to remember. But remembering is not enough.

Make a gift to the Regular Fund for our people in Israel, around the world and here at home; make a special gift to the Israel Emergency Fund for our people in Israel.

United Jewish Appeal — Federation of Jewish Philanthropies Joint Campaign
Campaign Headquarters: 220 West 58th Street, New York 10019

173
ART DIRECTOR Cathie Campbell
WRITER Richard Goodman
DESIGNER Cathie Campbell
PHOTOGRAPHER Sam Varnedoe
AGENCY Lord, Geller, Federico
CLIENT UJA Federation

YOU CAN'T TAKE A HEART ATTACK VICTIM TO JUST ANY HOSPITAL.

Half the hospitals in the Los Angeles area are not committed to the emergency heart care standards of the Heart Association.

Some of these hospitals don't have the proper equipment. Some of them don't always have the right personnel. Others only treat heart attacks if prior arrangements have been made by a staff physician.

That's why if you rush a heart attack victim to a hospital that's not set up to handle such emergencies, he may not get the immediate attention he needs.

Keeping a properly equipped emergency room staffed and open 24 hours a day is an extraordinarily expensive proposition. For that reason, in most communities only a small number of hospitals maintain such facilities.

The hospitals which are committed to Heart Association standards are listed below. They're ready at any time, day or night, to give heart attack victims fast professional care.

You should read this list carefully. Remember it. Save it.

Most people recover completely from a heart attack if treatment starts at once. So if you're with someone who has a steady pressure on the center of the chest lasting two minutes or more, it's important that you get that person to the right hospital fast.

Or better still, do what the Heart Association recommends. Call the Fire Dept. Rescue Squad. They'll come to you. That way you can't go wrong.

AMERICAN HEART ASSOCIATION
GREATER LOS ANGELES AFFILIATE

Save this list. It might save a life.

HOLLYWOOD-WILSHIRE
California Hospital Medical Center
1414 South Hope Street, LOS ANGELES
Hollywood Presbyterian Medical Center
1300 North Vermont Avenue, LOS ANGELES
Orthopaedic Hospital
2400 South Flower Street, LOS ANGELES
Queen of Angels Hospital
2301 Bellevue Avenue, LOS ANGELES
EAST LOS ANGELES
East Los Angeles Doctors Hospital
4060 East Whittier Boulevard, LOS ANGELES
Los Angeles County-USC Medical Center
1200 North State Street, LOS ANGELES
White Memorial Medical Center
1720 Brooklyn Avenue, LOS ANGELES
SOUTH CENTRAL LOS ANGELES
Los Angeles County-Martin Luther King, Jr. General Hospital
12021 South Wilmington Avenue, LOS ANGELES
Morningside Hospital
8711 South Harvard Boulevard, LOS ANGELES
West Adams Community Hospital
2231 South Western Avenue, LOS ANGELES
WESTERN
Dr. David M. Brotman Memorial Hospital
3828 Hughes Avenue, CULVER CITY
Marina Mercy Hospital
4650 Lincoln Boulevard, MARINA DEL REY
Santa Monica Hospital Medical Center
1225 Fifteenth Street, SANTA MONICA
UCLA Hospital & Clinics
10833 Le Conte Avenue, LOS ANGELES
CENTINELA-SOUTH BAY
Bay Harbor Hospital
1437 West Lomita Boulevard, HARBOR CITY
Carson Inter-Community Hospital
23621 South Main Street, CARSON
Centinela Valley Community Hospital
555 East Hardy Street, INGLEWOOD
Daniel Freeman Memorial Hospital
333 North Prairie Avenue, INGLEWOOD
Hawthorne Community Hospital
11711 Grevillea Avenue, HAWTHORNE
Imperial Hospital
11222 Inglewood Avenue, INGLEWOOD
Little Company of Mary Hospital
4101 Torrance Boulevard, TORRANCE
Los Angeles County-Harbor General Hospital
1000 West Carson Street, TORRANCE
Memorial Hospital of Gardena
1145 West Redondo Beach Boulevard, GARDENA
San Pedro and Peninsula Hospital
1300 West Seventh Street, SAN PEDRO

South Bay Hospital
514 North Prospect Avenue, REDONDO BEACH
Torrance Memorial Hospital
3330 West Lomita Boulevard, TORRANCE
SOUTHEASTERN
Beverly Hospital
309 West Beverly Boulevard, MONTEBELLO
Doctors Hospital of Compton
950 West Alondra Boulevard, COMPTON
Dominguez Valley Hospital
3100 Susana Road, COMPTON
Downey Community Hospital
11500 Brookshire Avenue, DOWNEY
La Mirada Community Hospital
14900 East Imperial Highway, LA MIRADA
Paramount General Hospital
16453 South Colorado Avenue, PARAMOUNT
Pico Rivera Community Hospital
5216 Rosemead Boulevard, PICO RIVERA
Presbyterian Intercommunity Hospital
12401 East Washington Boulevard, WHITTIER
St. Francis Hospital of Lynwood
3630 East Imperial Highway, LYNWOOD
Studebaker Community Hospital
13100 Studebaker Road, NORWALK
Whittier Hospital
15151 Janine Drive, WHITTIER
EAST SAN GABRIEL VALLEY
Baldwin Park Community Hospital
14148 Francisquito Avenue, BALDWIN PARK
Foothill Presbyterian Hospital
250 South Grand Avenue, GLENDORA
Glendora Community Hospital
638 South Santa Fe Avenue, GLENDORA
Inter-Community Hospital
275 West College Street, COVINA
Pomona Valley Community Hospital
1798 North Garey Avenue, POMONA
Queen of the Valley Hospital
1115 South Sunset Avenue, WEST COVINA
San Dimas Community Hospital
1350 West Covina Boulevard, SAN DIMAS
WEST SAN GABRIEL VALLEY
Alhambra Community Hospital
100 South Raymond Avenue, ALHAMBRA
Community Hospital of San Gabriel
218 South Santa Anita Street, SAN GABRIEL
Garfield Hospital
510 Hampton Street, MONTEREY PARK
Greater El Monte Community Hospital
1701 Santa Anita Avenue, SOUTH EL MONTE
Huntington Memorial Hospital
100 Congress Street, PASADENA

The Methodist Hospital of Southern California
300 West Huntington Drive, ARCADIA
Monterey Park Hospital
900 South Atlantic Boulevard, MONTEREY PARK
St. Luke Hospital of Pasadena
2632 East Washington Boulevard, PASADENA
Santa Teresita Hospital
1210 Royal Oaks Drive, DUARTE
VERDUGO
Antelope Valley Hospital Medical Center
1600 West Avenue J, LANCASTER
Burbank Community Hospital
466 East Olive Avenue, BURBANK
Glendale Adventist Medical Center
1509 East Wilson Terrace, GLENDALE
Memorial Hospital of Glendale
1420 South Central Avenue, GLENDALE
Palmdale General Hospital
1212 East Avenue "S", PALMDALE
Saint Joseph Medical Center
Buena Vista Street & Alameda Avenue, BURBANK
Verdugo Hills Hospital
1812 Verdugo Boulevard, GLENDALE
SAN FERNANDO VALLEY
Canoga Park Hospital
20800 Sherman Way, CANOGA PARK
Encino Hospital
16237 Ventura Boulevard, ENCINO
Granada Hills Community Hospital
10445 Balboa Boulevard, GRANADA HILLS
Hillside Community Hospital
21704 West Golden Triangle Road, SAUGUS
Holy Cross Hospital
15031 Rinaldi Street, SAN FERNANDO
Medical Center of Tarzana
18321 Clark Street, TARZANA
Northridge Hospital Foundation
18300 Roscoe Boulevard, NORTHRIDGE
Pacoima Memorial Lutheran Hospital
11600 Eldridge Avenue, LAKE VIEW TERRACE
Parkwood Community Hospital
7011 Shoup Avenue, CANOGA PARK
Riverside Hospital
12629 Riverside Drive, NORTH HOLLYWOOD
Serra Memorial Hospital
9449 San Fernando Road, SUN VALLEY
Valley Hospital
14500 Sherman Circle, VAN NUYS
West Hills Hospital
23023 Sherman Place, CANOGA PARK
West Park Hospital
22141 Roscoe Boulevard, CANOGA PARK
Westlake Community Hospital
4415 South Lake View Canyon Road, WESTLAKE VILLAGE

Emergency Heart Care 1975.

This sign identifies hospital emergency rooms committed to the standards of the Los Angeles County Heart Association.

No hospitals are listed for AVALON, HAWAIIAN GARDENS, LAKEWOOD, LONG BEACH and SIGNAL HILL. The American Heart Association-Greater Los Angeles Affiliate does not serve these communities. Residents and workers there and outside Los Angeles County should contact their local Heart Association for information. This list does not reflect on the adequacy of service of hospitals not listed. Reproduction of this list requires prior approval by the American Heart Association-Greater Los Angeles Affiliate.

174

174
ART DIRECTOR Mas Yamashita
WRITER Elizabeth Hayes
DESIGNER Mas Yamashita
AGENCY Doyle Dane Bernbach
CLIENT American Heart Association

THIS NOV. 4
YOU CAN DO A LOT MORE
THAN JUST CHANGE THE FACES.

It's a kind of election that's only happened twice in 100 years.

The candidate's a Revised City Charter. Kind of a working constitution for New York City, that fundamentally changes the way City Government works, accounts for itself, and spends our money.

Every Monday, in your paper, there's an ad with the details. Read it.
And take it with you when you vote.

This Nov. 4, New York is the underdog. Not some politician.

VOTE ON THE NEW YORK CITY CHARTER.
THE PROPOSED CHANGES ARE IN YOUR MONDAY NEWSPAPER, AND AT YOUR PUBLIC LIBRARY.
STATE CHARTER REVISION COMMISSION FOR NEW YORK CITY

THIS NOV. 4
NEW YORK IS THE UNDERDOG.
NOT SOME POLITICIAN.

It's a kind of election that's only happened twice in 100 years.

The candidate's a Revised City Charter. Kind of a working constitution for New York City, that fundamentally changes the way City Government works, accounts for itself, and spends our money.

Every Monday, in your paper, there's an ad with the details. Read it.
And take it with you when you vote.

This Nov. 4, vote for the kind of city you want. Not just the kind of politics.

VOTE ON THE NEW YORK CITY CHARTER.
THE PROPOSED CHANGES ARE IN YOUR MONDAY NEWSPAPER, AND AT YOUR PUBLIC LIBRARY.
STATE CHARTER REVISION COMMISSION FOR NEW YORK CITY

THIS NOV. 4
VOTE FOR THE KIND OF CITY YOU WANT.
NOT JUST THE KIND OF POLITICS.

VOTE ON THE NEW YORK CITY CHARTER.
THE PROPOSED REFORMS ARE IN YOUR NEWSPAPER ON MONDAYS.
STATE CHARTER REVISION COMMISSION FOR NEW YORK CITY

THIS NOV. 4
YOU CAN DO A LOT MORE
THAN JUST CHANGE THE FACES.

VOTE ON THE NEW YORK CITY CHARTER.
THE PROPOSED REFORMS ARE IN YOUR NEWSPAPER ON MONDAYS.
CHARTER REVISION COMMISSION FOR NEW YORK CITY

175

175
ART DIRECTORS E. Raul Almario
               Peter Bemis
WRITER   Geoffrey Frost
DESIGNER   E. Raul Almario
AGENCY   Grey Advertising
CLIENT   NYC Charter Revision
               Commission

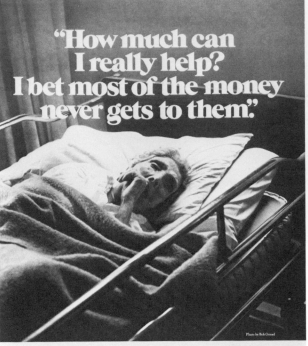

"How much can I really help? I bet most of the money never gets to them."

Sure, you're cynical. You've a right. You've heard those stories about the high costs of running charities.
Not United Fund of New York. We're kind of a rarity, actually. We ask for contributions only through offices—only where you work. So we don't need an enormous staff.

Indeed, most of our work is done by high-placed, unpaid volunteers. Which means costs are a low 9%. This is a fact: 91¢ of every dollar you

give really gets to "them."
And "them's" all kinds of people. The aged, young, crippled, sick and poor are helped through 425 Fund agencies, the Red Cross and Salvation Army.
So when you're asked at the office, remember: give once—and for all. The efficient way.

United Fund of Greater New York.

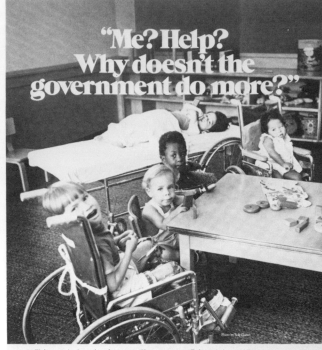

"Me? Help? Why doesn't the government do more?"

Washington is already something of a "big brother."
Do you want government underwriting more of your life? Taxing more?
Voluntary giving is necessary. (Good for the soul, too.)
And United Fund is the satisfying way. You give once—once a year—and you

give to 425 community agencies. To the Red Cross and Salvation Army, too.
You give to the young, the aged, ill, retarded, handicapped, forsaken.

And you give efficiently. 91¢ of every dollar donated really helps. The Fund runs its drive only where you work (and mostly with volunteers), so operating costs are a low 9%.
When you're asked at the office, dig deep. You'll give once—and for all. You'll feel good, too.

United Fund of Greater New York.

"Why should I get involved with the city? I only commute here."

Okay, so you'd rather live with grass and trees.
But you earn wages in these blocks. Keeping the city well and alive is important to you, too.
United Fund funds do good every day through 425 community agencies, the Red Cross and Salvation Army.

And the money isn't wasted. 91¢ of every dollar truly helps some person. They're persons stricken by poverty, emergencies, illness, handicaps.

People of all ages, all religions. And 1 out of 4 is a commuter.
So when you're asked to give at the office (we ask you only once a year), think: over 4 million people every year get a healthy boost from Fund services. But we all can benefit. Give once—and for all.

United Fund of Greater New York.

"Sure, life in the city is tough. But why ask me for help? I live in Rye."

Knock wood, you'll never need us. Hopefully, you'll never need emergency help.
Or special cancer or heart care. Or help with adoption, the aged, handicapped. Or be forsaken, senile or in despair.
But as United Fund of Greater New York, we don't discriminate. We'll help millions

this year through 425 community agencies, the Red Cross and Salvation Army.
Roughly 1 out of 4 will be a commuter. Actually our funds come only from

people like you. Working people. We ask for contributions only where you work. Only once a year.
And because our costs are only 9%, 91¢ of every Fund dollar really does do good. Isn't this the easiest way to help others? And maybe yourself?
Give once—and for all.

United Fund of Greater New York.

176
ART DIRECTOR Jim Brown
WRITER Camille Larghi
PHOTOGRAPHER Bob Gomel
AGENCY Doyle Dane Bernbach
CLIENT United Fund of Greater New York

SILVER

1975.
YOU MAY HAVE LESS TO GIVE, BUT WE ALL HAVE MORE TO LOSE.

Israel is so crippled by inflation, economic and social hardship in the aftermath of the Yom Kippur War, its people so beset with critical problems, that more than ever it is our responsibility to house, help and heal those who are already there.

And tens of thousands of new immigrants are expected to arrive in 1975.

In Arab and Eastern European lands the only sure way Jews will survive is if we help them. If we do not support the agencies that care for these Jews, what will become of them?

And what of those who have been waiting years to flee to freedom? If they don't get out in 1975, there may not be another opportunity. Once they arrive in Israel,

America, or wherever they are welcome, if we do not help make life livable for them, who will?

What of those in New York? What of the growing numbers of our fellow Jews living in poverty? What of the aged, especially those too sick or too poor to help themselves? What of our youth who need counseling and education to maintain their Jewish heritage? Without the funds to help fill their needs, what will happen to them?

In Israel, in New York, and all around the world, we must help Jews live as Jews. One gift does a world of good.

In 1975, give more. Because there is so much more to lose.

The Joint Campaign of the
United Jewish Appeal & Federation of Jewish Philanthropies
On behalf of the United Jewish Appeal beneficiaries: United Israel Appeal, Joint Distribution Committee, ORT (Organization for Rehabilitation through Training), New York Association for New Americans, United HIAS Service and National Jewish Welfare Board.
And on behalf of the Federation of Jewish Philanthropies' 130 local member agencies providing: Aged Care, Camping, Child Care, Community Centers, Family Welfare, Medical Services, Jewish Education and Rabbinical Services.
Campaign headquarters: 220 West 58th Street, New York 10019.

MUNICH KIRYAT SHEMONA MA'ALOT BEIT SHEAN.

The headlines screamed the story of horror. Israeli athletes murdered at Munich, schoolchildren shot at Ma'alot. Terrorism. Tragedy. A shocked world recoiled.

How does the world react now to such news? Is it with sympathy? Indignation? Grief? Or does indifference cover it over?

We live in an uncertain time in an uncertain world. New priorities replace older allegiances. Thirty years after the survivors of the Holocaust were freed from concentration camps, twenty-seven years after the State of Israel was established by the United Nations, the survival of the Jewish people is again being challenged.

In Israel the price of vigilance is high. Inflation, three times our own. Austerity. Relentless tension. And yet, human needs continue.

New immigrants must be housed, clothed, fed, trained, educated. The young, the old, the sick, the handicapped need help. Who will do that job, if we don't?

In too many countries Jews are harassed for their beliefs, oppressed by governments, and regarded as unwelcome aliens. Who will extend the hand of hope, if we do not?

In New York, too, there are very real problems. Old age, poverty, illness, family breakup, alienated children. The list is long. Who will answer these needs, if we turn away?

All over the world and here at home, there are Jews who cannot help themselves. Remember: what happens to a Jew anywhere, affects Jews everywhere. If we do not help, who will? This year, more than ever, one gift does a world of good.

THE JOINT CAMPAIGN OF THE
UNITED JEWISH APPEAL & FEDERATION OF JEWISH PHILANTHROPIES
On behalf of the United Jewish Appeal beneficiaries: United Israel Appeal, Joint Distribution Committee, ORT (Organization for Rehabilitation through Training), New York Association for New Americans, United HIAS Service and National Jewish Welfare Board.
And on behalf of the Federation of Jewish Philanthropies' 130 local member agencies providing: Aged Care, Camping, Child Care, Community Centers, Family Welfare, Medical Services, Jewish Education and Rabbinical Services.
Campaign headquarters: 220 West 58th Street, New York 10019.

THE PRICE OF SILENCE.

The price of silence was the Warsaw ghetto. Bergen-Belsen. Auschwitz. Dachau. Buchenwald.

The price of silence was horror, tragedy, cruelty. And, for six million Jews, for millions of others, the price of silence was death.

Long before the terrible price was paid, there were warnings. There were signs we did not want to recognize. Treaties were broken, pacts were dissolved, guarantees recanted, promises ignored. Inevitably, words of hate became deeds of savagery.

Now, in this month of April, thirty years after the horrible revelations of the death camps, words of hate are heard once again.

The signs can be seen. The warnings can be

heard. They must not be ignored. Silence can mean extinction. Freedom demands vigilance. Whatever happens to Jews anywhere can happen to Jews everywhere.

This is no time to be silent. This is the time to give voice to our concern and our compassion.

Speak through us and you address those human needs which demand attention. You bring help to newly arrived immigrants in Israel and America and other free lands. You bring hope and comfort to those who need us here in New York. Speak through us and you speak to all Jews everywhere who need help now.

Speak with a gift.

Speak now, so that we never again pay the price of silence.

UNITED JEWISH APPEAL & FEDERATION OF JEWISH PHILANTHROPIES
JOINT CAMPAIGN Campaign headquarters: 220 West 58th Street, New York 10019.
Make a gift to the Regular Fund for our people in Israel, around the world and here at home; make a special gift to the Israel Emergency Fund for our people in Israel.

NEXT YEAR MAY BE TOO LATE.

Thirty years ago the ravaged survivors of the Holocaust were liberated from the death camps. And the world wept. Twenty-seven years ago oppressed Jewish people found a haven; the State of Israel was established by the United Nations. And we rejoiced.

Last year we heard the United Nations applaud the assassins of children, the murderers of Olympic athletes, the terrorists of innocents.

Last year we watched, in disbelief, as UNESCO barred Israel from its cultural, scientific, and educational activities. Last year we heard words spoken that were strikingly, shiveringly reminiscent of Germany in the early Thirties.

The clouds have gathered and the wind is cold. New voices speak for old nations. New alliances replace traditional friendships. We have seen it before; we are one people with one past, one memory.

Here at home, there is rising anxiety due to business boycotts and other world-wide developments, and to anti-Jewish expressions

in our own country. There is apprehension, also, over the acute problems of our Jewish poor and aged, our youth, our troubled families.

This year the human needs of our fellow Jews everywhere are great, and growing ever greater. If we do not help them now, who will?

For centuries, Jew has helped Jew. Helped with the basics of life: with the requisites for human dignity. It meant survival. We inherit this tradition, a tradition which must continue as long as need exists anywhere.

This year, in this time and in this circumstance, we ask you to help Jews who are in need. Once again, it is a matter of survival. As a community we require unity in this effort, for we have never been so alone.

Through your support we can provide the human services so desperately needed by the people of Israel, by deprived and persecuted Jews in other lands, and by those who need us right here in New York.

This year, one gift does a world of good.

Next year may be too late.

UNITED JEWISH APPEAL & FEDERATION OF JEWISH PHILANTHROPIES
JOINT CAMPAIGN Campaign headquarters: 220 West 58th Street, New York 10019.
On behalf of the United Jewish Appeal beneficiaries: United Israel Appeal, Joint Distribution Committee, ORT (Organization for Rehabilitation through Training), New York Association for New Americans, United HIAS Service and National Jewish Welfare Board.
And on behalf of the Federation of Jewish Philanthropies' 130 local member agencies providing: Aged Care, Camping, Child Care, Community Centers, Family Welfare, Medical Services, Jewish Education and Rabbinical Services.

177
ART DIRECTOR   Cathie Campbell
WRITER   Dick Lord
DESIGNER   Cathie Campbell
AGENCY   Lord, Geller, Federico
CLIENT   UJA Federation

THIS DIABETIC CHILD HAS A BETTER CHANCE OF GOING BLIND, HAVING A HEART ATTACK OR KIDNEY FAILURE.

And taking insulin won't help.
Oh, it will control her diabetes.
But not its complications. Like a gradual weakening of blood vessels that eventually hemorrhage and cause blindness and heart failure. Or a steady disintegration of the urinary system that leads to eventual kidney failure.

Diabetes has become the biggest killer of children. It is the most frequent cause of blindness. A major cause of heart disease and kidney failure. And diabetes is growing. Claiming Americans at the rate of nine percent more every year.

So you can see controlling diabetes isn't enough. We want to cure it. There is a cure that's near. Almost in sight. But it will take money to reach it. Please help by helping the Juvenile Diabetes Foundation, Box 9999, New York, N.Y. 10011.

FOR AN "OKAY" DISEASE DIABETES KILLS A LOT OF PEOPLE.

 Juvenile Diabetes Foundation

FOR AN "OKAY" DISEASE DIABETES KILLS A LOT OF PEOPLE.

There are one million diabetic children in the United States who depend upon insulin. And at least eight million diabetic adults.

It's a leading killer of children. The most frequent cause of blindness. A major cause of heart disease and kidney failure. And diabetes is growing at an alarming rate. Claiming nine percent more Americans every year.

So you can see controlling diabetes isn't enough. We have to cure it. We're near to some cures. But it will take money. Please help by helping the Juvenile Diabetes Foundation. Box 9999, New York, N.Y. 10011.

FOR AN "OKAY" DISEASE DIABETES KILLS A LOT OF PEOPLE.

Juvenile Diabetes Foundation

178

178
ART DIRECTOR Richard Brown
WRITER Steve August
PHOTOGRAPHERS Robert Monroe
Steve Steigman
Joe Morello
DESIGNER Richard Brown
AGENCY McCann-Erickson
CLIENT Juvenile Diabetes Foundation

GOLD

City strikes:
San Francisco 2, Memphis 0.
Re-elect Mayor Chandler
Paid by Re-elect Chandler Campaign, James E. Harwood III, Treasurer

City income tax:
Cincinnati 2%, Memphis 0.
Re-elect Mayor Chandler
Paid by Re-elect Chandler Campaign, James E. Harwood III, Treasurer

Tax increases since 1971:
Birmingham 3, Memphis 0.
Re-elect Mayor Chandler
Paid by Re-elect Chandler Campaign, James E. Harwood III, Treasurer

City layoffs:
Detroit 4000, Memphis 0.
Re-elect Mayor Chandler
Paid by Re-elect Chandler Campaign, James E. Harwood III, Treasurer

New community centers:
Memphis 7, Dallas 2.
Re-elect Mayor Chandler
Paid by Re-elect Chandler Campaign, James E. Harwood III, Treasurer

Weekly garbage pickup:
Memphis 2, Atlanta 1.
Re-elect Mayor Chandler
Paid by Re-elect Chandler Campaign, James E. Harwood III, Treasurer

179

179
ART DIRECTOR Ed Bailey
WRITER John Malmo
DESIGNER Ed Bailey
ARTIST Jean Dondeville
AGENCY John Malmo
CLIENT Re-elect Chandler
Campaign

PHOTOGRAPHY
& ILLUSTRATION

180

182

	180		182
ART DIRECTOR	David Perkins	ART DIRECTORS	Frank Perry
WRITER	James Ens		Art Christy
DESIGNER	David Perkins	WRITERS	Paul Lippman
ARTIST	James Johnson		Art Christy
AGENCY	Johnson & Dean		Frank Perry
CLIENT	Second National Bank	DESIGNERS	Art Christy
			Frank Perry
		ARTIST	Richard I less
		AGENCY	Fuller & Smith & Ross
		CLIENT	Grumman Corporation

183

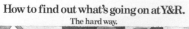

How to find out what's going on at Y&R.
The hard way.

The easy way.

See the Reel of the Month. March 1-5, 12-1 pm. Theatre A.

THEY'RE NOT
MOVIES OF THE WEEK ANYMORE.
THEY'RE MOVIES.

abc THE MOVIE PEOPLE.

184

	183		**184**
ART DIRECTORS	Jeff Witchel	**ART DIRECTOR**	Peter Bemis
	Steve Kasloff	**WRITER**	Geoffrey Frost
WRITER	Steve Kasloff	**PHOTOGRAPHER**	Carl Fischer
DESIGNERS	Jeff Witchel	**AGENCY**	Grey Advertising
	Steve Kasloff	**CLIENT**	American Broadcasting
AGENCY	Young & Rubicam		Co.
CLIENT	Young & Rubicam		

185

185
ART DIRECTOR David Perkins
WRITER James Ens
DESIGNER David Perkins
ARTIST James Johnson
AGENCY Johnson & Dean
CLIENT Second National Bank

186

186
ART DIRECTOR Hillen Smith
ARTIST Bart Forbes
AGENCY Bart Forbes
CLIENT U.S. Fidelity and
Guaranty
Insurance Co.

187

188

	187		**188**
ART DIRECTOR	Jay Loucks	**ART DIRECTORS**	Richard Brown
DESIGNER	Jay Loucks		Sue Weaver
PHOTOGRAPHER	Walter Nelson	**DESIGNERS**	Richard Brown
AGENCY	Robertson Advertising		Sue Weaver
CLIENT	Adler's Jewelry	**ARTIST**	Charles Santore
		AGENCY	Gardner Advertising
		CLIENT	Busch Gardens

Good Morning America

189

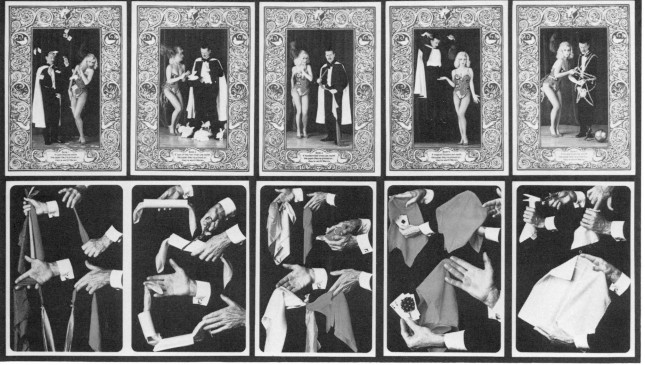

190

	189		**190**
ART DIRECTORS	Onofrio Paccione	ART DIRECTORS	Jim Witham
	Bo Costello		Ralph Moxcey
DESIGNERS	Onofrio Paccione	WRITER	Nelson Lofstedt
	Bo Costello	DESIGNERS	Jim Witham
PHOTOGRAPHER	Onofrio Paccione		Ralph Moxcey
AGENCY	Willis Case Harwood	ARTISTS	Izadore Seltzer
CLIENT	Mead Paper		Bob Peak
		PHOTOGRAPHER	Pete Turner
		AGENCY	Humphrey Browning
			MacDougall
		CLIENT	S. D. Warren Paper

SILVER

191

	191		192	
ART DIRECTORS	Jim Witham	**DIRECTOR**	Elmer Pizzi
	Ralph Moxcey	**WRITER**	Hank Inman
WRITER	Nelson Lofstedt	**DESIGNER**	Elmer Pizzi
DESIGNERS	Jim Witham	**ARTIST**	Jean Mulatier
	Ralph Moxcey	**AGENCY**	Gray & Rogers
ARTIST	John Burgoyne	**CLIENT**	Grit Publishing
PHOTOGRAPHER	Frank Foster		
AGENCY	Humphrey Browning		
	MacDougall		
CLIENT	S. D. Warren Paper		

Just because times are tough there's no reason the meat should be.

These days, your chances of serving a tough piece of meat are getting better all the time. Because, today things are tough all over.

Meat prices are up. Meat production is down. And meat eaters are caught in between. Trying to make each dollar work hard. In a year when a lot of people aren't working at all.

It isn't easy. And the higher meat prices continue to go, the cheaper the cut you tend to buy. Which can be pretty tough, any way you slice it.

Your family deserves better. A way you can serve them a steak that's easy to chew, at a price that's easy to swallow. And McCormick/Schilling can show you the way.

Every bottle of McCormick/Schilling Meat Tenderizer gives you something few butcher shops can. A tender, juicy cut of meat, every time you cut it.

You know it. The butcher knows it. And we know it.

But there may be a few facts about our tenderizers that might amaze you none-the-less.

Of course, you probably know that McCormick/Schilling Meat Tenderizer will tenderize just about any kind of meat. Rump roasts, rib roasts, chuck roasts, or pot roasts. Round steak or family steak. Pork loins and sirloins. Instantly. Just as easily as sprinkling salt.

But what you might not know is that McCormick/Schilling Tenderizer gives you up to 57% more tenderizer for your money than the other leading tenderizer you can buy.

So as long as you're economizing on your cuts of meat, why not economize on your tenderizer as well. Especially when the best costs less.

And with McCormick/Schilling "Seasoned" Tenderizer, you get more than just tender meat. You get McCormick/Schilling seasoning. And that can make all the difference in the world.

You see, McCormick/Schilling are the spice and flavor people. So when it comes to making sauces, tenderizers, or anything at all, they put a lot of good flavor into everything they make. Which can improve the good flavor of the meat you cook at home.

That way, if times should take a turn for the worse, your meat can always turn out better.

McCormick/Schilling flavor makes all the difference in the world.

McCormick/Schilling

193

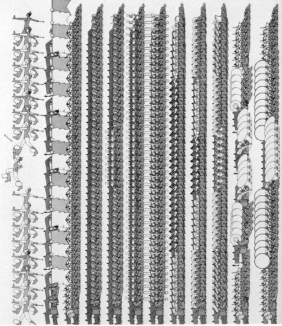

193
ART DIRECTOR Peter Coutroulis
WRITER Jim Weller
DESIGNER Peter Coutroulis
PHOTOGRAPHER Menken-Seltzer
AGENCY Clinton E. Frank
CLIENT McCormick/Schilling

194
ART DIRECTOR Lou Dorfsman
WRITER John Wilkoff
DESIGNER Akihiko Seki
ARTIST Akihiko Seki
AGENCY CBS/Broadcast Group
CLIENT CBS Television Network

SHEER MADNESS

195

THESE DREAMS NOW
IN YOUR STORE
BANANA FUDGE
BROWNIE FUDGE SWIRL
BUTTER PECAN
CHOCOLATE ALMOND
CHOCOLATE CHIP
FRENCH VANILLA
FRESH STRAWBERRY
GRASSHOPPER PARFAIT
OLD-FASHIONED MIXED NUTS
PINEAPPLE JULEP
TIN ROOF SUNDAE
BLACK WALNUT
CHOCOLATE
VANILLA
BUTTERNUT CRUNCH
CHOCOLATE MARSHMALLOW
RASPBERRY SUNDAE
BUTTERMINT FUDGE
CHICAGO BRICK
CHOCOLATE NESSELRODE
HEATH CANDY CRUNCH
NEAPOLITAN
SPUMONI
STRAWBERRY CHEESECAKE
SWISS STYLE CHOCOLATE
BUTTERSCOTCH SUNDAE
ICE MILK
CHOCOLATE FUDGE FUNDAE
ICE MILK
CHOCOLATE ICE MILK
NEAT NEAPOLITAN ICE MILK
VANILLA ICE MILK
PEACH SUNDAE ICE MILK
DREAMS TO COME
STRAWBERRY N CREAM
ROOT BEER FLOAT
PEPPERMINT FUDGE
CANDIED PECAN
ENGLISH TOFFEE
TROPICAL FRUIT
CARAMEL NUT CLUSTER
FUDGE VANILLA
CHOCOLATE PEANUTTY
TOASTED ALMOND
FUDGE NUT SUNDAE
WILD BLUEBERRY
BUTTER BRICKLE ICE MILK
DOUBLE CHOCOLATE ECLAIR
SCOTCH PECAN
CHOCOLATE PECAN
NEW YORK BRICK WALNUT
CRUNCH N FUDGE
RAINBOW SHERBET
NEW YORK CHERRY
PEANUT BRITTLE
COFFEE N CREAM FUDGE
DEVIL MINT ICE MILK
SWISS CHIP ICE MILK
DOUBLE CHOCOLATE CHIP
BLUEBERRY PATCH
GERMAN CHOCOLATE
BANANA CHOCOLATE CHIP

DEAN'S.
ALL YOUR ICE CREAM DREAMS COME TRUE

It's like an ice cream shop in your grocer's freezer. Dean's has dreamed up more flavors than you could imagine. 95 mouth-boggling, natural flavors. Just look at our partial listing. All that Dean's country-charm goodness. We start with fresh, whole, Grade A milk and cream. And use only tree-ripened fruit and the richest chocolate.

Luscious. One creamy scoop after another. Now in a constantly changing, always surprising rainbow of flavors. Let your imagination soar. Indulge. Enjoy. We're still dreaming up new flavors. So if you see an ice cream in your dreams that you don't see in our listing, tell us about it. We'll do our best to swing it.

196

	195		196
ART DIRECTOR	Joe Goldberg	ART DIRECTOR	David Bartels
WRITER	Bob Levey	WRITER	Pat McBride
DESIGNER	Joe Goldberg	DESIGNER	Maxfield Parrish
PHOTOGRAPHER	Henry Wolf	ARTISTS	Bruce Wolfe
AGENCY	Marsteller		Michael Doret
CLIENT	SLC Fashion Corp.		Bob Deschamps
		AGENCY	Clinton E. Frank
		CLIENT	Dean Foods

197
ART DIRECTOR Steven D. Clark
DESIGNER Marcus Hamilton
ARTIST Marcus Hamilton
AGENCY NCNB Advertising
CLIENT North Carolina National
Bank

In the bitter controversies over education some important things are being overlooked.

The kids.
For instance, when some parents debate the pros and cons of busing, politics and race are the issues. Not education.
When some teachers argue about "behavior modification" or "open schools," it becomes an argument about learning methodology. Not about learning.
And when some school administrators define "success", they talk about increasing last year's budget. Not improving last year's reading scores.

The Washington Star Stations feel this is deplorable.
So we've brought educators, parents and psychologists together for a number of in-depth discussions dealing with busing, methodology, reading scores, and the classroom environment.
And in all the discussions, we always ask one question: "How will this help the kids?"
We've even organized Neediest Kids, Inc. A non-profit corporation that gets books, lunches and even new shoes to

underprivileged children who wouldn't stay in school without them.
Some people praise us for getting involved. Others storm us for meddling. But we've learned something useful about education. When you deal with it continually, and from the right perspective, it's harder to overlook the essentials.
The Kids.

Washington Star Station Group
WMAL AM, FM, TV.

198

198

ART DIRECTOR J. Roger Vilsack
WRITER Drew Babb
DESIGNER J. Roger Vilsack
PHOTOGRAPHER Richard Noble
AGENCY Henry J. Kaufman
CLIENT The Washington Star
Station Group

19

	199		200
ART DIRECTOR	Jack Ophir	ART DIRECTORS	Richard Brown
WRITER	Jack Ophir		Al Landholt
ARTIST	Mariah Graham		Steve Williams
AGENCY	Amber Lingerie	DESIGNER	Richard Brown
CLIENT	Amber Lingerie	PHOTOGRAPHER	Robert Monroe
		AGENCY	Gardner Advertisin
		CLIENT	Busch Gardens

200

201
ART DIRECTOR Charles Piccirillo
WRITER Jane Talcott
DESIGNER Charles Piccirillo
ARTIST John Clift
AGENCY Doyle Dane Bernbac
CLIENT Olin Corp.

Before I discovered McCormick/Schilling, my family had no taste.

Around our house, you could always tell the nights I was making my famous Salisbury steak. You just couldn't tell my family. They had a way of coming up with excuses why they couldn't come home for dinner, whenever they knew I was making something special.

Like the time my husband called to tell me that he had to work late at the office. Until then, I never knew an organ grinder even had one.

Not that he didn't love me. He always said that I was the most important person in his life. And that's including the monkey. It's just that when it came to appreciating the food I made, my husband had no taste. In fact, no one in my family really did.

Oh I tried. Coq au Vin. Steak au Poivre. But no matter how hard I tried, my meals never tasted like much of anything at all.

Which is the kindest thing you could ever say about my gravy. As a matter of fact, my husband once said I was the only cook he knew, whose brown gravy could turn people green. And as far as the rest of the family was concerned, when it came time for dinner they usually were.

That is, until I discovered McCormick/Schilling. You know, McCormick/Schilling are the spice and flavor people. So when it comes to making sauces, seasonings, or anything at all, they put a lot of good taste into everything they make.

Take their gravies, for instance. With McCormick/Schilling Brown Gravy, Onion Gravy or Chicken Gravy Mix, you just open a package and you've got it made. Smooth, rich gravy. With just the right blend of spices and herbs, to make a great tasting gravy every time.

Which made a great difference in my famous Salisbury steak. And a noticeable difference in my life.

In fact, you could say McCormick/Schilling gave my family good taste. And believe me, it's all in their mouth.

My Famous Salisbury Steak.

1 egg, beaten; 2 tbsp water; 1 tbsp McCormick or Schilling Instant Minced Onion; 1½ tsp McCormick or Schilling Season-All; ⅓-cup uncooked oatmeal or fine, dry bread crumbs; 1½ lbs. ground beef; one ⅞-ounce package McCormick or Schilling Brown Gravy Mix; 1 cup water; 2 tbsp ketchup. Combine first five ingredients. Mix in ground beef with fork, just until blended.

Form into four 1" thick oval patties. Broil, 5" from heat, ten minutes on each side (for medium). In saucepan combine Gravy Mix with remaining ingredients. Cook, stirring until mixture comes to a boil. Serve over meat patties. Makes 4 servings.

Note: For flavor variation, use McCormick/Schilling Onion Gravy Mix or Mushroom Gravy Mix in place of Brown Gravy Mix.

McCormick/Schilling flavor makes all the difference in the world.

McCormick/Schilling

202

The Optimum Frog.

GRIT
THE NATIONAL SMALL-TOWN WEEKLY
Big frog in small towns

203

204

205

205
ART DIRECTOR Jack Ophir
WRITER Jack Ophir
ARTIST Mariah Graham
AGENCY Amber Lingerie
CLIENT Amber Lingerie

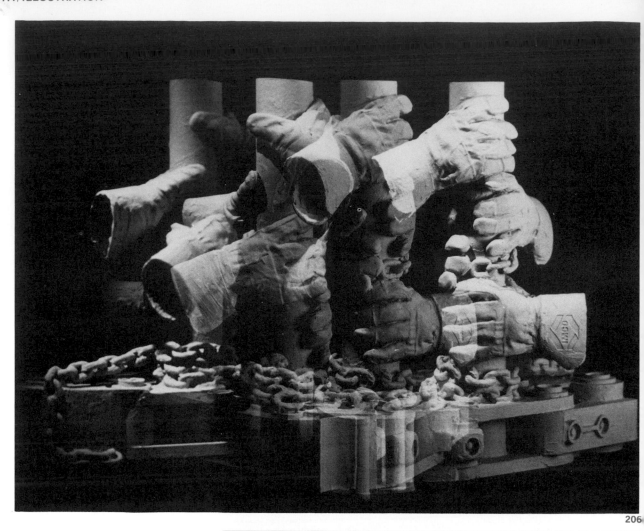

206

206
ART DIRECTOR James Wilkins
WRITER William F. Finn
DESIGNER William F. Finn
ARTIST Thomas Nachreiner
PHOTOGRAPHER Hurley Bradshaw
AGENCY William F. Finn & Assoc.
CLIENT Imco Services

207

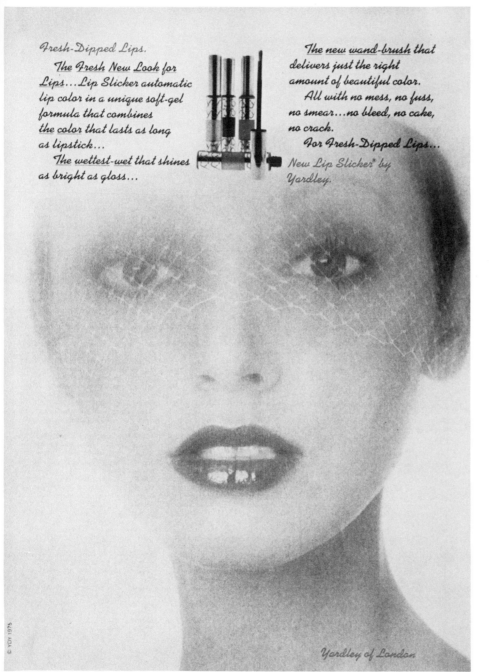

Fresh-Dipped Lips.

The *Fresh New Look* for *Lips*...Lip Slicker automatic lip color in a unique soft-gel formula that combines the color that lasts as long as lipstick...

The *wettest-wet* that shines as bright as gloss...

The *new wand-brush* that delivers just the right amount of beautiful color.

All with no mess, no fuss, no smear...no bleed, no cake, no crack.

For *Fresh-Dipped Lips*...

New Lip Slicker® by Yardley.

Yardley of London

208

	207	
ART DIRECTOR	Jean Srebnick	
DESIGNER	Jean Srebnick	
ARTIST	Janet McCaffery	
AGENCY	Altman, Stoller, Weiss	
CLIENT	Courtaulds North America	

	208	
ART DIRECTOR	Dave Pearl	
PHOTOGRAPHER	Henry Wolf	
AGENCY	Warren, Muller, Dolobowsky	
CLIENT	Yardley of London	

HAVE A FRUITFUL YEAR WITH CHIQUITA BANANAS AND THE COMPLETE LINE OF QUALITY FRUITS AND VEGETABLES AVAILABLE IN THE COMING MONTHS. Chiquita Brands, Inc.

209

209
ART DIRECTOR Janet Monte
WRITER Jim Johnston
DESIGNER Janet Monte
ARTIST Melinda Bordelon
AGENCY Young & Rubicam
CLIENT Young & Rubicam

Before I discovered McCormick/Schilling the only one who ate well was Ralph.

Each night when our family sat down to dinner, there was a lot of begging at the table. But it never made much difference. My family wouldn't touch my food with a ten-foot fork. No matter how much I begged.

Not that they complained, mind you. When it came to the subject of the dinners I made, my family generally kept their mouth shut. Especially between soup and dessert. But, whenever I told them to come and get it, the only one who did was Ralph. And Ralph never had any taste.

Of course, taste can be a relative thing. In fact, one of my relatives used to say that when it comes to judging taste, leave it to the tongue. Because the tongue always knows. Of course, the nose knows. But nothing knows as much as the tongue. And believe me, if my family's tongues could talk, they could tell you a lot about my cooking. Which was sometimes pretty hard for me to swallow.

Until I discovered McCormick/Schilling. You know, McCormick/Schilling are the spice and flavor people. So when it comes to great spices, seasonings, extracts, and flavors, they come from McCormick/Schilling.

Take their Season-All, for example. Season-All does a lot more than regular seasoning salts. Because it's a lot more than just seasoned salt. It's like a whole spice rack in a single bottle. With a delicate mixture of more than 11 different spices, herbs and special flavorings, that can add a special flavor to almost anything you make.

Raw or cooked vegetables. Salads. Soups and stews. Cheese or egg dishes. Sauces and gravies. Not to mention some of the important basics like seafood, poultry and meats. Just sprinkle a little Season-All, and you've got it made.

Which made a big difference in the meals I made. And the way my family ate. Except for Ralph, of course. He's still eating the way he always did. Sitting under the table.

McCormick/Schilling flavor makes all the difference in the world.

McCormick/Schilling

210

ART DIRECTOR	Peter Coutroulis
WRITER	Jim Weller
DESIGNER	Peter Coutroulis
PHOTOGRAPHER	Menken-Seltzer
AGENCY	Clinton E. Frank
CLIENT	McCormick/Schilling

RADIO & TELEVISION

SUMMER
60-second

MUSIC: (Caribbean)

ANNCR: Come with me and feel the warmth of our sunshine . . . and the sparkle of our fountains. This summer, spend your vacation like no other. Taste plump, ripe, tropical fruits . . . and delicacies of a hundred lands. Visit our market place and watch native craftsmen create things of beauty. See thousands of unique things to buy in our marvelous shops by day. Then dine in our gourmet restaurants . . . and laugh as you dance to the music in our discotheque. Come this summer . . . spend your vacation like no other. Spend your vacation . . . in Kansas City . . . at Crown Center.

SINGERS: Crown Center . . .
This summer . . .
The vacation you can walk to.

ANNCR: Come join us under our glorious roof . . . at Crown Center.

LILE VS. BLAZERS
60-second

ANNCR: You are about to hear something never before attempted in athletic competition.

SCHONELY: This is Bill Schonely . . . and right here . . . in front of our microphones . . . we've assembled two of the finest moving teams in the Northwest. On my right is a team from the Portland Trailblazers. . . . And on my left . . . is a team from Lile Moving & Storage. Both these fine teams will attempt to pack an entire roomful of furniture . . . and we'll find out who makes the best moves. Ready fellas?

FELLAS: Ready!

SHONELY: On your marks . . . get set . . . pack!

Quickly . . . Larry Steele grabs a lamp . . . hands it off to Lloyd Neal . . . and Lloyd can't find the handles. Back in the corner . . . LaRue Martin is packing a beautiful china cabinet . . .

. . . and LaRue gets called for unnecessary roughness.

Meanwhile . . . across court . . . the team from Lile is performing brilliantly . . . packing that furniture away . . . smoothly, carefully . . . folks, it's just no contest. . . . and that's it . . .

. . . the team from Lile Moving & Storage has defeated the team from the Portland Trailblazers . . . and man oh man . . . those guys at Lile really make some *great* moves.

SONG: Lile Moving & Storage . . . the northAmerican way . . .

ANNCR: When you're going places . . . call Lile northAmerican. They make some *great* moves.

SONG: Lile Moving and Storage

211
WRITER Radio Band of America
PRODUCER Michael Davenport
PRODUCTION CO. Radio Band of America
AGENCY Radio Band of America
CLIENT Crown Center

212
WRITER Dave Newman
DIRECTOR Dave Newman
PRODUCERS Dave Newman
Mike Carter
PRODUCTION CO. Spectrum Studios
AGENCY Cole & Weber
CLIENT Lile Moving & Storage

LAST INCA
60-second

MUSIC UNDER

ANNCR: You're standing on a remote mountain peak in the Andes. Before you sprawls the massive ruins of an ancient fortress that hid from the world for centuries. Above you, clouds pass close enough to make you believe you have entered another world.

You have.

You have entered the incredible world of Aero-Peru. You have passed through the barriers of time and the dimension of space to arrive in Machu Picchu.

The time is 500 years ago. And you are the last Inca on earth. You have helped build a civilization that will mystify man until the end of time. A civilization that carved strange markings into the earth over 5,000 years ago. Markings that make sense only when seen from the sky.

But who—or what—could have seen them from the sky—5,000 years ago? AeroPeru can now fly you from the United States to all the mysteries of Peru 7 days a week.

AeroPeru. The world's newest . . . and perhaps oldest airline.

MYSTERIOUS JOURNEY
60-second

MUSIC UNDER

ANNCR: You are about to begin a journey to the most unique and mysterious destination in the known universe.

A journey into your imagination.

Because only here—in your imagination—can you explain the incredible mysteries of Peru.

How, for example, could the ancient Incas have lifted 200-ton slabs of rock and fitted them into place—within l/l00th of an inch? Without the use of the wheel. Or mortar of any kind.

And why—5,000 years ago—did people in Peru carve markings into the ground . . . when those markings could only make sense when seen from the sky? Who—or what—could have seen them from the sky . . . 5,000 years ago?

AeroPeru can fly you and your imagination on another fantastic journey—to and through 21 destinations in the world's most mysterious country. Peru. To places like Machu Picchu. The Amazon Jungle. Cuzco. Sacsahuamán.

AeroPeru. The world's newest . . . and perhaps oldest airline.

213
WRITER Rick Breen
PRODUCER Mike Moss
PRODUCTION CO. MJ Productions
AGENCY Philip J. Taylor & Assoc.
CLIENT AeroPeru

214
WRITER Rick Breen
PRODUCER Mike Moss
PRODUCTION CO. MJ Productions
AGENCY Philip J. Taylor & Assoc.
CLIENT AeroPeru

OLD WOMAN IN SHOE
60-second

OLD WOMAN: Hello there. I'm the old woman who lived in a shoe. You know, the one with so many children she didn't know what to do.

Excuse me. Stevie! Stevie! Come into the shoe for lunch.

STEVIE: Is it soup yet?

OLD WOMAN: Almost!

How do you please the whole hungry herd and still stick to a budget? Thank goodness for Lipton Noodle Soup. Each box has two envelopes that make four servings each. That's eight bowls of soup at less than seven cents a serving. What with a shrinking dollar and a growing family, that really helps . . .

Matty, stop playing with the laces!

Besides, I feel good because I cook Lipton Noodle Soup up fresh. Just smell that real chicken broth simmering, and taste those fresh cooked noodles. Mmm, you can't get *that* from a can.

NADINE: Mommy, Matty made a double knot!

OLD WOMAN: Ohhh. Soup's on gang!

CHILDREN: Yay!

OLD WOMAN: Oh, what I wouldn't give for a nice, quiet little moccasin in the country.

ANNCR: Lipton Noodle Soup. At less than seven cents a serving, it lets you be good to your family. And kind to your budget.

FU-CHI MANOOLI
60-second

BERT: Sir, the Fu-Chi Manooli is the finest automobile in the world!

DICK: Oh, I know that. It's just—$89,000 is more money than I had in mind . . .

BERT: Look on the seat, here. What do you see?

DICK: A magazine.

BERT: This is not just a magazine, sir. This is the Fu-Chi Manooli of magazines . . . a *Time* magazine.

DICK: Oh, right. Someone leave it on the seat here?

BERT: We left it on the seat for you.

DICK: Oh—re—I love *Time* . . . Great!

BERT: It's our way of saying, here is expert craftsmanship . . .

DICK: Yes.

BERT: . . . Here is an experience that's fast moving and bright.

DICK: Right, bright.

BERT: . . . Just like the Fu-Chi Manooli.

DICK: Yes.

BERT: So, why don't you go ahead and take it?

DICK: Thank you. I love this *Time* magazine.

BERT: Good, good. Now, what about delivery?

DICK: I'll just stick it in my briefcase . . . I don't need to . . .

BERT: I meant the car.

DICK: Oh. You mean I have to take the 89 to get . . . to get . . . th' . . . I—I see. Oh. You know what? I think I read this issue. Excellent issue. I couldn't put it—uh . . .

BERT: Put it down, sir.

DICK: On the seat, here . . . you want . . .

BERT: Yes.

DICK: Fine. If I hadn't read it, uh, I'm sure this Fu-Chi Manooli would be s-s-sitting in my carport. Okay. I'll check you again when next week's *Time* magazine comes in.

BERT: . . . or, we'll call you.

DICK: Okay!! Okay!!

ANNCR: *Time* makes everything more interesting . . . including you!

215
WRITER Steve Kasloff
DIRECTOR Jim Coyne
PRODUCER Jim Coyne
PRODUCTION CO. Audio One
AGENCY Young & Rubicam
CLIENT Thomas J. Lipton

216
WRITERS Dick Orkin
Bert Berdis
Woody Woodruff
DIRECTORS Dick Orkin
Bert Berdis
PRODUCER Jim Coyne
PRODUCTION CO. Dick & Bert
AGENCY Young & Rubicam
CLIENT Time

 SILVER

AIRPLANE
60-second

STEW: Magazine, sir?

BERT: Ah, yes. *time* Magazine, please, stewardess.

STEW: Oh, golly, that man across the aisle just took the last copy of *Time* we have.

BERT: Oh . . .

STEW: Sorry! Magazines?

BERT: Uh, pardon me?

DICK: Yes?

BERT: I notice you haven't started reading your *Time* yet . . . could I . . .

DICK: No, you couldn't.

BERT: But, you haven't . . .

DICK: I'm writing a letter to my mother and when I'm finished, I'm going to enjoy *Time* . . . Don't try to peek inside of it, sir!

BERT: Stewardess!

STEW: Yes, sir?

BERT: This man isn't reading the *Time* magazine you gave him.

DICK: I'm writing a letter first . . .

BERT: To his *Mommy*

DICK: Don't be nasty.

BERT: All I want . . .

STEW: Sir, couldn't this gentleman here . . .

BERT: Just lemme glance at the theatre section?

DICK: No

BERT: Modern living?

DICK: No.

BERT: One little book review?

DICK: Look, I know how enjoyable *Time* magazine is to read. He'll start reading one article, then another, and by the time he's finished, we'll be in Budapest.

BERT: I have a speed reading diploma, sir!

CAPTAIN: Problem here, stewardess?

STEW: Not really, Captain . . . this man here has the last copy of *Time* magazine, but he's writing a letter to his mommy!

CAPTAIN: Sir, you'll have to give up one or the other.

BERT: Yes.

DICK: All right . . . here!

CAPTAIN: Dear mommy . . . I'm up in a big airplane . . .

ANNCR: *Time* makes everything more interesting, including you.

HOME IN MY HAND
60-second

MUSIC UNDER

SONG: Just another city
Just another place
Lonely streets, the same in any town.

Strangers that will pass you by
Could be from anywhere
Sometimes it can really get you down.

But they wrote me to say they love me
And I know they're trying hard
To understand
So for a while the distance falls away
And it's nice to hold again
A little bit of home here in my hand.

ANNCR: The gift of a letter . . . nothing brings you closer to home. P.S., write soon.

SONG: So for a while the distance falls away
And it's nice to hold again
A little bit of home, here in my hand

ANNCR: From your Postal Service.

217
WRITERS Dick Orkin
Bert Berdis
Woody Woodruff
DIRECTORS Dick Orkin
Bert Berdis
PRODUCER Jim Coyne
PRODUCTION CO. Dick & Bert
AGENCY Young & Rubicam
CLIENT Time

218
ART DIRECTOR Steve Salzburg
WRITERS John Ferrell
Larry Spector
DIRECTOR Jim Coyne
PRODUCERS Jim Coyne
Susan Hamilton
PRODUCTION CO. Herman Edel Assoc.
AGENCY Young & Rubicam
CLIENT U.S. Postal Service

GOLD

NOBODY CAN RESIST SARA LEE
60-second

GROUP: Who ate the Sara Lee?
Who ate the piece that I saved for me?
Who just couldn't resist?
Who ate the Sara Lee?
Who?
Was it you?
Or did I forget?
Was it me?
Nobody can resist Sara Lee.

Who ate the Sara Lee?
Who ate the piece that I saved for me?
Who just couldn't resist?
Who ate the Sara Lee?
Who?
Was it you?
Or did I forget?
Was it me?
Nobody can resist Sara Lee.

AUDITORIUM SALE
60-second

MUSIC UNDER

MAN: My wife. How does she do it? She always looks so neat, so attractive. How does she *do* it?

WOMAN: How do I do it? Easy. I take *care* of myself. There's only my husband and the twelve children. So there's plenty of time for me. I rest. Get lots of exercise. And twice a year I take in the auditorium fashion clearance at Carson Pirie Scott & Company.

MAN: What a woman.

WOMAN: I buy my dresses, my sweaters, my skirts, my sportswear. Everything. Because it's all marked down to half its original price.

MAN: My wife. How does she do it?

WOMAN: Today's the day you find out, darling.

MAN: Huh?

WOMAN: I'm going to Carson's clearance sale. So here. This is called a brush. This is a sponge. And this nice stuff is what we call . . . oven cleaner.

219
WRITER Radio Band of America
PRODUCER Roy Eaton
PRODUCTION CO. Radio Band of America
AGENCY Benton & Bowles
CLIENT Kitchens of Sara Lee

220
WRITER Jan Zechman
PRODUCER Janet Collins
PRODUCTION CO. Studio One
AGENCY Zechman Lyke Vetere
CLIENT Carson Pirie Scott

LINEN SALE
60-second

MUSIC UNDER

NARRATOR: Once upon a time, there lived a Sleeping Beauty. Alas, she had lain asleep for some time, until a dashing young prince happened by.

PRINCE: Ah, how long you say this dame's been in the rack?

NARRATOR: Three years, your grace.

PRINCE: Three years!? On the same sheets, three years?!

NARRATOR: Sheets are expensive, my lord.

PRINCE: Whatsamatta, you don't know about Carson's huge linen sale going on?

They got prices outta some fairy tale. 20, 30, 40% off. On Martex, Globe, Cannon.

I mean, c'mon, baby, this lady needs new sheets. And, if I'm not being too indiscreet, she could use a few wash cloths, towels, a shower curtain, they're all on sale.

C'mon, sweetheart, let's get down to Carson's linen sale.

NARRATOR: To awaken her, sire, thou must kiss her on the lips.

PRINCE: Whataya kidding? I never kiss on the first date.

FILMOSONIC DEALER
60-second

MUSIC UNDER

CHORUS: Hey, look around
Get high on what you see
Take it all in
'Cause it's a great country.
Open up your eyes
And capture what you see
And focus on America!

ANNCR: Throughout this land of ours, there are sights to see and sounds to remember. Now you can capture them both—with Bell & Howell Filmosonic super 8 sound movie cameras and projectors. If you've been waiting for home movies to sound as good as they look, this is what you've been waiting for. The Bell & Howell Filmosonic sound home movie system. See it—and hear it—at your Bell & Howell/Mamiya dealer.

221
WRITER Jeff Gorman
PRODUCER Janet Collins
PRODUCTION CO. Studio One
AGENCY Zechman Lyke Vetere
CLIENT Carson Pirie Scott

222
WRITER Jack Hartgen
PRODUCER Michael Paradise
PRODUCTION CO. Sequence Productions
AGENCY N W Ayer ABH International
CLIENT Bell & Howell

HIT BY A TRUCK
60-second

GIRL: I'm going to pat myself on all the perfect places with Clairol Herbal Essence Body Powder, and Tom will ask me to the dance, fall in love with me, and we will fly off to the Bahamas and drink exotic things in the moonlight.

MAN: What if Tom doesn't do that?

GIRL: I'll use it again! 'Cause if all that doesn't happen, I'll need a lift.

GIRL: Using Clairol Herbal Essence Body Powder will make the dude your date say: Sniff, sniff . . . hum mm.

GIRL: And if you're a shorter person, your old man will probably say:

CHILD VOICE: How do I love thee, let me count the ways.

WOMAN: I sprinkled Clairol Herbal Essence Body Powder all over me, and that fragrance of spring herbs and wild flowers—I was in heaven!

MAN: I didn't know Body Powder was the way into heaven!

WOMAN: Well, it could be that I have found the back door.

GIRL: It gives you so much poise that you're not afraid to go out with a hole in your underwear, even though you know you could get hit by a truck.

RUFFINO VERONESE—VALPOLICELLA
60-second

ANNCR: You're the guest at Sunday dinner with a European family. There's a chill in the air, so your host has just added another log to the fire. His flaxen-haired wife is serving you lamb simmered in a sauce as light as anything you've ever tasted.

Welcome to Italy. Northern Italy. Where it borders Austria, France, and Switzerland. Where they drink a wine called Valpolicella. A fresh ruby-red that's as different from other Italian wines as seasoned beef is from Saltenbocca.

And yet as different as Valpolicella is from other Italian wines, it does share something in common with the best of them. A classic Italian name. Ruffino. A name that's meant great wine since 1877.

So when you're looking for a robust wine that's perfect with roasts, lamb and veal, ask for Valpolicella. Ruffino Valpolicella.

223
WRITERS Chuck Blore
Don Richman
Lois Wyse
DIRECTOR Chuck Blore
PRODUCER Chuck Blore
PRODUCTION CO. Chuck Blore Creative Services
AGENCY Wyse Advertising
CLIENT Clairol

224
WRITERS Kay Kavanagh
Mark Yustein
PRODUCERS Lewis Kuperman
Suzanne De Plautt
PRODUCTION CO. National Recording
AGENCY Della Femina, Travisano & Partners
CLIENT Schieffelin & Co.

RUFFINO VERONESE—SOAVE
60-second

ANNCR: You're in a charming European restaurant. Outside there's a breathtaking view of snow-capped peaks. Inside a breathtaking blonde is serving you fresh trout in a light delicate sauce.

You're in Italy. Northern Italy, where it borders France, Austria, and Switzerland. So when they serve you a wine, you're not surprised that it's Soave. A white wine as smooth and as soft as its name. A white wine as different from other Italian wines as Sole in Lemon Sauce is from Lobster Fra Diablo.

And yet as different as Soave is from other Italian wines, it does share something in common with the best of them. A classic Italian name. Ruffino. A name that's meant great wine since 1877.

So when you're looking for a great white wine that's perfect with seafood and cold dishes, ask for Soave. Ruffino Soave.

RUFFINO VERONESE—BARDOLINO
60-second

ANNCR: In Northern Italy, where it borders Switzerland, France, and Austria you'll find a few surprises. The scenery is green and mountainous. The signorinas blonde and blue-eyed. And the pasta sauce light and delicate.

So when you're served a wine in Northern Italy, don't be surprised if it's Bardolino. A light, dry red that's as unique and different from other Italian wines as Veal Picata is from Veal Parmigiana.

And yet as different as Bardolino is from other Italian wines, it does share something in common with the best of them. A classic Italian name. Ruffino. A name that's meant great wine since 1877.

So when you're looking for the perfect wine to have with casseroles, hams, and light meat dishes, ask for Bardolino. Ruffino Bardolino.

225
WRITERS Kay Kavanagh
Mark Yustein
PRODUCERS Lewis Kuperman
Suzanne De Plautt
PRODUCTION CO. National Recording
AGENCY Della Femina, Travisano
& Partners
CLIENT Schieffelin & Co.

226
WRITERS Kay Kavanagh
Mark Yustein
PRODUCERS Lewis Kuperman
Suzanne De Plautt
AGENCY Della Femina, Travisano
& Partners
CLIENT Schieffelin & Co.

JAMES DEAN
60-second

MUSIC UNDER

GIRL: You goin' to the drag race tonight, Jimmy?

JIMMY: I got no choice, Kitten . . . Buzz called me a chicken.

GIRL: You drivin' the Merc'?

JIMMY: Hey, is Eisenhower the President?

ANNCR: Ever wonder what happened to that '49 Merc' James Dean drove in "Rebel Without A Cause"?

GIRL: You know, Jimmy, until I met you I thought I'd flunked the exam of love.

ANNCR: Right now, James Dean's '49 Merc' is at the Auto Show. Along with other famous cars. Al Capone's '29 Lincoln. Charlie Chaplin's Rolls Royce. Plus all those classic new '75 models. Ride with the famous and the infamous. Come to the '75 Detroit Auto Show, January 11 through 19 at Cobo Hall.

GIRL: Oh, Jimmy, I worry about you.

JIMMY: Well, Kitten, I guess I'm just a rebel without a cause.

GIRL: Good name for a movie, Jimbo.

SOUND ROOM/BLINDFOLDED
60-second

HANK: Wow, is it dark!

PHIL: That's because you're blindfolded, Hank, and have been for quite some time.

HANK: C'mon now, what is it? An all-day eclipse of the sun?

PHIL: No, you see, I've taken you to a very special mystery spot. And now I'm going to remove the blindfold. Okay—can you tell me where you are?

HANK: Yeah. All this great stereo equipment . . . I must be in the sound room at Tech Hi-Fi.

PHIL: Uh, uh.

HANK: Then it's gotta be the sound room at Audioland.

PHIL: wrong.

HANK: Stereoland?

PHIL: No, actually you're in the sound room at Highland Appliance.

HANK: Highland Appliance!?!?

PHIL: Wrong.

HANK: C'mon, where am I? Audioland? Stereoland?

PHIL: *High*-land. Highland Appliance.

HANK: Are you kidding me? Look at all these great names—Pioneer, Marantz, Sansui, Dual . . .

PHIL: That's right. And there's a complete sound room just like this inside every Highland store.

HANK: An appliance store like Highland?? C'mon, Highland just sells washers and dryers and refrigerators and stuff.

PHIL: Oh, yeah. Look through this door. What do you see?

PHIL: I see washers and dryers and refrigerators and stuff.

ANNCR: The Highland Appliance Sound Shops. Everything you never expected from an appliance store.

227

ART DIRECTOR	Edd Mangino
WRITER	Thom Sharp
DIRECTOR	Edd Mangino
PRODUCER	Thom Sharp
PRODUCTION CO.	Bell Sound Studios
AGENCY	W. D. Doner & Co.
CLIENT	Detroit Auto Dealers Assoc.

228

WRITER	Chato Hill
PRODUCER	Chato Hill
PRODUCTION CO.	Bell Sound Studios
AGENCY	W. B. Doner & Co.
CLIENT	Highland Appliance

AVERAGE AMERICAN FAMILY
60-second

ANNCR: The average American family consists of a father, mother, two-and-a-half children, and a dog.

The average Italian pizza consists of cheese, crust, pepperoni and a handful of mushrooms. . . .

Until now, the average American family was satisfied with the average Italian pizza because they really thought that was as good as pizza was going to get.

But now, Pizza Ring brings you the first truly American pizza. It's as good as any Italian pizza . . . and it's twenty-four square inches bigger, with thick crusts and a combination with thirteen ingredients to go on top.

Pizza Ring serves great lasagna and spaghetti, too. So come to any of our 13 locations, including Central Avenue, West Peachtree, and Stewart Avenue.

Compare our American pizza with any Italian pizza, and we think you'll find that when it comes to Italian food, we speak your language.

GENERIC: CENSORED II
60-second

ANNCR: Test drive the elegant new *beep*! today.

ANNCR: Yes-siree. You take this baby around the block and you'll wanna take her home.

ANNCR: Visit your neighborhood *beep*! dealer and test drive the exciting new *beep*!

ANNCR: Maybe the reason car dealers are so anxious to have you take a test drive is because they can't lose. After all, how bad can a car be with 12 miles on it? It'll be smooth . . . tight . . . rattle-free. But how do you know in a couple of years it won't be a rattle trap? That's why Volvo is introducing a more intelligent kind of test drive. We'll have you test drive two Volvos. A used Volvo that has at least 30,000 miles on it. And, a new Volvo of your choice. The new Volvo shows you how good a Volvo is when it's young. The used Volvo shows you how gracefully a Volvo can age. See for yourself. Look for the Volvo dealer who invites you to take "The Test Drive for People who Think."

229
WRITER Jim Paddock
PRODUCER Jim Paddock
PRODUCTION CO. Doppler Studios
AGENCY Paddock, Smith & Aydlotte
CLIENT Pizza Ring Restaurants

230
WRITER Larry Cadman
PRODUCER Tanya English
PRODUCTION CO. National Studio
AGENCY Scali, McCabe, Sloves
CLIENT Volvo

CONSUMER SINGLE

232

GENERIC: REMEMBER WHEN II?
60-second

ANNCR: Remember the day you test drove the car you now own? Terrific, wasn't it? Smelled new. Ran smooth as silk. No rattles. No mileage.

But today . . . it's hard to believe it's the same car . . . and you're ready to unload it. Well, this time, unload it at your Volvo dealers, and take a completely new kind of test drive. We'll have you test drive two Volvos. A used Volvo that has at least 30,000 miles on it. And, a new Volvo of your choice. The new Volvo shows you what you get today. The old Volvo shows you that after a lot of miles, all it seems to have lost is the new car smell.

See the Volvo dealer who invites you to take "The Test Drive for People who Think." Because you're going to want your next car to wear on and on . . . long after the novelty has worn off.

GENERIC: MAN VS. SALESMAN II
60-second

SALESMAN: Sir, you're gonna love this baby. Here take the keys. Go for a spin.

ANNCR: In a test drive around the block, any new car is terrific. But how do you know it won't be a rattling bucket of bolts in a couple of years?

Volvo gives you a chance to find out. We'll have you test drive two Volvos. A used one with at least 30,000 miles on it. And, a new Volvo of your choice. The new Volvo tells you what you're getting today. The used one gives you some idea of what to expect tomorrow.

At a time when the future seems uncertain, Volvo wants you to be more certain of your car's future. Look for the Volvo dealer who offers "The Test Drive for People who Think."

SALESMAN: Well, what did you think? Those 400 horses really move, don't they?

MAN: It felt a little stiff.

SALESMAN: Don't worry. She'll loosen up.

231
WRITER Larry Cadman
PRODUCER Larry Cadman
PRODUCTION CO. National Studio
AGENCY Scali, McCabe, Sloves
CLIENT Volvo

232
WRITER Larry Cadman
PRODUCER Larry Cadman
PRODUCTION CO. National Studio
AGENCY Scali, McCabe, Sloves
CLIENT Volvo

PAY WHAT YOU WEIGH
60-second

VOICE: Where's the grape?

MURRAY: If you come in here to a Lollipop store right now and step on a scale, you can buy a case of Lollipops and pay only what you weigh. Listen in . . .

FRED: Hmmm. Let's see here. Sir that'll be $1.40 plus deposit for you and 90 cents for you lady.

LADY: Oh, Terrific.

MURRAY: So come on in before July 5 and step on a scale and get a whole case of 12 oz. Lollipop Soft Drinks and pay only what you weigh plus deposit. All you need is a driver's license and your body to save a fortune. Take it away Fred.

FRED: Thank you, Murray. Ma'am. That'll be $1.28, plus deposit.

LADY: Hey, I only cost $1.24 at home.

FRED: Lady, look at the clothes you have on.

LADY: Well heck with the clothes. I'll take care of that right now. I'm not paying $1.28.

FRED: Give me the money. Ah, come on, lady.

MURRAY: Fred. Fred. Fred, give me the mike back. Come to the Lollipop's "pay what you weigh" promotion. Remember, only one case per customer, and we'll be open on the 4th.

LADY: See, I told you I only weigh 124.

FRED: Murray, Murray, Murray. Bring the camera, Murray.

SONG: Now everybody knows that Lollipop is
Well we melted it down, and we added the
 fizz
Now it's in the bottle and not on the stick
Take a sip. Not a lick.

MIAMI SMILE
60-second

MUSIC UNDER

SONG: I was born with a smile on my face
I know how to make life a holiday.
Come let me show you the ways
On Air Jamaica, you're sure to feel good.

ANNCR: There's a kind of smile that starts on your lips and spreads 'til it takes over your whole body. It's the Air Jamaica smile. And the air fare alone will make you smile.

Air Jamaica will fly you round trip to Jamaica for only $87 any day of the week. The minimum ground cost is only $39, and you can stay from three to fourteen nights enjoying the scenery, shopping, foods, and nightlife of another country.

Come—enjoy the Air Jamaica smile. It feels good all over.

SONG: Come let me show you the ways
On Air Jamaica you're sure to feel good.

233
WRITERS Doug Burford
Henry Waleczko
DIRECTOR Doug Burford
PRODUCER Doug Burford
PRODUCTION CO. Alpha Audio Recording
AGENCY Burford Company
CLIENT Lollipop Beverages

234
WRITER Geraldine Newman
PRODUCER Merl Bloom
PRODUCTION CO. Merl Bloom Assoc.
AGENCY Ketchum, MacLeod &
Grove
CLIENT Air Jamaica

THE INCREDIBLE MACHINE/BLOOD
30-second

ANNCR: The awesome sound of an incredible machine . . . it's the actual sound of blood, rushing endlessly throughout the human body.

This is E. G. Marshall. Tonight, journey with me into The Incredible Machine through the eyes of amazing cameras that actually made the trip.

Don't miss this exciting National Geographic special, brought to you on public television by a grant from Gulf Oil Corporation.

HEARTS
60-second

ANNCR: Every year there comes a time when a man's or woman's heart turns to hearts. Valentine's Day.

And nobody has more hearts than Fortunoff, the source.

Hearts from simply platonic,
to truly romantic,
to out-and-out lecherous.

Little silver "I like you" hearts. Big crystal "I adore you" hearts. Teeny, tiny 14-karat-gold "You're cute" hearts. And luscious sparkling diamond "run away with me" hearts.

Jade, ivory, enamel, and black onyx hearts. Neck hearts, wrist hearts, finger hearts. $5 hearts, $5,000 hearts.

Hearts that say, "You're wonderful." Hearts that say, "I can't live without you." Even hearts that say, "My apartment or yours?"

Hearts that express everything from mild pleasure to intense, crazy passion. Every kind of heart your heart desires. Fortunoff, the source.

More than you can imagine, for much less than you'd expect. Fortunoff, Westbury, Long Island. East 57th Street, Manhattan. Paramus Park Mall, New Jersey.

235
WRITER Susan McFeatters
PRODUCER John Runnette
PRODUCTION CO. Braverman Productions
AGENCY Ketchum, MacLeod & Grove
CLIENT Gulf Oil

236
ART DIRECTOR Arnie Arlow
WRITER Jennifer Berne
PRODUCER Barbara Gans
PRODUCTION CO. Judrac Recording Studio
AGENCY Martin Landey, Arlow
CLIENT Fortunoff

LYRIC
60-second

MUSIC: I love flyin' far and wide
To see the land I love
Climb to find the blue horizon
The sun and sky above.

ANNCR: American Airlines wants your next flight to be a pleasure. So we have comfortable planes . . . convenient schedules . . . and more than 35,000 dedicated people. When you get the best people doing what they do best—then you really have something to sing about . . .

MUSIC: From the sunrise in the East
To the sunset in the West
We're American Airlines
Doing what we do best.

MONSTER
60-second

MUSIC UNDER

DOCTOR: Look, my friend . . . I've brought you a treat.

MONSTER: Friend . . . good.

DOCTOR: Yes. And I've brought you something good to eat. Strawberry Twizzlers.

MONSTER: Twizzlers . . . good?

DOCTOR: Oh, they're delicious! Here . . . taste one and say, "Twizzlers taste good."

MONSTER: Twizzlers taste good.

DOCTOR: Yes . . . I knew you'd love them.

MONSTER: Friend taste good?

DOCTOR: No . . . no . . . no . . . n-o-o-o-o. . . .

ANNCR: Whenever you want to share a fun-to-eat treat with friends, have Twizzlers licorice candy around. Soft, chewy, delicious Twizzlers come in your favorite flavors—strawberry, chocolate, grape, and old-fashioned black licorice.

And Twizzlers come in two convenient packages. The regular size, that lets you share with a friend. And the family size, that lets you share with . . .

DOCTOR: . . . half the city of Scarsdale.

237
WRITERS Bob Mackall
Stevie Pierson
PRODUCER Paul Conti
PRODUCTION CO. S.D.C. Recording
AGENCY Doyle Dane Bernbach
CLIENT American Airlines

238
WRITERS Stephen Fenton
Larry Kenney
DIRECTORS Stephen Fenton
Dick Klein
PRODUCER Stephen Fenton
PRODUCTION CO. Studio 21 Sound
AGENCY Friedlich, Fearon & Strohmeier
CLIENT Y&S Candies

DIZZY GILLESPIE
60-second

MUSIC UNDER

DIZZY: This is the Diz . . . Dizzy Gillespie that is.
I'm not so much for ballet. Tu-tus and tights and
cats on tip-toe is not exactly where I'm at. Which
is why I really dig the Joffrey.

That's the Beach Boys. Now when you find a
ballet company that dances to the Beach Boys,
you've found a hip company. That's the Joffrey.
Sometimes they're camp, sometimes they're
classical, and sometimes they're pure JAZZ . . .
by which I mean far-out, far-flung and very fine.
You catch'em, you hear. Dig the Joffrey. The Diz
does!!

A CHORUS LINE
60-second

ANNCR: They come from God knows where
They stay, God knows why.

All they ask is to be a part of *A Chorus Line*.
Voted best musical of the year by the New York
Theatre Critics.

It moves to Broadway after a sold-out run at the
Public Theatre.

A CHORUS LINE.

Seats now at the Shubert Theatre on 44th Street,
the heart of Broadway.

239
WRITER Nancy Coyne
PRODUCER Nancy Coyne
AGENCY Blaine Thompson Co.
CLIENT Joffrey Ballet Co.

240
WRITER Nancy Coyne
PRODUCER Nancy Coyne
AGENCY Blaine Thompson Co.
CLIENT N.Y. Shakespeare
Festival

EDGAR KREPPS
60-second

INTERVIEWER: We're extremely lucky to be here today with world traveler and explorer, Fortunoff representative, and jewel seeker, Mr. Edgar Krepps. Welcome.

EDGAR KREPPS: Hi.

INTERVIEWER: Now, Mr. Krepps, or is it Dr.? When you venture into foreign lands, unexplored areas, savage environs, and meet the suspicious, perhaps even hostile, natives guarding the treasures after which Fortunoff has sent you, how do you make contact? I mean, what do you say to these fierce savages?

EDGAR KREPPS: Hi.

INTERVIEWER: And when you bring back sapphires from Ceylon, pearls from Hong Kong, turquoise from Arizona, and diamonds from Africa, you often have to cross rivers, traverse valleys, and climb mountains. Yes, take the mountains for example. Tell us, what are the mountains like?

EDGAR KREPPS: High.

INTERVIEWER: And when you come home, loaded with nap sacks, urns, and sachels filled with treasures—incredible things you bought for incredible prices, all for Fortunoff, how do you feel Mr. Krepps?

EDGAR KREPPS: High.

ANNCR: Fortunoff, the source. Westbury, Long Island. East 57th Street, Manhattan. Paramus Park, New Jersey.

FOG
60-second

ANNCR: Who knows what evil lurks in the Broadhurst Theatre? Sherlock Holmes knows! Step into the world of Sherlock Holmes. London fog, secret passages, gas chambers, trap doors, hidden elevators, and damsels in distress.

Meet Moriarity, the Napoleon of Crime. Your heart will pound, your eyes will pop. Spend an evening on the edge of your seat. Sherlock Holmes, the greatest sleuth in his greatest adventure. See it now!

241
ART DIRECTOR Arnie Arlow
WRITER Jennifer Berne
PRODUCER Barbara Gans
PRODUCTION CO. Judrac Recording Studio
AGENCY Martin Landey, Arlow
CLIENT Fortunoff

242
WRITER Nancy Coyne
PRODUCER Nancy Coyne
AGENCY Blaine Thompson Co.
CLIENT Nederlander Association

PAUL ANKA
60-second

MUSIC UP

ANNCR: And now, for Kodak, Paul Anka.

PAUL ANKA: Good morning, yesterday
You wake up and time has slipped
away
And suddenly it's hard to find
The memories you left behind
Remember
Do you remember.

The laughter and the tears
The shadows of misty yesteryears
You get the yearning now and then
To bring the moments back again
Remember
Do you remember
The times of your life.

ANNCR: Kodak film.
For the times of your life.

IN THE BEGINNING
60-second

MUSIC UNDER

ANNCR: In the beginning was the shower . . . cold and wet, but it got you clean.

Then somebody thought of hot water . . . which was a *big* improvement.

And *now* somebody's come up with the biggest improvement *yet*—the Shower Massage by Water Pik.

The unique, pulsating showerhead designed to give you a massage with every shower.

The Shower Massage by Water Pik . . . If you haven't discovered it yourself, you're missing out on some Good Clean Fun.

243
WRITER Bill Lane
PRODUCER Farlan Myers
AGENCY J. Walter Thompson
CLIENT Eastman Kodak

244
WRITER Nancy Foster
PRODUCTION CO. Imagination Inc.
AGENCY J. Walter Thompson
CLIENT Teledyne Water Pik

THE NEW YORK TIMES
60-second

ANNCR: Home delivery?

SONG: Did you know that you could get
The New York Times at home?
Did you know you don't have to miss it,
  Ever?
Never have to go out for it,
Have to go look for it,
Have to go find it, and
Find that they're out of it?

Did you know that you could have
The Times for breakfast,
That you could scan the world
While sipping your *cafe au lait*,
Thrilling to the sports in it,
The fashions and food in it,
The movies and news in it, and
All the who's whos in it?

ANNCR: Miss, *The Times*?

SONG: Can you bear not knowing
What the market's doing?
Can you bear not knowing
What the pundits say?
Can you stand it if *The Times*
Is quoted at you
Instead of just the other way?

ANNCR: Must you sit around regretfully without it?
Unthinkable!

Must you miss the latest talk about a play?
Intolerable!

Must you only hear what others say about it?
Impossible!

Good Heavens, Sir or Madam, call today!
800-325-6400

That's the splendid toll-free number
That you phone.
800-325-6400

And say, "By George,
I want *The New York Times* at home!"

ITEMS—HAT
60-second

ANNCR: This Fall, some wives in New York are finding they have less space for groceries in the refrigerator. Because it's being taken up by their husband's hat. The hat in question is a tweed classic from Ireland that New Yorkers have discovered can be shaped any way they like and then set in the refrigerator overnight. The idea is to make it look lived-in, even before it's worn.

The classic Irish hat is now at Barney's . . . along with a large collection of hats for Fall . . . such as hunting hats from South Africa and felt hats from the 30's . . . in new Fall colors such as putty and tan. In fact, for whatever hats suit your own tastes, even the hats found in the best refrigerators in New York, head for the one place that has them all . . . at room temperature. Barney's.

We're big enough to treat you as an individual. 7th Avenue and 17th Street. Open evenings till 9:30. Free parking and free alterations.

245
WRITER Paula Green
PRODUCER John Glucksman
AGENCY Green Dolmatch
CLIENT The New York Times

246
WRITER Joan McArthur
PRODUCER Joan McArthur
PRODUCTION CO. Howard Schwartz
AGENCY Scali, McCabe, Sloves
CLIENT Barney's

BEEF-MEAT THERMOMETER
60-second

ANNCR: As careful as we at BIG G are about the beef we buy, we don't know what's going to happen to it when you get it home. You can't trust cookbooks. They don't know if your oven is fast or slow. Gas or electric.

The only thing you can trust is a meat thermometer. When it gets to the right temperature, the meat's done.

If you don't have one, we'd like to encourage you to get one. So we've shopped around and found a good accurate meat thermometer. It usually costs $2.99. But we'll sell you one for $1.99. Because that's what it costs us.

We won't make any money on it. But we will make our beef come out of your oven as good as it was when you put it in. At BIG G, we shop as carefully as you do.

ITEMS—BOOTS
60-second

ANNCR: Since the fourteenth century, men's boots have doubled in popularity. That's because in the fourteenth century, it was the height of fashion to wear only *one*. It may have been the only time in history that men didn't have the problem of finding two matched socks in the morning.

Even so, boots have come a long way in six centuries . . . from the crudely sewn doeskin boot made then, to the few boots that are still hand-crafted today from the most luxuriously tanned leathers.

One of these few is the boot designed by Bruno Piatelli. The Piatelli boot is subtly tapered at the toe and hand-lasted from Italy's finest polished calf. And there's only one place in New York where you can find it: Barney's. Where you'll also find a whole collection of this Fall's newest shoes and boots that not only come in the finest leather and suede . . . but also in left and right.

Barney's. We're big enough to treat you as an individual. 7th Avenue and 17th Street. Open evenings till 9:30. Free parking.

247
WRITER Jon Coward
PRODUCER Jon Coward
PRODUCTION CO. Twelve East Recording
AGENCY Scali, McCabe, Sloves
CLIENT Big G

248
WRITER Joan McArthur
PRODUCER Joan McArthur
PRODUCTION CO. Howard Schwartz
AGENCY Scali, McCabe, Sloves
CLIENT Barney's

VEGETABLE COUNTERS
60-second

ANNCR: When we build a new BIG G, we build it better. Take our vegetable counters. A lot of stores let theirs get warm. BIG G vegetable counters are refrigerated. It keeps our fresh vegetables fresh.

And our frozen foods go into stand-up freezers. So you don't have to bend over and fish around for what you want. You open a door and take it out.

And when you get to our checkout counter, you don't have to unload everything. The cashier can empty our shopping carts. All you have to do is open the trunk to your car.

When it comes to anything that's going into a BIG G, we shop as carefully as you do.

MOVIE BUFF
60-second

MEARA: Tell me, Rupert, what did you think of tonight's movie? Did you ever see such symbolism, such subtleties, such technique?

STILLER: Talk about technique. Did you catch that couple in front of us?

MEARA: I understand it was filmed in cinema verité.

STILLER: No kidding. I thought it was filmed in Hollywood.

MEARA: I've always loved movies. You know, I was star-struck as a child.

STILLER: Oh yeah? I was almost hit by lightening when I was a kid.

MEARA: Did you ever see *The Garden of the Finzi Continis*?

STILLER: No, but the people next door grow eggplant on the roof, and speaking of food, I'm ordering steak.

MEARA: I'll have the lobster thermador. Lets have some wine.

STILLER: Terrific.

MEARA: What do you think of Blue Nun?

STILLER: The Blue Nun. Sure a classic. With Deitrich, right?

MEARA: No, Blue Nun is a wine. A delicious white wine.

STILLER: Even I know you don't have white wine with steak.

MEARA: Blue Nun is the white wine that's correct with any dish. It goes as well with meat as it does with fish.

STILLER: Gee, great food, great wine. Well, here's looking at you kid.

MEARA: Oh, you've seen *Casablanca*?

STILLER: No, but I once took a trip to Asbury Park.

ANNCR: Blue Nun. The delicious white wine that's correct with any dish. Another Sichel wine imported by Schieffelin & Co., New York.

249
WRITER Jon Goward
PRODUCER Jon Goward
PRODUCTION CO. Twelve East Recording
AGENCY Scali, McCabe, Sloves
CLIENT Big G

250
WRITERS Kay Kavanagh
Mark Yustein
PRODUCER Suzanne De Plautt
PRODUCTION COS. National Recording
Mack Anderson
AGENCY Della Femina, Travisano & Partners
CLIENT Schieffelin & Co.

POLYNESIAN RESTAURANT
60-second

MEARA: Aloha and welcome to Bali High Rise, where every meal is a cultured pearl.

STILLER: I'd like to make arrangements for a 40th wedding anniversary party.

MEARA: Why, sir, you must have been a child groom.

STILLER: No, it's for my parents. They honeymooned on the island.

MEARA: Maui or Coney?

STILLER: Coney.

MEARA: I think the Tacky Tacky room will be perfect.

STILLER: Is that the room with the primitive mask?

MEARA: I beg your pardon! That's a bust of my mother. She founded this restaurant.

STILLER: Oh, sorry.

MEARA: Well, let's discuss the menu. We have a choice of entree. Tuna Tanda Laya or Lava Liver. And may I suggest you include a little Blue Nun in your plans.

STILLER: Great idea. A missionary might be the perfect touch.

MEARA: No, Blue Nun is a wine. A delicious white wine.

STILLER: But we can't serve white wine to the people having meat.

MEARA: Certainly we can. Blue Nun is the white wine that's correct with any dish. It goes as well with meat as it does with fish.

STILLER: Wow, you really do things right here. I just tried one of your delicious clams. What was it stuffed with?

MEARA: A cigar. Sir, you just ate one of our ashtrays.

ANNCR: Blue Nun. The delicious white wine that's correct with any dish. Another Sichel wine imported by Schieffelin & Co., New York.

TENNIS CAMP
60-second

MEARA: Say aren't you Sancho Margolies, the tennis pro here?

STILLER: Yes, I am

MEARA: I couldn't help but admire your racquet.

STILLER: Why, thank you. It's a Wilcox 500.

MEARA: No, I mean teaching beautiful girls tennis all day. Now that's what I call a racquet.

STILLER: Well, it has its faults. Say you've got a lovely forehand.

MEARA: Oh, thank you, most people notice my eyes first.

STILLER: Well, maybe we could discuss your form over lunch.

MEARA: Love to. I'll start with the Wimbeldon fruit cup. And then I'll have the King Crab.

STILLER: And I'll have the mixed doubles salad and the singles steak. And perhaps we could share a bottle of wine.

MEARA: Aces!!

STILLER: I'll have a little Blue Nun sent over.

MEARA: I thought everyone had to wear regulation whites.

STILLER: No, no. Blue Nun is a wine. A delicious white wine.

MEARA: You can't have white wine with meat.

STILLER: Blue Nun is the white wine that's correct with any dish. It goes as well with meat as it does with fish.

MEARA: Wow, you really do things with class.

STILLER: Well, like I always say—what good is a tennis pro who can't serve well?

MEARA: Sanch, you've got a little gravy on your sweat band.

ANNCR: Blue Nun. The delicious white wine that's correct with any dish. Another Sichel wine imported by Schieffelin & Co., New York.

	251
WRITERS	Kay Kavanagh
	Mark Yustein
PRODUCER	Suzanne DePlautt
PRODUCTION COS.	National Recording
	Mack Anderson
AGENCY	Della Femina, Travisano
	& Partners
CLIENT	Schieffelin & Co.

	252
WRITERS	Kay Kavanagh
	Mark Yustein
PRODUCER	Suzanne De Plautt
PRODUCTION CO.	National Recording
AGENCY	Della Femina, Travisano
	& Partners
CLIENT	Schieffelin & Co.

JALAXY ONE
60-second

MUSIC UNDER

CHRISTOPHER PLUMMER: Japan Air Lines introduces "Jalaxy One" . . . its nonstop flight on the fastest route to Tokyo.

Nobody gets you to Tokyo faster than Jalaxy Flight One . . . as JAL cuts three and a half hours from flying time by taking the nonstop polar route.

Your arrival is timed to make excellent connections on to Hong Kong or Osaka.

Then, when you're ready, nobody gets you home faster than Jalaxy Flight Two . . . nonstop from Tokyo to San Francisco.

Even beyond the flight itself, a total Jalaxy of care is there to help you feel at home throughout your visit to JAL's Orient.

JALAXY GARDEN
60-second

JALAXY ONE FIRST CLASS
60-second

JALAXY ONE EXECUTIVE
60-second

HEAVENLY BODIES
60-second

MUSIC UNDER

ANNCR: There are 100 billion heavenly bodies in our universe. As far as we know, life exists on only one of them. A planet called earth.

On this planet, in a country known as Peru, scientists have discovered incredible markings that were carved into the earth more than 5,000 years ago. These markings form precise patterns. And yet, they only make sense when seen from the sky. But who—or what—could have seen them from the sky—5,000 years ago?

Some people say these markings were landing strips for ancient astronauts. Some people say we'll never know the answer. But we do know this.

AeroPeru can fly you to Peru. And to some of the most mysterious places on earth. Places like the Galapagos Islands. And Machu Picchu. And Sacsahuamán.

AeroPeru. The world's newest . . . and perhaps oldest airline.

AMAZON JUNGLE
60-second

MYSTERIOUS JOURNEY
60-second

TOUR ANNOUNCEMENT
60-second

LAST INCA
60-second

253
WRITER Arthur X. Tuohy
PRODUCER Carol Sernasie
PRODUCTION CO. Merl Bloom Assoc.
AGENCY Ketchum, MacLeod & Grove
CLIENT Japan Air Lines

254
WRITER Rick Green
PRODUCER Mike Moss
PRODUCTION CO. MJ Production
AGENCY Philip J. Taylor & Assoc.
CLIENT AeroPeru

 SILVER

CHOCOLATE ECLAIR
60-second

ANNCR: As you probably know, Pine State makes all kinds of tasty things to help people control their weight. We even invented a special diet to go with our Trim cottage cheese.

But you also know that every so often we do something that makes all those noble efforts look foolish, and we're pleased to announce that we've done it again. It's called Pine State Chocolate Eclair Ice Cream . . . our own rich chocolate just stuffed, like a French eclair with a whipped vanilla custard cream . . . and folks, if you're on a diet, you're in trouble.

There's no such thing as a small portion, and if you're the kind of person who can sort of take sweets or leave them alone, this new ice cream of ours is liable to strum your jaw like a guitar, because it's every bit as sweet and rich as it sounds. But it's also kind of elegant.

So if your figure can stand it and you're planning a party or a fancy dinner, you might plan on some Pine State Chocolate Eclair for dessert. Just do what most people do—don't use any cream in your coffee.

Pine State Chocolate Eclair Ice Cream. It's at your store right now, alongside our diet products.

JALAPENO HOLIDAY
60-second

ALMOST PAINLESS DIET
60-second

SWEET ACIWHATSIS
60-second

ANNCR: I guess you've been hearing a lot about Pine State's new milk. We've been calling it Nu-Trish, but it's still Sweet Acidophilus, and if you're anything like me, you'd just as soon not drink something you can hardly pronounce.

But John Wiley explained it so even I could get it. Now, an acidophilus is a bacteria. But now don't get antsy—there's bad germs and there's good germs, and just like you need good bugs like honeybees in your garden, you need good germs like aciwhatsis in your body; and the way a lot of us eat, you might not be getting all you need to feel right.

Only it took till now to develop a *sweet* strain that you could put in milk and still come out with something that Pine State'd want to put its name on. And it's really *better* than that: you can't tell it from our Trim-and-Tasty milk, that's how good it tastes, and for all the extra good it can do you, it doesn't cost a cent more than homogenized.

But you'll see it in the store and the story's on the package—it's the milk that sounds like the problem it's supposed to take care of.

But try it anyhow, it's good for you. And it's carrying our guarantee, so what've you got to lose? *I* tried some and I don't care *what* they call it—it's milk.

MAINTENANCE
60-second

ENDORSEMENTS
60-second

255
WRITER William Teitelbaum
PRODUCTION CO. Howard Schwartz
AGENCY McKinney Silver & Rockett
CLIENT Pine State Creamery

256
WRITER William Teitelbaum
PRODUCTION CO. Howard Schwartz
AGENCY McKinney Silver & Rockett
CLIENT Pine State Creamery

LEAPING
60-second

BERT: You grabbed *Time* magazine right out of my hand.

DICK: I know that, sir. I had to.

BERT: Why?

DICK: Because you're reading it wrong—all out of order.

BERT: What?

DICK: You should read it in order.

BERT: Read . . . .

DICK: See, you opened it to the book section in the back, then leapt forward to the people section, and *then* doubled back to science.

BERT: Well, that's how I read *Time*—by leaping here and there, see.

DICK: Acrobats flip, sir.

BERT: Each week, T-Time is . . . is filled with great stories of people, places and events, so I . . . .

DICK: In order! In order and by page number!

BERT: All right, but some stories *interest* me more than others, so I naturally dip into those stories, first, and then I—

DICK: Crackers dip, sir.

BERT: What?

DICK: Forget that one. My point is this. If you want to read Helter Skelter, Higgledy-Piggledy, read the Willy-Nilly weekly. Not *Time,* the weekly news magazine.

BERT: Look, I'll read—j-just don't grab my *Time* again!!

DICK: Then, stop page-jumping!

BERT: I'll jump if I want to!

DICK: Checkers jump!

BERT: I'm gonna jump you, right here on the bus.

DICK: This looks like my stop, here. Yes, this is my stop, definitely.

BERT: C'mon, put 'em up . . . c'mon, c'mon . . .

ANNCR: *Time* makes everything more interesting, including you.

FU-CHI MANOLI
60-second

AIRPLANE
60-second

PEN TO THE PAPER
60-second

MUSIC UNDER

SONG: Put the pen to the paper
Push it all around.
Fold the paper in the envelope
Lick the stamp down.

Put it in the mailbox
Where the man with the bag
Takes it to the building
Where they get it on a plane
And Old Uncle Henry
With the pipe in his mouth
Gets it in his mailbox
At his very own house.

And he reads it and he loves it.
And he says, "Wow!"
And he reads it and he loves it
And he says, "Now . . . I gotta
Put the pen to the paper
Push it all around.
Fold the paper in the envelope
Lick the stamp down."

And I get it on the spot
Where it falls to the floor,
Get it through a slot
That I got in the door.
And I read it and I love it
And I say, "Wow!"
And I read it and I . . . .

ANNCR: The gift of a letter . . . nothing brings you closer to someone special. P.S., write soon.

SONG: I gotta put the pen to the paper
Push it all around
Fold the paper in the envelope . . .

ANNCR: From your Postal Service.

SISTERS
60-second

HOME IN MY HAND
60-second

	257
WRITERS	Dick Orkin
	Bert Berdis
	Woody Woodruff
DIRECTORS	Dick Orkin
	Bert Berdis
PRODUCER	Jim Coyne
PRODUCTION CO.	Dick & Bert
AGENCY	Young & Rubicam
CLIENT	Time

GOLD

	258
ART DIRECTOR	Steve Salzburg
WRITERS	John Ferrell
	Larry Spector
DIRECTOR	Jim Coyne
PRODUCER	Jim Coyne
PRODUCTION CO.	Herman Edel Assoc.
AGENCY	Young & Rubicam
CLIENT	U.S. Postal Service (First Class)

PRICE CUTS
60-second

PHIL: Hey, Hank . . . did you hear about Highland Appliance's Sound Shops?

HANK: What's there to hear? A couple of Victrolas left over from the forties . . . the rinsing action of a washing machine?

PHIL: Highland has just announced across-the-board price cuts on every piece of stereo equipment in the place. Price cuts on Pioneer, Marantz, Dual, Sansui and more.

HANK: I didn't even know Highland carried Pioneer, Marantz, Dual, Sansui, and more.

PHIL: So right now, you can get the stereo of your dreams for just above wholesale at Highland. Listen to this:

(Insert)

HANK: That's amazing! How do they do that?

PHIL: The price? Well, they—

HANK: No, I mean, how do you get that other guy to come on and talk like that?

PHIL: Oh well, I just say "listen to this" and stay quiet for a few seconds. Here, I'll show you. Listen to this:

(Insert)

PHIL: There he was again!

HANK: The magic of radio.

ANNCR: The Highland Appliance Sound Shops. Everything you never expected from an appliance store.

MAYTAG
60-second

SOUND ROOM/BLINDFOLDED
60-second

QUEEN ELIZABETH
60-second

MUSIC: (Pomp and Circumstance)

QUEEN: Giles, bring my Daimler Limousine around, would you?

GILES: The *Daimler* limousine, your majesty?

QUEEN: Yes.

GILES: That would be a bit of a problem . . . you sold it.

QUEEN: I sold it . . . I can't have sold it . . . Where is it Giles?

GILES: I believe it's in the colonies. At a Motor Car Exposition?

ANNCR: Queen Elizabeth, it's at the Detroit Auto Show, to be precise. Your royally-appointed '49 Daimler limousine is on special display, along with other famous cars. Al Capone's '29 Lincoln, James Dean's '49 Merc from *Rebel Without A Cause*. Plus all those beautiful new '75 cars. Ride with the famous and the infamous. Come to the '75 Detroit Auto Show, January 11 through the 19 at Cobo Hall.

QUEEN: How could I have sold that car . . . I left my crown in the glove box.

JAMES DEAN
60-second

AL CAPONE
60-second

	259
WRITER	Chato Hill
PRODUCER	Chato Hill
PRODUCTION CO.	Bell Sound
AGENCY	W.B. Doner & Co.
CLIENT	Highland Appliance

	260
ART DIRECTOR	Edd Mangino
WRITER	Thom Sharp
DIRECTOR	Edd Mangino
PRODUCER	Thom Sharp
PRODUCTION CO.	Bell Sound Studios
AGENCY	W.B. Doner & Co.
CLIENT	Detroit Auto Dealers

NEW POOR
60-second

ANNCR: *New Times* is on the stands, and this week's issue is devoted to America's New Poor. Four million people—confident, secure—until events not of their making reduced them to poverty, despair, and worst of all, uncertainty.

Like publisher John Thompson, whose magazine was just breaking even when his bank changed its rules and foreclosed.

Or Don Stewart, who used to bring in a full day's catch of salmon *every* day until Russian trawlers made it a memory.

Or Jim Darneal, successful fieldhand until hard times made everybody a fieldhand. Now he picks less, earns less, and lives in an $84 tent.

If you've ever had to choose between paying rent and buying food—especially if you've *never* had to—*New Times'* July 25th issue is sobering. A human story told in human terms. It's going to be talked about tomorrow. Read it today.

OSWALD'S DOUBLE
60-second

COFFEE
60-second

MOVIE BUFF
60-second

MEARA: Tell me, Rupert, what did you think of tonight's movie? Did you ever see such symbolism, such subtleties, such technique?

STILLER: Talk about technique. Did you catch that couple in front of us?

MEARA: I understand it was filmed in cinema verité.

STILLER: No kidding. I thought it was filmed in Hollywood.

MEARA: I've always loved movies. You know, I was star-struck as a child.

STILLER: Oh yeah? I was almost hit by lightening when I was a kid.

MEARA: Did you ever see *The Garden of the Finzi Continis?*

STILLER: No, but the people next door grow eggplant on the roof, and speaking of food, I'm ordering steak.

MEARA: I'll have the lobster thermador. Let's have some wine.

STILLER: Terrific.

MEARA: What do you think of Blue Nun?

STILLER: The Blue Nun. Sure a classic. With Deitrich, right?

MEARA: No, Blue Nun is a wine. A delicious white wine.

STILLER: Even I know you don't have white wine with steak.

MEARA: Blue Nun is the white wine that's correct with any dish. It goes as well with meat as it does with fish.

STILLER: Gee, great food, great wine. Well, here's looking at you kid.

MEARA: Oh, you've seen *Casablanca?*

STILLER: No, but I once took a trip to Asbury Park.

ANNCR: Blue Nun. The delicious white wine that's correct with any dish. Another Sichel wine imported by Schieffelin & Co., New York.

TENNIS CAMP
60-second

POLYNESIAN RESTAURANT
60-second

261
WRITER Stephen Fenton
DIRECTOR Stephen Fenton
PRODUCER Stephen Fenton
PRODUCTION CO. ServiSound
AGENCY Friedlich, Fearon & Strohmeier
CLIENT New Times

262
WRITERS Kay Kavanagh
Mark Yustein
PRODUCER Suzanne De Plautt
PRODUCTION CO. National Recording
AGENCY Della Femina, Travisano & Partners
CLIENT Schieffelin & Co.

CONCERT
60-second

ED: Harriet?

HARRIET: What's the matter, Ed?

ED: I feel funny being here.

HARRIET: Ed, you like concerts.

ED: I know, but why did we have to bring our Umbrella Tree?

HARRIET: Oh, he likes music. Ed, we've discussed this.

ED: Well, you don't see anybody else here with a dumb Umbrella Tree sittin' next to 'em do you? And, why does he have to sit between us?

HARRIET: Well you know how jealous he is. And, you've probably hurt his feelings. Now apologize this minute.

ED: Harriet. I'm not apologizing to an Umbrella Tree. And that's final, Harriet . . . and that's . . .

HARRIET: Ed. If you don't apologize . . .

ED: No, no, no . . .

ANNCR: There are lots of theories about plant growing. Let's look at some facts. Fact . . . plants need light, water and nutrition. Fact . . . Precise Brand Timed Release Plant Food from the 3M Company is the easy way to feed your plants. One feeding last four months. And once in the soil, Precise's timed release beads provide daily nutrition to your plant roots.

HARRIET: Never mind, apologize or I'm leaving.

ED: Okay! Okay! I'm . . . sorry, Umbrella Tree.

HARRIET: I didn't believe that! Do it again, more sincerely.

ED: I'm sorry, Umbrella Tree.

HARRIET: One more time.

ED: I'm sorry, Umbrella Tree.

ANNCR: Light, water and Precise. One of those very good ideas from the 3M Company.

RHODA
60-second

CHERRY TOMATOES
60-second

RICHMOND ROBINS VS. ROCHESTER AMERICANS
60-second

SONG: What hockey team's so ruthless
Most opponents go home toothless?
The toughest birds on ice
Are fun but not so nice.

The Robins—Look out for the Robins.

INTERVIEWER: We're talking with Wally Wurtzel, P.R. man for the Rochester Americans. Wally, what kind of team do you guys have?

P.R. MAN: We're improving every game, Phil. Most of the boys are getting dressed by themselves, now. So we're usually out on the ice before the games start, and that's a help.

INTERVIEWER: Speaking of games, Wally, care to make a prediction on the Rochester-Richmond game?

P.R. MAN: Well, it's always tough on the road when you don't have your teddy bears to sleep with, Phil, but we won't suit up any thumbsuckers, I can tell you that.

SONG: The puck goes flying
The other team's crying
And everyone's yelling for more.
When the Robins are playing
Mothers are praying
Their sons will come back from the war.

The Robins—Look out for the Robins.
Tweet, tweet.

RICHMOND ROBINS VS. PROVIDENCE REDS
60-second

RICHMOND ROBINS VS. NOVA SCOTIA VOYAGEURS
60-second

RICHMOND ROBINS VS. NEW HAVEN NIGHTHAWKS
60-second

263
WRITER Craig Wiese
PRODUCER Craig Wiese
PRODUCTION CO. Dick Orkin Creative Services
AGENCY Campbell-Mithun
CLIENT 3M Company

264
ART DIRECTOR Harry Jacobs
WRITER Bill Westbrook
PRODUCER Bill Westbrook
PRODUCTION COS. Radio Band of America
Alpha Audio
AGENCY Jacobs Morgan & Westbrook
CLIENT Richmond Sports International

ITEMS—HACKING JACKET
60-second

ANNCR: Of all the arbiters of men's fashion, one can take credit for having influenced more fashion than any other: the horse. It was the horse that first put men in boots . . . in pants . . . and in the hacking jacket, a style which this fall is bigger than ever.

The hacking jacket has several distinctive details that separates it from the rest of the pack. Its closely fitted waist that flares out over the hips for a comfortable ride . . . even in a subway. And its slanted pockets, making them easy to get into while sitting on a saddle . . . or in a restaurant.

The place to go to find more hacking jackets than you'd see at the annual hunt at Devonshire, is Barney's English Room. And this fall, it's roomier than ever. Because it's just been expanded to accomodate the mounting interest in English clothing . . . including the fashions first dictated by the horse.

Barney's. We're big enough to treat you as an individual. 7th Avenue and 17th Street. Open evenings till 9:30. Free parking.

ITEMS—BOOTS
60-second

ITEMS—HAT
60-second

ANNE MURRAY
60-second

ANNCR: And now, for Kodak, Anne Murray:

ANNE MURRAY (SINGS): Good morning, yesterday
You wake up and time has slipped away
And suddenly it's hard to find
The memories you left behind
Remember
Do you remember

The laughter and the tears
The shadows of misty yesteryears
You get the yearning now and then
To bring the moments back again
Remember
Will you remember
The times of your life

ANNCR: Kodak film. For the times of your life.

PAUL ANKA
60-second

THE SPINNERS
60-second

265
WRITER	Joan McArthur
PRODUCER	Joan McArthur
PRODUCTION CO.	Howard Schwartz
AGENCY	Scali, McCabe, Sloves
CLIENT	Barney's

266
WRITER	Bill Lane
PRODUCERS	Paul Anka
	Farlan Myers
	Anne Murray
	Ray Fragasso
	Bill Artope
AGENCY	J. Walter Thompson
CLIENT	Eastman Kodak

HUMAN SENSUAL RESPONSE
60-second

GIRL: A clinical study of sensations felt while experiencing Clairol Herbal Essence Body Powder. Kathy-Ann F., Age 22, Married.

MAN: Subject had occasional pre-marital Clairol Herbal Essence Body Powder after developing an interest in a ski instructor. Her responses were similar to those she now enjoys since being married. She attributes that to the mountain fresh flower fragrance of Clairol Herbal Essence Body Powder and the fact that both men appreciated her mind.

We placed Kathy Ann in a room filled with Clairol Herbal Essence Body Powder, which Kathy Ann used to pat herself on all the perfect places. Her eyelids closed and her mind wandered to the Garden of Earthly Delights as she savored the bouquet of herbs and wild flowers and she smoothed the powder into her skin, raising goose-bumps on those of us conducting the test. A truly human response.

GIRL: Clairol Herbal Essence Body Powder should be kept out of the reach of children.

HIT BY A TRUCK
60-second

A COOL AND SILKY SONG
60-second

GOOD FRIENDS ARE FOR KEEPS—
THE CARPENTERS
60-second

SONG: Hey now don't let your empty room
Ever get you down, •
You can fill the silence with a smile.
And don't let the crowds on the
Street make you feel
Like you were just a stranger in town.

If you're feeling happy
Or if you want to weep
Or you want a warm word before you sleep.
Remember . . .
Good friends are forever.
Good friends are forever.
Good friends are for keeps.

ANNCR: The Carpenters sing for the Bell System.
Good friends are for keeps.
So, keep in touch.
Long Distance is the next best thing to being there.

SONG: Good friends are forever.
Good friends are forever.
Good friends are for keeps.

GOOD FRIENDS ARE FOR KEEPS—LORETTA LYNN
60-second

GOOD FRIENDS ARE FOR KEEPS—VALERIE SIMPSON
60-second

GOOD FRIENDS ARE FOR KEEPS—TONY BENNETT
60-second

267
WRITERS	Chuck Blore
	Don Richman
	Lois Wyse
DIRECTOR	Chuck Blore
PRODUCER	Chuck Blore
PRODUCTION CO.	Chuck Blore Creative Services
AGENCY	Wyse Advertising
CLIENT	Clairol

268
WRITER	Gerald Pfiffner
DIRECTOR	Gerald Pfiffner
PRODUCER	Gaston Braun
PRODUCTION CO.	Elliot Lawrence Productions
AGENCY	N.W. Ayer
CLIENT	AT&T Long Lines

SONICS—SLICK WATTS
60-second

BLACKBURN: This is Bob Blackburn . . . and to recap what just happened . . . a very impressive team from Lile Moving & Storage has defeated a team from the Seattle Supersonics . . . as both teams competed in a very moving *furniture*-packing contest. And our guest here on the Post Game Show is Slick Watts . . . from the Sonics. Slick, what would you say makes the people at Lile Moving & Storage so good at packing furniture?

SLICK: Well, Bob, it's a lot of things. It's dedication . . . it's desire . . . they just seem to have it all together, you might say.

BLACKBURN: Slick, I know one thing the fans want to know about is that crucial play where you were called for unnecessary roughness . . . when you dropped that beautiful Ming Vase. What happened on that play, Slick?

SLICK: Well, Bob, it's hard to say. All *I* know is . . . packing furniture is no job for amateurs. And those guys at Lile really make some great moves.

BLACKBURN: And those guys at Lile really make some great moves, don't they, Slick?

SLICK: They sure do, Bob.

BLACKBURN: Slick Watts . . . thank you very much for being our Post Game Guest.

SLICK: Thank *you*, Bob.

LILE VS. SONICS
60-second

SONICS—ARCHIE CLARK
60-second

EUGENE DAILEY
60-second

BARTON: On January 29, Eugene Dailey of Pittsburgh flew on American Airlines. And wrote this note . . .

MR. DAILEY: "Dear American:
I want to compliment you on your prompt departures and arrivals. However, this promptness really messes up travel, so you may have to run late to get in phase with everyone else.

All your people have been most courteous; they were especially helpful when I missed your Flight #64 yesterday."

BARTON: Being on time—and helping people who aren't—is one of the things we do best. We're American Airlines.

MUSIC: We're American Airlines. Doing what we do best.

JOSEPH WRIGHT
60-second

MARY JASON
60-second

269
WRITER   Dave Newman
DIRECTOR   Dave Newman
PRODUCERS   Dave Newman
Mike Carter
PRODUCTION CO.   Spectrum Studios
AGENCY   Cole & Weber
CLIENT   Lile Moving & Storage

270
WRITER   Stevie Pierson
PRODUCER   Paul Conti
PRODUCTION CO.   S.D.C. Recording
AGENCY   Doyle Dane Bernbach
CLIENT   American Airlines

NORTH CAROLINA HEART ASSOCIATION
60-second

SFX: (A STEADY HEARTBEAT)

ANNCR: This woman leads a perfectly normal, active life. She takes care of her three children. Has a good job. Feels fine. And is dying. The same way over 25,000 North Carolinians die every year. From high blood pressure.

High blood pressure leads to heart attack and stroke. But before that, there are no noticeable symptoms.

That's why most people with high blood pressure don't know it. And that's one out of every six adults.

If you're black, your chances are almost twice that. So have your blood pressure checked today. It's fast. Painless. And high blood pressure can be successfully treated in most cases.

If you don't have your blood pressure checked, you'll continue to lead a perfectly normal life until, perhaps on one of these beautiful days you're happy just to be alive . . .

I LIVE IN RYE
60-second

CYNICAL MAN: "Sure, life in the city is tough.
But why ask me for help?
I live in Rye."

WOMAN ANN: Hopefully, you'll never need help.
Hopefully, you'll never have an emergency.
Or need special cancer or heart care.
Or help with handicaps.
Or be abandoned, senile, or in despair.

But as United Fund of Greater New York, we don't discriminate. We'll help millions this year through 425 community agencies, the Red Cross, and Salvation Army. Roughly 1 out of 4 will be a commuter. Actually, our funds come only from working people.

We ask for contributions only through offices. And that's only once a year.
And because our costs are only 9%, 91¢ of every Fund dollar really does do good.

Doesn't this seem the easiest way to help others? And maybe yourself?
Give once . . . and for all.

Give to UNITED FUND of Greater New York.

271
WRITER George Dusenbury
PRODUCER George Dusenbury
PRODUCTION CO. Audio One
AGENCY Carmichael & Co.
CLIENT North Carolina Heart Assoc.

272
ART DIRECTOR Jim Brown
WRITER Camile Larghi
PRODUCER Elaine Morris
PRODUCTION CO. Superdupe Creations
AGENCY Doyle, Dane, Bernbach
CLIENT United Fund of Greater New York

GIVE A HAND
60-second

ANNCR: You're pretty lucky, friend,
Darn lucky, you'll find.
If you think you've got troubles,
Then you should see the real kind.

Kids that have no mom or dad,
Kids strung out on dope,
Old folks all alone and sad,
Families with no hope,
Men who've lost their jobs and pride,
The sick, the blind, the lame,
People trying suicide,
Homes gone up in flame.

Won't you give a hand to help them
Reach a brighter day.
They want a hand, not a handout
So give the United Way.

DO, RE, MI
30-second

MUSIC UNDER

ANNCR: If you think the New England Conservatory is strictly long hair, listen!

(Music up)

ANNCR: True, our alumni play with every major American symphony and represent a third of the Boston Symphony, but listen!

(Music up)

ANNCR: Trouble is, right now, financial obligations could simply drown us out.

(Music winds down to stop)

ANNCR: We need $1,500,000 by July.

(Music starts up and continues under)

ANNCR: Help the New England Conservatory raise a little do, re, mi.

273
WRITER	Don Mix
PRODUCER	Joe Sicurella
AGENCY	Burke Dowling Adams
CLIENT	United Way of Metro Atlanta

274
WRITERS	Tony Winch
	Jim Pappademas
PRODUCERS	Tony Winch
	Jim Pappademas
PRODUCTION CO.	Jay Rose Sound
AGENCY	Hill, Holliday, Connors, Cosmopulos
CLIENT	New England Conservatory

HIGHWAY SAFETY—MR. ADAMS
60-second

GROUP: Good news . . . Mr. Adams.
You have good friends
We laughed, we drank, and then we said good-by.

SOLO: Bad news.

You have no friends, Mr. Adams.
When they last saw you alive
They should've known you shouldn't drive but
they said:

MAN: He's only drinkin' beer.

GROUP: He's only drinking beer.

MAN: How drunk can you get on beer?

GROUP: How drunk can you get on beer?
How drunk can you get on beer?

ANNCR: Too much beer or wine can make your
friend too drunk to drive. And black coffee won't
really help. But you can. Drive him yourself. Or
call a cab. Friends don't let friends drive drunk.

SONG: Sad news, Mr. Adams . . .
        He's only drinking beer.
        You have bad friends, Mr. Adams . . .
        How drunk can you get.

ANNCR: Find out how else you can help. Write
Drunk Driver, Box 2345 Rockville, Maryland. A
public service message on behalf of the U.S. Department of Transportation.

KILLER
30-second

MUSIC UNDER

ANNCR: There's a killer in our midst. Its victims
include men, women, Blacks, whites, young, and
old. And every month, it's responsible for more
deaths in North Carolina than any other killer in
history.

The killer is high blood pressure. And one out of
every six adults has the disease. So have your
blood pressure checked today. It's your only de-
fense.

PROBLEM
30-second

TEST
30-second

BLACK PLAGUE
30-second

275
WRITERS Harold Karp
        Enid Futterman
PRODUCER Michael Cohen
PRODUCTION CO. Radio Band of America
AGENCY Grey Advertising
CLIENT U.S. Department of
        Transportation

276
WRITER George Dusenbury
PRODUCER George Dusenbury
PRODUCTION CO. Audio One
AGENCY Carmichael & Co.
CLIENT North Carolina Heart
        Assoc.

MARLON BRANDO/HIGHWAY
60-second

MUSIC UNDER

FENNIMAN: Welcome to YOU SAVE YOUR LIFE.

GROUCHO: If you're a dumb cluck you get a dead duck.

GROUCHO: OK. Today's category is motorcycles in Virginia. Now when you come to a railroad track, what's the safest way to cross—straight on or at a slight angle?

MARLON BRANDO: Oh, wow, man. I take 'em straight on.

GROUCHO: Correct.

FENNIMAN: Before the next question, let's hear a word from our sponsors.

SONG: The Highway Safety Division of Virginia and this station are here to say: When you're on your bike, please be bright. Burn your lights. Burn your lights. Night and day.

GROUCHO: In Virginia, where's the best place for motorcycles to pull up at a stop light? Behind the car or between the cars in front of you?

MARLON BRANDO: Well in Hollywood we always drive up between the cars and bug the first family we see.

GROUCHO: Oh no. You bug the first family of Virginia and the whole State will be agin' you.

FENNIMAN: Right Groucho. Same laws cars obey motorcycles obey. Tune in again to YOU SAVE YOUR LIFE.

MAE WEST
60-second

JOHN WAYNE
60-second

CARPOOLING EXPERT
60-second

ANNCR: The U.S. Department of Transportation, the Advertising Council, and this Station, remind you to Double-Up. Share a Ride with a Friend. Today we're talking to a carpooling expert.

EXPERT: That's right. I'm an expert in this. I've studied carpooling—forever.

ANNCR: Uh, huh. Who actually invented carpooling?

EXPERT: Way back, a Neanderthal man did it where he sat on a rock and he asked another person to sit on the rock. . .unfortunately the rock did not move. . .but he was not aware. . .

ANNCR: But that was kind of the very fundamental beginnings of carpooling. . .

EXPERT: That's right. That's right.

ANNCR: Well tell us, why is it important today to carpool?

EXPERT: Uh, because why take two cars? Why use energy with gasoline when you can go together . . .get to know each other. . .

ANNCR: Double-Up?

EXPERT: That's right. You can Share a Ride with a Friend. You know, somebody that works with you. You can talk and you get there in no time. . .

ANNCR: You get relaxed. . .

EXPERT: That's right! You won't be lonely. It's no fun being lonely. I was lonely last year. I went in the closet and played with my shoes.

ANNCR: Uh, huh. Do you have a specific friend that you carpool with?

EXPERT: Excellent friend. Yes.

ANNCR: How do we get the term "Carpool"? Where does that come from?

EXPERT: Ah. . .named after Mr. Henry Carpool.

ANNCR: Oh? There was actually a person named "Carpool"?

EXPERT: Carpool, yes. The New Hampshire Carpools.

ANNCR: Uh, huh.

WORLD'S FRIENDLIEST
60-second

NEWS TEAM
60-second

277
WRITER	Doug Burford
DIRECTOR	Doug Burford
PRODUCER	Ron Dunn
PRODUCTION CO.	Sound Images Recording Studio
AGENCY	Burford Co.
CLIENT	Highway Safety Division of Virginia

278
WRITER	Alan Barzman
DIRECTOR	Alan Barzman
PRODUCER	Sherie Levin
PRODUCTION CO.	Barzman & Co.
AGENCY	VanSant Dugdale & Co.
CLIENT	U.S. Department of Transportation

RESTAURANT
30-second

FATHER: Shrimps, lobster sauce . . .

HARRY: Spare ribs for me.

MOTHER-IN-LAW: I'll have won ton soup. He'll never remember all that.

ANNCR: If your business depends on getting orders right . . .

get yourself a Sony cassette-recorder.

This TC-55 has a built-in mike, 90 minutes of recording, and lots more.

And with a Sony recorder, if anyone ever questions you, you'll always have the answers.

MOTHER-IN-LAW: I didn't order that.

SUPER: *It's a Sony.*

279
ART DIRECTOR Don Slater
WRITERS Ron Berger
Dan Cohen
DIRECTOR Neil Tardio
PRODUCER Rob Ewing
PRODUCTION CO. Tardio, Lovinger, Melsky
AGENCY Rosenfeld, Sirowitz &
Lawson
CLIENT Sony

MEL BLANC
30-second

MEL BLANC: Do you know me? Would you believe I'm Bugs Bunny?

I'm also the voice of many other cartoon characters.

But in here they don't care if I'm Daffy Duck. Despicable!

So I carry an American Express Card . . . the one card I need for travel and entertaining, for business and pleasure.

Why, without this, the only way I'd get any attention is by saying:

"Badee! Badaa! That's all folks!"

ANNCR: To apply for a card, call 800 528-8000.

MEL BLANC: The American Express Card. Don't leave home without it.

280
ART DIRECTOR Mark Ross
WRITER Bill Taylor
DIRECTOR Dick Miller
PRODUCER Sue Paskoski
PRODUCTION CO. Wakeford/Orloff
AGENCY Ogilvy & Mather
CLIENT American Express

IT'S GOT TRADITION
30-second

FATHER: What's happened to tradition . . .

My son . . . I thought he'd be a doctor . . . he works on a herb farm.

My daughter's a doctor.

My wife's running for alderman . . . er . . . alderwoman.

Now Mogen David Concord Wine . . . there's tradition.

For generations, they've made it in the same traditional way for that great Mogen David taste.

Even they (looking at family) like Mogen David. Some traditions they've still got respect for!!!

SUPER: *It's got tradition.*

281
ART DIRECTOR Henry Hechtman
WRITER Norman Kantor
DESIGNER Henry Hechtman
DIRECTOR Dob Giraldi
PRODUCERS Norman Kantor
Henry Hechtman
PRODUCTION CO. Giraldi Productions
AGENCY Lee King & Partners
CLIENT Mogen David Wine

FLICK YOUR BIC-STEWARDESS
30-second

MUSIC UNDER

STEWARDESS: Coffee, tea, or a flick of my Bic?

OFFICER: Private! Don't you know to flick your Bic in the presence of an officer?

PRIVATE: Yessir, yessir, yessir.

GIRL: Phillip . . .

PHILLIP: Yes.

GIRL: Now that we're in the tunnel of love . . . could I have a flick of your Bic?

ANNCR: Why just light up when you can flick your Bic. It's smooth, easy on the thumb, and you get thousands of flicks from a single Bic. The Bic Butane.

MAN: Keep flicking your Bic, Marsha. There's got to be a ship within at least a thousand miles of us!

282
ART DIRECTOR Maurice Mahler
WRITER Adam Hanft
DIRECTOR Steve Horn
PRODUCER Dan Kohn
PRODUCTION CO. Steve Horn
AGENCY Wells, Rich, Greene
CLIENT Bic Pens

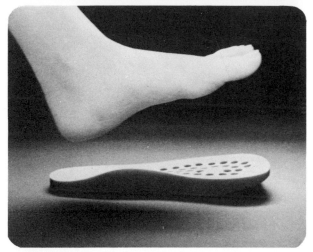

THIS INVENTION
30-second

ANNCR: This invention, when placed between the foot and the ground, guides you through a unique experience called "pure walking."

A path of motion designed to focus and concentrate your own natural forces so that you will walk, perhaps for the first time, with continuous, comfortable, easy power.

This invention is the Earth sole, the patented sole of the Earth Shoe.

The Earth brand shoe.

Sold only at Earth Shoe stores.

283
ART DIRECTOR Mel Platt
WRITER Jennifer Berne
DIRECTOR Toni Ficalora
PRODUCER Barbara Gans
PRODUCTION CO. Toni Ficalora Film Productions
AGENCY Martin Landey, Arlow
CLIENT Kalsø Systemet

CHEETA/USA
30-second

MUSIC UNDER

ANNCR: This elegant spotted cat flashes across the sundrenched African plains swifter even than the wind.

But if he were competing with another creature, as elegant and as wonderful, after several hundred yards, even the cheetah would be overtaken by the world record holder for the mile.

The Thoroughbred race horse, one of the fastest animals in the world.

Come out and see him at Belmont Park.

He's beautiful.

SUPER: *Belmont Park*

284
ART DIRECTOR Ira Madris
WRITER Nicholas Pisacane
PRODUCER Diane Maze
PRODUCTION CO. Independent Artists
AGENCY McCann-Erickson
CLIENT New York Racing Assoc.

TOBACCO STORE
30-second

LEADER: It is said there is still a good 10¢ cigar left in the world whose name is Muriel. You have such a cigar? Eh?

CLERK: Yes sir. Muriel Panatellas, Senators, Coronella Kings. They're . . .

. . . *really* good 10¢ cigars.

LEADER: Caramba. Only 10¢. How does Muriel do it? Eh?

LEADER: (Singing) Ees tough to put a Muriel down, ees tough to . . . put a Muriel down.

SUPER: *There's still a good 10¢ cigar.*

285
ART DIRECTOR Mike Withers
WRITER Barry Greenspon
DESIGNER Mike Withers
DIRECTOR Bob Giraldi
PRODUCER Joanne Michels
PRODUCTION CO. Giraldi Productions
AGENCY DKG
CLIENT Consolidated Cigar Corp.

BUREAU
30-second

ANNCR: This man has worked a long, hard day, and he's got a lot of money to show for it . . .

Other people's money.

He's a pickpocket.

His take . . . $700.

It's dangerous to carry cash. Carry American Express traveler's checks.

If they're lost or stolen, you can get them back.

Your vacation is protected.

American Express traveler's checks. Don't leave home without them.

286
ART DIRECTOR Mark Ross
WRITER Brendon Kelly
DIRECTOR Rick Levine
PRODUCER Lark C. Navez
PRODUCTION CO. Rick Levine Productions
AGENCY Ogilvy & Mather
CLIENT American Express

CAR BREAK-IN
30-second

HUSBAND: Hon, you know that fancy restaurant we drove by . . .

WIFE: Ahm.

HUSBAND: Let's go there tonight.

WIFE: Can we afford it?

HUSBAND: Can we afford it!

ANNCR: It's dangerous to carry cash. When you travel, carry American Express traveler's checks. Don't leave home without them.

287
ART DIRECTOR Mark Ross
WRITER Brendon Kelly
DIRECTOR Rick Levine
PRODUCER Lark C. Navez
PRODUCTION CO. Rick Levine Productions
AGENCY Ogilvy & Mather
CLIENT American Express

ENGLISH ROOM—HISTORY
30-second

MUSIC UNDER

ANNCR: The British have contributed more to men's fashion than any other nation in history.

The vest.

The Chesterfield.

The Blazer.

The Trenchcoat.

The Cardigan.

And today Barney's with America's most complete collection of British fashions is doing more than any other men's store to carry on this tradition.

Barney's English Room.

288
ART DIRECTOR Carl Stewart
WRITER Mike Lichtman
DIRECTORS Morty Gerstan
Steve Horn
PRODUCER Susan Scherl
PRODUCTION COS. Phil Kimmelman
Steve Horn
AGENCY Scali, McCabe, Sloves
CLIENT Barney's

TWIST ARMS
30-second

FRANK PERDUE: Everybody knows how tough it is to get kids to eat what's good for them.

But you don't have to twist their arms.

Just give them one of my legs. It's a perfect children's portion.

One Perdue drumstick and thigh has more protein value

than a hamburger, a hot dog, or some other things kids eat.

And kids love it.

Look. It's even got its own handle.

289
ART DIRECTOR Sam Scali
WRITER Ed McCabe
DIRECTOR Franta Herman
PRODUCERS Sam Scali
Ed McCabe
PRODUCTION CO. Televideo
AGENCY Scali, McCabe, Sloves
CLIENT Perdue Farms

FOREIGN CAR
30-second

ANNCR: Foreign cars are fun, but . . .

DRIVER: Hi. I need a new muffler.

OWNER #1: Where does it go? In the glove compartment?

DRIVER: Muffler?

OWNER #2: Four months. But you gotta leave the car.

THREE MEN: (Hysterical laughter)

SPOKESMAN: Foreign car mufflers aren't foreign to Midas. We now stock and install mufflers on most foreign cars the way we've been installing them on American cars for years.

DRIVER: I think I'll try Midas.

SUPER: *Midas. At Midas we're specialists. We have to do a better job.*

290
ART DIRECTOR Bob Kuperman
WRITER Pacy Markman
DIRECTOR Stan Dragoti
PRODUCER Bob Emerson
PRODUCTION CO. WRG/Dragoti
AGENCY Wells, Rich, Greene
CLIENT Midas International

LARGE EGG
30-second

ANNCR: One Dinner Bell wiener . . . has as much high-quality protein as one large egg.

But just try to give a kid an egg on a picnic. (Boy holds up hot dog roll with egg in it.)

Dinner Bell. We want you to know more about our wieners. To get our free booklet, write Dinner Bell. Defiance, Ohio.

SUPER: *We want you to know more about meat.*

291
ART DIRECTOR	Blaine Gutermuth
WRITER	Patricia Sierra
DIRECTOR	Mike Cowan
PRODUCER	Bob Long
PRODUCTION CO.	Johnson-Cowan
AGENCY	Howard Swink
CLIENT	Dinner Bell Foods

LEGROOM
30-second

ANNCR: Let's compare the legroom for passengers in the front seat of America's most luxurious cars.

Chrysler Imperial . . . 42.8 inches.

Lincoln Continental . . . 43.3 inches.

Cadillac Eldorado . . . 43.4 inches.

Fiat 128 . . . 43.8 inches. More than the Imperial, Continental, the Eldorado. Now that's luxury.

292
ART DIRECTOR	Amil Gargano
WRITER	David Altschiller
DIRECTOR	Michael Cuesta
PRODUCER	Maureen Kearns
PRODUCTION CO.	Griner/Cuesta
AGENCY	Carl Ally
CLIENT	Fiat Distributors

ARCHITECTURE
25-second

BUCKMINSTER FULLER: This is a Geodesic Dome. I invented them and been living in them for years.

I'm Buckminster Fuller. Architect. And advisor for the sections on design and engineering in Funk & Wagnalls new encyclopedia.

This latest edition is full of almost everything I've ever wanted to know about everything.

Yet it's low-priced because it's sold directly through super-markets, rather than salesmen who come knocking on your dome.

293
ART DIRECTOR Ray Alban
WRITER Steve Smith
DIRECTOR Steve Horn
PRODUCER Susan Scherl
PRODUCTION CO. Steve Horn
AGENCY Scali, McCabe, Sloves
CLIENT Funk & Wagnalls

FACTORY
30-second

ANNCR: Detroit, move over.

Make room for Mound, Minnesota, the trucking capital of the world.

Where scores of dedicated workers supply the nation's trucking needs

with incredibly rugged trucks that come in all kinds of models and go for all kinds of prices.

Which is why, year after year, more people buy Tonka trucks than any other truck in the world.

294
ART DIRECTOR Michael Tesch
WRITER Patrick Kelly
DIRECTOR Steve Horn
PRODUCER Vera Samama
PRODUCTION CO. Steve Horn
AGENCY Carl Ally
CLIENT Tonka Corp.

GENERIC—TEST DRIVE
30-second

ANNCR: If you could have test-driven your car with the mileage it has on it now, would you have bought it?

No?

That's why Volvo invented The Test Drive For People Who Think.

You take out a new Volvo . . . and one with at least 30,000 miles on it.

You'll see how well Volvos hold up from one that's already held up.

So look for the Volvo dealer who displays this sign.

Today when you buy a new car . . . you should know how good it can be as an old one.

295
ART DIRECTOR   Bob Reitzfeld
WRITERS   Ed McCabe
Tom Nathan
DIRECTOR   Barry Brown
PRODUCER   Tanya English
PRODUCTION CO.   Brillig Productions
AGENCY   Scali, McCabe, Sloves
CLIENT   Volvo

CLOCKS
30-second

ANNCR: Every weekday at five o'clock . . . all over California . . . something very special happens.

SFX: (Bell tower chimes five)

ANNCR: Long distance telephone rates go down.

By as much as one-third.

SUPER: *Talk is cheaper after five.*

TALK IS CHEAPER AFTER 5

(🔔) Pacific Telephone

Does not apply to calls
outside continental U.S., intra-state calls
40 miles & under, and operator-assisted calls.

296
WRITERS Ron Armstrong
Scott Deal
DIRECTOR Jack Cole
PRODUCER Ron Armstrong
PRODUCTION CO. N. Lee Lacy
AGENCY BBDO
CLIENT Pacific Telephone

TORTURE
30-second

ANNCR: After Homelite developed a chain saw for $109.95,

we tried to ruin it. By doing things you shouldn't do.

Because as America's largest maker of professional chain saws,

Homelite has a reputation to protect.

And we're not about to let a saw out that can't stand up.

So while the Homelite XL may be inexpensive . . .

it's not cheap.

Homelite. For the pro and the man who wants to cut like one.

And now the $109.95 Homelite is just $99.99.

297
ART DIRECTOR Paul Gulinar
WRITER Steve Smith
DIRECTOR Dave Quad
PRODUCTION CO. Dave Quad
AGENCY Scali, McCabe, Sloves
CLIENT Homelite

MR. JOHNSON
30-second

MECHANIC: You gotta trust me, Mr. Johnson. This muffler fits three hundred different cars. True, it's smaller than your muffler . . . But add an adapter here . . . Add a thingamabob over here . . . Add a washer . . . It's a beauty, huh?

ANNCR: Your car came with a specific muffler to help it run efficiently. That's why we at Midas stock 539 different mufflers. We have the right muffler for your car.

MR. JOHNSON: I think I'll go to Midas.

MECHANIC: They don't do work like this! Midas.

SUPER: *Midas. At Midas, we're specialists. We have to do a better job.*

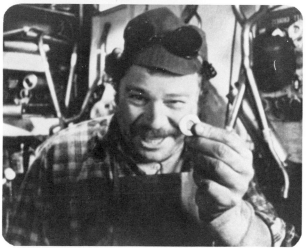

298
ART DIRECTOR Bob Kuperman
WRITER Pacy Markman
DIRECTOR Stan Dragoti
PRODUCER Bob Emerson
PRODUCTION CO. WRG/Dragoti
AGENCY Wells, Rich, Greene
CLIENT Midas

245 REVOLUTIONARY CARS
30-second

ANNCR: A lot of "revolutionary" new cars have been introduced this year.

But nothing like this.

This car has three windshield wipers. Five doors. Three breaking systems.

Front seats designed by an orthopedic specialist.

It's the same size as a Volvo . . . yet it holds five times as much.

The Volvo Wagon.

The only wagon as carefully thought out as a Volvo.

Volvo. The wagon for people who think.

299
ART DIRECTOR Earl Cavanah
WRITER Larry Cadman
DIRECTOR Barry Brown
PRODUCER Tanya English
PRODUCTION CO. Brillig Productions
AGENCY Scali, McCabe, Sloves
CLIENT Volvo

GUZZLE
30-second

MUSIC UNDER

ANNCR: This is Hi-C Fruit Drink. It contains 10% real fruit juices. And kids love to drink it.

This Hawaiian Punch. It contains 11% real fruit juices. And kids love it.

This is Seneca Frozen Apple Juice. It contains 100% real apple juice. And kids love it.

Which one would you rather have your kid guzzle down?

Seneca Frozen Apple Juice.

The kids' drink you'll both love.

300
ART DIRECTOR Bob Needleman
WRITER Mike Drazen
DIRECTOR Steve Horn
PRODUCER Susan Scherl
PRODUCTION CO. Steve Horn
AGENCY Scali, McCabe, Sloves
CLIENT Seneca Marketing Co.

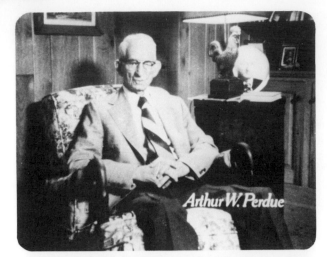

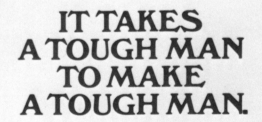

A.W. PERDUE
30-second

A.W. PERDUE: When you eat a Perdue Chicken, you have no idea how much work has gone into it.

My son, Frank, eats, sleeps and breathes chicken.

He works inhuman hours . . . Fifteen, sixteen hours a day . . . to bring you the quality you've come to expect from Perdue.

You might wonder what drives a man like this.

I'll tell you . . .

Me!

	301
ART DIRECTOR	Sam Scali
WRITER	Ed McCabe
DIRECTOR	Franta Herman
PRODUCERS	Sam Scali
	Ed McCabe
PRODUCTION CO.	Televideo
AGENCY	Scali, McCabe, Sloves
CLIENT	Perdue Farms

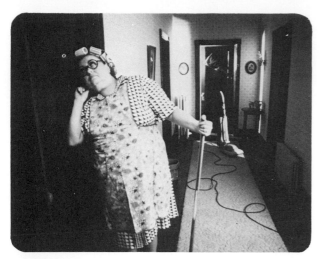

ALEXANDER
30-second

MOTHER: (Knocking on bathroom door) What are you doing in there, Alexander?

ALEXANDER: (Reply unintelligible—muffled by sound of shower)

MOTHER: My Alexander is 13. . . and I never used to be able to get him into a shower. But now . . . since we got the Shower Massage . . . I can't get him out of it.

ANNCR: The Shower Massage by Water Pik is good clean fun. Gives you a massage with every shower.

It'll get your kids into the shower . . . but you'll have to get them out.

There's only one Shower Massage . . . by Water Pik.

MOTHER: Alexander?

THE SHOWER MASSAGE
by Water Pik®

302
ART DIRECTOR John Trusk
WRITER Nancy Foster
DIRECTOR Joe Sedelmaier
PRODUCERS Ed Manser
Bob Gardner
John Trusk
PRODUCTION CO. Sedelmaier Film
Productions
AGENCY J. Walter Thompson
CLIENT Teledyne Water Pik

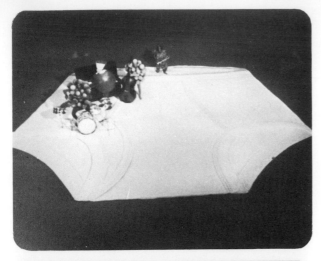

SINGING LOGO
30-second

APPLE: Hit it!!! For Fruit of the Loom. (Music)

APPLE: It's hard to be brief when it comes to our briefs.

ALL: So much value for what you pay.

LEAF: I'll say! They've got waistbands that keep their fit.

GRAPE #2: Strong elastic and soft knit.
A great buy in every way!

ALL: So if you're shoppin' for savings
We're the guys for you.
Get Fruit of the Loom briefs.
And get our Tee-shirts, too.

ANNCR: Our men's cotton briefs. Still under a dollar.

APPLE: Why'd you have to open your mouth?
You're not even in that part!

SUPER: *Our men's briefs still under a dollar.*

303
ART DIRECTOR Bill Gangi
WRITER Alan Barcus
DIRECTOR Dominick Rossetti
PRODUCER Ira Lassman
PRODUCTION CO. Rossetti Films
AGENCY Grey Advertising
CLIENT Union Underwear

LICK LIPS
30-second

MUSIC UNDER

ANNCR: If you have to lick your lips to keep them moist,

maybe your lipstick is dry.

Now discover the lipstick that never dries your lips.

'Moon Drops' Lipstick

With the special moisturizing formula in 77 beautiful shades.

With 'Moon Drops' you can purse your lips,

bite your lips,

pucker your lips,

even lick your lips. But it won't be because they're dry.

'Moon Drops' Moisturizing Lipstick.

By Revlon. Beautiful.

304
ART DIRECTOR Tom Wolsey
WRITER Ed McCabe
DIRECTOR Harold Becker
PRODUCTION CO. N. Lee Lacy
AGENCY Scali, McCabe, Sloves
CLIENT Revlon

164 CADILLACS
30-second

ANNCR: Visit a Volvo dealer these days and you might find something surprising . . . Cadillacs.

This year Cadillac is one of the cars most traded in . . .

for the luxurious Volvo 164.

Which we find . . . very gratifying.

After all, it's one thing for us to say the Volvo 164 is the most intelligently designed luxury car in the world.

But what's really nice is that a lot of Cadillac owners aren't disagreeing with us.

305
ART DIRECTOR	Earl Cavanah
WRITER	Larry Cadman
DESIGNER	Earl Cavanah
DIRECTOR	Rick Levine
PRODUCER	Tanya English
PRODUCTION CO.	Rick Levine
AGENCY	Scali, McCabe, Sloves
CLIENT	Volvo

PERFORMING
30-second

MUSIC UNDER
ANNCR: The Volvo 242.
The BMW 2002.
The Audi 100LS.
The new Fiat 131.
In handling, the Fiat is the equal of all of them.
In acceleration . . . the Fiat is faster than all of them.
But what's incredible,
. . . is that Fiat does all this about $2000 cheaper than all of them.

306
ART DIRECTOR Amil Gargano
WRITER David Altschiller
DIRECTOR Neil Tardio
PRODUCER Maureen Kearns
PRODUCTION CO. Lovinger, Tardio, Melsky
AGENCY Carl Ally
CLIENT Fiat Distributors

GOLD

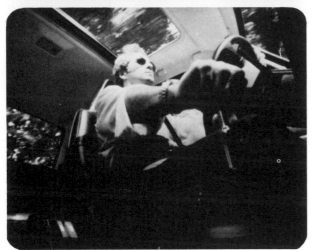

THE VOLVO 264

JEKYLL & HYDE
30-second

ANNCR: Send two men out with $10,000 and they won't come back with the same car.

While one seeks creature comforts like real leather . . . power windows and air conditioning,

another looks for rack-and-pinion steering and an overhead cam V 6.

The Volvo 264.

With what you pay for a fine car these days . . .

Volvo thinks you should get one that's two.

307
ART DIRECTOR John Danza
WRITER Tom Nathan
DIRECTOR Steve Horn
PRODUCER Tanya English
PRODUCTION CO. Steve Horn
AGENCY Scali, McCabe, Sloves
CLIENT Volvo

SIGNATURES
30-second

SUPER: *Pierre Cardin*
Yves St. Laurent
Carlo Palazzi

Bruno Piatelli
Bill Blass
Rafael

MUSIC UNDER:

ANNCR: Only a store that offers *all* of the most respected names in men's fashion,

SUPER: *R. Meledandri*
Phillipe Venet
Cacharel
Givenchy

ANNCR: Can allow you to assemble a wardrobe that truly has *your* signature on it . . .

SUPER: *Eugene Gooch*

ANNCR: Barney's International House. We're big enough to treat you as an individual.

308
ART DIRECTOR Sam Scali
WRITERS Ed McCabe
Mike Lichtman
DIRECTORS Morty Gerstan
Steve Horn
PRODUCER Susan Scherl
PRODUCTION CO. Phil Kimmelman
AGENCY Scali, McCabe, Sloves
CLIENT Barney's

Ruth Buzzi

Jimmy Connors

**The Dry Soft Drink
That's Not-Too-Sweet On You.**

**NOT TOO SWEET
IRELAND/BUZZI/CONNERS**
30-second

SUPER: *Presenting some not-too-sweet folks for the not-too-sweet soft drink*

JOHN IRELAND: It's not too sweet
It's dry, it's crisp, it's neat
Canada Dry Ginger Ale
It's not too sweet

RUTH BUZZI: It's not too sweet
I repeat it's not too sweet
Canada Dry cools your thirst
It's a taste that can't be beat

JIMMY CONNORS: It's not too sweet
It's a light, refreshing treat
Canada Dry Ginger Ale
It's not too sweet

ANNCR: It's the dry soft drink
that's not too sweet on you

SUPER: *The dry soft drink that's not too sweet on you*

309
ART DIRECTOR Bob Schlesinger
WRITERS Jeff Wolff
Bob Schlesinger
DESIGNER Bob Schlesinger
DIRECTOR Jeff Lovinger
PRODUCER Vinnie Infantino
PRODUCTION CO. Lovinger, Tardio, Melsky
AGENCY Grey Advertising
CLIENT Canada Dry

GIVE THE MAN A CHANCE
30-second

UDELL: Good evening, this is Paul Udell with the Channel 13 news.

(Man takes remote control and changes channel to old-time cowboy film)

SHE: Hey, that was the new anchorman, Fred.

(Woman takes her remote control and switches channel back to Udell)

SHE: Give the man a chance.

(He switches it away again)

SHE: Some chance!

(She switches it back again)

SHE: The man was an investigative reporter . . . a war correspondent.

(He switches it away)

(She switches it back)

SHE: He was anchorman in New York and Chicago.

(A short flurry where they switch back and forth so fast the channel hardly changes)

(She aims her control at his head like a gun)

SHE: Drop it, Fred.

ANNCR: There has never been an anchorman like Paul Udell in Indianapolis. Give the man a chance.

SUPER: *Paul Udell, Eyewitness News, 6 & 11 p.m.*

310
ART DIRECTOR Barry Vetere
WRITER Jeff Gorman
DIRECTOR Joe Sedelmaier
PRODUCER Janet Collins
PRODUCTION CO. Sedelmaier Film Production
AGENCY Zechman Lyke Vetere
CLIENT WTHR-TV

THE SHOWER MASSAGE
by Water Pik®

DEL CORONADO
30-second

ANNCR: Here at the Del Coronado Hotel, we got peoples' reactions to the Shower Massage by Water Pik . . .

LAURENNE SUE DELANNOY: Ha, ha, ha, hey this is too much!

PAUL DAVEY: . . . You have your own masseuse here!

ANNCR: the Shower Massage goes all the way from a regular shower to a brisk massage.

KATHY ROUNDS: . . . That would be so good after tennis!

LILLIAN SHOOK: Nice birthday present . . . Christmas present.

MARIE HARLEY/KATHLEEN HARLEY: Giggle, giggle, giggle . . .

VIRGINIA MULLER: How you doing?

ERNEST MULLER: Oh, this is terrific!!

ANNCR: There's only one Shower Massage by Water Pik.

311
ART DIRECTOR John Trusk
WRITER Robert Gardner
DIRECTOR Dick Snider
PRODUCERS Ed Manser
Robert Gardner
John Trusk
PRODUCTION CO. N. Lee Lacy
AGENCY J. Walter Thompson
CLIENT Teledyne Water Pik

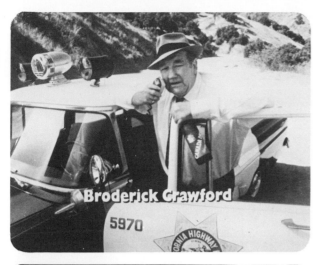

Broderick Crawford
5970

Isaac Hayes

The Dry Soft Drink
That's Not-Too-Sweet On You.

NOT TOO SWEET
ELAM/CRAWFORD/HAYES
30-second

SUPER: *Presenting some not-too-sweet folks for the not-too-sweet soft drink*

JACK ELAM: It's not too sweet
It's dry, it's crisp, it's neat
Canada Dry Ginger Ale
It's not too sweet

BRODERICK CRAWFORD: It's not too sweet
I repeat, it's not too sweet
Canada Dry cools your thirst
It's a taste that can't be beat

ISAAC HAYES: It's not too sweet
It's a light, refreshing treat
Canada Dry Ginger Ale
It's not too sweet

ANNCR: It's the dry soft drink
That's not too sweet on you

SUPER: *The dry soft drink that's not too sweet on you*

312
ART DIRECTOR Bob Schlesinger
WRITERS Jeff Wolff
Bob Schlesinger
DESIGNER Bob Schlesinger
DIRECTOR Jeff Lovinger
PRODUCER Vinnie Infantino
PRODUCTION CO. Lovinger, Tardio, Melsky
AGENCY Grey Advertising
CLIENT Canada Dry

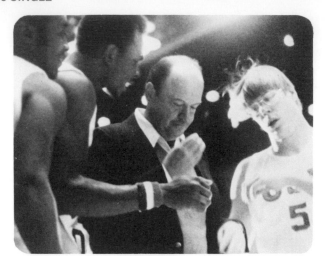

OLYMPIC TENSION
30-second

ANNCR: The tension of the Olympic Games. You can't know it unless you've been there.

And Converse All Stars have been there.

In Berlin. London. Helsinki. Melbourne. Rome. Tokyo. Mexico City. Munich.

Since basketball became an Olympic sport, Converse All Stars have been there.

And again this year in Montreal, Converse All Stars have been selected for use by the U.S. team.

Converse All Stars. The American basketball shoe.

313
ART DIRECTOR Ralph Moxcey
WRITER Derald Breneman
DESIGNER Ralph Moxcey
DIRECTOR Joseph Hainwright
PRODUCER Paul St. Germaine
PRODUCTION CO. Wakeford/Orloff
AGENCY Humphrey Browning MacDougall
CLIENT Converse Rubber Co.

MOTHER AND BABY
30-second
___

ANNCR: If you don't always take the time to eat right, Dannon yogurt is the right thing to eat.

Check the label. Dannon supplies many of the nutrients your body needs.

And since nobody knows yogurt like Dannon, nobody can make a yogurt quite like Dannon.

Dannon all natural yogurt.

If you don't always eat right, it's the right thing to eat.

314
ART DIRECTOR Joseph Goldberg
WRITER Peter Lubalin
DIRECTOR Bob Giraldi
PRODUCER Arlene Hoffman
PRODUCTION CO. Bob Giraldi Productions
AGENCY Marsteller
CLIENT Dannon Milk Products

Poolside - Del Coronado Hotel

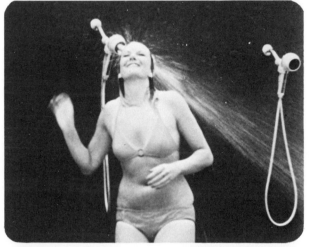

THE SHOWER MASSAGE
by Water Pik®

FREEZE FRAME
30-second

ANNCR: How do people react to the Shower Massage by Water Pik?

MR. & MRS. ACTON: Ha, ha, ha, ha, ha, ha . . .

MR. & MRS. B. HEPP: Ha! Feels like a vibrator!

RANDY LITTLETON: Ah . . . Wow!

LAURENNE SUE DELANNOY: Far out!

ROSE INNISS: It's ooh-la-la!!

BETTY GALLAGHER: I feel ten years younger!

TOSCA COMUCILIUS: . . . Kind of vibrating my muscles like a massage!

PAUL DAVY: This is invigorating!!

ERNEST & VIRGINIA MULLER: Boy, it's exhilarating!!

BEA BURRES: If the inventor is single, I would like to meet him!

ANNCR: There's only one Shower Massage and it's made by Water Pik.

JIM HARRIS: Can I stay in here a little longer? Ha, ha!!!

315
ART DIRECTOR John Trusk
WRITER Robert Gardner
DIRECTOR Dick Snider
PRODUCERS Ed Manser
Robert Gardner
John Trusk
PRODUCTION CO. N. Lee Lacy
AGENCY J. Walter Thompson
CLIENT Teledyne Water Pik

WHAT'S THAT
30-second

MUSIC UNDER

AUNT: Mr. Whitney, this is my niece, Sybil.

MR. WHITNEY: Hello!

SYBIL: How do you do!

MR. WHITNEY: (At opera) Won't you tell me what you have on?

MR. WHITNEY: (At posh night club) You aren't going to tell me what you have on, are you?

MR. WHITNEY: (In front of hotel room) Why won't you tell me what you have on?

SYBIL: (With a passionate kiss) Tweed! (Closes door)

ANNCR: Tweed succeeds. The classic fragrance.

SUPER: *Tweed Lentheric*

316
ART DIRECTOR	Bob Wall
WRITER	Rudy Fiala
DIRECTOR	Bill Helburn
PRODUCER	Bob Wall
PRODUCTION CO.	Chance Three
AGENCY	Lois Holland Callaway
CLIENT	Yardley of London

Larry Csonka

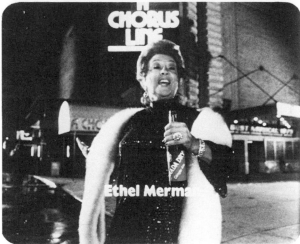

Ethel Merman

NOT TOO SWEET
GORDON/CSONKA/MERMAN
30-second

SUPER: *Some not-too-sweet folks for the not-too-sweet soft drink.*

BRUCE GORDON: It's not too sweet
It's dry, it's crisp, it's neat
Canada Dry Ginger Ale
It's not too sweet

LARRY CSONKA: Its not too sweet,
I repeat, it's not too sweet
Canada Dry cools your thirst
It's the taste that can't be beat.

ETHEL MERMAN: It's not too sweet
It's a light refreshing treat
Canada Dry Ginger Ale
It's not too sweet

ANNCR: It's the dry soft drink
That's not too sweet on you.

SUPER: *The dry soft drink that's not too sweet on you.*

**The Dry Soft Drink
That's Not-Too-Sweet On You.**

317
ART DIRECTOR Bob Schlesinger
WRITERS Jeff Wolff
Bob Schlesinger
DESIGNER Bob Schlesinger
DIRECTOR Jeff Lovinger
PRODUCER Vinnie Infantino
PRODUCTION CO. Lovinger, Tardio, Melsky
AGENCY Grey Advertising
CLIENT Canada Dry

FOOD
30-second

ANNCR: After spare ribs . . .

after veal parmigiana . . .

after potato pancakes . . .

glazed ham . . .

fried chicken . . .

there's nothing Americans like better . . .

than an S.O.S. soap pad.

Nothing makes cleaning easier . . . and cuts grease better.

That's why more people use S.O.S. than any other soap pad.

S.O.S. There's nothing better after a meal.

318
ART DIRECTOR Roy Grace
WRITER Diane Rothchild
DESIGNER Roy Grace
DIRECTOR Toni Ficalora
PRODUCER Jim deBarros
PRODUCTION CO. Toni Ficalora
AGENCY Doyle Dane Bernbach
CLIENT Miles Laboratories

THREADS
30-second

ANNCR: In 1850, Levi Strauss made the toughest pants the world has ever known . . . Levi's Blue Jeans.

SONG: (We put a little blue jean in everything we make)

ANNCR: Today, we're threading the spirit of those blue jeans through enough new fabrics, colors, and styles to last you a lifetime.

SONG: (We put a little blue jean in everything we make)

ANNCR: So if you want quality and comfort too, just remember that Levi's don't end with blue.

SONG: (We put a little blue jean in everything we make)

319

ART DIRECTOR	Chris Blum
WRITER	Mike Koelker
DESIGNER	Bob Peluce
ARTIST	Bob Peluce
PHOTOGRAPHERS	Bill Quinville
	John Dekderian
DIRECTOR	Bob Kurtz
PRODUCER	Bob Kurtz
PRODUCTION CO.	Kurtz & Friends
AGENCY	Honig-Cooper & Harrington
CLIENT	Levi Strauss

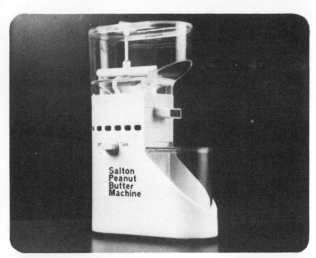

ADULT PEANUT BUTTER
30-second

ANNCR: Salton introduces an adult method of enjoying peanut butter.

The Salton Peanut Butter Machine.

Simply add peanuts, turn it on and it dispenses pure peanut butter that's actually warm and tastes infinitely better.

Nutritious for the offspring, but with a taste a sophisticated adult can appreciate.

320

ART DIRECTOR	Ron Brello
WRITER	Hy Abady
DESIGNER	Ron Brello
DIRECTOR	Henry Sandbank
PRODUCERS	Hy Abady
	Ron Brello
PRODUCTION CO.	Henry Sandbank Productions
AGENCY	Sacks and Rosen
CLIENT	Salton

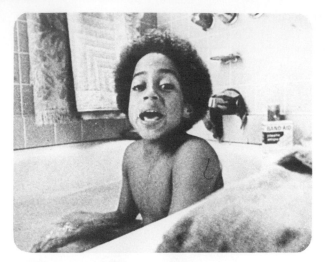

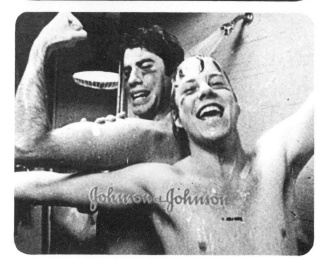

BENDED KNEE
30-second

BLACK KID: (Singing) I am stuck on BAND-AID Brand, 'cause BAND-AID stuck on me . . .

POLICE WOMAN: (Singing) I am stuck on BAND-AID 'cause BAND-AID stuck on me . . .

TEEN-GIRL: (Singing) 'Cause they really stick to your fingers, and they stick on bended knees . . .

ANNCR: Depend on the protection of America's number one bandage with the unique super stick adhesive.

Remember only JOHNSON & JOHNSON makes BAND-AID Brand Adhesive Bandages.

TEENAGE BOYS: (Singing) I am stuck on BAND-AID, 'cause BAND-AID stuck on me.

SUPER: *JOHNSON & JOHNSON*

321
ART DIRECTOR   Harry Webber
WRITER   Mike Becker
DIRECTOR   Bob Giraldi
PRODUCER   Phyllis Landi
PRODUCTION CO.   Bob Giraldi Films
AGENCY   Young & Rubicam
CLIENT   Johnson & Johnson

LA GRANDE BUG
30-second

ANNCR: Zsa Zsa talks about a new luxury car.

ZSA ZSA: Darling I love the seats—with corduroy . . . and I love the sexy carpeting . . .

. . . and the sunroof . . .

. . . and the metallic paint—I love it.

And mother loves getting 33 miles per gallon on the highway.

MAGDA: She's right. With daughters like mine, you learn the value of a dollar.

ANNCR: Presenting . . . La Grande Bug. A new limited edition of Volkswagen.

322

ART DIRECTOR	Charles Piccirillo
WRITER	Mike Mangano
DIRECTOR	Neil Tardio
PRODUCER	Rosemary Barre
PRODUCTION CO.	Lovinger, Tardio, Melsky
AGENCY	Doyle Dane Bernbach
CLIENT	Volkswagen

 SILVER

SPLIT WALL
30-second

MOOSE: I Moose.

LAURA: And I'm Laura in a La-Z-Boy Wall Recliner one inch from the wall. Ready to compare? Recline.

MOOSE: Moose chair no recline.

LAURA: La-Z-Boy reclines to any position, and the footrest operates only when you want it to.

MOOSE: No find footrest.

SFX: (Crash)

MOOSE: Next time Moose demonstrate La-Z-Boy.

LAURA: Comfortable, Moose?

MOOSE: Mmmmm.

LAURA: Do you play bridge?

MOOSE: Moose eat bridge.

323
ART DIRECTOR Richard B. Luden
WRITER Stig Wegge
DIRECTOR Sy Weissman
PRODUCER Evonne Kosover
PRODUCTION CO. Director's Circle
AGENCY Sweet & Company
CLIENT La-Z-Boy Chairs

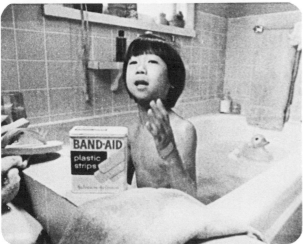

SOAPY SUDS
30-second

COUNTRY GIRL: (Singing) I am stuck on BAND-AID brand 'cause BAND-AID stuck on me . . .

ORIENTAL BOY: (Singing) 'cause they hold on tight in the bathutb, and they cling in soapy suds . . .

ANNCR: Remember, only JOHNSON & JOHNSON makes BAND-AID brand adhesive bandages.

SCOUT LEADER: (Singing) I am stuck on BAND-AID, 'cause BAND-AID stuck on me . . .

ANNCR: Depend on the protection of America's number one bandage with the unique super-adhesive.

SECOND BOY: (Singing) I am stuck on BAND-AID, 'cause BAND-AID stuck on me.

SUPER: *JOHNSON & JOHNSON*

324
ART DIRECTOR Harry Webber
WRITER Mike Becker
DIRECTOR Bob Giraldi
PRODUCER Phyllis Landi
PRODUCTION CO. Bob Giraldi
AGENCY Young & Rubicam
CLIENT Johnson & Johnson

FIBERGLASS SHELL OF PACER WITHOUT INTERNAL PARTS.

SHELL
30-second

ANNCR: Introducing the AMC Pacer . . . the first wide small car.

The pacer's so wide, and has so much room,

you can fit a Pinto, or a Comet, or a Maverick, or even a car as big as this Nova inside it.

And the Pacer's wide stance and isolated suspension system

give it an incredibly stable ride.

The AMC Pacer.

The first wide small car. Backed by the AMC buyer protection plan.

SUPER: *AMC Pacer. The first wide small car.*

325	
ART DIRECTOR	Gerald Sneed
WRITER	Michael Kahn
DIRECTOR	Dick Stone
PRODUCER	Dick Wotring
PRODUCTION CO.	Dick Stone Productions
AGENCY	Cunningham & Walsh
CLIENT	American Motors

IF YOU CAN'T FIND THE GLASSES
30-second

RESTAURANT LADY: At Meyrowitz you can find these simple unostentatious glasses for people who are excessively secure about themselves. They sold two pair last year.

FERRARI MAN: Exquisite racing glasses . . . not for the car . . . for the ladies.

SECRETARY: The only thing Christian Dior ever made to wear in the file room.

ARCHITECT: And this year's choice for the Hamptons—East, South, Bridge and Lionel.

ANNCR: If you can't find the glasses you want at Meyrowitz, you should have your eyes checked.

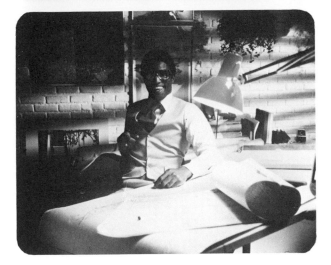

326
ART DIRECTORS Frank Attardi
Bruno Brugnatelli
WRITERS Frank Attardi
Marvin Watnick
DESIGNERS Frank Attardi
Bruno Brugnatelli
DIRECTOR Jeff Lovinger
PRODUCERS Bruno Brugnatelli
Frank Attardi
PRODUCTION CO. Lovinger, Tardio, Melsky
AGENCY The Creative Workshop
CLIENT E.B. Meyrowitz

HYPERTENSION
30-second

ANNCR: One of these men has high blood pressure. One in six American adults does.

It strikes the young, the old, black, white—physically fit, not so fit.

There are no symptoms. Yet high blood pressure can cause stroke, heart attack, kidney disease—a shortened life.

The man on the left has high blood pressure—

And he'd be the last to suspect it.

How about you? It only takes your doctor 30 seconds to find out.

SUPER: *A message in the public interest from Blue Cross and Blue Shield.*

327
ART DIRECTOR David Meador
WRITER Susan Procter
DIRECTOR Murray Bruce
PRODUCER Robert LaChance
PRODUCTION CO. Ampersand Productions
AGENCY J. Walter Thompson
CLIENT Blue Cross & Blue Shield

Jimmy Breslin, writer

JIMMY BRESLIN
30-second

BRESLIN: This is the new Olivetti Lexikon 82, the only electric portable in the world

that actually gives you a choice of different type styles.

Why different type styles? Why not!

It's also got a quick-change ribbon cartridge.

You can change to a fresh ribbon or a different color in a flash.

It costs less than $300, and it's available at your Olivetti dealer.

The Lexikon 82 by Olivetti. It'll bring out the writer in you.

SFX: Dear Norman: I am . . .

328
ART DIRECTOR Kurt Weihs
WRITER Wally Weis
DIRECTOR Kurt Weihs
PRODUCER Famous Commercials
PRODUCTION CO. Famous Commercials
AGENCY Lois Holland Callaway
CLIENT Olivetti Corp. of America

MAILBOX
30-second

ANNCR: Tonight, you can visit anyone you love.
By long distance.
And the cost is so very little,
when you dial direct without
operator assistance.
SFX: (Touchtone dialing)
ANNCR: Who's waiting for you to call tonight?
SUPER: *Direct dial and save*

329
ART DIRECTOR Dan Snope
WRITER Hal Newsom
DIRECTOR N. Lee Lacey
PRODUCER N. Lee Lacey
PRODUCTION CO. N. Lee Lacey
AGENCY Cole & Weber
CLIENT Pacific Northwest Bell
Telephone

SISTERS
30-second

WOMAN: Last year, my sister and her husband were killed in an accident.

Naturally, their four kids moved in with us, even though we didn't have the room or the money.

I suppose they should have had life insurance. But then, I guess I was their insurance.

MUSIC UNDER

ANNCR: Someone else may be able to provide your children with love. But you should provide the money.

Call us. We'll help plan for your life insurance needs.

Mutual of New York. MONY. For the Future.

SUPER: *MONY. Money for the future.*

330
ART DIRECTOR Andrew Langer
WRITER Marshall Karp
PRODUCER Diane Jeremias
PRODUCTION CO. Steve Horn
AGENCY The Marschalk Co.
CLIENT Mutual of New York

GENERAL WEEKEND #2
30-second

MUSIC UNDER

CHORUS: Let's take some more.
Let's find the stuff
they make happiness of . . .
and then we'll pass
around the pictures . . .
and share each other's love.

SPOKESWOMAN: Why not see pictures of the fun,
while the fun's still going on.
This weekend, shoot a pack of
Polaroid's new super color film.

CHORUS: Let's take some more.

331
ART DIRECTOR Robert Gage
WRITERS Jack Dillon
  Phyllis Robinson
DESIGNER Robert Gage
DIRECTOR Robert Gage
PRODUCER Cliff Fagin
PRODUCTION CO. Director's Studio
AGENCY Doyle Dane Bernbach
CLIENT Polaroid

KEVIN DELANEY
30-second

ANNCR: Announcing the 1976 Delaney.

Everything you've always wanted in a fine auto dealer.

The elegance and style of the wide-track Pontiac.

Or the economical, yet still tasty, Toyota.

Whichever; test drive all two 1976 Delaneys at Kevin Delaney Pontiac Toyota in Dorchester.

You'll find a good deal—more than you'd hoped for.

Get your hands on a Delaney—you'll never let go.

Kevin Delaney Pontiac Toyota.

GIRL: Does he come in green?

SUPER: *Delaney Pontiac Toyota*

332

ART DIRECTORS	Dick Pantano
	Tony Viola
WRITER	Seumas McGuire
DESIGNER	Paul Collins
DIRECTOR	John Purdy
PRODUCER	Beverly Monchun
PRODUCTION CO.	Videocom
AGENCY	Hill, Holliday, Connors,
	Cosmopulos
CLIENT	Kevin Delaney Pontiac

BUCK'S COUNTY
30-second

ANNCR: Recently, these regulars at a well-known Inn out in Buck's County. . .

decided to compare

Schmidt's—our Easy Beer—against famous Coors, the legendary beer from the West.

And may the best beer win.

BARTENDER: OK, fellows, which one did you like the best?

That's 7 Coors
. . .9 Schmidt's.

How about you, Leo, can't you make up your mind?

LEO: I'm thinkin'. . .I'm thinkin'. . .

ANNCR: Schmidt's does it again. You compare Schmidt's and Coors. We'll take our chances.

YOU CAN ALWAYS TELL A COORS
30-second

PROFESSOR
30-second

333
ART DIRECTORS Stan Block
Len Sirowitz
WRITER Ron Rosenfeld
DIRECTORS Gary Hall
Joe Devoto
PRODUCERS Magi Durham
Rob Ewing
PRODUCTION COS. Goodhue/Hall
Z Productions
AGENCY Rosenfeld, Sirowitz & Lawson
CLIENT C. Schmidt & Sons

FLICK YOUR BIC
30-second

FIRST MAN: (looking at two girls nearby) Hey, get a load of those two!!

SECOND MAN: I'll break the ice with a flick of my Bic.

MAN: (in back seat of Rolls Royce) When I want to call my chic. . .all I do is flick my Bic.

PARROT: (in elderly lady's pet shop) She's flicking her Bic. . .She's flicking her Bic. . .

BUTLER: (in men's club) Flick of the Bic, Sir? Oh . . .Flick of the Bic. . .?

ANNCR: Why just light up when you can flick your Bic. It's smooth, easy on the thumb. . .And you get thousands of flicks from a single Bic. The Bic Butane

LADY: (to man behind her in movie theatre) Shhh! Stop flicking your Bic.

334
ART DIRECTOR Maurice Mahler
WRITER Adam Hanft
DIRECTOR Steve Horn
PRODUCER Dan Kohn
PRODUCTION CO. Steve Horn
AGENCY Wells, Rich, Greene
CLIENT Bic Pens

CAR BREAK-IN/MALDEN
30-second

HUSBAND: Hon, you know that fancy restaurant we drove by. . .

WIFE: Ahm.

HUSBAND: Let's go there tonight.

WIFE: Can we afford it?

HUSBAND: Sure we can!

ANNCR: It's dangerous to carry cash. Carry American Express traveler's checks. Now, there are other traveler's checks, but they're not the same. If you lose these, not only can you get them replaced, you can even get an emergency refund on holidays. American Express traveler's checks. Don't leave home without them.

RACOON
30-second

BUREAU
30-second

335
ART DIRECTOR Mark Ross
WRITER Brendon Kelly
DIRECTOR Rick Levine
PRODUCER Lark C. Navez
PRODUCTION CO. Rick Levine Productions
AGENCY Ogilvy & Mather
CLIENT American Express

Broderick Crawford

5970

Isaac Hayes

NOT TOO SWEET
ELAM/CRAWFORD/HAYES
30-second

SUPER: *Some not-too-sweet folks*
for the not-too-sweet
soft drink.

JACK ELAM: It's not too sweet
It's dry, it's crisp, it's neat
Canada Dry Ginger Ale
It's not too sweet

BRODERICK CRAWFORD: It's not too sweet
I repeat it's not too sweet
Canada Dry cools your thirst
It's a taste that can't be beat

ISAAC HAYES: It's not too sweet
It's a light refreshing treat
Canada Dry Ginger Ale
It's not too sweet

ANNCR: It's the dry soft drink
That's not too sweet on you.

SUPER: *The dry soft drink*
that's not too sweet on you

GORDON/CZONKA/MERMAN
30-second

IRELAND/BUZZI/CONNORS
30-second

The Dry Soft Drink
That's Not-Too-Sweet On You.

336
ART DIRECTOR Bob Schlesinger
WRITERS Jeff Wolff
Bob Schlesinger
DESIGNER Bob Schlesinger
DIRECTOR Jeff Lovinger
PRODUCER Vinnie Infantino
PRODUCTION CO. Lovinger, Tardio, Melsky
AGENCY Grey Advertising
CLIENT Canada Dry

SHOWROOM
30-second

ANNCR: Last year was a rotten year for cars. Volkswagen sales were down.

Vega down.

Pinto down.

Toyota down.

Gremlin down.

Datsun down.

Capri, Opel, Mazda. . .down.

Of these leading small cars, last year. . .only one was up. Fiat. It was our best year ever.

LIVE WITH IT
30-second

337

ART DIRECTOR	Amil Gargano	**PRODUCERS**	Janine Marjollet
WRITER	David Altschiller		Vera Samama
DIRECTORS	Steve Horn		Maureen Kearns
	Steve Horn	**PRODUCTION COS**	Steve Horn Griner/Cuesta
	Michael Cuesta		Lovinger, Tardio, Melsky
	Neil Tardio	**AGENCY**	Carl Ally
		CLIENT	Fiat Distributors

GOLD

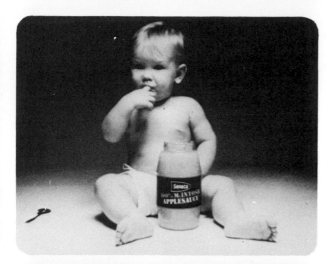

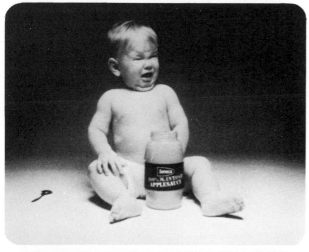

WAAAHHH APPLEBARREL
30-second

ANNCR: It's flavorful.

It's interesting.

It's full-bodied. It's crisp.

It's tangy.

It's rich.

It's. . .it's sophisticated.

Seneca Applesauce. It doesn't taste like baby food. (music)

338
ART DIRECTORS Sam Scali
Bob Needleman
WRITERS Ed McCabe
Mike Drazen
DESIGNERS Sam Scali
Bob Needleman
DIRECTOR Steve Horn
PRODUCER Karen Spector
PRODUCTION CO. Steve Horn
AGENCY Scali, McCabe, Sloves
CLIENT Seneca Food Corp.

BROTHERS
30-second

MUSIC UNDER

ANNCR: When the Holstein brothers, at the very last minute, had to substitute for the Strauss brothers,

they were lucky their agent had a new AMC Pacer.

The Pacer is the first wide small car,

so they had room to practice their most delicate melodies.

And since it has a wide, stable ride. . .

they never

did skip a beat.

The Pacer's room and ride. . .

make beautiful music together

SUPER: *AMC Pacer Backed by the AMC Buyer Protection Plan.*

339
ART DIRECTORS John Linder
Gerald Sneed
WRITER Michael Kahn
DIRECTORS Bob Giraldi
Alan Dennis
Dick Stone
PRODUCERS Arthur Wright
Dick Wotring
PRODUCTION COS. Bob Giraldi Productions
Cooper, Dennis, Vietro
Dick Stone Productions
AGENCY Cunningham & Walsh
CLIENT American Motors

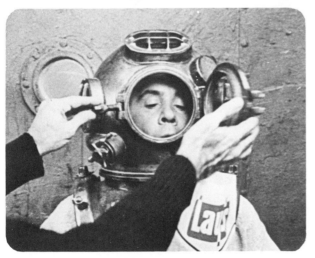

DIVER
30-second

ANNCR: Lay's Potato Chips are so thin,

so crisp,

so light. . .

No one can eat just one.

DIVER: (voice muffled—tries to eat potato chip through closed helmet)

SUPER: *No one can eat just one*

DIVER: Mmm. There's somebody in here.

SUPER: *No one can eat just one*

WILL POWER
30-second

STUCK
30-second

340
ART DIRECTOR   Don Ross
WRITER   Jim Johnston
DIRECTOR   Jack Desort
PRODUCER   John Clark
PRODUCTION CO.   Desort & Sam
AGENCY   Young & Rubicam
CLIENT   Frito-Lay

SILVER

PHONE
30-second

SFX: Phone rings. Cat knocks it off the hook.

VOICE: Hello. This is Fatty's Supermarket. We deliver 24 hours. What is your order today, Ma'm.

CAT: Meow.

VOICE: What was that?

CAT: Meow.

VOICE: Hold on. . .

ANNCR: There's one cat food that cats ask for by name. Meow Mix—a tasty combination of three flavors cats love. Tuna, liver, and chicken. Each a separate bite size morsel. So your cat gets a mouthful of variety in every bite.

VOICE: Ma'm, on that Meow Mix, was that the large bag or the 18 oz. box?

LETTERS
30-second

341
ART DIRECTOR Mark Yustein
WRITER Neil Drossman
DIRECTOR Steve Gluck
PRODUCER Joanne Diglio
PRODUCTION CO. Stan Lang
AGENCY Della Femina, Travisano
& Partners
CLIENT Ralston Purina

DAVE MAYNARD
30-second

DAVE MAYNARD: Do you realize that every morning on WBZ Radio we have Gary LaPierre with news, Gil Santos, sports, Don Kent to tell you about the weather, Joe Green in the "BZ 'copter and Pat Mitchel's reviews. There's music, Carl DeSuze and me, Dave Maynard. Now really, is there anything we've left out?

MAGICIAN: Magic tricks!

SONG: We please all of the people most all of the time on WBZ.

SUPER: *WBZ. Spirit of 103*

STEPHEN SMITH
30-second

342
ART DIRECTOR   Bob Curry
WRITERS   Geoff Currier
Terry MacDonald
PRODUCTION CO.   Carl E. Casselman
AGENCY   Pearson and MacDonald
CLIENT   WBZ-Radio

ANNCR: SAAB believes the roof over you. . .
should be able to support the car under you.

SAAB. It's what a car should be.

343

ART DIRECTORS	Michael Jackson
	Alan Zwiebel
WRITER	Michael Cox
DIRECTOR	A. Kane
PRODUCER	Ray Lofaro
PRODUCTION CO.	Associates Lofaro
AGENCY	Cox & Co.
CLIENT	Saab-Scania

GUARANTEE
10-second

ANNCR: Our cars need no gas,

never get a flat,

and are guaranteed for 10,000 pushes.
SUPER: *Matchbox*

UNCLE SAM
10-second
AUTO DUMP
10-second

344
ART DIRECTOR   Allan Beaver
WRITER   Larry Plapler
DIRECTORS   Mike Cuesta
Dick Stone
PRODUCERS   Shep Meyers
Don Trevor
PRODUCTION COS.   Griner/Cuesta
Richard Stone
AGENCY   Levine, Huntley, Schmidt,
Plapler, and Beaver
CLIENT   Lesney Products

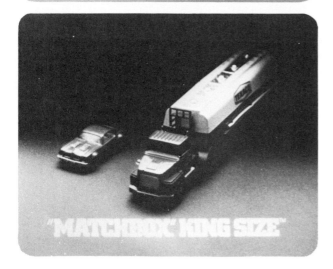

DETROIT
10-second

ANNCR: Detroit, famous for big cars, goes small.
Matchbox, famous for small cars, goes big.
SUPER: *Matchbox "King Size"*

345
ART DIRECTOR   Allan Beaver
WRITER   Larry Plapler
DIRECTOR   Dick Stone
PRODUCER   Don Trevor
PRODUCTION CO.   Richard Stone
Productions
AGENCY   Levine, Huntley, Schmidt,
Plapler, and Beaver
CLIENT   Lesney Products

CAR REPAIRS
10-second

MAN: Do you have any books on car repairs?

CLERK: Sorry, have you tried Barnes & Noble?

MAN: Barnes & Noble. Of course, of course!

SUPER: *Barnes & Noble*
Of course
Of course

DOG TRAINING
10-second

EARLY READERS
10-second

ELECTRICAL WIRING
10-second

346

ART DIRECTOR Jim Adair
WRITER Steve Olderman
DIRECTOR Mike Elliot
PRODUCER Doria Steedman
PRODUCTION CO. EUE/Screen Gems
AGENCY Geer, DuBois
CLIENT Barnes & Noble
Bookstores

GOLD

MONKS
90-second

MUSIC UNDER: (Baroque)

ANNCR: Ever since people started recording information, there's been a need to duplicate it.

FATHER: Very nice work, Brother Dominick.

BROTHER: Thank you.

FATHER: Now, I'd like 500 more sets!

BROTHER: (muttering painfully) 500 more sets?

STEPHENS: Brother Dominick, what can I do for you?

MONK: Could you do a big job for me?

ANNCR: Xerox has developed an amazing machine that's unlike anything we've ever made.

The Xerox 9200 Duplicating System. It automatically feeds and cycles originals. . .

Has a computerized programmer that coordinates the entire system.

Can duplicate, reduce, and assemble a virtually limitless number of complete sets. . .

And does it all at the incredible rate of 2 pages per second.

BROTHER: Here are your sets, Father.

FATHER: What?

BROTHER: The 500 sets you asked for.

FATHER: (glances upward) It's a miracle!

SUPER: *Xerox*

347
ART DIRECTOR Allen Kay
WRITER Steve Penchina
DIRECTOR Neil Tardio
PRODUCER Syd Rangell
PRODUCTION CO. Lovinger, Tardio, Melsky
AGENCY Needham, Harper & Steers
CLIENT Xerox

GOLD

BASEBALL—DEAN
60-second

ANNCR: Bottom of the ninth. Two out. The count's three and two. Dizzy Dean's one pitch away from his 30th win.

An American Dream of glory. To spend still summer afternoons running on finely manicured grass. To become part man, part myth, and part legend. To extend boyhood into manhood.

Dizzy checks the runner back on third.

To taste the joy of achievement reserved for those who can run, throw, and hit the round ball better than the millions of wide-eyed boys who ever played the game.

And it was this dream that enabled a farm boy from Arkansas, named Dizzy Dean, to become one of the greatest pitchers of his generation. To achieve fame, and a touch of immortality playing the summer game called baseball.

ANNCR: Around comes the arm.

The pitch.

He's out.

The game's over.

The Spirit of Achievement is the Spirit of America. This message was brought to you by Exxon in commemoration of the American Bicentennial.

SUPER: *The spirit of achievement is the spirit of America.*

348
ART DIRECTOR Don Tortoriello
WRITER Nick Pisacane
DESIGNERS Don Tortoriello
Bill Backer
DIRECTOR Steve Horn
PRODUCER John Jenkins
PRODUCTION CO. Steve Horn Production
AGENCY McCann-Erickson
CLIENT Exxon

SILVER

SAVER
60-second

OLDER MAN: You know my son is the president of this company.

I taught him how to save. When he was six years old I gave him twenty cents. . .he brought back a quarter.

Smart. Very smart kid.

He just got that Xerox 4500 copier. It copies on both sides. . .

of the *same* sheet of paper automatically!

It even takes out the old original and makes room for the new one.

(confidential tone). . .and then sorts what it copies.

That Xerox 4500 saves paper, filing space, mailing costs. . .time. . .AND money!

I tell you. . .my son, he really knows how to save.

You ought to see him play ball. (First young man leaves and another sits down.)

OLDER MAN: (proudly, to second young man) You know my son is the president of this company?

SUPER: *Xerox*

349
ART DIRECTOR Jeff Cohen
WRITER Lester Colodny
DIRECTOR Neil Tardio
PRODUCER Syd Rangell
PRODUCTION CO. Lovinger, Tardio, Melsky
AGENCY Needham, Harper & Steers
CLIENT Xerox

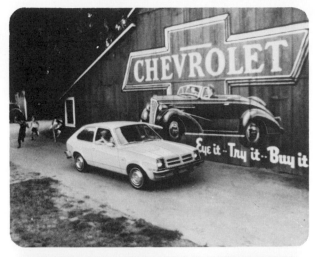

BASEBALL, HOTDOGS '76
60-second

MUSIC UNDER: (Labunski rag-time version of "Baseball, Hotdogs.")

SINGER: In the years that I've been living. A lot of things have surely changed.

A lot of things have come and gone, Some even came back again.

But through all the many changes, Some things are for sure. . .

. . .And you know that's a mighty fine feeling, Kind of makes me feel secure.

'Cause I love baseball, hotdogs, apple pie and Chevrolet. . .

. . .baseball, hotdogs, apple pie and Chevrolet.

They go together in the good ol' U.S.AAAA.

Baseball, hotdogs, apple pie and Chevrolet.

CHORUS: BASEBALL, hotdogs, apple pie and Chevrolet

ANNCR: In case you're wondering, this message is brought to you by baseball, hotdogs, applie pie and America's favorite car.

350
ART DIRECTOR Greta Clugston
WRITERS James W. Hartzell
Garry G. Neilsen
DIRECTOR Reid Miles
PRODUCER David E. Davis, Jr./Greta Clugston
PRODUCTION CO. Reid Miles Studio
AGENCY Campbell-Ewald Co.
CLIENT Chevrolet

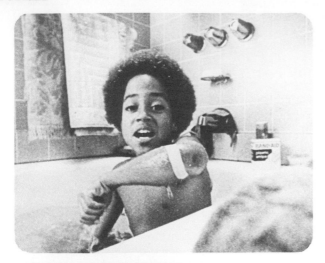

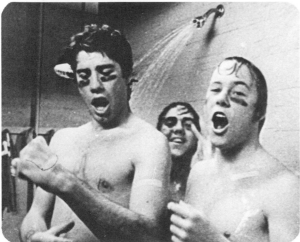

STUCK ON ME
60-second

COUNTRY GIRL: (singing) I'm stuck on Band-Aid Brand, 'cause Band-Aid stuck on me. . .

BOY: (singing) I'm stuck on Band-Aid, 'cause Band-Aid stuck on me. . .

BOY: (singing) 'Cause they hold on tight in the bathtub, and they cling in soapy suds. . .

BOY: (singing) I am stuck on Band-Aid, 'cause Band-Aid stuck on me. . .

TEENAGERS: (singing) Da-da-da-da-da-da-da. I am stuck on Band-Aid Brand 'cause Band-Aid stuck on me. . .

POLICEWOMAN: (singing) I am stuck on Band-Aid 'cause Band-Aid stuck on me. . .

TEEN GIRL: (singing) 'Cause they really stick to your fingers and they stick on bended knees. . .

COWBOY: (singing) I am stuck on Band-Aid, 'cause Band-Aid stuck on me. . .

ANNCR: Depend on the protection of America's number one bandage with unique super stick adhesive. Remember, only Johnson & Johnson makes Band-Aid Brand Adhesive Bandages.

BOY: (singing) I am stuck on Band-Aid, 'cause Band-Aid stuck on me.

SUPER: *Johnson & Johnson*

351
ART DIRECTOR Harry Webber
WRITER Mike Becker
DIRECTOR Bob Giraldi
PRODUCER Phyllis Landi
PRODUCTION CO. Bob Giraldi Films
AGENCY Young & Rubicam
CLIENT Johnson & Johnson

LEE TREVINO
60-second

GIRLS: (singing) We'll try to make you happy. . . and spread a little cheer. . .We've got Lee Trevino. . .

TREVINO: (singing) They paid me to appear.

ALL THREE: (singing) We'll dance if we have to. A thing to prove that we're sincere. . .

TREVINO: (singing) And sell some Dr Pepper. . .

ALL THREE: (singing) That is why we're here.

ALL THREE: (singing) Dr Pepper. . .

TREVINO: (singing) It's not a cola. . .it's something much, much more.

It's not a root beer.

ALL THREE: (singing) There are root beers by the score.

GIRLS: (singing) Drink Dr Pepper. . .

TREVINO: (singing) The joy of every boy and girl.

ALL THREE: (singing) It's the most original soft drink ever in the whole wide world. . .Dr Pepper . . .Dr Pepper.

352
ART DIRECTOR Jim Swan
WRITER Lou DiJoseph
DIRECTOR Ed Bianchi
PRODUCER Phyllis Landi
PRODUCTION CO. Ed Bianchi
AGENCY Young & Rubicam
CLIENT Dr. Pepper

PENTHOUSE
30-second

YOUNG WOMAN: (singing) I asked Melinda for a diet soft drink. . .She brought me a glass right away. Took one sip. . .suddenly knew, most likely it wasn't her day.

I looked at this drink in front of me. . .Took another sip and told her *No*. This just can't be. . .

DANCERS: (singing) This can't be a diet soft drink. It tastes too good to be true. . .It's Sugar Free Dr. Pepper. It tastes too good to be true. It really is a diet soft drink. . .It tastes too good to be true.

It's Sugar Free Dr. Pepper. . .It tastes too good to be. . .It tastes too good to be. . .It tastes too good to be true.

353
ART DIRECTOR David Kingman
WRITER Mara Connolly
DIRECTOR Ridley Scott
PRODUCER Linda Mevorach
PRODUCTION CO. Sunlight Pictures
AGENCY Young & Rubicam
CLIENT Dr. Pepper

AIRPORT
60-second

MAN: It's just my watch. It's just my watch.

WOMAN: Yes, sir.

VOICE: Flight 6 to Denver now boarding.

WOMAN: (Laughs)

MAN: OK.

WOMAN: Oh. . .

ANNCR: It has come to our attention that beer lovers have from time to time carried Stroh's Beer across state lines because it is not available in some parts of the country. It is our duty to inform you that state tax laws place a strict limit on the amount of beer you can transport even for personal use.

VOICE: Last call for Flight 6 to Denver.

SUPER: *Stroh's, For the real beer lover*

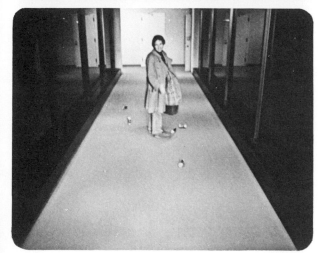

354
ART DIRECTOR Charles Piccirillo
WRITER David Reider
DIRECTOR Al Viola
PRODUCERS Joe Rein
Phil Bodwell
PRODUCTION CO. Viola, Aronson
AGENCY Doyle Dane Bernbach
CLIENT Strohs Brewing Co.

The Greater Denver Toyota Dealers

A low sticker price is just the beginning.

OLD BLUE
60-second

CUSTOMER: (meekly) How much is this going to cost me?

SALESMAN: Well, I can put you in this big beauty for a total of $493. . .(customer smiles) a month (customer gulps).

SFX: (in rundown gas station) Pump bell ringing to indicate gallonage.

CUSTOMER: How much is this going to cost me?

ATTENDANT: Hey Blue! Come over here. This guy wants to know how much this is going to cost him. (Attendant starts laughing and then totally breaks down laughing uncontrollably.)

(Customer in car attached to wrecker with front end still up in the air. Mechanic walks back and forth looking quizzically at car.)

CUSTOMER: How much is *this* going to cost me?

DEALERS
60-second

355
ART DIRECTOR Rick Brenkman
WRITER Jim Weller
DIRECTOR Joe Sedelmaier
PRODUCER Rick Brenkman
PRODUCTION CO. Sedelmaier Films
AGENCY Clinton E. Frank
CLIENT Denver Toyota
Dealers Assn.

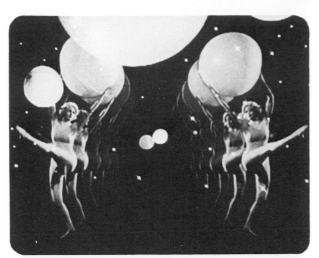

BUBBLES
60-second

MUSIC UNDER: (SEE THE LIGHT)

Series of zooms and dissolves of 7UP poster, neon girl holding bubble, chorus line holding bubbles, girl becoming butterfly, light show of 7UP graphics, the word UNCOLA, and finally a huge hot dog and bun in the midst of 7UP light show. Each sequence is keyed to appropriate music of the 30s, 40s, 50s, 60s, and 70s.

SUPER: *See the light*

356
ART DIRECTOR Robert Taylor
WRITERS Joel Slosar
Greg Obrzut
DESIGNERS Bob Abel
Bob Mitchell
ARTISTS Conn Pederson
Wayne Kimbell
Richard Taylor
DIRECTOR Bob Mitchell
PRODUCER Bob Abel
PRODUCTION CO. EUE/Screen Gems
AGENCY J. Walter Thompson
CLIENT Seven-Up

SAVER
60-second

OLDER MAN: You know my son is the president of this company.

I taught him how to save. When he was six years old I gave him twenty cents. . .he brought back a quarter.

Smart. Very smart kid.

He just got that Xerox 4500 copier. It copies on both sides. . .

of the *same* sheet of paper automatically!

It even takes out the old original and makes room for the new one.

(confidential tone). . .and then sorts what it copies.

That Xerox 4500 saves paper, filing space, mailing costs. . .time. . .AND money!

I tell you. . .my son, he really knows how to save.

You ought to see him play ball. (First young man leaves and another sits down.)

OLDER MAN: (proudly, to second young man) You know my son is the president of this company?

SUPER: *Xerox*

MIGRANT
90-second

MONKS
90-second

357

ART DIRECTORS Allen Kay
Jeff Cohen
WRITERS Lester Colodny
Lois Korey
Steve Penchina
DIRECTORS Ray Baker
Neil Tardio

PRODUCER Syd Rangell
PRODUCTION COS. Ansel Productions
Lovinger, Tardio, Melsky
AGENCY Needham, Harper &
Steers
CLIENT Xerox

SILVER

ANNE SULLIVAN
60-second

Anne Sullivan was a child without promise, orphaned and almost sightless. But she spent her adult life bringing understanding and illumination to those trapped in darkness and silence. She taught the deaf and the blind.

And her greatest achievement of all was that she enabled those minds cut off from sight and sound to find expression.

Her pioneering teaching methods brought the music of understanding to the ears of the deaf and the eyes of the blind.

Hers was a life of compassion, tenderness, patience and love.

And her most illustrious pupil, Helen Keller, went on to become one of the great women of our time. We salute Anne Sullivan for her great achievements in teaching and helping the handicapped.

The Spirit of Achievement is the Spirit of America.

This message was brought to you by Exxon in commemoration of the American Bicentennial.

SUPER: *The spirit of achievement is the spirit of America.*

SUPER: *Exxon*

MARK TWAIN
60-second

358

ART DIRECTOR Ken Demme
Don Tortoriello
John Jenkins
Gavino Sanna
WRITER Nick Pisacane
DIRECTORS Norm Griner
Steve Horn

PRODUCER John Jenkins
PRODUCTION CO. Griner/Cuesta
Steve Horn
AGENCY McCann-Erickson
CLIENT Exxon

GOLD

QUARTER HORSE
60-second

MUSIC UNDER

ANNCR: Now comes Miller Time.

You always said you had the fastest quarter horse in three states.

And you just proved it. Now's the time to head for the best tasting beer you can find.

America's quality beer. Miller High Life

HIGH IRON
60-second

359

ART DIRECTOR	Bob Lenz
WRITERS	Bob Meury
	Nick Pisacane
DIRECTORS	Neil Tardio
	Jeff Lovinger
PRODUCERS	Barney Melsky
	Sally Kellner
PRODUCTION CO.	Lovinger, Tardio, Melsky
AGENCY	McCann Erickson
CLIENT	Miller Brewing Co

TEDDY
60-second

MAN: I might be saving my buddy's life.

He was all ready to drive home when I said, "Teddy, I think you had too much to drink."

He says, "Come on, a couple of beers."

I said, "Teddy, nine beers. That could be like nine mixed drinks. I'll drive ya. Better yet park yourself on the couch."

He says, "Come on, give me a cup of coffee and I'll get out of here."

I said, "Teddy, your kidding yourself. Coffee's not gonna sober you up, no way."

So we talked it over some more. Finally I convinced him. Simple. I hid his car keys. Hey, I never did anything like this before.

Ya know, I figured he was gonna give me an argument. But then I thought, how many best friends does a guy have?

Sleeping beauty over there, he's gonna have some head in the morning. But me, I'm gonna feel terrific.

There are no more excuses.

Friends don't let friends drive drunk.

Find out how else you can help. Please write.

361
ART DIRECTOR Anthony Angotti
WRITER Harold Karp
DIRECTOR Judd Maze
PRODUCER Maura Dausey
PRODUCTION CO. Flickers
AGENCY Grey Advertising
CLIENT National Highway Traffic Safety Admin.

GOLD

**Act fast.
Call the Fire Dept.
Rescue Squad.**

AMERICAN HEART ASSOCIATION
GREATER LOS ANGELES AFFILIATE

PEARL BAILEY
60-second

PEARL: You know what I'm doing? Just sitting here, honey, thinking about a lot of stubborn people.

Let me tell you something. When I had my first heart attack, I said, "Heart attack for Pearl? No sir! Maybe I've got indigestion, maybe I'm getting a little nervous, but it couldn't be a heart attack."

And that's what the Heart Association calls the denial syndrome.

One out of every two people says, "Me? Not me." That's the denial.

Don't do it.

If a friend of yours is having about a, oh, a two-minute steady pressure on that chest, you'd better take some action fast.

Now don't just sit around, sweetheart, and wait for the person to fall down an' collapse. I'll tell you what to do.

Call the Fire Department Rescue Squad. They've got the right equipment, and they know what to do with it. And they move, and they move awful fast.

You know, I was thinking. . .this denial. . .I'm so glad that nobody listened to me.

Boy, am I glad, and am I alive. Ooh, am I ever!

362
ART DIRECTOR Si Lam
WRITER John Annarino
DIRECTOR Harry Hamburg
PRODUCER Mel Kane
PRODUCTION CO. McGraw-Hill
AGENCY Doyle Dane Bernbach
CLIENT American Heart Assoc.

 SILVER

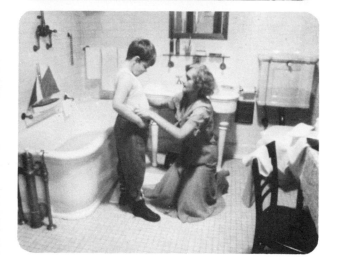

EVERY SATURDAY NIGHT
11-minute

ANNCR: I don't know you.

I mean, we've never met before. But I'm willing to bet you're just like me when it comes to at least one thing. How you get away from it all when it all gets to be too much. When your kids turn into temporary monsters and the dishwasher conks out. . .and the spider mites declare war on your asparagus fern. If you're like me, you just escape to a tub-full of steaming hot water. All you need is a few drops of perfumed bath oil and some nice, flower-scented soaps, a little music, and a lot of time, so you can lie there and relax and day-dream.

Don't you ever wonder how people managed before they invented hot running water? Or *why* your great-grandmother bathed only on Saturday night? Or how this wonderful, wet ritual started in the first place? Well, if you've nothing planned for the next ten minutes, I'll tell you. It's a fascinating story; besides it'll give me an excuse to lie here a little longer.

(Following is a history of bathrooms, sheared-terry towels and the Martex company)

363
ART DIRECTOR Peter Hirsch
WRITER Neil Calet
DESIGNER Peter Hirsch
DIRECTOR Gennaro Andreozzi
PRODUCER Arlene Hoffman
PRODUCTION CO. Gennaro Andreozzi Productions
AGENCY DKG
CLIENT West Point Pepperell

EDITORIAL

364

366

365

364
ART DIRECTOR Steve Heller
DESIGNER Steve Heller
EDITOR Charlotte Curtis
PUBLISHER The New York Times
AGENCY The New York Times

365
ART DIRECTOR Thaddeus A. Miksinski, Jr
DESIGNER Thaddeus A. Miksinski, Jr
PHOTOGRAPHER Leo Touchet
WRITER Robert Cochran
PUBLISHER U.S. Information Agency
AGENCY U.S. Information Agency

366
ART DIRECTOR Steve Heller
DESIGNER Steve Heller
ARTIST Brad Holland
EDITOR Charlotte Curtis
PUBLISHER The New York Times
AGENCY The New York Times

GOLD

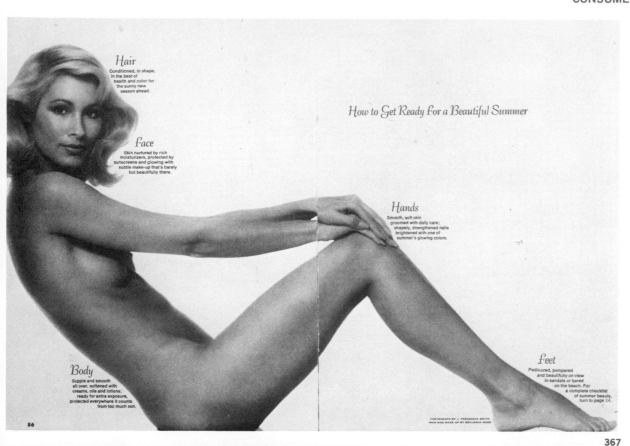

Hair
Conditioned, in shape, in the best of health and color for the sunny new season ahead.

How to Get Ready for a Beautiful Summer

Face
Skin nurtured by rich moisturizers, protected by sunscreens and glowing with subtle make-up that's barely but beautifully there.

Hands
Smooth, soft skin groomed with daily care; shapely, strengthened nails brightened with one of summer's glowing colors.

Body
Supple and smooth all over, softened with creams, oils and lotions; ready for extra exposure, protected everywhere it counts from too much sun.

Feet
Pedicured, pampered and beautifully on view in sandals or bared on the beach. For a complete checklist of summer beauty, turn to page 14.

PHOTOGRAPH BY J. FREDERICK SMITH
HAIR AND MAKE-UP BY BENJAMIN MOSS

86

367

ENJOYING THE FRUITS OF SUMMER

Summer brings forth a glorious profusion of fresh fruit. Luscious ripe peaches and nectarines, blushing apricots, plump blueberries and fragrant raspberries, cool melons and all the varieties of plums. Eat them raw, bake them into pies—but don't stop there. Fruit can be the basis of a whole array of splendid summer dishes. We've collected the most delicious ones we could find, and they start on page

IGNAZIO PARRAVICINI

368

	367		**368**
ART DIRECTOR	Bill Cadge	**ART DIRECTOR**	Alvin Grossman
DESIGNER	Ed Sobel	**DESIGNER**	Alvin Grossman
PHOTOGRAPHER	J. Frederick Smith	**PHOTOGRAPHER**	Ignazio Parravicini
EDITOR	Jean Adams	**EDITOR**	Mary Eckley
PUBLISHER	Redbook Publishing Co.	**PUBLISHER**	McCall Publishing Co.
AGENCY	Redbook Publishing Co.	**AGENCY**	McCall Publishing Co.

A Redbook Guide to
Good Food for Small Children
Is your preschool child eating
the right kinds of foods to grow on and
stay healthy on? For new ideas
about menus, recipes and serving—
and the latest advice from
nutritionists— turn to page

369

HOMEMADE
ICE CREAM
If you've never tasted
real homemade ice
cream, you've been
missing a great taste
experience. And you
can make delicious
ice cream yourself—
and ice milk and
sherbet and water ices—
whether you use an
old-fashioned, hand-
cranked tub, one of
the new electric models
or just your freezer.
Redbook serves the
latest scoop on different
methods, plus recipes
for old and new favorites.
Try Mellow Chocolate,
Double Espresso,
Pineapple Freeze,
Peppermint-Candy
and...and... Which
will you make first?
For directions and
recipes see page

YUM!

370

369
ART DIRECTOR Bill Cadge
DESIGNER Ed Sobel
ARTIST Miyo Endo
PHOTOGRAPHER Doug Corry
EDITOR Elizabeth Alston
PUBLISHER Redbook Publishing Co.
AGENCY Redbook Publishing Co.

370
ART DIRECTOR Bill Cadge
DESIGNER Ed Sobel
PHOTOGRAPHER Mort Mace
EDITOR Elizabeth Alston
PUBLISHER Redbook Publishing Co.
AGENCY Redbook Publishing Co.

THE ULTIMATE SOUFFLE

What goes into a superb, sweet soufflé like this one? Simple ingredients—eggs, flour, sugar, milk, a lacing of liqueur. What comes out of the oven is pure magic—a lofty, golden-crested creation as fragile as foam. The magic is in the way you mix, whip and fold. Find out how simple it is to make this fabulous dessert on page 113.

110

PHOTOGRAPH BY PHIL MARCO

371

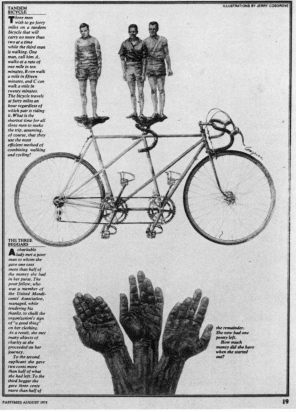

371
ART DIRECTOR Bill Cadge
DESIGNER Ed Sobel
PHOTOGRAPHER Phil Marco
EDITOR Elizabeth Alston
PUBLISHER Redbook Publishing Co.
AGENCY Redbook Publishing Co.

372
ART DIRECTOR B. Martin Pedersen
DESIGNER B. Martin Pedersen
ARTIST Jerry Cosgrove
PUBLISHER Pastimes Publications
AGENCY Pedersen Design

372

YOU CAN WEIGH WHAT YOU WANT TO WEIGH

...ALWAYS!

Redbook's Wise Woman's Diet... A plan for lifelong weight control begins on page

373

THE ELEGANCE OF WELFARE

More and more people are learning how to live well off the welfare system. *Your Legal Guide to Unemployment Insurance* by Peter Jan Honigsberg, recently published by the Golden Rain Press in Berkeley, gives a list of work-related reasons that have usually been of sufficient good cause for the employee to leave work and collect benefits:

Some General Work-Related Reasons

☐ Your wages are substantially reduced (usually more than 10%) or full-time work is reduced to part-time.

☐ Your wages are substantially less than the prevailing wage rate in the community for your kind of work (or below union wage rate if you are a member of the union) and you left as soon as you discovered the differences.

☐ Your religious morals are violated by your employer requiring you to work on your sabbath.

☐ Your employer violated your employment contract and you've tried to get him or her to follow the contract.

☐ Your employer promised you that though you were hired for one job, you would soon be taken into a training program or given some more important responsibilities and it hasn't happened though you've made a demand on him for it.

☐ You are told by your employer to perform work quite different from that for which you had originally been hired or had agreed to perform.

☐ Your employer demands you date him if you want to

keep your job or be promoted or he is always pawing you or making you uncomfortable and nervous all the time. The same would apply if it were a fellow employee who keeps making passes at you and this interferes with your work.

☐ You are a female and you must walk or even ride a bus through a rough part of town late at night on leaving work.

☐ You leave to take another job that is promised to you or to return to former employment or to join the Armed Forces (some states require you to actually work at the new job for a specified length of time before you can collect benefits).

☐ You have reached the age where you are required to retire from your job but you are still in the labor market, though this reason is accepted only in a few states.

When filling out your unemployment insurance forms, you may explain briefly why you voluntarily left work. You will be discussing your reasons in more detail during your interview. Be consistent.

It often happens that while you tell the unemployment insurance office that you quit for good cause, your employer, because he doesn't want to be taxed an additional amount as a result of your collecting benefits, may say either that he discharged you because of misconduct or that you left without good cause. Be prepared to argue against him or her, using witnesses and other evidence where necessary. In the case where you quit before he fires you these issues are especially likely to flare up, so document everything you can. Get your evidence and witnesses together.

374

373
ART DIRECTOR Bill Cadge
DESIGNER Ed Sobel
PHOTOGRAPHER Gordon E. Smith
EDITOR Elizabeth Alston
PUBLISHER Redbook Publishing Co.
AGENCY Redbook Publishing Co.

374
ART DIRECTOR Mike Salisbury
DESIGNER Mike Salisbury
PHOTOGRAPHER Ron Thal
WRITER Warren Hinckle
PUBLISHER City of San Francisco
AGENCY Salisbury/Ziff Design

Redbook's Quick and Easy Wise Woman's Diet

PHOTOGRAPHS BY JERRY SARAPOCHIELLO

This is a hearty Seasoup. For more—including delicious dieting desserts—turn the page.

Get Lost!

By Dolores Laschever

Connecticut is one of the few megalopolis states where a body can still get lost. Here are some suggestions about where to find the wilderness.

Between Canaan and South Canaan extends a wilderness area into which expert woodmen sometimes venture for the sport of getting lost.

This section of the Housatonic Forest is one of the few spots around where intrepid backpackers can get far from the maddening crowd; maybe even get lost for awhile, especially since the area's untapped iron deposits send a compass needle into a St. Vitus dance. Although Connecticut is nearly 80 percent forested, it's not easy to get lost for more than an hour or so before bumping into a road that eventually leads to civilization.

During the American Revolution the iron ore in this part of Northwestern Connecticut was turned into the cannons that helped General Washington—with considerable assistance from the French—send the Redcoats packing. Today's backpackers still stumble on the ruins of old iron foundries here. (At Kent, one has been restored adjacent to the intriguing Sloane-Stanley American Tool Museum.)

While stumbling upon an old iron foundry may be fun for the backpacker, stumbling upon other people is not. No one can guarantee that won't happen considering Connecticut is only 8,000 square miles and devoid of even one National Park or National Forest.

However, there are woods and trails aplenty, and an enterprising hiker can manage to avoid other human beings for many happy hours at a time. To do this, you'll find yourself tripping more over your tongue than feet when penetrating the leafy boughs of such state forest preserves as the Meshomasic, the Natchaug, Nehantic, Nipmuck, Pachaug, Quaddick, Shenipsit, Massacoe, Mattatuck, Nassahegon, Pootatuck, Tunxis, Wyantenock, Naugatuck, and Algonquin, not to mention the Cockaponset, Paugnut, and Paugussett—all respectable names that recall the days when the Indians held sway over this land of rolling hills and pleasant valleys.

There are other parks, forests, and sanctuaries in the state with such mundane names as Beaver Brook, George D. Seymour, Old Furnace, and Talcott Mountain. Then there's White Memorial. This 4,000-acre preserve—part of which is in Litchfield, part in Morris—was left to the people of this state by the late Alain C. White and his sister, May, for the preservation of fields, forests, and the waters of Bantam Lake.

Half of White Memorial borders on the lake. Sandy Beach, operated by Litchfield as a public swimming area, is leased to the town by the memorial. But beaches are for people, lots of them at one time in one place. For the wilderness buff, the woods of White Memorial have enough hiking and horseback riding trails to keep you in the shade for several days.

Start at Mr. White's former home, now a nature museum where you can gasp over a collection of 4,000 butterflies (exhibited on request only), watch a variety of birds dive for their meals at outdoor feeders, and obtain trail maps and booklets that will help you get lost for a while in White's woods' famous Devil's Plunge or in a grove of blight-resistant American chestnut trees, perhaps the only ones left after almost all American chestnuts were wiped out by a blight in the first half of the century. To this day tree scientists have been unable to grow the ordinary American chestnut on this continent.

During odd times of the year, a broad field adjacent to the museum is the scene of such nostalgic activities as horse-drawn sleigh or buggy wagon rallies and competitions.

When historic Litchfield celebrated its two-hundred and fiftieth anniversary a few years back, the First Litchfield Artillery shot off live cannons as the accom-

BILL BINZEN

375
ART DIRECTOR Bill Cadge
DESIGNER Ed Sobel
PHOTOGRAPHER Jerry Sarapochiello
PUBLISHER Redbook Publishing Co.
AGENCY Redbook Publishing Co.

GOLD

376
ART DIRECTOR Nancy V. Kent
DESIGNER Nancy V. Kent
PHOTOGRAPHER Bill Binzen
WRITER Dolores Laschever
EDITOR Prudence Brown
PUBLISHER Connecticut Magazine
AGENCY Connecticut Magazine

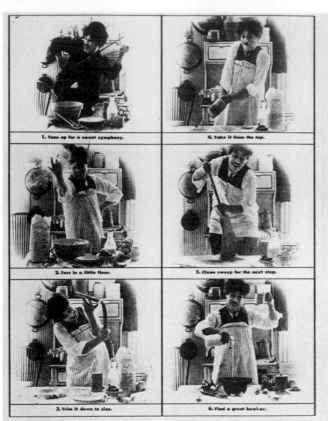

1. Tune up for a sweet symphony.

4. Take it from the top.

2. Toss in a little flour.

5. Clean sweep for the next step.

3. Trim it down to size.

6. Find a great bowl-er.

7. Beat with love.

8. A dash of creme de menthe.

9. Chocolate reaches its crescendo.

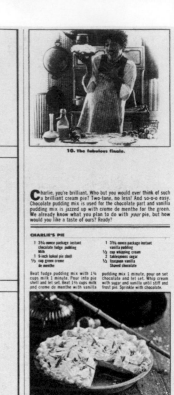

10. The fabulous finale.

Charlie, you're brilliant. Who but you would ever think of such a brilliant cream pie? Two-tone, no less! And so-o-o easy. Chocolate pudding mix is used for the chocolate part and vanilla pudding mix is jazzed up with creme de menthe for the green. We already know what you plan to do with *your* pie, but how would you like a taste of ours? Ready?

CHARLIE'S PIE

1 3¾-ounce package instant
  chocolate fudge pudding
  Milk
1 9-inch baked pie shell
⅓ cup green creme
  de menthe
	1 3¾-ounce package instant
	  vanilla pudding
	½ cup whipping cream
	2 tablespoons sugar
	½ teaspoon vanilla
	  Shaved chocolate

Beat fudge pudding mix with 1¾ cups milk 1 minute. Pour into pie shell and let set. Beat 1¾ cups milk and creme de menthe with vanilla pudding mix 1 minute, pour on set chocolate and let set. Whip cream with sugar and vanilla until stiff and frost pie. Sprinkle with chocolate.

A PIE FOR CHARLIE
BY ROSE DOSTI   REID MILES PHOTOGRAPHS

377

377
ART DIRECTOR Hans Albers
DESIGNER Reid Miles
PHOTOGRAPHER Reid Miles
WRITER Rose Dosti
PUBLISHER Home Magazine
AGENCY Los Angeles Times

SILVER

Town & Country
Visits the Daughters of the
First Families of Virginia

BY SOPHY BURNHAM · PHOTOGRAPHED BY JOEL BALDWIN

378
ART DIRECTOR Ed Hamway
DESIGNER Ed Hamway
PHOTOGRAPHER Joel Baldwin
EDITORS Mary Louise Ransdell
Anne Kampmann
PUBLISHER Town & Country
AGENCY Town & Country

It's called the new Low-High Cuisine—low fat, high pleasure. The greatest chefs in France are working on its techniques right now, and you can be the first to try it out. It isn't exactly simple or timesaving; it isn't a diet. But it allows you to eat lavishly and festively without gaining weight or feeling stuffed or guilty. Best of all, it is a celebration of natural flavors and textures; no masking, no artifice, no flour, no enrichment with butter or cream. Here is the first major change in French cooking—in terms of concept and technique—since Escoffier, with five recipes to start you going.

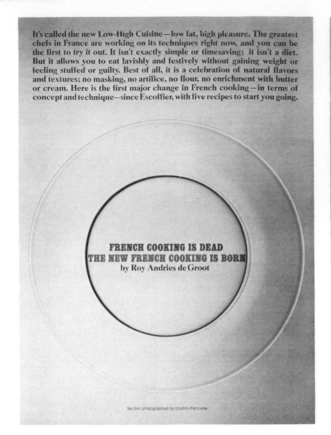

**FRENCH COOKING IS DEAD
THE NEW FRENCH COOKING IS BORN**
by Roy Andries de Groot

Section photographed by Onofrio Paccione

And, at last, a dessert with very little sugar and with an extremely high pleasure content. This is a sherbet made from Champagne adapted by Paul Haeberlin, one of the great three-star chefs of France. You'll need an electric or hand-turned ice-cream maker—described in the article—but it's simple to make if you have that. The better the French Champagne the better the taste, but the dish will work with good California or New York State bubbly. The sweetening added is a smidgen of maple syrup and some Sweet 'n Low or other sucre faux. Swim the sherbet in a glass of Champagne for the perfect grand finale.

Two of the most famous chefs in the world are Jean and Pierre Troisgros. Their idea for a Low-High main course is an adaptation of sukiyaki without the sautéing. They call it yakisuki. Six vegetables and a fruit are poached or steamed separately with their own flavorings and combined with four meats. The unifying element is a flavorful broth used to cook the chicken and in which the meats are poached. This same broth is poured over the dish and—in a new Low-High trick—is thickened with low-fat cheese to form a sauce. Clockwise from top: lamb, carrots with scallions, leeks, chicken, potatoes and mushrooms with mint, beef, apple slices, veal with parsley, yellow turnips. Center: anise or fennel. The result: dramatic coexistence.

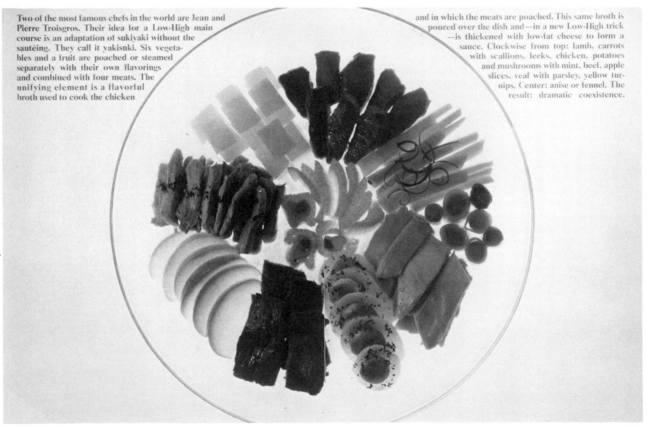

379

379
ART DIRECTOR Richard Weigand
Onofrio Paccione
DESIGNER Onofrio Paccione
PHOTOGRAPHER Onofrio Paccione
EDITOR Don Ericson
PUBLISHER Esquire
AGENCY Paccione Photography

Forgotten for nearly 50 years, the remarkable work of a Mormon photographer from Utah is rediscovered and published here nationally for the first time

G.E. Anderson. SPRINGVILLE & SPANISH FORK. UTAH.

BY RELL G. FRANCIS

Geo. Ed. Anderson.

Portrait and Landscape Photographer.

Headquarters: Springville, Utah.

Improved apparatus for Interior and Exterior work.

I make a specialty of outdoor Groups.

Duplicates made at reduced rates.

ne of the many wonderful and enchanting aspects of photography is that every so often a discovery is made that takes everybody by surprise and adds something of real value to our knowledge and understanding of the medium.

If the discovery is of a photographer who worked several generations ago and produced a large volume of esthetically outstanding pictures on a particular subject or theme of historical importance, but whose accomplishments lay buried and forgotten for years in some dusty cellar until found quite by accident, then the event is usually greeted with a genuine outpouring of astonishment and delight.

Those were exactly the sentiments expressed by POP PHOTO's picture editor, Charles Reynolds, when, during the course of his travels around the country visiting colleges and looking for fresh talent, he came across an exhibition of work by George Edward Anderson in the Springville, Utah, Museum of Art. And they were also my own sentiments when I happened upon them quite by chance about a year earlier as I was preparing a biography-catalog of a noted 19th-century Utah sculptor named Cyrus Dallin (page 89) and was looking for old-time pictures of him. A friend and local leader of the Mormon Church, Leo Crandall, told me he had taken possession of some 10,000 of Anderson's glass plates that had been found in the continued on page 113

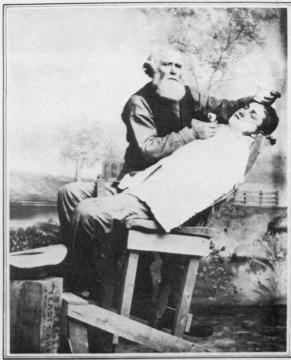

James Walker (barber) and young David Fullmer, Mt. Pleasant, c. 1900

JEX & SONS BROOM FACTORY

G.E.Anderson SPRINGVILLE & SPANISH FORK. UTAH.

Jex Broom factory, Spanish Fork, c. 1898

380

ART DIRECTOR Shinichiro Tora
DESIGNER Shinichiro Tora
PHOTOGRAPHER G.E. Anderson
WRITER Rell G. Francis
PUBLISHER Ziff Davis Publishing Co.
AGENCY Ziff-Davis Publishing Co.

381

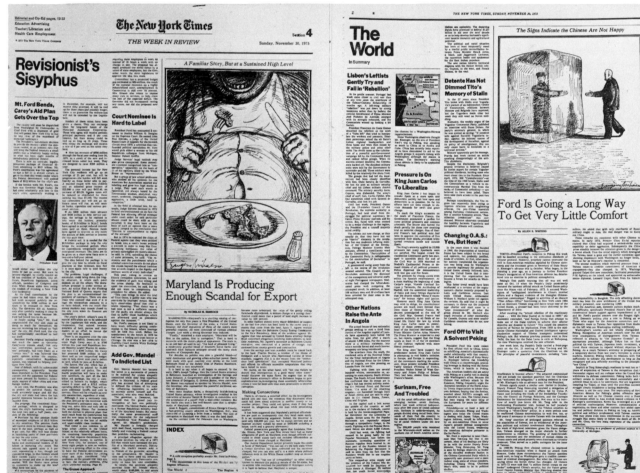

382

381
ART DIRECTOR Henry Wolf
DESIGNER Henry Wolf
PUBLISHER Children's Television
Workshop
AGENCY Henry Wolf Productions

382
ART DIRECTOR Eric Seidman
DESIGNER Eric Seidman
ARTIST Eugene Mihaesco
EDITOR Al Marlens
PUBLISHER The New York Times
AGENCY The New York Times

Anyone for Tennis ?

Clothes to stroke balls in

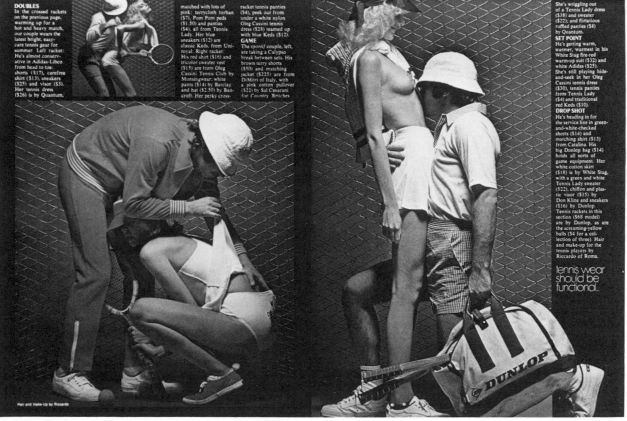

DOUBLES
In the crossed rackets on the previous page, warming up for a hot and heavy match, our couple wears the latest bright, easy-care tennis gear for summer. Left racket: He's almost conservative in Adidas-Libco from head to toe: shorts ($17), carefree shirt ($13), sneakers ($25) and visor ($3). Her tennis dress ($26) is by Quantum, matched with lots of pink: terrycloth turban ($7), Pom Pom peds ($1.50) and panties ($4), all from Tennis Lady. Her blue sneakers ($12) are classic Keds, from Uniroyal. Right racket: His red shirt ($16) and tricolor sweater vest ($15) are from Oleg Cassini Tennis Club by Munsingwear; white pants ($14) by Barclay and hat ($2.50) by Bancroft. Her perky cross-racket tennis panties ($4), peek out from under a white nylon Oleg Cassini tennis dress ($28) teamed up with blue Keds ($12).

GAME
The *sportif* couple, left, are taking a Calypso break between sets. His brown terry shorts ($50) and matching jacket ($225) are from DiMitri of Italy, with a pink cotton pullover ($22) by Sal Cesarani for Country Britches.

She's wriggling out of a Tennis Lady dress ($38) and sweater ($22); and flirtatious ruffled panties ($8) by Quantum.

SET POINT
He's getting warm, warmer, warmest in his White Stag fire-red warm-up suit ($32) and white Adidas ($25). She's still playing hide-and-seek in her Oleg Cassini tennis dress ($30), tennis panties from Tennis Lady ($4) and traditional red Keds ($10).

DROP SHOT
He's heading in for the service line in green-and-white-checked shorts ($14) and matching shirt ($13) from Catalina. His big Dunlop bag ($14) holds all sorts of game equipment. Her white cotton skirt ($18) is by White Stag, with a green and white Tennis Lady sweater ($22), chiffon and plastic visor ($15) by Don Kline and sneakers ($16) by Dunlop. Tennis rackets in this section ($68 model) are by Dunlop, as are the screaming-yellow balls ($4 for a collection of three). Hair and make-up for the tennis players by Riccardo of Roma.

tennis wear should be functional...

Hair and Make-Up by Riccardo

383

ART DIRECTOR Don Menell
DESIGNER Jean-Pierre Holley
PHOTOGRAPHER Francis Giacobetti
PUBLISHER Oui Magazine
AGENCY Playboy Publications

Congress Hall on Independence Square.

A WALK THROUGH HISTORIC
Philadelphia

Nowhere else in
America did
events of such
importance occur

BY CHRISTOPHER DAVIS

ILLUSTRATED BY
PAUL HOGARTH

20

In 1776 Philadelphia was a city of merchants and tradesmen, and it remains so 200 years later. Elizabeth Ross, an upholsterer's widow, lived in a little house on Arch Street, and it is appropriate that the commemorative plaque honoring Betsy's sideline of flag making was placed on the house in 1957 by the Upholsterers' International Union—trade and patriotism simultaneously honored. Beyond the lady's bedroom (canopy bed, sampler), across Arch at Fourth Street, stands the Friends Meeting House, the oldest still functioning in the city.

There were two sorts of Quakers in that first American war, as there have been in wars since. A dissenting faction, the Free Quakers, fought. The nonfighting ones (rather than support the war against the Indians in 1756 they had withdrawn from the legislature) were rounded up and, in the fall of 1777, shipped for safekeeping to Virginia—solid Philadelphia Emlens and Pembertons, Drinkers, Fishers and Whartons—where by resolution of Congress they were treated with respect and ". . . entertained agreeable to their rank and station in life." When houses of Philadelphians who "had not manifested their attachment to the American cause" were searched for firearms, the Tories were to be paid for their guns at fair appraised value. The Revolutionary War, we are reminded, was conducted with a certain amount of gentility and with due respect to the

Christopher Davis's most recent novel, The Sun in Mid-Career, is set in Philadelphia, where he was born and still resides.

canons of commerce. The proof of this is to be found not only in old documents, but in bricks and cobbles—the look and feel of the city itself.

The old part of the city is much the same today as it was 200 years ago, in appearance as well as character, thanks to restoration and urban redevelopment. It lies between the Delaware River and Tenth Street to the east and west, between Queen Street in the south and Vine in the north. The heart of it is Independence National Historical Park—the State House, Congress Hall, Carpenters' Hall, the first banks, the old Exchange, certain private houses. As monuments, these are vital places; but to the north and south (Betsy lived to the north; Society Hill, old Philadelphia resurrected, is to the south) was made the everyday history that began with William Penn's holy experiment and does not end even with you and me. All of it is well worth exploring.

One way to start is at the present City Hall, a Victorian mega-bastion apparently of kings but really, of course, of justice and rational city plans, and proceed east on Market toward the river. We are descending centuries. Now in the process of reconstruction at the corner of Seventh Street is a small bricklayer's house, in a room of which Jefferson drafted the Declaration of Independence. A few blocks farther on, the years fading, we find old Philadelphia still in use: warehouses, wholesalers, rug merchants, cabinetmakers, men and boys' wear, auctioneering houses, Leather City, Cheep Feet, Back Number Magazines. The handsome late 18th and early 19th-century structures serve trade. Between Third and Fourth south of Market is Franklin Court, the restored site of Franklin's last home. But sites for the moment aside, walk south down Bank Street and Strawberry Street, explore the alleys and ways to the north and east where they turn from the numbered streets to the river. They are there for us to discover, cobbled as they were 200 years ago, with a drainage gutter down the center of each. One encounters mounting blocks worn like the steps of a European church, hitching posts and tiny three-storied houses—two rooms below, two above, one above that—gardens the size of dollar bills behind. Down the street, glimpsed between warehouses, is the Delaware, from which sailors came rolling up to their homes after a voyage.

Here is Christ Church on Second north of Market on a warm midweek morning. Visitors drift in and find comfortable benches in the sun. Itchy schoolchildren form columns. Moravian women, hair in identical crocheted sacks, descend from a Gray Line bus. In pew number 70 inside the church, where Benjamin Franklin sat, we sit. We look up at the solid, soaring white bones of the 18th-century architecture, observe wealth and expensive

rectitude, and think, being Franklin distracted from a sermon he might better have written himself, that the young country would do very well indeed on its own two feet; we are solvent merchants and England can go whistle for all anyone cares.

The church was built between 1727 and 1754, is called the Nation's Church, and is beautiful, inside and out. Robert Morris and James Wilson are buried here; and here lies that Charles Lee who made the mistake of ordering a retreat at the Battle of Monmouth. Since Valley Forge was just past and since Washington had the need for victory like fire burning in his mind, the unlucky major general was disgraced. Here also on July 4, 1788, the bells rang all day to celebrate the ratification of the Constitution by ten of the thirteen states.

At 235 North Fourth Street is Old St. George's, the oldest Methodist church in the world. During that same bitter winter of 1777-78, with Tory Philadelphia dancing with the British, the banker Robert Morris prayed here for inspiration in his task of rais-

South Façade of Independence Hall.

384

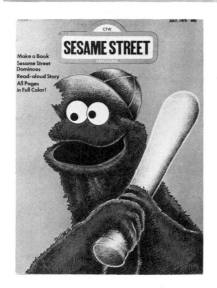

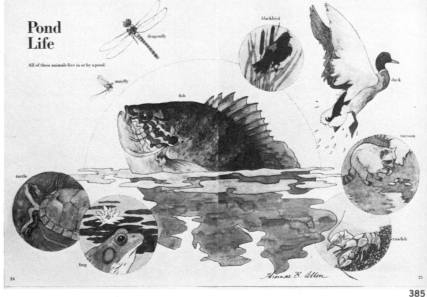

Pond Life

All of these animals live in or by a pond.

dragonfly
blackbird
duck
mayfly
raccoon
fish
turtle
crawfish
frog

Thomas B. Allen

24   25

385

384
ART DIRECTOR Norman S. Hotz
DESIGNER Gail Tauber
ARTIST Paul Hogarth
WRITER Christopher Davis
PUBLISHER American Express Publishing
AGENCY Travel & Leisure

385
ART DIRECTOR Henry Wolf
DESIGNER Henry Wolf
PUBLISHER Children's Television Workshop
AGENCY Henry Wolf Productions

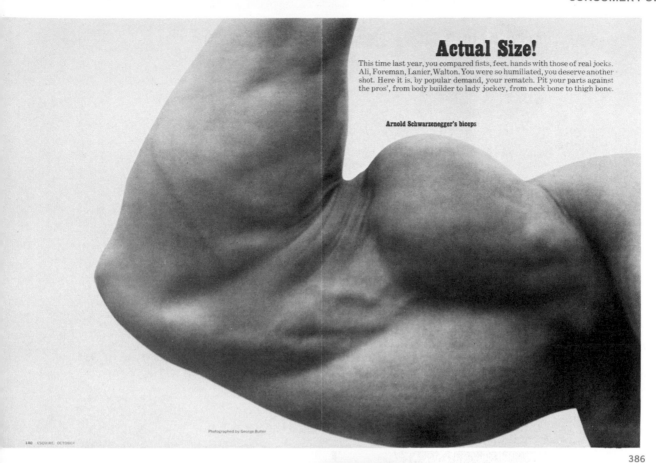

Actual Size!

This time last year, you compared fists, feet, hands with those of real jocks. Ali, Foreman, Lanier, Walton. You were so humiliated, you deserve another shot. Here it is, by popular demand, your rematch. Pit your parts against the pros', from body builder to lady jockey, from neck bone to thigh bone.

Arnold Schwarzenegger's biceps

Photographed by George Butler

140 ESQUIRE OCTOBER

386

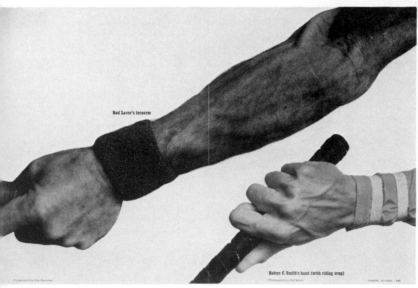

Rod Laver's forearm

Robyn C. Smith's hand (with riding crop)

Photographed by Dan Wynn

Photographed by Wai Janiece

ESQUIRE OCTOBER 141

386
ART DIRECTOR Richard Weigand
DESIGNER Richard Weigand
PHOTOGRAPHER George Butler
WRITER Lee Eisenberg
PUBLISHER Esquire
AGENCY Esquire

 SILVER

The forms of California:
The season's new body-defining black swimsuits
take shape against
the state's spectacular natural contours.

Photographs by Silano

The High Sierras

387

Redwood National Forest

THE FORMS OF CALIFORNIA

The High Sierras The great granite mass that cracks California from the rest of the continent. Their awesome beauty called forth in the poet's words now chiseled on the state capitol in Sacramento: "Bring me men to match my mountains." This is the eternal, unchanging California. A wonderland of peaks and gorges and high valleys. Once volcanic country, its convulsed past is recorded by pinkish, mauvish lava cones along the horizon. Here, a lone human form echoes the angles of the silent, legend-filled landscape at Owens Valley—once a well filled lake; today an almost totally dry stretch of earth with bristling branches and brittle bushes. The female shape is alluringly emphasized in a black swimsuit of clinging Lycra that's square cut at the neckline and bordered in black lace. Its shelter against winds: a little, hooded black beach dress with a drawstring waist. Outfit by Gottex of Israel. At Bergdorf Goodman; Harzfeld's; Bullock's-Wilshire; Neiman-Marcus. Silver coiled around the neck, by Georg Jensen.

Yosemite National Park The gem of the Sierras. "The range of light." Shouldering up in solemn splendor through some 1,182 square miles. Encompassing wild granite mountains, rushing silver-ribbon streams and frothy waterfalls, as well as the grand Sequoia groves with trees that begin their growth more than 1,500 years before the birth of Christ. Most of this ravishing territory—the famous El Capitan, Half Dome, Bridalveil, and Yosemite Falls—is still accessible only on foot or on horseback. Here, spanning the breathtaking sawn of Yosemite Valley is a dramatic definition of the quintessential dazzle of the female form. A one-piece Lycra bathing suit with surplice bodice and a rounded, very low back. By Cole of California. At Bergdorf Goodman; Swanson's; Robinson's.

Death Valley Sandblasted ground afire. The lowest, hottest, driest acreage of the Mojave Desert and of the United States. About 140 miles long, it is a solitary hades—190° at its febrile extreme. A land of freakish natural formations, blazingly colored canyons that are constantly changing from deep purple to fool's gold, rosy fawn to milky green at the whim of the passing sun overhead. The arid, furrowed sand dunes—actually the beachline of an ancient sea—are among the most geologically fascinating places on earth. Etched sharply in pure contour like the stark land itself is the black Lycra swimsuit in the foreground. It sleekly hugs the lines of a long, lissome torso and is decorated with a subtle gathering of diagonal clouds, not unlike those in the sky above the desert. By Catalina. At Altman's; Jordan Marsh, Miami; Hudson's; Robinson's. Necklace by V.J. Gerardo.

Diablo Range The heaving, breastlike green hills near Livermore, rolling over a wide swath of the California landscape about 30 miles east of Oakland. Under scudding clouds that signal the imminence of a drenching storm, the bald treeless terrain rises and falls and throbs with the regenerative qualities of the land, where heedless, venturesome, eclectic men once trekked in pursuit of quick fortunes. In the wake of nature's carving, a glorious curving of Lycra rounds and rights the figure in the foreground. It's the most wily, feminine swimsuit of black, with three strips of brilliant color dipping down the shoulder and across the bosom. By Jantzen. At Jordan Marsh, Miami; Titche's, Dallas.

Redwood National Forest The world's tallest trees, soaring into venerable silence. Compelling the spirit to reach upward —almost with religiosity—while the feet remain rooted in the rich humus below. Extending from just north of the Oregon border to the Big Sur coastline, these 58,000 acres of handsome virgin Redwoods are nurtured by the unique raw forces of the region—the white, fleecy-wooly coastal fogs and the relentlessly sizzling sun. Transparent shafts of light filter through the delicate foliage from above and fall upon a creamy-skinned, nearly bare body, its slender curves smoothly molded by a crisscross-strapped black swimsuit of Lycra. By Catalina Juniors. At Bloomingdale's; L.S. Ayres, Indianapolis; Robinson's. Adolfo hat. Silver bracelet by Robin Kahn. All bathing suits in Lycra, a Du Pont fabric.

71

387
ART DIRECTOR Ed Hamway
DESIGNER Ed Hamway
PHOTOGRAPHER Silano
EDITOR Mary Louise Ransdell
PUBLISHER Town & Country
AGENCY Town & Country

GOLD

JAMES ABBE

Armed with camera and great wit, this once famous, but recently overlooked photographer toured the world to capture celebrities and politicians of the '20s and '30s

BY MARGARETTA MITCHELL

Most of the photographs shown on the following pages were chosen from a new book titled Stars of the Twenties, observed by James Abbe. The Viking Press, Inc. $10.95.

With our current fascination for the 1920s and 1930s, it is no accident that we have found in the photographs of James Abbe our expectations of that era so perfectly contained. Through Abbe we rediscover in images the collective dream of Western culture much as we do in the writing of Fitzgerald and Hemingway.

Born in 1883, James Abbe was the foremost stage, screen, and society photographer of the early 20th century, bringing before his camera virtually every luminary of the entertainment world, among them Fred and Adele Astaire, Lillian and Dorothy Gish, Mary Pickford, Ann Harding, Katharine Cornell, Fanny Brice, Helen Hayes, Mae West, John Barrymore, Charlie Chaplin, Jackie Coogan, Pola Negri,

Theda Bara, Rudolph and Natasha Valentino, Irving Berlin, Noel Coward, and Gertrude Lawrence, to mention only a few. Indeed, his pictures reflect the glamor and urbane sophistication romantically associated with the theater. When the glitter was tarnished by the Depression of the early '30s he found himself on the political stage, capturing on film all the famous (or infamous) faces, among them Adolf Hitler, Joseph Stalin, Benito Mussolini, Hermann Göring, Francisco Franco, and Franklin Roosevelt.

Possessing great energy and a superb wit, Abbe was a man who had an insatiable curiosity for life and a love of living it. "Photography was a free pass through life," he told his assistant of continued on page 111

Dolly Sisters, Paris, 1927

JAMES ABBE

Katharine Cornell, New York City, 1920

Helen Hayes, New York City, 1921

388

ART DIRECTOR Shinichiro Tora
DESIGNER Shinichiro Tora
PHOTOGRAPHER James Abbe
WRITER Margaretta Mitchell
PUBLISHER Ziff Davis Publishing Co.
AGENCY Ziff Davis Publishing Co.

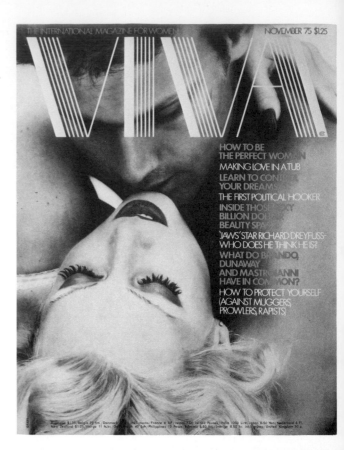

389

	389			**390**
ART DIRECTOR	Rowan Johnson		ART DIRECTOR	Rowan Johnson
DESIGNERS	Claire Victor		DESIGNERS	Claire Victor
	George Moy			George Moy
PHOTOGRAPHERS	Chris Callis		PHOTOGRAPHER	Richard L. Shaefer
	Bonnie Maller		PUBLISHER	Viva International
PUBLISHER	Viva International		AGENCY	Viva International
AGENCY	Viva International			

GOLD

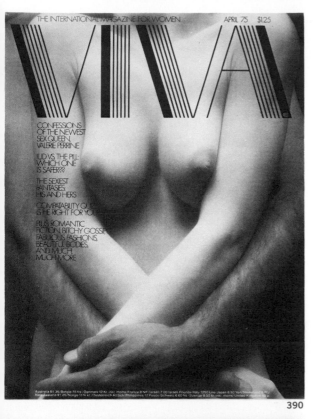

390

391

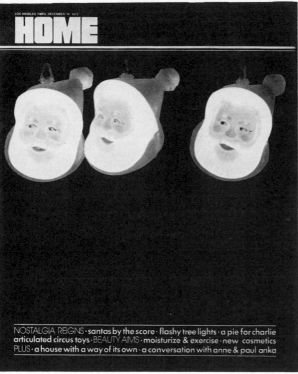

392

393

391
ART DIRECTOR Michael Salisbury
ARTIST Charles Shields
PUBLISHER City of San Francisco
AGENCY Daniele DeVerin

392
ART DIRECTOR Hans Albers
DESIGNERS Carolyn S. Murray
Gerard T. Brane
PHOTOGRAPHER Harry Chamberlain
PUBLISHER Home Magazine
AGENCY Los Angeles Times

393
ART DIRECTOR Ruth Ansel
DESIGNER Ruth Ansel
EDITORS Lewis Bergman
Jack Rosenthal
PUBLISHER The New York Times
AGENCY The New York Times

REHABILITATION

Two Perspectives

She looks like any other pretty sixteen year old girl—faded jeans, pink knit top, a red bandana covering her hair. Then she starts talking . . .

She was twelve when she started taking pills—uppers, downers, anything the schoolyard pusher had to offer. Last year she became addicted to heroin, ran away from home and turned to prostitution to support her habit. She was arrested and put into a cell with three other women prisoners. Before bail could be posted all the horror stories she had heard about being in jail came true.

But, terrible as they were, those few hours in jail did one thing that the desperation of a $150 a day habit and nine months on the street hadn't—she decided to get help.

As far removed from the lives of most people as this young woman's story may seem, she is not a unique case. Young alcoholics and drug abusers roam most city streets. Many say they do not want or need help. But a number of them do wake up and realize that they must straighten out their lives and that they can't do it alone. Once that decision is made, help has to be available—and fast—before the over-whelming desire for a drink or a fix erases the thought of getting help . . . maybe forever.

7

394

394
ART DIRECTOR Al Gluth
DESIGNER Al Gluth
PHOTOGRAPHER Joe Baraban
WRITER Charlie McBroom
PUBLISHER Exxon Chemical Magazine
AGENCY Baxter & Korge

GOLD

Progressive Architecture

July 1975 An [C] Reinhold publication

Douglas House

given his admiration for the buildings of the heroic period of modern architecture, whose authors were consciously responding to the vocabulary of steamships, industrial plants, and powerful machinery. If this vocabulary were used only for itself, merely as a fashion, any building expressive of it would have little significance. On the other hand, if it is used as a tool to support a valid theory of architecture, of architectonic space, and of architecture in relation to its context as it is here, then it is important. It is not, as is often the case, simply the application of some visual images from Aalto, Duiker or Le Corbusier. Instead, it represents an uncommon understanding and synthesis of modern architecture, of where it has been, and of where at least some of it is going. It represents a vision, regardless of the vocabulary, that is only Richard Meier's, and that could not have come from anyone else. [David Morton]

Deck at entry level (above), living-room-level staircase (opposite)

Skylight extends, through cutouts, to lower-level dining room (above)

West façade (detail above showing LR and DR) and east façade (below)

Data

Project: Douglas House, Harbor Springs, Mich.
Architect: Richard Meier & Associates, team: Richard Meier, Karl Born, John Colamarino, Sherman Kung, Tod Williams.
Program: a year-round residence for a family of five.
Site: a densely wooded, steeply sloping site on northern Lake Michigan.
Structural system: wood bearing wall and framing system enclose private portions of building; steel columnar structure used for public portions.
Mechanical system: forced warm and cold central air conditioning system.
Major materials: wood piles, wood frame and steel column structure; wood floors, wood roof and built-up roofing; redwood exterior siding; gypsum wall partitions; fiberglass insulation; fixed wood windows and steel operable sash; solid core wood doors.
Consultants: Richard Meier & Associates, interior designers; Dalton & Dunne, mechanical engineers; Severud, Perrone, Strum, Bandel, structural engineers.
Client: Mr. and Mrs. James E. Douglas, Jr.
Costs: withheld at request of client.
Contractor: Jordan Shepherd.
Photography: Ezra Stoller © ESTO, except p. 45, Richard Meier.

44 Progressive Architecture 7:75

395
ART DIRECTOR	George W. Coderre
DESIGNER	George W. Coderre
EDITOR	John Morris Dixon
PUBLISHER	Progressive Architecture
AGENCY	Reinhold Publishing Co.

"Pioneer, innovator, visionary . . . all describe Paul Rand, but none measures the
true meaning of his many contributions to the contemporary scene.
He was a graphic designer before the concept 'graphic design' existed.
He is an artist who has brought high standards of art to the world of business, and proved their value.
And he is a presence whose achievements prod all of us in the visual arts to do better.
There could be no more fitting subject for a graphic arts publication such
as The Printing Salesman's Herald than Paul Rand and his exciting work."

Edward Russell Jr., Vice President, Marketing Services, Champion Papers

Champion Papers
The Printing Salesman's Herald
Book 35

Special Issue on **Paul Rand**

396

396
DESIGNER Paul Rand
PHOTOGRAPHER Paul Rand
WRITER Paul Rand
PUBLISHER Champion Papers
AGENCY Champion Papers

GOLD

Preventing atherosclerosis—Lessons from pathogenesis

Bronchodilator
tablets, 5 mg.

BRETHINE
terbutaline sulfate

Geigy
Please see last page for full
Prescribing Information

The atherosclerotic plaque

Inheritance in coronary heart disease

397
ART DIRECTOR J. Ronald Vareltzis
DESIGNER J. Ronald Vareltzis
ARTISTS Rick McCollum
Norm Walker
Jose Reyes
Keith Batchiller
Mary Sherman
WRITERS Barbra Ramm
Linda Chadsey
PUBLISHER Geigy Pharmaceuticals
AGENCY Geigy Pharmaceuticals

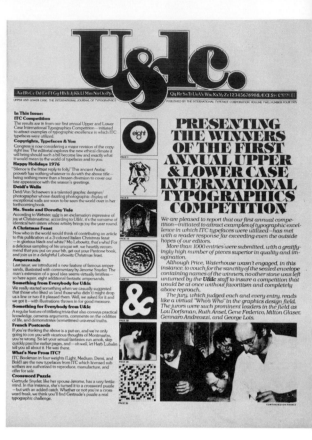

ART DIRECTOR **398**
ART DIRECTOR Herb Lubalin
DESIGNER Herb Lubalin
WRITERS Herb Lubalin
Jerome Snyder
Mo Lebowitz
Jack Finke
PUBLISHER International Typeface
Corp.
AGENCY Lubalin, Smith, Carnase &
Peckolick

SILVER

POETRY OF EARTH & SKY *a portfolio of living scenes*

Landscape, seascape, skyscape — the endless variety delights the eye, enchants the soul. The scientist gropes to find the laws that keep the great natural forces endlessly working; the artist perceives the designs forming and re-forming and is inspired; and the child in every one of us, young or old, simply exults . . .

What is a rock? What is a brook? What is a cloud? What caused the mountains? What gouged the valleys? Each question has its answer, each answer but leads to another question. Such is the road to knowledge. But the enjoyment of the sheer beauty requires only that the eye rove over scenes that the camera has caught. Wind, rain and erosion may already have altered their contours, but here they are transfixed forever.

Navajo sandstone, a compressed sand dune from earlier ages in Zion National Park, Utah. **Opposite page:** Reflections in a pothole at late evening in Canyonlands National Park, Utah.

5 by Dan McCoy

Boulders in Joshua Tree National Monument Park, Twentynine Palms, California. **Opposite page:** Desert holly in Death Valley lava bed, Mojave Desert, California.

399

ART DIRECTOR	Robert Sadler Design
DESIGNER	Robert Sadler
PHOTOGRAPHERS	Dan McCoy
	Bob Meyer
EDITOR	Louis Zara
PUBLISHER	Mineral Digest
AGENCY	Robert Sadler Design

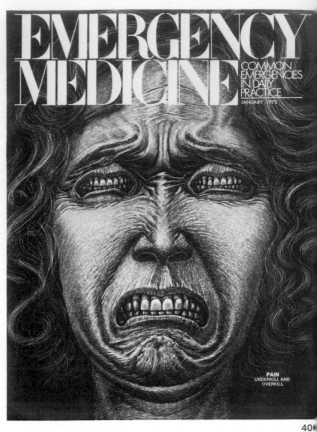

400

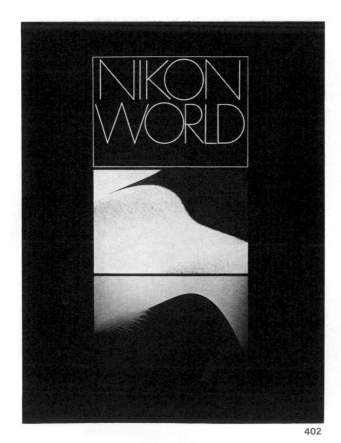

402

40

400
ART DIRECTOR Ira Silberlicht
              Tom Lennon
DESIGNER   Tom Lennon
ARTIST   Ed Soyka
EDITOR   Irving J. Cohen
PUBLISHER   Emergency Medicine
AGENCY   Fischer Medical
              Publications

GOLD

401
ART DIRECTOR Richard Coyne
DESIGNER   Richard Coyne
PHOTOGRAPHER Jay Maisel
EDITOR   Richard Coyne
PUBLISHER   Communication Arts
AGENCY   Coyne & Blanchard

402
ART DIRECTOR Ernest Scarfone
PHOTOGRAPHER Pete Turner
EDITOR   Pat May
PUBLISHER   Ehrenreich Phot
AGENCY   Pete Turner

SILVER

403

404

405

403
ART DIRECTORS Albert M. Foti
JoAnne Cassella
DESIGNER JoAnne Cassella
PHOTOGRAPHER Shig Ikeda
PUBLISHER RN Magazine
AGENCY Medical Economics Co.

404
ART DIRECTOR George W. Coderre
DESIGNER George W. Coderre
PHOTOGRAPHER Edmund H. Stocklein
EDITOR John Morris Dixon
PUBLISHER Progressive Architecture
AGENCY Reinhold Publishing Co.

405
ART DIRECTOR Stanley Stellar
DESIGNER Richard Schneider
PHOTOGRAPHER Peter Fürst
PUBLISHER Art Direction Magazine
AGENCY Schneider Studio

COMPLETE UNIT

406

SEPTEMBER 15
47.
MOURNING VIRGIN
GERMAN, SWABIAN, c. 1525.
LINDENWOOD, 14 in.
LENT BY THE METROPOLITAN MUSEUM
OF ART, NEW YORK CITY.
ROGERS FUND, 1909.

In the ninth century originated the popular veneration of Mary on Saturdays. This practice appears to have grown out of the ancient weekly memorial of Christ's Passion. The books of that time motivate it by the thought that while the Lord's body rested in death Mary alone did not doubt or despair, but firmly adhering to the faith in her Divine Son. She was thus believed to deserve more devotion and honor on Saturday than on other weekdays. The authorities of the Church not only provided a votive Mass (which now has five different texts according to the seasons of the ecclesiastical year), but also a special office in honor of Mary to be recited on "free" Saturdays.

Francis X. Weiser, Handbook of Christian Feasts and Customs

People who could not read, and among them especially the lay brothers in the monasteries, substituted for the written texts a certain number of familiar prayer formulas which they knew by heart. Thus, for instance, one hundred and fifty Ave Marias were substituted for the one hundred and fifty psalms, and the mysteries of Christ's life (taken from ancient responsories), were inserted in the Hail Marys. It was in this way that the rosary gradually developed during the High Middle Ages. Saint Dominic (1221) is credited with the spreading of this particular exercise among the lay population of Italy.

Francis X. Weiser, Handbook of Christian Feasts and Customs

406
ART DIRECTOR Joseph Erceg
DESIGNER Joseph Erceg
WRITER Francis J. Newton
EDITOR Robert Peirce
PUBLISHER Portland Art Museum
AGENCY Joseph Erceg Graphic Design

What do you call a clean, neat, hardworking, kind, intelligent, and friendly monster? **A failure.**

What does a werewolf put on at the beach? **Moon-tan lotion.** How can you make a witch scratch? **Take away its W.**

Where does a vampire plant flowers? **In a bat-tanical garden.**

407

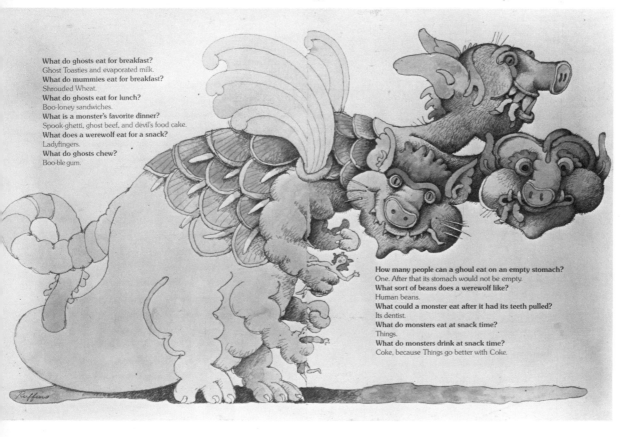

What do ghosts eat for breakfast?
Ghost Toasties and evaporated milk.
What do mummies eat for breakfast?
Shrouded Wheat.
What do ghosts eat for lunch?
Boo-loney sandwiches.
What is a monster's favorite dinner?
Spook-ghetti, ghost beef, and devil's food cake.
What does a werewolf eat for a snack?
Ladyfingers.
What do ghosts chew?
Boo-ble gum.

How many people can a ghoul eat on an empty stomach?
One. After that its stomach would not be empty.
What sort of beans does a werewolf like?
Human beans.
What could a monster eat after it had its teeth pulled?
Its dentist.
What do monsters eat at snack time?
Things.
What do monsters drink at snack time?
Coke, because Things go better with Coke.

407

ART DIRECTOR	Jane Zalben
DESIGNER	Reynold Ruffins
ARTIST	Reynold Ruffins
WRITER	Jane Sarnoff
PUBLISHER	Charles Scribner's Sons
AGENCY	Charles Scribner's Sons

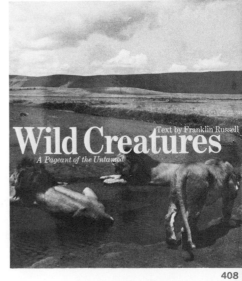

408
ART DIRECTOR Massimo Vignelli
DESIGNER Massimo Vignelli
WRITER Franklin Russell
PUBLISHER Simon and Schuster
AGENCY Chanticleer Press

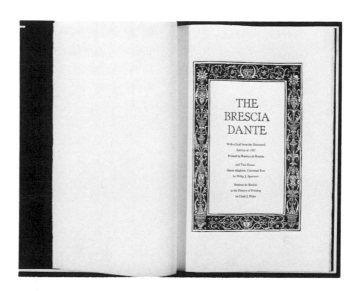

409

ART DIRECTOR McRay Magleby
WRITERS Louise Hansen
Philip J. Spartano
Chad J. Flake
PUBLISHER Brigham Young
University Library
AGENCY Graphic Communications
Dept.

GOLD

COMPLETE UNIT

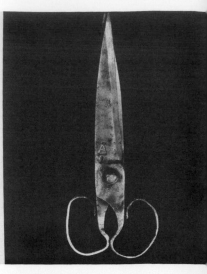

Shears

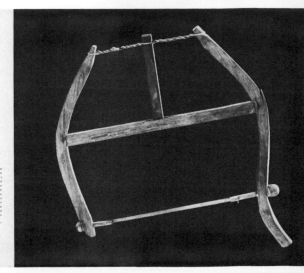

Bow Saw

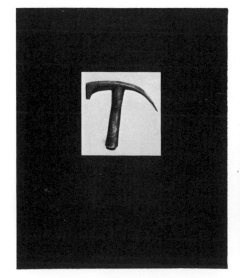
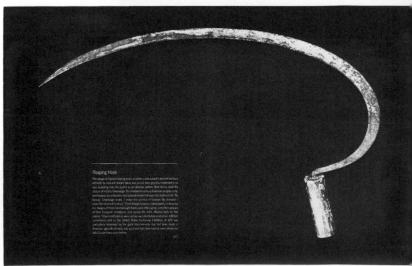

Reaping Hook

410
ART DIRECTOR Irwin Glusker
DESIGNER Irwin Glusker
PHOTOGRAPHER Hans Namuth
WRITER Marshall B. Davidson
PUBLISHER Olivetti Corp. of America
AGENCY Olivetti Corp. of America

411

411
ART DIRECTOR Paul Gamarello
DESIGNER Paul Gamarello
WRITER Carol Wald
AGENCY Pantheon

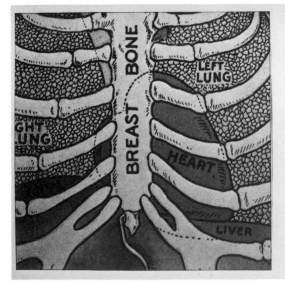

412
ART DIRECTOR Seymour Chwast
DESIGNERS Seymour Chwast
Bob Conrad
PUBLISHER Avon Books
AGENCY Avon Books

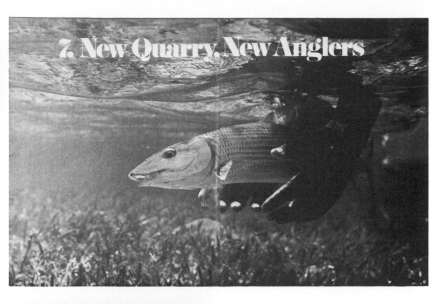

7. New Quarry, New Anglers

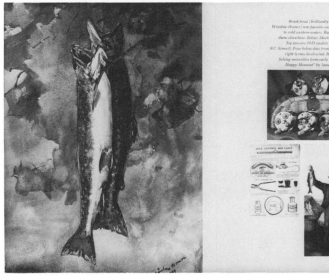

Brook trout (brilliantly depicted by Winslow Homer) was favorite eastern fish transplanted to cold western waters. Below: Meek bait-casting reels. Top two are 1845 models handmade by B.C. himself. Four below date from 1890 to 1940. Farther eight is rare level-wind. Bottom: Page of fishing novelties from early catalog, and "The Happy Moment" by James G. Clonney.

Opening page: Tournament tuna team proudly displays 518-pounder caught off Nebraska Shoals, between Point Judith and Block Island. Below: Fishing for the purist—Atlantic salmon on a fly rod, taken on St. Mary's River in Nova Scotia. Canadian government has recognized that income from sportsmen is greater than from commercial catch and has prohibited netting of salmon at river mouths.

N

ations and their navies have quarreled for hundreds of years over ownership of the sea's fish, the problems becoming more and more complex as food requirements and sporting values increased.

The development of commercial fishing techniques made it possible to catch more fish from a smaller stock, and exploitation could not keep pace with the harvest. But the issues were clouded by fundamental ignorance of the supply. While some scientists said the sea was the future food source of the world, others argued that it had already been overexploited and that fish populations had declined as human population increased. Another conflict emerged when sport fishing became an industry in itself. In some cases, at least, a fish was worth more at the end of a sportsman's line than in the net of a commercial fisherman. Thus there was conflict among the fishing nations and conflict between sporting interests and commercial operators. There also was conflict between the sport fishermen of one country and commercial fishermen of another, a sort of double discord.

American commercial fishermen were outdistanced in technology after World War II. It was not that other nations invented more practical fishing apparatus, but simply that the fishing enterprises of other governments were on a larger scale, a matter of national support and an urgent need for seafood. The Soviet "factory ships" were an unmistakable factor in the cold war—floating processing plants which could serve the smaller vessels that did the actual fishing. American fleet noted that the fishing boats were equipped with complex electronic gear that was unnecessary for any kind of fishing, and the American news media called these "spy ships" in the belief they were monitoring naval and aerial activity. It was

also reported that the Russian ships were equipped to track American rocket experiments.

There always had been reports that certain oceanic grounds were being fished out, but now it was being suggested that the entire salt-water population of fish could be depleted through concentrated attacks.

The Atlantic salmon situation became the outstanding example of a conflict of interests. As a sporting fish the salmon was primarily a fresh-water quarry. Commercial fishing in the upper reaches of salmon rivers had been banned for a long while. The supply had dwindled and New England salmon fishing was almost completely finished for both sporting and commercial interests by 1930. Restocking began in 1958 and there was improvement, although it was considered a token fishery. With new funds and new projects under way in the seventies the future looked better.

Americans spent a great deal of money on sport fishing for salmon in the Maritime Provinces of Canada, but until the nineteen-seventies they competed with Canadian netters. Then the Canadians decided sport fishing was more valuable than the commercial catch, and prohibited netting at the river mouths.

But many mature American salmon never came home. Adult fish roaming the deeps of the Atlantic gathered in staging areas before returning to their native streams and there they were vulnerable to the sophisticated methods of European fishermen. Not only was a large percentage of the population caught, but migrants of a particular river might be so concentrated that they could be trapped as a group a thousand miles from their spawning grounds.

197

413

ART DIRECTOR Albert Squillace
DESIGNER Albert Squillace
WRITER Charles Waterman
PUBLISHERS Ridge Press
Holt Rinehart Winston
AGENCY Ridge Press

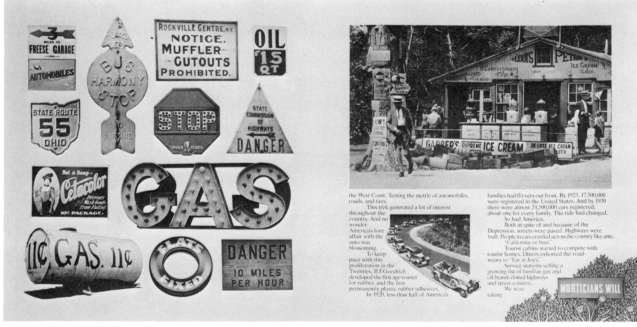

the West Coast. Testing the mettle of automobiles, roads, and tires.

This trek generated a lot of interest throughout the country. And no wonder. America's love affair with the auto was blossoming.

To keep pace with this proliferation in the Twenties, B.F.Goodrich developed the first age-resister for rubber, and the first permanently plastic rubber adhesives.

In 1920, less than half of America's

families had flivvers out front. By 1925, 17,500,000 were registered in the United States. And by 1930 there were almost 24,500,000 cars registered, about one for every family. The tide had changed. So had America.

Both in spite of and because of the Depression, streets were paved. Highways were built. People in cars crawled across the country like ants. "California or bust."

Tourist cabins started to compete with tourist homes. Diners exhorted the road-weary to "Eat at Joe's."

Service stations selling a growing list of familiar gas and oil brands dotted highways and street corners.

We were taking

414

414
ART DIRECTOR Tom Smith
DESIGNER Tom Smith
ARTIST Elwyn Mehlman
PHOTOGRAPHERS Brown Brothers
Elwyn Art Works
Bob Bender
WRITER Mike Atwell
PUBLISHER B. F. Goodrich
AGENCY Griswold Eshleman

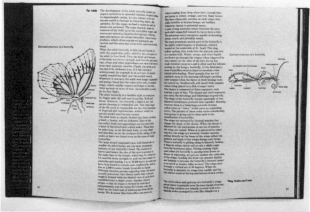

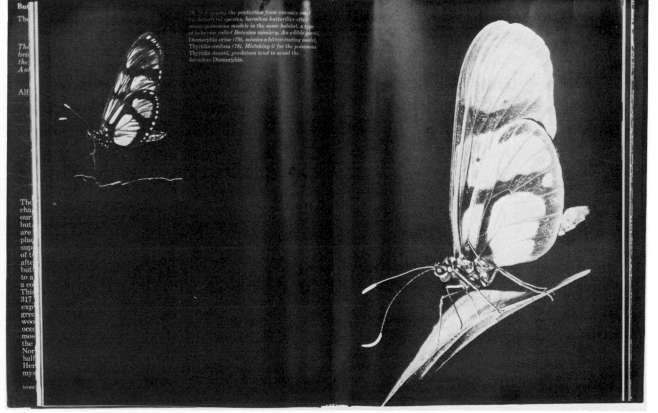

415
ART DIRECTOR Massimo Vignelli
DESIGNER Massimo Vignelli
WRITER Thomas C. Emmel
PUBLISHER Alfred A. Knopf
AGENCY Chanticleer Press

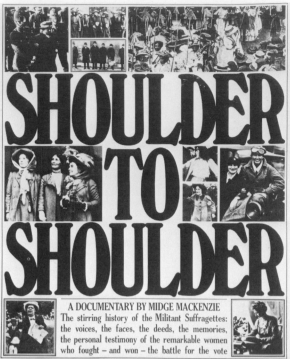

417

BOSTON

Engravings on Wood by *Rudolph Ruzicka*
With Text by *Walter Muir Whitehill*

XVII

A View of University Hall,

Harvard University, Cambridge, 1924

After a dozen years, the keepsakes moved to Cambridge to depict the building by which during the War of 1812 Harvard College attempted to catch up with the latest elegances of Boston. When Charles Bulfinch undertook the construction of Stoughton Hall in 1804, he obeyed orders and modelled the new dormitory closely, in dimensions and style, upon its neighbor, Hollis Hall, which had been built in 1763. Consequently Stoughton, although built in the nineteenth century, presented no startling contrast to its eighteenth-century neighbors, Massachusetts, Harvard, and Hollis Halls and Holden Chapel. With University Hall, however, Bulfinch moved out of red brick into Chelmsford granite, which caused a conservative tutor to call the new building 'the white spectre.'

Although the building was to provide a 'Common Hall' for dining, it seemed prudent in the interest of public order to have individual rooms for the four classes, rather than a single great hall that would accommodate the entire undergraduate body. Bulfinch submitted three alternative designs late in 1812, of which the simplest was chosen. An elegant cupola was omitted because of expense, as well as two flights of stairs on the east façade. Because of the war, the beginning of construction was delayed until the summer of 1813; nevertheless the building was completed the following year at a cost of $65,000. Its material and its ele-

416

	416		417
ART DIRECTOR	John Anderson	**ART DIRECTOR**	R. D. Scudellari
DESIGNER	John Anderson	**DESIGNER**	Louise Fili
ARTIST	Rudolph Ruzicka	**WRITER**	Midge MacKenzie
WRITER	Walter Muir Whitehill	**PUBLISHER**	Alfred A. Knopf
PUBLISHER	David R. Godine	**AGENCY**	Alfred A. Knopf
AGENCY	David R. Godine		

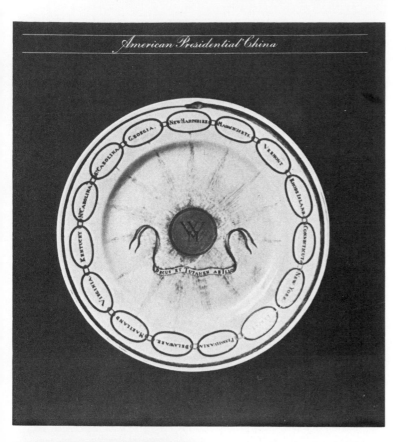

American Presidential China

Andrew Jackson 1829-1837

William Howard Taft 1909-1913

418

418

ART DIRECTOR David Ashton
DESIGNER David Ashton
PHOTOGRAPHER Richard Anderson
WRITER Susan Detweiler
PUBLISHER Smithsonian Institution
Traveling Exhibition
Service
AGENCY Ashton-Worthington

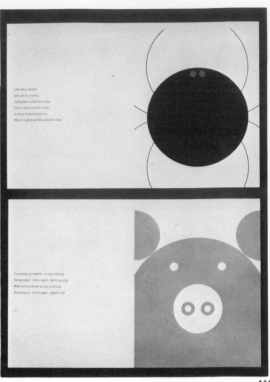

419

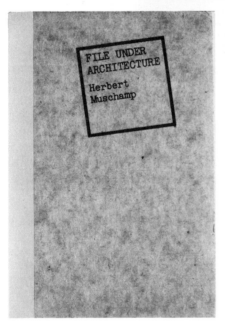

420

419
ART DIRECTOR Robert A. Propper
DESIGNER Robert A. Propper
ARTIST Robert A. Propper
EDITOR Sandra Glasser
PUBLISHER The Museum of Modern Art
AGENCY Propper/Elman

420
ART DIRECTOR Muriel Cooper
DESIGNERS Muriel Cooper
Sylvia Steiner
WRITER Herbert Muschamp
EDITOR Kathy Bayliss
PUBLISHER The MIT Press
AGENCY The MIT Press

SAPPHO THE ART OF LOVING WOMEN

THE POETRY OF SAPPHO   PHOTOGRAPHY BY J. FREDERICK SMITH

From the sound of cool waters heard through the green boughs
Of the fruit-bearing trees,
And the rustling breeze,
Deep sleep, as in a trance, down over me flows

For your sake, Aphrodite, I will burn
The rich fat of a white she-goat...
And drink a libation to thee.

421

421
ART DIRECTOR Susan Lusk
DESIGNER Susan Lusk
PHOTOGRAPHER J. Frederick Smith
EDITOR Susan Lusk
PUBLISHER Chelsea House
AGENCY Chelsea House

422

423

422
ART DIRECTOR K.K. Merker
DESIGNER K.K. Merker
TRANSLATOR Kate Franks
PUBLISHER The Windhover Press
University of Iowa
AGENCY The University of Iowa

423
ART DIRECTOR Arthur Boden
DESIGNER Arthur Boden
ARTIST Arthur Boden
PHOTOGRAPHERS John Tanski
Tom Rabstenek
Arthur Boden
WRITER John Woodside
PUBLISHER Two Continents
Publishing Group
AGENCY Arthur Boden

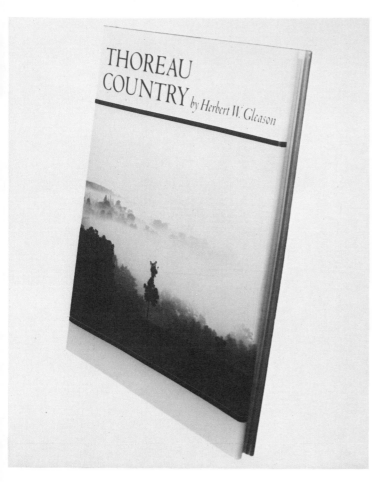

424
ART DIRECTOR Klaus Gemming
DESIGNER Klaus Gemming
PHOTOGRAPHER H. W. Gleason
EDITOR Mark Silber
PUBLISHER Sierra Club Books
AGENCY Charlsen & Johansen & Others

A therapeutic session without the therapist—it's an uncommon approach.

third groups. The results of the experiment were impressive. All four experimental groups were superior with regard to creative productivity to a control group who received none of these instructions. The fourth group, however—that is, the one with a combination of role instruction and reinforcement—proved most effective in increasing the rate of uncommon word associations. At the end of this task, subjects in each group were asked to rate the role of the person that they were being asked to copy. All groups rated this role as being more imaginative, better adjusted, and more original than did the subjects in the control group.

This investigation suggests a number of interesting points relevant to psychotherapy, and a strong similarity between the efforts to train for creative thinking and the psychiatrist's efforts to assist the patient in coping with stress. First, role model. This is a very direct "do as I do" approach. In most cases, in therapy, this instruction is left unstated, but remains implicit in the approach of the psychotherapist. It is not uncommon for a patient to say to his therapist: "I got into this tough situation, I knew I wouldn't see you for a while. I started pretending you were there and talking to you as though we were sitting here together." At such moments, the patient is most likely trying to review for himself the nature of the overt and covert cues the therapist might be giving as a role model, trying to picture, in his mind, what type of attitude the therapist might display at that time, suggesting, perhaps, that this is a correct and effective role for him to take in the situation as well.

Secondly, role instruction. Many times this is also left implicit by the psychotherapist. But it is probably reflected in such questions to the patient as: "Did you tell him you were angry with him?" and "What were you feeling at the time?" (not "Were you feeling anything at the time?").

Thirdly, reinforcement. This may vary in psychotherapy from a comment—similar to that used in Levy's study, such as "good," "fine," or "right"—to a smile or response of pleasure and approval on the part of the therapist to an idea or action by the patient. Naturally, the reward offered by the therapist must eventually be reinforced by rewards taking place outside the treatment setting, or else the responses learned would be limited to the consulting room. For instance, in choosing a situation for "assertive training"—a technique advocated by certain behavior therapists—it is important there be a

Creative Psychiatry

5

Creativity and the Ability to Cope
Daniel S. P. Schubert, M.D., Ph.D.

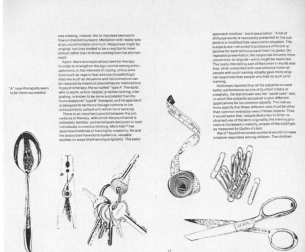

"A" type therapists seem to be more successful.

was missing. Instead, the id impulses seemed to flow unchecked outward. Mediation with reality was at an uncomfortable minimum. Responses might be original, but they tended to be a reaction to inner stimuli rather than to those coming from the environment.

Again, there are implications here for therapy. In order to strengthen the ego control among schizophrenics, in the interests of coping, unfixe emotions such as rage or fear and psychopathologic features such as delusions and hallucinations can be reduced by means of phenothiazine medications. In psychotherapy, the so-called "type A" therapist, who is warm, active, helpful, problem-solving, integrating, is known to be more successful than the more analytical "type B" therapist, and his approach is designed to reinforce the ego controls in the schizophrenic patient with whom he is working.

There is an important parallel between the procedures of therapy, with which the psychiatrist is intimately familiar, and techniques designed to train individuals in creative thinking. Maltzman has described methods of training for creativity. He and his associates have done numerous, valuable studies on ways of enhancing originality. The basic

approach involves "word association." A list of stimulus words is repeatedly presented to the subjects in a modified free-association situation. The subjects are instructed to produce a different response for each stimulus each time it is given. On repeated presentation, the responses became more uncommon or original—which might be expected. The really interesting part of Maltzman's results was that, when presented with new stimulus material, people with such training reliably gave more original responses than people who had no such prior training.

Maltzman reported that all his subjects showed better performance on one of Guilford's tests of creativity, the test chosen was the "usual uses" test, in which the subjects are asked to give different applications for six common objects. The instructions specify that these different uses must be other than common everyday uses of these objects. Thus it would seem that, despite Maltzman's rather restrained use of the term originality, his training procedure increased creativity, at least of the cold type, as measured by Guilford's test.

Ward found that incentive effects would increase creative responses among children. The children

Table I

Guilford's Tests of Creativity

Test Name	Example Item
1. Word Fluency	Write words starting with a given letter.
2. Figural Units	Combine two-line elements to make a larger number of figures.
3. Semantic Units (listing of class members)	Name kinds of fish.
4. Figural Classes (e.g., alternate letter groups based on structure of figural property of letters)	A, H, P—all have horizontal lines.
5. Symbolic Class	Words with similarities, such as number of syllables.
6. Associational Fluency; simile completion	"His smile was as wide as a _____." (The blank to be filled as many times as possible.)
7. Semantic System	Write sentences starting with the letters W, C, E, N.
8. Semantic Transformation	Unusual quick response to word association; clever plot titles—short story is presented and subject asked to give clever titles.

425

425
ART DIRECTORS Ken Jordan
John DeCesare
DESIGNER Ken Jordan
ARTIST Joe Harris
EDITORS Frederic Flach
Robert Boswell
PUBLISHER Geigy Pharmaceuticals
AGENCY Geigy Pharmaceuticals

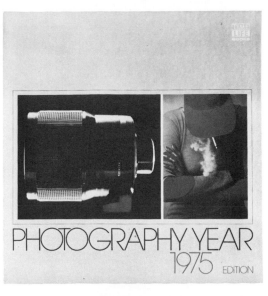

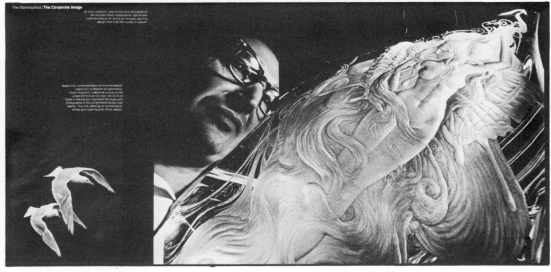

426

426
ART DIRECTOR Sheldon Cotler
DESIGNER Thomas S. Huestis
EDITOR Fred R. Smith
PUBLISHER Joan D. Manley
Time Life Books
AGENCY Time Life Books

A Sparkling, Informal History of the Black Man in Baseball
ART RUST, JR.

427

428

429

430

	427		**428**		**429**
ART DIRECTOR	Barbara Cohen	**ART DIRECTOR**	Lidia Ferrara	**ART DIRECTOR**	Harris Lewine
DESIGNER	Alan Peckolick	**DESIGNER**	Ira Teichberg	**DESIGNER**	Herb Lubalin
ARTIST	Lubalin Smith Carnase	**WRITER**	Louis J. Weichmann	**ARTIST**	Herb Lubalin
PUBLISHER	Delacorte Press	**EDITOR**	Angus Cameron	**PUBLISHER**	Harcourt Brace
AGENCY	Lubalin Smith Carnase &	**PUBLISHER**	Alfred A. Knopf		Jovanovich
	Peckolick	**AGENCY**	Alfred A. Knopf	**AGENCY**	Lubalin, Smith, Carnese &
					Peckolick

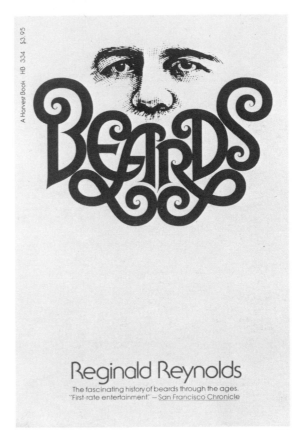

431

A Harvest Book   HB 334 $3.95

Reginald Reynolds

The fascinating history of beards through the ages.
"First-rate entertainment." — San Francisco Chronicle

432

A CRIME CLUB SELECTION
E. X. FERRARS

Alive & DEAD

433

430
ART DIRECTOR Harris Lewine
DESIGNER Seymour Chwast
ARTIST Haruo Mayauchi
PUBLISHER Harcourt Brace Jovanovich
AGENCY Push Pin Studio

431
ART DIRECTOR Alex Gotfryd
DESIGNER Gene Federico
ARTIST Gene Federico
PUBLISHER Doubleday and Co.
AGENCY Doubleday and Co.

432
ART DIRECTOR Harris Lewine
DESIGNER Alan Peckolick
ARTIST Alan Peckolick
PUBLISHER Harcourt Brace Jovanovich
AGENCY Lubalin, Smith, Carnese & Peckolick

GOLD

433
ART DIRECTOR Rallou M. Hamshaw
DESIGNERS Nancy & Tom Tafuri
ARTISTS Nancy & Tom Tafuri
PUBLISHER Doubleday & Co.
AGENCY Doubleday & Co.

GRAPHIC DESIGN

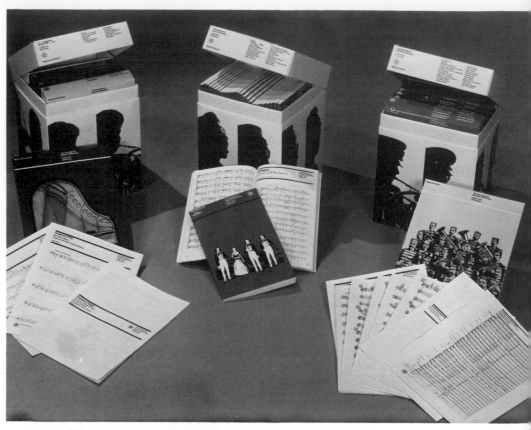

434

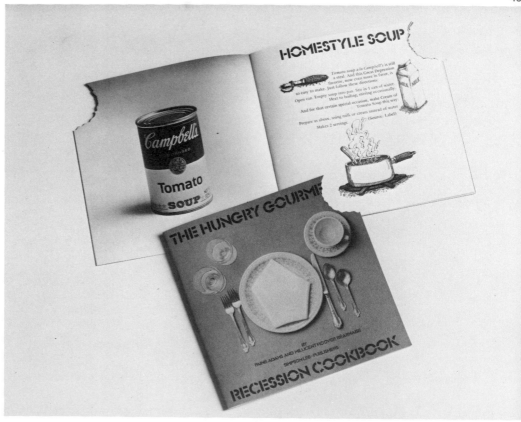

435

	434		**435**
ART DIRECTOR	Robert P. Gersin	**ART DIRECTOR**	Steve Jacobs
DESIGNERS	Paul Hanson	**DESIGNERS**	Jennie Chien
	Ken Cooke		Steve Jacobs
PHOTOGRAPHER	Melabee Miller	**ARTIST**	Jack Tom
WRITER	Edward Chasins	**PHOTOGRAPHER**	William Arbogast
AGENCY	Robert P. Gersin Assoc.	**WRITER**	Maxwell Arnold
CLIENT	J. C. Penney Co.	**AGENCY**	Steven Jacobs Design
		CLIENT	Simpson Lee Paper Co.

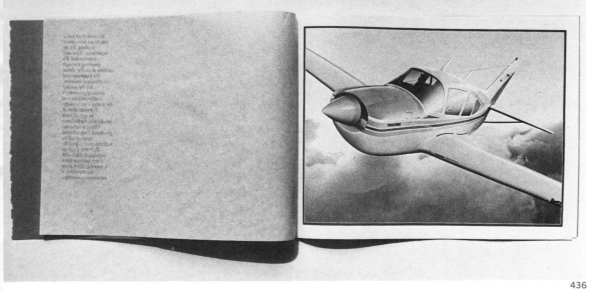

436
ART DIRECTOR James Lotter
PHOTOGRAPHER Charles Schmid
WRITERS Duane Johnson
Jim Barnum
AGENCY Carmichael/Lynch
CLIENT Bellanca Aircraft Corp.

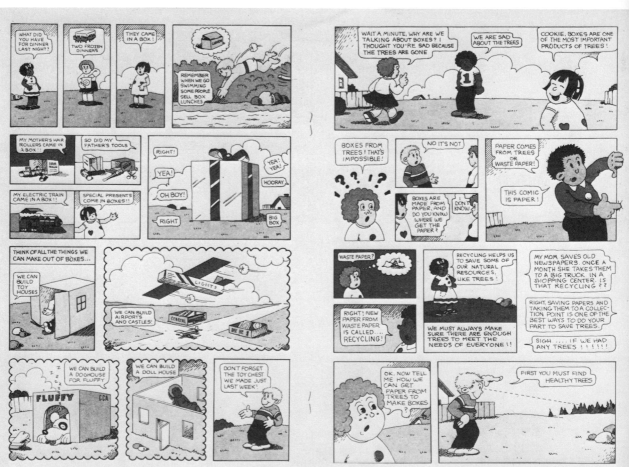

437
ART DIRECTOR Bill Bonnell
ARTIST Bob Zoell
EDITOR Sue Black
AGENCY Container Corp. of America
CLIENT Container Corp. of America

Litholinn & Printing

Electronics

Utilities

Travel

Its proven printability is perfect for pretty faces
and pretty places.

Because it takes to 4-color like a fish takes to
water, it's always got something in store for you.

Food

438

438

ART DIRECTORS	Richard Burns
	Doug Akagi
DESIGNERS	Richard Burns
	Doug Akagi
	John Clark
ARTIST	Doug Akagi
PHOTOGRAPHERS	George Selland
	Craig Simpson
	Richard Burns
	John Andersen
WRITER	David Johnson
AGENCY	Crown Zellerbach
CLIENT	Crown Zellerbach

God loves an idle rainbow no less than laboring seas.

Ralph Hodgson — *"A Wood Song"*

439
ART DIRECTOR John Casado
DESIGNER John Casado
PHOTOGRAPHER Charles Weckler
WRITER The Light Opera Studio
AGENCY Casado Design
CLIENT The Light Opera Studio

440

440

ART DIRECTOR	Don Moravick
DESIGNER	Don Moravick
ARTISTS	Judy Cohen
	Harley Shelton
	Roger Harvey
WRITER	Don Moravick
AGENCY	Don Moravick & Assoc.
CLIENT	Richard-Allan Medical
	Industries

44

442

441
ART DIRECTOR Blaine Gutermuth
DESIGNER Dick Moulton
PHOTOGRAPHER Spectrum Div.
WRITER John J. Folger
AGENCY Howard Swink Advertising
CLIENT Owens-Illinois Glass

442
ART DIRECTORS Robin Rickabaugh
Heidi Rickabaugh
DESIGNER Robin Rickabaugh
ARTIST Robin Rickabaugh
PHOTOGRAPHER Rick Rappaport
WRITERS Judith Spannegel
Ann Granning Bennet
AGENCY Robin & Heidi Rickabaugh
CLIENT Oregon Episcopal School

The FMC Approach To
Agro-industrial Development.

FMC

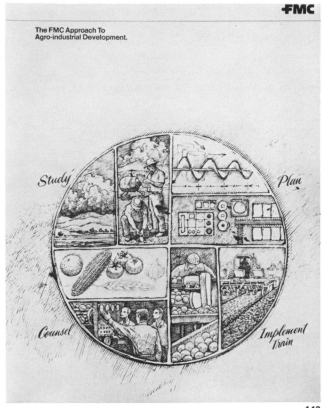

Study

Plan

Counsel

Implement
Train

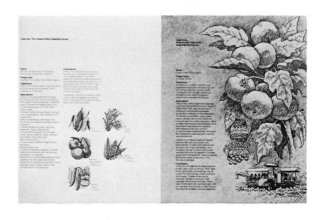

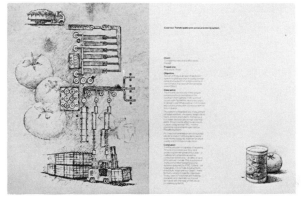

443

Stock Trade Marks

Dear corporation president, public
relations director or agency art
buyer: Are you in need of a
dynamic new image to replace the
smoking smoke stacks you or your
client is now using as a trade
mark? Well, I'm sure the answer
to that question is YES! But you're
hesitant to act because of the
time, expense and uncertainty of
selecting an image to represent
you or your client.
 That is precisely why Herring
Design Studio of Houston, Texas
has gone to the effort of preparing
this collection of Stock Trade
Marks. Long a leader in the design
of trade marks and logotypes,
HDS now draws on this vast
experience to offer trade marks
that are not only inexpensive,
but can be used for almost
any company.
 So why not order a trade mark
today? You may want to order
one for yourself and all your
subsidiaries.
 When ordering, specify the full
name of the company and
whether you want the trade mark
centered over the name or to the
right side. All the designs are
available in black, green and blue.
A few are available in red. Allow
2-3 weeks for delivery.

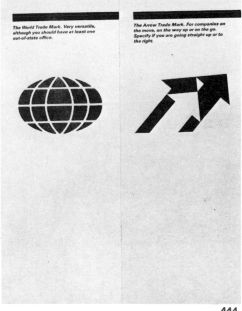

*The World Trade Mark. Very versatile,
although you should have at least one
out-of-state office.*

*The Arrow Trade Mark. For companies on
the move, on the way up or on the go.
Specify if you are going straight up or to
the right.*

444

443
ART DIRECTOR N. Jack Jannes
DESIGNER Jack McKee
ARTIST Chuck Eckart
WRITER David S. Hill
AGENCY Dancer Fitzgerald Sample
CLIENT FMC Corporation

444
ART DIRECTOR Jerry Herring
ARTIST Jerry Herring
WRITER Jerry Herring
AGENCY Herring Design
CLIENT Herring Design

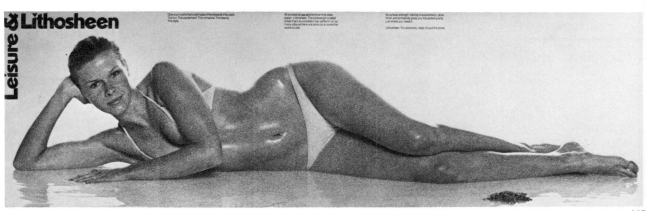

445

445
ART DIRECTORS Richard Burns
Doug Akagi
DESIGNERS Richard Burns
Doug Akagi
John Clark
ARTIST Doug Akagi
PHOTOGRAPHER Craig Simpson
WRITER David Johnson
AGENCY Crown Zellerbach
CLIENT Crown Zellerbach

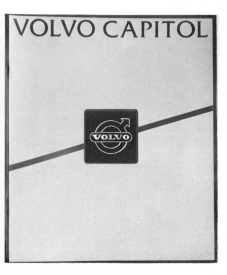

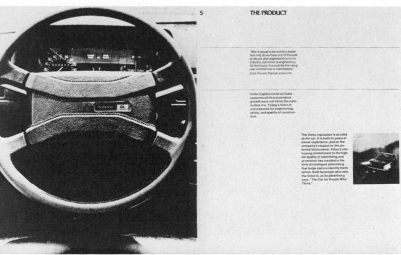

5   THE PRODUCT

"We're proud to be a Volvo dealer. Not only do we have one of the best products and organizations in the industry, but Volvo is engineering for the future. It should be the rising star of tomorrow's marketplace."
Dick Parrish, Parrish Volvo, Inc.

Volvo Capitol could not have experienced its tremendous growth were not Volvo the automobile it is. Today's Volvo is unsurpassed for engineering, safety, and quality of construction.

The Volvo reputation is as solid as the car. It is built on years of owner experience, and on the company's respect for the potential Volvo owner. Volvo's continuing commitment to the highest quality of advertising and promotion has resulted in the kind of intelligent advertising that helps owners identify themselves. Built by people who care, the Volvo is, as its advertising says, "The Car for People Who Think."

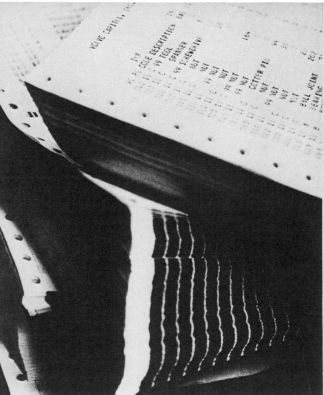

3   THE COMPANY

Volvo Capitol is dedicated to the traditional business philosophy that profit is a basic motive.

The profitability of Volvo dealers depends not only on the capability of the dealers themselves, but upon the committed resources and talents of the dealer organization that serves them.
Cy Shelton, President

Volvo Capitol, Inc., is one of five Volvo Distributing companies in the United States. All are wholly owned by Volvo of America, Inc., which in turn is owned by AB Volvo of Sweden. These companies provide dealers with Volvos, Volvo parts, service back-up, and counsel in marketing and business management.

Incorporated in 1972, Volvo Capitol employs 160 persons in its Columbia, Maryland, headquarters. The Columbia facility is the administrative center for the nine-state distributorship—providing financial and accounting services, and computerized distribution and billing of cars and parts. The 50,000-square foot facility will double its floor area during 1976.

The map shows the nine states in which Volvo Capitol operates. In three years, dealerships in these states increased from 65 to 119. During the same period, sales volume grew from under $40 million to more than $85 million.

446

446	
ART DIRECTOR	Bernice Thieblot
DESIGNER	Robert Shelley
ARTIST	Robert Shelley
PHOTOGRAPHER	Burgess Blevins
WRITER	Bernice Thieblot
AGENCY	The North Charles Street Design Organization
CLIENT	Volvo Capitol

447

STOCKHAM BALL VALVES
A 70-year-old comes of age.

SBM/Loews
Monte-Carlo Casino Guide

Blackjack / Craps

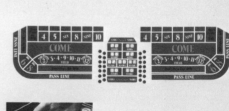

448

447
ART DIRECTOR Clyde Hogg
DESIGNER Clyde Hogg
ARTIST Lisa Johnson
PHOTOGRAPHER Parish Kohanim
WRITER Clyde Hogg
AGENCY Daniel, Riley & Hogg
CLIENT Stockham Valves and Fittings

448
ART DIRECTOR John Cavalieri
DESIGNERS John Cavalieri
Marion Schneider
ARTISTS Sal Murdocca
B. P. Grimaud
PHOTOGRAPHER Jules Alexander
WRITER Robert Pearlman
AGENCY Cavalieri, Kleier, Pearlman
CLIENT Loews Hotels

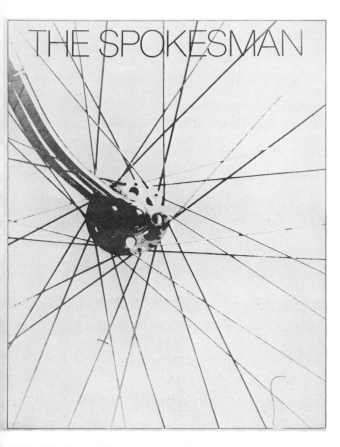

449

449
ART DIRECTORS	Richard Burns
	Doug Akagi
DESIGNERS	Richard Burns
	Doug Akagi
	John Clark
ARTIST	John Clark
PHOTOGRAPHER	George Selland
WRITER	David Johnson
AGENCY	Crown Zellerbach
CLIENT	Crown Zellerbach

DANSK HATCHES
SOME FRESH IDEAS
IN FLATWARE

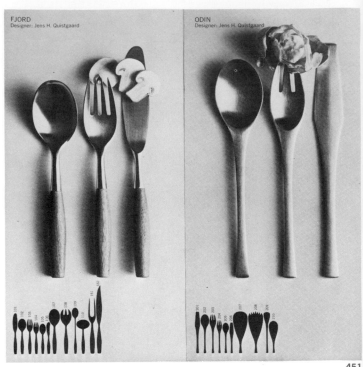

FJORD
Designer: Jens H. Quistgaard

ODIN
Designer: Jens H. Quistgaard

451

450

450

ART DIRECTORS Kit Hinrichs
Linda Hinrichs
DESIGNERS Paul Hardy
Linda Hinrichs
Kit Hinrichs
ARTISTS Nancy Stahl
Frank Mayo
Kit Hinrichs
Carveth Kramer
Skip Andrews
George Masi
Marvin Mattelson
Tim Lewis
John Clarke
Phillipe Weisbecker
Christoph Blumrich
Guy Billout
PHOTOGRAPHERS Ken Korsh
Bettmann Archives
WRITER Linda Hinrichs
AGENCY Hinrichs Design Assoc
CLIENT Hinrichs Design Assoc

451

ART DIRECTOR Lou Dorfsman
DESIGNER Lou Dorfsman
ARTIST Akihiko Seki
PHOTOGRAPHER Peter Roth
WRITER Lou Dorfsman
AGENCY Lou Dorfsman
CLIENT Dansk Design

452

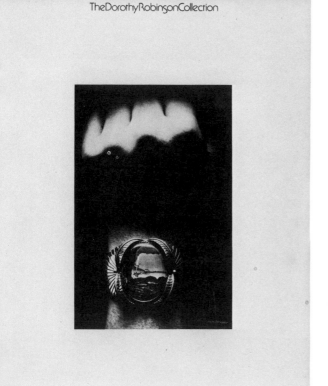

453

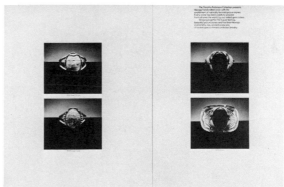

452
ART DIRECTOR W. Chris Gorman
DESIGNER W. Chris Gorman
ARTIST W. Chris Gorman
WRITER Stan Bratskeir
AGENCY Martin E. Janis & Co.
CLIENT N. Merberg & Son

453
ART DIRECTOR John Casado
DESIGNER John Casado
PHOTOGRAPHER Sherman Weisburd
WRITER Casado Design
AGENCY Casado Design
CLIENT The Dorothy Robinson Collection

454

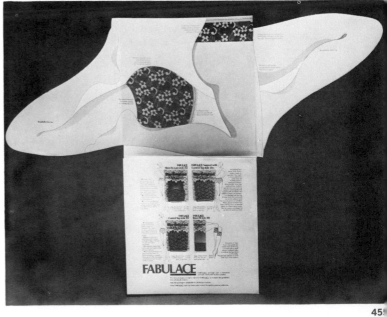

455

	454		**455**
ART DIRECTOR	Bob Wilkinson	**ART DIRECTOR**	Peter Mariotti
DESIGNER	Al Hutt Associates	**DESIGNER**	Peter Mariotti
PHOTOGRAPHER	Mike Brady	**ARTIST**	Peter Mariotti
WRITER	John Lapp	**WRITER**	Terry Alvarez
AGENCY	Stone & Simons	**AGENCY**	deKrig Advertising
	Advertising	**CLIENT**	Burlington Hosier
CLIENT	Sinclair Manufacturing		

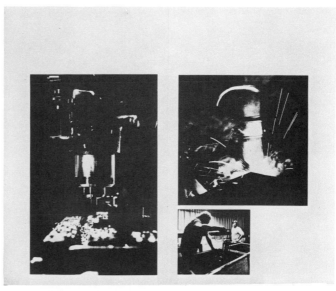

456

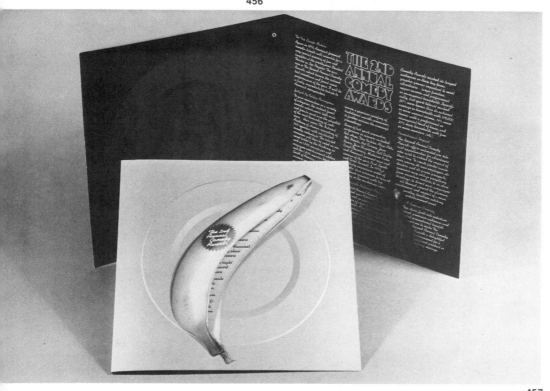

457

456
ART DIRECTOR   Lowell Williams
DESIGNER   Lowell Williams
PHOTOGRAPHER   Joe Baraban
WRITER   Lowell Williams
AGENCY   Lowell Williams Design
CLIENT   Lowell Williams

457
DESIGNER   C. Leah Becker
PHOTOGRAPHER   Nobumitsu Iwasawa
WRITER   Al Cohen
AGENCY   ABC Corporate Art
Department
CLIENT   American Broadcasting
Companies

4

4

458
ART DIRECTOR Mike Eakin
DESIGNER Mike Eakin
PHOTOGRAPHER John Paul Endress
WRITER Jan Zechman
AGENCY Zechman Lyke Vetere
CLIENT Nunn Bush Shoe Co.

459
ART DIRECTOR Steve Jacobs
DESIGNER Jennie Chien
ARTIST Bunny Carter
PHOTOGRAPHERS Carol Fulton
Mark Gottlieb
WRITER Mark Fulton
AGENCY Steven Jacobs Desig
CLIENT Simpson Lee Paper C

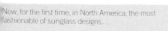
Now, for the first time, in North America, the most fashionable of sunglass designs…

460

Introducing Polaroid Sunglasses. Now, everything else is something less.

POLAROID

461

	460		461
ART DIRECTOR	John Milligan	ART DIRECTOR	Louis Nelson
DESIGNER	John Milligan	DESIGNERS	Ronald Wong
ARTIST	Roy Hughes		Paul Hanson
PHOTOGRAPHERS	Bruno Joachim		Robert P. Gersin
	Phil Porcella	PHOTOGRAPHER	Melabee M. Miller
WRITER	Cameron Foote	WRITER	Bruce Hart
AGENCY	Polaroid Corp.	AGENCY	Robert P. Gersin Assoc.
CLIENT	Polaroid Corp.	CLIENT	American Telephone & Telegraph Co.

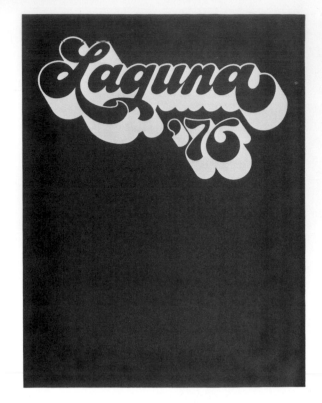

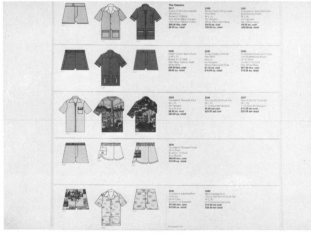

466

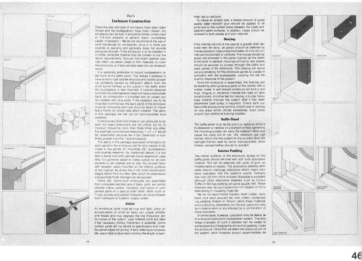

466

465
ART DIRECTOR John Anselmo
DESIGNER Thomas Bloch
PHOTOGRAPHER Herbert Kravitz
WRITER Chip Potter
AGENCY John Anselmo Design Assoc.
CLIENT Laguna Sportswear

466
ART DIRECTOR Dennis S. Juett
DESIGNER Dennis S. Juett
ARTISTS Dennis S. Juett
Dan Hanrahan
PHOTOGRAPHER Dave Holt
WRITER Garry Margolis
AGENCY Dennis S. Juett & Assoc
CLIENT George Hartley
James B. Lansing Soun

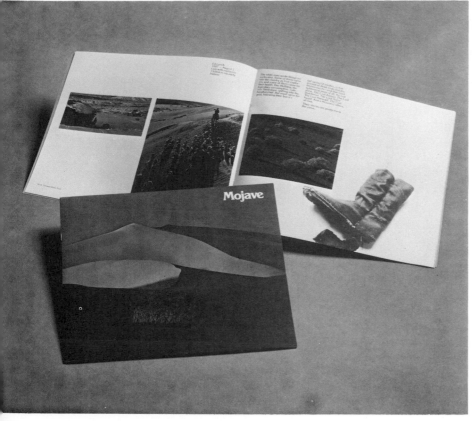

467

468

	467		**468**
ART DIRECTOR	Steve Jacobs	ART DIRECTOR	John Casado
DESIGNER	Jennie Chien	DESIGNERS	John Casado
PHOTOGRAPHERS	David Muench		Barbara Casado
	William Arbogast	WRITER	Casado Design
WRITER	Maxwell Arnold	AGENCY	Casado Design
AGENCY	Steven Jacobs Design	CLIENT	Casado Design
CLIENT	Simpson Lee Paper Co.		

462
ART DIRECTOR	George Tscherny
DESIGNER	George Tscherny
PHOTOGRAPHER	George Tscherny
WRITER	George Tscherny
AGENCY	George Tscherny
CLIENT	Monadnock Paper Mill

463

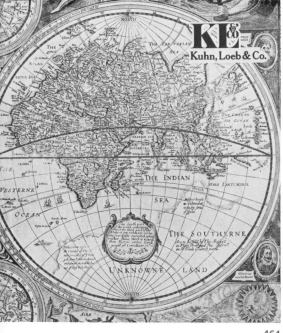

464

	463		**464**
ART DIRECTOR	Keith Bright	ART DIRECTOR	J. M. Moriber
DESIGNER	Keith Bright	DESIGNER	J. M. Moriber
ARTISTS	Joanne Hirose	PHOTOGRAPHER	Bill Farrell
	Patrick Soo Hoo	WRITERS	Kuhn, Loeb, and Staff
WRITER	Edmund Cohen	AGENCY	Hill and Knowlton
AGENCY	Berry, Cullen, Cohen	CLIENT	Kuhn, Loeb & Co.
CLIENT	New Markets		

No thanks. I don't smoke.

46

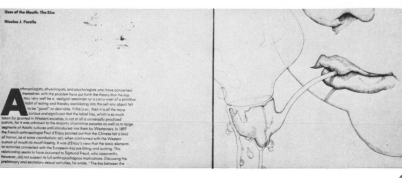

47

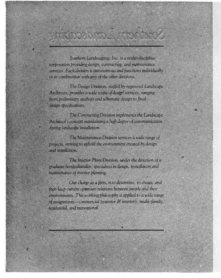

47

469
ART DIRECTOR Henry Wolf
DESIGNER Henry Wolf
PHOTOGRAPHER Henry Wolf
AGENCY Henry Wolf Productions
CLIENT Parsons School of Design

470
ART DIRECTOR Seymour Chwast
DESIGNER Seymour Chwast
ARTISTS Seymour Chwast
Joyce Mac Donald
Haruo Miyauchi
Milton Glaser
George Stavrinos
Victor Kotowitz
PHOTOGRAPHERS Arnold Rosenberg
Benno Friedman
WRITER Phyllis Levine
AGENCY Push Pin Studios
CLIENT Push Pin Studios

471
ART DIRECTOR Lowell Williams
DESIGNER Lowell Williams
PHOTOGRAPHER Joe Baraban
WRITER Grant Halter
AGENCY Lowell Williams Design
CLIENT Southern Landscaping

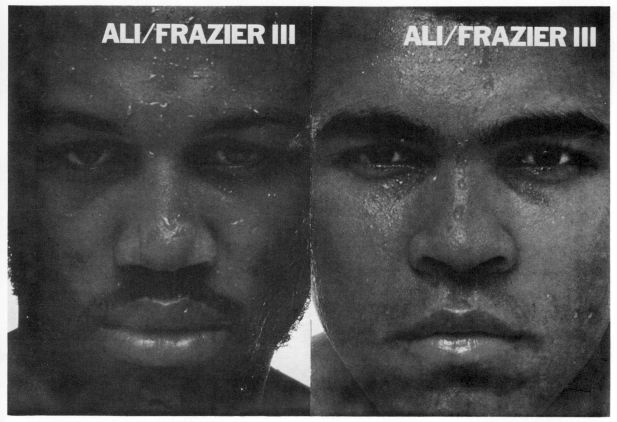

472

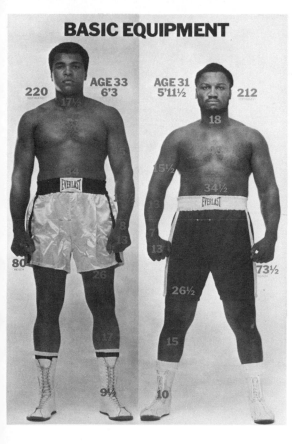

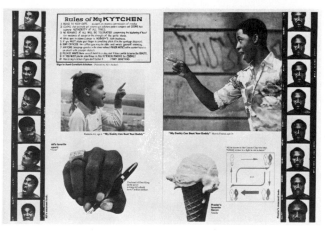

472
ART DIRECTORS George Lois
               Kurt Weihs
DESIGNERS   George Lois
               Kurt Weihs
PHOTOGRAPHER   Carl Fischer
WRITER   Harold Hayes
AGENCY   Lois Holland Callaway
CLIENT   Don King Productions

Bring us $25 from your sugar bowl and get some beautiful tableware. Free.

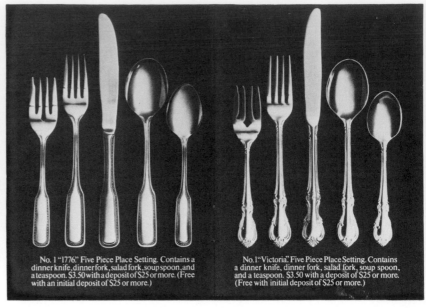

No. 1 "1776." Five Piece Place Setting. Contains a dinner knife, dinner fork, salad fork, soup spoon, and a teaspoon. $3.50 with a deposit of $25 or more. (Free with an initial deposit of $25 or more.)

No. 1 "Victoria." Five Piece Place Setting. Contains a dinner knife, dinner fork, salad fork, soup spoon, and a teaspoon. $3.50 with a deposit of $25 or more. (Free with initial deposit of $25 or more.)

474

	473		474
ART DIRECTOR	C. J. Overholser	ART DIRECTOR	Pam Roseburg
DESIGNER	C. J. Overholser	DESIGNER	Pam Roseburg
PHOTOGRAPHER	Lee Batlin	PHOTOGRAPHERS	Francisco & Booth
WRITER	John Siddall	WRITER	Pat Stehr
AGENCY	Cargill, Wilson & Acree	AGENCY	Nieman-Marcus
CLIENT	Planters National Bank	CLIENT	Nieman-Marcus Mail Order

475

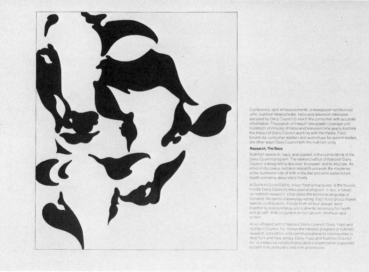

476

	475		**476**
ART DIRECTORS	Lou Dorfsman	ART DIRECTOR	Carla Barr
	David November	DESIGNER	Carla Barr
DESIGNER	David November	ARTIST	Carla Barr
WRITERS	John Wilkoff	WRITERS	Lorraine W. Shafer
	William Soden		Margaret Pettingell
AGENCY	CBS/Broadcast Group	AGENCY	Carla Barr
CLIENT	CBS Television Network	CLIENT	Dairy, Food, and Nutrition Council

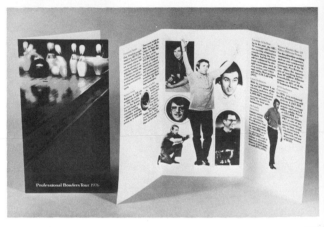

477

478

477
ART DIRECTOR Henry Epstein
DESIGNER William D. Duevell
ARTIST Tony DiSpigna
PHOTOGRAPHERS Nobumitsu Iwasawa
William Duevell
AGENCY ABC Corporate Art
Department
CLIENT ABC-TV Sales
Development

478
ART DIRECTORS Richard Burns
Doug Akagi
DESIGNERS Richard Burns
Doug Akagi
John Clark
ARTISTS George Selland
Richard Burns
PHOTOGRAPHERS David Johnson
AGENCY Crown Zellerbach
CLIENT Crown Zellerbach

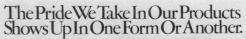

The Pride We Take In Our Products Shows Up In One Form Or Another.

At Nucor Steel, we put a lot into making our steel. And take a lot of pride in the angles, rounds, channels, flats, forging billets and special structural shapes that are our final products.

We make both carbon steel grades and alloy steel grades at Nucor. In standard lengths of 20, 40 and 60 feet. (Special lengths can be furnished.)

Nucor's pride shows up in another form too. Service. Because Nucor will go to great lengths to give you what you need, when you need it.

In fact, more than half the time our customers can get the steel they need right away, from our inventory.

If we don't have all the steel you need on hand, we can get it to you in two to four weeks. Thanks to Nucor Steel's flexible rolling schedules and quick gear-up time.

Once our products are ready for delivery, truck or rail facilities will get them to you fast because Nucor Steel is close to home, with mills in the Southeast, Midwest and Southwest. And that can mean potential savings on shipping costs.

479

SICK BAG

A little something to keep handy while watching the new network shows.

TV 6 The healthy independent in Miami.

480

479		**480**	
ART DIRECTOR	Frank Rogers	ART DIRECTOR	Fred Caravetta
DESIGNER	Frank Rogers	WRITER	Ray Allen
PHOTOGRAPHER	Gary Ludwick	AGENCY	Caravetta Allen
WRITER	Roger Feuerman		Kimbrough
AGENCY	Cargill, Wilson & Acree	CLIENT	WCIX-TV 6
CLIENT	Nucor Corporation		

484

485

	484		485
ART DIRECTOR	Raymond Waites	ART DIRECTOR	Bruce Johnson
DESIGNER	Jill Ying	DESIGNER	Bruce Johnson
PHOTOGRAPHER	Raymond Waites	ARTIST	Bruce Johnson
AGENCY	Design Group: Design	PHOTOGRAPHER	Susan Johnson
	Research	WRITER	Jay Edsal
CLIENT	Design Research	AGENCY	Jay D. Edsal Company
		CLIENT	Cornu Corp.

486

DESIGNER Miho
PHOTOGRAPHER Miho
WRITER David Brown
AGENCY Champion Papers
CLIENT Champion Papers

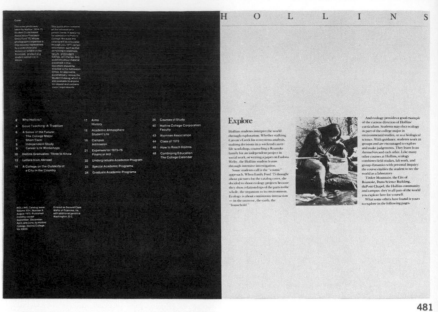

Explore

Hollins students interpret the world through exploration. Whether stalking Carvin's Creek for ecosystems analysis, making decisions in a weekend career-life workshop, counseling a Roanoke family for an independent project in social work, or writing a paper on Eudora Welty, the Hollins student learns through intensive investigation.

Some students call it the "cosmic" approach. When Emily Ford '75 thought about pictures for the catalog cover, she decided to shoot ecology projects because they show relationships of the parts to the whole, the organism to its environment. Ecology is about continuous interaction — in the universe, the earth, the "household."

And ecology provides a good example of the current direction of Hollins' curriculum. Students may elect ecology as part of the college major in environmental studies, or as a biological science. With guidance, students work in groups and are encouraged to explore and make judgements. They learn from themselves and each other. Like many other courses at Hollins, ecology combines field studies, lab work, and group dynamics with personal inquiry; the course enables the student to see the world as a laboratory.

Tinker Mountain, the City of Roanoke, Dana Science Building, duPont Chapel, the Hollins community and campus: they're all part of the world you explore here for yourself.

What some others have found is yours to explore in the following pages.

481

The Great Hall and The Cooper Union

Few auditoriums have a history equal to that of the Great Hall. It was where in 1860, Lincoln delivered his famous "right makes might" address in which he enunciated his opposition to slavery and which was to lead him to the presidency. It was from meetings in the Great Hall that the American Red Cross and the National Association for the Advancement of Colored People were born. And it was where Peter Cooper's ideal of education as a vital and continuing force in the lives of all people was vigorously pursued. From the opening of the Foundation Building, the Great Hall has been the scene of lectures and cultural events of every variety. And through the years the Great Hall has become a symbol of intellectual and cultural vitality and the ideals of The Cooper Union.

Today in the Great Hall, The Cooper Union Forum presents programs of variety and of the highest quality. In accordance with the principles of Peter Cooper no admission fee is ever charged. Programs may consist of a series of lectures on public affairs or the creative arts. Another series might concentrate on music — recitals and concerts — and on dance. With the Great Hall now fully renovated and the stage enlarged, it is one of the most attractive and versatile halls in the city. The Encounter Program, a series of free concerts by members of the New York Philharmonic, is now held there.

The Cooper Union Forum is under the aegis of the Division of Adult Education which offers every year a wide variety of adult education courses in the evening. These courses are viewed as a central responsibility of The Cooper Union,

482

481
ART DIRECTOR Bernice Thieblot
DESIGNER Robert Rytter
ARTIST Robert Rytter
PHOTOGRAPHERS Don Carstens
Emily Ford
Lynn Davis
Rigby Robinson
WRITERS Lynn Davis
Bernice Thieblot
AGENCY The North Charles Street Design Organization
CLIENT Hollins College

482
ART DIRECTOR Peter Adler
DESIGNER Peter Adler
ARTIST Joel Levirne
PHOTOGRAPHER Stanley Seligson
WRITER Fred English
AGENCY Adler, Schwartz & Connes
CLIENT Cooper Union

483

Tree farming is now such a widely accepted idea that it is difficult to imagine the skepticism that greeted Weyerhaeuser's establishment of the Clemons Tree Farm just a generation ago. Today there are more than 30,000 privately owned tree farms in America, ranging from 20 acres to 1.5 million acres. Weyerhaeuser alone planted 157 million new trees last year.

The broad acceptance of the tree farm concept is perhaps surprising when one considers the long-range nature of tree farming. A new batch of Douglas fir seedlings planted today, for example, will not be ready for complete harvest for almost half a century.

Tree farming is far from the entire company story in the period from 1941 to 1967. The company continued to grow and diversify. It became a manufacturer of laminated beams and arches, hardwood plywood and veneers, particleboard and hardboard.

It expanded into packaging, shipping containers, milk cartons and folding boxes. Another research laboratory was set up to develop products and processes for wood-based building materials and to find new uses for bark. One result of this activity has been more and more efficient use of trees. During the last 25 years the volume of useful products from an acre has more than doubled. And the company continues to strive for increased utilization of waste for fuel.

Still, from this period, tree farming is the development in which Weyerhaeuser takes greatest pride. It is the thing that tells the most about the company.

483

ART DIRECTOR	Elmer Pizzi
DESIGNERS	Mandala, Inc.
	Allan Hill
ARTISTS	Kenneth Callahan
	Stan Galli
	James Hayes
WRITER	Hank Inman
AGENCY	Gray & Rogers
CLIENT	Weyerhauser Co.

487

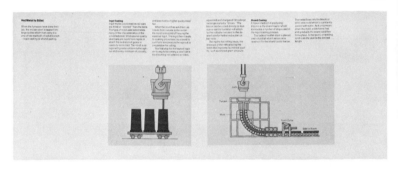

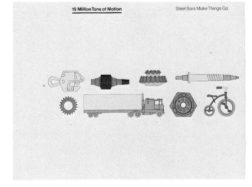

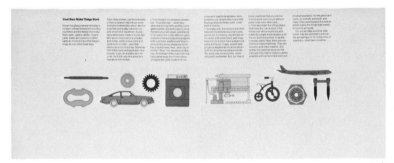

488

	487		**488**
ART DIRECTOR	Al Gluth	**ART DIRECTOR**	Marie Christine Lawrence
DESIGNER	Al Gluth	**DESIGNER**	Marie Christine Lawrence
PHOTOGRAPHER	Joe Baraban	**ARTIST**	Ed Duchene
WRITER	Larry Landmesser	**WRITER**	William Hitchcock
AGENCY	Baxter & Korge	**AGENCY**	Hill and Knowlton
CLIENT	Christiana Corp.	**CLIENT**	American Iron & Steel Institute

489

490

489
ART DIRECTOR John Cavalieri
DESIGNERS John Cavalieri
Marion Schneider
PHOTOGRAPHERS Chuck Bangert
Jules Alexander
WRITER Robert Pearlman
AGENCY Cavalieri, Kleier,
Pearlman
CLIENT Loews Hotels

490
ART DIRECTOR Steve Jacobs
DESIGNER Ed Jaciow
ARTIST Rick von Holdt
WRITER Maxwell Arnold
AGENCY Steven Jacobs Design
CLIENT Simpson Lee Paper Co.

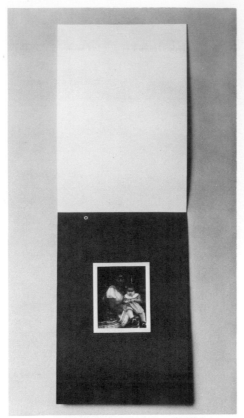

Polaroid's ultra-brilliant Polacolor 2.

492

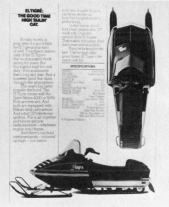

491

	491		492
ART DIRECTOR	James Lotter	ART DIRECTOR	John Milligan
DESIGNER	Bill Hogan	DESIGNER	John Milligan
PHOTOGRAPHERS	Vern Hammarlund	ARTIST	Stan Malcolm
	Dick Nielund	WRITER	Ted Voss
WRITER	Duane Johnson	AGENCY	Polaroid Corp.
AGENCY	Carmichael/Lynch	CLIENT	Polaroid Corp.
CLIENT	Arctic Enterprises		

494

493

	493		494
ART DIRECTOR	Louis Nelson	ART DIRECTOR	Onofrio Paccione
DESIGNERS	Ronald Wong	DESIGNER	Onofrio Paccione
	Robert P. Gersin	PHOTOGRAPHER	Onofrio Paccione
AGENCY	Robert P. Gersin Assoc.	AGENCY	Paccione Photography
CLIENT	American Telephone & Telegraph Co.	CLIENT	Paccione Photography

SILVER

495

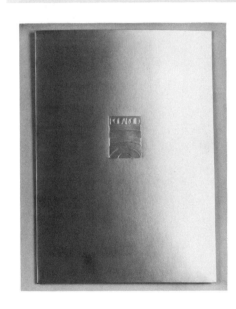

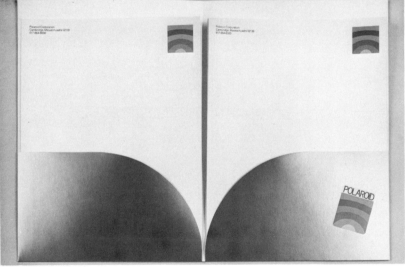

496

	495		496
ART DIRECTOR	Mark Norrander	ART DIRECTOR	John Milligan
DESIGNER	Mark Norrander	DESIGNER	John Milligan
ARTIST	Newman Myrah	ARTIST	Stan Malcolm
PHOTOGRAPHERS	Warren Morgan	WRITER	Ted Voss
	Brian Lanker	AGENCY	Polaroid Corp.
WRITER	Dave Newman	CLIENT	Polaroid Corp.
AGENCY	Cole & Weber		
CLIENT	University of Oregon		

497

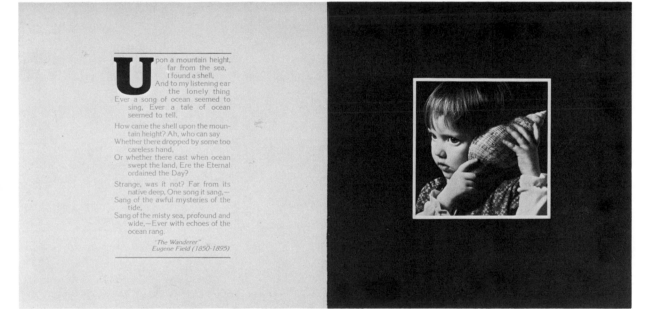

497
ART DIRECTOR Terry Lesniewicz
DESIGNER Terry Lesniewicz
PHOTOGRAPHERS Dave McKenna
John Fong
WRITER Dolores Sullwold
AGENCY Flournoy & Gibbs
CLIENT The Toledo Hearing and
Speech Center

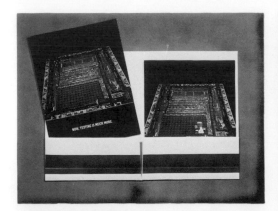

499

498

498
ART DIRECTOR Louis Nelson
DESIGNERS Ronald Wong
Robert P. Gersin
AGENCY Robert P. Gersin Assoc.
CLIENT American Telephone &
Telegraph Co.

499
ART DIRECTOR Douglas Hoppe Stone
DESIGNER Douglas Hoppe Stone
ARTISTS Randy Chewning
Art Banuelos
Larry McAdams
Dan Laws
Darleen McElvoy
Pamela Ann Smith

PHOTOGRAPHERS Harry Chamberlain
Stan Sholik
WRITERS John Joss
E. D. Rose
AGENCY Rose & Stone Advertising
CLIENT Fairchild Systems
Technology

500

501

	500		501
ART DIRECTOR	Joan Cassidy	**ART DIRECTOR**	Louis Nelson
DESIGNER	Joan Cassidy	**DESIGNERS**	Ronald Wong
ARTISTS	Joan Cassidy		Robert P. Gersin
	Richard Waxberg	**AGENCY**	Robert P. Gersin Assoc.
PHOTOGRAPHER	Lawrence Mayea	**CLIENT**	American Telephone &
AGENCY	Texasgulf		Telegraph
CLIENT	Texasgulf		

502

502
ART DIRECTOR Richard Stack
DESIGNERS Richard Stack
Herb Rogalski
PHOTOGRAPHER Steve Hansen
WRITER Richard Stack
AGENCY Richard Stack
CLIENT Wintergreen

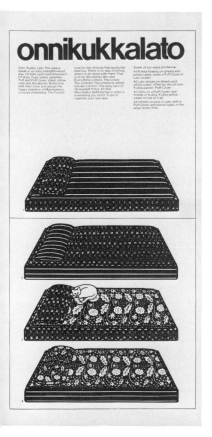

	503		**504**
ART DIRECTOR	Raymond Waites	**ART DIRECTOR**	Tamoko Miho
DESIGNER	Joel Fuller	**DESIGNER**	Tamoko Miho
ARTIST	Barbara Bascove	**WRITER**	David Brown
WRITER	Kay Tyller	**AGENCY**	Champion Papers
AGENCY	Design Group: Design Research	**CLIENT**	Champion Papers
CLIENT	Design Research		

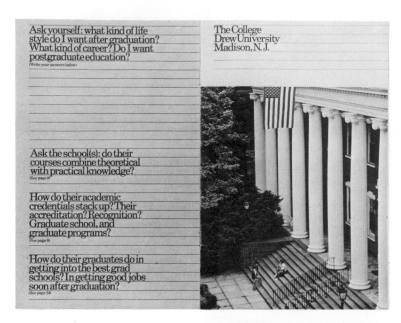

Before you finally decide on
a college or university,
ask yourself the key questions
shown inside.

Ask yourself: what kind of life
style do I want after graduation?
What kind of career? Do I want
postgraduate education?
(Write your answers below)

Ask the school(s): do their
courses combine theoretical
with practical knowledge?
(See page 6)

How do their academic
credentials stack up? Their
accreditation? Recognition?
Graduate school, and
graduate programs?
(See page 8)

How do their graduates do in
getting into the best grad
schools? In getting good jobs
soon after graduation?
(See page 24)

The College
Drew University
Madison, N.J.

Then ask the school(s) you're
considering for their answers
to corollary questions.

Most people can change their mind about
most things time and time again, with no
ill effects.
But college isn't one of those things:
Most people decide on a college once, and—
for better or worse—that decision holds.
Since it's unlikely that you're an expert at
selecting a college, we've prepared some
questions that can provide criteria for your
decision. These yellow pages are for you to
write the answers on. Answers about Drew
University. And about other schools as well.
Please use them for notes until you've made
your decision.
Remember:
Before you start your college education,
you must start your education about college.
The College, Drew University, Madison,
New Jersey 07940.

505

Craftsmanship thrives at
Deerwood.
We found something
remarkable in the garden
townhomes of Deerwood. The kind of
craftsmanship you just don't find
today. And the kind of beauty.

You'll enter your home in a most
welcoming way. Protected from the
elements by roofing canopies and
greeted by greenery, chandeliers and
sparkling skylights. You may feel
you're in the Old French Quarter of
New Orleans. But once inside your
home, you'll know the conveniences
are totally today.

Refrigerators are frost-free and
ranges are self-cleaning. Dishwashers
and disposals are sound-insulated, to
keep things peaceful for you.

Foyers are the finest wood parquet.
Carpeting is wall-to-wall luxury. And
the kitchen and bathroom wall
covering is easy-to-live-with vinyl,
color coordinated. We've carpeted
your balcony, too, to take you
comfortably into our great outdoors.

Air conditioning is individually
controlled.

Closets are walk-in and oversized.
But just in case, you'll have extra
exterior storage space, too.

Parking is covered. And the
Deerwood security patrol is on guard
at all times to protect you and
your property.

You'll have a front entrance. A rear
entrance. A fireplace, if you choose.
And a skylight in most second-floor
bathrooms. More space, more
comforts, more living.

A Colony Called Deerwood

506

505
ART DIRECTORS Ellen Shapiro
Lawrence Miller
DESIGNER Lawrence Miller
PHOTOGRAPHER Barnett Studio
WRITERS Steven Paradis
Lawrence Miller
AGENCY The Barton-Gillet
Company
CLIENT Drew University

506
ART DIRECTOR Anna Wingfield
DESIGNER Jack Amuny
ARTIST Art City
PHOTOGRAPHER Larry Payne
WRITER Anna Wingfield
AGENCY Goodwin, Dannenbaum
Littman & Wingfield
CLIENT Deerwood Garden
Townhomes

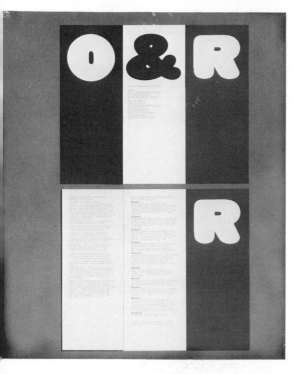

507

508

507
ART DIRECTOR W. Chris Gorman
DESIGNER W. Chris Gorman
WRITER William G. O'Donnell
AGENCY W. Chris Gorman Assoc.
CLIENT American Business Press

508
ART DIRECTOR Peter Teubner
DESIGNER Peter Teubner
WRITER Thomas Eads
AGENCY Teubner & Assoc.
CLIENT Fred S. James & Co.

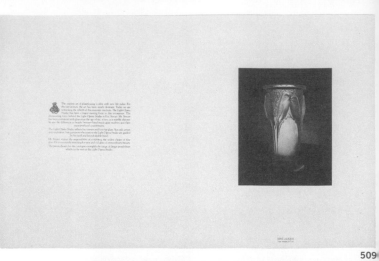

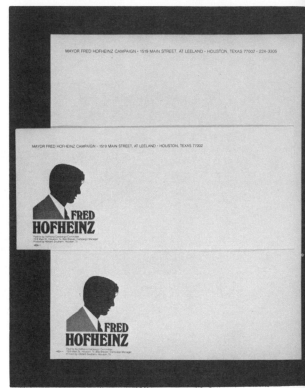

Since 1974
Houston has recruited
581 new police officers,
spent 6.5 million dollars
on crimefighting equipment,
bought 100 new buses,
added half a million miles of
new bus routes, lowered
fares and ended up as the
only major American city
with money in the bank.

	509		510
ART DIRECTOR	John Casado	**ART DIRECTOR**	Jim Culberson
DESIGNER	John Casado	**DESIGNER**	Jim Culberson
ARTISTS	John Casado	**ARTIST**	Jim Culberson
	Jackie Jones	**PHOTOGRAPHER**	Joe Baraban
PHOTOGRAPHER	Rudy Legname	**WRITER**	Rick Barthelme
WRITER	The Light Opera Studio	**AGENCY**	Goodwin, Dannenbaum
AGENCY	Casado Design		Littman & Wingfield
CLIENT	The Light Opera Studio	**CLIENT**	Hofheinz Campaign
			Committee

512

The Rookery

For some time, "progress" has been synonymous with new building. However, increasing awareness of the need to protect and conserve the resources of our environment has placed a new responsibility upon the architect. He must respond to the need to preserve the richness of the past and at the same time creatively adapt landmark buildings such as The Rookery to today's requirements.

511

	511		512
DESIGNER	Ron Coates	**ART DIRECTOR**	Louis Nelson
PHOTOGRAPHER	Hedrich-Blessing	**DESIGNERS**	Ronald Wong
WRITER	Pat Sieben		Paul Hanson
AGENCY	Ron Coates Design		Robert P. Gersin
	Consultant	**AGENCY**	Robert P. Gersin Assoc.
CLIENT	Graham, Anderson,	**CLIENT**	American Telephone &
	Probst, White		Telegraph

51

 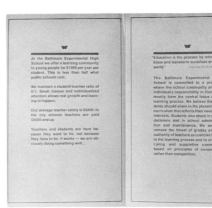

51

	513		514
ART DIRECTOR	John Milligan	ART DIRECTOR	Pete Traynor
DESIGNER	John Milligan	DESIGNER	Pete Traynor
ARTIST	Roy Hughes	ARTIST	Pete Traynor
PHOTOGRAPHER	Bruno Joachim	PHOTOGRAPHER	Richard Anderson
WRITER	Ted Voss	WRITER	Howie Evans
AGENCY	Polaroid	AGENCY	Ashton-Worthington
CLIENT	Polaroid	CLIENT	Baltimore Experimental High School

515

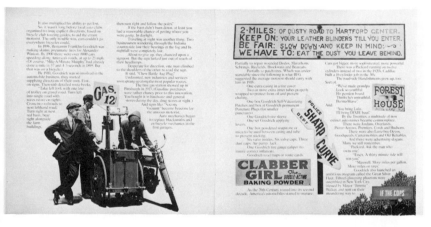

515
ART DIRECTOR Tom Smith
DESIGNER Tom Smith
ARTIST Elwyn Mehlman
WRITER Mike Atwell
AGENCY Griswold-Eshleman
CLIENT B.F. Goodrich

THE 1975 ORANGE BOWL ANNUAL REPORT. CHEERS.

STAFF CELEBRATES COMPLETION OF FOUR PAGES OF BORING FINANCIAL NOTES.

ORANGE BOWL REPORTS RECORD EARNINGS.

516

ART DIRECTOR	Ron Sullivan
DESIGNER	Ron Sullivan
PHOTOGRAPHER	Greg Booth
WRITER	Ed Wattenbarger
AGENCY	The Richards Group
CLIENT	Data Point

517

ART DIRECTOR	Frank Schulwolf
DESIGNER	Frank Schulwolf
PHOTOGRAPHER	Robert Panuska
WRITER	Richard Maender
AGENCY	Frank Schulwolf
CLIENT	The Orange Bowl Cor

To the Shareholders:

A great deal of uncertainty exists in the financial community related to offshore drilling companies and yet, by almost any standard of measurement, fiscal year 1975 was the finest year in SEDCO's history. The popular scenario that there are too many rigs under construction, while true, is simplistic and misses the mark. Contract drilling has always been competitive and SEDCO can compete effectively with any company in the business. We have experienced people, first-class equipment, the best technology and a record of performance.

SEDCO's biggest problem today is the lack of worldwide political stability and its effect on the willingness of our customers to spend exploration money. In making an investment decision, the international oil companies consider many factors, but none are more important than political/economic stability and the sanctity of a contract. Unfortunately, during the past several years, international contracts have been breached, assets confiscated without compensation and leases assessed retroactively. Even in our own country we have seen long-standing investment incentives eliminated and natural market forces distorted with ill-conceived government controls. The resulting confusion has understandably caused oil companies to draw back and selectively defer additional investments. In the final analysis, no progress can be made toward solving the free world's energy problems until political stability returns to the domestic and international scene.

Although these political problems have not yet affected SEDCO financially, it is becoming more difficult to obtain long-term drilling contracts. However, during the past year SEDCO's Drilling Division was able to sign new contracts ranging from one to three years for the SEDCO K, SEDCO 702, SEDCO H.I., SEDCO 135, SEDCO 135-A, SEDCO 135-E and SEDCO 135-F. Construction of the SEDCO 704 was completed in October 1974 and it began working for Mobil Oil Corporation in the North Sea under a two-year drilling contract. In April 1975 the SEDCO 470 was canceled during the early stages of construction, but it was replaced by the SEDCO 472, another dynamically stationed drill ship, which upon completion will work for Exxon under a three-year contract. This contract is important in that it establishes a direct relationship between SEDCO and Exxon, one of the few major international oil companies which was not a SEDCO customer.

Our backlog of Drilling Division equipment under construction presently totals $378 million, of which up to $304 million will be financed by SEDCO. The balance of the financing will be handled by our partners through joint-ownership companies without the use of SEDCO's credit lines.

The consolidated revenues of SEDCO, Inc. during fiscal year 1975 rose 35 percent to $229,675,000, while net income increased 57 percent to $37,594,000, the equivalent of $3.49 per share. All of these financial results represent record highs.

The Construction Division in particular made an impressive turnaround during 1975 as divisional profits rose to $1,700,000 after tax, compared to last year's $570,000 loss. The Construction Division presently has a backlog of approximately $190,000,000 consisting of pipeline work in Iran, Brazil, Nigeria, Peru and Alaska. We expect profits from pipeline construction to continue to grow for several years based on contracts in hand and our forecast of pipeline activity worldwide.

In planning for the future, your Management has tried to extend SEDCO's offshore engineering capabilities into new areas with such ventures as an offshore drilling unit for the Canadian arctic, a semi-submersible service/firefighting unit and deep-ocean mining. We are pleased to report good progress during 1975 on all these projects. The SCOPA, a dynamically stationed semi-submersible drilling unit capable of working continuously in shifting offshore ice, was model tested in the arctic last spring. These expensive tests, primarily funded by a group of Canadian oil companies led by Sun Oil, were successful and further testing is scheduled for 1976.

Our efforts in obtaining a long-term commitment for a semi-submersible oil field service/firefighting unit were brought to a successful conclusion in August of 1975 when Phillips Petroleum Company Norway signed a five-year contract for the use of this unique $45 million unit. The Phillips SS, as it is named, will be a self-propelled, semi-submersible unit outfitted and staffed to supply North Sea offshore production platforms with

With North Sea waters swirling below him, this roughneck makes adjustments to the riser tensioner line so that drilling operations can continue.

They Race to Meet Schedules
Every step in the production process must be tightly programmed. A Moroccan worker selects the best nursery seedlings for transfer to the tomato fields as company managers supervise construction of a factory that will be finished in time to process the first crop.

H.J. Heinz Company   Annual Report 1975

They Cater to Various Palates
Heinz became an international force by learning how to satisfy local tastes in food. A Dutch foreman inspects green tomatoes destined to go into a familiar spread. In Britain, a machine operator feeds lids to a canning line for popular oxtail soup.

518
ART DIRECTOR Jack Summerford
DESIGNER Jack Summerford
PHOTOGRAPHER Sedco Employees
WRITERS B. Gill Clements
Jeanne Archer
Steve Mahood
AGENCY The Richards Group
CLIENT Sedco

519
ART DIRECTOR Alicia Landon
DESIGNER Alicia Landon
PHOTOGRAPHER Bruce Davidson
WRITER Oscar Schefler
AGENCY Corporate Annual Reports
CLIENT H.J. Heinz Co.

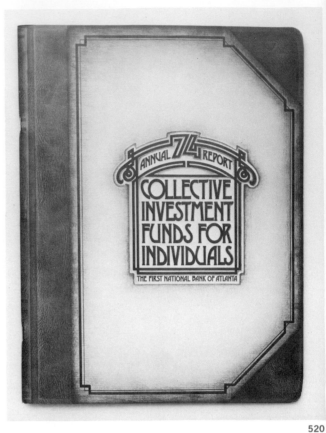

520

ART DIRECTOR Bob Wages
DESIGNER The Workshop, Inc.
ARTIST The Workshop, Inc.
AGENCY McDonald & Little
CLIENT The First National Bank of Atlanta

GOLD

Colonial Penn Group, Inc.   1974 Annual Report

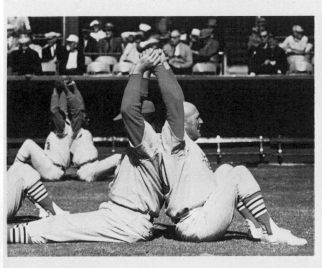

"Sure there are lots of things wrong with this country, but committed to us everyone else is second place."

Gnorie Pasagar, major league baseball coach

with Action for Independent Maturity (AIM), a pre-retirement division of AARP, and is coordinated with employer pre-retirement programs.

During this period of economic downturn, Mature Temps will effect prudent economies and concentrate on the most stable sources of demand for temporary services in order to minimize operating losses in 1975.

Colonial Penn Communities
Colonial Penn Communities, our retirement housing subsidiary, dedicated its pilot mobile home retirement community, Hawthorne at Leesburg, in March of 1974.

Since the summer of 1972 when the company acquired this mid-Florida site of approximately 300 acres with access to fresh water lakes, construction has proceeded substantially on schedule. The project provides a full package of amenities specifically designed for older Americans. The community, which can eventually house 1,300 families, includes a 24,000 square foot recreational building. It is the center of a recreational complex that includes a swimming pool and a marina with slips for 125 boats. The community also features 24-hour security and fire protection.

At year-end, the total project in terms of permanent land improvements and facilities was virtually completed; 520 sites had been leased with 404 of them occupied. About 65% of the more than 800 residents are actively participating in one or more activities that they themselves have planned and organized with the assistance of a full-time program director of

recognized standing and experience in the field of aging.

In sum, Hawthorne at Leesburg is now a functioning retirement community. Its reasonably priced, high-quality housing situated in esthetically pleasant surroundings has set a standard of excellence for other retirement communities.

At the same time, the rate of sales at Hawthorne at Leesburg was and continues to be adversely affected by the economy, causing this project to operate at a loss in 1974. In periods of economic uncertainty, people, and especially older persons, are inclined to "wait-and-see" before committing to a major move in life. More particularly, a shortage of mortgage funds has made it difficult for older persons to find qualified buyers for their current residences. The vast preponderance of home sales at Hawthorne at Leesburg are cash purchases from the sale proceeds of a former residence.

It is anticipated that in the absence of an early favorable change in the economic environment, home sales at Hawthorne at Leesburg will proceed at a slow pace. However, the gradual increase in site rental income as homes are occupied, coupled with improved operating efficiencies, should help to control losses in 1975 at a level under those of 1974. There are no plans at this time for the development of new retirement communities.

21

insurance coverages and other services to their members.

These capabilities rest to a large extent on the use of self-contained, in-house resources to plan, test, and market your company's services through an economical distribution system.

Your company believes that this distribution system facilitates the extension of its programs to increasing numbers of older Americans over a broader income range. In addition, although members of the principal older persons organizations remain Colonial Penn's primary customer group, the company also serves the membership of some 90 other organizations which, together with NRTA/AARP, represent access to a potential customer group of more than 13 million individuals. This population segment, more diverse by age and income, can also be reached by the proven distribution system of your company.

To further broaden its understanding of its customer groups, Colonial Penn has intensified its market research activities. The growing importance of market research in your company is reflected in the threefold increase in annual budgeted expenditures for this function between 1970 and 1974.

New products jointly developed by representatives of the company's actuarial, underwriting, marketing, administrative and legal staffs are normally tested on a pilot basis before being offered on a national scale.

The Marketing Division offers Colonial Penn full-line advertising services—from copywriting and production to media selection—all tailored to the company's customer groups.

Other essential marketing tools—from the most advanced electronic data processing facilities to mail-house operations geared to handle large volumes of varied solicitation packages—are also part of the company's centralized resource base.

The Business of the Company
As in years past, during 1974 Colonial Penn was primarily engaged through its subsidiaries in the business of soliciting, administering and insuring policies of health, life, automobile and other insurance written principally for members of various organizations on either a group or individual basis. In addition, other subsidiaries of the company arrange and conduct group travel tours for older people, place older persons in temporary employment, operate a retirement community in Florida and conduct a list brokerage business.

Life and Health Insurance Operations
Colonial Penn's life and health insurance operations achieved excellent production results for 1974.

Premium income from health insurance—your company's principal line of business—amounted to $177,335,000, up 38% from 1973.

Health premium income results for 1974 reflected to a significant extent a marked upswing in new written health premiums during the last two years. The production highs of three successive NRTA/AARP group health insurance enrollment periods from the fall of 1973 to the summer of 1974 were due in some measure to coverage liberalizations that proved attractive

"I like color. It gives me the gaiety that life doesn't always provide."

Eddie Heckeger, retired teacher

10

521

ART DIRECTOR George Tscherny
DESIGNER George Tscherny
PHOTOGRAPHER Bill Binzen
WRITER Corporate Affairs Dept.
AGENCY George Tscherny
CLIENT Colonial Penn Group

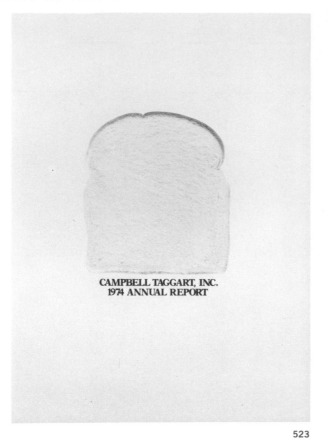

CAMPBELL TAGGART, INC.
1974 ANNUAL REPORT

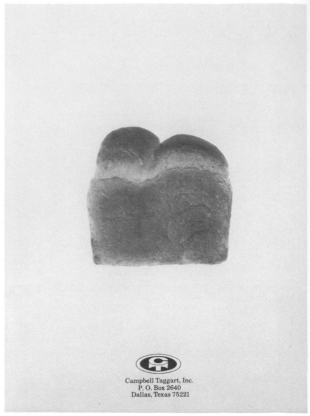

Campbell Taggart, Inc.
P. O. Box 2640
Dallas, Texas 75221

523

H. J. Heinz Company   Annual Report 1975

522

hng

CUBIC FEET

524

522
ART DIRECTOR   John Weaver
DESIGNER   John Weaver
PHOTOGRAPHER   Ron Scott
WRITER   Barbara Shook
AGENCY   Baxter & Korge
CLIENT   Houston Natural Gas

523
ART DIRECTOR   Ad Directors
DESIGNERS   Don Crum
Tom Melnichek
Jack Reed
ARTIST   Don Crum
PHOTOGRAPHER   Gary Blockley
WRITER   Mike Moon
AGENCY   Ad Directors
CLIENT   Campbell Taggart

GOLD

524
ART DIRECTOR   Alicia Landon
DESIGNER   Alicia Landon
PHOTOGRAPHER   Bruce Davidson
WRITER   Oscar Schefler
AGENCY   Corporate Annual Reports
CLIENT   H.J. Heinz

SILVER

525

526

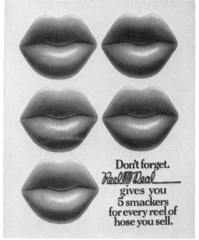

527

525
DESIGNER Richard Hess
PHOTOGRAPHER Richard Hess
WRITER Richard Hess
AGENCY Champion Papers
CLIENT Champion Papers

526
ART DIRECTOR Henry Wolf
DESIGNER Henry Wolf
PHOTOGRAPHER Henry Wolf
WRITER Anne Stegemeyer
AGENCY Henry Wolf Productions
CLIENT Saks Fifth Ave.

527
ART DIRECTOR Bob Kwait
DESIGNER Bob Kwait
ARTIST Elwyn Mehlman
WRITER Walt Woodward
AGENCY Griswold-Eshleman
CLIENT B.F. Goodrich

 SILVER

528

529

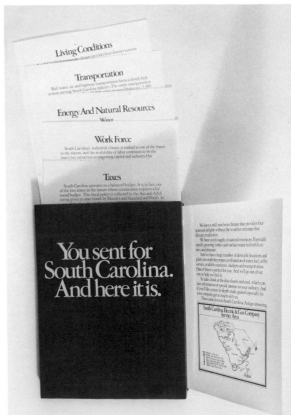

530

	528		529		530
ART DIRECTOR	Terry Mutzel	DESIGNER	Bill Farrell	ART DIRECTOR	Jerry Torchia
DESIGNER	Terry Mutzel	PHOTOGRAPHER	Bill Farrell	DESIGNER	Jerry Torchia
ARTIST	Terry Mutzel	AGENCY	Bill Farrell	ARTIST	Jim Scancarelli
WRITER	Richard Stites	CLIENT	Bill Farrell	WRITER	Barbara Ford
AGENCY	Case-Hoyt			AGENCY	Cargill, Wilson & Acree
CLIENT	Case-Hoyt			CLIENT	South Carolina Electric & Gas

FJORD
Designer: Jens H. Quistgaard

ODIN
Designer: Jens H. Quistgaard

DANSK HATCHES
SOME FRESH IDEAS
IN FLATWARE

531

Our Problem

To create
a bottle for
Cutty Sark's
12 year old
Scotch
that dramatizes
its lightness,
distinguishes
it from
regular
Cutty Sark,
yet maintains
the traditional
Cutty Sark
'feel'.

Our Solution

First the name:
Cutty 12.
A swift
separation from
Cutty Sark.
Next:
Maintaining
the traditional
'feel' of
Cutty Sark.
We delved
into
nautical lore
and adapted
the most
exciting use
of glass
that involves
ships:
the brilliant
prisms that
send light
flashing from
lighthouses.

And here's
what our
prismatic bottle
accomplishes.

1. It looks
unlike
Chivas Regal,
Johnnie
Walker Black,
or any other
Scotch bottle.

2. The prisms
actually gather
in light,
then reflect
it out,
in a
sparkling,
multifaceted
demonstration
of
Cutty 12's
lightness.

3. The
jewel-like
look supports
the necessarily
higher price
of a
12 year old
Scotch.

Finally,
we enriched
the familiar
Cutty Sark
yellow label
with an
elegant
embossed print
on a luxurious
gold foil.

Note

The ecstasy
(and the agony)
of designing
glass bottles
is in finding
fresh,
original
expressions
that make
economic
sense,
can stand
the rigors
of automated
conveyors,
and be
labelled with
existing
machinery.
We passed
every
aesthetic,
practical and
monetary test.

532

	531		532
ART DIRECTOR	Lou Dorfsman	**ART DIRECTOR**	Kurt Weihs
DESIGNER	Lou Dorfsman	**DESIGNER**	Kurt Weihs
ARTIST	Akihiko Seki	**PHOTOGRAPHER**	Tom Weihs
PHOTOGRAPHER	Peter Roth	**WRITER**	Ron Holland
AGENCY	Lou Dorfsman	**AGENCY**	Lois Holland Callaway
CLIENT	Dansk Designs	**CLIENT**	Buckingham Corp.

GOLD

533

534

533
ART DIRECTOR Tom Smith
DESIGNER Tom Smith
ARTIST Elwyn Mehlman
WRITER Mike Atwell
AGENCY Griswold-Eshleman
CLIENT B.F. Goodrich

534
ART DIRECTOR Marvin Mitchneck
DESIGNER Marvin Mitchneck
ARTIST Paul Davis
WRITER Jack Keane
AGENCY David, Oksner &
Mitchneck
CLIENT Consolidated Cigar Corp

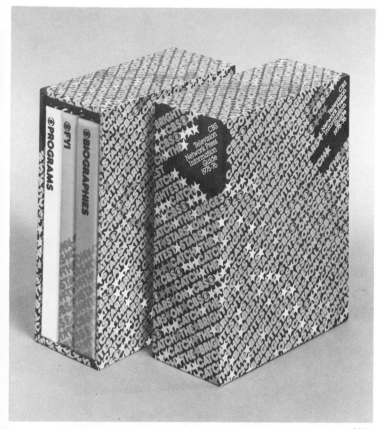

536

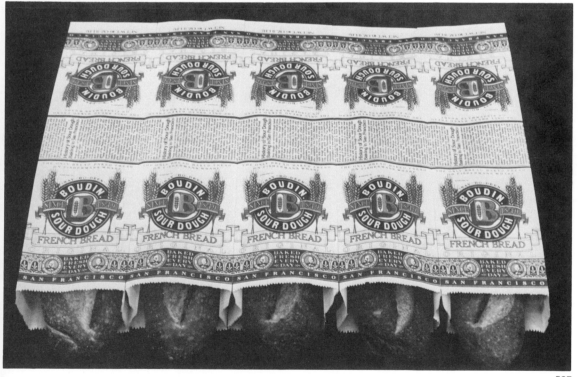

537

	536		537
ART DIRECTOR	Lou Dorfsman	ART DIRECTORS	Primo Angeli
DESIGNER	Kathy Palladini		Roger Shelly
AGENCY	CBS/Broadcast Group	DESIGNER	Primo Angeli
CLIENT	CBS Television Network	ARTISTS	Primo Angeli
			Tandy Belew
		AGENCY	Steedman, Cooper &
			Busse
		CLIENT	Boudin Bakeries

GOLD

538

540

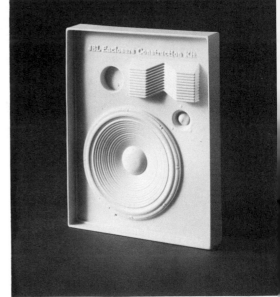

539

538
ART DIRECTOR Ford, Byrne & Assoc.
DESIGNER Ford, Byrne & Assoc.
ARTIST Ford, Byrne & Assoc.
AGENCY Ford, Byrne & Assoc.
CLIENT Pennwalt Corporation

539
ART DIRECTOR Dennis S. Juett
DESIGNER Dennis S. Juett
ARTISTS Dave Holt
Dennis S. Juett
Alan Williams
PHOTOGRAPHER Dave Holt
AGENCY Dennis S. Juett & Assoc.
CLIENT James B. Lansing Sound

540
ART DIRECTOR Keith Bright
DESIGNER Keith Bright
ARTIST Glenn Vilppu
WRITER Edmund Cohen
AGENCY Keith Bright & Assoc.
CLIENT Filice Winery

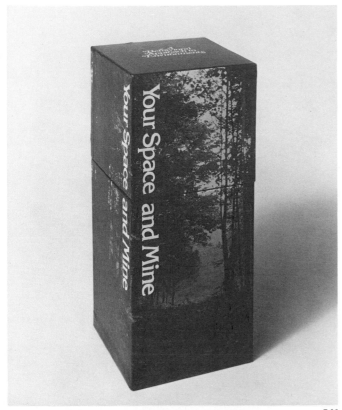

541

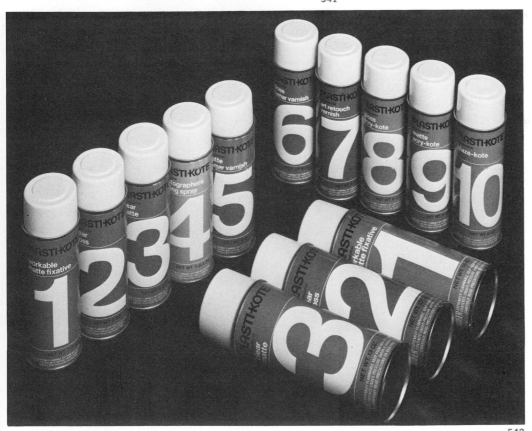

542

	541		**542**
ART DIRECTOR	Ed Brodsky	**ART DIRECTOR**	F.E. Smith & Assoc.
DESIGNERS	Ed Brodsky	**DESIGNER**	F.E. Smith & Assoc.
	Janice Hermansen	**ARTIST**	F.E. Smith & Assoc.
PHOTOGRAPHER	Freelance Photographers	**AGENCY**	F.E. Smith & Assoc.
	Guild	**CLIENT**	Plasti-Kote Co.
WRITERS	Peggy Haney Pyle		
	Alisun Smith		
AGENCY	Brodsky Graphics		
CLIENT	J.C. Penny		

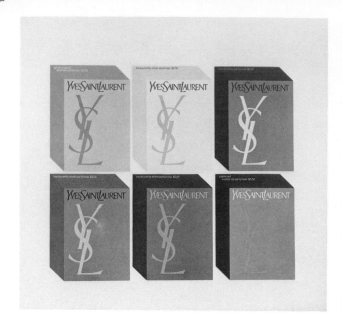

543

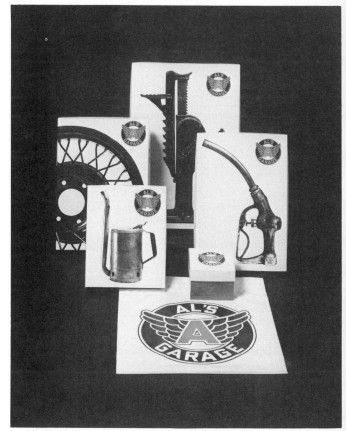

544

543
ART DIRECTOR Robert P. Gersin
DESIGNERS Kenneth Cooke
Paul Hanson
AGENCY Robert P. Gersin Assoc.
CLIENT Kayser-Roth Hosiery

544
ART DIRECTOR John Follis
DESIGNERS Wayne Hunt
Connie Beck
PHOTOGRAPHER Scott Slobodian
AGENCY John Follis & Assoc.
CLIENT At-Ease (Al's Garage)

545

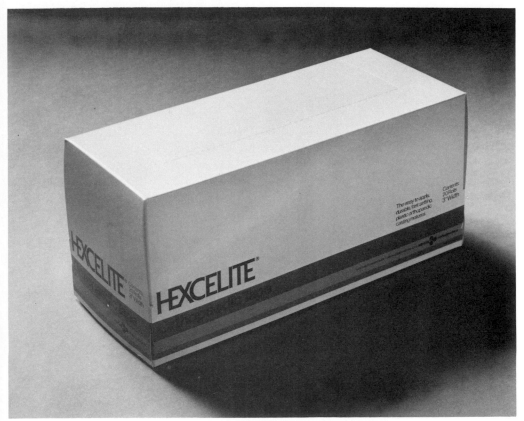

546

	545		546
ART DIRECTORS	Dan Bittman	ART DIRECTOR	Steve Jacobs
	George Tassian	DESIGNER	Steve Jacobs
DESIGNER	Dan Bittman	AGENCY	Steven Jacobs Design
ARTIST	Maurice Delegator	CLIENT	Hexcel Medical Products
WRITER	Edward S. Nemo		
AGENCY	The George Tassian Org.		
CLIENT	Meiers Wine Cellars		

547

548

<table>
<tr><td>547</td><td></td><td>548</td></tr>
</table>

ART DIRECTOR	Fred Podjasek	**ART DIRECTOR**	Raymond Waites
DESIGNERS	Jack Kellbach	**DESIGNER**	Bruce McIntosh
	Fred Podjasek	**AGENCY**	Design Group: Design
AGENCY	Racila & Vallarta Assoc.		Research
CLIENT	Johnson Products	**CLIENT**	Design Research

549

550

551

	549		**550**		**551**
ART DIRECTOR	Don Stone	**ART DIRECTOR**	James Stitt	**ART DIRECTOR**	Marilyn Lowther
DESIGNER	Kathleen Clark	**DESIGNER**	James Stitt	**DESIGNER**	Marilyn Lowther
ARTIST	Kathleen Clark	**ARTIST**	James Stitt	**ARTIST**	Marilyn Lowther
PHOTOGRAPHER	Bill Braly	**AGENCY**	James Stitt & Co.	**PHOTOGRAPHER**	Bob Maxham
WRITER	David Warford	**CLIENT**	Steam Beer Brewing	**WRITER**	David Ham
AGENCY	Lenac, Warford, Stone			**AGENCY**	Atkins and Assoc.
CLIENT	Interbath			**CLIENT**	Natural Oxygen Products

552

553

554

	552		553		554
ART DIRECTOR	Harry Millyard	ART DIRECTOR	Dave Reid	ART DIRECTORS	Tom Knott
DESIGNER	Harry Millyard	DESIGNER	James Stitt		Steve Miller
ARTIST	Dawson Design	ARTIST	James Stitt	DESIGNERS	Woody Pirtle
PHOTOGRAPHER	Mel Goldman	AGENCY	James Stitt & Co.		Jack Summerford
WRITER	Adrian VanDorpe	CLIENT	Browne Vintners	ARTISTS	Tom Knott
AGENCY	Polaroid				Steve Miller
CLIENT	Polaroid				Woody Pirtle
					Jack Summerford
				PHOTOGRAPHER	Chuck Untersee
				AGENCY	The Bloom Agency
				CLIENT	Campbell Taggart

555

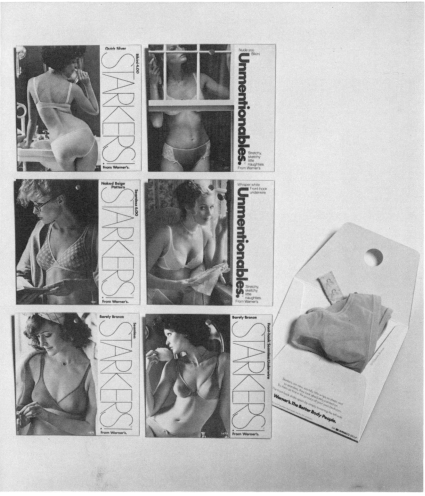

556

	555		556
ART DIRECTOR	Keith Bright	ART DIRECTOR	Murray Jacobs
DESIGNER	Keith Bright	DESIGNER	Murray Jacobs
ARTIST	Glenn Vilppu	PHOTOGRAPHER	Jacques Malignon
WRITER	Edmund Cohen	WRITER	Cay Gibson
AGENCY	Keith Bright & Assoc.	AGENCY	Gardner Advertising
CLIENT	Filice Winery	CLIENT	Warnaco
			Warner's Division

557

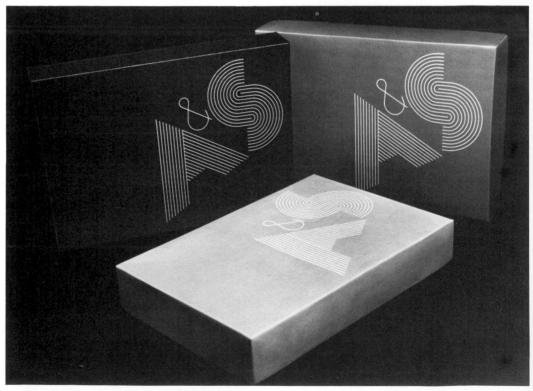

558

	557		**558**
ART DIRECTOR	James Stitt	**ART DIRECTORS**	Howard Chanler,
DESIGNER	James Stitt		Thomas H. Geismar
ARTIST	Ann Williams Stitt	**DESIGNER**	Thomas H. Geismar
AGENCY	James Stitt & Co.	**ARTIST**	Hoi Ling Chu
CLIENT	Steam Beer Brewing Co.	**AGENCY**	Chermayeff & Geismar
		CLIENT	Abraham & Straus

 SILVER

559

560

561

	560		561		559
ART DIRECTOR	John Berg	ART DIRECTOR	Ed Lee	ART DIRECTOR	Tom Wilkes
DESIGNER	Teresa Alfieri	DESIGNER	Ed Lee	DESIGNER	Tim Bryant
AGENCY	CBS Records	ARTIST	Peter Lloyd	PHOTOGRAPHER	Ron Slenzak
CLIENT	CBS Records	AGENCY	CBS Records	AGENCY	ABC Records
		CLIENT	CBS Records	CLIENT	ABC Records

562

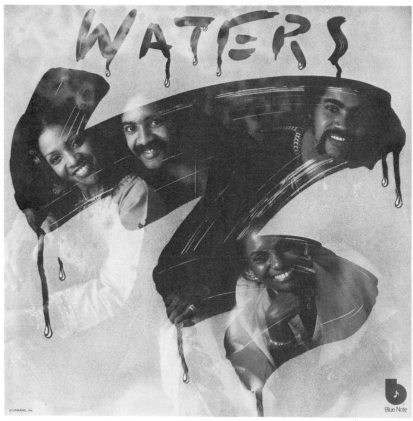

563

	562		**563**
ART DIRECTOR	Tom Wilkes	**ART DIRECTOR**	Lloyd Ziff
DESIGNER	Tom Wilkes	**DESIGNERS**	John Kehe
ARTIST	John Diele		Mick Haggerty
AGENCY	ABC Records	**ARTIST**	Mick Haggerty
CLIENT	ABC Records	**PHOTOGRAPHER**	Doug Metzler
		AGENCY	United Artists Artists
		CLIENT	Blue Note Records

564

565

564
ART DIRECTOR Martin Donald
DESIGNER Martin Donald
AGENCY ABC Records
CLIENT ABC Records

565
ART DIRECTOR John Berg
DESIGNER John Berg
PHOTOGRAPHER Joel Baldwin
AGENCY CBS Records
CLIENT CBS Records

GOLD

566

567

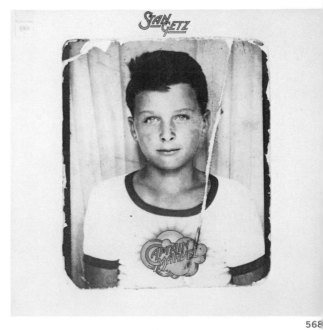

568

	566		**567**		**568**
ART DIRECTOR	Ed Thrasher	ART DIRECTOR	Bob Defrin	ART DIRECTOR	John Berg
DESIGNER	Ed Thrasher	DESIGNER	Bob Defrin	DESIGNERS	Teresa Alfieri
ARTISTS	John Casado	ARTIST	Stanislaw Zagorski		John Berg
	Barbara Casado	AGENCY	Atlantic Records	ARTIST	Gerard Huerta
WRITER	Barry Hansen	CLIENT	Atlantic Records	AGENCY	CBS Records
AGENCY	Warner Bros. Records			CLIENT	CBS Records
CLIENT	Warner Bros. Records				

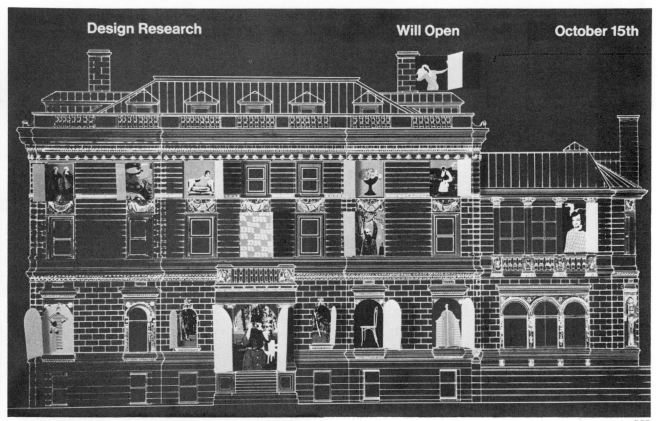

Design Research   Will Open   October 15th

569

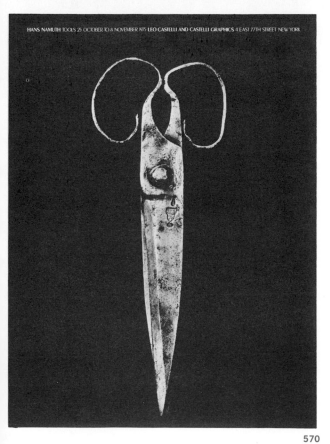

HANS NAMUTH TOOLS 25 OCTOBER TO 8 NOVEMBER 1975 LEO CASTELLI AND CASTELLI GRAPHICS 4 EAST 77TH STREET NEW YORK

570

	569		**570**
ART DIRECTOR	Raymond Waites	**ART DIRECTOR**	David Smoak
DESIGNER	Lou Brooks	**DESIGNER**	David Smoak
ARTIST	Adrienne Turnbull	**ARTIST**	Hans Namuth
PHOTOGRAPHERS	Thomas Ballantyne	**PHOTOGRAPHER**	Hans Namuth
	Raymond Waites	**AGENCY**	Marcus Ratliff
AGENCY	Design Group: Design	**CLIENT**	Castelli Graphics
	Research		
CLIENT	Design Research		

573

572

"Let
he who is
without sin,
cast."

This spring semester the Fresno State University Art Department
enters the Bronze Age – offering classes in the art of metal casting for
the very first time. Let he or she who is interested enroll now.
It'd be a real sin to miss it.

571

	571		572		573
ART DIRECTOR	Charles Fillhardt	ART DIRECTORS	Ria Lewerke	ART DIRECTOR	Bernice Thieblot
DESIGNER	Charles Fillhardt		Thom Williams	DESIGNER	Robert Shelley
WRITERS	Charles Fillhardt	DESIGNERS	Bill Naegels	ARTIST	Robert Shelley
	Curtis Wright		Rod Dyer	WRITER	Bernice Thieblot
AGENCY	Bergthold, Fillhardt &	AGENCIES	United Artists Records	AGENCY	The North Charles Street
	Wright		Rod Dyer		Design Organization
CLIENT	Professor John Stewart	CLIENT	United Artists Records	CLIENT	Corcoran School of Art

574

575

576

ART DIRECTOR 574
Keith Bright
DESIGNER Keith Bright
ARTIST Ignacio Gomez
WRITER Edmund Cohen
AGENCY Berry, Cullen, Cohen
CLIENT Endevco

ART DIRECTOR 575
Bob Nyitray
DESIGNER Bob Nyitray
WRITER Jerry Hubschman
AGENCY Beber, Silverstein & Partners
CLIENT Arvida Corp.

ART DIRECTOR 576
Kit Hinrichs
DESIGNER Paul Hardy
ARTISTS Guy Billout
Nancy Stahl
AGENCY Hinrichs Design Assoc.
CLIENT Crum & Forster Insurance Cos.

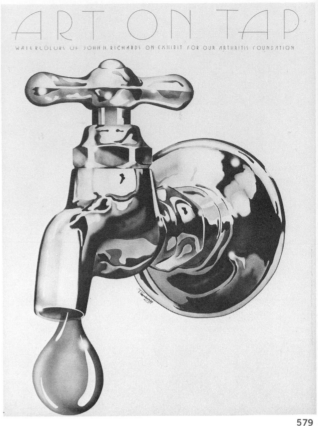

579

578

	577		578		579
ART DIRECTOR	Stephen Frykholm	**ART DIRECTOR**	Bill Bonnell	**ART DIRECTOR**	Terry Lesniewicz
DESIGNER	Stephen Frykholm	**DESIGNER**	Bill Bonnell	**DESIGNER**	Terry Lesniewicz
ARTIST	Stephen Frykholm	**PHOTOGRAPHER**	Stan Jorstad	**ARTIST**	Terry Lesniewicz
AGENCY	Herman Miller	**AGENCY**	Container Corp. of America	**WRITER**	Al Navarre
CLIENT	Herman Miller	**CLIENT**	Container Corp. of America	**AGENCY**	Flournoy & Gibbs
				CLIENT	Arthritis Foundation

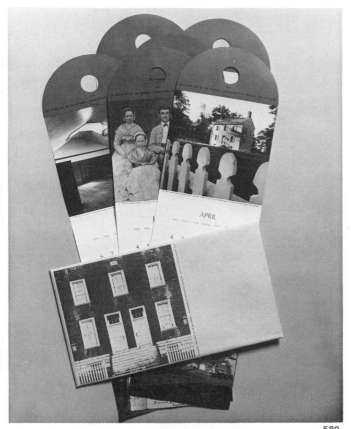

580

581

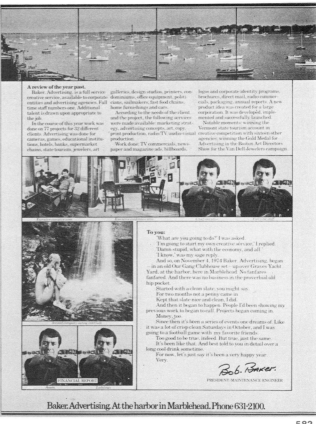

582

	580		581		582
ART DIRECTOR	Susan Jackson Keig	**ART DIRECTOR**	Seymour Chwast	**ART DIRECTOR**	Bob Baker
DESIGNER	Susan Jackson Keig	**DESIGNER**	Seymour Chwast	**DESIGNER**	Florrie Everett
ARTIST	Susan Jackson Keig	**PHOTOGRAPHER**	Arnold Rosenberg	**PHOTOGRAPHERS**	John Holt
PHOTOGRAPHER	James L. Ballard	**WRITER**	Phyllis Flood		Steve Haesche
WRITER	Susan Jackson Keig	**AGENCY**	Push Pin Studios	**WRITER**	Bob Baker
AGENCY	Susan Jackson Keig	**CLIENT**	Push Pin Studios	**AGENCY**	Baker Advertising
CLIENT	Shakertown at			**CLIENT**	Baker Advertising
	Pleasant Hill				

585

583

go fly
a kite.

584

583
ART DIRECTOR Bob Farber
DESIGNER Bob Farber
WRITER Bob Farber
AGENCY Typographic Innovations
CLIENT Typographic Innovations

584
ART DIRECTOR Arnold Saks
DESIGNERS Arnold Saks
Tomas Nittner
PHOTOGRAPHER Barnett Studio
AGENCY Arnold Saks
CLIENT Go Fly A Kite

585
ART DIRECTOR Carol Moore
DESIGNER Carol Moore
PHOTOGRAPHER Photo Media
AGENCY Davis-Delaney-Arrow
CLIENT Xerox Education
Publications

Bon Vivant Soup Can, after Andy Warhol

586

587

586

ART DIRECTORS	Michael Gross	PHOTOGRAPHERS	Arky & Barrett
	Bob Pellegrini		David Kaestle
DESIGNER	Bob Pellegrini	WRITERS	Chris Cerf
ARTISTS	Randy Enos		Henry Beard
	Michael Gross		Bill Efros
	Jeff Jones	AGENCY	Pellegrini, Kaestle & Gross
	David Kaestle	CLIENT	National Lampoon
	Raymond Kursar		
	Mara McAfee		
	Alan Rose		
	W.T. Vinson		

587

ART DIRECTOR	Dan Smith
DESIGNER	Dan Smith
ARTISTS	Dan Smith
	Don Webster
	Graham Assoc.
AGENCY	U.S. Information Agency
CLIENT	U.S. Information Agency

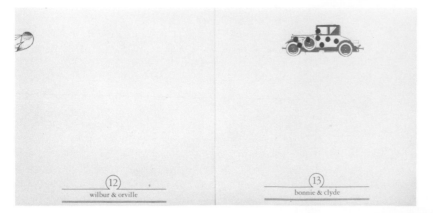

(12)
wilbur & orville

(13)
bonnie & clyde

(16)
pairs

588

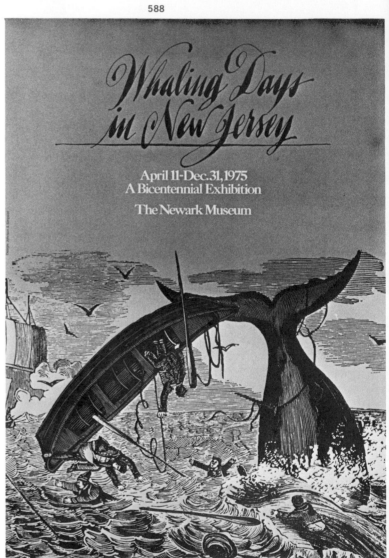

589

588
ART DIRECTOR Larry Sons
DESIGNER Larry Sons
ARTISTS Larry Sons
Ann Wright
WRITER Larry Sons
AGENCY The Richards Group
CLIENT Mr. & Mrs. Michael R.
Levy

589
ART DIRECTOR Milt Simpson
DESIGNER Johnson & Simpson
Graphic Designers
ARTISTS Virginia Puzon
Larry Ottino
WRITER Bill Bartle
AGENCY Johnson & Simpson
Graphic Designers
CLIENT The Newark Museum

590

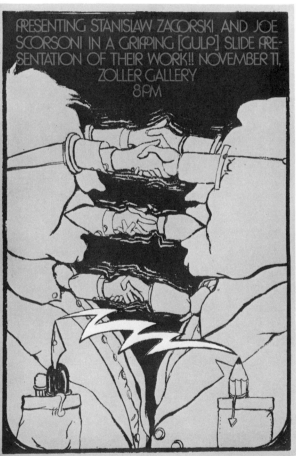

591

	590		591
ART DIRECTOR	Jim Lienhart	**ART DIRECTOR**	Lanny B. Sommese
DESIGNER	Jim Lienhart	**DESIGNER**	Lanny B. Sommese
AGENCY	Murrie, White,	**ARTIST**	Lanny B. Sommese
	Drummond, Lienhart &	**AGENCY**	Lanny Sommese Design
	Assoc.	**CLIENT**	Penn State University
CLIENT	Chicago Communications		
	Collaborative		

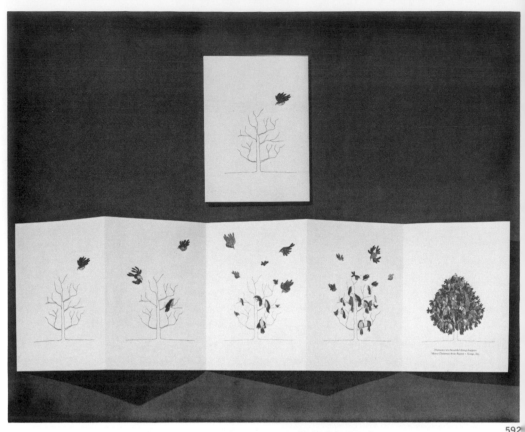

592

593

	592		**593**
ART DIRECTOR	Alice Campbell	**ART DIRECTOR**	Dick Chodkowski
DESIGNER	Alice Campbell	**DESIGNER**	Keith Bright
ARTIST	Alice Campbell	**ARTISTS**	Various
WRITER	Alice Campbell	**WRITERS**	Dick Chodkowski
AGENCY	Baxter & Korge		Paul Mimiagn
CLIENT	Baxter & Korge		Barbara Scharlebois
		AGENCY	Ogilvy-Mather
		CLIENT	Baskin Robbins

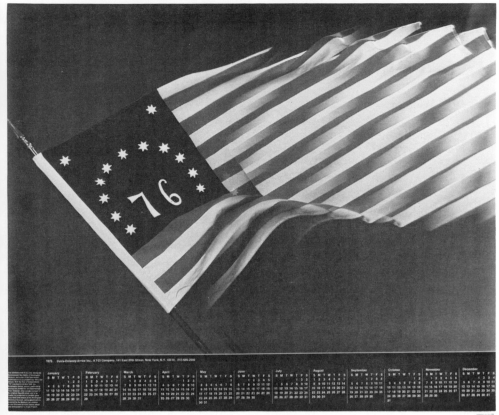

594

595

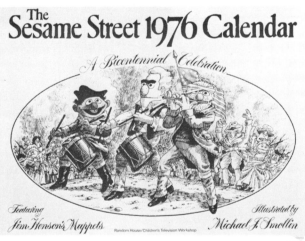

596

594
ART DIRECTOR Carol Moore
DESIGNER Carol Moore
PHOTOGRAPHER Roger Prigent
AGENCY Davis-Delaney-Arrow
CLIENT Davis-Delaney-Arrow

595
ART DIRECTOR Herb Lubalin
DESIGNER Herb Lubalin
ARTIST Tom Carnase
AGENCY Lubalin, Smith, Carnase
& Peckolick
CLIENT Carol Anthony

596
ART DIRECTOR Ole Risom
DESIGNER Michael J. Smollin
ARTIST Michael J. Smollin
WRITERS Ole Risom,
Christopher Cerf
AGENCY Children's T.V. Workshop
CLIENT Children's T.V. Workshop

597

598

599

597
ART DIRECTOR Keith Bright
DESIGNER Keith Bright
ARTIST Ignacio Gomez
WRITER Edmund Cohen
AGENCY Berry, Cullen, Cohen
CLIENT Endevco

598
ART DIRECTOR Dick Pantano
DESIGNER Dick Pantano
ARTIST Stavros Cosmopulos
PHOTOGRAPHER George Petrakes
WRITERS Jay Hill
Dick Pantano
AGENCY Hill, Holliday,
Connors, Cosmopulos
CLIENT Hill, Holliday,
Connors, Cosmopulos

599
ART DIRECTOR William L. Sweney
DESIGNER William L. Sweney
WRITER James P. Cole
AGENCY Cole, Henderson, Drake
CLIENT Cole, Henderson, Drake

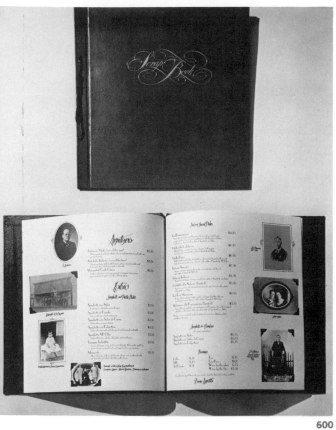

600

601

600
ART DIRECTOR John Weaver
DESIGNER John Weaver
ARTIST Kick Sherman
WRITER Larry Landmesser
AGENCY Baxter & Korge
CLIENT Mama Rizzo Restaurant

SILVER

601
ART DIRECTOR Harry M. Jacobs
WRITER Bill Westbrook
AGENCY Jacobs Morgan & Westbrook
CLIENT National Bank and Trust Co.

"I got my job through the Washington Post."

602

604

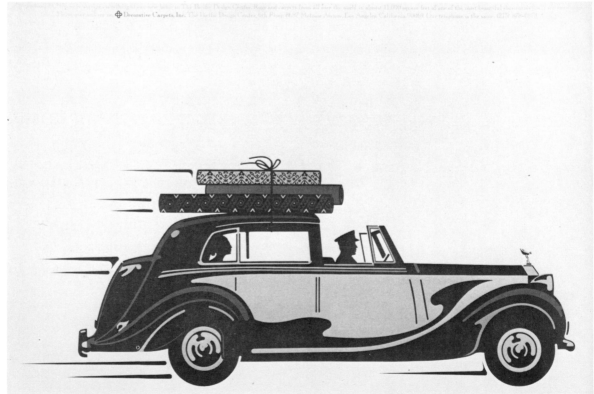

603

	602		**603**		**604**
ART DIRECTOR	Bill Caldwell	ART DIRECTOR	Keith Bright	ART DIRECTOR	Bob Farber
DESIGNER	Bill Caldwell	DESIGNERS	Keith Bright	DESIGNER	Bob Farber
ARTIST	Bill Caldwell		Patrick Soo Hoo	WRITER	Bob Farber
WRITER	Bill Caldwell	ARTIST	Steve Miller	AGENCY	Typographic Innovations
AGENCY	Bill Caldwell Graphics	AGENCY	Keith Bright & Assoc.	CLIENT	Typographic Innovations
CLIENT	Corcoran School of Art	CLIENT	Decorative Carpets		

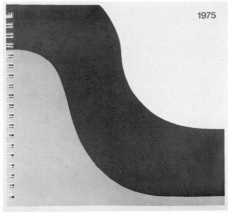

1975

605

606

DESIGNER 605 Tamoko Miho
AGENCY Champion Papers
CLIENT Champion Papers

ART DIRECTOR 606 Jim Lienhart
DESIGNER Jim Lienhart
PHOTOGRAPHER Jean Moss
WRITERS John Bissinger
Jim Lienhart
AGENCY Murrie White Drummond
and Lienhart Associates
CLIENT Chicago Communications
Collaborative

607

608

609

	607		608		609
ART DIRECTOR	Keith Bright	ART DIRECTOR	Terry Lesniewicz	ART DIRECTORS	William Lyons
DESIGNER	Keith Bright	DESIGNER	Terry Lesniewicz		William Reynolds
ARTIST	Ignacio Gomez	ARTIST	Terry Lesniewicz	DESIGNER	William Reynolds
WRITER	Edmund Cohen	AGENCY	Terry Lesniewicz	ARTISTS	Kenneth Alliston
AGENCY	Berry, Cullen, Cohen	CLIENT	Amy Jo Lesniewicz		Deby Schroeder
CLIENT	Endevco			WRITER	William Lyons
				AGENCY	RL Advertising Studio
				CLIENT	Art Directors Club of N.J

611

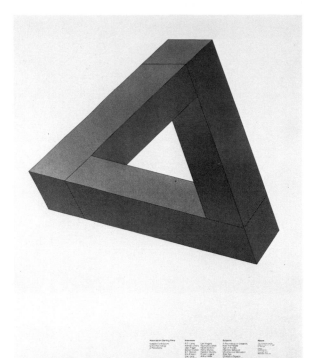

612

613

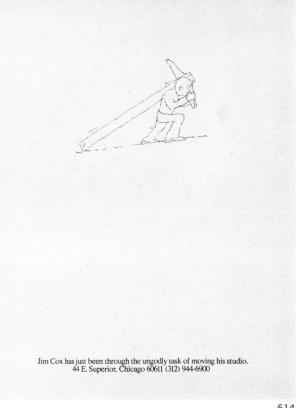

614

Filmfeast

The Event

Mark January 21 on your calendar! It's the one day we've been waiting for all year... the day when we see the best of the best in international television commercials and public service announcements... the day when ACT and the American Marketing Association join forces to present... the 1975 Clio Awards.

This year's award-winning performance will be emceed by Jeff Heitz, WTOL's popular anchorman.

Join us for one last, happy look at 1975 and a toast to a great 1976. It all happens Wednesday, January 21 in the Crystal Room of the Commodore Perry Motor Inn. Cocktails at 11:30, lunch at 12 and the 1975 Clio Awards program at 12:45. Don't miss it!

The Award

The Clio Award for advertising excellence worldwide is the finest recognition of quality achievement that is attainable by individuals and organizations in advertising and communications. Nationally and internationally, the annual presentations of Clio Awards are widely reported via major news-weeklies, wire services, newspapers, advertising and communications journals, local and network radio and television.

The Clio is called the cousin of the Oscar. So intense is the quality of competition and the judging process that selection as a finalist in the Clio competition ranks as an exceptionally high honor throughout the world's advertising and communications communities. As one of the winners put it, "You haven't won an advertising award until you have 'won a Clio.'

Clio winners are selected by 450 judges from 15 countries around the world, in small groups per judging session. This creative panel's size and geographic dispersion effectively blunts any hope of politicking. The judging process itself is as stringent and uncompromising as any pursuit of excellence demands. Judges' votes are confidential and results are tabulated by an independent auditing firm. Clio awards are not given for the sake of giving awards and it is not unusual for competitive categories to come up winnerless.

615

nothi ng

I love to talk a lot and say

New Year's Resolution
Children's Christmas Competition
for kids 8 thru 12.

Check the bulletin board
for contest details.

Entry blanks available from your
personnel manager.

Deadline for entries
Oct. 1

Write a Story   Win a Bike

616

617

615
ART DIRECTOR Al Navarre
DESIGNER Al Navarre
ARTIST Al Navarre
PHOTOGRAPHERS John Fong
Visualforms
WRITERS Mike Lutton
Dennis Beck
AGENCY Al Navarre
CLIENT Advertising Club of Toledo

616
ART DIRECTOR Bob Farber
DESIGNER Bob Farber
WRITER Bob Farber
AGENCY Typographic Innovations
CLIENT Typographic Innovations

617
ART DIRECTOR Bill Bonnell
DESIGNER Bill Bonnell
AGENCY Container Corp. of
America
CLIENT Container Corp. of
America

618

619

	618		**619**
ART DIRECTORS	Lou Dorfsman	**ART DIRECTORS**	Woody Pirtle
	Ira Teichberg		Gayl Ware
DESIGNER	Ira Teichberg	**DESIGNER**	Woody Pirtle
ARTIST	Tim Lewis	**ARTIST**	Woody Pirtle
WRITER	John Wilkoff	**WRITERS**	Dick Smith
AGENCY	CBS/Broadcast Group		Woody Pirtle
CLIENT	CBS Television Network	**AGENCY**	Smith, Smith, Baldwin &
			Carlberg
		CLIENT	Atascocita Country Club

620

621

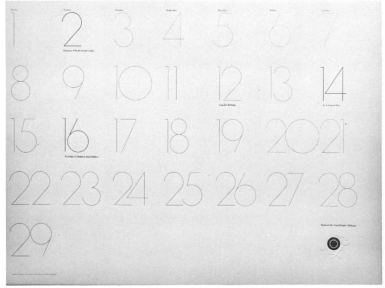

622

	620		621		622
ART DIRECTOR	Judith Kovis Stockman	**ART DIRECTOR**	Bob Feldgus	**ART DIRECTOR**	Vance Jonson
DESIGNER	Judith Kovis Stockman	**DESIGNER**	Bob Feldgus	**DESIGNER**	Vance Jonson
AGENCIES	Stockman & Manners Assoc. Ferguson Sorrentino Design	**ARTIST**	Peter Palombi	**AGENCY**	Vance Jonson Design
		AGENCY	Scholastic Book Services	**CLIENT**	Modern Litho
		CLIENT	Scholastic Book Services		
CLIENT	The First Women's Bank				

623

624

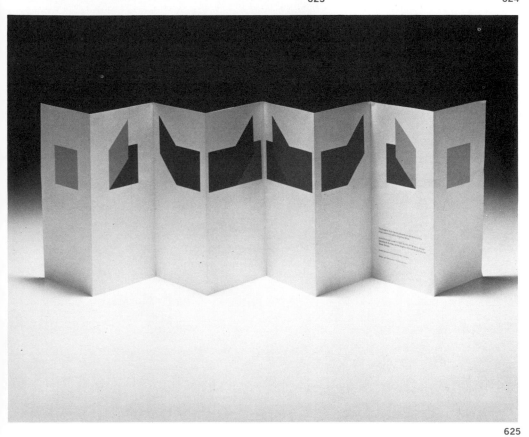

625

	623		624		625
ART DIRECTOR	Phelps K. Manning	**ART DIRECTOR**	Keith Bright	**ART DIRECTOR**	Jack Summerford
DESIGNER	William R. Tobias	**DESIGNER**	Keith Bright	**DESIGNER**	Jack Summerford
WRITER	Phelps K. Manning	**ARTIST**	Ignacio Gomez	**ARTIST**	Jack Summerford
AGENCY	BirthdayBook	**WRITER**	Edmund Cohen	**WRITER**	Olmsted-Kirk Paper
CLIENT	BirthdayBook	**AGENCY**	Berry, Cullen, Cohen	**AGENCY**	The Richards Group
		CLIENT	Endevco	**CLIENT**	Olmsted-Kirk Paper

626

627

629

628

	626		**627**		**629**
ART DIRECTOR	Bob Farber	ART DIRECTOR	Joseph Boggs	ART DIRECTOR	Walter Ender
DESIGNER	Bob Farber	DESIGNER	Joseph Boggs	DESIGNER	Walter Ender
WRITER	Bob Farber	ARTIST	Joseph Boggs	ARTIST	Walter Ender
AGENCY	Typographic Innovations	WRITER	Irene Rubens	PHOTOGRAPHER	Jack Caspary
CLIENT	Typographic Innovations	AGENCY	Realty Hotels	AGENCY	Ruder & Finn
		CLIENT	Realty Hotels	CLIENT	Commonwealth National Bank

628
ART DIRECTOR Jeff Gorman
DESIGNER Mike Eakin
ARTIST David Kasper
WRITER Jeff Gorman
AGENCY Epiphany
CLIENT Pete & Karin Johnson

630

CHARLES AND LINDA ARE FINISHED!

After a year-and-a-half of trying to work things out, we're finished—with the house and yard. Well, almost finished.

So, for lack of a better reason, we've decided to celebrate before we start doing everything over.

Join us, please, on September 20th at 8 p.m. or thereabouts for an evening of drinking, talking, and hors d' oeuvreing. RSVP by the 17th of September, please.

631

McCall's: a 100 year dialogue with the American Woman 1876–1976

632

	630		631		632
ART DIRECTOR	Robert Cipriani	ART DIRECTOR	Charles Fillhardt	ART DIRECTOR	Richard Selby
DESIGNER	Robert Cipriani	DESIGNER	Charles Fillhardt	DESIGNER	Richard Selby
WRITER	Paul McDermott	WRITER	Charles Fillhardt	ARTIST	Richard Selby
AGENCY	Gunn Associates	AGENCY	Bergthold, Fillhardt & Wright	WRITER	Marie Conklin
CLIENT	Advertising Club of Greater Boston	CLIENT	Charles & Linda Fillhardt	AGENCY	McCall's Promotion Dept.
				CLIENT	McCall's Magazine

633

634

633
ART DIRECTOR Guglielmo Nardelli
DESIGNER Guglielmo Nardelli
ARTIST Guglielmo Nardelli
PHOTOGRAPHER Guglielmo Nardelli
WRITER Forest Hills Village
Improvement Society
AGENCY Forest Hills Village
Improvement Society
CLIENT Forest Hills Gardens

634
ART DIRECTORS Richard Burns
Doug Akagi
DESIGNERS Richard Burns
Doug Akagi
ARTIST Doug Akagi
AGENCY The GNU Group
CLIENT The SWA Group

635

636

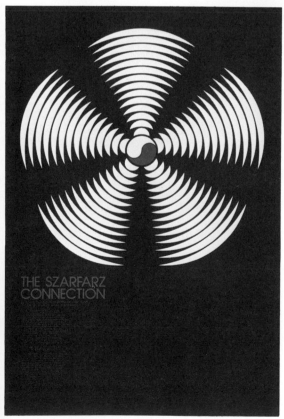

637

635
ART DIRECTOR Keith Bright
DESIGNER Keith Bright
ARTIST Ignacio Gomez
WRITER Edmund Cohen
AGENCY Berry, Cullen, Cohen
CLIENT Endevco

636
ART DIRECTOR Carol Deitz
DESIGNER Carol Deitz
ARTIST Carol Deitz
WRITER Richard Wilde
AGENCY School of Visual Arts
CLIENT School of Visual Arts

637
ART DIRECTOR George Canciani
DESIGNER George Canciani
ARTIST George Canciani
PHOTOGRAPHER George Canciani
AGENCY George Canciani
Graphic Design
CLIENT Art Directors Club
of Boston

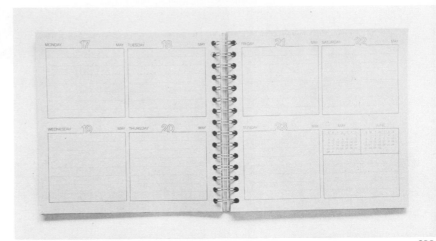

638

ONLY IN AMERICA
COULD A WORKING PERSON
SEND A FOUR COLOR
CHRISTMAS CARD.

639

638
DESIGNERS Howard Auerbach,
& ARTISTS Jan Esteves
Irwin Fleminger
Michael Meyerowtiz
Bill Ronalds
Tom Rummler
G. Clark Sealy
George Stavrinos
CLIENT The Artists

639
ART DIRECTOR Paul Collins
DESIGNER Paul Collins
PHOTOGRAPHER Jeff Stein
WRITER Seumas McGuire
AGENCY Hill, Holliday, Connors,
Cosmopulos
CLIENT McGuire/Seeto/Burns/Marcelle

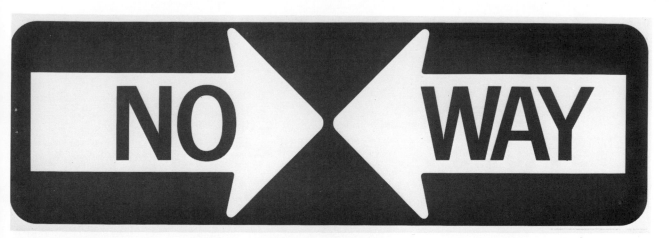

640

642

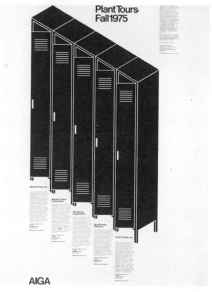

	640		641		643
ART DIRECTOR	Brian O'Neill	**ART DIRECTORS**	Vance Jonson	**ART DIRECTOR**	David L. Romanoff
DESIGNER	Michael Schacht		Bob Ross	**DESIGNER**	David L. Romanoff
ARTIST	Susan Newton	**DESIGNER**	Vance Jonson	**ARTIST**	David L. Romanoff
AGENCY	Davis-Delaney-Arrow	**AGENCY**	Vance Jonson Design	**WRITER**	Suzanne Livornese
CLIENT	Xerox Education	**CLIENT**	Steelcase	**AGENCY**	David Romanoff Design
	Publications			**CLIENT**	American Institute
					of Graphic Arts

	642	
ART DIRECTOR	Arthur Eisenberg	
DESIGNER	Arthur Eisenberg	
WRITER	Arthur Eisenberg	
AGENCY	Eisenberg& Pannell	
CLIENT	Chuck Untersee	

644

644
ART DIRECTOR Charlie Clark
DESIGNER Charlie Clark
WRITER Adrienne Cohen
AGENCY Weltin Advertising Agency
CLIENT Atlanta Ad Club

645

647

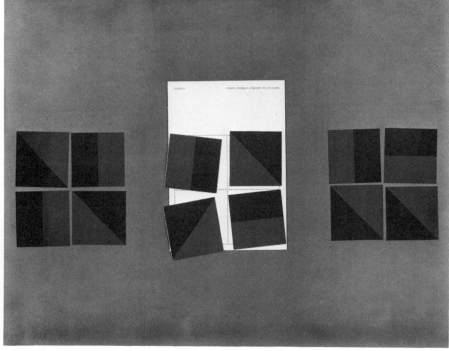

646

645		**646**		**647**	
ART DIRECTOR	Keith Bright	ART DIRECTOR	John deCesare	ART DIRECTOR	John Casado
DESIGNER	Patrick Soo Hoo	DESIGNER	John deCesare	DESIGNER	John Casado
ARTIST	Bob Maile	WRITER	Moira deCesare	ARTIST	John Casado
PHOTOGRAPHER	Peter James Samerjan	AGENCY	deCesare Design	AGENCY	Casado Design
AGENCY	Keith Bright & Assoc.	CLIENT	The deCesare family	CLIENT	Kaye Bernstein
CLIENT	G.P. Color				

648

649

650

	648		**649**		**650**
ART DIRECTOR	Bob Farber	**ART DIRECTOR**	Bob Defrin	**ART DIRECTOR**	Lou Dorfsman
DESIGNER	Bob Farber	**DESIGNER**	Paula Scher	**DESIGNER**	Lou Dorfsman
AGENCY	Typographic Innovations	**PHOTOGRAPHER**	Giuseppe Pino	**ARTIST**	Akihiko Seki
CLIENT	Typographic Innovations	**AGENCY**	Atlantic Records	**PHOTOGRAPHER**	Peter Roth
		CLIENT	Atlantic Records	**WRITER**	Lou Dorfsman
				AGENCY	Lou Dorfsman
				CLIENT	Dansk Designs

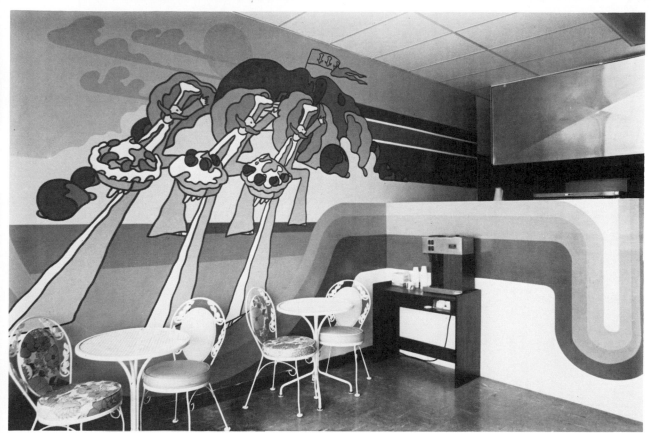

651

DANCING IN THE BLUE ROOM   DICK STABILE & ORCHESTRA   FEATURING KIKI CARR
7PM-1PM MONDAY THRU SATURDAY   ONLY $1.50   COCKTAILS & DINNER AVAILABLE

BLUE ROOM

652

	651		**652**
ART DIRECTOR	Jon Dahlstrom	**ART DIRECTOR**	Jay Loucks
DESIGNER	Jon Dahlstrom	**DESIGNERS**	Stephen Walsh
AGENCY	Larson/Bateman		Chris Hill
CLIENT	Slimland	**ARTIST**	Stephen Walsh
		AGENCY	Robertson Advertising
		CLIENT	Fairmont Hotel

653

654

655

	653		654		655
ART DIRECTOR	Murray Jacobs	ART DIRECTOR	Michael Kiernan	ART DIRECTOR	Warren Kass
DESIGNER	Linda Wachner	DESIGNER	Michael Kiernan	DESIGNER	Warren Kass
WRITER	Cay Gibson	ARTIST	Michael Kiernan	ARTIST	Warren Kass
AGENCY	Gardner Advertising	AGENCY	Dailey & Assoc.	AGENCY	Warren Kass Graphics
CLIENT	Warnaco	CLIENT	Granny Goose Foods	CLIENT	Ruth Scharf Ltd.
	Warner's Division				

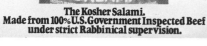

657

658

656

	656		657		658
ART DIRECTOR	Tom Wilkes	ART DIRECTOR	Steve Kasloff	ART DIRECTOR	James Stitt
DESIGNERS	Tom Wilkes	DESIGNER	Steve Kasloff	DESIGNER	James Stitt
	Martin Donald	PHOTOGRAPHER	Dan Katz	ARTIST	James Stitt
ARTIST	Joe Heiner	WRITER	Steve Kasloff	AGENCY	James Stitt & Co.
AGENCY	ABC Records	AGENCY	Frieze Advertising	CLIENT	Steam Beer Brewing Co.
CLIENT	ABC Records	CLIENT	Shofar Kosher Foods		

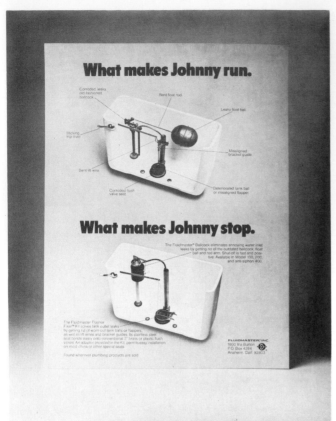

659

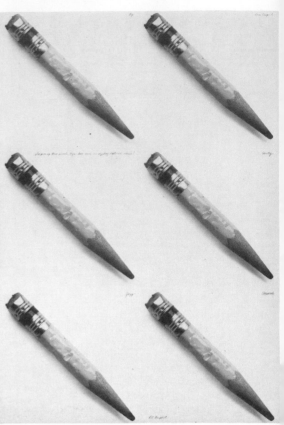

661

660

	659		661		660
ART DIRECTOR	Ralph Lenac	**ART DIRECTOR**	Tom Wilkes	**ART DIRECTOR**	Lou Dorfsman
PHOTOGRAPHERS	Bill Braly	**DESIGNERS**	Tim Bryant	**DESIGNER**	Lou Dorfsman
	Al Namura		Tom Wilkes	**PHOTOGRAPHER**	Peter Roth
WRITER	David Warford	**PHOTOGRAPHER**	Ron Slenzak	**WRITER**	Lou Dorfsman
AGENCY	Lenac, Warford, Stone	**AGENCY**	ABC Records	**AGENCY**	Lou Dorfsman
CLIENT	Fluidmaster	**CLIENT**	ABC Records	**CLIENT**	Dansk Designs

662

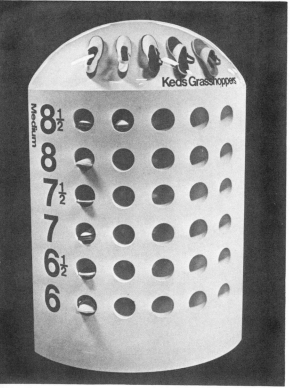

663

	662		**663**	
ART DIRECTORS	Ed George	**ART DIRECTOR**	Bob Salpeter
	Paul Francis	**DESIGNER**	Bob Salpeter
ARTIST	Rudy Laslo	**AGENCY**	Lopez Salpeter
WRITER	Kin Essington	**CLIENT**	Uniroyal
AGENCY	J. Walter Thompson		
CLIENT	Champion Spark Plug Co.		

SILVER

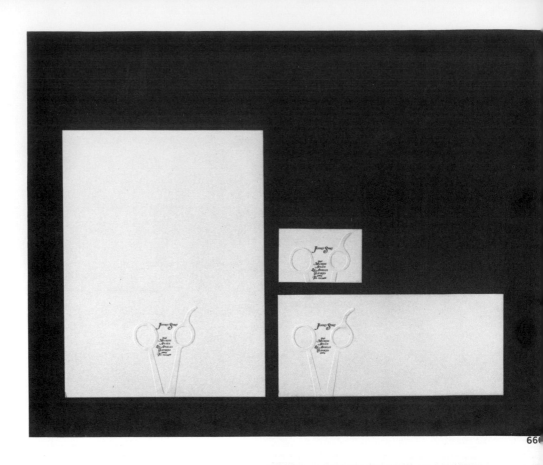

666

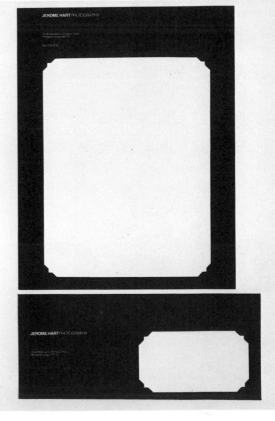

664

666

	664		665		666
ART DIRECTOR	Michael Doret	ART DIRECTORS	Robin Rickabaugh	ART DIRECTOR	Cheri Ramey
DESIGNER	Michael Doret		Heidi Rickabaugh	DESIGNER	Cheri Ramey
ARTIST	Michael Doret	DESIGNER	Robin Rickabaugh	ARTIST	Sheri Herman
AGENCY	Michael Doret	ARTIST	Robin Rickabaugh	AGENCY	Ramey Communication
CLIENT	Michael Doret	AGENCY	Robin& Heidi Rickabaugh	CLIENT	Jeffrey Spirit
		CLIENT	Jerome Hart		

667

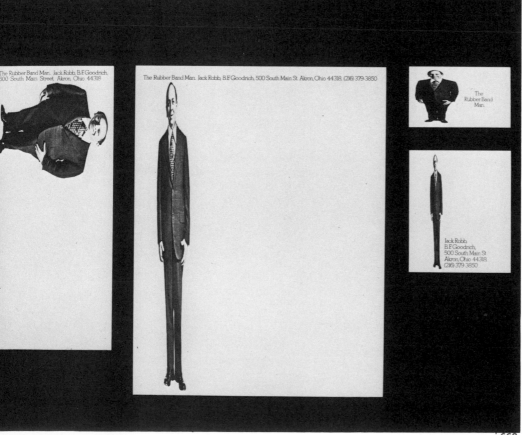

668

667
ART DIRECTOR Lou Dorfsman
DESIGNER Lou Dorfsman
ARTIST Lou Dorfsman
WRITERS Lou Dorfsman
Jerome Snyder
AGENCY Lou Dorfsman
CLIENT Jerome Snyder

668
ART DIRECTOR Bob Kwait
DESIGNER Bob Kwait
PHOTOGRAPHERS Bob Bender
Geoff Whittaker
AGENCY Griswold-Eshleman
CLIENT B.F. Goodrich

GOLD

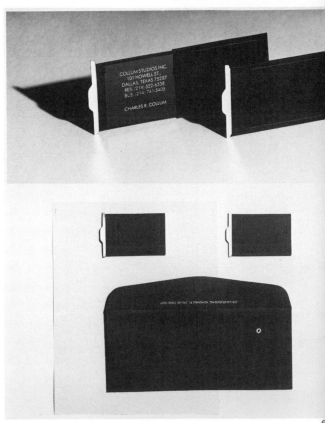

	669		670
ART DIRECTOR	John Pringle	**ART DIRECTOR**	Morgan L. Ziller
DESIGNER	Lee Bonner	**DESIGNER**	Morgan L. Ziller
ARTIST	Lee Bonner	**ARTIST**	Morgan L. Ziller
AGENCY	The Top Banana	**AGENCY**	The Bloom Agency
CLIENT	The Top Banana	**CLIENT**	Collum Studios

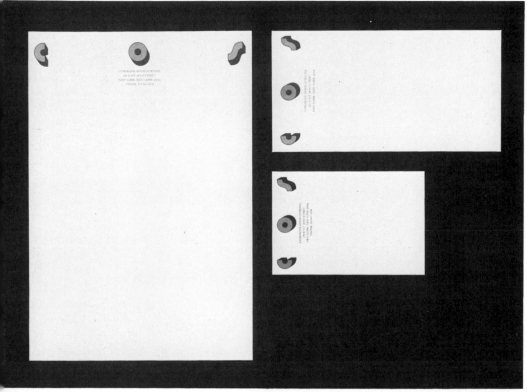

671

672

	671		**672**
ART DIRECTOR	Jerry Cosgrove	ART DIRECTOR	Bob Warkulwiz
DESIGNER	Jerry Cosgrove	DESIGNER	Bob Warkulwiz
ARTIST	Cosgrove Assoc.	ARTIST	Bob Warkulwiz
AGENCY	Cosgrove Assoc.	PHOTOGRAPHER	Richard Hamill
CLIENT	Cosgrove Assoc.	WRITER	Gerry Reimel
		AGENCY	Baseline Studio
		CLIENT	Baseline Studio

 SILVER

Alfred Zelcer 2009 Green Street
San Francisco, CA 94123 415/567-3259

673

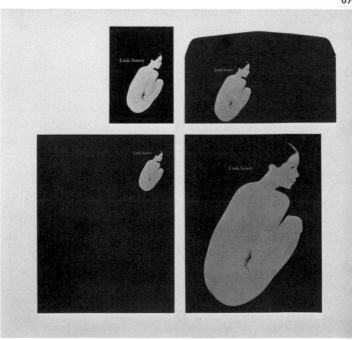

674

	673		674
ART DIRECTOR	Francois Robert	ART DIRECTOR	Douglas Boyd
DESIGNER	Francois Robert	DESIGNER	Douglas Boyd
ARTIST	Francois Robert	ARTIST	Gordon Tani
AGENCY	Francois Robert Assoc.	PHOTOGRAPHER	Moshe Brakha
CLIENT	Alfred Zelcer	AGENCY	Douglas Boyd Desi
		CLIENT	Linda Somers

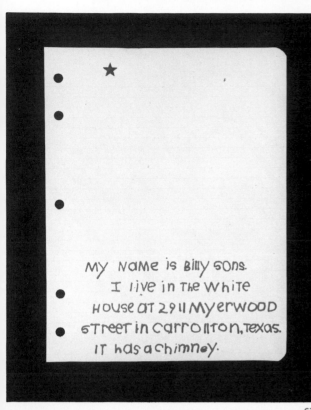

★

My name is Billy Sons.
I live in the white
house at 2911 Myerwood
street in carrollton, texas.
It has a chimney.

675

677

676

	675		676		677
ART DIRECTOR	Larry Sons	**ART DIRECTOR**	Terry Lesniewicz	**ART DIRECTOR**	John Casado
DESIGNER	Larry Sons	**DESIGNER**	Terry Lesniewicz	**DESIGNER**	John Casado
ARTIST	Billy Sons	**ARTIST**	Terry Lesniewicz	**ARTIST**	Casado Design
WRITER	Billy Sons	**AGENCY**	Terry Lesniewicz	**AGENCY**	Casado Design
AGENCY	The Richards Group	**CLIENT**	Barry Spoon	**CLIENT**	Sid Avery & Assoc.
CLIENT	Billy Sons				

678

679

680

	678		**679**		**680**
ART DIRECTORS	Kit Hinrichs	**ART DIRECTORS**	Lance Wyman	**ART DIRECTOR**	Bobbie Hazeltine
	Carveth Kramer		Bill Cannan	**DESIGNER**	Bobbie Hazeltine
DESIGNER	Gerard Huerta	**ARTISTS**	Lance Wyman	**ARTIST**	Bobbie Hazeltine
ARTIST	Gerard Huerta		Brian Flahive	**AGENCY**	Metzdorf Advertising
AGENCY	Hinrichs Design Assoc.	**AGENCY**	Wyman & Cannan Co.	**CLIENT**	Women's Christian Home
CLIENT	McCall's Magazine	**CLIENTS**	National Zoological Park		
			National Endowment		

681

683

682

681
DESIGNER Marty Neumeier
AGENCY Marty Neumeier
CLIENT Real Estate Masters

682
ART DIRECTOR Keith Bright
DESIGNER Patrick Soo Hoo
ARTIST Bob Maile
AGENCY Berry, Cullen, Cohen
CLIENT Clover Productions

683
ART DIRECTOR Don Ervin
DESIGNER Don Ervin
ARTIST Don Ervin
AGENCY Siegel & Gale
CLIENT New Canaan Library

684

686

684
ART DIRECTOR Michael O. Kelly
DESIGNER Michael O. Kelly
ARTIST Michael O. Kelly
AGENCY BBDM
CLIENT Audio Archives

686
ART DIRECTOR John Follis
DESIGNERS Connie Beck
Wayne Hunt
ARTIST Connie Beck
AGENCY John Follis & Assoc.
CLIENT At Ease (Al's Garage)

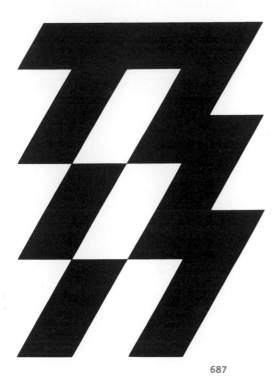

687

ALL AMERICAN NUT CO.

688

687
ART DIRECTOR Wayne Kosterman
DESIGNER Wayne Kosterman
ARTIST Wayne Kosterman
AGENCY RVI Corporation
CLIENT Federated Media

688
ART DIRECTOR Don Stone
DESIGNER Don Stone
AGENCY Lenac, Warford, Stone
CLIENT All-American Nut Co.

689

690

691

	689		690		691
ART DIRECTOR	Steven Sessions	ART DIRECTOR	Hoi Ling Chu	ART DIRECTORS	Saul Bass
DESIGNER	Steven Sessions	DESIGNER	Hoi Ling Chu		Art Goodman
ARTIST	Steven Sessions	AGENCY	Hoi Ling Chu Design	DESIGNERS	Saul Bass
AGENCY	Steven Sessions Design	CLIENT	Hoi Ling Chu Design		Art Goodman
CLIENT	International Motorcycle				Saul Bass & Assoc.
	Award Show			AGENCY	Saul Bass & Assoc.
				CLIENTS	Otto Preminger
					Sigma Productions

DELAWARE LEAGUE FOR PLANNED PARENTHOOD, INC.

692

693

694

	692		693		694
ART DIRECTOR	Norman Tomases	ART DIRECTOR	Yoshi Sekiguchi	ART DIRECTOR	Denis Johnson
DESIGNER	Gerald Robertson	DESIGNER	Yoshi Sekiguchi	DESIGNER	Denis Johnson
ARTIST	Saul Sophrin	ARTIST	Yoshi Sekiguchi	ARTIST	Denis Johnson
AGENCY	Reese, Tomases & Ellick	AGENCY	Rising Sun Design	WRITER	Phil Adams
CLIENT	Delaware League for Planned Parenthood	CLIENT	U.S. Ski Writers Assoc.	AGENCY	Adams & Adams Advertising
				CLIENT	The Holmstad

695

696

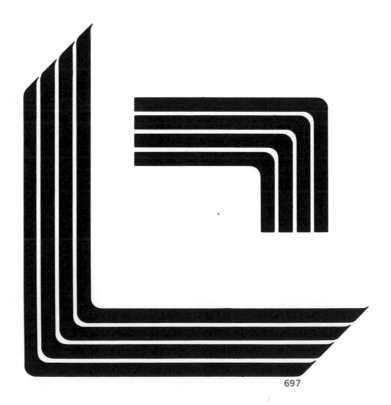

697

	695		696		697
ART DIRECTOR	Bruce Johnson	ART DIRECTORS	Mike Quon	ART DIRECTORS	Wally Roberts
DESIGNER	Bruce Johnson		Bruce Kaump		John McEown
ARTIST	Bruce Johnson	DESIGNER	Mike Quon	DESIGNER	John McEown
WRITER	Jay Edsal	ARTIST	Mike Quon	ARTIST	Bill Suman
AGENCY	Jay D. Edsal Co.	AGENCY	Mike Quon Graphic	AGENCY	The Roberts Group
CLIENT	Cornu Corp.		Design	CLIENT	Slides Limited
		CLIENT	Sentry Medical Products		

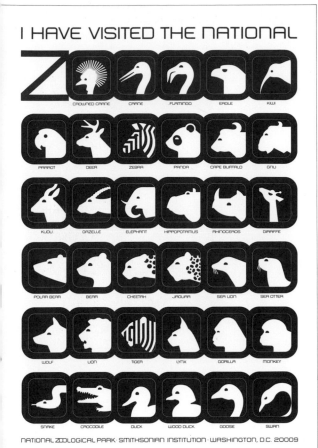

698

699

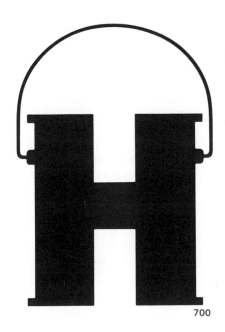

700

	698		699		700
ART DIRECTORS	Lance Wyman	**ART DIRECTOR**	Steven Sessions	**ART DIRECTORS**	George McGinnis
	Bill Cannan	**DESIGNER**	Steven Sessions		Mark Howard
ARTISTS	Lance Wyman	**ARTIST**	Steven Sessions	**DESIGNER**	George McGinnis
	Brian Flahive	**AGENCY**	Steven Sessions Design	**ARTIST**	Taro Hiroshi Yamashita
	Tucker Viemeister	**CLIENT**	The Racquet Club	**AGENCY**	Image Factory
	Ernesto Lehfeld			**CLIENT**	Harrad Paint
AGENCY	Wyman & Cannan Co.				
CLIENTS	National Zoological Park				
	National Endownment				

701

702

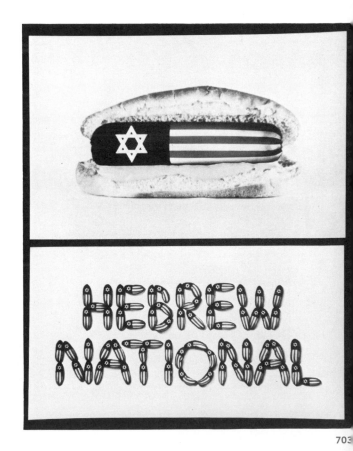

703

	701		702		703
ART DIRECTORS	Primo Angeli	ART DIRECTOR	Warren Kass	ART DIRECTOR	Herb Lubalin
	Roger Shelly	DESIGNER	Warren Kass	DESIGNER	Herb Lubalin
DESIGNER	Primo Angeli	ARTIST	Warren Kass	ARTIST	Barbra Bergman
ARTISTS	Primo Angeli	AGENCY	Warren Kass Graphics	PHOTOGRAPHER	Simon Cherpitel
	Tandy Belew	CLIENT	Ruth Scharf Ltd.	AGENCY	Lubalin, Smith, Carnase & Peckolick
AGENCY	Steedman, Cooper & Busse			CLIENT	Lubalin, Smith, Carnase & Peckolick
CLIENT	Boudin Bakeries				

704

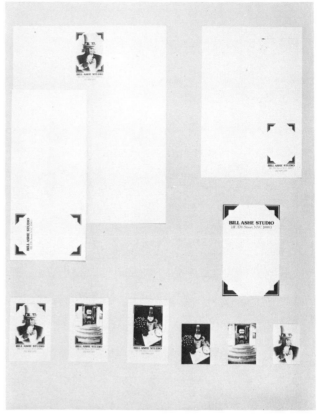

706

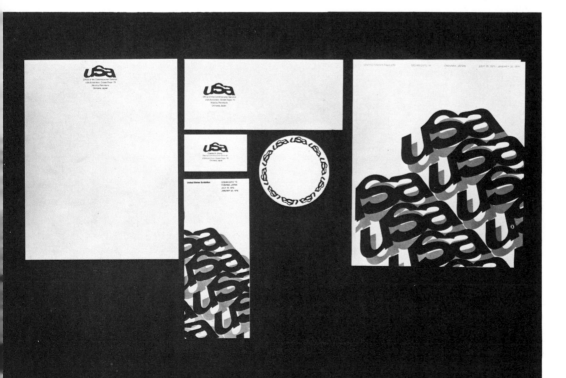

705

	704		**705**		**706**
ART DIRECTOR	Fred Marcellino	**ART DIRECTOR**	Ethel K. Freid	**ART DIRECTOR**	Marty Goldstein
DESIGNER	Fred Marcellino	**DESIGNER**	Ethel K. Freid	**DESIGNER**	Harold Aber
ARTIST	Fred Marcellino	**ARTIST**	Ethel K. Freid	**ARTIST**	Harold Aber
AGENCY	Marcellino	**PHOTOGRAPHERS**	Graham Assoc.	**PHOTOGRAPHER**	Bill Ashe
CLIENT	Passport Records		Don Webster	**AGENCY**	Bill Ashe Studio
		AGENCY	U.S. Information Agency	**CLIENT**	Bill Ashe Studio
		CLIENT	U.S. Information Agency		

PHOTOGRAPHY & ILLUSTRATION

20

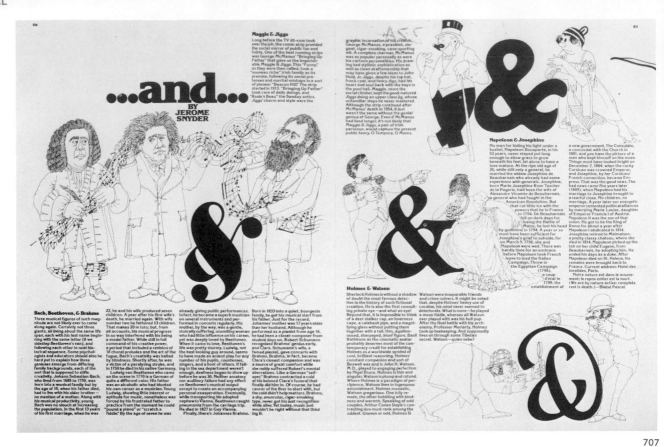

...and...

BY JEROME SNYDER

Maggie & Jiggs

Long before the TV sit-com took over the job, the comic strip provided the social mirror of public fun and foible. One of the best running strips was George McManus' "Bringing Up Father" that gave us the imperishable Maggie & Jiggs. This "Funny," as they were then called, took a "nouveau riche" Irish family as its premise, following its social pretenses and marital mishaps in a sort of pioneer "Beacon Hill." The strip started in 1913. "Bringing Up Father" took care of daily doings, and "Rosie's Beau" the Sunday antics. Jiggs' charm and style were the graphic incarnation of his creator, George McManus, a prankish, elegant, cigar-smoking, cane-sporting wit. A complete charmer, McManus was as popular personally as were his cartoon personalities. His drawing had stylistic sophistication as well as clean draftsmanship that may have given a few ideas to John Held, Jr. Jiggs, despite his top hat, frock coat, and fancy digs, had his heart and soul back with the boys in the pool hall. Maggie, more the social climber, kept the good-natured Jiggs doing an upper class jig, whose unfamiliar steps he never mastered. Although the strip continued after McManus' death in 1954, it just wasn't the same without the genial genius of George. Even if McManus had lived longer, it's not likely that Maggie & Jiggs, a pair of Irish parvenus, would capture the present public fancy. O Tempora, O Mores.

21

Bach, Beethoven, & Brahms

Three musical figures of such magnitude are not likely ever to come along again. Certainly not three giants, all living about the same life span, each with his last name beginning with the same letter (if we sidestep Beethoven's van), and following each other in neat historical sequence. Some psychologists and educators should also be hard put to explain how three geniuses emerge from differing family backgrounds, each of the sort that is supposed to stifle creativity. Johann Sebastian Bach, who lived from 1685 to 1750, was born into a musical family but by the age of 10, when his father died, had to live with his elder brother—no mention of a mother. Along with his musical productivity, young Bach was no slouch at increasing the population. In the first 13 years of his first marriage, when he was 22, he and his wife produced seven children. A year after his first wife's death, he married again. With wife number two he fathered 13 children. That makes 20 in toto; but, from all accounts, his musical progress in no way interfered with his being a model father. While still in full command of his creative power, a period that included a revision of 18 choral preludes and the art of the fugue, Bach's creativity was halted by blindness. Shortly after, he was a victim of a paralyzing stroke, and in 1750 he died in his native Germany.

Ludwig van Beethoven who came on the scene in 1770 is a German of quite a different color. His father was an alcoholic who had blunted his own career as a musician. Young Ludwig, showing little interest or aptitude for music, nonetheless was forced by his frustrated father to practice from the moment he could "pound a piano" or "scratch a fiddle." By the age of seven he was already giving public performances. In fact, he became a superb musician on several instruments and performed in concerts regularly. His mother, by the way, was a gentle, stoically suffering, unsmiling woman who had little influence on his career, yet was deeply loved by Beethoven. When it came to love, Beethoven's life was pretty stormy. Ludwig, not the best looking guy around, seems to have made an ardent play for any number of his pupils, countesses, singers, and a host of others. If failing in the sex department weren't enough, deafness began to show up before he was 30. Neither amatory nor auditory failure had any effect on Beethoven's musical output except to create an accompanying personal exasperation. Eventually, while transporting his adopted nephew to Vienna, Beethoven caught pneumonia from the carriage trip. He died in 1827 in Gay Vienna.

Finally, there's Johannes Brahms. Born in 1833 into a quiet, bourgeois family, he got his musical start from his father. Just for the record, Johannes' mother was 17 years older than her husband. Although he performed as a pianist from age 16, he had been a closet-composer from student days on. Robert Schumann recognized Brahms' genius early, and Clara, Schumann's wife, a famed pianist, gave concerts with Brahms. Brahms, in fact, became Clara's closest companion and was a source of great comfort while she nobly suffered Robert's mental aberrations. Like a German "self-oper," Brahms contracted a cold at his beloved Clara's funeral that finally did him in. Of course, he had cancer of the liver to start with, but the cold didn't help matters. Brahms, a shy, avuncular, cigar-smoking type, never got his just recognition while alive. Yet today, music just wouldn't be right without that third big B.

Napoleon & Josephine

No man for hiding his light under a bushel, Napoleon Bonaparte, in his 52 years, never stayed put long enough to allow grass to grow beneath his feet, let alone to have a love mature. At the ripe old age of 26, while still only a general, he married the widow Josephine de Beauharnais who already had some experience with generals. Josephine, born Marie Josephine Rose Tascher de la Pagerie, had been the wife of Alexandre Vicomte de Beauharnais, a general who had fought in the American Revolution. But that cut little ice with the powers that be in France in 1794. De Beauharnais fell on dark days for, losing the Battle of Mainz, he lost his head by guillotine in 1794. A year or so must have been sufficient for Josephine's grief to subside, for on March 9, 1796, she and Napoleon were wed. There was hardly time for an embrace before Napoleon took French leave to lead the Italian Campaign. Throw in the Egyptian Campaign (1798), a coup d'etat in 1799, the establishment of a new government, The Consulate, a concordat with the Church in 1801, and you have the picture of a man who kept himself on the move. Things must have looked bright on December 2, 1804, when the cocky Corsican was crowned Emperor, and Josephine, by her Corsican/French connection, became Empress. That was the good news. The bad news came five years later (1809), when Napoleon had his marriage to Josephine brought to a tearful close. No children, no marriage. A year later our energetic emperor cemented political alliances by marrying Marie Louise, daughter of Emperor Francis I of Austria. Napoleon II was the son of that union. He got to be the King of Rome for about a year after Napoleon I abdicated in 1814. Josephine retired to Malmaison, a pretty classy chateau, where she died in 1814. Napoleon picked up the tab on her child Eugene, from Beauharnais, by adopting him. He ended his days as a duke. After Napoleon died on St. Helena, his remains were brought back to France. Current address: Hotel des Invalides, Paris.

Notre nature est dans le mouvement; le repos entier est la mort. (We are by nature active; complete rest is death.)—Blaise Pascal.

Holmes & Watson

Sherlock Holmes is without a shadow of doubt the most famous detective in the history of such fictional creation. He is also the first consulting private eye—and what an eye! Beyond that, it is impossible to think of a deer stalker cap, an Inverness cape, a calabash pipe, and a magnifying glass without putting them together with a tall, thin, aquiline-nosed, sharpeyed, aloof figure. Basil Rathbone as the cinematic avatar probably deserves most of the contemporary credit for establishing Holmes as a worldwide symbol of cool, brilliant reasoning. Holmes' constant companion and sort of Boswell was and is John H. Watson, M.D., played to engaging perfection by Nigel Bruce. Holmes is thin and angular, Watson is plump and rotund. Where Holmes is a paradigm of percipience, Watson lives in ingenuous astonishment. Holmes monastic, Watson gregarious. One icily remote, the other bubbling with kindness and warmth. Speaking of odd couples, Arthur Conan Doyle's contrasting duo must rank among the oddest. Uneven or odd, Holmes & Watson were inseparable friends and crime-solvers. It might be noted that, despite Holmes' heavy use of cocaine, his mind never seemed to deteriorate. What is more—he played a mean fiddle, whereas all Watson ever played with was his bull pup. After the final battle with his arch-enemy, Professor Moriarty, Holmes took up beekeeping. And supposedly lives on through some Tibetan secret. Watson—quien sabe?

707

Sober–yet drinking too much

New research suggests that three-martini-a-day or four-highball-a-day drinkers (including baboons) may be damaging their hearts and brains, as well as their livers.

By Arthur Fisher

Alcohol is man's original tranquilizing drug and has been used for some 200 million years. But until recently, there has been precious little information on precisely how it affects the human body and brain. Over the last several years, however, scientists have been conducting experiments into the relationships between alcohol and virtually every aspect of human physiology, with a series of ominous results.

For years, doctors believed that nutritional deficiencies were the prime causes of alcohol-related diseases. After all, everybody knows that alcoholics are notorious for their haphazard eating habits. But the new research shows that harmful effects of heavy drinking can be produced in animals and humans who are following nutritious diets, and it has led researchers to speculate that alcohol may be harmful to anyone who drinks substantially and regularly—whether or not he can be considered an alcoholic. (There are almost as many definitions of alcoholism as there are brands of bourbon. One, widely, if loosely, agreed to, is that an alcoholic is dependent on alcohol to the extent that it impairs his relations with other people, his work or his health.)

Exactly how much drinking is dangerous? The recent research indicates that a daily ration of more than half a pint of 86-proof whisky—the equivalent of three martinis or four highballs—can result in physical damage over a long period of time. Dr. Morris E. Chafetz, director of the National Institute on Alcohol Abuse and Alcoholism, suggests that drinkers who wish to preserve their health should follow the advice offered in 1862 by the English physician Francis Anstie: Drink no more than one and one-half ounces of alcohol per day, only with food, and only in dilute form. That translates into three ounces of 100-proof bourbon, about a half-bottle (12 ounces) of wine or three 12-ounce bottles of beer. Anstie's test, clearly, is one that a great many self-described "moderate" drinkers would fail miserably.

As I interviewed experts in alcohol research, I was assured over and over that drinking alcohol should not now be considered a health hazard for most people. The problem, the researchers emphasize, lies in defining safe quantities for each individual. But for some, a safe quantity of alcohol is very, very small.

"What we really have to be clear about," says Dr. Emanuel Rubin, chief of pathology at Mount Sinai School of Medicine, "is that we're dealing with a drug that is poisonous in certain quantities. It is not poisonous when consumed in less than those amounts—but there are many other substances in that category, and we treat them with great respect."

The most provocative new research focuses on three organs of the body: the liver, the heart and the brain.

ALCOHOL AND THE LIVER. Alcoholic liver disease, especially cirrhosis, is one of the world's chief public health problems. In large U.S. cities, alcoholic cirrhosis is the fourth leading cause of death between ages 25 and 45, and in New York City, it is the third leading cause of death (after heart disease and cancer, in that order) between ages 25 and 65. Most liver specialists believe that cirrhosis is the culmination of changes in the liver marked by several stages, the first being a usually harmless condition called fatty liver. In his Mount Sinai Hospital office, Dr. Rubin sat surrounded by stacks of liver specimens representing various stages of decrepitude. Under a microscope, the appearance of fatty liver—in contrast with a normal liver—is unmistakable, even to a layman. It seems to have been invaded by an army of large, pale marbles—fat globules.

The whole question of who gets alcoholic liver disease and why has been hotly debated for many years, but in 1949, Dr. C. H. Best, a major figure in metabolic studies (he was one of the discoverers of insulin), fired off what was intended to be a finishing salvo in the controversy: Experiments with rats, he wrote, showed "no more evidence of a specific toxic effect of pure ethyl alcohol on liver cells than there is for one due to sugar."

But that theory has been decisively overturned by a series of experiments—culminating in an ongoing test using baboons as subjects—demonstrating the direct, toxic effects of alcohol on the liver. The experiments were initiated by Dr. Charles S. Lieber, who is chief of the Section of Liver Disease and Nutrition at Bronx Veterans Administration Hospital and professor of medicine at Mount Sinai School of Medicine. Since 1967, the experiments have been a joint project of Dr. Lieber, Dr. Rubin and their colleagues.

Dr. Lieber had noticed that some of his alcoholic patients developed liver troubles even though their diets were adequate. He wondered if alcohol might be a factor. Between 1959 and 1968, he and his colleagues conducted research in test tubes and with alcoholic volunteers and found that alcohol had a number of startling effects on liver metabolism. It would stop the liver from burning its normal fuel—fat—in order to burn alcohol instead. The result was that fat accumulated in the liver. The alcoholics, even on a good diet, developed not only fatty liver but elevated levels of blood lipids (fatty substances such as cholesterol and triglycerides) and uric acid, which is associated with gout.

"But people don't die of fatty liver," Dr. Lieber said. "They die of alcoholic hepatitis or cirrhosis. So we needed an animal model in which we could induce these conditions." The animal they chose was the baboon; the doctors set up an experimental colony of them in a trailer in the Sterling Forest, N.Y., headquarters of LEMSIP—the Laboratory for Experimental Medicine and Surgery in Primates—and under controlled conditions, they plied them with drink as well as adequate diet for prolonged periods, sometimes more than four years. They succeeded in producing fatty liver, alcoholic hepatitis and cirrhosis. Of 15 baboons, all got fatty liver, five got alcoholic hepatitis, and another five went on to get cirrhosis. This was the first time alcoholic cirrhosis had been produced in an experimental animal. "The appearance of the cirrhotic baboon liver was so similar to that of a human cirrhotic liver that the two were hard to distinguish under the microscope," Dr. Lieber said. "Now for the first time we can answer yes to the question: Can you produce all aspects of alcoholic liver disease despite an adequate diet? Dr. L. Feinman and I have found that alcohol use leads to an accumulation of collagen in the livers of both rats and baboons, and collagen is the chief component of fibrous tissue, which is what builds up in cirrhosis. If we can understand this mechanism, we may be able to do something about it."

Statistical evidence from Europe shows a direct correlation between liver disease and the total amount of alcohol consumed, the kind of dose-time relation that applies to many drugs. In the studies of both Dr. W. K. Lelbach *(Continued on Page 65)*

Arthur Fisher is the science editor of Popular Science.

16

708

	707
ART DIRECTOR	Herb Lubalin
DESIGNER	Herb Lubalin
ARTIST	Jerome Snyder
WRITER	Jerome Snyder
PUBLISHER	International Typeface Corp.
AGENCY	Lubalin, Smith, Carnase & Peckolick

	708
ART DIRECTOR	Ruth Ansel
DESIGNER	Ruth Ansel
ARTIST	Seymour Chwast
EDITORS	Lewis Bergman Jack Rosenthal
PUBLISHER	The New York Times
AGENCY	The New York Times

709

Opportunity for America: The Negro

This is excerpted from "An American Dilemma: The Negro Problem and Modern Democracy." The book was written by Gunnar Myrdal, the Swedish social scientist and a 1974 co-recipient of the Nobel Memorial Prize in Economic Science, with the assistance of Richard Sterner and Arnold Rose. It was published originally in 1944.

By Gunnar Myrdal

America feels itself to be humanity in miniature. When in this crucial time the international leadership passes to America, the great reason for hope is that this country has a national experience of uniting racial and cultural diversities and a national theory, if not a consistent practice, of freedom and equality for all. What America is constantly reaching for is democracy at home and abroad. The main trend in its history is the gradual realization of the American Creed.

In this sense the Negro problem is not only America's greatest failure but also America's incomparably great opportunity for the future. If America should follow its own deepest convictions, its well-being at home would be increased directly. At the same time America's prestige and power abroad would rise immensely. The century-old dream of American patriots, that America should give to the entire world its own freedoms and its own faith, would come true. America can demonstrate that justice, equality and cooperation are possible between white and colored people.

In the present phase of history this is what the world needs to believe. Mankind is sick of fear and disbelief, of pessimism and cynicism. It needs the youthful moralistic optimism of America. But empty declarations only deepen cynicism. Deeds are called for. If America in actual practice could show the world a progressive trend by which the Negro became finally integrated into modern democracy, all

mankind would be given faith again —it would have reason to believe that peace, progress and order are feasible. And America would have a spiritual power many times stronger than all her financial and military resources— the power of the trust and support of all good people on earth. *America is free to choose whether the Negro shall remain her liability or become her*

opportunity.

The development of the American Negro problem during the years to come is, therefore, fateful not only for America itself but for all mankind. If America wants to make the second choice, she cannot wait and see. She has to do something big and do it soon.

For two generations after the na-

tional compromise of the 1870's between the North and the South on the Negro problem, the caste status of the Negro was allowed to remain almost unchanged. It was believed by most well-meaning people that self-healing would work, that the Negro problem would come to solve itself by the lapse of time. George Washington Cable wrote in the eighties:

There is a vague hope, much commoner in the North than in the South, that somehow, if everybody will sit still, *"time"* will bring these changes.

Two decades later, Ray Stannard Baker reported from the South:

All such relationships will work themselves out gradually, naturally, quietly in the long course of the years: and the less they are talked about the better.

Most of the literature on the Negro problem continues to this day to be written upon this same static assumption.

We have given the reasons why we believe that the *interregnum,* during which the forces balanced each other fairly well, is now at an end. The equilibrium, contrary to common belief, was unstable and temporary. As American Negroes became educated and culturally assimilated, but still found themselves excluded, they grew bitter.

Meanwhile the whites were in the process of losing their caste theory. The international upheavals connected with the two World Wars and the world depression brought these developments to a crisis. American isolation was lost. Technical developments brought all nations to be close neighbors even though they were not trained to live together.

We are now in a deeply unbalanced world situation. Many human relations will be readjusted in the present world revolution, and among them race relations are bound to change considerably. As always in a revolutionary situation when society's moorings are temporarily loosened, there is, on the one hand, an opportunity to direct the changes into organized reforms and, on the other hand, a corresponding risk involved in letting the changes remain uncontrolled and lead into disorganization. To do nothing is to accept defeat.

710

	709		710
ART DIRECTOR	Ernest Scarfone	**ART DIRECTOR**	Steve Heller
DESIGNER	Ernest Scarfone	**DESIGNER**	Steve Heller
PHOTOGRAPHER	Naomi Savage	**ARTIST**	Brad Holland
EDITOR	Julia Scully	**EDITOR**	Charlotte Curtis
PUBLISHER	Modern Photography	**PUBLISHER**	The New York Times
AGENCY	ABC Leisure Magazines	**AGENCY**	The New York Times

 SILVER

"'Nick Wilder is the most important art dealer in town,' says one supporter. 'He's always giving young artists his time.'"

celebrated.

"Serious" art lovers bemoan the fact that Wilder's opening-night guests care less about art. But, as one rather plastered feminist painter phrased it to me one evening, "Now that the revolution is over, what are you going to do? *Party!*

"By the way," she added, "do you know of any parties after this one is over?"

"Nicholas Wilder's gallery continues to provide strength [in Los Angeles]," wrote *Art in America* recently. "Wilder is a cool, 'smart' dealer who established an attractive beachhead in the sixties. His taste is eclectic but his choices (both new and old) are almost always the right ones."

The best galleries of New York and Europe are constantly in touch with Wilder about the Los Angeles scene. Top local collectors, including Robert Rowan and Norton Simon, often confer with him about purchases.

Next to some of the best contemporary art in museum collections of special exhibitions is a tiny card reading, "Loaned by Nicholas Wilder Gallery, Los Angeles."

Elyse Grinstein, a kind of den mother to the Los Angeles art scene and the wife of an owner of the city's prestigious Gemini Editions Limited, calls Wilder "the most important art dealer in town because of what he does for the total community. Every week he goes to a dozen artists' studios. He's always giving young artists his time. He's supportive. He's always promoting art."

He must be doing something right. Wilder's gallery is grossing $100,000 per month in sales this year, most of which is going to the artists that he shows. His roster includes Chuck Arnoldi, Don Bachardy, Billy Al Bengston, Helen Frankenthaler, Sam Francis, Joe Goode, George Herms, Ed Moses, Bruce Nauman, Jules Olitski, Peter Zecker—and a lot more.

Artists like him.

"He's good," says Joe Goode. "He doesn't try to fuck artists. Other dealers sell things and don't pay. They tell you they've lost your art or something. Nick's gallery has an identity. The list of people he shows is staggering. He's better than any gallery in Europe. He's probably as good as the top two or three in New York."

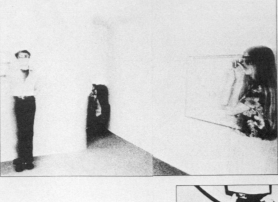

"He's like no other dealer I've dealt with before," says Don Bachardy. "He's enthusiastic. Beautifully supportive. He pays such attention to the most minute detail of your opening. Artists are very nervous about exhibitions, you know. He's with you—holding your hand all the way."

A former Stanford law student and a failed artist, Wilder opened his gallery with barely enough money to last five months.

He has been in business for ten years—six on La Cienega Boulevard's "art row," four in his present location. In the back room of his gallery he has personally amassed a $1.2-million collection of art. ("I'm not a Pontiac dealer," he says. "The goal isn't to sell everything off the lot as fast as I can. I only want to sell enough to pay for what I keep.") He meets a monthly overhead of $10,000 for each show he puts on (rent, $2250; 'phones, $1000; payroll, $2000; plus travel, parties, etc.).

"Most people think I'm very rich," he says. "But that's just not true. There isn't some wealthy person behind all this. . . . So I wish they'd stop asking me for a $25,000 painting for charity every other week."

And what *does* he have?

"The gallery, the gallery, the gallery," he says. "It's just become my whole life."

"There are very few people like him," says his friend, Christopher Isherwood. "He's my idea of a millionaire, or at least what a millionaire should be. He has the taste of a true aristocrat. Anyone could bring anything before him and he sees it from their whole frame of reference. He's a real romantic character. If you have to relate him to someone from the past it would be Scott Fitzgerald. That whole scene. He's a great celebrity. He's got fantastic style."

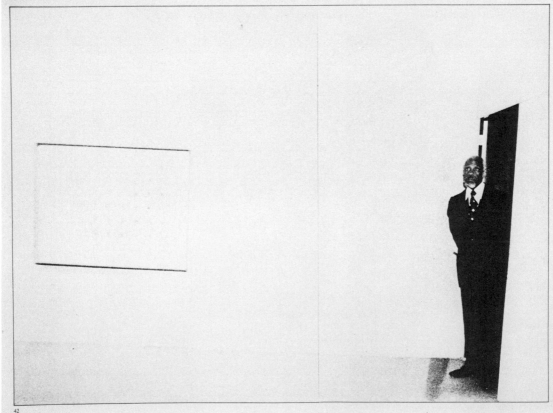

712
ART DIRECTOR Don Owens
DESIGNER Don Owens
PHOTOGRAPHER Antonin Kratochvil
PUBLISHER Coast Magazine
AGENCY Antonin Kratochvil

CAMBRIDGE, MASS.

When someone suffers a severe personal loss, they experience grief. All the purposes attached to the lost relationship seem to have become unrealizable. The bereaved are at first numbed and unbelieving, then despairing, angry, guilty, sleepless, as they restlessly seek release from their distress.

They are torn between conflicting impulses — to cling to the past, or to escape into a future where the loss can be forgotten and new purposes will make life meaningful again.

Each impulse checks the other: The comfort of remembered security soon recalls the anguish of loss, while to forget seems to deny all that the relationship meant, and arouses anxieties of betrayal.

As they struggle with these conflicted emotions, the bereaved gradually and painfully begin to restore a sense of continuity in their lives, which both accepts the loss, yet rescues the essential meaning and purpose of the past, so that without repudiating their deepest attachments life can make sense again.

Bereavement is therefore a crisis of meaning. Grief is the expression of an exhausting effort of reintegration, as much emotional as practical. A similar ambivalence has to work itself out in any transition that disrupts our familiar expectations and attachments — divorce, retirement, loss of home or job — sometimes even when we desire the change but are bewildered by its consequences.

The crisis may not be provoked by personal misfortune at all, but by a disintegration of our assumptions about the world in which we seek to fulfill our purposes.

Such a disintegration may be so gradual that we cannot say how or where it began, nor when we at last came to acknowledge it. But we then undergo a collective bereavement, which will arouse reactions analogous to grief, both in our private lives and projected as a social drama.

As I ride to work, for instance, I read in my paper that the recession is the worst since the Great Depression. At a departmental meeting, the talk is of financial cuts, of permanent positions threatened and even worse news, perhaps, next week. Passing by the supermarket, I cannot believe the price of a few bags of routine groceries. In the evening paper, a former director of the Central Intelligence Agency admits that he deliberately misled Congress.

Each of these experiences reinforces a nagging doubt about the reliability of the familiar assumptions on which I base my life — that my money will always be worth what it seems to promise, that my talents will always earn me a living, that government is an open system under democratic control.

In the back of my mind is a deeper anxiety that my way of life depends on a careless exhaustion of the world's resources, which is already driving the weakest to starvation. As such common experiences accumulate, the mood grows into a shared, bewildering uncertainty about our ability to foresee and control events, which demoralizes our sense of purpose.

All our instincts of self-preservation urge us to

The Meaning of Grief

By Peter Marris

deny this loss of meaning. For if our assumptions collapse, none of the skills by which we have learned to manage our lives are any longer trustworthy. We cling to the hope that a new President, more adroit economic management, luck and technological resourcefulness will set the problems to rights in predictable ways.

But the more events undermine the complacency of this underlying conservatism, the more it shades into a grief reaction — a retreat into a past we cannot recover, whose nostalgic security only makes the reality of the present more unbearable.

At the same time, radical movements that seek a total reconstruction of society broaden their appeal, for they offer an escape into a coherent future, to which our present confused and corrupted purposes are irrelevant.

This growing ideological polarization represents the contradictory impulses of grieving, but it cannot resolve them, and so becomes abortive and destructive, like a morbid grief. It displaces the conflict into a political struggle, which no longer recognizes the personal search for meaning in a confused social context.

We cannot work out our ambivalence by alternating between these ideological refuges as the bereaved alternate, because each has externalized and made an enemy of the impulse it cannot contain, and demands an unwavering loyalty. Hence we need to find social expressions of the ambivalence of loss, which neither deny it nor displace it, but articulate a common search for meaning.

Tribal institutions have evolved in contemporary Africa, for instance, which both reassert the traditional ideals of tribal society and yet organize their activities around the problems of modern urban life. They do not resolve the contradiction. But they provide a supportive framework of principles and relationships, through which people can begin to find a sense of identity amid the confusion of profound social transitions, without self-destructively repudiating their cultural inheritance.

In much the same way, minorities in the United States have looked back to rediscover their cultural roots, searching for a separate identity more meaningful than an American identity that contradicts its own promise, and more faithful to their experience; yet this separatism is organized about demands for recognition and acceptance by society at large.

Hence these movements admit an ambiguous and troubled search for identity, whose statements and symbolic demonstrations are, like rituals of mourning, both displays of grief and expressions of the attachments which must be ultimately reconciled in a viable reintegration.

The women's movement, too, contains a corresponding ambivalence. It expresses a profound grief at the loss of loving relationships in a world that seems to impose on women a choice between nonentity and the frustration of their sexuality, and at its extremes it both rejects men altogether and demands equality in masculine terms.

This exclusiveness, the apparently self-contradictory demands, the outraged challenge to conventional assumptions are necessary qualities of any movement that can support a shared experience of loss. Since grief is intrinsically ambivalent, it must articulate its contradictions before they can be worked through: And since each of us is searching for the personal meaning of our lives, we can only look for it with those whose experiences and emotional reactions match our own.

Those who think they understand, prescribing resolutions to a loss they have not felt, only stand in the way, however rational their advice may seem. And when loss arises from the disintegration of a social context, it cannot be resolved without making everyone confront this disintegration.

The instinct of adaptability, which looks for solutions within the framework of familiar institutions and assumptions, is more powerfully repressive of grief than the strident conservatism which at least acknowledges its vulnerability. Hence grief must sometimes be outrageous to overwhelm the complacency of well-meaning but obtuse gestures of reform.

If we can recognize how, when the social context of life loses its meaning, people will share a sense of bereavement, we can begin to understand and respect the movements that articulate their grief. But if we refuse to acknowledge this grief in others, clinging to assumptions that deny the reality of change, or prescribing radical alternatives that deny that there is anything to grieve for, we will stultify the difficult and painful process of reintegration in ways that will be destructive for everyone.

Peter Marris, author of "Loss and Change," is visiting professor of sociology at the University of Massachusetts.

713

Movies

The Greatest Ape

By Joseph Gelmis

Can a middle-aged gorilla from Skull Island find happiness with Fay DunnaWray atop New York's World Trade Center?

The predator spirit of King Kong lives on—in the hearts and the minds of the men skirmishing to claim the right to remake the classic movie. Kong may wear a two-button, Italian-cut suit and Gucci loafers now, instead of basic jungle. But don't let the white collar respectability fool you. He's the same old gorilla. Prehensile instincts, even in corporate garb, are unmistakable. "King Kong," one of the most popular motion pictures in history since its initial release in April 1933, is up for grabs.

A full two-page advertisement in the May 14 issue of *Variety*, the weekly trade paper, announced "Dino De Laurentiis and Paramount Pictures are proud to bring you . . . 'King Kong,' the legend reborn . . . for release in 1976." The words "King" and "Kong" were printed so big that each nearly filled a tabloid page. It was, surely, some kind of joke. How could they mess with Kong, the pride of Skull Island and the scourge of New York? Unable to take the idea seriously, many laughed.

But Universal Pictures—the studio that won the "special effects" Oscar this year for its Sensurround theatre-shaking device used in "Earthquake"—wasn't amused. Somewhere in the talking stage at Universal was a plan to remake "King Kong" using the Sensurround process. Universal decided to do battle with Paramount for Kong rights in court.

There are few hard facts forthcoming, understandably, until the winner of the Kong fight is declared. Strategies and details are still obscured by a smokescreen of legalese. Meanwhile we can speculate on why after forty-two years two of the most savvy-to-public-tastes movie outfits think the time has come for a new version of "King Kong." And, with the help of a new book, we can use the occasion as an opportunity to understand some of the effort that went into making "King Kong" a classic.

The most obvious parallel between 1933 and 1975 is hard times and a psychological public need for scary entertainment. It is part of the same sort of thinking that led 20th Century-Fox and Warner Brothers, which jointly bankrolled "The Towering Inferno," to prize the services of producer Irwin Allen so highly that each studio recently announced it signed Allen for unprecedented amounts of money for nonexclusive multi-picture contracts. Allen's previous disaster movie was another box office champ, "The Poseidon Adventure."

"Jaws," which Universal estimates will be the leading moneymaker of all time, can be seen as a latter-day King Kong versus the imaginary island of Amity, an idyllic vacation refuge as corrupt and unsafe as any metropolis. "Jaws," like "King Kong," is a monster movie. And all of the monster movies of the Depression—from "Frankenstein" to "Dracula" to "The Werewolf of London" or "Jekyll and Hyde"—were ultimately about monsters from the id.

It doesn't pay to get too analytical in looking for significance in popular culture, you understand. Because it leads to the kind of criticism that emphasizes ink-blot interpretations of "King Kong"—*i.e.*, that Kong is a symbol of the black slave forcibly brought in chains to the United States and struggling to be free (or the phallic symbolism of the world's tallest erection, as mentioned in former *New York Times* critic Bosley Crowther's book on the fifty greatest films ever made).

"King Kong" definitely belongs to the genre of monster movie that, as in "Jaws" and "The Exorcist," pits a superhuman adversary against a specialized team and the public at large. And genres didn't die out with the nonnarrative films of the 1960s (like "Five Easy Pieces"), any more than the novel was kaput a half-century

Illustration by James Luft

47

714

713
ART DIRECTOR Steve Heller
DESIGNER Steve Heller
ARTIST Brad Holland
EDITOR Charlotte Curtis
PUBLISHER The New York Times
AGENCY The New York Times

714
ART DIRECTOR Nancy V. Kent
DESIGNER Nancy V. Kent
ARTIST James Luft
EDITOR Prudence Brown
WRITER Joseph Gelmis
PUBLISHER Connecticut Magazine
AGENCY Connecticut Magazine

715

716

	715		716
ART DIRECTOR	B. Martin Pedersen	ART DIRECTOR	Ernest Scarfone
DESIGNER	B. Martin Pedersen	DESIGNER	Ernest Scarfone
ARTIST	Jerry Cosgrove	PHOTOGRAPHER	Ernst Haas
PUBLISHER	Pastimes Publications	EDITOR	Julia Scully
AGENCY	Pedersen Design	PUBLISHER	Modern Photography
		AGENCY	ABC Leisure Magazines

717

718

	717		718
ART DIRECTOR	Ernest Scarfone	**ART DIRECTOR**	Arthur Paul
PHOTOGRAPHER	Pete Turner	**DESIGNER**	Robert Post
PUBLISHER	Ehrenreich Photo	**ARTIST**	Ignacio Gomez
AGENCY	Pete Turner	**PUBLISHER**	Playboy Enterprises
		AGENCY	Playboy Magazine

Robert Coles talks with Ken Woodward about the American family, the resourcefulness of the tradition-bound poor, the uncertainties of the mobile rich, and how therapists have become preachers to the shopping-center community. "There is no final answer this side of Heaven or Hell."

Survival Drill in the Suburbs

THE COLD, TOUGH WORLD OF THE AFFLUENT FAMILY

Kenneth Woodward: For the last 15 years, you've been living with all kinds of American families — poor and rich, white, black and red — to see how they cope. Do you think the American family has a future?

Robert Coles: I am not one of those "experts" who thinks that the American family is about to disappear. Anyway, there are so many different kinds of families. What I've been studying, first in the South and then in the North and West, is how specific families in certain places are getting along at a particular time in American history. I have written up the work I did in New Mexico and Alaska with Chicano, Indian and Eskimo families for volume four of *Children of Crisis*. Before that I tried to write up, in the first three volumes of *Children of Crisis*, how black and white children in the rural South, and those in Appalachia and our northern ghettos manage to live. I am also trying to write up my work with the upper-middle-class suburban families I've met in all parts of the country, families I've gotten to know in connection with my observations of migrant workers, mountaineers and so on.

Woodward: How do the rich white families compare with poor families?

Coles: It's hard to compare an Eskimo family with, say, a suburban Massachusetts family on a $40,000 income or on up — except in the ways these very different families meet their particular challenges.

As a clinician, I guess I can pick out anxiety and despair fairly well. In some of the young children in rural parts of this country, whether they be black or white or Indian or Eskimo or Chicano, I see less anxiety, less fearfulness than I see in upper-middle-class children. These rural children have sources of support from within the extended family, from the church or from certain other cultural or social traditions. These supports, I think, have made for a certain steadiness in child-rearing which — for a while — means a lot.

Woodward: Just for a while?

Coles: Yes, you get a curve in the family life of poor rural children. They start strong, then hit trouble outside the family. Early on, there is a rising sense of hopefulness and contact in a large family unit — a sense of steadiness, of calmness about the world. It often seems crazy to outside observers from the middle class to find so much hope among kids who are poor and often malnourished. Not all such children, of course, have that hope, but a surprisingly substantial number do. And I say that *not* to romanticize poverty.

Poverty is no paradise, it can be hell. But many poor people can be, and are, very kind and loving parents to their small children.

But then when these children reach nine, 10 or 11 years old, they begin to find school useless at best. They're often insulted by teachers who have no real feeling for them. They begin to see no future for themselves. They get older and they find themselves both jobless and scorned, pushed around by sheriffs and other authorities because of race, of family background and.

Woodward: And what about upper-middle-class suburban kids?

Coles: The opposite kind of curve, often a bad start but a rise later. Children raised in the wealthier suburbs tend to experience a different sequence of hopefulness. I think that to be a parent in an upper-middle-class suburb is often to be without the sources of traditional family support. Suburban children are often brought up by troubled, worried parents who frequently have no real faith in much of anything, parents who are handed about from one child-rearing expert to another, from one fad to another, from one secular creed to the next.

But at about the same age that poor children begin to feel an erosion of hope, suburban kids find it. After having gone through what may well be a tense, difficult childhood, they begin to gain all kinds of strength and confidence. They see older brothers or neighbors getting the stereo, the motorcycle, the car they want. They learn that they belong to a well-to-do family that is highly regarded, or feared, by teachers, neighbors, camp counselors and so on. They see that promises made to them are going to be kept. About the same time, these upper-middle-class kids begin to show independence, effectiveness and authority.

Woodward: Where does this psychological strength come from, if not from traditional family sources?

Coles: I think of it as a continuity in authority transferred to the children by parents, by the schools they go to, the attitudes teachers take toward their well-to-do pupils. To be blunt about it,

719
ART DIRECTOR Richard Coyne
DESIGNER Richard Coyne
PHOTOGRAPHER Jay Maisel
EDITOR Richard Coyne
PUBLISHER Coyne & Blanchard
AGENCY Jay Maisel Photography

720
ART DIRECTOR Neil Shakery
DESIGNER Neil Shakery
ARTIST Wilson McLean
PUBLISHER Ziff-Davis Publishing Co.
AGENCY Ziff-Davis Publishing Co.

721

722

	721		722
ART DIRECTOR	Charles O. Hyman	ART DIRECTOR	Ernest Scarfone
DESIGNERS	Charles O. Hyman	DESIGNER	Ernest Scarfone
	Allan Porter	PHOTOGRAPHER	Sam Haskins
	Hans Peter Renner	EDITOR	Julia Scully
PHOTOGRAPHER	Fred J. Maroon	PUBLISHER	Modern Photography
WRITER	Hugh Sidey	AGENCY	ABC Leisure Magazines
PUBLISHER	EPM Publications		
AGENCY	Fred J. Maroon Photography		

What Rocky Did for New York,
He Can Do for America:

GENERALISSIMO ROCKEFELLER

I used to believe that Nelson Rockefeller was a moral vacuum surrounded by a huge body of money, that he had an absolutely insatiable longing for power. But as I watched him shift first this way, then that, in his fifteen years as governor of New York and presidential candidate I came to believe he couldn't be all bad because both the far right and the far left hated him so much.

Right-wingers think he's a Communist. Worse than that, they think he's a One-World Communist without a shred of loyalty to the United States. According to this school of thinking, he is also a tax dodger, a draft dodger, and murders little babies in the womb.

The left hates Nelson Rockefeller because they believe he is a fascist, that he is loyal only to the multinational corporations, that he believes in "destabilizing" governments like Chile's which are uppity about American capitalist expansion, that he is anti-democratic and a militarist. Both right and left are convinced that Rockefeller and his family are deeply involved in international plots to screw the American people.

Wouldn't you think with all this hate radiating from the political poles that the folks in the middle would recognize him as one of their own? Well, as it happens, Louis Harris published a poll on September 11, 1975, after Rockefeller had been vice president for almost a year. Here is what Harris reports: the American public opposes Rockefeller's nomination for vice president in 1976 by 47 percent to 34 percent. In other words, after watching Rocky on the job for almost a year, most average Americans don't even want him for vice president—let alone the top job!

Why don't middle-of-the-road Americans like Rockefeller? It may be because they know that he has as much contempt for them as he has for all others—except for those in his own economic class. During the reign of Nelson Rockefeller, the New York State income tax doubled, and the total state tax load quintupled—even as he developed ever more ingenious methods for helping the rich to escape it. As governor, Nelson Rockefeller proved himself a master at spending other people's money. That money didn't come from the poor, large numbers of whom, after all, were on welfare (partly because thousands of

BY MARY PEROT NICHOLS

SOFT SCULPTURE BY JUDITH JAMPEL/COSTUME BY EAVES, N.Y.C.

47

723

"bodyscapes"

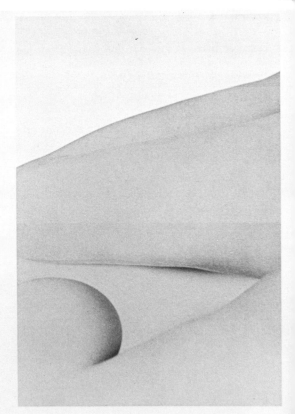

72

723
ART DIRECTOR   Joe Brooks
DESIGNER   Frank De Vino
ARTIST   Judith Jampel
PHOTOGRAPHERS   Klaus Lucka
Linda Moss
PUBLISHER   Penthouse International
AGENCY   Penthouse International

724
ART DIRECTOR   Shinichiro Tora
PHOTOGRAPHER   Dick Kranzler
PUBLISHER   Popular Photography
AGENCY   Ziff-Davis Publishing C

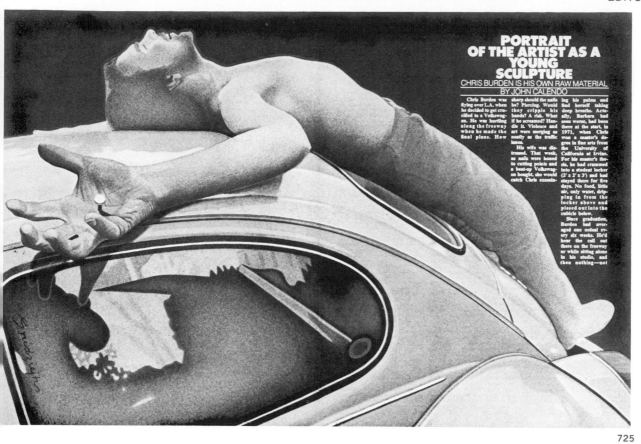

725

726

725
ART DIRECTOR Don Menell
DESIGNER Don Menell
ARTIST Alex Gnidziejko
PUBLISHER Oui Magazine
AGENCY Playboy Publications

726
ART DIRECTOR Arthur Paul
DESIGNER Len Willis
ARTIST Melinda Bordelon
PUBLISHER Playboy Magazine
AGENCY Playboy Enterprises

727
ART DIRECTOR Arthur Paul
DESIGNER Len Willis
ARTIST Frank Root
PUBLISHER Playboy Magazine
AGENCY Playboy Enterprises

728
ART DIRECTOR Ernest Scarfone
DESIGNER Ernest Scarfone
PHOTOGRAPHER Richard W. Brown
WRITER Julia Scully
PUBLISHER Modern Photography
AGENCY ABC Leisure Magazines

Mountains, seacoast, and a living legacy

NEW HAMPSHIRE

VERMONT

MASSACHUSETTS

RHODE ISLAND

CONNECTICUT

CLOSE-UP: U.S.A.

New Hampshire
Vermont
Massachusetts
Rhode Island
Connecticut

NATIONAL GEOGRAPHIC

729
ART DIRECTOR Charles O. Hyman
DESIGNERS Fred Otnes
Charles O. Hyman
ARTIST Fred Otnes
WRITER Jules B. Billard
PUBLISHER National Geographic
AGENCY National Geographic
Society

THE END OF THE AMERICAN DREAM

BY JEFF GREENFIELD

America has always equated freedom with abundance. But the old order changeth —and as we enter the Age of Shortages we'd better take care that our liberty isn't one of them.

Something is happening to America—something that has never happened before; something that may change our country's government and society beyond recognition and accomplish what no enemy nation, no army, no domestic tyrant or subversive ever managed to do: eradicate the freedom and liberty of American citizens. The first evidence is already around us—the persistent joblessness, the cost of food and fuel, the steadily eroding real value of the dollar, the sporadic shortages at the supermarket, and the continuing uneasiness about the availability of gasoline and other fuels. But we are still probably a

Photograph By Cosimo

730

730
ART DIRECTOR Joe Brooks
DESIGNERS Frank De Vino
Linda Moss
PHOTOGRAPHER Cosimo
PUBLISHER Penthouse Magazine
AGENCY Penthouse International

Back to Nature

A great explorer tells the story of a
great adventure: how he and his wife survived a year
on a primitive South Pacific island

BY THOR HEYERDAHL

The islands we had dreamed of rose from the sea like the morning sun. The rising sun glowed red to the east, and the first Marquesas island was pale blue like the shadows of fingers on the northern horizon. Steep, rugged and menacing, the mountain masses hurled themselves ever higher as we sailed on, until they were soaring like rock fortresses high above the ocean. Tumbling, frothing and rumbling like a distant thunderstorm, the endless sea beat wildly against these fixed obstacles in a world of living water. As one island rose from the sea another sank and disappeared, for there is a great distance between the islands in the Marquesas group. The Pacific stretched between them in many tints of blue, but around each island the water was as green as grass, due to masses of microscopic plankton that thrive upon an incessant rain of minerals gnawed from the brittle rocks by the perpetual surf. Shoals of fish were attracted to this evergreen marine pasture, with dolphins and birds in visible pursuit. Swarms of seabirds followed the little schooner and plunged after the fish that repeatedly struggled on the line we were towing astern.

We were much nearer the equator now, and as we came inshore we could verify that here the Pacific reached its highest degree of fertility. One valley after the other opened in front of us and closed behind as we sailed past, all formed as deep wild gorges cutting into the central mass of ridges and peaks. Only truly vertical precipices had managed to shake off the jungle and rise as naked red rock above the chaos of luxuriant greenery that flowed down the steep ridges and bluffs to the palm-studded valley bottom.

The tropical heat alone was not responsible for this extravagant fertility. In the interior of the islands the towering peaks intercept the westward course of the sparse but ever-present little trade wind clouds and squeeze the rain out of them before they manage to proceed westward. Therefore, fresh rainwater always pours down from the mountains in rushing torrents and rivers, through dark jungles and friendly valleys, into the green sea. The tooth of time had gnawed greedily everywhere into

As the storm clouds of World War II began to gather over Europe, Thor Heyerdahl, then a 22-year-old University of Oslo biology graduate, and his 20-year-old bride sailed for the South Pacific, where they intended to turn their backs on the materialism of a civilization they thought doomed to destruction. The article that begins on this page is excerpted from the book Fatu-Hiva so be published in the United States this month by Doubleday & Company, Inc. (Copyright© 1974 by George Allen and Unwin Ltd.)

ILLUSTRATED BY ROBERT GIUSTI   23

731

ART DIRECTOR	Norman S. Hotz
DESIGNER	M. Jane Heelan
ARTISTS	Robert Giusti
	David Wilcox
WRITER	Thor Hyerdal
PUBLISHER	American Express
	Publications
AGENCY	Travel & Leisure

731

RICHARD FEGLEY

Photographer Richard Fegley and
Associate Art Director Tom
Staebler cooked up the idea for
this one. Which was, simply, to
show legs in a relatively natural,
uncontrived setting. "So," says
Fegley, "I just put the girl in
bed and shot her." Makes sense.

732

These
United
States

Near Tubac,
Arizona

733

	732		733
ART DIRECTOR	Arthur Paul	ART DIRECTOR	Shinichiro Tora
DESIGNER	Tom Staebler	PHOTOGRAPHER	Fred J. Maroon
PHOTOGRAPHER	Richard Fegley	PUBLISHER	Popular Photography
PUBLISHER	Playboy Magazine	AGENCY	Ziff-Davis Publishing Co.
AGENCY	Playboy Enterprises		

ARTHUR PAUL

Up against the wall, or how to liven up a decadent but dull soiree. Our satin doll and her Mr. Right (at least for the evening) find that "sitting this one out" can use up as much energy as the boogie. As choreographed by photographers Bob Keeling and Francois Robert, it's a Last Tangoish routine you won't learn at Arthur Murray's. Above and right: PLAYBOY Art Director Arthur Paul turned cameraman for these studies, which carry realism to a point beyond reality—first, as a female leg, viewed from above, acquires an abstractly sculptural quality; second, as a foot —with the aid of a stiletto heel, some black nail polish and a mysteriously missing shoe—takes on the potent role of fetish.

734

735

	734		735
ART DIRECTOR	Arthur Paul	DESIGNER	Jacqueline Schuman
DESIGNER	Tom Staebler	PHOTOGRAPHER	André Kertész
PHOTOGRAPHERS	Paul Gremmler	WRITER	Daniel Okrent
	Robert Keeling	PUBLISHER	Grossman Publishers
	Francois Robert	AGENCY	Grossman Publishers
	Arthur Paul		
	Don Azuma		
	Bill Arsenault		
	Ken Marcus		
	Richard Fegley		
	Pompeo Posar		
PUBLISHER	Playboy Magazine		
AGENCY	Playboy Enterprises		

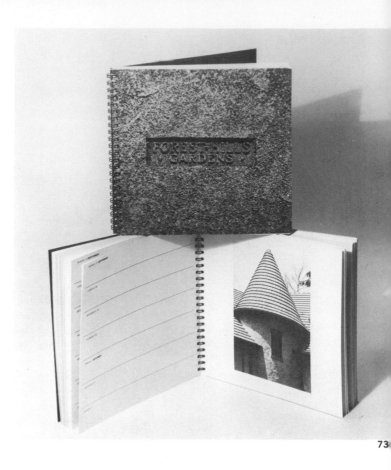

73

73

736
ART DIRECTOR Guglielmo Nardelli
DESIGNER Guglielmo Nardelli
ARTIST Guglielmo Nardelli
PHOTOGRAPHER Guglielmo Nardelli
WRITER Forest Hills Village
Improvement Society
AGENCY Forest Hills Village
Improvement Society
CLIENT Forest Hills Gardens

737
ART DIRECTOR Ivan Chermayeff
DESIGNER Elaine Rooney
ARTIST Helen Federico
AGENCY Chermayeff & Geisma
CLIENT Mobil Oil Corp.

Photographed by Henry Wolf

9

10

738

738
DESIGNER | Henry Wolf
PHOTOGRAPHER | Henry Wolf
AGENCY | Henry Wolf Productions
CLIENT | Henry Wolf

SILVER

741

73

740

740

	739		740		741
ART DIRECTOR	Frank Wagner	ART DIRECTOR	William Rivelli	ART DIRECTORS	Ria Lewerke
DESIGNERS	Frank Wagner	DESIGNERS	William Rivelli		Thom Williams
	Mark English		Lore Baer	DESIGNERS	Bill Norgels
			Alex MacLeod		Rod Dyer Inc.
ARTIST	Mark English	PHOTOGRAPHER	William Rivelli	ARTISTS	Various
WRITER	Diane Cooney	AGENCY	Rivelli Photography	PHOTOGRAPHERS	Various
AGENCY	Sudler & Hennessey	CLIENT	Rivelli Photography	AGENCY	United Artists Record
CLIENT	Pfizer Laboratories			CLIENT	United Artists Record

May

S	M	T	W	T	F	S
						1
2	3	4	5	6	7	8
9	10	11	12	13	14	15
16	17	18	19	20	21	22
23	24	25	26	27	28	29
30	31					

"Whenever in the course of the daily hunt the red hunter comes upon a scene that is strikingly beautiful or sublime – a black thundercloud with the rainbow's glowing arch above the mountain, a white waterfall in the heart of a green gorge, a vast prairie tinged with the blood red of sunset – he pauses for an instant in the attitude of worship."

Ohiyesa, Santee Dakota, 1911

742

744

743

	742		**743**		**744**
ART DIRECTOR	Greg Wilder	**ART DIRECTOR**	Jerry Friedman	**ART DIRECTOR**	Don Weller
DESIGNER	Bart Forbes	**DESIGNER**	Rinaldo Frattolillo	**DESIGNER**	Don Weller
ARTIST	Bart Forbes	**PHOTOGRAPHER**	Jerry Friedman	**ARTIST**	Don Weller
AGENCY	Sun Graphics	**AGENCY**	Jerry Friedman Studio	**AGENCY**	The Weller Institute for the Cure of Design
CLIENT	Sun Graphics	**CLIENT**	Jerry Friedman Studio	**CLIENT**	Picante Press

745

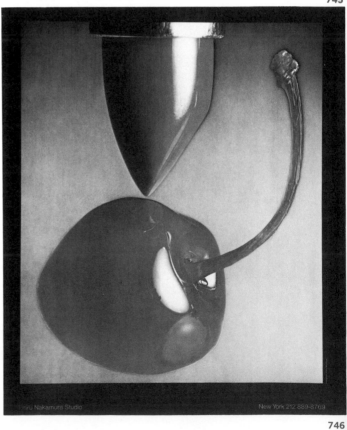

746

	745		**746**
ART DIRECTOR	Sue Llewellyn	**ART DIRECTOR**	Tohru Nakamura
DESIGNER	Sue Llewellyn	**DESIGNER**	Richard Moore
ARTIST	Sue Llewellyn	**PHOTOGRAPHER**	Tohru Nakamura
AGENCY	Sue Llewellyn	**AGENCY**	Tohru Nakamura Studio
CLIENT	Sue Llewellyn	**CLIENT**	Tohru Nakamura Studio

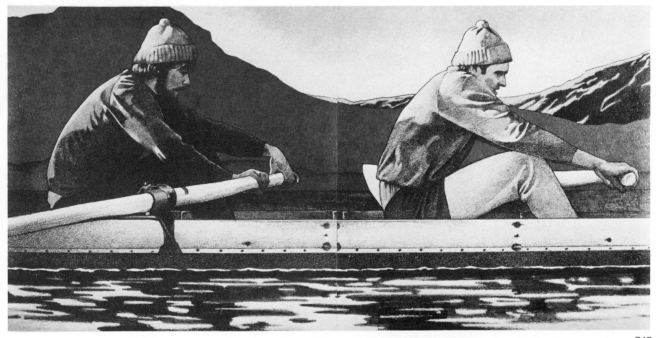

747

748

	747		**748**	
ART DIRECTORS	Howard Auerbach	ART DIRECTOR	Richard Stack	
	Jan Esteves	DESIGNERS	Richard Stack	
	Irwin Fleminger		Steve Hansen	
	Michael Meyerowitz		Herb Rogalski	
	Bill Ronalds	PHOTOGRAPHER	Steve Hansen	
	Tom Rummler	WRITER	Richard Stack	
	G. Clark Sealy	AGENCY	Cabot Cabot & Forbes	
	George Stavrinos	CLIENT	Wintergreen	
ARTIST	George Stavrinos			
AGENCY	Push Pin Studios			
CLIENT	Push Pin Studios			

749

750

751

749		**750**		**751**	
ART DIRECTOR	Joan Peckolick	**ART DIRECTOR**	Randy Miller	**ART DIRECTOR**	Don Weller
DESIGNER	Joan Peckolick	**DESIGNER**	Randy Miller	**DESIGNER**	Don Weller
ARTIST	Bascove	**PHOTOGRAPHER**	Randy Miller	**ARTIST**	Don Weller
WRITER	Joan Peckolick	**WRITER**	Randy Miller	**AGENCY**	The Weller Institute for
AGENCY	Joan Peckolick Design	**AGENCY**	Randy Miller		the Cure of Design
CLIENT	Joan Peckolick Design	**CLIENT**	Randy Miller	**CLIENT**	Picante Press

SILVER

752

January

S	M	T	W	T	F	S
				1	2	3
4	5	6	7	8	9	10
11	12	13	14	15	16	17
18	19	20	21	22	23	24
25	26	27	28	29	30	31

753

Brush up on O'Neill's latest work.

To see Michael O'Neill's portfolio call Joe DiBartolo at (212) 677-3449.

754

	752		753		754
ART DIRECTOR	William Rivelli	**ART DIRECTOR**	Greg Wilder	**DESIGNER**	Ray Alban
DESIGNERS	William Rivelli	**DESIGNER**	Bart Forbes	**PHOTOGRAPHER**	Michael O'Neill
	Lore Baer	**ARTIST**	Bart Forbes	**WRITER**	Tom Nathan
	Alex MacLeod	**AGENCY**	Sun Graphics	**AGENCY**	Michael O'Neill
HOTOGRAPHER	William Rivelli	**CLIENT**	Sun Graphics	**CLIENT**	Michael O'Neill
AGENCY	Rivelli Photography				
CLIENT	Rivelli Photography				

LIGHTEN
SUFFERING
BY
EXCHANGING
BAD
FOR GOOD.
CONFUCIUS

755

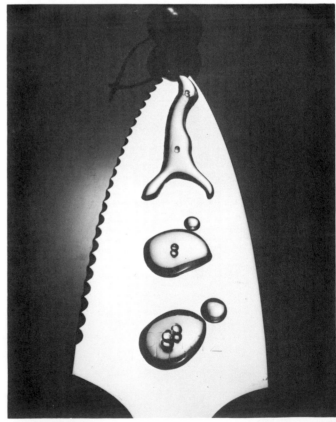

756

	755		756
ART DIRECTOR	Frank Wagner	**ART DIRECTOR**	Jerry Friedman
DESIGNERS	Frank Wagner	**DESIGNER**	Rinaldo Frattolillo
	Mark English	**PHOTOGRAPHER**	Jerry Friedman
ARTIST	Mark English	**AGENCY**	Jerry Friedman Studio
WRITERS	Diane Cooney	**CLIENT**	Jerry Friedman Studio
	Mary Powers		
AGENCY	Sudler & Hennessey		
CLIENT	Pfizer Laboratories		

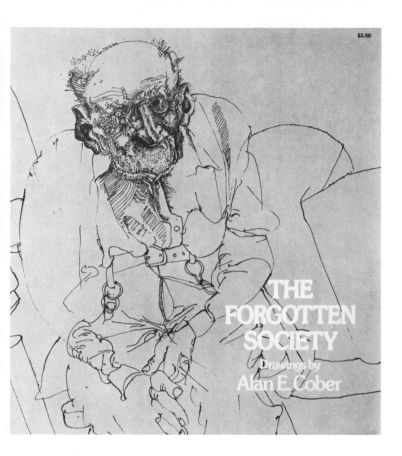

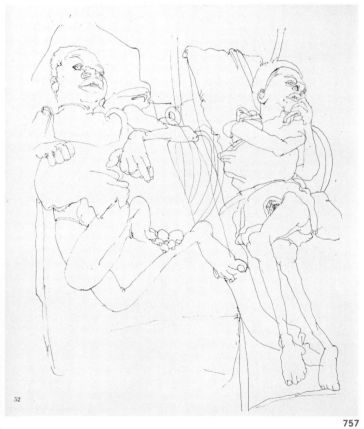

757

757

ART DIRECTOR Paul Kennedy
DESIGNERS Sam Antupit
Alan E. Cober
ARTIST Alan E. Cober
PUBLISHER Dover Publishing
AGENCY Alan E. Cober

758

	758		759
ART DIRECTOR	Uli Boege	ART DIRECTOR	Don Weller
DESIGNER	Uli Boege	DESIGNER	Don Weller
PHOTOGRAPHER	Robert Sommer	ARTISTS	Don Weller
WRITER	Robert Sommer		Alan Williams
PUBLISHER	Quick Fox	PHOTOGRAPHER	Roger Marshutz
AGENCY	Quick Fox	WRITER	Sheldon Weinstein
		PUBLISHER	Standard Brands Paint Co.
		AGENCY	The Weller Institute for the Cure of Design

 GOLD

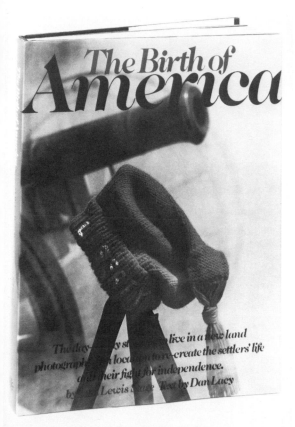

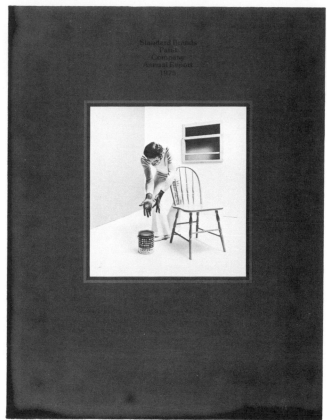

760

759

760
ART DIRECTOR Albert Squillace
DESIGNER Albert Squillace
PHOTOGRAPHER John Lewis Stage
WRITER Dan Lacy
PUBLISHERS Ridge Press
Grosset and Dunlap
AGENCY Ridge Press

 SILVER

the
real
cowboy

Until September in 1867, the cowboy was just another over-worked ranch hand with a bad reputation. But in that month, Joseph G. McCoy opened his cattle pens in Abilene, Kansas, to Texas longhorns, and the image began to change. The cowboy who drove the steers northward to market over the Chisholm Trail rapidly attracted attention in a country recovering from a bitter civil war and looking westward for relief.

"This kind of life seems to have an inexpressible charm for the young men," exclaimed a San Antonio reporter. "It is an exciting scene to see them in full chase, with their lariats whirling over their heads, their mustangs as much excited by the race as themselves."

"Cowboys are a much misrepresented set of people," Theodore Roosevelt told a New York **Tribune** reporter in 1884. "I have taken part with them in roundups, have eaten, slept, hunted and herded cattle with them, and have never had any difficulty. If you choose to enter rum shops or go on drinking sprees with them, it is easy to get into difficulty as it would be in New York, or anywhere else . . . and there are many places in our cities where I should feel less safe than I would among the wildest cowboys in the West."

The cowboy had not always been so well thought of. The word "cowboy" had evolved from the Tory guerrillas who roamed New York State during the Revolution and cropped up again in the Texas Revolutionary Army company of 1842, but the image denoted by the word was that of "rough men with shaggy hair and wild, staring eyes." Some ranchers even refused to use the word, preferring instead the antiseptic "hands." Writers for **Harper's Weekly** and **Leslie's Illustrated**, the two most widely read weeklies of the nineteenth century, reported that the cowboy was considered "a constant source of peril to the settler and tradesman," a man with "no fear," who "respects no law." Even after the cowboy had won almost universal admiration as an American folk hero, there were outbreaks of violence that recalled their lawless days. As late as 1881, Arizona cowboys became nationally known for bandit raids, and President Chester A. Arthur denounced them as "armed desperadoes" in a message to Congress after frightened citizens of the territory telegraphed him for assistance.

But when McCoy established a market for cattle at Abilene, he gave the haphazard ranching business a large part of the stability it needed to become a viable industry, and the hard-working, hard-riding cowboy began to become respectable. By 1879, his image had picked up some of the "hero" gloss it has today. Most westerners realized that the cowboy was "just a plain, everyday bow-legged human," but his double conquest of the rangy, wild Texas longhorn and the "Great American Desert," as the Great Plains was called, imbued him with a superhuman reputation.

"There is perhaps no class of civilized beings whose characteristics are more marked than the Texas cow boy," boasted the editor of the Victoria (Texas) **Advocate**. "Accustomed to the saddle from infancy, he grows up familiar with his native prairies, and a love for them develops with his manhood, which appears to the stranger an infatuation. What the broad

Preceding pages:
Moving a thousand
head of cattle
into Big Horn mountains
of Wyoming for summer
grazing. Opposite: Gary
Morton, cowboy of
Bell Ranch— "I'm working
for the Bells"—near
Tucumcari, NM. He wears
chink chaps more common
to buckaroos of
Northwest. Unlike wide
batwings, straight-
leg shotguns, and
woolly angoras, chink
chaps end at knee.

761

761
ART DIRECTOR Albert Squillace
DESIGNER Albert Squillace
PHOTOGRAPHER Bank Langmore
WRITER Ron Tyler
PUBLISHERS Ridge Press
William Morrow & Co. Inc
AGENCY Ridge Press

762

ALI'S PEOPLE

FRAZIER'S PEOPLE

762
ART DIRECTOR George Lois
PHOTOGRAPHER Carl Fischer
WRITER Harold Hayes
PUBLISHER Buckingham Corp.
AGENCY Lois Holland Calloway

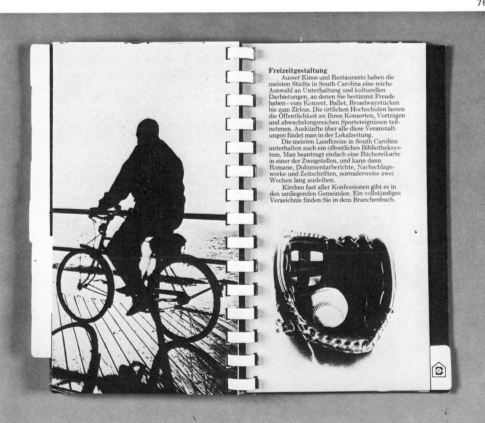

763
ART DIRECTOR Ed Martel
DESIGNER Ed Martel
PHOTOGRAPHER John Bilecky
WRITER John Davis
PUBLISHER The Citizens and
Southern National Bank
AGENCY Doran Stein Grey

764

764
ART DIRECTOR Onofrio Paccione
DESIGNER Onofrio Paccione
ARTIST Onofrio Paccione
PHOTOGRAPHER Onofrio Paccione
PUBLISHER Collier Graphic Services
Co.
AGENCY Paccione Photography

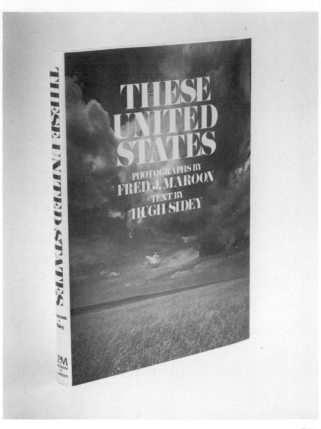

765

765
ART DIRECTOR Charles O. Hyman
DESIGNERS Charles O. Hyman
Allan Porter
Hans Peter Renner
PHOTOGRAPHER Fred J. Maroon
WRITER Hugh Sidey
PUBLISHER EPM Publications
AGENCY EPM Publications

Schlumberger Employees Credit Union

Schlumberger Suggestion System

766

767

	766		767
ART DIRECTOR	Al Gluth	**ART DIRECTOR**	Bob Nemser
DESIGNER	Al Gluth	**DESIGNER**	Bob Nemser
ARTISTS	Al Gluth	**PHOTOGRAPHER**	Dennis Yeandle
	Joe Romano	**WRITER**	G.A. Kraut Co.
AGENCY	Baxter & Korge	**AGENCY**	Nemser & Howard
CLIENT	Schlumberger	**CLIENT**	Keystone International

768

769

768		769	
ART DIRECTOR	B. Martin Pedersen	**ART DIRECTOR**	Joan Cassidy
DESIGNER	B. Martin Pedersen	**ARTISTS**	Joan Cassidy
ARTIST	Daniel Maffia		Richard Waxberg
AGENCY	Pedersen Design	**PHOTOGRAPHER**	Lawrence Mayea
CLIENT	Eastern Airlines	**AGENCY**	Texasgulf
		CLIENT	Texasgulf

770

771

770
ART DIRECTOR Barbara Bertoli
DESIGNERS Push Pin Studios
Richard Nebiolo
ARTIST Nicholas Gaetano
PUBLISHER Avon Books
AGENCY Avon Books

771
DESIGNER O. Paul Slaughter
PHOTOGRAPHER Leonard Ross
AGENCY Bethlehem Steel Corp.
CLIENT Bethlehem Steel Corp.

773

774

772
ART DIRECTOR Ace Lehman
DESIGNERS Ace Lehman
Frank Mulvey
ARTIST Norman Miller
AGENCY RCA Records
CLIENT RCA Records

773
ART DIRECTORS Richard Weigand
Onofrio Paccione
DESIGNER Onofrio Paccione
PHOTOGRAPHER Onofrio Paccione
WRITER Don Ericson
AGENCY Paccione Photography
CLIENT Esquire Magazine

774
ART DIRECTOR Brian O'Neill
DESIGNER Brian O'Neill
ARTIST Barbara Nessim
AGENCY Davis, Delaney, Arrow
CLIENT International Flavors
& Fragrances

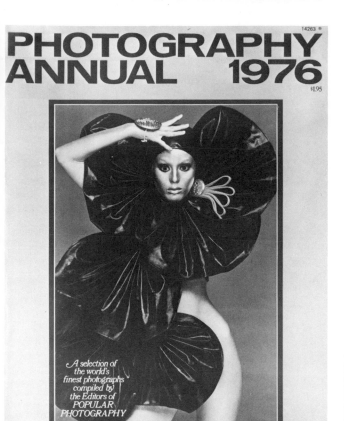

775

776

	775		776		777
ART DIRECTOR	Thomas Ridinger	**ART DIRECTOR**	Ruth Ansel	**ART DIRECTOR**	Steve Phillips
DESIGNER	Thomas Ridinger	**DESIGNER**	Ruth Ansel	**DESIGNER**	Steve Phillips
PHOTOGRAPHER	Hideki Fujii	**PHOTOGRAPHER**	Evelyn Hofer	**ARTIST**	Bill Nelson
WRITER	Jim Hughes	**EDITORS**	Lewis Bergman	**WRITER**	Jon Larsen
PUBLISHER	Ziff-Davis Publishing		Jack Rosenthal	**PUBLISHER**	New Times
CLIENT	Ziff-Davis Publishing	**PUBLISHER**	The New York Times		Communications
		CLIENT	The New York Times	**CLIENT**	New Times
					Communications

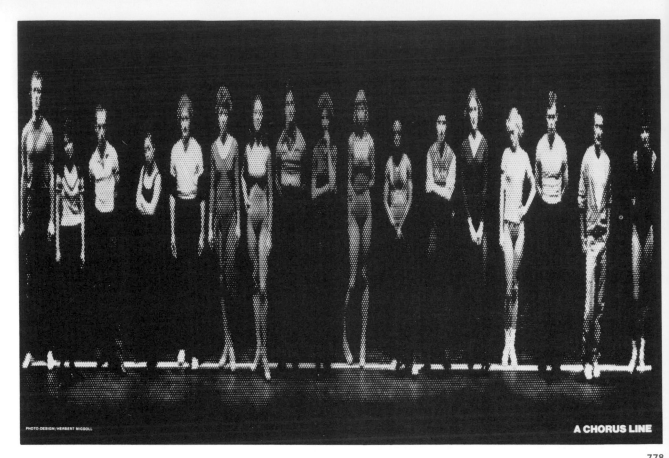

778

779

	778		779
ART DIRECTOR	Herbert Migdoll	ART DIRECTOR	Andrew Kner
DESIGNER	Herbert Migdoll	DESIGNER	James Grashow
PHOTOGRAPHER	Herbert Migdoll	ARTIST	James Grashow
WRITER	Nancy Heller	AGENCY	Print Magazine
AGENCY	N.Y. Shakespeare	CLIENT	Print Magazine
	Festival Plum		
	Productions		
CLIENT	N.Y. Shakespeare		
	Festival Plum		
	Productions		

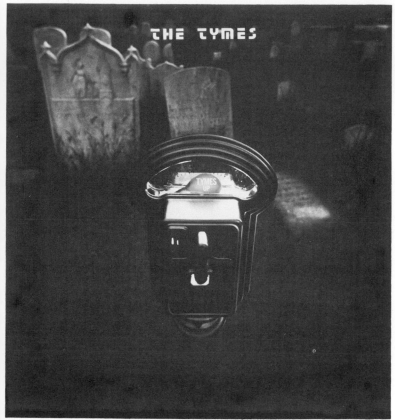

780

781

	780		781
ART DIRECTOR	Joseph Stelmach	**ART DIRECTOR**	Andrew Kner
DESIGNER	Joseph Stelmach	**DESIGNER**	Pierre Le-Tan
PHOTOGRAPHER	Nick Sangiamo	**ARTIST**	Pierre Le-Tan
AGENCY	RCA Records	**PUBLISHER**	Print Magazine
CLIENT	RCA Records	**CLIENT**	Print Magazine

782

783

784

	782		**783**		**784**
ART DIRECTORS	Richard Weigand	**ART DIRECTOR**	Frances McCullough	**ART DIRECTOR**	Ace Lehman
	Onofrio Paccione	**DESIGNER**	Brad Holland	**DESIGNER**	Mick Rock
DESIGNER	Onofrio Paccione	**ARTIST**	Brad Holland	**PHOTOGRAPHER**	Mick Rock
PHOTOGRAPHER	Onofrio Paccione	**WRITER**	Craig Nova	**AGENCY**	RCA Records
WRITER	Don Ericson	**AGENCY**	Brad Holland	**CLIENT**	RCA Records
AGENCY	Paccione Photography	**CLIENT**	Harper & Row		
CLIENT	Esquire Magazine				

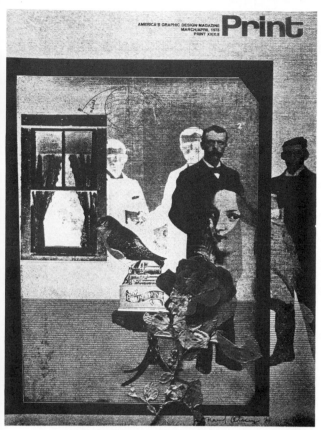

785

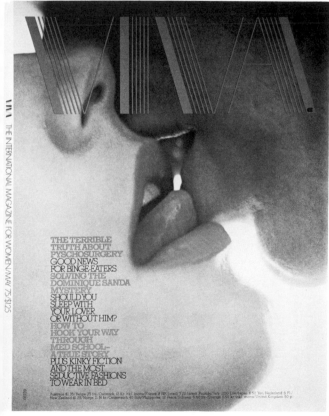

786

	785		786
ART DIRECTOR	Andrew Kner	ART DIRECTOR	Rowan Johnson
DESIGNER	Fred Otnes	DESIGNER	Onofrio Paccione
ARTIST	Fred Otnes	PHOTOGRAPHER	Onofrio Paccione
PUBLISHER	Print Magazine	PUBLISHER	Paccione Photography
CLIENT	Print Magazine	CLIENT	Viva Magazine

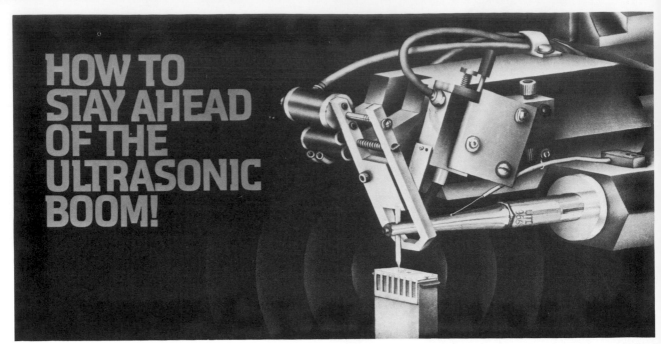

HOW TO
STAY AHEAD
OF THE
ULTRASONIC
BOOM!

787

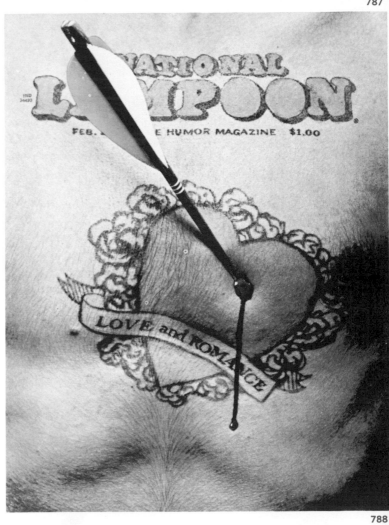

788

	787		788
ART DIRECTOR	David Gauger	ART DIRECTOR	Peter Kleinman
DESIGNER	David Gauger	DESIGNER	Peter Kleinman
ARTIST	David Gauger	ARTIST	Peter Kleinman
WRITER	Larry J. Silva	PHOTOGRAPHER	Neil Selkirk
AGENCY	Gauger Sparks Silva	WRITER	Doug Kenney
CLIENT	Uthe Technology	PUBLISHER	National Lampoon
	International	CLIENT	National Lampoon

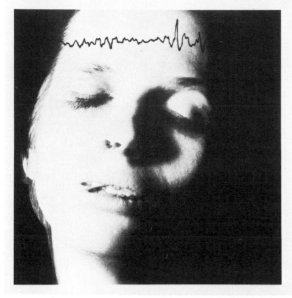

789

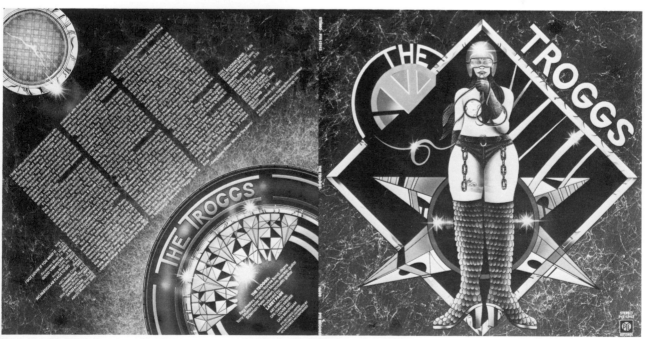

790

	789		790
ART DIRECTOR	John deCesare	**ART DIRECTOR**	David Krieger
DESIGNERS	Hank Gans	**DESIGNER**	Ted Amber
	Claude Emile Furones	**ARTIST**	Don Brautigam
PHOTOGRAPHER	Hank Gans	**AGENCY**	DFK Sales Promotions
WRITER	Barbara Ramm	**CLIENT**	ATV Records
AGENCY	Geigy Pharmaceuticals		Incorporated
CLIENT	Geigy Pharmaceuticals		

791

792

	791		792
ART DIRECTORS	Arnold Kushner	ART DIRECTOR	John Berg
	Andrew Kner	DESIGNERS	John Berg
DESIGNER	Arnold Kushner		Andy Engel
ARTIST	Allen Welkis	ARTIST	Roger Huyssen
PHOTOGRAPHER	Bill Aller	AGENCY	CBS Records
WRITER	Jane Klein	CLIENT	CBS Records
PUBLISHER	The New York Times		
CLIENT	The New York Times		

 SILVER

793

794

	793		**794**
ART DIRECTOR	Ed Lee	**ART DIRECTOR**	Ed Lee
DESIGNER	Ed Lee	**DESIGNER**	Ed Lee
ARTIST	Peter Lloyd	**ARTIST**	Clifford Condak
AGENCY	CBS Records	**AGENCY**	CBS Records
CLIENT	CBS Records	**CLIENT**	CBS Records

795

796

	795		796
ART DIRECTOR	Ed Lee	ART DIRECTOR	John Berg
DESIGNER	Ed Lee	DESIGNER	John Berg
ARTIST	Robert Giusti	ARTIST	Robert Weaver
AGENCY	CBS Records	AGENCY	CBS Records
CLIENT	CBS Records	CLIENT	CBS Records

 SILVER

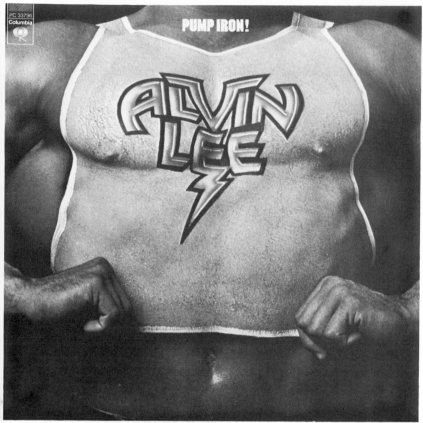

797

798

	797		**798**
ART DIRECTOR	John Berg	**ART DIRECTOR**	John Berg
DESIGNER	John Berg	**DESIGNERS**	John Berg
ARTISTS	Roger Huyssen		Henrietta Condak
	Gerard Huerta	**ARTIST**	Edward Sorel
HOTOGRAPHER	Richard Davis	**AGENCY**	CBS Records
AGENCY	CBS Records	**CLIENT**	CBS Records
CLIENT	CBS Records		

INTERNATIONAL

HOW TO ECONOMISE:
CUT OUT HEINZ TOMATO KETCHUP.

799
ART DIRECTOR Derrick Hass
DESIGNER Derrick Hass
PHOTOGRAPHER Stak Aivaliotis
WRITERS Derrick Hass
Simon Risley
AGENCY Doyle Dane Bernbach
England
CLIENT H.J. Heinz Co.

THE FUDGEE-O OBSERVATION:

If it weren't for the thick, creamy fudge, the chocolate wafers would bump into one another.

WITHOUT FUDGE:

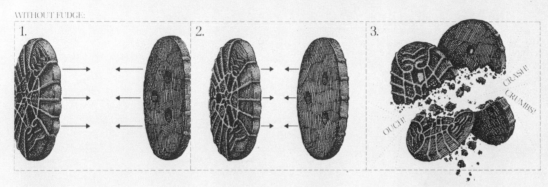

WITH FUDGE:

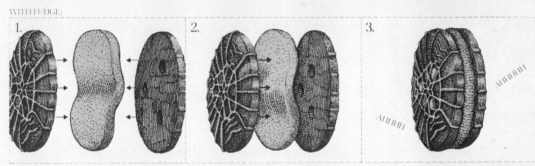

A FURTHER OBSERVATION:

One day Mr. Christie had a very bad cold and couldn't come to work to make his thick, creamy fudge for his Fudgee-o Cookies. So he phoned the bakery and told the chocolate wafers to hold everything until the next day. But, as you can imagine, those frisky wafers just couldn't sit still. And when Mr. Christie returned to work two days later, there were crumbs all over the place from those crazy wafers running around and bumping into each other. And boy, was Mr. Christie mad.

A FINAL OBSERVATION:

Mr. Christie, you make good cookies.

800
ART DIRECTOR Brian Harrod
WRITER Allan Kazmer
DESIGNER Brian Harrod
ARTIST Tony Kew
AGENCY McCann-Erickson
Canada
CLIENT Christie, Brown

FILL OUT THIS TOMATO AND WE'LL SEND YOU 25 WAYS TO EAT IT.

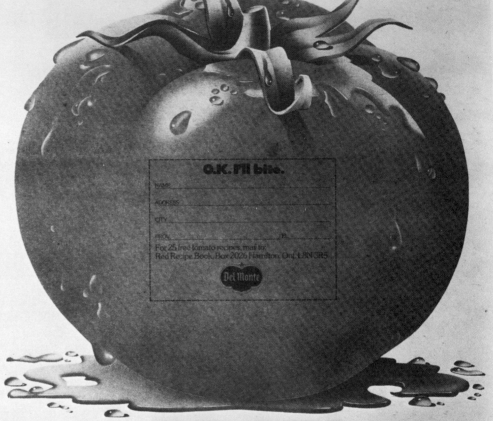

O.K. I'll bite.

NAME

ADDRESS

CITY

PROV. P.C.

For 25 free tomato recipes, mail to:
Red Recipe Book, Box 2026 Hamilton, Ont. L8N 3R5

Del Monte

FREE!

You'll get hungry just reading our little tomato recipe book. Because there are some absolutely delicious things going on between its pages.

And not only that, everything in it is easy to make: Unheard of dishes like Tomatoed Potatoes. Exotic delicacies like Gazpacho.

the little red recipe book

Here are 25 new recipes to help you create memorable meals.

There are even recipes that turn the hum drum into the yum yum. Like Speedy Spaghetti Sauce.

Altogether, you'll find out how to make 25 new goodies. And all this know-how is yours merely for the asking. Just fill out the tomato.

And we'll fill you in.

801

ART DIRECTOR	David Purser
WRITER	Mike Stillman
DESIGNER	David Purser
ARTIST	Roger Hill
AGENCY	McCann-Erickso Canada
CLIENT	Canadian Canne

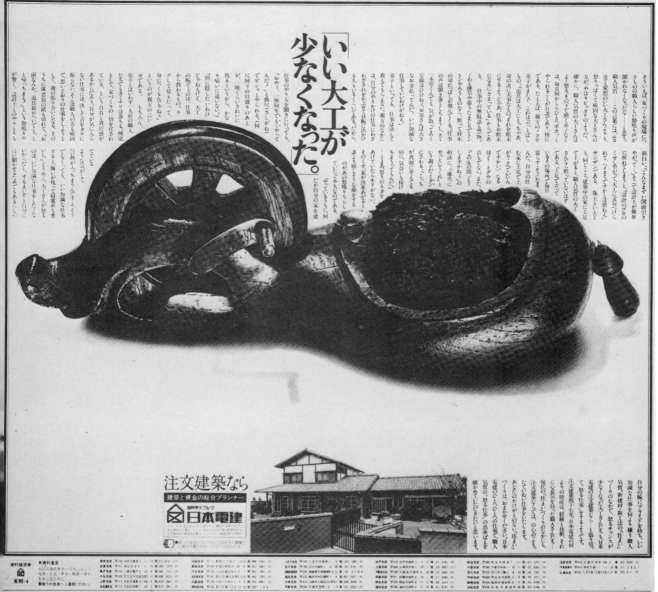

Tops.

Show it off muscle T-shirt top. Super rib cotton trimmed with tartan. Red, navy, French blue. $10.50. Elegant coral shell necklace. $5.00. Tonal bangles at various prices.
Sportsgirl

Exclusive skimpy tie up in the front top. Cotton rib, muscle sleeves in red, white, navy, French blue, green. $8.00. exclusive Italian straw hat. Sportsgirl super sunshades.
Sportsgirl

Exclusive tube top in kenzo stripes. Boat neck, square sleeves. Red/white, Navy/white, French blue/green, French blue/white. $10.00. Exclusive Italian straw hat.
Sportsgirl

Exclusive tight top. Cut like men's basketball singlet. Red/White/Navy, Navy/Red/White. $6.00. Imitation Puka shell necklaces. $1.95. Italian printed Sun Visor hats $4.50.
Sportsgirl

Exclusive not a lot on the back, little in the front halter top. Square neck, tie back. Red/blue, French blue/red, navy/red. $3.00. Italian straw hat. Various shapes and prices.
Sportsgirl

The Boob Tube. Gathered front, halter strap. Red/White, Navy/White, Black/White. Hangs in there. $4.00. Sportsgirl super sunshades, various shapes and prices.
Sportsgirl

Exclusive clingy striped, muscle top. Shows off all kinds of muscles. French blue/green, Navy/red, White/navy, French blue/white. $7.00.
Sportsgirl

Exclusive bare back, tie back, T-shirt top. The rest is front. Red, White, Navy. $5.00. Exclusive imported Italian straw bags.
Sportsgirl

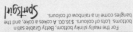

Sportsgirl Miniscule recycled patch work denim bottoms. No running in required. $13.50. Sportsgirl super sunshades, and Eve's apple.

Sportsgirl For the really slinky bottom, Betty Grable satin bottoms. Lots of colours. $16.00. A cokes a coke, and the bangles come in a rainbow of colours.

Sportsgirl Especially when you remember her ankles. Betty Grable gaberdine bottoms. Red, white, navy, cream. $14.00. Tons of zippy sox, in all kinds of colour combinations.

Sportsgirl The pleats are in the front but the prints are all over these Betty Grable bottoms. Lots of prints. $10.00. Exclusive Italian straw bags. Various colours and prices.

Sportsgirl Betty Grable knew about legs when she gave her name to these front pleat bottoms. Denim blue. $14.00.

Sportsgirl Overalls that start at the bottom, and work up to a lace up effect front. Denim blue, white drill. $18.00. Use your own paintbrush.

Sportsgirl Plenty of leg, and everything, in skimpy denim cut off exclusive bottoms. $8.00.

Sportsgirl Tiny bottom of cheeky blue denim, with turnups. for tan to the top. $9.50. Exclusive cotton cotton triangle printed scarf $6.00.

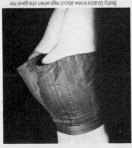
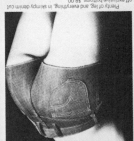

Bottoms.

80

804
ART DIRECTOR Gordon Trembath
WRITER Lionel Hunt
DESIGNER Gordon Trembath
ARTIST Pat Mason
PHOTOGRAPHER Angie Heinl
AGENCY The Campaign Palace
Australia
CLIENT Sportsgirl

At around 90°F, workers evaporate.

65°F. He's okay.

72°F. He's feeling warm.

78°F. He's hot and bothered.

80°F. He can't concentrate.

85°F. He's fading fast.

90°F. He's disappeared.

It's a sad fact of life that the 'Disappearing Workers' actually exist in large numbers throughout Britain.

And if you're in any doubt about it, try spending an hour or two on the factory floor one sunny afternoon.

The chances are, you'll find that a number of employees aren't to be seen. And of those who are, many will be present in body but not in spirit.

The reason will hit you full blast the moment you step in the door. It is, quite simply, the hot, sweltering atmosphere caused by bad ventilation.

It's unpleasant to walk around in, it's damned near impossible to work in. And if you subject a man to these conditions, his will to work dies.

His productivity drops like a stone, his attitude to management takes a very fast turn for the worse. In his eyes, you actually become the cause of his misery – for it's an industrial fact he can only work at his best in a temperature of 60°F to 72°F.

So what's to be done about it? The answer that over 60,000 British companies have found is to call us at Colt.

We carry out a detailed survey at your factory, then report in full and without charge, showing how the right use of ventilation can create healthier, safer, altogether better working conditions (and, incidentally, help to keep you within the Act).

It can only do good for your company's profits – and even the tax-man shoulders a fair share of the capital outlay.

Write or phone. It's the one sure way you have of making a very real problem disappear.

Colt International Limited (Heating, Ventilation and Industrial Access). Havant, Hants. Havant 6411. Telex 86219.

People work better in Colt conditions.

805

805
ART DIRECTOR John Wood
WRITER Geoff Horne
DESIGNER John Wood
HOTOGRAPHER John Thornton
AGENCY Davidson, Pearce,
Berry & Spottiswoode
England
CLIENT Colt International

 GOLD

The expensive motor car we made for our president and others like him.

When your president tells you that he wants a motor car in keeping with his position, your initial reaction may well be to panic.

However, if the president you're talking to happens to be our president you have no cause for alarm.

If you want a designer with the reputation of Pininfarina, or a V6 3.2 litre motor like you'd find in a Dino Ferrari, it can be arranged.

If you want wall-to-wall carpets, electrically operated windows, a steering wheel that can be adjusted for height and reach, the mention of the president's name can make a lot of things possible.

And when people try to tell you that independent suspension, disc brakes, rack and pinion steering and air conditioning cost a lot of money, you can afford to smile.

As can the president when he sees that the car you have made for him will be eminently suitable for Presidents, Chairmen and Managing Directors of other companies.

Now you can drive the Fiat 130 Saloon we made for our president, or if you prefer, the Fiat 130 Coupe.

They're exactly like his except for one little detail:

Unlike our president, you won't have the name of your company on the front grille.

F I A T

806
ART DIRECTOR Tony Stewart
WRITERS Peter Carey
Terry Durack
PHOTOGRAPHER Bob Bourne
AGENCY Grey Advertising Pty
Australia
CLIENT Fiat of Australia Pty.

COMPANIES THAT GOBBLE UP PEOPLE END UP WITH FAT PAYROLLS AND LEAN PROFITS. Today, scarcity and rising costs don't only apply to raw material. They also apply to people. Especially skilled people. For this reason, we at Olivetti have been applying ourselves to the people problem. Our successes to date include a word processing machine that can replace two typists. And an invoicing machine that can replace three invoice clerks and a bookkeeper. And on-line computer and visible data processing systems that can replace a horde of clerks, storemen and accounting staff. Don't get the wrong idea though. We're not just interested in replacing people with machines. Our main concern is better systems within a company, so that the whole company can operate more rationally and efficiently. If your company is high on people, but low on operating efficiency, come talk to Olivetti. And we'll show you how to turn your fat frog of a company into a rich and handsome prince.

olivetti
These days we're a heck of a lot more than typewriters.

Grey-Phillips, Bunton, Mundel & Blake 52821

807

807

ART DIRECTOR Ian Blake
WRITER David Said
DESIGNER Ian Blake
ARTIST Ian Blake
AGENCY Grey, Phillips, Bunton,
Mundel & Blake
South Africa
CLIENT Olivetti Africa, Pty.

SILVER

Out of school. Into Peaches.

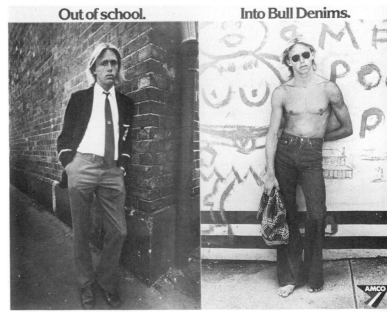

Out of school. Into Bull Denims.

80

ART DIRECTOR Lindsay Crethar
WRITER Garry Murphie
DESIGNER Lindsay Crethar
PHOTOGRAPHER Brian Morris
AGENCY Crethar, Murphie
Australia
CLIENT AMCO

808

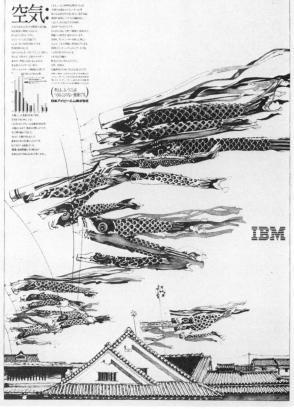

809

809
ART DIRECTORS Masao Katsura
Hideo Mori
WRITER Shosuke Matsuo
DESIGNERS Hideo Mori
Yasunobu Asoh
ARTIST Akira Mohri
AGENCY Hakuhodo Inc.
Japan
CLIENT IBM Japan

1720 Royal Exchange   1802 Essex & Suffolk   1805 Caledonian   1808 Atlas   1821 Guardian   1835 Union of Canton

1881 Reliance Marine   1890 Licenses & General   1891 State   1906 Motor Union   1915 United British   1968 Guardian Royal Exchange

We've been called many names in our time.

If Guardian Royal Exchange Assurance is a name that conjures up Dickensian images of clerks in wing collars scratching away with quill pens, perhaps we should point out that we'll soon be celebrating our 7th birthday.

But for such a new company, our history goes back a remarkably long way.

To 1720 to be exact, when Royal Exchange Assurance first saw the light of day.

Over the next couple of hundred years or so it did very well.

So well, in fact, that it was able to take half a dozen other insurance companies under its wing, many of whose names you'll recognise above.

Meanwhile, back in the City, the respected Guardian Assurance Company was likewise taking other well-known companies into its fold.

Which brings us to 1968, and leaves us with two prosperous and very old insurance companies. Now what could be more natural than a merger?

The result was Guardian Royal Exchange Assurance. A company with the size, experience and financial stability to give policyholders a really good deal.

Which, together with our name, is something worth remembering next time you want a good insurance policy.

Guardian
Royal Exchange
Assurance
A good name to insure with.

810

810

ART DIRECTOR David Harrison
WRITER Chris O'Shea
DESIGNER David Harrison
PHOTOGRAPHER John Gladwin
AGENCY C. Vernon & Sons
England
CLIENT Guardian Royal
Exchange Assurance

TOSSING A COIN IS NO WAY TO PICK AN ASIAN HOLIDAY.

CBA TRAVEL.

811

811

ART DIRECTOR Gordon Trembath
WRITER Lionel Hunt
DESIGNER Gordon Trembath
PHOTOGRAPHER Peter Gough
AGENCY The Campaign Palace
Australia
CLIENT C.B.A. Travel

Why older whisky isn't necessarily better whisky.

If you think spending time in a barrel helps make a Canadian rye better, you're right.

But only up to a point.

Because rye whisky, like everything else in life, reaches one point in time when it's at its peak.

When it's in its "Prime."

Before that it can be pale, harsh and still unmatured.

After that it begins to get darker and take on a stronger "woody" taste.

Most of our competitors settled for whisky that's 6 years old or less.

Not us.

In our opinion, 8 is the "Prime" year for OFC.

When it couldn't be better. Smooth.

Mellow.

And full-bodied.

And yet still light enough to have a taste that takes no getting used to.

We make OFC 8-Year Old, and only 8 years old, because that's the best year.

Frankly those two extra years of aging, cost us extra money.

But that's the price we were willing to pay to create the only whisky ever to win three consecutive gold medals in the World's toughest competition "The Olympics of Food and drink" Monde Sélection.

Yes, there are younger whiskies.

Yes, there are older whiskies.

No, there is no other whisky "Picked in its Prime."

OFC 8-Year Old.

The Prime Canadian.

2 years
4 years
6 years
O.F.C.
8 years
10 years
12 years

CANADIAN SCHENLEY DISTILLERIES LTD.
Sponsors of the Canadian Schenley Football Awards since 1953.

812
ART DIRECTOR Pierre Leduc
WRITER Pete Mathieu
DESIGNER Pierre Leduc
PHOTOGRAPHER Bill Stettner
AGENCY Châles, Gerfen, Leduc & Mathieu
Canada
CLIENT Canadian Schenley Distilleries

As luck would have it, our fire insurances were very popular in San Francisco just before the earthquake.

At 5.15 am on Wednesday April 18th 1906 a tremendous earthquake shook the city of San Francisco, causing fires to break out in the damaged buildings.

Shattered water mains hindered the Fire Brigade, and after 3 days the city centre was just a collection of smouldering ruins.

Not surprisingly, the various insurance companies who had issued fire cover on the gutted buildings weren't exactly overjoyed.

They faced colossal claims. And so did many of the companies that now make up Guardian Royal Exchange Assurance.

But unlike those who couldn't meet their liabilities and went to the wall, we paid up. What's more we did it quickly and without quibbling.

In all, it set us back £1,750,000, a tidy sum in those days.

But looking back, it was one of the shrewdest investments we ever made.

It proved to the world that we had the strength to withstand a major disaster.

Consequently the business started pouring in and we've not looked back since.

In fact, today we're one of the very largest insurance companies in Britain.

(Last year alone, we paid out over £257 million in claims.)

But solid and stable as we are, we don't intend to rest on our laurels.

We're determined not to lose sight of the fact that every policy we offer, whether it be for a modest car or a vast industrial complex, must be what the customer wants.

And to our way of thinking, that means the best possible cover at the most reasonable price.

If you agree, we suggest you have a word with your broker and mention our name. It's Guardian Royal Exchange Assurance.

Guardian Royal Exchange Assurance

A good name to insure with.

813

813
ART DIRECTOR David Harrison
WRITER Chris O'Shea
DESIGNER David Harrison
PHOTOGRAPHER Library Material
AGENCY C. Vernon & Sons
England
CLIENT Guardian Royal
Exchange Assurance

Creme 21 pflegt die Haut und schützt die Haut. Creme 21 gibt es als Lotion. Sie läßt sich leicht auf dem Körper verteilen. Und Creme 21 gibt es als Schaumcreme. Sie zieht besonders schnell ein.

Creme 21 gehört auf die Haut, wie die Nase zum Gesicht.

Creme 21. Die Haut für die Haut.

Creme 21

815

Die meisten nehmen eine Hautcreme nur fürs Gesicht. Als ob sie sonst keine Haut hätten.

Creme 21. Die Haut für die Haut.

Creme 21

Creme 21 pflegt die Haut und schützt die Haut und gibt ihr Feuchtigkeit. Creme 21 gibt es auch als Lotion. Sie läßt sich leicht auf dem Körper verteilen. Und Creme 21 gibt es als Schaumcreme. Sie zieht besonders schnell ein. Ⓧ Henkel-Khasana

815
ART DIRECTOR Jürgen Pilger
WRITERS Michael Schirner
Diethardt Nagel
Berthold Schmidt
PHOTOGRAPHERS Christa Peters
Will McBride
Christian von Avensleben

AGENCY GGK Düsseldorf
West Germany
Henkel-Khasana

SILVER

Parmi toutes les bières du monde–et Dieu sait si elles sont nombreuses et souvent appréciables–il en est une réputée excellente: Beck's Bier. Et pourtant lors qu'elle est tant appréciée dans le pays qui l'a vue naître– l'Allemagne–le malheur veut qu'elle demeure, sous nos cieux, une rareté. Très chers experts de la distribution, ne nous aiderez-vous pas à changer cela?

Brauerei Beck & Co. 2800 Bremen, RFA, Am Deich 45

816

816
ART DIRECTOR Uwe Duvendack
WRITER Mike Camesasca
ARTIST Uwe Duvendack
PHOTOGRAPHER Mane Weigand
AGENCY TBWA GmbH
West Germany
CLIENT Brauerei Beck & Co.

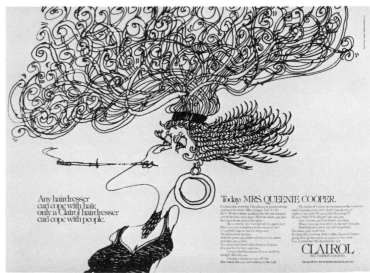

817

817
ART DIRECTOR Barry Chemel
WRITER Ian Mirlin
DESIGNER Barry Chemel
ARTIST Barry Chemel
AGENCY Grey-Phillips, Bunton,
Mundel & Blake
South Africa
CLIENT Clairol

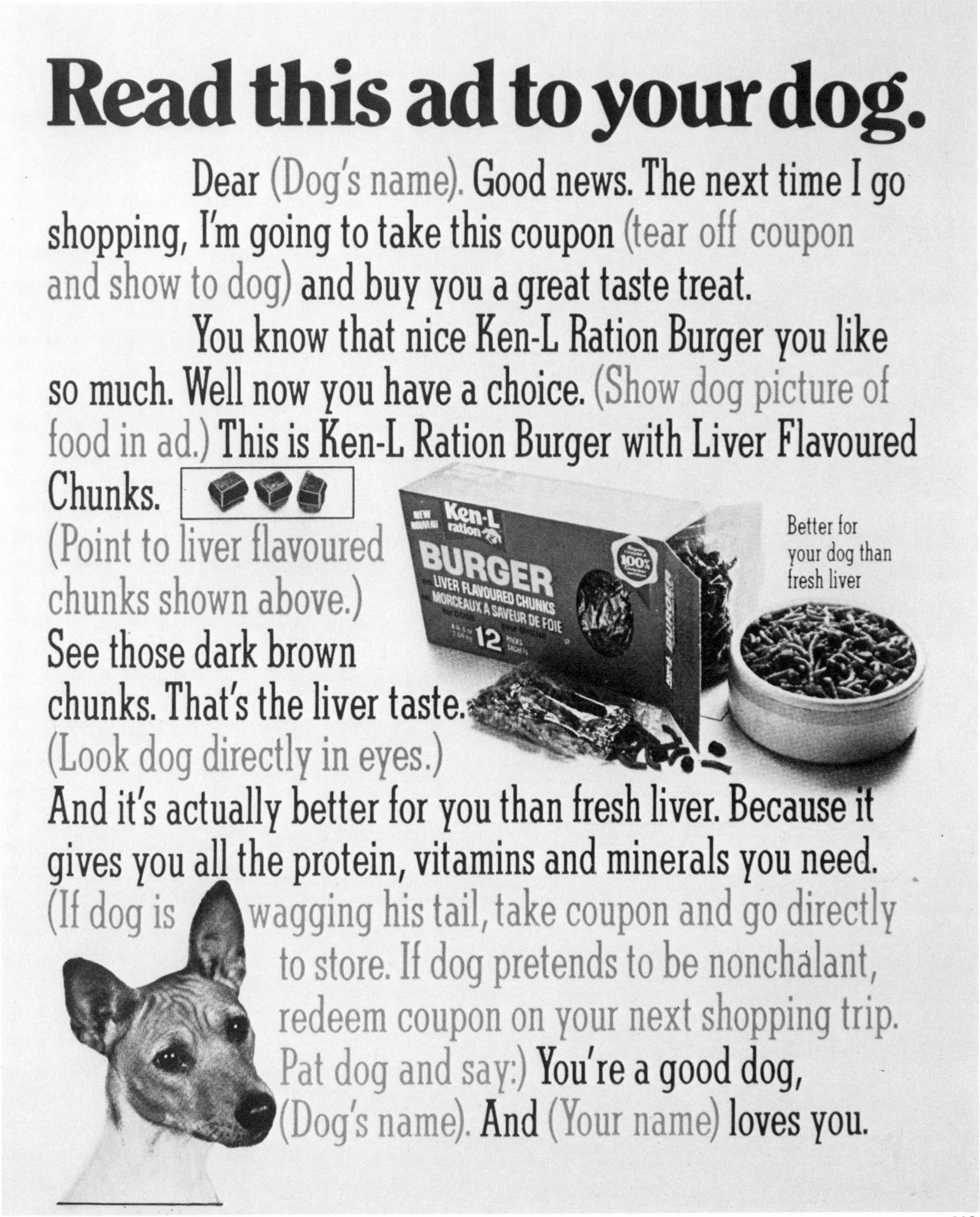

Read this ad to your dog.

Dear (Dog's name). Good news. The next time I go shopping, I'm going to take this coupon (tear off coupon and show to dog) and buy you a great taste treat.

You know that nice Ken-L Ration Burger you like so much. Well now you have a choice. (Show dog picture of food in ad.) This is Ken-L Ration Burger with Liver Flavoured Chunks. (Point to liver flavoured chunks shown above.) See those dark brown chunks. That's the liver taste. (Look dog directly in eyes.) And it's actually better for you than fresh liver. Because it gives you all the protein, vitamins and minerals you need. (If dog is wagging his tail, take coupon and go directly to store. If dog pretends to be nonchalant, redeem coupon on your next shopping trip. Pat dog and say:) You're a good dog, (Dog's name). And (Your name) loves you.

Better for your dog than fresh liver

818

818
ART DIRECTOR Brian Harrod
WRITER Allan Kazmer
DESIGNER Brian Harrod
PHOTOGRAPHER David Allan
AGENCY McCann-Erickson
Canada
CLIENT The Quaker Oats Co.

819

820

	819		**820**
ART DIRECTOR	Brian Harrod	**ART DIRECTOR**	Peter Harold
WRITER	Allan Kazmer	**WRITER**	Barbara Nokes
DESIGNERS	Brian Harrod	**DESIGNER**	Peter Harold
	Allan Kazmer	**PHOTOGRAPHER**	Tony May
ARTIST	Tony Kew	**AGENCY**	Doyle Dane Bernbach
AGENCY	McCann-Erickson		England
	Canada	**CLIENT**	K Shoemakers
CLIENT	Tootsie Roll		

Rund 400 Mark unter Preis.

Jeans zum Fahren.

821

ART DIRECTOR Feico Derschow
WRITER Rainer Baginski
AGENCY GGK Düsseldorf
West Germany
CLIENT Volkswagenwerke AG

THE 7th SUMMER JAZZ FESTIVAL

サマージャズ

8月31日(日)

正午〜午後9時

日比谷野外大音楽堂

雨天決行

指定席2300円

前売自由席1500円

当日自由席1800円

出演

池田芳夫カルテット

今田勝トリオ

今村裕司クインテット

ジョージ大塚クインテット

ジョージ川口・松本英彦とビッグ4

鈴木宏昌トリオ

高橋達也と東京ユニオン

土岐英史カルテット

外山喜雄とデキシーランドセインツ

中村誠一トリオ

日野元彦グループ

水橋孝カルテット

峰厚介クインテット

宮間利之とニューハード

向井滋春クインテット

山口真文カルテット

ボーカル

後藤芳子

戸谷重子

司会

いソノてルヲ

行田よしお

50音順

主催／文化放送

後援／スイングジャーナル

提供／TCP(株)

都内各プレイガイド・有名ジャズ喫茶にて好評前売中

お問合せ

TCP(株)208-1011

文化放送コンサート係357-1111

822

822
ART DIRECTOR Takenobu Igarashi
DESIGNER Takenobu Igarashi
ARTIST Takenobu Igarashi
AGENCY Takenobu Igarashi Design Institute
Japan
CLIENT Bunka Broadcasting Co.

MOTORBIKES
60-second

CONDUCTOR: Right. German motorbike owners . . .all together please.

GERMAN VOICE: One, two, three (in German)

GERMAN CHORUS: (Sound of motorbike to tune of "Wooden Heart")

CONDUCTOR: Sloppy, sloppy. . .again, please.

GERMAN VOICE: One, two, three (in German)

GERMAN CHORUS: (Singing sound of motorbikes to tune of "Wooden Heart")

CONDUCTOR: Good, good. Now English bikes, annunciate please.

ENGLISH CHORUS: (Singing sound of motorbike to tune of "English Country Garden" together with German chorus)

CONDUCTOR: Japanese bikes. . .er. . .no need to bow, just sing.

JAPANESE CHORUS: (Singing sound of motorbikes to oriental tune together with German and English chorus)

ANNCR: Nowdays, there are as many different kinds of motorbike people as there are motorbikes. Some enthusiasts are turned on by racing . . .some try trail riding. . .touring. . .scrambling. Whatever your interest. . .the latest bikes, accessories, overseas news, club news. . .you'll find it in the *Advertiser* comprehensive motorbike section. If motorbikes are music to your ears, check out the *Advertiser* every Friday, 'cause now we're big on motorbikes.

824
WRITER Street Remley
Creative Services
DIRECTOR Street Remley
Creative Services
PRODUCER Street Remley
Creative Services
PRODUCTION CO. Pepper Studios
AGENCY Street Remley
Creative Services
Australia
CLIENT Advertiser Newspapers

PY-CO-PAY
45-second

MAN: Presenting the Py-Co-Pay jingle:

FEMALE GROUP SINGING:
Py-Co-Pay jingle, jingle, jingle,
Py-Co-Pay jingle, jingle, jingle,
Py-Co-Pay jingle, jingle, jingle,

MAN: (Shouting through song) Hear that jingle! It's telling you that the Py-Co-Pay toothbrush has rounded ends on the bristles so they won't scratch teeth enamel.

And Py-Co-Pay has a gum massager on the handle.
And Py-Co-Pay costs more than most toothbrushes.
But although Py-Co-Pay is hard on your pocket, it's certainly gentle on your teeth.

You can find the Py-Co-Pay toothbrush at chemists everywhere.

But don't listen to me. Listen to that jingle.

825
WRITERS Peter Carey
Tony Stewart
Terry Durack
PRODUCERS Pat Aulton
Terry Durack
PRODUCTION CO. United Sound Studios
AGENCY Grey Advertising Pty.
Australia
CLIENT Stafford-Miller

 SILVER

OLD MAN
60-second

OLD MAN: Like to tell you about a mistake I made back in 1907...9...8. Got married, bought a big beautiful house, working like a mule, and the payments would go out every month. But—she's paid off now, and we can really start living. Yep! (sound of body falling to floor)

ANNCR: Look. . .save some money for living. Highcraft Homes are big, full brick and tile homes that cost less. See the award-winning Highcraft Home of The Year. Choose one of the three superb designs. . .and leave some money for living.

SISTINE CHAPEL
60-second

MICHAELANGELO: Is this the Sistine Chapel?

HIS GRACE: Yes.

MICHAELANGELO: Hi, my name is Michaelangelo and you wanted me to stop by and give you an estimate on fixing the place up a little.

HIS GRACE: Yes, I wanted you to look at the main chapel. Right this way.

MICHAELANGELO: Nice place you got here.

HIS GRACE: We like it. Ah, here we are.

MICHAELANGELO: Wow—that's some floor!

HIS GRACE: I beg your pardon.

MICHAELANGELO: That's a great floor.

HIS GRACE: Oh.

MICHAELANGELO: But, you're right. You do need a new floor covering. I'd recommend GAFSTAR Sheet Vinyl Flooring. It comes in hundreds of patterns and colours and never needs scrubbing or waxing. It's made by GAF.

HIS GRACE: That's G-A-F.

MICHAELANGELO: No, it's GAF, G-A-F spells GAF.

HIS GRACE: Are you arguing with us?

MICHAELANGELO: No, no, no, of course not, your Grace. Uh?

HIS GRACE: Good, then it's settled. It's G-A-F. Now, what do you think about the ceiling?

MICHAELANGELO: Well, the ceiling. See, I don't do ceilings, I do floors. No ceilings, no windows, and half a day on Saturday.

HIS GRACE: Are you arguing with us again?

MICHAELANGELO: No, no, I—I'll start in the morning, your Grace.

MUSIC: Capture your great moments—great moments with G-A-F)

826
WRITER Street Remley
Creative Services
DIRECTOR Street Remley
Creative Services
PRODUCER Street Remley
Creative Services
PRODUCTION CO. Pepper Studios
AGENCY Barraclough & Beynon
Australia
CLIENT Highcraft Homes

827
WRITERS Miles Ramsay
Doug Linton
PRODUCERS Miles Ramsay
Evelyn Arthur
PRODUCTION CO. Griffiths, Gibson
AGENCY Goodis, Goldberg, Soren
Canada
CLIENT GAF Canada

GOLD

LADY GODIVA
60-second

ANNCR: There is quite a crowd gathered here waiting for Lady Godiva. And I'll try to talk to some of the simple peasants. Could you tell us your name sir?

PIPPIN: I'm Tom Pippin.

ANNCR: And what do you do sir?

PIPPIN: I'm a simple peasant.

ANNCR: I see you have a camera Mr. Pippin. Are you planning to photograph Lady Godiva?

PIPPIN: Well of course. I mean it's not every day you get the opportunity to snap royalty in the buff.

ANNCR: What kind of camera is it sir?

PIPPIN: Well, it's an electronic 35mm single lens reflex; it has a 55mm lens. . .a bright viewing system, and a blue silicone metering system: it's called the LES—fully automatic made by GAF.

ANNCR: That's G-A-F.

PIPPIN: Look pal, I can read. It says GAF.

ANNCR: No, no, sir, those are letters, you see, G-A-F.

PIPPIN: Oh well, if they're letters, then why don't they put periods behind them. I mean, what kind of letters are. . .oh, wait a minute. . .here she is. (Click)

ANNCR: There she goes.

PIPPIN: I think that was Lady Godiva.

ANNCR: Are you sure?

PIPPIN: Well, I don't know, there's been so much streaking going on around here.

ANNCR: First time I've seen it on a horse though.

PIPPIN: Yeh, you're right. Here, help me with the tripod.

ANNCR: I'm sorry buddy, wrong union.

MUSIC: (Great moments with G-A-F)

EAR
60-second

WIFE: George, I got to get some sleep.

HUSBAND: Hold still.

WIFE: I can't hear you, George.

HUSBAND: Of course you can't hear me. I just filled up your ear with plaster of paris.

WIFE: Can't hear you, George.

HUSBAND: Your ear's full of plaster of paris.

WIFE: Huh?

HUSBAND: If we want Atlantis Pools to build us a pool shaped like your ear. . .we have to give them the shape of your ear.

WIFE: Huh?

HUSBAND: Your ear's the perfect prototype for a swimming pool. It should be set by now. . .hold still.

HUSBAND: Look at that fabulous detail.

WIFE: Fabulous.

HUSBAND: Yes. See the point bit? Diving board goes there. And the ear lobe? That's where the patio will be. And here, where you had your ear pierced?. . .Guess what goes there?

WIFE: What goes there, George?

HUSBAND: Barbeque pit!

WIFE: Oh, my God!

ANNCR: Atlantis Pools can build almost any shape pool you want. And Atlantis will pay a hard cash penalty if your pool's not finished when promised. Drive out to the Atlantis Display Centre at 9 Springvale Road, Springvale—seven days a week.

HUSBAND: Sorry, love. I took the mould from the wrong ear.

WIFE: Get away from me, George.

HUSBAND: We can't use your left ear. . .we have a right hand back yard.

WIFE: Don't touch me, George.

828
WRITERS Miles Ramsay
Doug Linton
PRODUCERS Miles Ramsay
Evelyn Arthur
PRODUCTION CO. Griffiths, Gibson
AGENCY Goodis, Goldberg, Soren
Canada
CLIENT GAF Canada

829
WRITER Street Remley
Creative Services
DIRECTOR Street Remley
Creative Services
PRODUCER Street Remley
Creative Services
PRODUCTION CO. Pepper Studios
AGENCY Hansen, Rubensohn,
McCann-Erickson
Australia
CLIENT Atlantis Pools

CHIKO ROLLS
90-second

MUSIC UNDER

ANNCR: Back in 1955 when I was a lad with a lusting after young ladies (I was different then), there were a whole lot of really good things they don't seem to have anymore.

You could walk into the Golden Wattle takeaway on a Saturday night and order a hamburger that was made from real steak, and it was about an inch and a half thick and it tasted of. . .hamburger. And you could go down the street to the Billabong Milk Bar and order a chocolate malted that tasted of. . .chocolate. And if ya think you're drinking chocolate milkshakes *now,* maybe you should walk across the road to 1955 and see how they used to taste. And even the Chiko Rolls. You could buy a girl a Chiko Roll in 1955 without her punchin' you in the face (which is another story), because the Chiko Rolls were really good then.

But what's happened. Well, we've all gotten older and sadder, and the hamburgers have got thin and mean, and the chocolate milkshakes taste like someone forgot what chocolate is, and the Chiko Rolls have gone down-hill.

The only ray of hope in this whole sad mess is that the Chiko Roll company has seen the error of its ways and has walked across the road back to 1955 and now it's making Chiko Rolls that taste as good as they did *way* back then.

So tonight if you're feelin' a little peckish, keep your eyes skinned for a shop that sells the 1955 Chiko Roll.

CHORUS: You can walk across the road back to 1955 and get yourself a decent Chiko Roll.

CHIKO ROLLS
30-second

WIZARD WILLIE
60-second

SHE: Hi. Was there a particular record you're looking for?

HE: (Abruptly) Yes.

SHE: Uh. . .good. A single or an LP perhaps?

HE: Yes.

SHE: Sir. . .you're not. . .being very helpful.

HE: Doesn't matter. You won't have it anyway.

SHE: Try me. We have just about everything here at Allan's.

HE: Huh. You won't have the foggiest notion. . . "Wizard Willie and the Unchained Lovepersons." They once cut a disc called. . .

SHE: "Peaches and Scream"?

HE: Lucky guess.

SHE: Wizard Willie's from Bendigo. Blows piano. Threw in with Paul Fred and Rosie after a gig on the Gold Coast. . .April '71. "Peaches and Scream" was their first single. . .followed by. . .

HE: "Passion in the Graveyard".

SHE: Right on! That was the number where. . .

HE: . . .Rosie blew 4/4 percussion using human skulls and a butcher's mallet. You Allan People know where it's *at!*

SHE: Dig. And Fred carved himself a flute out of a thigh bone. . .remember. . .

ANNCR: Allan's Music Stores. When you're ready to explore the world of music—we'll get you goin'.

SONG: Allan's gotcha goin'. . .Allan's Music Store

MOTHER GREEB
60-second

AXE
60-second

830
WRITERS Peter Carey
Terry Durack
PRODUCERS Peter Best
Terry Durack
PRODUCTION CO. Armstrong Audio,
Video Pty.
AGENCY Grey Advertising Pty.
Australia
CLIENT Provincial Traders Pty.

831
WRITER Street Remley
Creative Services
DIRECTOR Street Remley
Creative Services
PRODUCER Street Remley
Creative Services
PRODUCTION CO. Pepper Studios
AGENCY Leo Burnett Pty.
Australia
CLIENT Allans Music Stores

THE SQUARE HEAD
30-second

ANNCR: You are now watching. . .a square-headed shaver. . .shave a square head.

You are now watching. . .the new Philips XTR shaver with the shaped head, shave a shaped head.

The new Philips XTR. The extremely thin shaving head. . .gives you an extremely close shave. The shaped head. . .at the perfect shaving angle gives you an. . .extremely comfortable shave.

The new Philips XTR. Because the human face is a bumpy place.

SUPER: *The new Philips XTR.*
Because the human face
is a bumpy place.

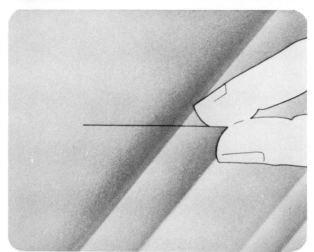

The new Philips XTR.

Because the human face is a bumpy place.

832
ART DIRECTOR Brian Harrod
WRITER Allan Kazmer
DIRECTOR Vladimir Goetzleman
PRODUCER Karen Hayes
PRODUCTION CO. Cinera Productions
AGENCY McCann-Erickson Canada
CLIENT Philips Electronics

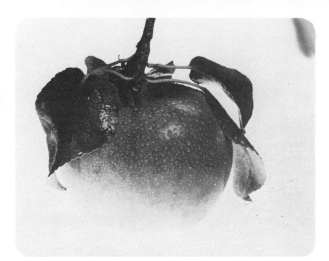

SOME PRODUCTS
30-second

ANNCR: Some products move off the shelf
quickly.

And some don't.
Maybe it's the advertising.

SUPER: *Fresh, creative marketing ideas. Krohn
Advertising.*

833
ART DIRECTOR Peter M. Krohn
WRITER Peter M. Krohn
PHOTOGRAPHER Peter Van der Linden
DIRECTOR Jed Falby
PRODUCTION CO. Falby Blum (Quebec)
AGENCY Krohn Advertising
Canada
CLIENT Krohn Advertising

ADULTS ONLY
30-second

HER: C'mon, try some Pauls Private Bin Banana Passionfruit.

HIM: Er, no thanks.

HER: It's delicious. It's made from real cream and fresh succulent fruit. How about Rum and Raisin?

HIM: I. . .ah. . .I'm driving.

HER: Coffee Walnut? (he shakes head) Rock Melon? Chocolate Mint Julep, y'all? Tropical Mango?

HIM: Do you have. . .er. . .vanilla?

HER: Sure, Private Bin French Vanilla.

HIM: French? Ah, do you think I'm ready for that?

ANNCR: Pauls Private Bin Adults Only Ice Creams.

SUPER: *Adults Only Ice Creams*

834
ART DIRECTOR Dennis Hearfield
WRITER Gary Graf
DIRECTOR Fred Schepisi
PRODUCTION CO. The Film House
AGENCY Young & Rubicam Pty. Australia
CLIENT Q.U.F. Industries

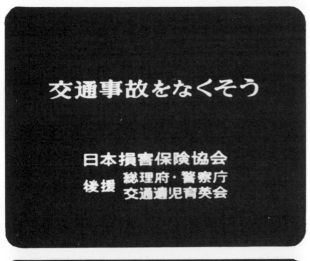

THE ACCIDENT
30-second

ANNCR: This man is unable to look others in the face.

If only it had not been raining that day.

If only he had been insured.

But now it is too late.

That traffic accident cannot be undone.

This figure could be you tomorrow.

835
WRITER Akira Ando
DIRECTOR Masami Kurihara
PRODUCERS Akira Ando
Mamoru Torimoto
PRODUCTION CO. Tokyo Publicity Center Co.
AGENCY Dentsu Advertising Ltd. Japan
CLIENT The Marine and Fire Insurance Assoc.

ROBOT
30-second

MAN: National Dry Batteries Hi-Tops are tough and long lasting. You can run a transistor radio for more than 150 hours on the energy in this tiny storage battery.

For clocks, tape recorders, flashlights, shavers, and toys.

I use Hi-Tops myself. (opens his chest to reveal himself as a mechanical man powered by Panasonic Dry Batteries. He takes one out and keels over with a crash.)

836
WRITERS Kuniharu Yamamoto,
Hideki Tsukinari
DIRECTOR Akira Imamura
PRODUCERS Akio Hirai
Toshiaki Takahashi
PRODUCTION CO. Dentsu Motion Picture Co.
AGENCY Dentsu Advertising
Japan
CLIENT Matsushita Electric
Industrial Co.

FLY AWAY HOME
30-second

CHILDREN: Ladybug, Ladybug, fly away home.
Your house is on fire. Your children are alone.

WOMAN: There's a new species of ladybug that's
going around. It's a Ladybug that makes a lady's
legs and underarms very soft and very smooth to
the touch. It's the Ladybug Shaver by Philips.

ANNCR: Why not give a Ladybug to a lady you like.

The Ladybug Shaver by Philips.

SUPER: *Philips*

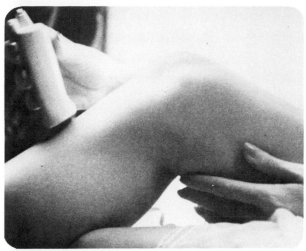

837
ART DIRECTOR Brian Harrod
WRITER Allan Kazmer
DESIGNERS George Pastic
  Andrew Welsh
DIRECTOR George Pastic
PRODUCER Karen Hayes
PRODUCTION CO. Sincinkin
AGENCY McCann-Erickson
  Canada
CLIENT Philips Electronics

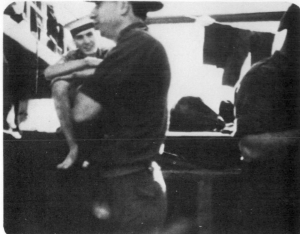

HOMECOMING
30-second

MUSIC UNDER: (Bless 'Em All)

ANNCR: In 1945 and '46 when our diggers were steaming home. . .

there was something so important to 'em, they'd queue up for hours. . .

. . .for their daily ration. . . two pints of Flag Ale.

Toohey's Flag Ale. It's still good to come home to.

SUPER: *Toohey's Flag Ale It's still good to come home to.*

838

ART DIRECTORS   Lou Principato
                Warwick Majcher
WRITER   Gary Graf
DIRECTOR   Ray Lawrence
PRODUCTION CO. Window
AGENCY   Young & Rubicam Pty.
                Australia
CLIENT   Tooheys

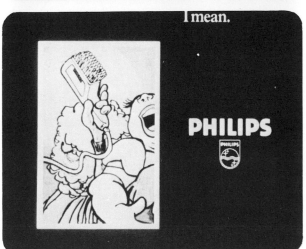

PHILIPS

RAPUNZEL
30-second

ROLLING SUPER:
Rapunzel, Rapunzel

Let down your hair

*I can't. I just
washed it.*

*That's okay, I bought
you a new Philips Hairdryer.*

*Wow! Dry it as you
climb.
Philips dries hair in
a hurry. With powerful
drying. . .and gentle
styling.*

*What a magnificent
machine.*

*Rapunzel, with this new
Philips Hairdryer you can
let your hair down more
often. If you know what
I mean.*

SUPER: Philips

PRINCE: (singing) Rapunzel, me
Rapunzel, see

Damni Capelli
Bella mia

RAPUNZEL: (singing) No, no, no, no, no, no, no.
PRINCE: (singing) No problema, compratto e
Philips Hairdryer.

PRINCE: (singing) Conforza

RAPUNZEL: (singing) Conforza

PRINCE: (singing) Gentille

RAPUNZEL: (singing) Gentille

RAPUNZEL: (singing) Macchina
magnifica

PRINCE: (singing) Rapunzel. . .
capisci.

TOGETHER: (singing) Winkie, winkie,
winkie, winkie
. . .winkie. . .

839
ART DIRECTOR Brian Harrod
WRITER Allan Kazmer
DIRECTOR Dino Kotopoulis
PRODUCER Karen Hayes
PRODUCTION CO. Dino Kotopoulis
AGENCY McCann-Erickson
Canada
CLIENT Philips Electronics

SILVER

840
ART DIRECTOR Wolfgang Haetman
WRITER Ross Jarvis
DIRECTOR Gene Beck
PRODUCER Lorre Jensen
PRODUCTION CO. Rabko Productions
AGENCY Doyle Dane Bernbach
Canada
CLIENT Cadbury Schweppes
Powell

THE TRAIN
30-second

MUSIC UNDER

GIRL: He's still looking at me. . .
I can feel his eyes. . .
What if he speaks to me?
How would I be?
Distant?
Warm?
Or would I fall in love with him?
Silly, I'm only going to talk to him.
Or am I?

MAN: Courant. . .it says what you feel.

Courant. . .a perfume by Helena Rubinstein.

841
WRITER Martha Everds
DIRECTOR Adrian Lyne
PRODUCER Charlotte Rosenblatt
PRODUCTION CO. Jennie and Company
AGENCY Kenyon & Eckhardt
Advertising
New York
CLIENT Helena Rubinstein

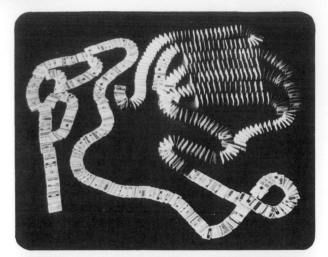

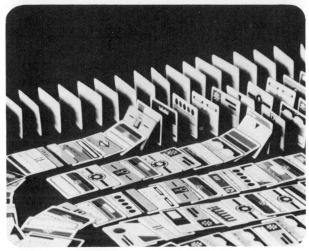

DOMINOES
30-second

ANNCR: There are a lot of credit cards in the line-up these days.

Cards that will get you clothes, but not gas. . .
cards that will get you gas, but not meals. . .
cards that will get you meals, but not furniture. . .
cards that will get you furniture, but not clothes.
And then, there's a card that will get you just about anything.

Master Charge. It's number one. . .because it's used by more people, for more things, than any other card in the world.

SUPER: *No. 1 in the world.*

842
ART DIRECTORS Barry Stringer
Barry Olson
WRITERS Kearney Freeman
Mary-Lynn Durrant
Barry Olson
DESIGNER Barry Smith
DIRECTOR Rick Okada

PRODUCERS Barry Smith
Barry Olson
PRODUCTION CO. Falby-Blum
AGENCY Vickers & Benson
Canada
CLIENT Bank of Montreal

GOLD

BLACK HORSE
30-second

SUPER: *What can Lloyds Bank do for you?*

MUSIC UNDER

ANNCR: What can Lloyds Bank do for you?

WE can give you freedom. Freedom from worry about remembering to pay your regular bills on time. We can advise you on things like insurance and tax. We can even help you save. But, above all, everything we do will help to set you free from so many of the things which make money such a problem.

You get a lot more than money with Lloyds Bank.

At the sign of the Black Horse.

SUPER: *At the Sign of the Black Horse*

843
ART DIRECTOR John Batty
WRITER Peter Hodgson
DIRECTOR Gerry Poulson
PRODUCER Roy Galloway
PRODUCTION CO. GPA
AGENCY McCann-Erickson
England
CLIENT Lloyds Bank

I CAN GET BY WITHOUT. . .
30-second

GIRL: I can get by without make-up. . .
I can get by without a bra. . .
I can get by without my boyfriend.

WOMAN: Is there anything you can't get by without?

GIRL: I can't get by without my Mum.

SUPER: *Every girl needs her Mum.*

ANNCR: Mum spray. An extra dry deodorant, and anti-perspirant all in one. Every girl needs her Mum.

GIRL: I can't really get by without my boyfriend.

844
ART DIRECTOR	Dennis Hearfield
WRITER	Friday Stevens
DIRECTOR	Ray Lawrence
PRODUCER	Ivan Robinson
PRODUCTION CO.	Window
AGENCY	Young & Rubicam Australia
CLIENT	Bristol-Myers

CIRCUS
30-second

ANNCR: Ladies and gentlemen!
Now, now. . . !
Will they be able to make it at one go?
The Bic lighter
And now for the most difficult moment! They are getting into their fantastic positions in the air.
The Bic special challenge
They are approaching
They've done it!
They've done it!

Look at his proud face
Really splendid.
And they did it with a flick of the lighter
This is a Bic-uri (surprise in Japanese)
It's the Bic

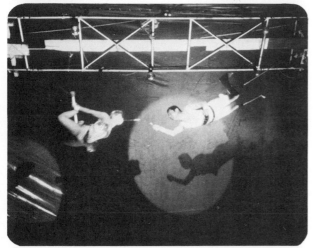

845
ART DIRECTORS Masanobu Yoshii
Minato Ishikawa
WRITER Minoru Kawase
DESIGNERS Masanobu Yoshii
Minato Ishikawa
DIRECTOR K. Kawanaka
PRODUCER Akira Hasegawa
PRODUCTION CO. T.C.J.
AGENCY Young & Rubicam
Japan
CLIENT Bic International

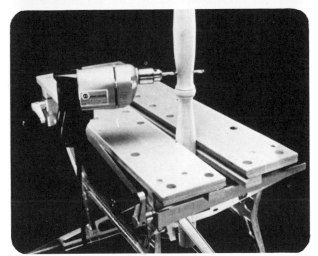

MAGICIAN
30-second

ANNCR: Work-mate is here from Black & Decker.
It holds anything
And it's versatile.
Circles. . .
Triangles. . .
Anything.

Makes your dreams come true.
Makes your work easy.
It's a workroom all of its own.

Work-mate from Black & Decker.
Price:

846
ART DIRECTOR Masanobu Yoshii
WRITER Minoru Kawase
DESIGNER Masanobu Yoshii
DIRECTOR K. Suzuki
PRODUCER Takao Seki
PRODUCTION CO. T.F.C.
AGENCY Young & Rubicam
Japan
CLIENT Nippon Black & Decker

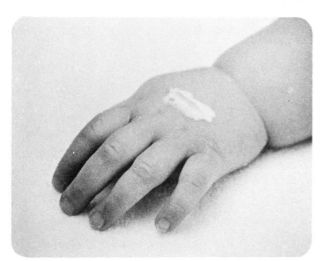

BABY
30-second

ANNCR: Creme 21
is a hand cream,
a shoulder cream,
a back cream,
a bottom cream,
a face cream for the daytime
and one for the night-time.

Creme 21 cares for your skin
and protects your skin.

Creme 21.
The skin for your skin.

Die Haut für die Haut.

847
ART DIRECTOR Jürgen Pilger
WRITER Michael Schirner
DIRECTOR Michael Schirner
PRODUCER Manfred Plapp
PRODUCTION CO. Radio Pictures
AGENCY GGK Düsseldorf
West Germany
CLIENT Henkel-Khasana

TAPESTRY
30-second

1½ seconds silence

MUSIC UNDER: "There's No Place Like Home"

Red thread starts to appear and sew itself into the shape of a tomato.

Green leaves are sewn on. These grow into a border that moves around the screen.

A bottle is sewn into the bottom right of screen. It is Heinz Tomato Ketchup.

The words "There's No Taste Like Heinz" are sewn on.

SONG: There's no taste like Heinz.

848
ART DIRECTOR Derrick Hass
WRITER Stuart Blake
DESIGNER Derrick Hass
ARTIST Shirt Sleeve Studio
DIRECTOR Charlie Jenkins
PRODUCER Nicky West
PRODUCTION CO. Trick Films
AGENCY Doyle Dane Bernbach England
CLIENT H.J. Heinz Co.

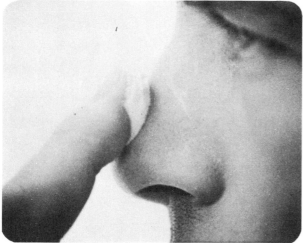

Die Haut für die Haut.

849
ART DIRECTOR Jürgen Pilger
WRITER Michael Schirner
DIRECTOR Michael Schirner
PRODUCER Manfred Plapp
PRODUCTION CO. Radio Pictures
AGENCY GGK Düsseldorf
West Germany
CLIENT Henkel-Khasana

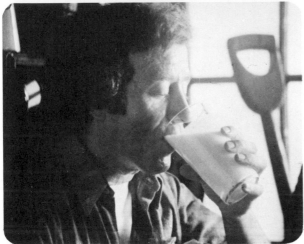

LIFE
45-second

SONG THROUGHOUT
Got my hair
Got my head
Got my brains
Got my ears
Got my eyes
Got my nose
Got my mouth
Got my smile
Got my tongue
Got my chin
Got my neck
Got my hips
Got my heart
Got my soul
Got my back
Got myself
Got my arms
Got my hands
Got my fingers
Got my legs
Got my feet
Got my toes
Got my liver
Got my blood
I've got life
Got my freedom
Yea . . . .
I Got Milk. I Got Life.

SINGER: I've got life.
I've got life.
I've got life.

SUPER: *I got milk*
I got life

850
ART DIRECTOR Roger Manton
WRITER Nigel Gordon
DIRECTOR Robin Tasker
PRODUCERS Andy Rork
Roger Manton
PRODUCTION CO. Illustra Films
AGENCY McCann-Erickson
England
CLIENT Milk Marketing Board

EVERY BUBBLE'S PASSED ITS FIZZICAL.

FIZZICAL
30-second

CHIEF BUBBLE: (Phil Silvers' voice) C'mon, c'mon, move, move, move!!

These aren't just any old bubbles getting into this bottle of Corona. No sir! Are they fizzy!!!

Every one has passed the Corona Fizzical.

SFX: Grunts and groans from the bubbles.

CHIEF BUBBLE: Boy it's really tough back there!

No, no, no! (To bubble who fails to get into the bottle of Corona)

ANNCR: Corona. Every bubble's passed its Fizzical.

CHIEF BUBBLE: That's it boys, let's see you fizz, fizz, fizz!

SUPER: *Every bubble's passed its Fizzical.*

851
ART DIRECTOR Ken Hoggins
WRITER Steve Grounds
DESIGNER Ken Hoggins
ARTIST John Perkins
DIRECTOR John Perkins
PRODUCER Nicky West
PRODUCTION CO. Richard Williams Animation
AGENCY Doyle Dane Bernbach England
CLIENT Corona Soft Drinks

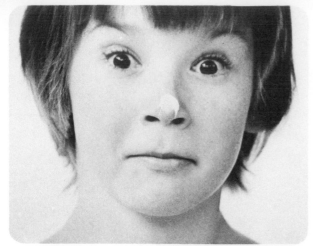

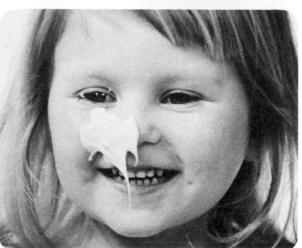

Die Haut für die Haut.

FAMILY
30-second

Creme 21
is the skin
for your skin
for your skin
for your skin
and for your skin.

Creme 21 cares for your skin
and protects your skin.

Creme 21.
The skin for your skin.

852
ART DIRECTOR Jürgen Pilger
WRITER Michael Schirner
DIRECTOR Michael Schirner
PRODUCER Manfred Plapp
PRODUCTION CO. Radio Pictures
AGENCY GGK Düsseldorf
CLIENT Henkel-Khasana

HOUSE OF CARDS
30-second

ANNCR: Do you know how many credit cards there are. . .in the whole world? Hundreds. Now, of all the cards there are to choose from. . .if you could choose only one. . .which one would it be? Well, if you're like most people, you'd probably want the one card that's number one in the world.

Master Charge. It's number one. . .because it's used by more people, for more things, than any other card in the world.

SUPER: *No. 1 in the world*

WALLET
30-second

HOUSE OF CARDS
30-second

853
ART DIRECTORS   Barry Stringer
                Ed Ward
                Barry Olson
WRITERS   Ed Ward
                Barry Olson
                Kearney Freeman
                Mary-Lynn Durrant
DESIGNER   Barry Smith
DIRECTOR   Rick Okada

PRODUCERS   Barry Smith
                Barry Olson
PRODUCTION CO. Falby-Blum
AGENCY   Vickers & Benson
                Canada
CLIENT   Bank of Montreal

BRIDGESTONE SNOW TIRES
10-second

ANNCR: The couple who forgot to put snow tires on their car have to stop to fit them on, on a narrow mountain road. Everyone else has to wait while they do so.

Bridgestone would like to remind us to put on snow tires *before* we need them.

854
ART DIRECTOR Tadaaki Suzuki
WRITER Mitsuru Takahama
DESIGNER Yuji Kataoka
ARTIST Masao Tanaka
PHOTOGRAPHER Tadanori Tajima
DIRECTOR Naoya Honma
PRODUCER Tohoru Konishi
PRODUCTION CO. Tōyō Cinema Co.
AGENCY Hakuhodo
Japan
CLIENT Bridgestone Tire Co.

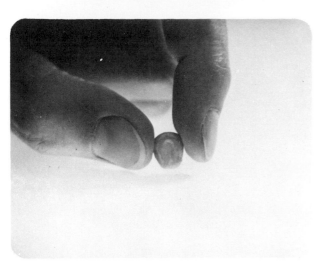

GROWING SEED
45-second

ANNCR: Inside this corn is something extremely valuable. It is called germ.

Inside the germ, which is inside the corn, there are substances essential to human health.

But that's not all: Inside the germ, which is inside the corn, there is the key to life and growth.

After two generations, this one single germ can produce so many of thousands of grandchildren that we can make this: A whole bottle of Mazola corn oil.

Mazola: good health from the germ of the corn.

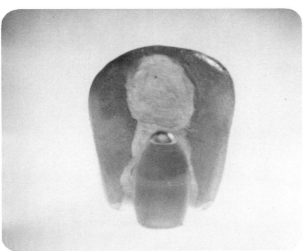

855
ART DIRECTOR Peter Wilke
WRITERS Peter Wilke
Klaus Peter Erxleben
PHOTOGRAPHER Dr. Walter Brandau
DIRECTOR Dr. Walter Brandau
PRODUCER Peter Wilke
PRODUCTION COS. Dr. Walter Brandau TV
Filmgestaltung
AGENCY Troost Campbell-Ewald
West Germany
CLIENT Maizena Markenartikel
GmbH

PLASTICINE
60-second

ANNCR: Corco produces gasoline. . .but that's only the beginning.

Corco has one of the world's most important petrochemical complexes right here in Puerto Rico. The petrochemicals we produce will one day enable our island to make the raw materials to manufacture thousands of things.

We'll be able to make all these products, every step of the way. From crude oil to finished products.

That's why we are expanding our petrochemical facilities. . .every day.

And downstream companies are being set up to further refine Corco petrochemicals. This activity has created over 3,000 jobs already. It will create more than 40,000 when we are done.

All based on Corco. . .the cornerstone of the petrochemical industry of Puerto Rico.

856
ART DIRECTOR Reinaldo Rivera
WRITER Dick Harrison
ARTIST Estudios Rosellon Staff
PHOTOGRAPHER Estudios Rosellon Staff
DIRECTOR César Rosellon

PRODUCER Dick Harrison
PRODUCTION CO. Estudios Rosellon
AGENCY Badillo/Compton Puerto Rico
CLIENT Commonwealth Oil Refining Co.

 SILVER

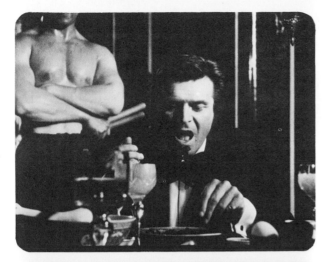

SECRET AGENT
70-second

DR. SING: Well Mr. Jonathan Lester, have you decided to accept my offer?

LESTER: Your offer, Dr. Sing? You're lucky I even accept your hospitality.

DR SING: A common Western weakness. . .your manners are revolting.

LESTER: But only as revolting as your food.

DR. SING: What is eating you Mr. Secret Agent?

LESTER: It's not what's eating me, it's what I'm eating. . .

DR. SING: Not surprising, when you consider you're eating lamb. . . .Rodney Lamb, the man you were sent to replace.

LESTER: (Revolting grimace) Don't pull my leg.

DR. SING: On the contrary, it's you who are pulling at the leg, ha ha. Yen, give this Secret Agent your special nightcap.

(Lester is hit on the head, with Kung Fu elegance)

ANNCR: Sometimes your stomach declares war on your body. Sometimes your head declares war on your body. And sometimes they join forces and attack together.

Whichever way the trouble hits you, speedy Alka Seltzer hits back with double action. Its unique formulation brings immediate relief to upset stomachs and exploding heads.

SUPER: *Alka Seltzer.*
It works for heads.
It works for stomachs.
It works for heads and stomachs.

857
ART DIRECTOR Ian Blake
WRITER Jonathan Harries
DIRECTOR Lynton Stephenson
PRODUCER Jeremy Watt
PRODUCTION CO. James Garrett & Partners
AGENCY Grey-Phillips, Bunton, Mundel & Blake South Africa
CLIENT Miles Laboratories

STRANGE LEGEND
60-second

SUPER: *The legend of chipmonks*

ANNCR: Long before they even had black-and-white TV, all the monks in the monasteries made something. . .like jam, or bread, or bagels, or wine. It seems they all had some kind of schtick . . .except one. All they had was potatoes. . . which ain't exactly earth shattering.

Now one day, one of the bright young monks was fooling around with some potatoes when he suddenly discovered something terrific to eat. So he named them "chips" after his dog. He tried them on a few of his pals; they were a big hit. . .

And in no time they were cranking them out.

Pretty soon, the place was in the chips.

Now naturally, it's a very old secret recipe only recently made available to the general public. . . that's you.

You get two whole stacks in every package and somehow or other every potato chip is perfectly formed. . .which is weird.

Today you can ask for them just the way they did centuries ago. . .

ABBOT: "Gimme a chip, monk."

ANNCR: Ye olde Chipmonks, from Christie's.

858
ART DIRECTORS Brian Harrod
Mel McKelvie
WRITER Alan Marr
DIRECTOR Paul Herriott
PRODUCER Karen Hayes
PRODUCTION CO. Paul Herriott Productions
AGENCY McCann-Erickson
Canada
CLIENT Christie, Brown

GOLD

SPOON
60-second

ANNCR: Oil. It's hard to imagine that there could be a shortage in Canada. Right now there's no shortage of fuel for our cars or for heating our homes.

And there's no shortage of any of the things that oil helps provide. There's no shortage of oil to make medicine or adhesives or synthetic fibres. Or oil to make film or plastics. *But there could be an oil shortage in 10 years, if we don't find new reserves.*

We've had a silver spoon in our mouths up to now, here in this country, but our present oil supplies can't last forever.

That's why Gulf Canada reinvested almost 80% of its 1974 earnings in Canada.

So Gulf is spending millions of dollars again this year looking for new oil.

Gulf—*working against time to find new energy.*

SUPER: *Gulf. Working against time to find new energy.*

859
ART DIRECTOR   Stewart Hood
WRITERS   Judy Samson
Stewart Hood
CAMERAMAN   Fritz Speiss
DIRECTOR   Fritz Speiss
PRODUCER   Chris Sanderson
PRODUCTION CO.   T.D.F. Productions
AGENCY   Vickers & Benson
Canada
CLIENT   Gulf Oil Canada

WARMBATH'S ROAD
90-second

FARMER: I found him on the Warmbath's road. A mongrel. Suffering from heat exhaustion, malnutrition, bleeding feet. I think if I'd had my shotgun with me, I'd have put him out of his misery.

As a farmer, I've seen some pretty grim things happen to animals. But Patchy was one of the saddest things I ever saw. I took him home and phoned the vet. "Put him down," the vet said. "I don't want to," I told him. The vet said, "Well, try giving him Epol Gravied Chunks. But if he doesn't eat, you'd better put him down."

Patchy was just strong enough to eat. But man, he didn't eat much. Even my fowls have a better appetite.

After a few weeks, though, he started eating and acting more like a dog. And I knew he was getting better when he jumped over the kitchen door and started chasing the chickens around the yard.

Man, there's nothing like the right food and a bit of affection to give you a dog you can depend on. Today Patchy goes with me everywhere. He's a good watchdog, but affectionate. Always with one eye open, looking at me even when he's resting. I get a funny feeling he's trying to say dankie.

ANNCR: Epol Gravied Chunks with Vitagen is a major scientific breakthrough in the field of animal nutrition.

SUPER: *All a dog needs*
is love and Epol.

860

ART DIRECTOR	Ian Blake
WRITER	Evert Celliers
PHOTOGRAPHER	David Goldblatt
DIRECTOR	Lynton Stephenson
PRODUCER	Jeremy Watt
PRODUCTION CO.	James Garrett & Partners
AGENCY	Grey, Phillips, Bunton, Mundel & Blake South Africa
CLIENT	The Premier Milling Group

MOSQUITO
60-second

ANNCR: Pana-Arm, like your arm.

SYNOPSIS: Stressing the ease of handling through personification of the lamp. With flexible movements, the lamp chases an annoying mosquito.

In the last scene an ambulance rushes to the fallen mosquito.

Pana-Arm like Your-Arm.
National Pana-Arm

861
WRITERS	Nobukazu Enami
	Hitoshi Hayashi
ARTISTS	Hirotsugu Horii
	Hitoshi Hayashi
DIRECTOR	Tsutomu Iwamoto
PRODUCERS	Minoru Chikuma
	Yoshinori Nagata
PRODUCTION CO.	Creative Ad Production
AGENCY	Dentsu Advertising
	Japan
CLIENT	Matsushita Electric
	Industrial Co.

THE CEMENT BALLOON
60-second

ANNCR: Cement is poured into a rubber balloon. The ultra-rapid hardener Denka QT has been added to this cement.

In a twinkling the cement hardens. (The balloon bursts)

Denka QT—the fast-working cement hardener. Denka—the chemical company always creating new materials.

863
WRITER Sakuro Kimura
PHOTOGRAPHER Rentaro Kawakami
DIRECTOR Sakuro Kimura
PRODUCERS Sakuro Kimura
Rentaro Kawakami
PRODUCTION CO. Rensei Creative Film
Production
AGENCY Dentsu Advertising Ltd.
Japan
CLIENT Denki Kagaku Kogyo
Kabushiki Kaisha

GIRL
45-second

She does all the company's payroll accounting.
She handles all the orders.
She figures all the prices and discounts.
She does all the billing.
She keeps exact track of stock.
She does all the ordering.
She does the entire bookkeeping.
She gets up all the statistics and figure breakdowns for the boss.
She has the inventory count in less than no time.

And because the System/32—the new small computer from IBM—helps her do her work, she still has time to take a coffee break every now and then.

IBM. For everyone who figures and writes.

864
ART DIRECTOR	Helmut Rottke
WRITER	Michael Schirner
DIRECTOR	Michael Schirner
PRODUCER	Manfred Plapp
PRODUCTION CO.	Falby, Blum International
AGENCY	GGK Dusseldorf West Germany
CLIENT	IBM Deutschland

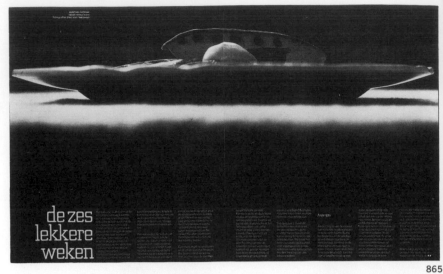

865

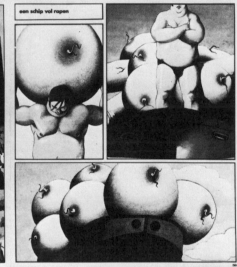

866

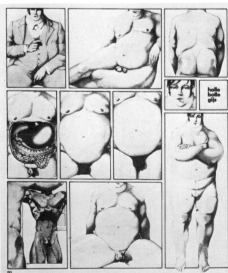

865
ART DIRECTOR Dick de Moei
DESIGNER Hans von Blommestein
PHOTOGRAPHER Pliet van Leeuwen
WRITER Wina Born
PUBLISHER Illustrated Press
AGENCY Avenue Magazine
Holland

866
ART DIRECTOR Dick de Moei
DESIGNER Martijn van der Jagt
ARTIST Martijn van der Jagt
PUBLISHER Illustrated Press
AGENCY Avenue Magazine
Holland

Karikaturen mit bösem Biß waren jahrelang das Markenzeichen des Elsässers Tomi Ungerer. Jetzt hat er einen neuen Ton gefunden. In seinem »Großen Liederbuch« erinnert er sich seiner Jugend und bebildert mit sanfter Ironie die schönsten deutschen Volksweisen. Der Prachtband für Kinder und Erwachsene ist ein Bestseller dieses Herbstes

Ein Traum von fernen Kindertagen

867

867

ART DIRECTOR Wolfgang Behnken
DESIGNERS Otmar Goller
Wolfgang Behnken
ARTIST Tomi Ungerer
WRITER Peter Meyer
PUBLISHER Stern Magazine
AGENCY Stern Magazine
West Germany

ISLAND

»Eisland« nannten die Wikinger die öde Insel im Nordatlantik. Die ersten Siedler flohen zurück nach Norwegen, weil die Fjorde noch im Sommer voller Eisberge waren. Den Christen des Mittelalters galt das feuerspeiende Vulkan-Eiland als »Maul zur Hölle«. Heute kommen immer mehr Touristen nach Island, allen voran die Deutschen – auf der Suche nach einer hellen Welt

E in Schiffswrack an der schwarzen Lava-Küste Südislands – Winterstürme in Orkanstärke haben den Frachter entzweigeschlagen und die Trümmer auseinandergetrieben. Die Südküste mit ihren sanften Wiesen ist schon Hunderten von Schiffen zum Verhängnis geworden. In den von Horizont zu Horizont reichenden flachen Sand- und Geröllstränden gibt es keine schützende Bucht, keinen natürlichen Hafen. Hier konnten nur die Wikinger und die norwegischen Frühsiedler mit ihren kleineren Drachenbooten einigermaßen gefahrlos landen.

868

868
ART DIRECTOR Rolf Gillhausen
DESIGNER Franz Braun
PHOTOGRAPHER Hans Feurer
WRITER Hannes-Peter Lehmann
PUBLISHER Stern Magazine
AGENCY Stern Magazine
West Germany

SILVER

Gegen 1850 saß dieses Mädchen einem Photographen Modell. Anschließend wurde die Aufnahme kunstvoll koloriert.

869

ART DIRECTOR Rolf Gillhausen
DESIGNER Max Lengwenus
PHOTOGRAPHER Sammlung Bokelberg
WRITER Axel Hecht
PUBLISHER Stern Magazine
AGENCY Stern Magazine
West Germany

SILVER

CONSUMER PUBLICATION (COLOR)

**Sind die
Frösche noch
zu retten?**

870

ART DIRECTOR Wolfgang Behnken
DESIGNER Max Lengwenus
WRITER Wolfgang Schraps
PUBLISHER Stern Magazine
AGENCY Stern Magazine
West Germany

871

871
ART DIRECTORS Martin Pollard
              Garry Emery
DESIGNER   Garry Emery
ARTIST   Garry Emery
PHOTOGRAPHER Martin Pollard
WRITER   K.M. Campbell
AGENCY   K.M. Campbell Pty.
              Australia
CLIENT   Associated Pulp and
              Paper Mills

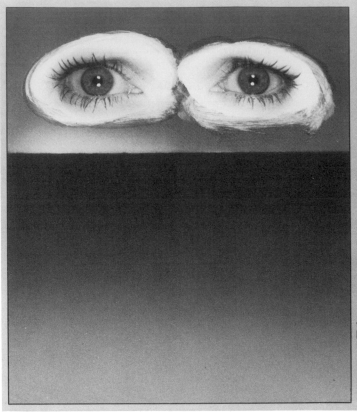

872

THE FOLLOWING STATEMENTS CONCERNING
CLINICAL EXPERIENCE WITH TRANXENE ARE AUTHORS
SUMMARIES OF THEIR PUBLISHED REPORTS

Magnus R V (1973) Once-a-day Potassium
Clorazepate in Anxiety. Brit. J. Clin. Pract. 1973, 27, 449.
Summary In two double-blind crossover studies the
effectiveness of a new anxiolytic agent, potassium
clorazepate, already shown to be effective when given
as a divided daily dose, was assessed when taken as
a once-a-day dose of 15 mg. In 30 anxious patients
clorazepate 15 mg was compared with diazepam 10 mg
as a single equimolar dose and in 29 patients with
diazepam 5 mg tds. In both trials clorazepate was as
effective as either diazepam dose, assessed by
improvement in mean scores for global assessment
of anxiety and target symptom evaluation. Significantly
more patients reported side-effects, especially
sleepiness/drowsiness, lassitude and loss of libido,
with both diazepam doses than with either clorazepate
or placebo. The administration of potassium
clorazepate at a dose of 15 mg once a day, while
reducing the total daily dose previously used,
has retained the clinical effectiveness and has further
decreased the incidence of side-effects.
Ricca J J (1972) Clorazepate Dipotassium in Anxiety:
A Clinical Trial with Diazepam and Placebo Controls.
J. Clin. Pharmacol. 1972, 286.
Summary Clorazepate dipotassium (4306CB,
Tranxene), a new member of the benzodiazepine series,
was administered to 17 patients with anxiety
neurosis in a double-blind trial. Similar groups received
a reference drug, diazepam (17 patients), and placebo
(16 patients) to serve as controls. Clorazepate
dipotassium was given at daily doses of 22.5 to 45 mg
and diazepam at daily doses of 15 to 30 mg.
The duration of treatment was 28 days. Among the
16 patients who received clorazepate, 14 had a
clinically satisfactory overall therapeutic response
(excellent or good). This compares with 12 of 17
patients on diazepam and 6 of 14 patients on placebo.
The difference between the response to clorazepate
dipotassium and the response to diazepam, while
favouring the former slightly, was without statistical
significance. On the other hand, the difference between
clorazepate dipotassium and placebo was statistically
significant ($p < 0.003$). Side effects were reported
by five patients on clorazepate dipotassium, three on
diazepam and five on placebo. There was no evidence

of toxicity clearly attributable to any of the test
preparations.
Kasich A M (1973) Chlorazepate Dipotassium
in the Treatment of Anxiety Associated with Chronic
Gastrointestinal Disease. Curr. Ther. Res. 1973, 15, 83.
Summary Clorazepate dipotassium (Tranxene®)
was administered to 43 patients with moderate anxiety
associated with chronic gastrointestinal disease.
Comparable groups on diazepam (39 patients) and
on placebo (43 patients) served as controls in this
double-blind study. Matching capsules of clorazepate
dipotassium (7.5 mg), diazepam (5.0 mg) and placebo
were administered orally at a daily dose of 3 or 4
capsules for 28 days.
On the basis of the overall (global) therapeutic
response, reduction of the average total Hamilton
Anxiety Rating Scale score, and the average reduction
of the Kellner-Sheffield Symptom Rating Test score,
clorazepate dipotassium was shown to be superior
to placebo to a statistically significant degree. While
the percentage of patients showing a clinically
satisfactory (excellent or good) response to clorazepate
dipotassium (85%) was greater than the percentage
showing such a response to diazepam (72%), the
difference was not statistically significant. Scale
reductions, on the other hand, were slightly greater
on clorazepate dipotassium, were essentially identical
on the two active test preparations.
The percentage of patients reporting side effects
on clorazepate dipotassium (37%) was comparable with
the percentage reporting side effects to the placebo
(33%), but significantly ($p < 0.05$) lower than that
on diazepam (77%). As judged by the necessity to
reduce the dose or discontinue treatment, the severity
of the side effects reported was similar on all three
test preparations. There was no evidence of drug-induced
toxicity revealed by physical, ophthalmoscopic or
laboratory examinations done before and after treatment.
On the basis of these data it is concluded that
clorazepate dipotassium is therapeutically effective
and safe for use in the management of manifest anxiety
associated with chronic gastrointestinal disease.
Wheatley D (1975) A Single-dose Anti-anxiety Drug.
A Report from the General Practitioner Research Group.
The Practitioner, 1975, 215, 98.

872
ART DIRECTOR   Garry Emery
DESIGNER   Garry Emery
ARTIST   Ulrich Lehmann
PHOTOGRAPHER   Martin Pollard
WRITER   Tony Geeves
AGENCY   Interact Communications
Australia
CLIENT   Glaxo

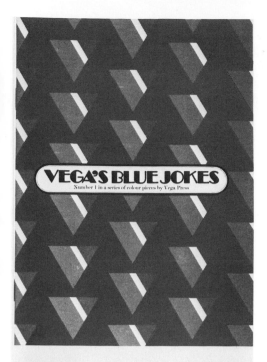

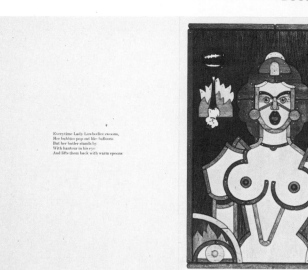

Everytime Lady Lewhotice swoons,
Her bubbies pop out like balloons
But her butler stands by
With hauteur in his eye
And lifts them back with warm spoons

A bather whose clothing was strewed
By breezes that left her quite nude
Saw a man come along,
And, unless I am wrong,
You expected this line to be lewd

Oh Sir Terence, do not touch me
Oh Sir Terence, do not touch
Oh Sir Terence, do not
Oh Sir Terence, do
Oh Sir Terence,
Oh Sir
Oh

873

873
ART DIRECTOR Cato Hibberd Hawksby
              Design
DESIGNER   Cato Hibberd Hawksby
              Design
ARTISTS   Alex Stitt
              Ray Condon
              Ian Dalton
              Cato Hibberd
WRITER   David Webster
AGENCY   Cato Hibberd Hawksby
              Australia
CLIENT   Vega Press

874

874
ART DIRECTOR Henry Steiner
DESIGNER Henry Steiner
PHOTOGRAPHERS Various
EDITOR Lucy Leeming
AGENCY Graphic Communications
Hong Kong
CLIENT The Hong Kong &
Shanghai Banking Corp.

875

876

878

875		876		878	
ART DIRECTOR	Henry Steiner	ART DIRECTOR	Chuck Carlberg	ART DIRECTOR	Naoyuki Satoh
DESIGNER	Henry Steiner	DESIGNER	Chuck Carlberg	DESIGNERS	Yoshiko Kitagawa
ARTIST	Hon Bing Wah	ARTISTS	Larry Keith		Naoyuki Satoh
AGENCY	Graphic Communication		Chuck Carlberg	ARTIST	Yoshiko Kitagawa
	Hong Kong	WRITER	Jim Killinger	AGENCY	Package Boutique
CLIENT	Jardine Fleming & Co.	AGENCY	Smith, Smith, Baldwin &		Jack and Betty
			Carlberg		Japan
			Texas	CLIENT	Package Boutique
		CLIENT	Gerald D. Hines Interests		Jack and Betty

880

881

	880		881
ART DIRECTOR	Yoshiko Kitagawa	**ART DIRECTOR**	Cato Hibberd Hawksby Design
DESIGNER	Yoshiko Kitagawa		
ARTIST	Yoshiko Kitagawa	**DESIGNER**	Cato Hibberd Hawksby Design
AGENCY	Package Boutique Jack and Betty Japan	**ARTIST**	Cato Hibberd Hawksby Design
CLIENT	Package Boutique Jack and Betty	**AGENCY**	Cato Hibberd Hawksby Design Australia
		CLIENT	Philip Morris

882

883

	882		883
DESIGNER	Landor Associates	ART DIRECTOR	Yoshiko Kitagawa
AGENCY	Landor Associates	DESIGNER	Yoshiko Kitagawa
	California	ARTIST	Yoshiko Kitagawa
CLIENT	Industria Italiana Petroli	AGENCY	Package Boutique
			Jack and Betty
			Japan
		CLIENT	Package Boutique
			Jack and Betty

884

885

	884		885
ART DIRECTOR	Annegret Beier	**ART DIRECTOR**	John McConnell
DESIGNER	Annegret Beier	**DESIGNER**	Howard Brown
PHOTOGRAPHER	Sarah Moon	**AGENCY**	Pentagram
AGENCY	D. Communications		England
	France	**CLIENT**	Face Photosetting
CLIENT	Cacharel		

Mille neuf cent soixante seize

886

887

	886		887
ART DIRECTOR	Annegret Beier	**ART DIRECTOR**	Michael Pacey
DESIGNER	Annegret Beier	**DESIGNER**	Michael Pacey
PHOTOGRAPHER	Sarah Moon	**ARTIST**	Michael Pacey
AGENCY	D. Communications France	**AGENCY**	Agency Press Canada
CLIENT	Cacharel	**CLIENT**	Ammo Power Tool Rentals

Eis bedeckt im Winter ein
afghanisches Naturwunder:
in 3000 Meter Höhe nord-
westlich der Hauptstadt Kabul
ist durch stete Ablagerung
von Mineralien ein Damm ent-
standen, der das Wasser
eines Bergstromes zu einem
See gestaut hat. Die Afghanen
nennen die natürliche
Staumauer Band-i-Amir —
Damm des Heiligen

**DER BERGSTROM,
DER SICH SELBER STAUTE**

**FLIRT AM
HINDUKUSCH**

Frauen wagen sich nur
tiefverschleiert auf die Straße.
Wichtigstes Zahlungsmittel sind vielerorts
noch Schafe, Ziegen und Kamele. 17 Millionen
Afghanen leben am Hindukusch, dem öden
Hochland Zentralasiens, wie im Mittelalter. Seit vor
zwei Jahren der König gestürzt und Afghanistan
Republik wurde, wird das ärmste Land der Welt —
es ist mehr als doppelt so groß wie die
Bundesrepublik und hat soviel Einwohner wie
Nordrhein-Westfalen — von seinen
mächtigen Nachbarn Iran und
Sowjetunion umworben

Alle Fotos: Roland und Sabrina Michaud

888

888
ART DIRECTOR Rolf Gillhausen
DESIGNERS Otmar Goller
Günther Meyer
PHOTOGRAPHERS Roland Michaud
Sabrina Michaud
WRITER Karl-Robert Pfeffer
AGENCY Stern Magazine
West Germany

>>Ook voor de ouderdom, grijs als een avond die overgaat in de nacht, hield hij de hele make-up zeer ingetogen. Het haar is glad en eenvoudig. De schaduwen zijn grijs en antraciet. De lippen enigszins bruin. De vingers van de ouderdom tooide hij met veel diamanten, saffieren en edelstenen. Als make-up nam hij weer Rire de Lune en Poudre Translucine. Als lipstick Brun Caché. En voor op en om de ogen oogschaduw Gel Gris Vosves en oogschaduw Poudre Beasie & Rouges. Verder zware mascara en potlood ••

889
ART DIRECTOR Dick de Moei
DESIGNER Hans van Blommestein
PHOTOGRAPHER Serge Lutens
AGENCY Avenue Magazine
Holland

FALTEN FÜR DIE BRAUT

Der Modemacher Kenzo Takada hält nichts von Abendkleidern, denn er meint, sie seien überflüssig. Wenn er für seine Jap-Modelle dennoch mal ein Gewand entwirft, das aussieht wie eine gro-Be Abendrobe — dann ist es als Brautkleid gedacht. Dieses Hochzeits-kleid aus zart-rosa Seidenstoff ist zweiteilig, ganz und gar in kleine Falten gelegt und mit einer Riesen-kapuze ausgestat-tet. Der Unterrock ist aus schwerem, goldfarbenem Sa-tin gearbeitet, die Strümpfe passen in der Farbe dazu

stern 111

890

891

	890		891
ART DIRECTOR	Rolf Gillhausen	ART DIRECTOR	Phil Snyder
DESIGNER	Detlef Conrad	WRITER	Rita Patterson
PHOTOGRAPHER	Hans Feurer	DESIGNER	Phil Snyder
WRITER	Barbara Larcher	ARTIST	Richard Hess
AGENCY	Stern Magazine	AGENCY	J. Walter Thompson
	West Germany		New York
		CLIENT	Pan American World
			Airways

892

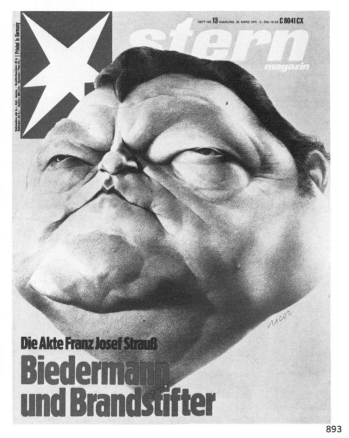

893

	892		893
ART DIRECTOR	Zanders Advertising Dept.	**ART DIRECTOR**	Wolfgang Behnken
PHOTOGRAPHER	Albrecht Ade	**ARTIST**	Patrice Ricor
AGENCY	Zanders Advertising Departement West Germany	**WRITER**	Peter Koch
		AGENCY	Stern Magazine West Germany
CLIENT	Zanders Feinpapiere GmbH		

THE HALL OF FAME

1972
M. F. Agha
Lester Beall
Alexey Brodovitch
A. M. Cassandre
René Clarke
Robert Gage
William Golden
Paul Rand
1973
Charles Coiner
Paul Smith
Jack Tinker
1974
Will Burtin
Leo Lionni
1975
Gordon Aymar
Herbert Bayer
Heyworth Campbell
Alexander Liberman
L. Moholy-Nagy
Cipe Pineles
1976
E. McKnight Kauffer
Herbert Matter

HOW THE HALL OF FAME BEGAN

Nineteen seventy-one was a year of change for The Art Directors Club. That year, the Club's new leadership felt that the ADC should be strengthened with more meaningful and far-reaching programs.

They believed that young and brash as it is, our profession has matured sufficiently to recognize the giants, the innovators, the bold craftsmen of the past. They sought to honor them not only because they had everything to do with making graphic communication a respectable craft but because they were recognized as powerful allies of business, publishing, broadcasting, education, and government.

Moreover, it had been demonstrated that this craft in the hands of a master could be elevated, at times, to an art form.

The Art Directors Hall of Fame began with the election of its first eight members. Basic criteria for selection to the Hall is that a candidate's efforts throughout an entire career will have made a lasting contribution to the field of art direction and graphic design.

Each year, the nominating committee elected by the Club's membership has added more names to that first group and in 1976, with the addition of E. McKnight Kauffer and Herbert Matter, The Art Directors Club Hall of Fame has come of age—it has reached 21.

Cipe Pineles
Chairman, 1976 Hall of Fame

1976 HALL OF FAME NOMINATING COMMITTEE

Bob Bach
William Brockmeier
Bill Buckley
Aaron Burns
Seymour Chwast
Dave Davidian
Lou Dorfsman
Gene Federico
Carl Fischer
Robert Gage
George Giusti
Bob Greenwell
Art Hawkins
George Krikorian
Helmut Krone
Leo Lionni
Bert Littmann
George Lois
Herb Lubalin
Onofrio Paccione
Cipe Pineles
Paul Rand
Eileen Hedy Schultz
Bill Taubin
Bradbury Thompson

E. McKNIGHT KAUFFER

In 1915, E. McKnight Kauffer, an impeccable, young American illustrator just arrived in London, was commissioned for his first poster for the city's Underground Railways, which was starting an adventurous corporate campaign treating stations like shops and advertising the delights found en route with the work of fine artists and painters and 'new' typography.

Kauffer's revolutionary work for the Underground, a client he retained for some years along with many prestigious others, precipitated a brilliant London career—one which comprised the largest portion of his life before his return to the U.S. in 1941.

He was born in Great Falls, Montana, and studied painting in Chicago (he was greatly influenced by the European art seen in the Armory Show there); he studied in Munich and Paris. Kauffer had style. He had a shock of red-brown hair, a tall frame, slightly stooped shoulders, and a hawk-like nose. A man of parts, he made an indelible impression on all who came in contact with him as he combined creative ability with an elegant demeanor. In London, Sir Franciscis Meynell of Nonesuch Press, who early became a patron and life-long friend, described him as "exquisite in face and figure and manners."

E. McKnight Kauffer can rightfully claim membership in the Hall of Fame for perhaps one overall contribution which affects a great body of our work today and one specific milieu. First the overview: he was a pioneer. In *Print* Magazine's tribute to Kauffer as 'one of the great graphic designers of the 20th century', we are reminded that he was an artist in the "world of commerce" before there was a graphic profession. He would prove that "complete creative fulfillment could be achieved without personal compromise by working with industry," wrote Keith Murgatroyd in *Print*. His special contribution was in posters where, in paintings and design, he reduced complex material to forceful, economical, expressive modern statements, his only rival the great Cassandre who was innovating at the same time in France.

As a young man still in America, he had been employed in a San Francisco bookstore where he did a lot of reading and, and as fortuitous chance would have it, a customer became a sponsor and sent him to art school. While at school odd jobs included, among others, washing dishes; he later painted scenery with a traveling theater company. He was twenty-four when he arrived in London following his painting studies. It was the outbreak of World War I.

Kauffer had had hard times as a youth but his career and influence began to blossom. One of the few extant examples of the early work of Kauffer is a poster for the Labour Party's *Daily Herald* (he disavowed ownership of the typography). Of triangles and parallelograms, in three colors, it is considered the first Cubist poster. A variety of posters, many experimental, emerged to delight the public during a decade for such clients as Derry and Toms, a store in Kensington. In 1928, he was commissioned for Burton's "Anatomy of Melancholy," his first book for Sir Meynell's quality Nonesuch Press. During the years of the '20s as a freelancer he had also put his hand to everything from booklets, ads, timetables, wine lists, Christmas cards, even scenery for ballet. In 1929, he was asked to join Crawfords, the great London agency, and worked with Ashley Havinden as his art director.

After leaving Crawfords in 1931 he was commissioned by Shell-Mex for a lorry bill. Shell-Mex and BP Limited consolidated and Jack Beddington, later Ministry of the Interior, became another valued friend. And perhaps Kauffer's most famous works are for the London Underground, Shell-Mex, and BP, Ltd.

McKnight Kauffer was made an honorary Fellow and sat on the Council of the Society of Industrial Arts in London. He became a member of the faculty of the newly-formed Royal Designers for Industry (1936), and his citation read: "for eminent services to commercial art".

He was part of the group of artists in the early part of our century steadfastly committed to new and experimental design principles. Many feel, more than any other American artist, he understood the avant garde painting of the time. In the 1930s, considered by many the golden era of the poster, Londoners in the 'tubes' would recognize Kauffer's posters. One of the aspects of his extraordinary oeuvre was his interpretation of machine forms but his was an organic style, not easy to define as he changed his approach continually. And at the heart of the work was a personal integrity which added immeasurably to the teamwork between artist and client.

He returned to the U.S. and never really received the recognition in his own country he had found earlier in England. He did, however, work for many American companies. He died in New York City in 1954.

In 1936, the Museum of Modern Art had given a one-man exhibition to this great and fascinating American talent. A tribute to Kauffer after his death was mounted in a commemorative show by the Royal Society of Arts by the British design profession. T. S. Eliot opened the exhibition which was at the Victoria and Albert Museum, where so much of Kauffer's work really belongs.

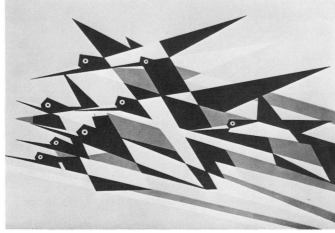

Untitled, Lithograph 1919

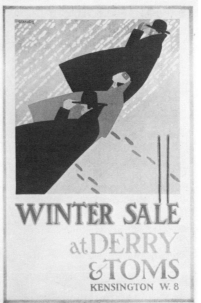

Poster for Derry & Toms 1919

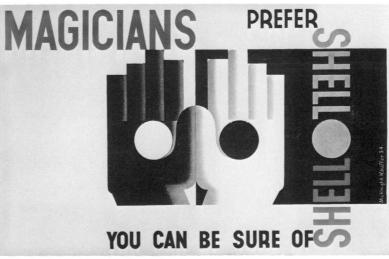

Poster for the Shell Oil Company 1934

Poster for the London Underground 1930

Poster for the London Underground 1922

HERBERT MATTER

Herbert Matter taught himself how to shoot pictures with a camera left in the Paris apartment where he was staying while a young painting student. We can be grateful because Matter, a life-long experimenter, probably would not have fared as well if he had adhered to a single school or approach. Instead, he went his own way and we're the better for it.

He has helped replenish our vision of the world with his own and images often exist only because of Matter's camera. With great pictorial imagination, he has added a new synthesis in editorial, ads, fashion, and especially in photographs and films on the art of artists, on the aesthetic experience itself. As a teacher and in graphic design for clients, he has seldom given less than his whole for it seems impossible for him to create anything casual. Rich in range and quality, his work is completely original.

Swiss born, he studied painting at the L'Ecole des Beaux Arts, Geneva, then in Paris, where he came under the guidance of Fernand Leger. Influenced by the internationalization of art fermenting in the city in the '20s as well as the Bauhaus, he was absorbed by all the forms of graphic expression. He worked with A.M. Cassandre on posters, with Le Corbusier on architecture and displays, and the Studio Deberny Peignot hired the talented youth as photographer-typographer-layout man.

He owes his career, in part, to a lady with long legs—Marlene Dietrich. His Paris stay ended one night after attending a Dietrich film at an art theater. It was law that foreign students renew their visas which Matter had neglected to do. When the theater was raided by authorities and Matter was found without his, he was put on a train for home.

Now in Zurich, his posters for the Swiss National Tourist office, were immediately to bring him recognition outside his own country. He pioneered photomontage techniques, a specialty. Before color photography, this darkroom perfectionist could achieve a freshness and harmony in his colors and photographic surfaces by dyeing various elements photochemically.

He came to America in 1936, and as a photographer worked for *Harper's Bazaar, Vogue,* most of the magazines, and New York ad agencies. He designed for the Swiss and Corning Glass Pavillions at the '39 World's Fair. His photography was soon the subject of a one-man show at the Pierre Matisse Gallery, and part of exhibits at the Art Institute of Chicago and Art Museum in Los Angeles.

He took on two long-term associations in 1946. As Design and Advertising Consultant for Knoll Associates, his agile and structured photos and sales promotion designs—whether of Barcelona chairs or new silverware—were avant garde as the furnishings. As staff photographer for Condé Nast Publications, he sealed his reputation as a master of motion. He would find the pattern of form, to make a new statement—experimenting with light as it moved to reveal a face, a jewel. In fashion and all his work, he used the same tools, darkroom, compass, drafting board, paste pot, scissors, type, picture files.

Design clients have included the New Haven and Boston & Maine Railroads for corporate programs, symbols, styling of engines, equipment, and the Cummins Engine Corporation. A Matter graphic mural adorns a floor in New York's Seagram's building.

This Hall of Famer has exhibited enormous gifts for intepreting art works. He has handled displays for the Museum of Modern Art, Solomon R. Guggenheim Museum, and Houston Museum of Fine Arts. A sustained effort of much of his life has been exploring the mysteries of the creative process.

Soon to be a book are photos of the sculptures of his friend, Alberto Giacometti. Wrote Louis Finkelstein in his introduction to his show at the American Institute of Graphic Arts: "Matter is an artist who can cross the gap which imprisons each of us in our limited awareness to make the essence of another personality real. He uses the medium not to record facts but understanding."

Earlier, Matter's innovating color film on Alexander Calder and his mobiles revealed the same imaginative shooting and meticulous editing, and his additional films are an educational series on R. Buckminister Fuller, a film on Segovia, and animation for Universal's movie "Guns of August."

Matter has lectured at the New York Studio School since 1964. He has been a Professor of Photography and Graphic Design at Yale University since 1952 when Josef Albers asked him to help create the department which today lists distinguished graduates Ivan Chermayeff, Bruce Davidson, Tom Geismar, Arnold Saks.

Herbert Matter says he has remained a student, and with his attitude combining passion, tact, and discipline has been able to enrich our professional life throughout his own.

Poster for Alberto Giacometti exhibition, Guggenheim. 1974

Knoll promotion, 1955

Harper's Bazaar Cover

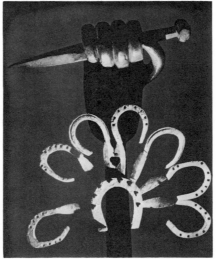

Symbol of salesmanship, Oxford Paper program

THE ADC, INC.

THE PRESIDENT'S MESSAGE JUNE 1976

Eileen Hedy Schultz

Looking ahead to a second term in the office of Presidency of The Art Directors Club is both inspiring and challenging: inspiring in the work that must be accomplished if our Industry is to continue its positive growth, and challenging in just how much one can accomplish in a short span of time with so much more to be done.

With the continued determination, perseverance, and downright hard work of our Board of Directors and dedicated Club members, along with the cooperative efforts of allied Clubs, our strides can be even greater this year.

The accomplishments of this past year were highly rewarding. It was a year which concentrated heavily on our membership—comprised of some of the finest talents in our Industry today: the year of the waiver for the return of former members; the initiation of member participation in the selection of our Hall of Fame candidates; the initiation of a Member Relations Committee; and the initiation of innumerable membership benefits.

It was a year where our work in education alone brought us the distinguished School Art League Youth's Friends Community Service Award medal for our determined efforts during the crisis over disproportionate cuts in art education in our public schools, and it was the first solid cooperative effort of 14 allied communications organizations (with over 7000 members collectively), to pull together in the signing of a document stating our joint concern; the first nationwide Educators Conference in our Club's history geared to investigate the problems of art education and opening the road to help solve them together; numerous meetings with officials at the Board of Education to further develop programs on behalf of art students and art education; the continuation of educational programs including well-developed Encounter Sessions which encourage dialogue between students and professionals, a successful portfolio review program, and a one-to-one adoption program matching students and professionals; scholarship monies designated to needy and talented art students; and finally my newly developed curriculum in Graphic Communications available as a guide for Institutions interested in reviewing the latest requirements in our field from the professional's point of view.

Along with our efforts in the education area, the following programs continued to flourish: The Art Directors Club Hall of Fame function held in November at the United Nations; our annual awards presentation held at the Americana in May of this year, and our annual exhibition held at One Dag Hammarskjold Plaza (which was attended by more than 1500 viewers); our annual One Show traveling exhibition now touring around the world; and our in-house activities including our Club exhibitions, Members' Exhibition, and diversified weekly luncheon programs.

In retrospect, it's been a very positive and progressive year and hopefully our momentum will carry us to the point to which we've been striving with such dedication: a new era of full recognition and total respect for all Graphic Communicators.

THE ONE SHOW ANNUAL EXHIBITION

Tony Cappiello
Kurt Haiman

One Show Director: Kurt Haiman
Editorial Chairman: Ernie Scarfone
Graphic Design Chairman: Rudi Wolf
Print Chairman: David Altschiller
Radio Chairman: Stephen Fenton
Television Chairmen: Dick Jackson, Richard Luden
International Chairman: Tony Cappiello

1976 marked the 55th annual awards competition for the Art Directors Club. It was also the fourth annual "One Show," and joint effort of The Art Directors Club and The Copy Club of New York.

This year a closer working relationship between the two clubs was established through a set of guidelines drawn up at summit-style meetings. The guidelines were agreed upon and approved by the directors of both clubs.

A committee chaired by members of the two clubs then studied the rules and categories of the previous One Show competitions and recommended several changes in the entry requirements. The recommendations were designed to simplify judging and the presentation of awards.

The 1976 "call for entries" included most, if not all, the committee suggestions and were mailed out in early December, 1975. Closing dates were January 30 for domestic entries, February 12 for international entries.

A study of the entries received indicated a small reduction in print but a heavy increase in television and radio categories.

The judging went smoothly and was completed during the first two weeks of March.

International entries were judged separately from domestic entries this year by a special group of internationally oriented judges.

Out of thousands of entries the judges selected 890 finalists. Of these 43 received gold medals and 42 received silver medals.

Medal winners were announced at the annual awards presentation which was held at the Americana on May 17.

The complete exhibition, designed by Miguel Velez, opened officially May 18 with the cutting of the ribbon by Administrator Alfred E. Eisenpreis, Economic Development Administration at One Dag Hammarskjold Plaza.

The 1976 Exhibition Chairman was Kurt Haiman with Ernie Scarfone, Dick Luden and Rudi Wolf serving as Co-chairmen for The Art Directors Club with Dick Jackson, David Altschiller and Marty Solow serving for The Copy Club.

GRAPHIC DESIGN
JURORS
Sam Antupit
Peter Belliveau
Greg Bruno
Thomas Carnase
Lou Dorfsman
Dave Epstein
G. Euring
Warren Kass
Andrew Kner
Helmut Krone
Irene Osborn
Tony Palladino
Robert Reed
J. Simpson
Kurt Weihs

GRAPHIC DESIGN
GOLD MEDAL JUDGING
INTERNATIONAL
JURORS
Ramona Bechtos
Nick Canetti
Bob Gill
Klaus Schmidt
Shinichiro Tora
Constance Von Collande
Hidehito Yamamoto
Alisa Zamir

PRINT ADVERTISING
JURORS
Peter Adler
Arnie Arlow
Lee Epstein
Joel Harrison
Peter Hirsch
Alan Kupchick
Marce Mayhew
Helen Nolan
Bob Pasqualine
Robert Reitzfeld
Marty Solow
Mel Stabin
Mike Tesch
Howard Title

EDITORIAL
JURORS
Ruth Ansel
Ernest Costa
Bob Crozier
Pasquale Del Vecchio
Carl Fischer
Len Fury
Al Greenberg
Al Grossman
Marilyn Hoffner
Anthony La Rotonda
Rudy Muller
Bob Pliskin
Otto Storch

RADIO
JURORS
Steve Fenton
Lee Gardner
Ken Howard
Walter Joyce
Kip Kaplan
Dick Klein
Dick Mendelsohn
Jackie Mirabel
Bob Vernon
John Zukowski

TELEVISION
JURORS
Hy Abady
Allan Beaver
Ron Becker
Richard Brown
Dick Calderhead
Rocco Campanelli
Robert Cole
Herman Davis
Gene Federico
Ms. Enid Futterman
Harvey Gabor
Michael Kahn
Steve Kambanis
Marshall Karp
Fred Kittel
William McCaffery
Tom Nathan
Bernard Owett
Eleonore Pepin
Joseph Toto
Alex Tsao

AWARDS PRESENTATION

Bill Brockmeier

The One Show is the "most prestigious" of the advertising awards competitions. Yet, despite the highest standards of excellence of the work accepted its awards presentations, more often than we care to admit, have been something less than professional. In the fifty-five years since its inception as The Art Directors Annual Exhibition, it has grown from a simple luncheon affair to a four to five hour extravaganza. Every attempt (and I've been a party to many) to cut into the boredom and the time of the presentation has been unsuccessful.

This year the Advisory Board was requested to produce the Presentation which included a delightful dinner selected through the expertise of Art Hawkins. We were determined to produce an affair befitting the excellence of the award winners. The heroes of the night were to be the award winning work and those who produced it . . . and the presentation was to last no longer than three hours.

The result was a *one hour and ten* minute, unhurried, professional presentation which featured the award winning work and those who produced it. Slides, film, and tape of the award winning work was skillfully blended with live video projected on three 14' x 10' screens of the winners receiving their awards.

It takes a professional to do a professional job. Our thanks go to Jim Sant' Andrea and the team of communicators he assembled. Their unselfish donation of time, talents, and hardware made it happen: Concept and Production: Jim Sant'Andrea Productions, Inc., Production Coordinator: Howard Hirsch, Nova Communications, Lighting Designer: Imero Fiorentino, Imero Fiorentino Associates, Music Composer/Arranger: Ted Simons, Writer: Roy Lampe, Electronic Animation: Allan Stanley, Dolphin Productions Inc., Video/Film Transfer: Ron Gunning, Image Transform, Inc., Art Services: Dick Ross/Paul Pento, Ross & Pento, Inc., Film Editor: Pat De Rosa, PDR Productions, Eidophor Projection: Fred Landman, Magna Verde Productions, Mobile Video System: Allan Rosenstein, Video Camera Services Ltd., Phototypography: George Sohn, Photo Lettering, Inc., Slide Photography: Ted Kraskow, Color Slides, Inc., Xerography Graphic Design: Dennis Wheeler, Wheeler Communications, Film/Slide Projection Equipment: Randy Will, Staging Techniques, Inc., Still Photography Coverage: Lynn Karlin.

P.S. The meal was excellent too! Not enough bars for cocktails, though!
Sic – nobody's perfect!

COMMUNICATIONS CONFERENCE

Walter Kaprielian

The 1976 version of the Art Directors Club Communications Conference is one that will have ramifications well into the 1980's and was born from questions raised by many in the industry who criticized the caliber and quantity of entrants into our field for the past 10 years.

Is it the fault of the schools, the students, the economy, the industry, or the teachers?

Unlike conferences of previous years, the Art Directors Club decided to act as a catalyst for such a discussion, and knowing full well that there is more than one side to a story, have invited leading Educators from all over the nation to attend, and tell their side.

The Conference will take place on July 21, 22 and 23, at the Parsons School of Design.

The Chairman of the event will be John Sellers of Syracuse University. His Co-Chairman is Peter Blank of Newsweek Magazine. Both are Art Directors Club members.

The program will be such that on the first day, both Educators and Professionals in the field can speak their minds about the situation as they see it.

The second and part of the third day will be devoted to Educators discussing their own varying programs, innovations, ideas, and problems, all leading to a closing panel discussion with a mixed group of Professionals.

The program in itself has a wide spectrum of "stars" in both fields of endeavor, which will lead to some exciting and stimulating discussions that will hopefully create a constructive atmosphere within which the industry, the schools, and students can benefit.

Many things will be discussed, and many questions will be raised. Many things will remain unanswered when this first Conference on Education is over, but one thing should come out very clearly to all concerned: the Art Directors Club is committed to education in our industry and we hope that this Conference becomes the first of many Conferences by many people on this most serious aspect of our professional lives.

The Art Directors Club, Inc.

Steinhauser Hess Levy Gangel Gargano

Scali Kobalin Kaprielian

HAIRLINE
RULES/PRINT
BLACK ON
WHITE
SCHOOL HAS
MORE COLOR

EDUCATION

The 1976 ADC Education Program had four basic parts this year: Curriculum, Education Encounters, Portfolio Reviews, and Adoption . . . each separate and each with their own Chairpeople.

I. Curriculum Development
Eileen Hedy Schultz, President.

In order to better prepare our upcoming Graphic Communicators in today's competetive market, a vital project in the area of education was undertaken by this year's Club President, Eileen Hedy Schultz.

After a two and half year intensive study of hundreds of graphic curriculums both here and abroad, a basic core curriculum was prepared by her, reviewed by professionals, and called "Graphic Communication."

This thesis is available to all interested in reviewing it for whatever purpose it will best serve their Educational Institutions.

II. Education Encounters
chairman Robert A. Propper

The Education Encounter series for 1976 took place 7 Wednesday evenings April and May at the ADC from 6 to 8:30 P.M.

36 top-flight talents from the

entire field were included in panels devoted to answering students' quandries as they approached graduation time. Panels were art directors, photographers, Illustrators, clients, editors, personnel people. Panels were fashioned on an intradisciplinary basis. Key questions which were taken up: What are the kinds of jobs in the field and what do you do on them? How do you hire a printer, photographer, and so forth? What do clients expect from creative people? How should you present work in an interview?

The Format included the following:
Ourselves, Our Future, Our Colleagues, Our Clients, Our Services, Our Guardians, Our Jobs.

In the words of Chairman Propper at the opening session:

"In a few short months, you will have to put away your esthetic fantasies and face the grim reality of today's job market. I don't have to tell you what kind of reality it is.

"This year's education encounter program is a departure from years past, and it is a departure from the old to the new. There is nothing wrong with the past. It serves us faithfully in turbulent times—allows us to sit back untroubled by the peripheral winds of change—that is until those winds become a hurricane.

"If we are not prepared, and our house is not in order, our future will rush by us leaving in its wake the still-born communications professional who never had a chance.

"Our Encounter sessions, all seven of them, were conceived to help bridge that awful chasm between student and professional. In these times, that chasm is very wide and dangerously deep.

"It seems to me, and to many of my fellow practitioners, that the academic world is substantially out of touch with the needs and realities of our society. There is a tendency on the part of schools toward romantic interpretation of the design/ communications world. Romantic interpretation according to 19th century painterly ideals, which are O.K., providing you don't have to earn a living according to 1970's requirements. These requirements won't go away, they won't disappear, you will . . ."

III. Portfolio Review
chairman Gladys Barton

Again this year, the Portfolio Review program was coordinated in a detailed fashion in order to broaden its reach. From the plans as they moved along: the chairman enlisted as much help and input as possible from a committee of about 9 and given assignments to help in getting the program moving.

Eight schools in the New York area were called. Schools received a covering letter explaining the program and reservation cards (for students to fill out), and flyers for bulletin boards. The reservation sets the program apart from past year's because it ensures the student's seriousness and the responsibility of the school, which must verify that information as given is correct. Reservations include area of interest.

Difference No. 2 in this program is that members were being matched with students with special disciplines who wished to work in special fields.

Difference No. 3. The plan is that each school had its own day. If enough students signed on from Pratt, there was a "Pratt Day at the ADC"—cutting down on trafficking and giving the students perhaps more attention than they have ever received in this program.

Portfolio took place Mondays and Fridays at lunchtime from mid-April through to late May.

Schools who participated were: Pratt, Cooper U.; SVA; Parsons; NYC Community; Keene; NY Institute of Technology; Fash. Instit. of Technology.

IV. Adoption Program
chairman Jessica Weber

The chairman received from the last chairman John Okladek a detailed analysis, and to avoid last year's problems, students were carefully matched and the schools were contacted to verify each selection. A one-to-one relationship between student and professional has proven a highly beneficial program and worthy of continuation in the coming years.

Other smaller educational endeavors took place during the year, for instance, hosting a group of intern students from the Memphis Art Academy and arranging some agency visits for them. Staff answers student letters on papers or careers.

An institution is the lengthened shadow of one man

WEDNESDAY SPEAKERS LUNCHEONS

Bob Greenwell

The purpose of the Club's Wednesday Speakers Luncheons has always been to stimulate, educate and entertain. This past year luncheons guests were treated to a magic show, wine-tasting seminar, sketch class, old-time vaudeville show, gastronomic tour of the Mid-East, British TV commercials, a Christmas sing-a-long, films, slide shows, discussion panels, etc.

Guest speakers included Dong Kingman, Herbert Bayer, Carol Wald, Bob Gill, Abril Lamarque, Lanny Ross, Jerry Robinson, Dave Hermann, Horn-Cuesta, Phil Peyton, Milt Glaser, Dan Wynn, Daniel Schwartz, Carl Fischer, Marcia Keegan, Cipe Pineles, Jerome Snyder, Fred Danzig, Helmut Krone, David Deutsch, Gene Federico, Hans Fuchs, Jill Krementz, Fritz Eichenberg, Judith Lowry and more.

The reasonably priced buffet plus always interesting programs make "Wednesday At The Club" the best luncheon deal in NYC. These luncheons are open to the general public if space is available and visiting Art Directors from out of town are expressly welcome.

GALLERY EXHIBITIONS

The House Exhibition Committee headed by Frank Pastorini, kept the walls of the penthouse exciting with a wide variety of material this past year.

Exhibit titles were Brainstorming Advertising 100 years, Theater Posters, Members' Art Exhibition, Art Weavers Guild Exhibit, Ulc Typography Exhibit.

Cocktail receptions formally opened each exhibition with a good member, student, and public attendance. The Art Weavers Guild Exhibit attracted considerable public interest in the unusual and beautifully crafted material not often seen on display.

THE ADVISORY BOARD

Bill Brockmeier

Somebody said "Profit by the mistakes of others." This quote alone is good reason for having a group of ex-presidents called the Advisory Board. The officers and Boards' members are able to turn for advice to this experienced group. At the same time they provide a continuity from one administration to another.

Special projects using their individual talents and experience are assigned at the Executive Board's discretion. They have become involved in real estate problems, legal and constitutional questions, and special functions such as this years' first Hall of Fame dinner and the One Show Awards Dinner. These are individual and collective undertakings of the Advisory Board, but most importantly their function is as advisors.

We on the Advisory Board would like to thank the present administration for its faith in our experience and for following through on our suggestions.

MEMBERSHIP

Arnold C. Holeywell

The Art Directors Club does not run an annual membership drive. Its growing membership seems to come spontaneously.

Arnold Holeywell, Chairman of the Membership Committee, nevertheless reminds members that you may well know of associates who would like to join and know about us. In a sense, he defines the Club here:

"Our basic purpose is to promote the highest standard in all forms of visual communications and to promote greater recognition of the art director within the business community. You can build a stronger organization by recommending to your fellow professionals that they join us. A continued growth of new membership is essential to maintain the force to carry us forward."

One of the industry's longtime hot talents—a man who is a photographer and sometime Art Director—happened by the Club the other day. In conversation, we asked him why he never became a member. He was surprised to learn that he *could* join. What came out of this is that we will probably add a lively new member to our roster and we think the present is a very good time to reiterate the classifications of membership in the ADC.

Regular Members.

Individuals who have been Art Directors for two years are eligible. Dues are $130 yearly and initiation fees are $50.

Associate Members.

Individuals who work within related creative endeavors (illustrators, photographers, journalists, copywriters). The fees are the same as those of Regular members.

Out-of-Town Members.

People who work and live outside the 75-mile radius of New York City. (Note: this is an exellent membership for individuals who want to stay in touch with what's going on in communications in New York as it includes all privileges including an Annual. A growing number of out-of-town members in the U.S. and overseas find the membership also provides them with a home-away-from-home when they do visit the city.) Dues are $65 and initiation dues $25.

Junior Members.

A young person must fill only two requirements: be 25 years or less; have a year's working experience. Dues are $25 and there is no initiation fee.

Affiliate Members: Corporate:

A company must be engaged in a communications-oriented business. (Two members of the Corporation carry the Club's membership card and receive all privileges.) Fees are $500 dues yearly and the initiation fee is $250.

Educational or Institutional:

This classification is for schools and museums. (The same privileges apply as above.) Dues are $250 a year, initiation fees $125.

Professional Organization:

This classification opens up group memberships for related graphic professional or trade groups in a wide range such as out-of-town Art Director organizations, printing clubs, etc. (Privileges and fees are the same as Corporate, Educational or Institutional.)

SCHOLARSHIP
Walter Kaprielian

In the past two years, the Scholarship Committee has remained active despite the financial strains the club has been under.

This committee has worked within the confines of existing budgets and has in the past year made two donations to tuition-free schools in the New York area.

The donations of $500 each were made to the Cooper Union Art School, and to the Commercial Art Department of the New York City Community College.

In each instance the monies were earmarked for art materials so as to offset the high cost of supplies that have had a limiting creative influence on the financially hard-pressed students.

New York City Community College for instance, used the money to purchase Minolta 35 mm cameras that students can take out on loan to do their photography and advertising design projects.

The committee also earmarked a percentage of the profits from the Hall of Fame Dinner and the forthcoming "Advertising 1920 and Today" show to be held at Lever House for Scholarship.

We are also planning a benefit affair with all proceeds going to Student help. The final stage of this particular affair are not far enough along to report in greater detail.

Likewise, a percentage of any profits derived from the July Educators Conference has also been earmarked for Scholarship.

We are pleased to report that the amount set aside from the Hall of Fame affair comes to $2,000 which will again be donated to schools for student use.

TRAVELING SHOW
Ray Robertson

The basic reason for offering this show is to aid groups wishing to inform their audience on various aspects of our culture, which come through rather vividly in "The One Show," also as an aid to professionals wishing to be better informed on U.S. ideas and methods of communicating sales or editorial messages to the public. Our Club did not wish to profit by this show, but at the same time, it did not wish to incur debt, so we try to break even.

First, as in past year, the U.S.I.A. (United States Information Agency) took the "One Show" which was then broken into smaller shows to be presented to open audiences in embassies and galleries in many countries around the world. Our committee felt that this was a good way to promote the excellence of U.S. advertising and promotional efforts and at the same time draw some attention to the club itself. Up to now, our information indicates that designers in communities where these shows were presented have not been informed of its availability. This concerns us so we are meeting with a representative of the U.S.I.A. to see what can be done to remedy this situation.

A large show was sent to Norberto Leon, a member of the Art Directors Club of Spain. This show was seen in Spain by professional people during the month of January, 1976.

A small print show selected by Mr. Tora, a member of the N. Y. A. D. Club was sent on a scheduled tour throughout Japan. This tour was under the sponsorship and direction of such groups as Nippon Designers and Idea Magazine.

A carefully selected print show was also sent to Westmore Paper Co. in Houston.

Any materials left over were offered to various New York Schools with Graphic Arts programs.

I wish to thank Jo Yanow, Dick MacFarlane and Dave MacInnes for their patience and untiring energy in helping to put these shows on the Road.

ADC Members

A

Adamec, Donald
Adams, Gaylord
Adams, George C.
Addiss, Patricia
Adler, Jane
Adler, Peter
Adorney, Charles S.
Agha, M.F.
Aldoretta, Warren P.
Allen, Lorraine
Allner, Walter H.
Ammirati, Carlo
Andreozzi, Gennaro R.
Andresakes, Ted
Anthony, Al
Anthony, Robert
Arlow, Arnold
Aronson, Herman
Asano, Tadashi
Aymar, Gordon C.

B

Bach, Robert O.
Baer, Priscilla
Baily, Li
Baker, Frank
Barbini, Edward
Barile, Carl
Barr, Carla
Barron, Don
Bartel, Clyde W.
Barton, Gladys
Baile, Matthew
Bassett, Karen L.
Bastian, Rufus A.
Beaver, Allan
Beckerman, Jay
Bee, Noah
Bell, James Jr.
Belliveau, Peter
Bennett, Edward J.
Benson, Laurence Key
Berenter, William
Berg, John
Berkowitz, Seymour
Berliner, Saul
Bernstein, Ted
Berry, Park
Biondi, Aldo
Birbrower, Stewart
Blank, Peter
Blattner, Robert H.
Blend, Robert
Blattner, Robert H.
Blend, Robert

Block, David S.
Blod, Francis
Blomquist, Arthur T.
Bloom, Stan
Bode, Robert W.
Bonder, Ronnie
Boothroyd, John Milne
Boroff, Sanford
Bossert, William T.
Boudreau, James
Bostrum, Thor F.
Bourges, Jean
Bowman, Harold A.
Boyd, Douglas
Braguin, Simeon
Brandt, Joan
Bratteson, Alfred
Brattinga, Pieter
Brauer, Fred J.
Braverman, Al
Brockmeier, William P.
Brody, Ruth
Brody, Marc
Brooke, John
Brodsky, Ed
Bruce, Robert E.
Brugnatelli, Bruno E.
Brussel-Smith,
  Bernard
Brzoza, Walter C.
Bua, Charles
Buckley, William H.
Bunzak, William
Burns, Aaron
Burns, Herman F.
Burtin, Cipe Pineles

C

Cadge, William
Campanelli, Rocco E.
Campbell, Stuart
Canetti, Nicolai
Cappiello, Tony
Carlu, Jean
Carnase, Thomas
Cerullo, C. Edward
Cherry, John V.
Chiesa, Alfred F.
Chin, Kay
Church, Stanley
Chwast, Paula Scher
Chwast, Seymour
Ciano, Robert
Civale, Frank, Sr.
Clark, George P.
Clark, Herbert
Clarke, George P.
Clemente, Thomas F.
Cline, Mahlon A.
Clive, Robert

Closi, Victor
Coiner, Charles T.
Collins, Benjamin
Confalonieri, Giulio
Conley, John
Corvington, Mark A.
Cook, John
Costa, Ernest
Cotler, Sheldon
Cottingham, Edward
  M.
Counihan, Thomas J.
Craddock, Thomas J.
Craig, James Edward
Crane, Meg
Cranner, Brian
Crozier, John Robert
Cummings, Richard
Cummins, Jerry
Cupani, Joseph
Cutler, Charles

D

Dadmun, Royal
Dane, Norman R.
D'Anna, Russell
DaRold, Thierry L.H.
David, Stephanie
Davidian, David
Davis, Herman A.
Davis, Philip
deCesare, John
Defrin, Bob
Del Sorbo, Joseph R.
Del Vecchio, Pat
Demner, Marius
Demony, Jerry C.
Deppe, Florian R.
Deutsh, David S.
Diehl, Carolyn
Diehl, Edward P.
Dignam, John F.
Dixon, Kenwood
Dolobowsky, Robert
Donald, Peter
Donatiello, Michael
Dorfsman, Louis
Dorion, Marc
Doyle, J. Wesley
Dubin, Morton
Duffy, Donald H.
Duffy, William
Dusek, Rudolph
Duskin, Ken
Dymond, Joanna

E

Eckstein, Bernard
Edelson, Carol Herman

Edgar, Peter
Egensteiner, Don
Eidel, Zeneth
Eisenman, Stanley
Elton, Wallace
Emory, Rod A.
Engler, Elliot
Enock, David
Epstein, David
Epstein, Henry
Epstein, Lee
Erikson, Rolf
Ermoyan, Suren
Essman, Robert N.

F

Farber, Bob
Farrell, Abe
Federico, Gene
Feiter, Bea
Fenga, Michael
Fenton, Timothy
Fernandez, George R.
Fertik, Samuel A.
Finegold, Rupert J.
Finn, William
Fiorenza, Blanche
Firpo, Gonzalo
Fischer, Carl
Fitzgerald, John E.
Flack, Richard
Flock, Donald
Flynn, J. Walter
Foster, Robert
Fraioli, Jon M.
Francis, Robert D.
Frankel, Ted
Franfurt, Stephen O.
Franzick, Philip E.
Freedman Mel
Freyer, Fred
Friedman, Martin
Frost, Oren S.
Fujii, Satoru
Fury, Leonard W.

G

Gabor, Harvey
Gage, Robert
Garlander, Gene
Gatti, David
Gauss, Joseph T.
Gavasci, Alberto P.
Geoghegan, Walter B.
Georgi, Carl H.
Gering, Joseph
Germakian, Michael
Giammalvo, Nick
Gibbs, Edward

Gillis, Richard B.
Giusti, George
Glaser, Milton
Glessman, Louis R.
Gluckman Eric
Guennel, Heidi
Goff, Seymour R.
Gold, William
Goldberg, Irwin
Goldgell, Hazel
Goldman, Edward
Goldowsky, Eli
Golub, William
Grace, Roy
Graham, John
Green, Arnie
Greenberg, Albert
Greenberg, Nancy
Greene, Bert
Greenwell, Robert
Greller, Fred
Griffin, John J.
Griner, Norman
Grotz, Walter
Grupper, Nelson
Guffey, Dione M.
Guild, Lurelle, V.A.
Guild, S. Rollins

H

Hack, Robert H.
Haiman, Kurt
Halpern, George
Halvorsen, Everett
Handelman, Michael
Hanson, Thurland
Hartman, George
Harris, Kenneth D.
Hartelius, Paul V. Jr.
Hautau, Janet
Hawkins, Arthur
Hayes, Dorothy
Heff, Saul
Heiffel, Eugene
Helleu, Jacques
Hemmick, Bud
Herman, Harvey
Heyman, Wesley F.
Hipwell, Grant I.
Hirsch, Peter M.
Hoashi, Jitsuo
Hodes, Ronald
Hoffman, Wallace R.
Hoffner, Marilyn
Holeywell, Arnold C.
Holtane, George
Hopkins, William P.
Horn, Steve
Hovanec, Joe

Howard, Hoyt
Howard, Kenneth M.
Howard, Mark
Hurd, Jud
Hulburt, Allen F.
Hyatt, Morton

I

Iger, Martin
Irwin, William A.

J

Jaccoma, Edward G.
Jackson, Robert T.
Jacobs, Harry M.
Jaggi, Moritz S.
Jagisch, Ronald A.
Jamison, John
Johnson, D. Carzell
Jones, Bob
Joslyn, Roger
Jossel, Leonard
Julia, Christian

K

Kambanis, Aristedes S.
Kambourian, Ron
Kanai, Kiyoshi
Kaprielian, Walter
Karsakov, Leonard
Katsui, Mitsuo
Katzen, Rachel
Kaufmann, M.R.
Keegan, Marcia
Keil, Tom S.
Kelley, Kenneth Roy
Kent, Nancy V.
Kenzer, Myron W.
Kittel, Fredrick H.
Kleckner, Valerie
Klein, Gerald
Klein, Judith
Kner, Andrew
Knoepfler, Henry O.
Komai, Roy
Koos, John
Kosarin, Norman
Krauss, Oscar
Krikoritan, George
Kurnit, Shep

L

LaGrone, roy E.
Laird, James E.
Lamarque, Abril
Lambray, Maureen
Lampert, Harry
Larkim, John J.

LaMicela, Sebastian N.
LaRotonda, Anthony
Lavey, Kenneth H.
Lazzarotti, Sal
Lee, Daniel S.
Leeds, Don
Leon, Norberto
Leonard, Jack
Leslie, Dr. Robert
Leu, Olaf
Levin, David T.
Levin, Irving
Levine, Richard
Levinson, Julian P.
Levy, Dean David
Leydenfrost, Robert
Liberman, Alexander
Liebert, Victor
Lipton, Shelli
LiPuma, Sal
Littlewood, Beverly
Littmann, Bert W.
Lockwood, Richard
Lois, George
Longo, Vincent R.
Longyear, William L.
Lotito, Rocco
Lowry, Alfred
Lubalin, Herbert
Ludekins, Fred
Luden, Richard B.
Luria, Richard
Lurin, Larry
Lyon, Robert W., Jr.

M

MacDonald, John
MacFarlane, Richard
MacInnes, David H.
Macri, Frank
Madia, Anthony
Madris, Ira B.
Magdoff, Samuel
Magnani, Louis
Malone, Martin J.
Mancino, Anthony
Manzo, Richard
Marinelli, Jack
Marshall, Al F.
Martin, Raymond M.
Martinott, Robert T.
Massey, John
Matyas, Theodore S.
Matsubara, Masaki
Maxmov, George
Mayhew, Marce
Mazzella, Dennis
McCaffery, William A.
McCallum, Robert

McCauley, Rita
McCoy, Kevin G.
McFadden, Keith
McGinnis, George
McOstrich, Priscilla
Medler, James V.
Meeker, Albert
Menell, Don
Merlicek, Franz
Mesnick, Eve
Messina, Joseph
Missina, Vincent N.
Metzdorf, Lyle
Michael, Jan
Milbauer, Eugene
Miller, Larry
Minko, William
Mohr, Sven
Mohtares, Alexander
Moore, William
Morang, Kenneth E.
Morgan, Burton A.
Morgan, Wendy Jo
Moriber, Jeffrey M.
Morrison, William R.
Morton Thomas Throck
Moss, Tobias
Moy, George
Murray, John R., Jr.
Mutter, Ralph

N

Nappi, Nick
Newman, Charles A.
Nicholas, Mary Ann
Nicolo, Frank
Nissen, Joseph
Nissenbaum, Judith
Noda, Ko
November, David
Nussbaum, Edward

O

O'Dell, Robert
Odette, Jack
O'Hehir, Joseph
Okladek, John
Olivo, Gary
Orr, Garrett P.
Osborn, Irene Charles
Otter, Robert David
Ottino, Larry
Owett, Bernard S.

P

Paccione, Onofrio
Pachman, David
Palladino, Tony
Parker, Paul E., Jr.

Parenio, Ralph
Paslavsky, Ivan
Pasternack, Bob
Pastorini, Frank
Peckolick, Alan
Peltola, John J.
Pento, Paul
Perel, Jules
Peter, John
Petrocelli, Robert H.
Peyton, Philip
Pfeffer, Elmer
Phelps, Stewart J.
Philiba, Allan
Philips, Gerald M.
Philpotts, Randy
Pioppo, Ernest
Piotrowsky, Eugene
Pittman, Stuart
Platt, Melvin
Pliskin, Robert
Podeszwa, Raymond
Polenberg, Myron
Pompiean, Thomas
Ponzian, Joel
Popcorn, Faith
Portuesi, Louis
Posnick, Paul
Post, Anthony
Pride, Benjamin
Propper, Robert
Prusmack, A. John
Pulise, Santo

Q

Queryroy, Anny

R

Rada, George A.
Radtke, Gary
Rafalaf, Jeffrey S.
Raffel, Samuel
Rand, Paul
Read, C. Richard
Redler, Harry
Reed, Robert C.
Reed, Samuel
Reed, Samuel
Reed, Sheldon
Reeves, Patrick A.
Reinke, Herbert O.
Reinke, Fred
Reisinger, Dan
Ricotta, Edwin C.
Ritter, Arthur
Rizzo, Dominic G.
Robbins, Morris
Roberts, Kenneth
Robertson, Raymond

Robinson, Clarke L.
Rocker, Harry
Rockwell, Harlow
Rofheart, Edward
Romagna, Leonard A.
Rondell, Lester
Rosenblum, Morris L.
Rosenthal, Herbert
Rosner, Charles
Ross, Andrew
Ross, Dick
Ross, James Francis
Roston, Arnold
Rothman, Irwin
Rubenfeld, Lester
Ribetti, Robert
Romano, Andy
Romero, Olga
Rubenstein, Mort
Rubin, Randee
Russell, Henry N.
Russo, John
Rustom, Mel
Ruther, Donald
Ruzicka, Thomas

S

Sadiq, Ahmad
St. Louis, Leonard A.
Saks, Robert
Salpeter, Robert
Santandrea, James, Jr.
Sauer, Hans
Scali, Sam
Scarfone, Ernest G.
Scheck, Henry
Schenk, Roland
Schiller, Lawrence
Schleider, Iren
Schneider, Richard M.
Schneider, William H.
Schreiber, Martin
Schultz, Eileen Hedy
Scocozza, Victor
Segal, Leslie
Seide, Allan
Seide, Ray
Seidler, Sheldon
Sellers, John L.
Shakery, Neil
Shear, Alexander
Sahw, Wesley
Sheldon, William
Shipenberg, Myron
Shomer, Harvey
Shutak, Sandra
Siano, Jerry J.
Sieger, Donald J.
Silverberg, Sanford
Silverstein, Louis
Simkin, Blanche

Simpson, Milton
Sirowitz, Leonard
Skolnik, Jack
Smith, Robert Sherrick
Smith, Paul
Smikler, Jerold
Sohmer, Steve
Solomon, Martin
Sosnow, Harold
Spelman III, Hoyt
Spiegel, Ben
Staperfeldt, Karsten
Stauf, Alexander
Stech, David H.
Stehling, Wendy
Steinbrenner, Karl H.
Stenzel, Alfred B.
Stern, Charles
Stevens, Martin
Stillman, Linda
Stone, Bernard
Stone, Loren B.
Storch, Otto
Strosahl, William
Sturtevant, Ira
Suarex, Jean-Claude
Sussman, Abie
Sutnar, Ladislav
Sweret, Michael
Sykes, Philip

T

Tanaka, Soji
Tanassy, Tricia
Tarallo, Joseph
Tashian, Melcon
Taubin, William
Tauss, Jack George
Taylor, Arthur R.
Tesoro, Ciro
Thomas, Lamont
Thomas, Richard
Thompson, Bradbury
Thorner, Lynne
Tillotson, Roy W.
Tinker, John Hepburn
Toledo, Harold
Tollin, Helaine Sharon
Tompkins, Gilbert
Tora, Shinichiro
Tortoriello, Don
Toth, Peter
Trasoff, Victor
Treidler, Adolph
Trumbauer, J. Rober
Tsao, Alex

U

Urbain, John A.
Urrutia, Frank

V

Vargas, Daniel O.
Velez, Miguel
Venti, Tony
Vitale, Frank A.
Von Collande,
  Constance

W

Wagener, Walter A.
Wagner, Charles W.
Waivada, Ernest
Wall, Robert
Wallace, Joseph O.
Wallace, Robert G.
Wallis, Harold
Wassyng, Sy
Watt, James C.
Watts, Ron
Wayne, Joel
Weber, Jessica Margot
Weihs, Kurt
Weinstein, Stephen
Weissberg, Robert
Weithas, Art
Wells, Sidney A.
Welti, Theo
Wheaton, Ned
Wheeler, Dennis
White, Cortland
  Thomas
White, Peter A.
Wickham, Ronald V.
Wilbur, Gordon M.
Wilde, Richard
Wilkison, David E.
Wilvers, Robert
Winkler, Horst
Winnick, Karen B.
Witalis, Rupert
Wolf, Henry
Wollman, Michael
Wurtzel, William K.

Y

Yablonka, Hy
Yamamoto, Hidehito
Yonkovig, Zen
Yuranyi, Steve

Z

Zahor, Bruce
Zalon, Alfred
Zlotnick, Bernard
Zweibel, Alan H.

Index

Designers

Editors

Publishers

Artists and Photographers

Production Companies

Agencies

Clients